Supply Chain Optimization, Design, and Management:
Advances and Intelligent Methods

Ioannis Minis
University of the Aegean, Greece

Vasileios Zeimpekis
University of the Aegean, Greece

Georgios Dounias
University of the Aegean, Greece

Nicholas Ampazis
University of the Aegean, Greece

BUSINESS SCIENCE REFERENCE
Hershey · New York

Senior Editorial Director: Kristin Klinger
Director of Book Publications: Julia Mosemann
Editorial Director: Lindsay Johnston
Acquisitions Editor: Erika Carter
Development Editor: Joel Gamon
Production Coordinator: Jamie Snavely
Typesetters: Keith Glazewski & Natalie Pronio
Cover Design: Nick Newcomer

Published in the United States of America by
Business Science Reference (an imprint of IGI Global)
701 E. Chocolate Avenue
Hershey PA 17033
Tel: 717-533-8845
Fax: 717-533-8661
E-mail: cust@igi-global.com
Web site: http://www.igi-global.com/reference

Library of Congress Cataloging-in-Publication Data

Supply chain optimization, design, and management : advances and intelligent methods / Ioannis Minis ... [et al.], editors.
p. cm.
Includes bibliographical references and index.
Summary: "This book presents computational intelligence methods for addressing supply chain issues, emphasizing techniques that provide effective solutions to complex supply chain problems and exhibit superior performance to other methods of operations research"--Provided by publisher.
ISBN 978-1-61520-633-9 (hbk.) -- ISBN 978-1-61520-634-6 (ebook) 1. Business logistics. 2. Production control. 3. Operations research. 4. Computational intelligence. I. Minis, Ioannis. II. Title.

HD38.5.S896154 2010
658.5--dc22

2010043662

British Cataloguing in Publication Data
A Cataloguing in Publication record for this book is available from the British Library.

Table of Contents

Detailed Table of Contents

This chapter proposes a new method to perform assignment of service requests (calls) with some flexibility taking into account expected routes in a multi-period horizon. The problem is solved on a rolling horizon basis in order to address the dynamics of arriving calls. The method is tested through several theoretical examples, as well as in an extensive industrial case, and appears to be superior to current methods used in practice.

This chapter discusses the prediction results generated by two travel time estimation methods that use historical and real-time data respectively. The first method follows the k-nn model, which relies on the non-parametric regression method, whereas the second one relies on an interpolation scheme which is employed during the transmission of real-time traffic data in fixed intervals.

Preface

THE ROLE OF QUANTITATIVE METHODS IN SUPPLY CHAIN MANAGEMENT

Introduction

The supply chain of both manufacturing and commercial enterprises comprises a highly distributed environment, in which complex processes evolve in a network of companies (see Figure 1). Such processes include materials procurement and storage, production of intermediate and final products, warehousing, sales, customer service, and distribution. The role of the supply chain in a company's competitiveness is critical, since the supply chain affects directly customer satisfaction, inventory and distribution costs, and responsiveness to the ever changing markets. This role becomes more critical in today's distributed manufacturing environment, in which companies focus on core competencies and outsource supportive tasks, thus creating large supply networks. Within this environment, there are strong interactions of multiple entities, processes, and data. For each process in isolation, it is usually feasible to identify those decisions that are locally optimal, especially in a deterministic setting. However, decision making in supply chain systems should consider intrinsic uncertainties, while coordinating the interests and goals of the multitude of processes involved.

Operational Research-based Management Science (OR/MS) methods as well as Computational Intelligence (i.e. nature inspired techniques), offer effective techniques for modelling, analyzing and

Figure 1. The flow of materials and information in the supply chain

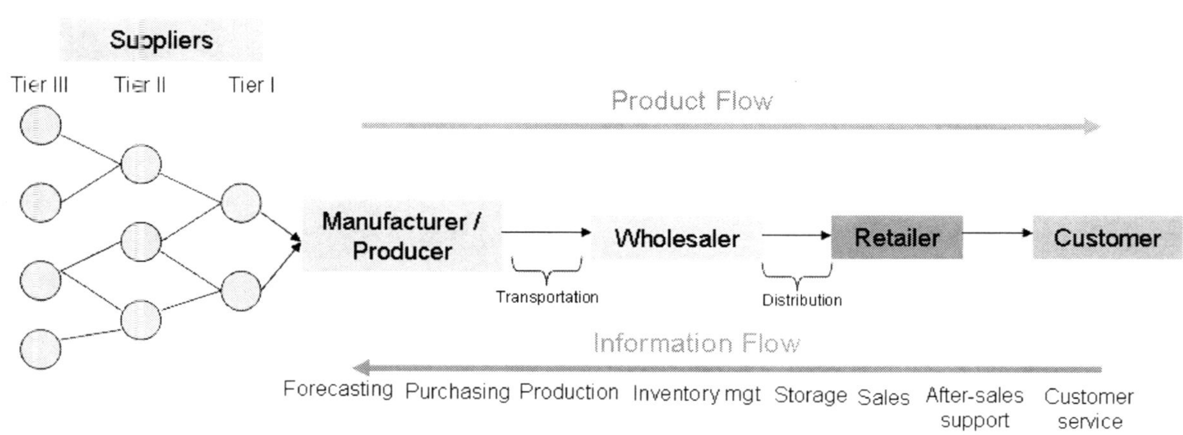

optimising operations in the uncertain environment of the supply chain, especially since these techniques are capable of handling complex interdependencies.

Operations Research and Computational Intelligence

The well-known and widely applied area of operational research (Churchman *et al.,* 1957; Hillier & Liebermann, 2005) offers powerful tools that enable optimal or near-optimal decision making in complex problems. Operational Research (OR) work may be classified into three major focus areas:

1. Probability, optimization, and dynamical systems theory (Luenberger, 1979; Kelly, 1994; Pinter, 2005)
2. Modeling (including construction and mathematical analysis of models, implementation and solution using computers, validation of models with data), (Jensen & Bard, 2003; Williams, 1999).
3. OR Applications in engineering and economics' disciplines that use models to make a practical impact on real-world problems (Thomson, 1982; Pinney & McWilliams, 1987).

Typical problems addressed successfully by OR include, optimal search, critical path analysis or project planning, floor planning, network optimization, allocation problems, production planning and scheduling, supply chain management, efficient messaging and customer response tactics, automation, transportation, distribution, etc.

Computational Intelligence (CI) is a term corresponding to a new generation of algorithmic methodologies in artificial intelligence, which combines elements of learning, adaptation, evolution and approximate (fuzzy) reasoning to create programs that -in a way- can be considered intelligent. Various editions can be found in modern literature around the fundamentals of CI, such as (Nilsson, 1998; Chen, 2000; Zimmermann *et al.,* 2001; Engelbrecht, 2002). CI has emerged as a rapid growing field in the past few years. Its variety of intelligent techniques emulate human intelligence and processes found in natural systems such as adaptation and learning, planning under large uncertainty, coping with large amounts of data, etc.

Computational intelligence methodologies can be generally classified into three major areas:

1. Standard widely acknowledged and applied intelligent techniques, such as neural networks (Haykin, 1994; Chen & Wang, 2006), fuzzy systems (Zadeh, 1965; Dubois & Prade, 1980), genetic algorithms and genetic programming (Holland, 1975; Koza, 1992) and other machine learning algorithms (Michalski, *et a.,l* 1983; Mitchell, 1997). These methods manage to successfully perform association, generalization, function approximation, rule induction, etc. in difficult multivariate domains of application.
2. Hybrid and Adaptive Intelligence (Negoita *et al.,* 2005; Abbod *et al.,* 2002), i.e. efficient combinations of the above mentioned intelligent techniques, with other intelligent or conventional methodologies for handling complex problems. Usually one of the methods combined within a hybrid or adaptive scheme, is used either to filter or to fine tune special operations of another methodology. Most popular hybrid methodologies are neuro-fuzzy systems, evolving-fuzzy systems, neuro-genetic approaches and genetic-fuzzy ones.
3. Nature Inspired Intelligence (NII) such as swarm intelligence, ant colony optimization, bee-algorithms, artificial immune systems etc., (Kannan *et al.,* 2004; Dorigo, 2005). Usually these

methodologies represent simultaneous exploration and exploitation of the search space in a smart manner (i.e. local and global search), analogously to the way natural systems or societies perform similar tasks (e.g. swarm flying or swimming, food search and identification, etc.)

Recent collections of research papers or textbooks demonstrate the potential of CI methods to address applications in transportation (Teodorovic, 2008), production planning (Voß and Woodruff, 2006), and supply chain management (Chaib-draa & Müller, 2006).

Scope and Contents of this Volume

This edited volume presents intelligent OR/MS and CI approaches for addressing the significant activities along the entire spectrum of the supply chain i.e. from forecasting, planning for production and distribution to actual implementation, including production and inventory control, warehouse management, management of transportation, and distribution. Emphasis is given to those methods and techniques that provide effective solutions to complex supply chain problems. The edited volume also includes integrated case studies that describe the solution to actual problems of high complexity. All concepts, ideas, methods and techniques, as well as integrated applications, presented in this volume aim in illustrating the significant value of CI and OR in resolving complex supply chain issues and providing breakthrough results.

Figure 2 classifies the contents of the current volume with respect to both the area of supply chain management addressed, as well as the type of method used. The volume contents are grouped in three sections:

- Section 1 focuses on the synthesis, or design, of supply chains.
- Section 2 focuses on planning, including forecasting and inventory management, in large supply chains.
- Section 3 focuses on supply chain operations, including warehouse management, production scheduling, as well as transportation and distribution.

Figure 2. Chapter classification

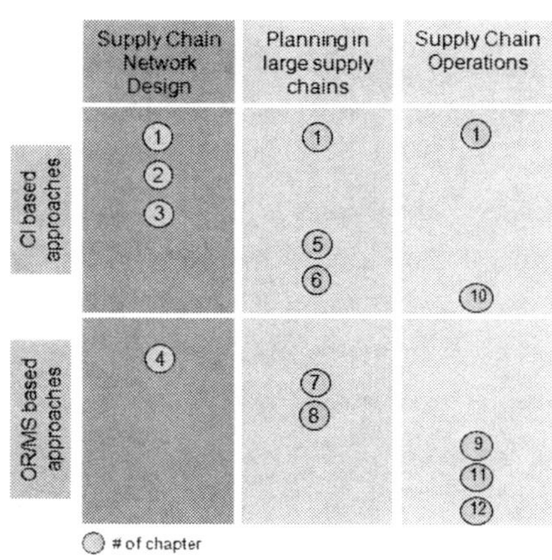

Prior to these three sections, Chapter 1 presents a survey of the available literature, regarding the use of nature-inspired (NI) methodologies to address supply chain management problems. The chapter presents initially the main characteristics and issues in a supply chain. In addition, some NI algorithms as well as their underlying natural principles are analyzed followed by findings from the literature review. The chapter concludes with a future research agenda in the area of NI in Supply Chain Management.

As mentioned before, Section 1 focuses on the synthesis, or design, of supply chains in order to address market opportunities on both an opportunistic or long-term basis.

Chapter 2 recognizes the significant contribution that e-marketplaces may offer to supply chain integration, and especially in areas such as enhanced information sharing among partners, reduction of administrative costs, streamlining of transactions, and improvement of transparency. Building upon these strengths, the research addresses the case of coalitions of small and medium-size suppliers, which are formed to respond effectively to significant customer requests, and to share the related risk. Specifically, the work focuses on key steps of coalition management, including the selection of the partners, synthesis of customer proposals, and profit sharing among partners. To address the latter, the authors combine game theory (Sharpley value), simulation experiments and a multi-agent architecture, for coalition management and profit sharing among partners in neutral e-marketplaces.. They have also developed a simulation environment based on multi agent architecture to test their approach and to support the competitiveness of SMEs. The test results show that in this environment, suppliers that form coalitions gain more benefits than the customers.

Chapter 3 also addresses aspects of collaboration among independent supply chains in the context of co-opetition, in which firms cooperate and compete at the same time. The researchers investigate sharing of production capacity in inter-firm networks. Specifically they focus on the issue of capacity investments under two models: In the first model there is no sharing of information in the inter-firm network, while in the second there is a periodic information exchange among firms concerning production capacity. The proposed models have been simulated and tested using a Multi Agent Architecture. The simulation results indicate that under the Information Sharing model the capacity investments can be drastically reduced, maintaining a high level of profit (at the same level as in the no information sharing model).

Chapter 4 addresses the design of supply chain networks comprising multiproduct production facilities with shared production resources, warehouses, distribution centers, and customer zones. Furthermore, demand uncertainty is considered through a number of likely scenarios. The problem is formulated as a mixed-integer linear programming problem, which aims to assist senior operations management in decision making about production allocation, production capacity per site, purchase of raw materials and network configuration. The proposed model is solved to global optimality using standard branch-and-bound techniques. The results of a significant case study indicate the value of a model that considers the complex interactions of such networks. Furthermore, the computational cost was found to be relatively low, thus making the overall model attractive for the solution of large-scale problems.

Section 2 focuses on planning, including forecasting and inventory management, in large supply chains.

Chapter 5 explores the potential of computational intelligence approaches as forecasting mechanisms for end product sales to the customer. It proposes a multivariate forecasting methodology that uses advanced training methods (Optimized Levenberg-Marquardt with Adaptive Momentum) in Artificial Neural Networks (ANNs), while exploring the potential of the powerful Support Vector Machines theory in this area. The proposed approach has been evaluated using public data from the Netflix movie rental online DVD store in order to predict the demand for movie rentals during the critical, for sales, Christmas holiday season. All ANNs tested performed quite well, while the winner exhibited reasonable prediction capability. These results illustrate the value of advanced multivariate models in capturing the complex interactions that influence SC demand in uncertain environments.

Chapter 6 addresses the problem of developing ordering policies that minimise the overall supply chain cost, while mitigating the bullwhip effect, in which demand variance at the customer end is amplified along the chain upstream. The researchers extend work in Evolutionary Algorithms and simulation to develop effective ordering policies. The extension comprises of capitalising on the Quantum Inspired Genetic Algorithm (QIGA) and on Grammatical Evolution (GE). Both the standard supply chain of the Beer Game, and arborescent supply chains have been investigated under stochastic demand distributions and lead times, and capacitated inventory. The results indicate that GE, with an appropriate grammar, can outperform other EA approaches over a range of supply network topologies and constraints. This does not appear to hold, in general, for QIGA in its current implementation. Thus, GE may effectively support a decision support system for ordering.

Chapter 7 overviews recent trends for risk management in extended supply chains. Risk and disruptions of operations are becoming significant issues as supply chains become globalised. Within this context, the chapter focuses on the area of quantifying the impact of supply chain disruptions on optimal determination of inventory control policies in a stochastic environment with unreliable sourcing. Specifically, single period (newsvendor-type) problems are examined, analyzing typical methodologies for systems with multiple unreliable suppliers due to production or distribution disruptions. Several promising directions for future research are also discussed, including extensions to multiple types of products, to more than two suppliers, as well as the explicit inclusion of service level concerns.

Chapter 8 deals with modelling and solution approaches for both the problem of prepositioning emergency supplies prior to a disaster, as well as the problem of their distribution after the disaster onset. Initially, some key aspects that are critical to the design and operations of effective relief distribution networks are discussed followed by a review of different algorithmic approaches reported in the literature of pre-disaster prepositioning of emergency supplies. A non-exhaustive survey of solution approaches for the post-disaster distribution of supplies is also presented. Chapter 8 reviews also a series of exact and heuristic methods that can be applied to tackle the aforementioned problems. In addition, the advantages and limitations of each of these two classes of approaches are discussed. The chapter concludes with a methodological framework for addressing the design and operation of relief distribution networks and some interesting research avenues.

Section 3 focuses on supply chain operations, including warehouse management, production scheduling, as well as transportation and distribution.

Chapter 9 deals with the development of an analytical parametric model for the order picking process in a modular warehouse. The research attempts to address three distinct, yet relevant, areas: (i) to produce a generic and analytical framework to model the order picking process, (ii) to define practical performance measures for the order picking process, and (iii) to provide the tools for a warehouse manager to set goals, measure performance and identify areas of improvement in his area of responsibility. In addition to these, the Chapter sets the foundations to further expand on other warehouse processes, such as loading/unloading, products receipt, etc., that pass the boundaries of order picking. The analysis is corroborated by a case study, accompanied by ABC analysis of the warehouse operation and a presentation of a fair frame to measure workers' performance.

Chapter 10 addresses the coordination of internal production supply chains in serial manufacturing lines. The model line examined comprises a set of unreliable machines linked with buffers, and the objective is to resolve the trade-off between minimizing holding costs and maintaining a high service rate. The work analyzes the performance of six important pull production control policies using discrete event simulation and setting the control parameters of each policy through a hybrid Genetic Algorithm (GA). Two types of penalty functions have been explored for constraint handling: A "death penalty" function and an exponential penalty function, which is synthesized using the results of the GA with the "death penalty" function. The latter exhibits superior results. Furthermore, the sensitivity analysis of significant system parameters offers considerable insight to the underlying mechanics of the JIT control policies examined.

Chapter 11 addresses a problem related to the courier environment in which a fleet of vehicles serves a set of customers using a hybrid service policy that includes (a) mandatory and (b) flexible requests (calls). The authors propose a new method to perform assignment of service requests (calls) with some flexibility taking into account expected routes in a multi-period horizon. The problem is solved on a rolling horizon basis in order to address the dynamics of arriving calls. The method is tested through several theoretical examples, as well as in an extensive industrial case, and appears to be superior to current methods used in practice.

Chapter 12 presents two travel time prediction methods that are embedded in a real-time fleet management system applied in fleets that execute urban freight deliveries. The author discusses the prediction results generated by the two methods that use historical and real-time data, respectively. The first method follows the *k-nn* model, which relies on the non-parametric regression method, whereas the second one relies on an interpolation scheme, which is employed during the transmission of real-time traffic data in fixed intervals. The study focuses on exploring the interaction of factors that affect prediction accuracy by modelling both prediction methods. The data employed are provided by real-life scenarios of a freight carrier and the experiments follow a 2-level full factorial design approach.

Standard operational research is now a mature and widely recognized field of applied mathematics and high-level computation. The ever-growing realm of applications and the computing power explosion of the last two decades are driving related research in new exciting directions, continuing to play an important role in modern management engineering. A pioneering position of those real world OR applications holds for supply chain management, a fast growing topic combining computing algorithms either based on discrete mathematics and heuristics, or related to computational intelligence based on evolution, learning and adaptation. To this end, we hope that the present Volume contributes towards the advancement of high quality research in CI solutions for real world OR problems.

As a final note to this introduction , the authors would like to express their sincere appreciation to all authors, contributors and external reviewers of the papers submitted for this edition.

REFERENCES

Engelbrecht, A. P. (2002). *Computational Intelligence: An Introduction*. John Wiley & Sons Ltd.

Abbod, M.F., Linkens, D.A., Mahfouf, M., & Dounias, G. (2002). Survey on the use of Smart and Adaptive Engineering Systems in Medicine. *Artificial Intelligence in Medicine*, *26*(3), 179-209.

Chaib-Draa, B., & Müller, J. (2006), *Multiagent based Supply Chain Management*, Studies in Computational Intelligence, Springer Publications

Chen, K., & Wang, L. (2006). *Trends in Neural Computation* (Studies in Computational Intelligence). Springer Publications

Chen, Z. (2000). *Computational Intelligence for Decision Support.* CRC Press

Churchman, C. W., Ackoff, R. L., & Arnoff, E. L. (1957). *Introduction to Operations Research.* New York: J. Wiley and Sons.

Dorigo, M., & Blum, C. (2005). Ant colony optimization theory: A survey. *Theoretical Computer Science, 344*(2-3), 243-278

Dubois, D., & Prade, H. (1980). *Fuzzy Sets and Systems: Theory and Applications.* London: Academic Press.

Hillier, F. S., & Lieberman, G. J. (2005). *Introduction to Operations Research* (8th . (International) Ed.). Boston: McGraw-Hill.

Holland, J.H. (1975). *Adaptation in Natural and Artificial Systems*. Cambridge, MA: MIT Press.

Jensen P. A., & Bard, J.F. (2003). *Operations Research: Models and Methods*. Chichester, UK: Wiley Press.

Kelly, F. P. (1994). *Probability, Statistics and Optimization, A Tribute to Peter Whittle*. Chichester, UK: Wiley Press.

Koza J. R. (1992). *Genetic Programming – On the Programming of Computers Means of Natural Selection.* Cambridge, MA: MIT Press,

Luenberger, D. G. (1979). *Introduction to dynamic systems.* New York: Wiley Press.

Michalski, R.S., Carbonell, J.G., & Mitchell, T.M. (1983). *Machine Learning: An Artificial Intelligence Approach*. Morgan Kaufmann Press

Mitchell, T.M. (1997). *Machine Learning.* New York: McGraw-Hill.

Negoita, M., Neagu, D., & Palade V. (2005). *Computational Intelligence: Engineering of Hybrid Systems*. Berlin-Heidelberg: Springer-Verlag.

Nilsson, N. (1998). *Artificial Intelligence: A New Synthesis*. Morgan Kaufmann.

Pinney, W. E., & McWilliams, D. B. (1987). *Management Science: An Introduction to Quantitative Analysis for Management*. Harper & Row Press

Pintér, J. D. (2005) *Applied Nonlinear Optimization in Modeling Environments: Using Integrated Modeling and Solver Environments*. Boca Raton, FL: CRC Press.

Haykin, S. (1994). *Neural Networks: A comprehensive foundation*. Prentice Hall

Teodorovic, D. (2008). Swarm intelligence systems for transportation engineering: Principles and applications. *Transportation Research Part C* (Vol. 16, pp. 651-667).

Thompson, G. E. (1982). *Management Science: An Introduction to Modern Quantitative Analysis and Decision Making*. New York: McGraw-Hill.

Voß, S., & Woodruff, D.L. (2006). *Introduction to Computational Optimization Models for Production Planning in a Supply Chain* (2nd ed.). Springer

Williams, H. P. (1999) *Model Building in Mathematical Programming* (4th ed.). New York: Wiley.

Zadeh, L.A. (1965). Fuzzy Sets. *Information Control, 8*(3), 338-353

Zimmermann, H-J., Tselentis, G., Van Someren, M., & Dounias, G. (Eds.). *Advances in Computational Intelligence and Learning: Methods and Applications*. Kluwer Academic Publishing.

Acknowledgment

We would like to thank Mr Joel A. Gamon, Development Editor (Editorial Content Department, IGI Global) for his assistance and support to the whole edition process during the last two years. In addition, our colleagues E. Ferneda (Catholic University of Brasília, Brazil), B. A. Mello (University of Brasília, Brazil), J. D. A. S. Diniz, (University of Brasilia, Brazil), and A. S. Figueiredo (Catholic University of Brasília, Brazil), are greatly acknowledged for contributing work, reviews and opinions for the current edition. Finally, we would like to thank the research staff of the following laboratories of the Department of Financial & Management Engineering, University of the Aegean, for providing all necessary additional reviews to the papers submitted for this book:

- Management & Decision Engineering Laboratory (MDE-Lab)
- Design Operations & Production Systems Laboratory (DEOPSys)
- Intelligent Data Exploration & Analysis Laboratory (IDEAL)

Ioannis Minis
University of the Aegean, Greece

Vasileios Zeimpekis
University of the Aegean, Greece

Georgios Dounias
University of the Aegean, Greece

Nicholas Ampazis
University of the Aegean, Greece

Chapter 1
Nature-Inspired Intelligence in Supply Chain Management: A Review of Selected Methods and Applications

Vassilios Vassiliadis
University of the Aegean, Greece

Georgios Dounias
University of the Aegean, Greece

ABSTRACT

Supply chain management is a vital process for the competitiveness and profitability of companies. Supply chain consists of a large and complex network of components such as suppliers, warehouses, customers etc. which are connected in almost every possible way. Companies' main aim is to optimize the components of these complex networks to their benefit. This constitutes a challenging optimization problem and often, traditional mathematical approaches fail to overcome complexity and to converge to the optimum solution. More robust methods are required sometimes in order to yield to the optimal. The field of artificial intelligence offers a great variety of meta-heuristic techniques which specialize in solving such complex optimization problems, either accurately, or by obtaining a practically useful approximation, even if real time constraints are imposed. The aim of this chapter is to present a survey of the available literature, regarding the use of nature-inspired methodologies in supply chain management problems. Nature-inspired intelligence is a specific branch of artificial intelligence. Its unique characteristic is the algorithmic imitation of real life systems such as ant colonies, flock of birds etc. in order to solve complex problems.

INTRODUCTION

Nowadays, most firms face difficulties in obtaining a competitive advantage over other companies due to the fact that most of their underlying processes have become complex. A remedy to this issue is to adopt the organizational scheme of supply-chains: an international network of external partners such as suppliers, warehouses, distribution centres. A starting point of this functional chain can be considered the collection of raw materials and an

DOI: 10.4018/978-1-61520-633-9.ch001

ending point the preparation of the final product and the delivery to its final destination (customer or any other terminal) (Silva et al. 2002). Logistics is a particular part of this process and deals with the planning, handling and control of the storage of goods between the manufacturing and the consumption point. One crucial challenge for decision makers is to satisfy all customers, using the available transportation fleet, while at the same time minimizing any intermediate costs (storage costs, transportation costs, delivery time etc.). The above problem can get very complex, especially in the case where various real life constraints regarding time, cost, availability etc. are imposed. A general term that characterizes these kinds of problems is the term "scheduling problems" (Silva et al. 2002).

A wide range of methodologies has been used to solve this optimization problem. However, traditional mathematical methods have proven insufficient in tackling the requirements rising from the development of market competition (Silva et al. 2003). Nature-inspired intelligent techniques are considered to be quite efficient in handling NP-hard problems (i.e. optimization problems in which the optimum cannot be found in polynomial time). The main characteristic of these methods is the imitation of the way natural systems function and evolve in order to deal with real-world situations (Vassiliadis and Dounias 2009). For example, natural ant colonies cooperate so as to find high-quality food source, a flock of birds implements a scheme of indirect communication with the aim of finding the optimal direction, etc. Some examples of nature-inspired algorithms are the following:

- *Ant Colony Optimization (ACO)*
- *Particle Swarm Optimization (PSO)*
- *Genetic Algorithms*
- *Genetic Programming*
- *Memetic Algorithms*
- *Artificial Immune Systems*
- *DNA Computing*

All of the above methods have been applied to hard optimization problems. However, literature indicates that only some of them have been applied to the optimization of logistic processes.

The main aim of this chapter is to present a literature review of the application of nature-inspired algorithms in supply chain management. Specifically, the focus is on certain parts of the supply chain, where certain processes need to be optimized such as finding the optimal route for a fleet. Academic research indicates that the use of NI methods is beneficial in dealing with this kind of problems. The contribution of this study is to collect the majority of academic work regarding the application of NI algorithms in logistic processes and to give a clear presentation of the usefulness and applicability of these techniques for future research projects.

The chapter is organized as follows. In section 1, an introduction of this chapter is given. In section 2, the main characteristics of the supply chain management problem are presented. In section 3, some NI algorithms as well as their natural principles are analyzed. In the next section, findings from the literature review are presented. Finally, in section 5, the main conclusions steaming from the review are summarized.

SUPPLY CHAIN MANAGEMENT OPTIMIZATION PROBLEM

Supply chain planning is adopted by more and more modern enterprises in order to upgrade performance. Their main aim is to organize and manage all different partners of this integral process in a coordinated manner so as to fulfil the customers' expectation (Silva et al. 2005). What is more, these different partners operate under different sets of constraints and objectives. However, high interdependency of the various parts of the supply chain system implies that optimization of one part may influence considerably the performance of the remaining parts.

The supply chain is a distributed system comprising of several parallel and independent optimization problems and coherence among different decision makers can be accomplished using a multi-agent based framework, whose constituent agents control multiple procedures. A typical supply chain has at least two parts. The logistic system deals with customers' orders, external supply centres for product components and organization of cross-docking centres. The distribution system deals with the collection and delivery of goods to the final clients.

Due to the way the concept of supply chain has been used by various sources, there is a lack of universal definition. On the contrary, the concept of supply chain has been considered from various points of view. However, an acceptable definition can be found in (Croom et al. 2000), which thoroughly presents an analytical framework for the supply chain process. So, supply chain management deals with materials/supply management from the supply of raw materials to the formation and delivery of the final product, including possible situations of re-use or recycling. Supply chain management focuses on how firms utilize their suppliers' processes, technology and capability to enhance competitive advantage. It can be also considered a management philosophy whose aim is to extend traditional intra–enterprise processes by bringing trading partners together with the common goal of optimization and efficiency (Croom et al. 2000).

In order to shed some light in the basics of supply chain management, it is desirable to present the main functions of a simplified supply chain (Silva et al. 2009). The modelling approach consists of three parts, the logistic, the supplying and the distribution system, namely.

- *Logistic system*: receives orders from customers and places orders to the suppliers as far as the raw materials are concerned. The purchased materials are going to be used in the manufacturing process. At this stage, the main objective is to minimize the tardiness time, i.e. the difference between the completion date and the desired delivery date, regarding the product. However, there are two disturbances. Firstly, suppliers might not respect the delivery date of raw materials. Secondly, clients might ask for delivery dates which are not compatible with the suppliers' services. The logistic problem can be formulated by using the general assignment optimization approach.
- *Supplying system*: consists of a network of different suppliers or manufacturers, each one of which deals with producing the requested product component for the logistic system. In this case, the minimization of the total tardiness time, as defined above, can be considered as the objective function. The supply problem can be thought as a scheduling optimization problem.
- *Distribution system*: delivers the complete products to the corresponding clients. Clients might be described by their geographical location. A simple realistic model of the distribution problem is the vehicle routing problem (or sometimes the travelling salesman problem). This is a minimization problem which considers the transportation cost of the fleet of available vehicles. For this kind of problem, a common constraint is that each customer is visited by one vehicle, and all customers have to be satisfied.

Finally, a simplified diagram is presented in Figure 1, which shows the overall process of supply chain (Silva et al. 2009).

In what follows, the general framework of nature-inspired methodologies is going to be analyzed. Literature indicates that the use of certain nature-inspired intelligent techniques, namely ant colony optimization algorithm (ACO), particle swarm optimization algorithm (PSO) and

Figure 1. A simplified supply chain

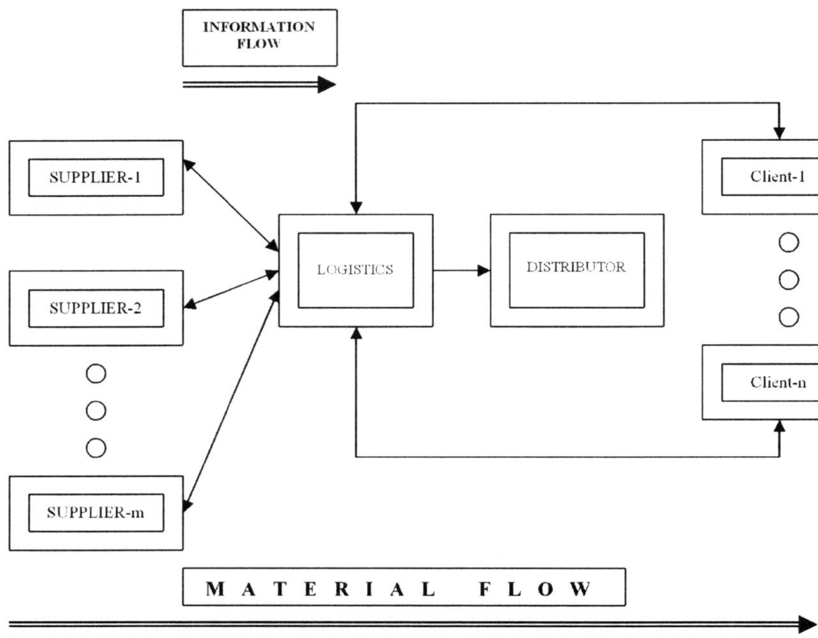

genetic algorithms, yields quite satisfactory results.

NATURE-INSPIRED INTELLIGENCE: GENERAL FRAMEWORK AND CERTAIN TECHNIQUES

Nature-inspired methodologies, which are part of the general field of artificial intelligence, are based on the way natural systems and biological networks function and evolve (Vassiliadis and Dounias 2009). Insect colonies, swarm of birds and of course basic functionalities of the human body have unique characteristics, which are applied in real life situations. For example, ant colonies have a unique searching ability of the space around their nest, a fact of vast importance in the process of finding high-quality food sources. Moreover, when a flock of birds decides to emigrate to a far destination, it has to continuously adjust the parameters of direction and speed. For each member of the swarm, this is achieved by adjusting its position and speed according to the best-so-far member of the population.

A special kind of problems which can be handled by nature-inspired techniques are optimization problems. The goal of an optimization issue is to find the best possible elements x^* from a space set X according to a set of criteria $F = \{f_1, f_2, \ldots, f_n\}$. The possible elements x^* are called decision variables, and the set of criteria F, which are usually expressed as mathematical functions, are called objective functions (Weise 2009). One of the difficult parts of optimization problems is the exploration of the solution space. Sometimes, the solution space, i.e. the space containing values for the decision variables, might be very complex. Furthermore, optimization problems can get very difficult if complex and ambiguous real life constraints are imposed. The supply chain management problem, described above, can be categorized as a complex optimization problem, with many decision variables and real life constraints. Many traditional methodologies fail to converge to the optimum solution. However, nature-inspired algorithms own some unique characteristics which can assist them in searching the solution space efficiently such as parallel exploration ability, exploitation of good solutions already found, indirect communication between artificial agents and implementation of certain search operators in order to converge to better quality solutions.

In what follows, an attempt in briefly presenting the most commonly used nature-inspired algorithms is made. More specifically, the study focuses on the main function and unique characteristics of these methods.

ANT COLONY OPTIMIZATION (ACO) ALGORITHM

ACO algorithms were first introduced by Dorigo in the 1990's (Dorigo et al. 1996). Their main characteristics come from properties of real ant colonies:

- Social behavior of real ants
- Foraging behavior of real ants, i.e. how and can efficiently explore the space around their nest in order to find the shortest path towards high-quality food sources.
- Indirect communication pattern between ants (stigmergy).

The development of ant colony algorithms was inspired by the observation of real ant colonies. When searching for food, ants initially explore the area surrounding their nest in a random way. While they move, they deposit an initial amount of pheromone (chemical component), which can be detected by other members of the colony. As soon as an ant comes up against a food source, it evaluates its quality and quantity and carries some of it back to the nest. During the return trip, based on the evaluation the ant made, it leaves a certain amount of pheromone. These pheromone trails, formed by the entire colony, will eventually guide all ants to the best food source.

Generally, ACO is suitable in solving hard optimization problems by iterating the following steps:

- Candidate solutions are constructed using a pheromone model, which is nothing more than a parameterized probability distribution over the solution space (discrete or continuous).
- The candidate solutions found are used to modify the pheromone values through a pheromone update formula, which is deemed to bias future sampling towards high quality solutions.
- Finally, the pheromone update aims at concentrating the search in regions of the search space containing high quality solutions.

PARTICLE SWARM OPTIMIZATION (PSO) ALGORITHM

The first PSO algorithm was proposed by Kennedy and Eberhart in 1995 (Kennedy and Eberhart 1995). It is considered a biologically inspired algorithm which models the social dynamics of bird flocking. Some of its basic properties are the following:

- Natural metaphor
- Stochastic move
- Adaptivity
- Positive feedback

The main function of a flock of real birds is that they fly in large swarms in a synchronous manner, change direction suddenly, scatter and regroup iteratively, and finally perch on a target. The PSO technique facilitates simple rules simulating bird flocking and serves as an optimizer tool. The general principles of the PSO algorithm are:

- *Particle representation*: each particle in the PSO is a candidate solution to the underlying problem and moves iteratively in the solution space.
- *Swarm*: PSO explores the solution space by flying in large number of particles
- *Personal best experience and swarm's best experience*: one unique characteristic of the algorithm, it stores the best position visited so far by each particle. Particularly, each particle remembers the best position among those it has visited and the best position by its neighbors.
- *Particle movement*: the swarm of particles flies iteratively about the solution space until the stopping criterion is met.
- *Stopping criterion*: the algorithm is terminated with a maximal number of iterations or if the best particle position of the entire swarm cannot be improved further after a sufficiently large number of iterations.

GENETIC ALGORITHMS (GA)

Genetic algorithms were firstly introduced by Holland back in the mid 70's (Holland 1975). They are mainly inspired by the concept of evolution and improvement of the descendants in a population. The solution to a given problem is represented in the form of strings called chromosomes. Each string consists of a set of elements called genes, which represent the decision variables of the optimization process.

The main steps of the genetic algorithm are the following:

- A random population of solutions-chromosomes is produced.
- The fitness value of each chromosome corresponds to its value of objective function.
- To simulate natural survival of the fittest, which is the main idea behind the genetic algorithms, best chromosomes exchange information to produce offspring for the next generation. The two operators that are used in the information exchange among the chromosomes are crossover and mutation.
- The offspring solutions are then evaluated and used to evolve the population only if they provide better solutions.
- The process is continued for a large number of generations so as to obtain a best-fit solution.

GENETIC PROGRAMMING (GP)

The framework of Genetic Programming (GP) was introduced by Koza (Koza, 1990). Genetic Programming is a domain independent, problem-solving approach in which computer programs are evolved to find solutions to several real-world problems. The solution strategy is based on the Darwinian principle of "survival of the fittest" (Sivanandam & Deepa, 2007). Specifically, GP is combining biologically inspired operators like mutation and crossover in a quite unique way.

The main characteristics of GP are the following (Sivanandam & Deepa, 2007):

- *Representation*: Genetic Programming overtly conducts its search for a solution to the given problem in program space.
- *Role of point-to-point transformations in the search*: Genetic programming conducts its search by transforming a set of points into another set of points.
- *Role of hill climbing in the search*: Genetic Programming allocates a certain number of trials, in a principled way, to choices that are known to be inferior.

- *Role of determinism in the search*: Genetic Programming conducts its search probabilistically.

DNA COMPUTING

DNA Computing was first introduced by Adleman (Adleman 1994) and it is a relatively new computing paradigm that proposes using molecular biology tools to solve mathematical problems. The key idea is that data can be encoded in DNA strands, while molecular biology laboratory techniques that involve manipulation of DNA strands in test tubes can be used to imitate arithmetical and logical operations.

Some unique characteristics of DNA computing are the following (Ezziane 2007):

- High memory capacity.
- Massive parallelism.
- Acceptable power requirements.

ARTIFICIAL IMMUNE SYSTEMS (AIS)

Artificial Immune Systems (AIS) were first introduced in 1986 (Farmer et al. 1986). AIS are techniques based on the features of antigen-antibody bindings in the immune system. In the natural immune system, local binding of immune cells and molecules to antigenic peptides is based generally on the behavior of surface proteins. Particularly, immune cells contain proteins on their receptors, and apparently, these proteins play the key role both in immune response and recognition process (Takaranov & Dasgupta 2000).

AIS use four main properties from natural immune systems (Bouckere et al. 2004):

- *Detection*: recognition of chemical components between pathogen fragments and receptors on the surface of the lymphocyte occurs in an immune system.
- *Diversity*: detection in the immune system is related to non-self elements of the organism, thus the immune system must have diverse receptors to ensure that at least some of the lymphocytes will react to the pathogenic element.
- *Learning*: the immune system must be capable of detecting as quickly as possible the pathogen and eliminating it. So, it includes a principle which allows lymphocytes to learn and adapt themselves to specific foreign protein structures, and to "remember" these structures as soon as possible when needed.
- *Tolerance*: the molecules that mark a cell as a self gene are contained in the chromosome sections also known as Major Histocompatibility Complex.

So far, the main framework of the nature-inspired intelligence has been presented. Moreover, some basic algorithms, which are mostly used in supply chain management problem, are roughly mentioned. In the following section, the main results of the literature review are presented and analyzed.

BASIC LITERATURE REVIEW AND FINDINGS

In this part, the main findings from the literature review related to nature –inspired intelligence in supply chain, are presented and analyzed. The search strategy followed for this literature survey is also described.

Search Strategy and Main Aim of the Survey

The survey of the literature presented in this chapter might not be considered exhaustive however it provides a representative picture of the existing trends in the application of NI algorithms in supply chain management. The works selected were mainly acquired by web databases such as the ScienceDirect, the SpringerLink, the IEEE and the EmeraldLibrary.

Specifically, the keywords which guided our search were the following, matched properly in meaningful combinations of two or three, with appropriate use of AND/OR logical operators:

{ACO AND Supply AND chain} OR {PSO AND supply AND chain} OR

{nature AND inspired AND intelligence AND supply AND chain} OR

{ant AND colony AND TSP} OR {particle AND swarm AND TSP} OR

{ant AND colony AND VRP} OR {particle AND swarm AND VRP} OR {genetic AND algorithm AND supply AND chain} OR {genetic AND algorithm AND [TSP OR VRP]} OR {ant AND colony AND inventory AND management} OR {particle AND swarm AND inventory AND management} OR {artificial AND immune AND systems AND inventory AND management} OR {genetic AND algorithm AND inventory AND management} OR {genetic AND algorithm AND bullwhip AND effect} OR {genetic AND programming AND supply AND chain AND management}

The main motives for performing this survey were:

- The large number of publications concerning the application of NI algorithms in supply chain management.
- Supply chain management problems such as, TSP, VRP, logistic processes, job scheduling etc. are considered as NP-hard optimization problems, especially in the case where a lot of constraints are imposed. Nature–inspired intelligent algorithms have some unique characteristics, which can assist them in searching the solution space in a fast and efficient manner.
- Nature-inspired intelligent techniques seem to perform highly efficient, both in computational time and identification of the optimal solution, opposed to traditional methodologies, e.g. from the field of operational research (mathematical programming methodologies).

BASIC RESULTS AND FINDINGS FROM LITERATURE REVIEW

In this part of the study, the basic findings of the literature survey are presented. It has to be noticed again, that this literature review is by no means exhaustive. However, it succeeds in giving a better insight in the applicability of NII techniques in supply chain management issues, which can prove very assisting to the potential researchers of this field. The bibliographical results are summarized in two tables.

Table 1 summarizes those publications related to NII algorithms which are presented in this chapter, based on a classification by subject (i.e. specific category of NII approaches implemented) and date published, while Table 2 is a digest of the nature-inspired application papers shown in this work classified by subject and task (i.e. specific content of research in the domain of supply chain management application).

In Table 1, it can be observed that the use of NII techniques in supply chain management performed an increase in the last 4-5 years. It seems that an increasing number of research groups explore further the efficiency and applicability of NII algorithms in logistic processes. What is more, a large number of works have dealt particularly with the application of genetic algorithms and ant colony optimization techniques in this problem. The searching ability of these algorithms, especially in the case of discrete solution space problems, proved to be quite interesting. Another fact that is worth mentioning is the increase of the number of publications of PSO algorithms in 2009. Finally, there is a considerable number of publications concerning the application of other methodologies such as genetic programming, evolutionary strategies, artificial immune systems,

Table 1. Publications referring to applications of NII in supply chain issues by subject and date

	≤1996	1997	1998	1999	2000	2001	2002	2003	2004	2005	2006	2007	2008	≥2009	Total
ACO	-	1	-	1	-	-	2	4	7	5	10	13	8	12	63
PSO	-	-	-	-	-	-	-	-	-	-	2	8	10	15	35
GA/MA	3	-	3	2	2	4	7	4	3	7	12	14	14	7	82
Other	1	2	2	-	1	-	4	-	7	4	7	6	11	2	47
Total	4	3	5	3	3	4	13	8	17	16	31	41	43	26	

bee-colony optimization algorithms, grammatical programming etc. in the field of supply chain management.

Findings from Table 2 indicate a considerable interest in applying NII techniques, especially ACO, to the traveling salesman (TSP) and vehicle routing (VRP) problem. These kinds of problems refer to the distribution part of the general supply chain management problem, which can be considered as a complex optimization problem, mainly with a discrete solution space (customers and other clients). ACO algorithms specialize in such routing problems, where the aim lies in finding the shortest path. On the other hand methodologies such as genetic algorithms, genetic programming, evolutionary strategies, artificial immune systems etc. are properly applied to other areas of supply chain management such as cost minimization/management, managing the bullwhip effect, inventory control (warehouse management), which are mainly optimization problems. However, the objective function in these kinds of problems refers to other managerial issues other than minimizing certain paths in a route.

To sum up the findings of the literature review, ACO algorithms have been vastly used to this area of expertise, especially in various formulations of the TSP problem. Another important methodology that has been drawn interest from the academia in the last years is genetic algorithm. Other methodologies such as PSO, genetic programming etc. have been also applied in various domains of the supply chain management problem. As far as the specific application domain is concerned, traveling salesman and vehicle routing problems have been dealt by ACO-based techniques, whereas general supply chain management problems have been tackled by genetic-based methodologies.

APPLICATIONS OF ACO ALGORITHMS ON SUPPLY CHAIN MANAGEMENT PROBLEMS

Literature survey indicated that many studies have been done concerning the application of the ACO metaheuristic in supply chain management. General supply chain management problems refer

Table 2. Publications related to NII techniques, summarized by subject and task

	TSP	VRP	System design / scheduling	Supply chain management (general)	Total
ACO	15	27	8	12	62
PSO	5	5	9	16	35
GA / MA	21	17	10	32	80
Other	5	9	10	27	51
Total	46	58	37	87	

to all three components of the supply chain, i.e. logistics, supply and distribution. In (Srinivas et al. 2005), a variation of ACO, namely an evolutionary cooperative multi ACO algorithm, is used to efficiently solve the balanced allocation problem. The aim is to minimize the workload disparities among various distribution centers with a goal of minimizing the total shipping cost. The proposed algorithm performs better than a genetic algorithm. In (Wang, H. S. 2009), the study concentrates in designing a defective supply chain network system, i.e. supply chain system with losses in production lines. A germane mathematical model is developed for solving this problem. However, due to the high complexity of the problem in hand, and in order to find a near-optimal solution with great speed, ant colony optimization metaheuristic is proposed. Results indicate that ant colony algorithm yields satisfactory results comparing to those of the proposed mathematical model. In (Silva et al. 2005), the application of a distribution-based ACO algorithm is presented so as to manage all components of a supply chain in an efficiency way. Finally, in (Silva et al. 2008) an algorithmic solution, based on Ant Systems metaheuristic, is proposed for an industrial-inventory problem in a steel continuous-casting plant. The aim of this problem is to find the most profitable production schedule in steel billets. However, two real-time constraints are imposed: (a) parameters of the finite-capacity of the productive system, (b) the make-to-order production environment, which is a phase similarly to the maturing in food production. Results indicate that the proposed algorithmic approach may provide good solutions in acceptable computation times, thus fulfilling the industrial needs. Other findings from this literature show the efficiency of ACO algorithm in various problems of the supply chain management such as scheduling and system design.

However, the majority of studies concern the application of ACO metaheuristic in traveling salesman and vehicle routing problems, which can be formulated as optimization problems. This component of the supply chain is considered central both by academia and enterprises because it deals with the efficient delivery of goods and services to final customers and customer satisfaction. An optimized management of the distribution system may enhance the profitability of the company. What is more, these kinds of problems contain many real-time constraints, due to the fact that it is related to real–life situations.

In (Li, X. and Tian 2006), an ant colony optimization algorithm is used for the traveling salesman problem. The traveling salesman problem can be stated in a simple manner as follows. A salesman has to visit n cities (nodes). In a single tour he visits one city just once, and finishes up where he started. One of his basic aims is to find the optimal route in which he visits all cities in a way that minimizes the distance travelled. Results indicate that the ACO metaheuristic performs very well. However, in (Cheng, C. and Mao 2007), a specific variation of the TSP problem is studied, i.e. the traveling salesman problem with time windows, which involves finding the minimum cost tour in which all cities are visited exactly once within their requested time windows. ACO algorithm is used to solve this NP-hard problem. Two local heuristic rules are used to manage the time-window constraints. The numerical results obtained for a series of benchmark problem instances verifies the efficiency of ACO. In (Chitty and Hernadez 2004), the dynamic vehicle routing problem is studied. The vehicle routing problem consists in the determination of the optimal set of routes to serve a given set of customers using a fixed fleet of vehicles. In dynamic vehicle routing problem, the time needed to traverse each city is uncertain. This problem can be expressed as a bi-criterion optimization with the mutually exclusive aims of minimizing both the total mean transit time and the total variance in transit time. A hybrid scheme, combining ACO and pareto fronts, is used to solve this combinatorial problem. Results are quite promising and show that the new technique can yield better quality solutions. In (Pellegrini et al. 2007), two variants of the ACO algorithm are used to solve the rich vehicle routing problem, which is characterized by the presence of multiple time windows, the availability of different types of vehicles, the requirement of multiple visits to some customers and the limitation of the duration of each sub-tour. The objective of this problem is twofold: the first one is the minimization of the number of vehicles used, and the second one is the minimization of the total time required by the sub-tours. The two variants of the ACO meta-heuristic are: the ant colony system and the Max-Min system. Result indicate that the two NII techniques very efficient and appear satisfactory with respect to the ones achieved by the firm.

APPLICATIONS OF GA ALGORITHMS ON SUPPLY CHAIN MANAGEMENT PROBLEMS

Genetic algorithms are another class of intelligent meta-heuristic techniques, which have been vastly implemented in supply chain management applications. As it can be shown from Table 2, above, the majority of works refer to the distribution part of the supply chain, i.e. TSP and VRP. In (Baker and Ayechew 2003), a genetic algorithm is applied to the basic vehicle routing problem, in which customers of known demand are supplied from a single depot. Vehicles are subject to a weight limit and, in some cases, to a limit on the distance travelled. Also, only one vehicle is allowed to supply each customer. As it can be seen from the formulation of the problem, this is one of the simplest cases in VRP. Simulations' results from tabu search and simulation annealing have been used as benchmark. Results from the study indicate that the genetic algorithm is quite competitive compared to the benchmark methods in terms of solution time and quality. In (Tan, K.C. and Chew 2006), a hybrid multi-objective evolutionary algorithm, which incorporates various heuristics for local exploitation, is proposed for solving a vehicle routing problem with time windows. This approach is featured with specialized genetic operators and variable-length chromosome representation to accommodate the optimization process of the vehicle routing problem. Results show that the proposed hybrid scheme improves the routing solutions in many aspects, such as lower routing cost etc. The proposed algorithmic scheme yields better solution compared to those published in literature, for a specific data set. In (Jeong et al. 2002), a computerized system for implementing the forecasting activities required in a supply chain management system is presented. For building the generic forecasting model, a linear causal forecasting model is proposed and its coefficients are efficiently determined using the proposed genetic algorithms, canonical genetic algorithms and guided genetic algorithms. Results obtained from two case studies show that the proposed guided genetic algorithm provides the best forecasting accuracy and greatly outperforms the regression analysis and canonical genetic algorithm methods. In (Ip et al. 2003) a risk-based partner selection problem is described and formulated where risk of failure, due date and the precedence of sub-project are considered. To solve this problem, a rule-based genetic algorithm with embedded project scheduling is applied. What is more, fuzzy factors-based rules are proposed in order to modify the partner selection according to different situations.

In (Bontoux et al. 2009), a memetic algorithm is used for solving the generalized TSP. In the generalized TSP, the set of cities is divided into mutually exclusive clusters and the objective consists in visiting each cluster exactly once in the tour, while minimizing the sum of the routing costs. Memetic algorithms are genetic algorithms embedded with local search operators. The proposed memetic operator applies a crossover procedure that uses a large neighborhood search. This algorithm is compared with other algorithms on a set of 54 test problems from the literature with a complexity of up to 217 clusters and 1084 cities. The proposed algorithmic scheme yield better solutions both in terms of quality and computational time efficiency. In (Liu, S. et al. 2009), a genetic algorithm is used to solve a mix vehicle routing problem, in which the fleet is heterogeneous and its composition is to be determined. Results from simulations on a set of twenty benchmark problems show that the algorithmic approach reaches the best-known solution in 14 cases and also find one new best solution. In (Liu, F. and Zeng 2009), an improved genetic algorithm with reinforcement mutation is used to solve the TSP. The core of this technique lies in the use of heterogeneous pairing selection instead of random pairing selection and the construction of a reinforcement learning mutation operator. The experimental results on small and large size TSP problems have shown that the proposed algorithm could almost get optimal tour every time in reasonable time and thus outperformed the known genetic algorithms in the quality of solutions and the running time.

APPLICATIONS OF PSO ALGORITHMS ON SUPPLY CHAIN MANAGEMENT PROBLEMS

PSO algorithms have not been widely applied in supply chain problems, as the literature survey indicates. However, an increasing interest seems to rise from the academic field regarding the use of PSO algorithms for these kinds of problems in the last 2-3 years.

In (Guner and Sevkli 2008), a PSO algorithm for solving discrete optimization problems is employed for the uncapacitated facility location problem which is considered as hard combinatorial optimization problem. Three metaheuristics, namely continuous particle swarm optimization, genetic algorithm and evolutionary simulated annealing, were used for comparison reasons. All algorithms were tested to the same benchmark suites collected from OR-library. Results from the proposed algorithm were slightly better than the benchmark methods. In (Onut et. al. 2008), an interest application concerning warehouse operation and management is studied. Generally, warehouse layout design models attempt to optimize different objectives such as the orientation of storage racks, the allocation of space among competitive uses, the number of cranes, the overall configuration of the facility etc. In this study, a distribution-type warehouse is considered that various type products are collected from different suppliers for storing in the warehouse for a determined period and for delivery to different customers. The aim is to design a multiple-level warehouse self configuration which minimizes the annual carrying costs. This is a NP-hard optimization problem. A particle swarm optimization algorithm is proposed for determining the optimal layout.

In (Bachlaus et al. 2008), the objective is to design a multi-echelon supply chain network considering agility as the key criterion. Specifically, five echelons of supply chains are considered including suppliers, plants, distribution centers, cross-docks and customer zones. This is a multi-objective optimization problem with the specific aim to minimize the cost (fixed and variable) and maximize the plant flexibility and volume flexibility. In order to solve this problem, a hybrid Taguchi-particle swarm optimization algorithm is proposed that incorporates the characteristics of statistical design of experiments and random search techniques. The main idea is to integrate the fundamentals of Taguchi method in the PSO meta-heuristic so as to minimize the effect of the causes of variations. Results from extensive simulations reveal that the proposed solution methodology is an effective approach to solve the underlying problem. In (Domoto et al. 2007) a model of mass customization about production and inventory planning is proposed. This model can be used when demand quantity is an unknown parameter of the problem. Particle Swarm Optimization algorithm is applied to this problem.

In (Marinakis and Marinaki 2009), a hybrid scheme combining a genetic and a particle swarm optimization algorithm for the vehicle routing problem is proposed. More specifically, the evolution of each individual solution of the total population, which consists of the parents and the offspring, is realized with the use of a particle swarm optimizer where each of them has to improve its physical movement following the basic principles of PSO until the point it obtains the requirements to be selected as a parent. This idea was applied to two instances of the vehicle routing problem and the results were satisfactory. In (Tasgetiren et al. 2007), a discrete particle swarm optimization algorithm is used to solve the generalized traveling salesman problem where the set of nodes is divided into clusters and the objective is to minimize the total cost of the tour. The proposed PSO algorithm is hybridized with a local search mechanism, a variable neighborhood descend algorithm, to further improve the solution quality. This algorithmic scheme was tested on a set of benchmark instances with symmetric distances up to 442 nodes from the literature. Computational results are quite promising. In (Ai and Kachitvichyanukul 2009), a formulation of the vehicle routing problem with simultaneously pickup and deliver and a particle swarm optimization algorithm to solve it, is proposed. The problem formulation is a generalization of three existing VRP formulations and the metaheuristic technique is base on a PSO algorithm with multiple social structures. The test set consists of three benchmark data sets available from the literature. Computational results show that the proposed method is competitive with other published results for solving the same problem. What is more, some new best known solutions of the benchmark problem are also found.

APPLICATIONS OF OTHER NII TECHNIQUES ON SUPPLY CHAIN PROBLEMS

Apart from the presented studies, concerning the implementation of ACO, PSO and Genetic algorithms in supply chain management issues, there exist a considerable amount of studies in which other NII algorithms such as bee colony optimization and artificial immune system are applied. In (Masutti and Castro 2008), hybrid algorithmic technique combining neural networks and artificial immune system is used to solve the capacitated vehicle routing problem. The main characteristic of this combinatorial optimization problem is that each vehicle has a restriction in its capacity. Also, the basic characteristics of the artificial immune system come from the way the human immune system operates in order to face a potential hostile organism. The set of tests conducted with the proposed approach indicates a good performance of the algorithm when compared with similar works from the literature and the known best solutions available. In (Lee, J. Y. et al. 2004), a DNA encoding method for the representation of numerical values and a biased molecular algorithm based on the thermodynamic properties of DNA is introduced. DNA strands are designed to encode real values by variation of their melting temperature. The thermodynamic properties of DNA are used for effective local search of optimal solutions using biochemical techniques such as denaturation temperature gradient polymerase chain reaction and temperature gradient gel electrophoresis. The proposed scheme is applied to the traveling salesman problem. The main contribution of this study is to extend the capability of DNA computing to solve solving numerical optimization problems. In (Phelan and McGarraghy 2007) a relatively new evolutionary algorithm in computer science, grammatical evolution, is introduced. This method is applied in a problem of supply chain dynamics and bullwhip mitigation. As a proof of concept experiments are conducted to derive optimal ordering policies for agents in multi-tier supply chain. Results indicate that the proposed grammatical evolution algorithm successfully discovers the optimal ordering policies similar to the genetic algorithm approach, and in some cases outperforms this benchmark. In (Fogel 1993), an evolutionary programming algorithm is applied to selected travelling salesman problems. In three test cases, solutions that are equal to or better than previously known best routings were discovered. What is more, in a 1000-city problem, the best evolved routing is about 5% longer than the expected optimum. In (Kleinau and Thonemann 2004) an alternative approach for solving inventory-control problems that is based on genetic programming is proposed. Genetic programming is an optimization method that applies the principles of natural evolution to optimization problems. Inventory control determines which quantity of a product should be ordered when to achieve some objective, such as minimizing cost. In (Kumar et al. 2006) a new hybrid evolutionary algorithm named endosymbiotic-psychoclonal algorithm is proposed to decide what and how much to stock as a semi-product in inventory. In the proposed theory, the ability of previously proposed psychoclonal algorithms to exploit the search space has been increased by making antibodies and antigen more co-operative interacting species. The efficacy of the proposed algorithm has been tested on randomly generated datasets and the results compared with other evolutionary algorithms such as genetic algorithms (GA) and simulated annealing (SA). The comparison of ESPC with GA and SA proves the superiority of the proposed algorithm both in terms of quality of the solution obtained and convergence time required to reach the optimal/near optimal value of the solution.

CONCLUSION

In this section, basic findings, drawn from the literature survey, are briefly summarized. The aim of this chapter was to outline the significance of NII techniques in the field of supply chain management, as well as the applicability of NII algorithms in this kind of problems. The unique attributes of natural systems can be used to solve difficult real-life problems, such as system design issues, job scheduling and vehicle routing problems.

Regarding the applicability of NII algorithms in supply chain management problems, the following could be stated. Firstly, supply chain management problems are divided into three major categories: (a) logistic, (b) supply and (c) distribution problems. Each of these categories has some unique real-life characteristics, which make them complex. Findings from the literature have shown that traditional mathematical techniques as well as simple heuristic rules are unable to solve these problems, especially in the case where demanding goals and real-life complex constraints are imposed. However, NII techniques have shown very good performance in dealing with these problems. In some cases new best solutions are found by these techniques. The nature of these metaheuristic algorithms can prove very efficient in dealing with complex formulations of supply chain management problems, handling in an effective way multiple objectives and various rigid constraints. One clear point from the literature is that the application of NII techniques focuses on difficult optimization problems such as the TSP and VRP. A lot of studies deal with various formulations of these two problems and how intelligent algorithms can solve them. Another important point is the efficiency of NII methodologies such as genetic algorithms, genetic programming and other to various supply chain management issues like cost and inventory management.

As far as the NII techniques are concerned, ACO and GA algorithms are vastly used. The main attributes of these intelligent metaheuristics may deal with difficult optimization problems very efficiently. Many studies are based on the application of these algorithms. However, there is an increasing interest, mainly in the last years, in using other NII techniques, such as PSO, AIS and DNA Computing in solving problems from the domain of supply chain management. As mentioned above, the main focus of these algorithms is on distribution problems, i.e. finding the optimal route, using the available vehicle fleet, so as to satisfy all customers under various constraints. Finally, there are few studies which combine characteristics from two or more intelligent techniques (hybrid schemes) in order to solve the aforementioned problems. Results are quite promising.

Future research should attempt hybrid intelligent approaches in order to effectively combine advantages of different methods in complex supply chain management problems. Generally, the use of NII algorithms should be encouraged by all means, due to the fact that intelligent approaches often yield high quality solutions in a reasonable time i.e. produce interesting solutions in terms of profitability and efficiency.

REFERENCES

Abdelmaguid, T. F., & Dessouky, M. M. (2006). A genetic algorithm approach to the integrated inventory-distribution problem. *International Journal of Production Research, 44*(21), 4445–4464. doi:10.1080/00207540600597138

Adachi, N., & Matsuo, K. (2006). Ecological dynamics under different selection rules in distributed and iterated prisoner's dilemma game. In *Parallel Problem Solving from Nature* (*Vol. 496*, pp. 387–394). Berlin, Heidelberg: Springer. doi:10.1007/BFb0029780

Adleman, L. M. (1994). Molecular computation of solutions to combinatorial problems. *Journal of Science, 266*(5187), 1021–1024. doi:10.1126/science.7973651

Agapitos, A., Dyson, M., Kovalchuk, J., & Lucas, S. M. (2008). On the genetic programming of time-series predictors for supply chain management. In *Proceedings of the 10th annual conference on Genetic and evolutionary computation* (pp. 1163-1170).

Ai, T. J., & Kachitvichyanukul, V. (2009). A particle swarm optimization for the vehicle routing problem with simultaneous pickup and delivery. *Computers & Operations Research, 36*, 1693–1702. doi:10.1016/j.cor.2008.04.003

Ai, T. J., & Kachitvichyanukul, V. (2009). Particle swarm optimization and two solution representations for solving the capacitated vehicle routing problem. *Computers & Operations Research, 56*, 380–387.

Alba, E., & Dorronsoro, B. (2008). A hybrid cellular genetic algorithm for the capacitated vehicle routing problem. In *Engineering Evolutionary Intelligent Systems* (pp. 379–422). Berlin, Heidelberg: Springer. doi:10.1007/978-3-540-75396-4_14

Aliev, R. A., Fazlollahi, B., Guirimov, B. G., & Alien, R. R. (2007). Fuzzy-genetic approach to aggregate production-distribution planning in supply chain management. *Information Sciences, 177*(20), 4241–4255. doi:10.1016/j.ins.2007.04.012

Altiparmak, F., Gen, M., Lin, L., & Karaoglan, I. (2009). A steady-state genetic algorithm for multi-product supply chain network design. *Computers & Industrial Engineering, 56*(2), 521–537. doi:10.1016/j.cie.2007.05.012

Altiparmak, F., Gen, M., Lin, L., & Paksoy, T. (2006). A genetic algorithm approach for multi-objective optimization of supply chain networks. *Computers & Industrial Engineering, 51*(1), 196–215. doi:10.1016/j.cie.2006.07.011

Amodeo, L., Prins, C., & Sanchez, D. R. (2009). Comparison of metaheuristic approaches for multi – objective simulation – based optimization in supply chain inventory management. In *Applications of Evolutionary Computing* (Vol. 5484, pp. 798-807).

Arora, V., Chan, F. T. S. & Tiwari, M. K. (2009). An integrated approach for logistic and vendor managed inventory in supply chain. *Expert Systems with Applications.*

Bachlaus, M., Pandey, M. K., Mahajan, C., Shankar, R., & Tiwari, M. K. (2008). Designing an integrated multi–echelon agile supply chain network: a hybrid tagushi – particle swarm optimization approach. *Journal of Intelligent Manufacturing, 19*, 747–761. doi:10.1007/s10845-008-0125-1

Baker, B. M., & Ayechew, M. A. (2003). A genetic algorithm for the vehicle routing problem. *Computers & Operations Research, 30*, 787–800. doi:10.1016/S0305-0548(02)00051-5

Banerjee, S., Dangayach, G. S., Mukherjee, S. K., & Mohanti, P. K. (2008). Modeling Process and Supply Chain Scheduling Using Hybrid Meta – heuristics. In *Metaheuristics for Scheduling in Industrial and Manufacturing Applications* (pp. 277–300). Berlin, Heidelberg: Springer. doi:10.1007/978-3-540-78985-7_11

Baraglia, R., Hidalgo, J. I., & Perego, R. (2001). A parallel hybrid heuristic for the TSP. In *Applications of Evolutionary Computing* (*Vol. 2037*, pp. 193–202). Berlin, Heidelberg: Springer. doi:10.1007/3-540-45365-2_20

Bashiri, M. & Tabrizi, M. M. (2009). Supply chain design: a holistic approach. *Expert Systems with Applications.*

Baykasoglu, A., Dereli, T., & Sabuncu, I. (2006). An ant colony algorithm for solving budget constrained and unconstrained dynamic facility layout problems. *Omega: the International Journal of Management Science, 34*, 385–396. doi:10.1016/j.omega.2004.12.001

Bell, J. E., & McMullen, P. R. (2004). Ant colony optimization techniques for the vehicle routing problem. *Advanced Engineering Informatics, 18*, 41–48. doi:10.1016/j.aei.2004.07.001

Bianchi, L., Gambardella, L. M., & Dorigo, M. (2002). An ant colony optimization approach to the probabilistic traveling salesman problem. In *Proceedings of the PPSN – VII, 7th International Conference on Parallel Problem Solving from Nature* (pp. 883-892).

Bontoux, B., Antigues, C. & Feillet, D. 2009, 'A memetic algorithm with a large neighborhood crossover operator for the generalized traveling salesman problem', *Computers & Operations Research.*

Boudia, M., Prins, C., & Reghioui, M. (2007). An effective memetic algorithm with population management for the split delivery vehicle routing problem. In *Hybrid Metaheuristcs* (*Vol. 4771*, pp. 16–30). Berlin, Heidelberg: Springer. doi:10.1007/978-3-540-75514-2_2

Bouhafs, L., Hajjam, A., & Koukam, A. (2006). A combination of simulated annealing and ant colony system for the capacitated location – routing problem. In *Knowledge-Based Intelligent Information and Engineering Systems* (pp. 409–416). Berlin, Heidelberg: Springer. doi:10.1007/11892960_50

Boukerche, A., Juca, K. R. L., Sobral, J. B., & Notare, M. S. M. A. (2004). An artificial immune based intrusion detection model for computer and telecommunication systems. *Parallel Computing, 30*, 629–646. doi:10.1016/j.parco.2003.12.008

Boysen, N., Fliender, M., & Scholl, A. (2007). Sequencing mixed-model assembly lines to minimize part inventory cost', in *OR Spectrum, 30*(3), 611-633.

Branke, J., & Guntsch, M. (2003). New ideas for applying ant colony optimization to the probabilistic TSP. In *Applications of Evolutionary Computing* (*Vol. 2611*, pp. 127–134). Berlin, Heidelberg: Springer. doi:10.1007/3-540-36605-9_16

Branke, J., & Guntsch, M. (2004). Solving the probabilistic TSP with ant colony optimization. *Journal of Mathematical Modelling and Algorithms, 3*, 403–425. doi:10.1023/B:JMMA.0000049380.86987.d4

Braysy, O., Dullaert, W., & Gendreau, M. (2004). Evolutionary algorithms for the vehicle routing problem with time windows. *Journal of Heuristics, 10*, 587–611. doi:10.1007/s10732-005-5431-6

Bullnheimer, B., Hartl, R. F., & Strauss, C. (1999). An improved ant system algorithm for the vehicle routing problem. *Annals of Operations Research, 89*, 319–328. doi:10.1023/A:1018940026670

Buriol, L., & Franca, P. M. (2004). A new memetic algorithm for the asymmetric traveling salesman problem. *Journal of Heuristics, 10*, 483–506. doi:10.1023/B:HEUR.0000045321.59202.52

Caldeira, J., Azevedo, R., Silva, C. A., & Sousa, M. C. (2007). Beam – ACO Distributed Optimization Applied to Supply – Chain Management. In *Foundations of Fuzzy Logic and Soft Computing* (*Vol. 4529*, pp. 799–809). Berlin, Heidelberg: Springer. doi:10.1007/978-3-540-72950-1_78

Cao, Q., & Leggio, K. B. (2008). Alleviating the bullwhip effect in supply chain management using the multi-agent approach: an empirical study. *International Journal of Computer Applications in Technology, 31*(3-4), 225–237. doi:10.1504/IJCAT.2008.018159

Carter, A. E., & Ragsdale, C. T. (2006). A new approach to solving the multiple traveling salesperson problem using genetic algorithms. *European Journal of Operational Research, 175*, 246–257. doi:10.1016/j.ejor.2005.04.027

Chan, C. C. H., Cheng, C. B., & Huang, S. W. (2006). Formulating ordering policies in a supply chain by genetic algorithm. *International Journal of Modelling and Simulation, 26*(2), 129–136. doi:10.2316/Journal.205.2006.2.205-4158

Chan, C. K., Cheung, B. K. S., & Langevin, A. (2003). Solving the multi-buyer joint replenishment problem with a modified genetic algorithm. *Transportation Research Part B: Methodological, 37*(3), 291–299. doi:10.1016/S0191-2615(02)00015-2

Chan, F. T. S., Kumar, V., & Mishra, N. (2007). A CMPSO algorithm based approach to solve the multi – plant supply chain problem. In *Focus on Ant and Particle Swarm Optimization* (p. 532). Australia: Itech Education and Publishing.

Chandrasekaran, C., Chandrasekharan, R., Krishnaian, O. V. C., & Hanumanna, D. (2007). Metaheuristics for solving economic lot scheduling problems (ELSP) using time-varying lot-sizes approach. *European Journal of Industrial Engineering, 1*(2), 152–181. doi:10.1504/EJIE.2007.014107

Chang, P. C., Huang, W. H. & Ting, C. J. (2009). Dynamic diversity control in genetic algorithm for mining unsearched solution space in TSP problems. *Expert Systems with Applications*

Chang, Y. H. (in press). Adopting co-evolution and constraint-satisfaction concept on genetic algorithms to solve supply chain network design problems. *Expert Systems with Applications*.

Chatterjee, S., Carrera, C., & Lynch, L. A. (1996). Genetic algorithms and traveling salesman problems. *European Journal of Operational Research, 93*, 490–510. doi:10.1016/0377-2217(95)00077-1

Chen, C. H., Ting, C. J., & Chang, P. C. (2005). Applying a hybrid ant colony system to the vehicle routing problem. In *Computational Science and Its Applications-ICCSA 2005* (*Vol. 3483*, pp. 417–426). Berlin, Heidelberg: Springer.

Chen, S. H., & Ni, C. C. (1999). Using Genetic Algorithms to Simulate the Evolution of an Oligopoly Game. In *Simulated Evolution and Learning* (Vol. 1585, pp. 293-300).

Cheng, C. B., & Mao, C. P. (2007). A modified ant colony system for solving the traveling salesman problem with time windows. *Mathematical and Computer Modelling, 46*, 1225–1235. doi:10.1016/j.mcm.2006.11.035

Chitty, D. M., & Hernandez, M. L. (2004). A hybrid ant colony optimization technique for dynamic vehicle routing. In *Genetic and Evolutionary Computation-GECCO 2004* (*Vol. 3102*, pp. 48–59). Berlin, Heidelberg: Springer. doi:10.1007/978-3-540-24854-5_5

Croom, S., Romano, P., & Giannakis, M. (2000). Supply chain management: an analytical framework for critical literature review. *European Journal of Purchasing & Supply Management, 6*, 67–83. doi:10.1016/S0969-7012(99)00030-1

Daniel, J. S. R., & Rajendran, C. (2005). A simulation-based genetic algorithm for inventory optimization in a serial supply chain. *International Journal in Operational Research, 12*(1), 101–127. doi:10.1111/j.1475-3995.2005.00492.x

Dellaert, N., Jeunet, J., & Jonard, N. (2000). A genetic algorithm to solve the general multi-level lot-sizing problem with time-varying costs. *International Journal of Production Economics, 668*(3), 241–257. doi:10.1016/S0925-5273(00)00084-0

Dimopoulos, C., & Mort, N. (2001). A hierarchical clustering methodology based on genetic programming for the solution of simple cell-formation problems. *International Journal of Production Research, 39*(1), 1–19. doi:10.1080/00207540150208835

Ding, C., Cheng, Y., & He, M. (2007). Two – level genetic algorithm for clustered traveling salesman problem with application in large – scale TSPs. *Tsinghua Science and Technology, 12*(4), 459–465. doi:10.1016/S1007-0214(07)70068-8

Disney, S. M., Naim, M. M., & Towill, D. R. (2000). Genetic algorithm optimization of a class of inventory control systems. *International Journal of Production Economics, 68*(3), 259–278. doi:10.1016/S0925-5273(99)00101-2

Doerner, K. F., Gutjahr, W. J., Hartl, R. F., & Lulli, G. (2008). Stochastic local search procedures for the probabilistic two – day vehicle routing problem. In *Advances in Computational Intelligence in Transport, Logistics, and Supply Chain Management* (*Vol. 144*, pp. 153–168). Berlin, Heidelberg: Springer. doi:10.1007/978-3-540-69390-1_8

Doerner, K. F., Hartl, R. F., Kiechle, G., Lucka, M., & Reimann, M. (2004). Parallel ant systems for the capacitated vehicle routing problem. In *Evolutionary Computation in Combinatorial Optimization* (*Vol. 3004*, pp. 72–83). Berlin, Heidelberg: Springer. doi:10.1007/978-3-540-24652-7_8

Domoto, E., Okuhara, K., Ueno, N., & Ishii, H. (2007). Production Planning System with Multi-Stages for Controlling Bullwhip Effect by Using Particle Swarm Optimization. *Journal of Advanced Mechanical Design, Systems and Manufacturing, 1*(3), 319–327. doi:10.1299/jamdsm.1.319

Donati, A. V., Darley, V., & Ramachandran, B. (2007). An Ant – bidding Algorithm for Multistage Flowshop Scheduling Problem: Optimization and Phase Transitions. *Advances in Metaheuristic for Hard optimization* (pp. 111- 136).

Donati, A. V., Montemanni, R., Casagrande, N., Rizzoli, A. E., & Gambardella, L. M. (2008). Time dependent vehicle routing problem with a multi ant colony system. *European Journal of Operational Research, 185*, 1174–1191. doi:10.1016/j.ejor.2006.06.047

Dorigo, M., & Gambardella, L. M. (1997). Ant colonies for the travelling salesman problem. *Bio Systems*, *43*, 73–81. doi:10.1016/S0303-2647(97)01708-5

Dorigo, M., Maniezzo, V., & Colorni, A. (1996). Ant system: optimization by a colony of cooperating agents. *IEEE Transactions on Systems, Man, and Cybernetics*, *26*(1), 29–41. doi:10.1109/3477.484436

Eriksson, R., & Olsson, B. (1997). Cooperative coevolution in inventory control optimization. In *Proceedings of the Third International Conference on Artificial Neural Networks and Genetic Algorithms*.

Ezziane, Z. (2007). Artificial Intelligence and DNA Computing. In *Intelligent Computing Everywhere* (pp. 195–209). London: Springer. doi:10.1007/978-1-84628-943-9_10

Falcone, M. A., Lopes, H. S., & Coelho, L. D. S. (2008). Supply chain optimization using evolutionary algorithms. *Int. J. Comput. Appl. Technol.*, *31*(3-4), 158–167. doi:10.1504/IJCAT.2008.018154

Fang, L., Chen, P., & Liu, S. (2007). Particle swarm optimization with simulated annealing for TSP. In *Proceedings of the 6th WSEAS International Conference on Artificial Intelligence* (pp. 206-210).

Farahani, R. Z., & Elahipanah, M. (2008). A genetic algorithm to optimize the total cost and service level for just-in-time distribution in a supply chain. *International Journal of Production Economics*, *111*(2), 229–243. doi:10.1016/j.ijpe.2006.11.028

Farmer, J. D., Packard, N. H., & Perelson, A. S. (1986). The immune system, adaptation, and machine learning. *Physica D. Nonlinear Phenomena*, *22*(1-3), 187–204. doi:10.1016/0167-2789(86)90240-X

Ferretti, I., Zanoni, S., & Zavanella, L. (2006). Production – inventory scheduling using ant system metaheuristic. *International Journal of Production Economics*, *104*, 317–326. doi:10.1016/j.ijpe.2005.01.008

Fogel, D. B. (1993). Applying evolutionary programming to selected traveling salesman problems. *Cybernetics and Systems*, *24*(1), 27–36. doi:10.1080/01969729308961697

Fuellerer, G., Doerner, k. F., Hartl, R. F. & Iori, M. (2009). Metaheuristics for vehicle routing problems with three – dimensional loading constraints. *European Journal of Operational Research.*

Fuente, De La D. & Lozano, J. (2007). Application of distributed intelligence to reduce the bullwhip effect. *International Journal of Production Research, 45*(8), 1815-1833.

Gajpal, Y., & Abad, P. L. (2009). Multi – ant colony system (MACS) for a vehicle routing problem with backhauls. *European Journal of Operational Research*, *196*, 102–117. doi:10.1016/j.ejor.2008.02.025

Gambardella, L. M., Rizzoli, A. E., Oliverio, F., Casagrande, N., Donati, A. V., Montemanni, R., & Lubicello, E. (2003). Ant Colony Optimization for vehicle routing in advanced logistics systems. In *Proceedings of the International Workshop on Modelling and Applied Simulation (MAS 2003)* (pp. 3-9).

Ghariani, S., & Furnon, V. (2006). Constraint programming and ant colonies applied to vehicle routing problems. In *Metaheuristics for Hard Optimization* (pp. 307–326). Berlin, Heidelberg: Springer. doi:10.1007/3-540-30966-7_11

Goldbarg, E. F. G., Sousa, G. R., & Goldbarg, M. C. (2006). Particle swarm for the traveling salesman problem. In *Evolutionary Computation in Combinatorial Optimization* (*Vol. 3906*, pp. 99–110). Berlin, Heidelberg: Springer. doi:10.1007/11730095_9

Gong, M., Jiao, L., & Zhang, L. (2006). Solving traveling salesman problems by artificial immune response. In *Simulated Evolution and Learning* (*Vol. 4247*, pp. 64–71). Berlin, Heidelberg: Springer. doi:10.1007/11903697_9

Gonsalves, T., & Itoh, K. (2008). Cost Minimization in Service Systems Using Particle Swarm Optimization. In *Software Engineering, Artificial Intelligence, Networking and Parallel* []. Berlin Heidelberg: Springer.]. *Distributed Computing, 149*, 151–161.

Guner, A. R. & Sevkli, M. (2008). A discrete particle swarm optimization algorithm for uncapacitated facility location problem. *Journal of Artificial Evolution and Applications*.

Guo, Y. W., Li, W. D., Mileham, A. R., & Owen, G. W. (2009). Applications of particle swarm optimization in integrated process planning and scheduling. *Robotics and Computer-integrated Manufacturing, 25*, 280–288. doi:10.1016/j.rcim.2007.12.002

Gupta, R. K., Bhunia, A. K., & Goyal, S. K. (2009). An application of genetic algorithm in solving an inventory model with advance payment and interval valued inventory costs. *Mathematical and Computer Modelling, 49*(5-6), 893–905. doi:10.1016/j.mcm.2008.09.015

Guvenir, H. A., & Erel, E. (1998). Multicriteria inventory classification using a genetic algorithm. *European Journal of Operational Research, 105*(1), 29–37. doi:10.1016/S0377-2217(97)00039-8

Han, C., & Damrongwongsiri, M. (2005). Stochastic modeling of a two-echelon multiple sourcing supply chain system with genetic algorithm. *Journal of Manufacturing Technology Management, 16*(1), 87–108. doi:10.1108/17410380510574103

Han, Y., Tang, J., Kaku, I., & Mu, L. (2009). Solving uncapacitated multilevel lot-sizing problems using a particle swarm optimization with flexible inertial weight. *Computers & Mathematics with Applications (Oxford, England), 57*(11-12), 1748–1755. doi:10.1016/j.camwa.2008.10.024

Hanshar, F. T., & Berman, B. M. O. (2007). Dynamic vehicle routing using genetic algorithms. *Applied Intelligence, 27*, 89–99. doi:10.1007/s10489-006-0033-z

Ho, W., Ho, G. T. S., & Lau, H. C. W. (2008). A hybrid genetic algorithm for the multi – depot vehicle routing problem. *Engineering Applications of Artificial Intelligence, 21*, 548–557. doi:10.1016/j.engappai.2007.06.001

Holland, J. (1975). *Adaptation in natural and artificial systems*. Ann Arbor, MI: University of Michigan Press.

Hong, S. P., & Kim, Y. H. (2009). A genetic algorithm for joint replenishment based on the exact inventory cost. *Computers & Operations Research, 34*(1), 167–175. doi:10.1016/j.cor.2007.08.006

Hou, C., Du, H., & Jiao, L. (2005). An algorithm based on antibody immunodominance for TSP. In *Advances in Natural Computation* (*Vol. 3611*, pp. 876–879). Berlin, Heidelberg: Springer. doi:10.1007/11539117_123

Hsu, C. M., Chen, K. Y., & Chen, M. C. (2005). Batching orders in warehouses by minimizing travel distance with genetic algorithms. *Computers in Industry, 56*(2), 169–178. doi:10.1016/j.compind.2004.06.001

Huang, S. H. & Lin, P. C. (2010). A modified ant colony optimization algorithm for multi-item inventory routing problems with demand uncertainty. *Transportation Research Part E: Logistics and Transportation Review*.

Hwang, H., Choi, B., & Lee, M. J. (2005). A model for shelf space allocation and inventory control considering location and inventory level effects on demand. *International Journal of Production Economics*, *97*(2), 185–195. doi:10.1016/j.ijpe.2004.07.003

Hwang, H. S. (2002). An improved model for vehicle routing problem with time constraint based on genetic algorithms. *Computers & Industrial Engineering*, *42*, 361–369. doi:10.1016/S0360-8352(02)00033-5

Hwang, H. S. (2002). Design of supply-chain logistics system considering service level. *Computers & Industrial Engineering*, *43*(1-2), 283–297. doi:10.1016/S0360-8352(02)00075-X

Ip, W. H., Huang, M., Yung, K. L., & Wang, D. (2003). Genetic algorithm solution for a risk-based partner selection problem in a virtual enterprise. *Computers & Operations Research*, *30*(2), 213–231. doi:10.1016/S0305-0548(01)00092-2

Izquierdo, J., Minciardi, R., Montalvo, I., Robba, M., & Tavera, M. (2008). Particle swarm optimization for the biomass supply chain strategic planning. In *Proceedings of the International Congress on Environmental Modeling and Software* (pp. 1272 – 1280).

Jeon, G., Leep, H. R., & Shim, J. Y. (2007). A vehicle routing problem solved by using a hybrid genetic algorithm. *Computers & Industrial Engineering*, *53*, 680–692. doi:10.1016/j.cie.2007.06.031

Jeong, B., Jung, H. S., & Park, N. K. (2002). A computerized causal forecasting system using genetic algorithms in supply chain management. *Journal of Systems and Software*, *60*(3), 223–237. doi:10.1016/S0164-1212(01)00094-2

Katayama, K., Sakamoto, H., & Narihisa, H. (2000). The efficiency of hybrid mutation genetic algorithm for the traveling salesman problem. *Mathematical and Computer Modelling*, *31*, 197–203. doi:10.1016/S0895-7177(00)00088-1

Kennedy, J., & Eberhart, R. (1995). Particle Swarm Optimization. In *Proceedings of the IEEE international conference on neural networks* (Vol. 4, pp. 1942 -1948).

Khouja, M., Michalewicz, Z., & Wilmot, M. (1998). The use of genetic algorithms to solve the economic lot size scheduling problem. *European Journal of Operational Research*, *110*(3), 509–524. doi:10.1016/S0377-2217(97)00270-1

Kim, M. C., Kim, C. O., Hong, S. R., & Kwon, I. H. (2008). Forward-backward analysis of RFID-enabled supply chain using fuzzy cognitive map and genetic algorithm. *Expert Systems with Applications*, *35*(3), 1166–1176. doi:10.1016/j.eswa.2007.08.015

Kimbrough, S. O., Wu, D. J., & Zhong, F. (2002). Computers play the beer game: can artificial agents manage supply chains? *Decision Support Systems*, *33*(3), 323–333. doi:10.1016/S0167-9236(02)00019-2

Kleinau, P., & Thonemann, U. W. (2004). Deriving inventory-control policies with genetic programming. *OR-Spektrum*, *26*(4), 521–546. doi:10.1007/s00291-004-0159-5

Kochel, P., & Nielander, U. (2005). Simulation-based optimization of multi-echelon inventory systems. *International Journal of Production Economics*, *93-94*, 505–513. doi:10.1016/j.ijpe.2004.06.046

Kochel, P., & Theim, S. (in press). Search for good policies in a single-warehouse, multi-retailer system by particle swarm optimization. *International Journal of Production Economics*.

Koza, R. J. (1992). *Genetic Programming: On the Programming of Computers by means of Natural Selection*. Cambridge, MA: MIT Press.

Kubiak, M., & Wesolek, P. (2007). Accelerating local search in a memetic algorithm for the capacitated vehicle routing problem. In *Evolutionary Computation in Combinatorial Optimization* (*Vol. 4446*, pp. 96–107). Berlin, Heidelberg: Springer. doi:10.1007/978-3-540-71615-0_9

Kumar, R., & Singh, P. K. (2007). Pareto evolutionary algorithm hybridized with local search for biobjective TSP. In *Hybrid Evolutionary Algorithms* (*Vol. 75*, pp. 361–398). Berlin, Heidelberg: Springer. doi:10.1007/978-3-540-73297-6_14

Kumar, V., Prakash, Tiwari, M. K. & Chan, F. T. S. (2006). Stochastic make-to-stock inventory deployment problem: an endosymbiotic psychoclonal algorithm based approach. *International Journal of Production Research*, *44*(11), 2245–2263. doi:10.1080/00207540500459678

Labadi, N., Prins, C., & Reghioui, M. (2008). An evolutionary algorithm with distance measure for the split delivery capacitated arc routing problem. In *Recent Advances in Evolutionary Computation for Combinatorial Optimization* (*Vol. 153*, pp. 275–294). Berlin, Heidelberg: Springer. doi:10.1007/978-3-540-70807-0_17

Lacomme, P., Prins, C., & Cherif, W. R. (2004). Cooperative memetic algorithms for arc routing problems. *Annals of Operations Research*, *131*, 159–185. doi:10.1023/B:ANOR.0000039517.35989.6d

Lan, Y. F., Liu, Y. K., & Sun, G. J. (2009). Modeling fuzzy multi – period production planning and sourcing problem with credibility service levels. *Journal of Computational and Applied Mathematics*, *231*, 208–221. doi:10.1016/j.cam.2009.02.009

Lee, C. Y., Lee, Z. J., Lin, S. W., & Ying, K. C. (2008). An enhanced ant colony optimization (EACO) applied to capacitated vehicle routing problem. *Applied Intelligence*, *32*(1), 88–95. doi:10.1007/s10489-008-0136-9

Lee, H. L., Padmanabhan, V., & Whang, S. (1997). Information distortion in a supply chain: The bullwhip effect. *Management Science*, *43*(4), 546–558. doi:10.1287/mnsc.43.4.546

Lee, J. Y., Shin, S. Y., Park, T. H., & Zhang, B. T. (2004). Solving traveling salesman problems with DNA molecules encoding numerical values. *Bio Systems*, *78*, 39–47. doi:10.1016/j.biosystems.2004.06.005

Lee, Y. H., Jeong, C. S., & Moon, C. (2002). Advanced planning and scheduling with outsourcing in manufacturing supply chain. *Computers & Industrial Engineering*, *43*(1-2), 351–374. doi:10.1016/S0360-8352(02)00079-7

Li, L., & Zhang, Y. (2007). An improved genetic algorithm for the traveling salesman problem. In *Advanced Intelligent Computing Theories and Applications. With Aspects of Contemporary Intelligent Computing Techniques* (*Vol. 2*, pp. 208–216). Berlin, Heidelberg: Springer. doi:10.1007/978-3-540-74282-1_24

Li, S. G., & Kuo, X. (2008). The inventory management system for automobile spare parts in a central warehouse. *Expert Systems with Applications*, *34*(2), 1144–1153. doi:10.1016/j.eswa.2006.12.003

Li, S. G., & Rong, Y. L. (2009). The reliable design of one – piece flow production system using fuzzy ant colony optimization. *Computers & Operations Research*, *36*, 1656–1663. doi:10.1016/j.cor.2008.03.010

Li, X., & Tian, P. (2006). An ant colony system for the open vehicle routing problem. In *Ant Colony Optimization and Swarm Intelligence* (*Vol. 4150*, pp. 356–363). Berlin, Heidelberg: Springer. doi:10.1007/11839088_33

Li, Y., & Gong, S. (2003). Dynamic ant colony optimization for TSP. *International Journal of Advanced Manufacturing Technology*, *22*, 528–533. doi:10.1007/s00170-002-1478-9

Liang, W. Y., & Huang, C. C. (2006). Agent-based demand forecast in multi-echelon supply chain. *Decision Support Systems*, *42*(1), 390–407. doi:10.1016/j.dss.2005.01.009

Liu, A., Deng, G. & Shan, S. (2006). Mean contribution ant system: an improved version of ant colony optimization for travelling salesman problem (Vol. 4247, pp. 489 – 496).

Liu, B., Wang, L., & Jin, Y. H. (2007). An effective hybrid particle swarm optimization for no – wait flow shop scheduling. *International Journal of Advanced Manufacturing Technology*, *31*, 1001–1011. doi:10.1007/s00170-005-0277-5

Liu, F., & Zeng, G. (2009). Study of genetic algorithm with reinforcement learning to solve the TSP. *Expert Systems with Applications*, *36*, 6995–7001. doi:10.1016/j.eswa.2008.08.026

Liu, H., & Abraham, A. (2007). An hybrid fuzzy variable neighborhood particle swarm optimization algorithm for solving quadratic assignment problems. *Journal of Universal Computer Science*, *13*(9), 1309–1331.

Liu, S., Huang, W., & Ma, H. (2009). An effective genetic algorithm for the fleet size and mix vehicle routing problems. *Transportation Research Part E, Logistics and Transportation Review*, *45*, 434–445. doi:10.1016/j.tre.2008.10.003

Liu, X., Qi, H., & Chen, Y. (2006). Optimization of special vehicle routing problem based on ant colony system. []. Berlin Heidelberg: Springer.]. *Computational Intelligence*, *4114*, 1228–1233. doi:10.1007/978-3-540-37275-2_153

Loreto, T., & Martinelli, G. (2007). Novel pheromone updating strategy for speeding up ACO applied to VRP. In *Biological and Artificial Intelligence Environments* (pp. 175–182). The Netherlands: Springer.

Lu, J., Humphreys, P., McIvor, R., & Maguire, L. (2007). Emplying genetic algorithms to minimize the bullwhip effect in a supply chain. In *Proceedings of the IEEE International Conference on Industrial Engineering and Engineering Management* (pp. 1527-1531).

Mahnam, M., Yadollahpour, M. R., Dasdashti, V. F., & Hejazi, S. R. (2009). Supply chain modeling in uncertain environment with bi – objective approach. *Computers & Industrial Engineering*, *56*, 1535–1544. doi:10.1016/j.cie.2008.09.038

Maiti, A. K., Bhunia, A. K., & Maiti, M. (2006). An application of real-coded genetic algorithm (RCGA) for mixed integer non-linear programming in two-storage multi-item inventory model with discount policy. *Applied Mathematics and Computation*, *183*(2), 903–915. doi:10.1016/j.amc.2006.05.141

Maiti, M. K., & Maiti, M. (2007). Two-storage inventory model with lot-size dependent fuzzy lead-time under possibility constraints via genetic algorithm. *European Journal of Operational Research*, *179*(2), 352–371. doi:10.1016/j.ejor.2006.03.029

Malmborg, C. J. (1996). A genetic algorithm for service level based vehicle scheduling. *European Journal of Operational Research*, *93*, 121–134. doi:10.1016/0377-2217(95)00185-9

Manfrin, M., Birattari, M., Stultze, T., & Dorigo, M. (2006). Parallel ant colony optimization for the traveling salesman problem. In *Ant Colony Optimization and Swarm Intelligence* (*Vol. 4150*, pp. 224–234). Berlin, Heidelberg: Springer. doi 10.1007/11839088_20

Mansouri, S A. (2005). Coordination of set-ups between two stages of a supply chain using multi-objective genetic algorithms. *International Journal of Production Research, 43*(15), 3163–3180. doi 10.1080/00207540500103821

Marinakis, Y., & Marinaki, M. (2008). A particle swarm optimization algorithm with path relinking for the location routing problem. *Journal of Mathematical Modelling and Algorithms, 7*, 59–78. doi:10.1007/s10852-007-9073-6

Marinakis, Y. & Marinaki, M. (2009). A hybrid genetic – particle swarm optimization algorithm for the vehicle routing problem. *Expert Systems with Applications*.

Marinakis, Y., & Marinaki, M. (2009). A hybrid multi – swarm particle swarm optimization algorithm for the probabilistic traveling salesman problem. *Computers & Operations Research, 37*, 432–442. doi:10.1016/j.cor.2009.03.004

Marinakis, Y, Marinaki, M., & Dounias, G. (2008). Honey bees mating optimization algorithm for the vehicle routing problem. In *Nature Inspired Cooperative Strategies for Optimization (NISCO 2007)* (Vol. 129, pp. 139 – 148). Berlin Heidelberg: Springer.

Marinakis, Y., Migdalas, A., & Pardalos, P. M. (2007). A new bilevel formulation for the vehicle routing problem and a solution method using a genetic algorithm. *Journal of Global Optimization, 38*, 555–580. doi:10.1007/s10898-006-9094-0

Martinez, C. G., Gordon, O., & Herrera, F. (2007). A taxonomy and an empirical analysis of multiple objective ant colony optimization algorithms for the bi – criteria TSP. *European Journal of Operational Research, 180*, 116–148. doi:10.1016/j.ejor.2006.03.041

Massim, Y., Yalaoui, F., Amodeo, L., Chatelet, E., & Zeblah, A. (2010). Efficient combined immune-decomposition algorithm for optimal buffer allocation in production lines for throughput and profit maximization. *Computers & Operations Research, 37*(4), 611–620. doi:10.1016/j.cor.2009.06.016

Masutti, T. A. S., & Castro, L. N. (2008). A neuro – immune algorithm to solve the capacitated vehicle routing problem. In *Artificial Immune Systems* (*Vol. 5132*, pp. 210–219). Berlin, Heidelberg: Springer. doi:10.1007/978-3-540-85072-4_19

Matos, A. C., & Oliveira, R. C. (2004). An experimental study of the ant colony system for the period vehicle routing problem. In *Ant Colony, Optimization and Swarm Intelligence* (*Vol. 3172*, pp. 286–293). Berlin, Heidelberg: Springer. doi:10.1007/978-3-540-28646-2_26

Min, H., Ko, H. J., & Ko, C. S. (2006). A genetic algorithm approach to developing the multi-echelon reverse logistics network for product returns. *Omega, 34*(1), 56–69. doi:10.1016/j.omega.2004.07.025

Moghadam, M. R. S., Afsar, A., & Sohrabi, B. (2008). Inventory lot-sizing with supplier selection using hybrid intelligent algorithm. *Applied Soft Computing, 8*(4), 1523–1529. doi:10.1016/j.asoc.2007.11.001

Montemanni, R., Gambardella, L. M., Rizzoli, A. E., & Donati, A. V. (2005). Ant colony system for a dynamic vehicle routing problem. *Journal of Combinatorial Optimization, 10*, 327–343. doi:10.1007/s10878-005-4922-6

Moon, C., Kim, J., Choi, G., & Seo, Y. (2002). An efficient genetic algorithm for the traveling salesman problem with precedence constraints. *European Journal of Operational Research, 140*, 606–617. doi:10.1016/S0377-2217(01)00227-2

Moon, C., Kim, J., & Hur, S. (2002). Integrated process planning and scheduling with minimizing total tardiness in multi-plants supply chain. *Computers & Industrial Engineering, 43*(1-2), 331–349. doi:10.1016/S0360-8352(02)00078-5

Moon, I., Silver, E. A., & Choi, S. (2002). Hybrid genetic algorithm for the economic lot-scheduling problem. *International Journal of Production Research, 40*(4), 809–824. doi:10.1080/00207540110095222

Moore, S. A., & DeMaagd, K. (2006). Using genetic programming to search for supply chain reordering policies. In *Genetic Programming Theory and Practice II* (*Vol. 8*, pp. 207–223). Springer. doi:10.1007/0-387-23254-0_13

Murata, T., & Itai, R. (2007). Local search in two – fold EMO algorithm to enhance solution similarity for multi – objective vehicle routing problems. In *Evolutionary Multi-Criterion Optimization* (*Vol. 4403*, pp. 201–215). Berlin, Heidelberg: Springer. doi:10.1007/978-3-540-70928-2_18

Naso, D., Surico, M., Turchiano, B., & Kaymak, U. (2007). Genetic algorithms for supply-chain scheduling: A case study in the distribution of ready-mixed concrete. *European Journal of Operational Research, 177*(3), 2069–2099. doi:10.1016/j.ejor.2005.12.019

Noorul, H. A., & Kannan, G. (2006). Effect of forecasting on the multi-echelon distribution inventory supply chain cost using neural networks, genetic algorithm and particle swarm optimization. *International Journal of Services Operations and Informatics, 1*(1-2), 1–22.

O'donell, T., Maguire, L., Mclvor, R., & Humphreys, P. (2006). Minimizing the bullwhip effect in a supply chain using genetic algorithms. *International Journal of Production Research, 44*(8), 1523–1543. doi:10.1080/00207540500431347

Ochi, L. S., Vianna, D. S., Drummond, L. M. A., & Victor, A. O. (1998). A parallel evolutionary algorithm for the vehicle routing problem with heterogeneous fleet. *Future Generation Computer Systems, 14*(5-6), 285–292. doi:10.1016/S0167-739X(98)00034-X

Onut, S., Tuzkaya, U. R., & Dogac, B. (2008). A particle swarm optimization algorithm for the multiple – level warehouse layout design problem. *Computers & Industrial Engineering, 54*, 783–799. doi:10.1016/j.cie.2007.10.012

Pang, H., Wei, Y., Wang, S., & Liu, X. (2009). Research on multi – time period production plan of supply chain under demands uncertainty. *Proceedings of the 6th International Symposium on Neural Networks on Advances in Neural Networks* (Vol. 5551, pp. 1098-1106).

Pankratz, G. (2005). A grouping genetic algorithm for the pickup and delivery with time windows. *OR-Spektrum, 27*, 21–41. doi:10.1007/s00291-004-0173-7

Parsopoulos, K. E., Skouri, K., & Vrahatis, M. N. (2008). Particle swarm optimization for tackling continuous review inventory models. In *Applications of Evolutionary Computing* (*Vol. 4974*, pp. 103–112). Berlin, Heidelberg: Springer. doi:10.1007/978-3-540-78761-7_11

Pasandideh, S. H. R., & Niaki, S. T. A. (2008). A genetic algorithm approach to optimize a multi-products EPQ model with discrete delivery orders and constrained space. *Applied Mathematics and Computation, 195*(2), 506–514. doi:10.1016/j.amc.2007.05.007

Pasia, J. M., Doerner, K. F., Hartl, R. F., & Reimann, M. (2007). Solving a bi – objective vehicle routing problem by pareto – ant colony optimization. In *Engineering Stochastic Local Search Algorithms. Designing, Implementing and Analyzing Effective Heuristics* (*Vol. 4638*, pp 187–191). Berlin, Heidelberg: Springer. doi:10.1007/978-3-540-74446-7_15

Pellegrini, P., Favaretto, D., & Moretti, E. (2007). Multiple ant colony optimization for a rich vehicle routing problem: a case study. In *Knowledge-Based Intelligent Information and Engineering Systems* (*Vol. 4693*, pp. 627–634). Berlin, Heidelberg: Springer. doi:10.1007/978-3-540-74827-4_79

Perboli, G., Pezzella, F., & Tadei, R. (2008). EVE-OPT: a hybrid algorithm for the capacitated vehicle routing problem. *Mathematical Methodologies in Operational Research*, *68*, 361–382. doi:10.1007/s00186-008-0236-7

Phelan, M., & McGarraghy, S. (2007). Mitigating the bullwhip effect in supply chains using grammatical evolution. In *Proceedings of the Systems Dynamics Society Conference*.

Pinto, P. C., Runkler, T. A., & Sousa, J. M. (2007). *Ant Colony Optimization and its Application to Regular and Dynamic MAX – SAT Problems* (pp. 285–304). Advances in Biologically Inspired Information Systems.

Pinto, P. C., Runkler, T. A., & Sousa, J. M. C. (2009). Ant colony optimization and its application to regular and dynamic MAX – SAT problems. *Studies in Computational Intelligence*, *69*, 285–304.

Pop, P. C., Pintea, C. M., & Sitar, C. P. (2007). An ant based heuristic for the railway traveling salesman problem. In *Applications of Evolutionary Computing* (*Vol. 4448*, pp. 702–711). Berlin, Heidelberg: Springer.

Prestwich, S. Tarim, S. A., Rossi, R. & Hnich, B. (2008). A steady-state genetic algorithm with resampling for noisy inventory control. in *Parallel Problem Solving from Nature-PPSN X* (Vol. 5199, pp. 559-568). Berlin Heidelberg: Springer.

Prins, C. (2004). A simple and effective evolutionary algorithm for the vehicle routing problem. *Computers & Operations Research*, *31*, 1985–2002. doi:10.1016/S0305-0548(03)00158-8

Prins, C., & Bouchenoua, S. (2006). A memetic algorithm solving the VRP, the CAPR and general routing problems with nodes, edges and arcs. In *Studies in Fuzziness and Soft Computing* (*Vol. 166*, pp. 65–85). Berlin, Heidelberg: Springer.

Prins, C., Prodhon, C., & Calvo, R. W. (2006). A memetic algorithm with population management (MA|PM) for the capacitated location – routing problem. In *Evolutionary Computation in Combinatorial Optimization* (*Vol. 3906*, pp. 183–194). Berlin, Heidelberg: Springer. doi:10.1007/11730095_16

Puris, A., Bello, R., Martinez, Y., & Nowe, A. (2007). Two – stage ant colony optimization for solving the traveling salesman problem. In *Nature Inspired Problem-Solving Methods in Knowledge Engineering* (*Vol. 4528*, pp. 307–316). Berlin, Heidelberg: Springer. doi:10.1007/978-3-540-73055-2_33

Qu, L., & Sun, R. (1999). A synergetic approach to genetic algorithms for solving traveling salesman problem. *Information Sciences*, *117*, 267–283. doi:10.1016/S0020-0255(99)00026-2

Rao, R. V. (2007). Vendor selection in a supply chain using analytic hierarchy process and genetic algorithm methods. *International Journal of Services and Operations Management*, *3*(3), 355–369. doi:10.1504/IJSOM.2007.013097

Reimann, M. (2007). Guiding ACO by problem relaxation: a case study on the symmetric TSP. In *Hybrid Metaheuristics* (*Vol. 4771*, pp. 45–56). Berlin, Heidelberg: Springer. doi:10.1007/978-3-540-75514-2_4

Reimann, M., Doerner, K., & Hartl, R. F. (2004). D-Ants: Savings Based Ants divide and conquer the vehicle routing problem. *Computers & Operations Research, 31*, 563–591. doi:10.1016/S0305-0548(03)00014-5

Reimann, M., & Ulrich, H. (2006). Comparing backhauling strategies in vehicle routing using Ant Colony Optimization. *Central European Journal of Operations Research, 14*, 105–123. doi:10.1007/s10100-006-0163-8

Reyes, L. C., Orta, J. F. D., Barbosa, J. J. G., Jimenez, J. T., Huacuja, H. J. F., & Cruz, B. A. A. (2008). An ant colony system algorithm to solve routing problems applied to the delivery of bottled products. In *Foundations of Intelligent Systems* (*Vol. 4994*, pp. 329–338). Berlin, Heidelberg: Springer. doi:10.1007/978-3-540-68123-6_36

Rezaei, J., & Davoodi, M. (2008). A deterministic, multi-item inventory model with supplier selection and imperfect quality. *Applied Mathematical Modelling, 32*(10), 2106–2116. doi:10.1016/j.apm.2007.07.009

Rezg, N., Xie, X., & Mati, Y. (2004). Joint optimization of preventive maintenance and inventory control in a production line using simulation. *International Journal of Production Research, 42*(10), 2029–2046. doi:10.1080/00207540310001638235

Rice, M. (2004). Computational Intelligence Algorithms for Optimized vehicle routing applications in Geographic information systems. Thesis Proposal.

Rizzoli, A. E., Oliverio, F., Montemanni, R. & Gambardella, L. M. (2004). Ant Colony Optimization for vehicle routing problems: from theory to applications. IDSIA, Technical Report.

Samanlioglu, F., Ferrell, W. G. Jr, & Kurz, M. E. (2008). A memetic random – key genetic algorithm for a symmetric multi – objective traveling salesman problem. *Computers & Industrial Engineering, 55*, 439–449. doi:10.1016/j.cie.2008.01.005

Schmitt, L. J., & Amini, M. M. (1998). Performance characteristics of alternative genetic algorithmic approaches to the traveling salesman problem using path representation: An empirical study. *European Journal of Operational Research, 108*, 551–570. doi:10.1016/S0377-2217(97)00206-3

Schneider, J., Froschhammer, C., Morgenstern, I., Husslein, T., & Singer, J. M. (1996). Searching for backbones – an effective parallel algorithm for the traveling salesman problem. *Computer Physics Communications, 96*, 173–188. doi:10.1016/0010-4655(96)00062-8

Scholz-reiter, B., Delhoum, S., Zschintzsch, M., Jagalski, T., & Freitag, M. (2006). Inventory Control in Shop Floors, Production Networks and Supply Chains Using System Dynamics. In *Proceedings of the 12th ASIM Conference on Simulation in Production and Logistics* (pp. 273-282)

Sena, G. A., Megherbi, D., & Isern, G. (2001). Implementation of a parallel genetic algorithm on a cluster of workstations: traveling salesman problem, a case study. *Future Generation Computer Systems, 17*, 477–488. doi:10.1016/S0167-739X(99)00134-X

Shi, X. H., Liang, Y. C., Lee, H. P., Lu, C., & Wang, Q. X. (2007). Particle swarm optimization – based algorithms for TSP and generalized TSP. *Information Processing Letters, 103*, 169–176. doi:10.1016/j.ipl.2007.03.010

Silva, C. A., Runkler, T., & Sousa, J. M. (2007). Optimization of logistic systems using fuzzy weighted aggregation. *Fuzzy Sets and Systems, 158*, 1947–1960. doi:10.1016/j.fss.2007.04.008

Silva, C. A., Runkler, T., & Sousa, J. M. (2008). Rescheduling and optimization of logistic processes using GA and ACO. *Engineering Applications of Artificial Intelligence, 21*, 343–352. doi:10.1016/j.engappai.2007.08.006

Silva, C. A., Runkler, T., Sousa, J. M., & Palm, R. (2002). Optimization of logistic processes using ant colonies. In. *Proceedings of Agent-Based Simulation, 3*, 143–148.

Silva, C. A., Runkler, T., Sousa, J. M., & Palm, R. (2005). Soft Computing optimization methods applied to logistic processes. *International Journal of Approximate Reasoning, 40*, 280–301. doi:10.1016/j.ijar.2005.06.004

Silva, C. A., Runkler, T. A., Sousa, J. M., & Palm, R. (2002). Ant Colonies as Logistic Processes Optimizers. In *Proceedings of the ANTS 3rd International conference on Ant Algorithms* (Vol. 2463, pp. 76-87).

Silva, C. A., Runkler, T. A., Sousa, J. M., & Sa da Costa, J. M. (2003). Optimization of Logistic Processes in Supply-Chains Using Meta-heuristics. In *Progress in Artificial Intelligence* (*Vol. 2902*, pp. 9–23). Berlin, Heidelberg: Springer. doi:10.1007/978-3-540-24580-3_9

Silva, C. A., Sousa, J. M., Runkler, T., & Sa da Costa, J. M. G. (2005). Ant-based distributed optimization for supply chain management. In *Adaptive and Natural Computing Algorithms* (pp. 357–360). Vienna: Springer. doi:10.1007/3-211-27389-1_86

Silva, C. A., Sousa, J. M., Runkler, T., & Sa da Costa, J. M. G. (2009). Distributed supply chain management using ant colony optimization. *European Journal of Operational Research, 199*, 349–358. doi:10.1016/j.ejor.2008.11.021

Sim, E., Jung, S., Kim, H., & Park, J. (2004). A generic network design for a closed-loop supply chain using genetic algorithm. In *Genetic and Evolutionary Computation-GECCO 2004* (Vol. 3103, pp. 1214-1225).

Sivanandam, S. N., & Deepa, S. N. (2007). Introduction to Genetic programming. In *Genetic Programming* (pp. 131–163). Berlin, Heidelberg: Springer.

Skaruz, J., Seredynski, F., & Gamus, M. (2006). Nature – inspired algorithms for the TSP. In *Intelligent Information Processing and Web Mining* (*Vol. 31*, pp. 319–328). Berlin, Heidelberg: Springer.

Srinivas, D. Y., Choudhary, A. K., Harding, J. A. & Tiwari, M. K. (2005). A Cooperative Multi Colony Ant Optimization Based Approach to Efficiently Allocate Customers to Multiple Distribution Centers in a Supply Chain Network. In *Computational Science and Its Applications-ICCSA 2005* (Vol. 3483, pp. 680 – 691). Berlin Heidelberg: Springer.

Strozzi, F., Bosch, J., & Zald, J. M. (2007). Beer game order policy optimization under changing customer demand. *Decision Support Systems, 42*(4), 2153–2163. doi:10.1016/j.dss.2006.06.001

Su, C. T., & Wong, J. T. (2008). Design of a replenishment system for a stochastic dynamic production / forecast lot – sizing problem under bullwhip effect. *Expert Systems with Applications, 34*, 173–180. doi:10.1016/j.eswa.2006.08.010

Syarif, A., Yun, Y. S., & Gen, M. (2002). Study on multi-stage logistic chain network: a spanning tree-based genetic algorithm approach. *Computers & Industrial Engineering, 43*(1-2), 299–314. doi:10.1016/S0360-8352(02)00076-1

Tan, K. C., & Chew, Y. H. (2006). A hybrid multiobjective evolutionary algorithm for solving vehicle routing problem with time windows. *Computational Optimization and Applications, 34*, 115–151. doi:10.1007/s10589-005-3070-3

Taniguchi, K., & Terano, T. (2004). Analyzing dynamics of a supply chain using logic-based genetic programming. In *Knowledge-Based Intelligent Information and Engineering Systems* (*Vol. 3213*, pp. 464–471). Berlin, Heidelberg: Springer.

Tarakanov, A., & Dasgupta, D. (2000). A formal model of an artificial immune system. *Bio Systems*, *55*, 151–158. doi:10.1016/S0303-2647(99)00093-3

Tarantilis, C. D., Ioannou, G., & Prastacos, G. (2005). Advanced vehicle routing algorithms for complex operations management problems. *Journal of Food Engineering*, *70*, 455–471. doi:10.1016/j.jfoodeng.2004.09.023

Tasgetiren, M. F., Suganthan, P. N., & Pan, Q. K. (2007). A discrete particle swarm optimization algorithm for the generalized traveling salesman problem. In *Proceedings of the 9th annual conference on Genetic and evolutionary computation* (pp. 158 – 165).

Teodorovic, D. (2008). Swarm intelligence systems for transportation engineering: Principles and applications. *Transportation Research Part C, Emerging Technologies*, *16*, 651–667. doi:10.1016/j.trc.2008.03.002

Ting, C. J., Tsai, C. Y., & Yeh, L. W. (2007). The use of particle swarm optimization for order allocation under multiple capacitated sourcing and quantity discounts. *Proceedings of the IEMS*, *6*(2), 136–145.

Tsai, C. Y., & Yeh, S. W. (2008). A multiple objective particle swarm optimization approach for inventory classification. in *International Journal of Production Economics, 114*(2), 656-666.

Tsou, C. S. (2008). Multi-objective inventory planning using MOPSO and TOPSIS. *Expert Systems with Applications*, *35*(1-2), 136–142. doi:10.1016/j.eswa.2007.06.009

Tsou, C. S. (2009). Evolutionary pareto optimizers for continuous review stochastic inventory systems. *European Journal of Operational Research*, *195*, 364–371. doi:10.1016/j.ejor.2008.02.039

Ugur, A., & Aydin, D. (2009). An interactive simulation and analysis software for solving TSP using Ant Colony Optimization algorithms. *Advances in Engineering Software*, *40*, 341–349. doi:10.1016/j.advengsoft.2008.05.004

Urban, T. L. (1998). An inventory-theoretic approach to product assortment and shelf-space allocation. *Journal of Retailing*, *74*(1), 15–35. doi:10.1016/S0022-4359(99)80086-4

Vassiliadis, V., & Dounias, G. (2009). Nature – Inspired Intelligence: A review of selected methods and applications. *International Journal of Artificial Intelligence Tools*, *18*(4), 487–516. doi:10.1142/S021821300900024X

Wang, G., Liu, Y. & Zheng, M. (2009). Fuzzy two – stage chain problem and its intelligent algorithm (Vol. 5552, pp. 15 – 24).

Wang, H. S. (2009). A two – phase ant colony algorithm for multi – echelon defective supply chain network design. *European Journal of Operational Research*, *192*, 243–252. doi:10.1016/j.ejor.2007.08.037

Wang, H. S., Che, Z. H. & Wu, C. (2009). Using analytic hierarchy process and particle swarm optimization algorithm for evaluating product plans. *Expert Systems with Applications*.

Wang, J. Q., Tong, X. N., & Li, Z. M. (2007). An improved evolutionary algorithm for dynamic vehicle routing problem with time windows. In *Computational Science-ICCS 2007* (*Vol. 4490*, pp. 1147–1154). Berlin, Heidelberg: Springer. doi:10.1007/978-3-540-72590-9_171

Wang, K., & Wang, Y. (2008). Applying Genetic Algorithms to Optimize the Cost of Multiple Sourcing Supply Chain Systems-An Industry Case Study. In *Success in Evolutionary Computation* (*Vol. 92*, pp. 355–372). Berlin, Heidelberg: Springer. doi:10.1007/978-3-540-76286-7_16

Wang, K. J., & Chen, M. J. (2009). Cooperative capacity planning and resource allocation by mutual outsourcing using ant algorithm in a decentralized supply chain. *Expert Systems with Applications*, *36*, 2831–2842. doi:10.1016/j.eswa.2008.01.089

Wang, W., Wu, B., Zhao, Y., & Feng, D. (2006). Particle swarm optimization for open vehicle routing problem. In *Computational Intelligence* (*Vol. 4114*, pp. 999–1007). Berlin, Heidelberg: Springer. doi:10.1007/978-3-540-37275-2_126

Wei, J. D., & Lee, D. T. (2006). Priority – based genetic local search and its application to the traveling salesman problem. In *Simulated Evolution and Learning* (*Vol. 4247*, pp. 424–432). Berlin, Heidelberg: Springer. doi:10.1007/11903697_54

Weise, T. (2009). Global Optimization Algorithms: Theory and Applications (2nd ed.). Retrieved from http://www.t-weise.de

Wong, J. T. (2009). The distribution processing and replenishment policy of the supply chain under asymmetric information and deterioration: Insight into the information value. *Expert Systems with Applications*.

Xie, J., & Dong, J. (2002). Heuristic genetic algorithms for general capacitated lot-sizing problems. *Computers & Mathematics with Applications (Oxford, England)*, *44*(1-2), 263–276. doi:10.1016/S0898-1221(02)00146-3

Xing, L. N., Chen, Y. W., Yang, K. W., Hou, F., Shen, X. S., & Cai, H. P. (2008). A hybrid approach combining an improved genetic algorithm and optimization strategies for the asymmetric traveling salesman problem. *Engineering Applications of Artificial Intelligence*, *21*, 1370–1380. doi:10.1016/j.engappai.2008.01.003

Yang, J. (2005). Using Immune Algorithms for Inventory Model with Reverse Logistics. Master Thesis.

Yang, J., Shi, X., Marchese, M., & Liang, Y. (2008). An ant colony optimization method for generalized TSP problem. *Progress in Natural Science*, *18*, 1417–1422. doi:10.1016/j.pnsc.2008.03.028

Yang, J., Wu, C., Lee, H. P., & Liang, Y. (2008). Solving traveling salesman problems using generalized chromosome genetic algorithm. *Progress in Natural Science*, *18*, 887–892. doi:10.1016/j.pnsc.2008.01.030

Yang, L., & Stacey, D. A. (2001). Solving the traveling salesman problem using the enhanced genetic algorithm. In *Advances in Artificial Intelligence* (*Vol. 2056*, pp. 307–316). Berlin, Heidelberg: Springer. doi:10.1007/3-540-45153-6_30

Yang, M. F. & Lin, Y. (2009). Applying the linear particle swarm optimization to a serial multi – echelon inventory model. *Expert Systems with Applications*.

Yao, M. J., & Chu, W. M. (2008). A genetic algorithm for determining optimal replenishment cycles to minimize maximum warehouse space requirements. *Omega*, *36*(4), 619–631. doi:10.1016/j.omega.2007.01.007

Yao, M. J., & Hsu, H. W. (2008). A new spanning tree-based genetic algorithm for the design of multi-stage supply chain networks with nonlinear transportation costs. *Optimization and Engineering*, *10*(2), 219–237. doi:10.1007/s11081-008-9059-x

Yeh, W. C. (2004). A hybrid heuristic algorithm for the multistage supply chain network problem. *International Journal of Advanced Manufacturing Technology*, *26*(5-6), 675–685. doi:10.1007/s00170-003-2025-z

Zegordi, S. H., & Nia, M. A. B. (2009). Integrating production and transportation scheduling in a two-stage supply chain considering order assignment. *International Journal of Advanced Manufacturing Technology*, *44*(9-10), 928–939. doi:10.1007/s00170-008-1910-x

Zhang, G. Q., & Lai, K. K. (2006). Combining path relinking and genetic algorithms for the multiple-level warehouse layout problem. *European Journal of Operational Research*, *169*(2), 413–425. doi:10.1016/j.ejor.2004.08.007

Zhang, J. L., Zhao, Y. W., Peng, D. J., & Wang, W. L. (2008). A hybrid quantum – inspired evolutionary algorithm for capacitated vehicle routing problem. In *Advanced Intelligent Computing Theories and Applications. With Aspects of Theoretical and Methodological Issues* (*Vol. 5226*, pp. 31–38). Berlin, Heidelberg: Springer. doi:10.1007/978-3-540-87442-3_5

Zhang, T., Tian, W. X., Zhang, Y. J. & Liu, S. X. (2008). Improved ant colony system for VRPSPD with maximum distance constraint. *Systems Engineering – Theory & Practice, 28*(1).

Zhang, X., & Tang, L. (2009). A new hybrid ant colony optimization algorithm for the vehicle routing problem. *Pattern Recognition Letters*, *30*, 848–855. doi:10.1016/j.patrec.2008.06.001

Zhao, F., Li, S., Sun, J., & Mei, D. (2009). Genetic algorithm for one – commodity pickup-and-delivery traveling salesman problem. *Computers & Industrial Engineering*, *56*, 1642–1648. doi:10.1016/j.cie.2008.10.014

Zhou, G., Min, H., & Gen, M. (2002). The balanced allocation of customers to multiple distribution centers in the supply chain network: a genetic algorithm approach. *Computers & Industrial Engineering*, *43*(1-2), 251–261. doi:10.1016/S0360-8352(02)00067-0

Section 1
Synthesis and Design of Supply Chain

Chapter 2
Coalitional Added Services in a Linear Neutral e-Marketplace:
An Approach Based on the Shapley Value

Paolo Renna
University of Basilicata, Italy

Pierluigi Argoneto
University of Basilicata, Italy

ABSTRACT

The increase of transactions by electronic commerce (e-commerce) in Business to Business applications has a constant trend during last years. Many research reports have focused on negotiation and auction mechanisms in this context, but a smaller number of related research attempts, has chosen to develop coalition approaches This research attempt tries to overcome this gap by an innovative coalition model for a private neutral linear e-marketplace that combines a full integration between customer's request and supplier's planning activity. The Shapley value approach is proposed to manage the profit sharing activity among the coalition participants. The Shapley value is an approach of game theory used to share a gain in coalition games. A proper simulation environment has been designed and modeled in order to measure the "stay-together economy" achievable within the proposed innovative e-marketplace. The simulation results highlight how the proposed approach increases the performance level of the e-marketplace: specifically the suppliers gain more benefits than the customers through the possibility of establishing coalitions.

INTRODUCTION

The increasing growth of transactions of e-commerce leads to focus the interest on e-commerce related applications, as the e-marketplaces. Especially in Business to Business (B2B) applications they are the most innovative tools to support procurement actions utilizing Internet and, more generally, the Web technologies. Among the several definitions of e-marketplace, a basic definition has been proposed by Grieger (2003): "*an e-marketplace brings multiple buyers and sellers together (in a "virtual" sense) in one central market space. If it also enables them to buy and sell from each other at a dynamic price*

DOI: 10.4018/978-1-61520-633-9.ch002

which is determined in accordance with the rules of exchange, it is called an electronic exchange; otherwise it is called a portal". The benefits of implementing an e-procurement approach for both buyers and sellers are the following (Yu, 2008):

- it reduces the transaction costs; among several researches, Tully (2000) point out that e-procurement can achieve gross saving of 5% to 40%; in particular small firms can gain 15-25% reduction in prices in online marketplaces compared with those negotiated by the business itself (Ash, 2006);
- it reduces the cycle time of the procurement process; firm that implement an e-procurement approach are forced to standardize the process and therefore some steps are automated. Moreover, the paperwork is eliminated and the time to decision is reduced;
- it increases the geographical boundary; particularly for small firms, e-procurement allows to increase the visibility and therefore the enterprises contacted. In this way, the searching activity of new buyers/sellers is faster and cheaper;
- minimize maverick (unplanned) buying; the improvement of the information flow and process standardized leads to mitigate this effect. The same motivations lead to reduce human errors in buying or shipping process.

During the last decade the role of e-marketplaces in supply chain management becomes more relevant. Eng (2004) summarized the contributions of e-marketplace to Supply Chain Management are examined in three dimensions: unit cost reduction, increased efficiency, and streamlined operations.

The main processes where Business To Business e-marketplaces are important can be the following (Murillo, 2001; Khosrow-Pour, 2005):

- the increase of information across the supply chain partners can improve the decision making processes;
- bargaining models among customers and suppliers can get benefit to the customers with reducing the price of transactions;
- the order management such as: placement and tracking activities;
- the integration of different logistic activities such as: warehouse management and transport;
- the reduction of costs for the financial transactions.

An exploration study (Wang and Archer, 2007) on the different collaboration in Supply chains by e-markteplace (EM). The study highlighted that supply chain collaboration tends to be supported more than buying groups by existing EMs, and a high percentage of EMs now offers supply chain coordination and integration. Among online buying groups, the exchange-catalogue model is the most popular, possibly since it puts fewer burdens on members and coordinators.

Min (2009) explored various sub-fields of Artificial Intelligence that are most suitable for solving practical problems relevant to Supply Chain Management. The most popular tools can be subdivided in three categories: agent-based system, genetic algorithm and expert systems.

The research presented in this chapter regards the agent-based negotiation in Business To Business applications that are one of the most important Artificial Intelligence area of research for Supply Chain Management.

Many Small and Medium Enterprises (SMEs) handle procurement through an inefficient combination of manual processes, including paper records, phone calls, e-mails and faxes. This can lead to problems such as limited financial reporting, lack of readily accessible management information, lower levels of vendor compliance and unauthorized spending. The e-procurement solutions can address these issues, but most of these tend to be expensive, complex, require technical expertise to install and maintain and are usually oriented towards larger firms. In justifying implementation of e-procurement, cost control is generally ranked as the highest motivator, followed by competitiveness and supplier requests, with strategic decision ranked the lowest. At the same time lack of standardization, social barriers and managers' limited understanding of e-procurement solutions and vendor offerings leads medium-sized firms more favorably disposed than small firms to e-procurement. This chapter proposes an integrated approach able to reduce some of these difficulties for small enterprises, reducing their cost burden by considering alliances among them by using a coalition support system as a value added services in an e-marketplace, together with Multi Agent Architecture and simulative performances evaluation through simulation. Coalition may be a big chance for small and medium suppliers not able to respond to the customer request by themselves: that means that this approach could be a basic topic in a "stay-together" economy, since it provides the business reasons to share the risk in an e-marketplace. Generally speaking, a coalition is a set of self-interested agents that agree to cooperate to execute a task or achieve a goal. Such coalitions were thoroughly investigated within game theory. There, issues of solution stability, fairness and payoff splitting were discussed and analyzed. The formal analysis in there provided can be used to compute multi-agent coalitions, however only in a centralized manner and with exponential complexity. Distributed Artificial Intelligence (DAI) researchers have adopted some of the game theoretical concepts and, upon them, developed coalition formation algorithms to be used by agents within a multi-agent system. These algorithms concentrate on distribution of computations, complexity reduction, task allocation and communication issues. Nevertheless, some of the underlying assumptions of the coalition formation algorithms, which are essential for their implementation, do not hold in real-world multi-agent systems. In this chapter, we propose an approach to manage the phases of coalition: selection of the partners, how the coalition formulates the proposal to the customer and when the coalition win a negotiation how the profit is shared among the partners. The main innovative contribution regards the application of the shapley value approach to share the profit among the partners of the coalition. Moreover, a simulation environment based on multi agent architecture has been developed to test the proposed approach. This tool can be most promising for SMEs that can be competitive in an e-marketplace respect the large enterprises. The remainder is organized as follows: Section 2 gives a brief overview on the state of the art on the coalition in the e-marketplace environment. The research context is described in Section 3. Section 4 presents the proposed agent based model for negotiation and coalition formation. Section 5 presents the coalition approaches, while the simulation case study is shown in Section 6. The simulative results are discussed in Section 7, while conclusions and future path research are illustrated in Section 8.

LITERATURE OVERVIEW

Many studies have been developed to study game theoretic properties of coalitions. The main topics of these works have been coalition stability, fairness, payoff distribution, methods for efficient formation of coalitions, as well as methods for manipulating results of coalition processes. However, most of these ones have concentrated on theoretical aspects of coalitions and thus there is currently limited research or system implementation activity in the context of concrete seller coalition formation. In this chapter, the considered coalition is a set of self-interested agents that agree to cooperate to achieve a goal (the agreement) with the considered buyer (Peleg 1984, Jeffrey and Zlotkin, 1994, Sandholm et al. 1999). A primary motivation for players in a game to form coalitions is to improve their surplus. Starting from this, three basic problems in coalition formation in a given game have to be considered: whether a stable coalition exists, how to share profit among the participants and who should be in which coalition. Among various theoretic developments, the core introduced by Gillies (Gillies 1953) is the earliest and most well accepted approach for coalition formation problems. The core is the set of all feasible payoffs to the players that no player or group of players could improve upon by acting unilaterally. The existence of a nonempty core implies that the game will have a stable solution and the players will have incentive to form the grand coalition. For the detailed discussion on the core, refer to Kannai (1992), Peleg (1992), Anderson (1992) and Gabszewicz and Shitovitz (1992). The literature on core game typically considers the stability of the grand coalition in a game and does not offer practical solution for coalition formation. Lerman and Shehory (2000) proposed a new model of coalition formation and applied it to coalition formation among buyer agents in an e-marketplace. Yamamoto and Sycara (2001) describe global behaviour of a set of agents from the macroscopic view point by differential equations and simulate how buyer coalitions evolve and reach the steady state. However, the model does not assist individual agents to form a coalition nor to negotiate surplus distribution. In this work, in order to overcome the above cited limitations and to obtain a fair allocation of gains obtained by cooperation among agents (Laruelle and Valenciano, 2008), we use the Shapley value approach From his seminal paper (Shapley, 1953b) a copious family of 'solutions' for transferable utility (TU) games has grown in different directions with many ramifications. Among others, weighted Shapley values (Shapley, 1953a), (Weber, 1988), probabilistic values (Weber, 1979), semi-values (Dubey et al., 1981), weak semi-values and weighted weak semi-values (Calvo and Santos, 2000), as well as non transferable utility (NTU) and non-atomic extensions of some of these notions, or their restriction to special sub domains as, e.g., simple games. Most of these extensions have been born out of axiomatic explorations: dropping axioms, finding weaker or more appealing ones, recombining already existing ones, etc. This leads to heterogeneous families of objects, of which the Shapley value is an omnipresent particular case. Our study differs from these papers in three main aspects. One important difference, as discussed above, is that we assist individual agents to form a coalition and to negotiate surplus distribution using the Shapley value approach. Another main difference is that, while other papers primarily investigate the existence of stable coalition structures from theoretical aspects, we are interested in its application to concrete cases of e-marketplace in which SMEs try to compete with bigger companies. Finally, our chapter differs from the above papers because of the agent based structure, related to the production planning of each single agent, capable to support the decision making procedure and to evaluate different performances in order to obtain a quantitative methodologies able to appraise different market scenarios.

RESEARCH CONTEXT

E-marketplace can be classified, according to the buying behavior, in *MRO Hubs*, *Catalogue*, *Yield Managers* and *Exchange*. According to whom the buyers are in *Horizontal* and *Vertical* e-marketplace and, on the centricity base, in *Buyer Centric*, *Seller Centric*, *Neutral linear* and *Neutral exponential* (Greiger, M. 2003 and Barratt, 2002). In particular, this chapter is concerned with a private neutral linear e-marketplace owned by a third part where a set of registered buyers and a set of registered sellers are allowed to play procurement actions. Examples of such e-marketplace are CPGmarket, Tribon Marketplace and ChemConnect.

Figure 1 shows the "*neutrality*" of the e-marketplace from the centricity point of view.

Figure 1. A private neutral linear e-marketplace

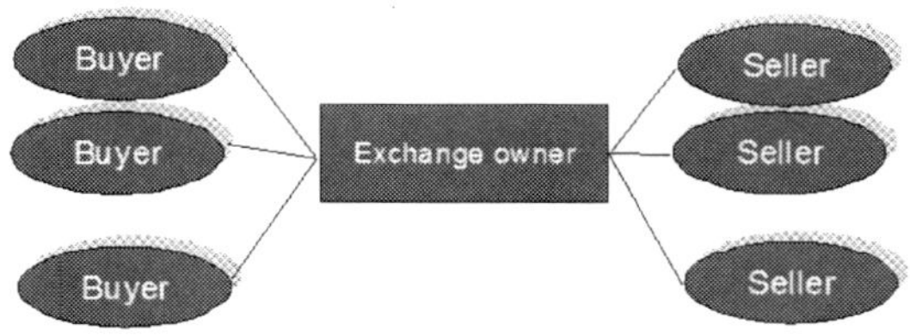

This kind of e-market sites are suitable for context in which operate highly fragmented industries. In this environment, the knowledge base is the same for buyers (also named customers) and sellers (also named suppliers); that means that all the involved typologies of agents have the same *market power*. Buyers or sellers do not establish such marketplaces, which are usually set-up by an independent company, such as an ICT provider or a bank, whose aim is to put together separate group of agents in order to establish a sort of "procurement virtual district". The exchange owner usually gets his income from the transaction fees and eventually from some added value service fees such as secure transactions or financial services. In such e-marketplaces, procurement actions are usually order-based (Hoffman, 2002).

MULTI AGENT ARCHITECTURE

One of the methodologies used to develop Value Added Services in B2B e-marketplace is the multi agent system technology (Turowski, 2002; Kurbel and Loutchko, 2005; Louta et al. 2008).

The agent technology is quite useful for e-marketplace for the following reasons: the agents can act in an autonomous manner and proactively; agents can analyze the situations and select the most appropriate behavior to perform actions; the robustness of the architecture based on agents allow the system to operate if some agents are in failure state; the flexibility of the architecture allows to introduce or remove agents quickly; the distribution approach of multi agent architectures is able to implement the e-marketplaces that are composed by actors distributed physically.

The Multi Agent System supporting the considered e-marketplace (proposed in Argoneto and Renna, 2009), consists of a Customer Negotiation Agent (CNA), who is in charge for negotiating the parameters of the order with the sellers, and a set of agents representing each seller:

- the *Supplier Negotiation Agent* (SNA), who is in charge to negotiate with the customer;
- the *Supplier Coalition Agent* (SCA), who is in charge to evaluate the possibility to make a coalition with other suppliers;
- the *Coalition and Negotiation Agent* (CoNa), who is in charge to represent the suppliers' coalition during the negotiation.

Finally, the e-marketplace owner provides a *Scheduler Agent* who is in charge for allowing communication and coordination among suppliers' and customers' agents. The UML activity diagram of Figure 2 shows the agents' interaction workflow. As the reader can notice five swim lines, corresponding to the above-described agents, have been located in the diagram. Very briefly, the workflow can be summarized as follows:

- *Step 1*: The customer submits the order through the CNA;
- *Step 2*: The customer's order activates the Scheduler who selects the negotiation policy and transmits order data to the SNA;
- *Step 3*: The SNA is activated; it verifies whether the round of negotiation is $r=2$, because coalitions are not allowed in the first step; if this condition is verified the SNA sends a coalition request to the SCA, otherwise it negotiates directly with the CNA;
- *Step 4:* The SCA is activated; it evaluates the availability of other suppliers to make a coalition as described in Section 4; if a

Figure 2. Agents' interaction workflow

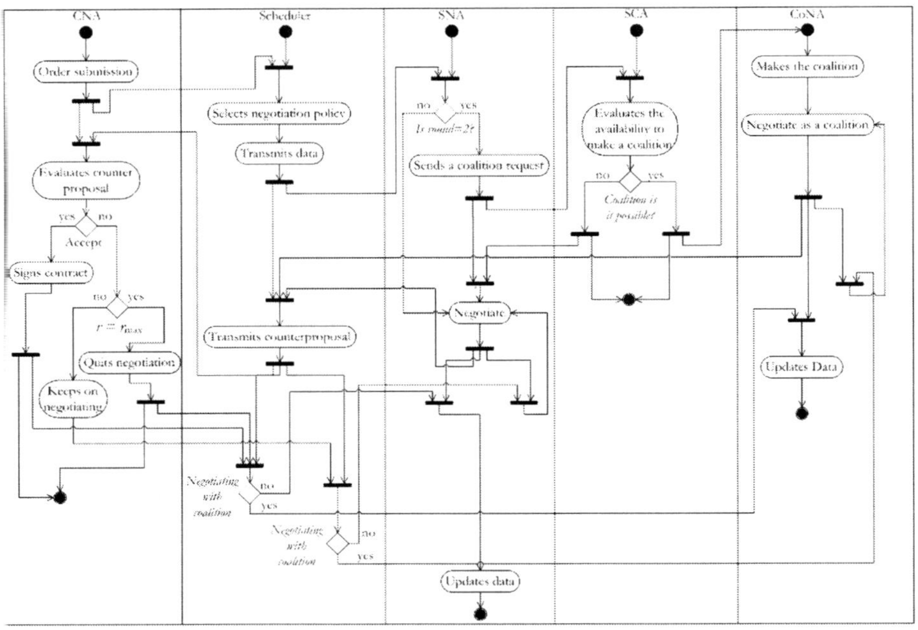

coalition is possible the SCA activates the CoNA, otherwise it calls again for the SNA for a one-to-one negotiation; in any case the SCA returns to its initial state;

- *Step 5*- In case it is impossible to have a coalition among sellers, or in case round $r=1$, the SNA starts the negotiation with the CNA by preparing a counter-proposal as described in Section 4; on the other hand, if a coalition is possible, the CoNA forms the coalition and it elaborates a counter-proposal as described in next the section; in both cases the counter-proposal is transmitted to the Scheduler;
- *Step 6:* The Scheduler is activated; it transmits the counter-proposal to the CNA;
- *Step 7:* The CNA is activated; it evaluates the supplier's or coalition's counter-proposal; if the counter-proposal meets the requirements described in next the section, the CNA accepts the proposal and it signs the contract; on the other hand, if the CNA does not find the counter-proposal satisfying, it evaluates the number of negotiation rounds; if round $r = r_{max}$, it quits the negotiation, otherwise it asks the SNA for another counter-proposal; in any case the CNA evaluation is transmitted to the Scheduler;
- *Step 8:* The Scheduler is activated; it transmits customer's decision either to the supplier or to the suppliers' coalition;
- *Step 9:* Either SNA or CoNA are activated; if the negotiation is over, because of an agreement or an unsuccessful termination, the agents update their negotiation database and they return on their initial state; if negotiation continues, they build another counter-proposal for the customer and the workflow starts again from *step 6*.

The negotiation process starts with the order submission of the customer. The order consists of the array *(i, V*, dd*, p*)*, being *i* the part type, *V** the required volume, *dd** the required due date and *p** the related price. The generic supplier *s* computes the counter proposal constraints, i.e.

a feasible range of the required price (Δp) and due date (Δdd). Such constraints are determined according to a production planning algorithm proposed in Argoneto and Renna (2009). Within the given ranges, a collection of potential *due date* (W) and *price* (Q) values are considered to generate a set of alternative counter proposals j ($j=1, 2, \ldots, W \times Q = J$), where the alternative j is the combination of the dd_w and p_q ($w=1, 2, \ldots, W$ and $q = 1, 2, \ldots, Q$). Furthermore, the supplier computes the minimum level of profit (Pr_{min}), with respect to the maximum achievable profit (Pr_{max}), that can be considered acceptable (see equation 1). At each alternative counter proposal, the following two matrixes are associated:

- a profit matrix $\boldsymbol{P} = \{Pr_j(dd_w, p_q)\}$, whose generic element $Pr_j(dd_w, p_q)$ returns the profit associated with the j-th counter proposal alternative;
- a volume ratio matrix $\boldsymbol{V} = \{V_j\ (dd_w, p_q)\}$ whose generic element $V_j\ (dd_w, p_q)$ returns the volume ratio, respect the required V^*, associated with each combination of offered due date (dd_w) and price (p_q). Indeed, for example, if $V_j\ (dd_w, p_q) = 0.9$ it means that the *j-th* alternative is able to satisfy the 90% of the required volume V^*.

Among all the possible alternatives, at first round $r = 1$ the supplier offers to the customer the most profitable ones. It first builds the set of alternatives $\bar{J}_{(r=1)}$ by maximizing the expected profit as explained in equation (1):

$$\bar{J}_{(r=1)} = \left\{Pr_{max}\right\} \equiv \max_{j=1,\ldots,J} \left\{ Pr_j \right\}, \text{ being } \bar{J}_{(r=1)} \subseteq J. \quad (1)$$

At this point, within the set of alternatives $\bar{J}_{(r=1)}$, the algorithm seeks those alternatives able to better satisfying the customer request, that is the alternative $j^* \in \bar{J}_{(r=1)}$ minimizing the distance from the requested parameters:

$$j^* = \min_{j \in \bar{J}_{(r=1)}} \left(\frac{\left|dd_w - dd^*\right|}{"\ dd} + \frac{\left|p_q - p^*\right|}{p^*} + \left|V_j - 1\right| \right) \quad (2)$$

On the other hand, if $r>1$, the supplier applies a profit reduction strategy, depending on the negotiation round, searching for those alternatives whose profit is according to the equation (3):

$$Pr\left(r\right) = Pr_{max} - \frac{Pr_{max} - Pr_{min}}{r_{max}} \cdot r \quad (3)$$

being $Pr_{min} = \min_{j=1,\ldots,J} \left\{ Pr_j \right\}$ and $Pr_j \geq Pr\left(r\right)\ \forall j \in \bar{J}_{(r)}$ (4)

Among the possible alternatives that have been found, the supplier searches for the alternative j^* satisfying relation (2) with $j \in \bar{J}_{(r)}$. The alternative j^*, both in cases $r = 1$ and $r > 1$, determines the *rth* supplier's counter-proposal: $V_s(r), dd_s(r), p_s(r)$. At each round, the customer computes the utility function threshold according to the following expression (5):

$$Thu(r) = Thu_{max} \cdot \left(1 - \frac{r-1}{r_{max}-1}\right)^2 + F \cdot \left(\frac{r-1}{r_{max}-1}\right) \cdot \left(1 - \frac{r-1}{r_{max}-1}\right) + Thu_{min} \cdot \left(\frac{r-1}{r_{max}-1}\right)^2 \quad (5)$$

The above expression shows how the customer utility threshold value decreases throughout the negotiation process: the customer is more willing to accept the supplier proposal when the negotiation proceeds toward its end. Thu_{min} and Thu_{max} respectively represent the minimum and maximum threshold values: they are correspondingly used when $r = r_{max}$ and $r = 1$. The parameter F represents the utility function slope and it models the customer willingness to find an agreement. Afterwards, the customer evaluates its satisfaction by computing the counter-proposal utility as follows:

$$U(r) = U_v(r) + U_{dd}(r) + U_p(r) \tag{6}$$

being $U_v(r)$, $U_{dd}(r)$, $U_p(r)$ respectively the utilities of the volumes, due date and price, computed at round r, as showed in the following equations 7 to 9:

$$U_v(r) = Max\left(\left(\frac{V_s(r) - V_{\min}}{V^* - V_{\min}}\right); 0\right) \tag{7}$$

$$U_{dd}(r) = Max\left(Min\left(\frac{dd_s(r) - dd_{min}}{dd^* - dd_{min}}; \frac{dd_{max} - dd_s(r)}{dd_{max} - dd^*}\right); 0\right) \tag{8}$$

$$U_p = Max\left(Min\left(\left(1 - \frac{p_s(r) - p^*}{p_{max} - p^*}\right); 1\right); 0\right) \tag{9}$$

being V_{min}, P_{max}, dd_{min}, and dd_{max} respectively the minimum quantity of volume, the maximum price and the due date interval that the customer can accept (see Table 3). Three cases can occur:

1. $U(r) \geq Thu(r)$: the customer accepts the counter-proposal of the supplier s and it signs the contract. Both agents update their database;
2. $U(r) < Thu(r)$ and $r < r_{max}$: the customer asks for a new counter-proposal,
3. $U(r) < Thu(r)$ and $r > r_{max}$: the customer rejects the proposal and quits the negotiation.

See the following workflow (Figure 2) for a deep explanation of the agents' interaction.

COOPERATIVE GAME THEORY AND SHAPLEY APPROACH

Generally speaking, a cooperative game consists of two elements: a set of players and a characteristic function specifying the value created by different subsets of the players in the game. Formally, let $N = \{1, \ldots, n\}$ be the (finite) set of players and i is the index of the generic player of the set. The characteristic function is a function, denoted v, that associates a number denoted $v(S)$ to every subset S of N, a number. The number $v(S)$ is interpreted as the value created when the members of S come together and interact. In sum, a cooperative game is a pair (N,v), where N is a finite set and v is a function mapping subsets of N to numbers. Given a cooperative game (N,v), the quantity $v(N)$ specifies the overall amount of value created. An important question is how this overall value is divided up among the various players. A solution is a mapping that assigns a set of payoff vectors in $v(N)$ to each characteristic function game (N,v). Thus, a solution in general prescribes a set, which can be empty or a singleton (when it assigns a unique payoff vector as a function of the fundamentals of the problem). Research on cooperative decision making from a cooperative game theory perspective provides axiomatic solution concepts for surplus (cost) sharing of coalitions. These include the Core, Shapley Value and Nucleolus among other concepts (Osborne and Rubinstein, 1994). The stability of a coalition requires that the distribution of surplus among the coalition members is immune to groups of agents refusing to participate and forming their own coalition and the *core* is the most commonly used concept to characterize this property. In this section, we discuss an approach to determine imputations of the gain attained by a coalition, namely, using the game core concept and calculating the Shapley vector (Belenky, 2002).

Coalition Mechanism

As deeply discussed in Tombuş and Bilgiç (2004) the coalition formation problem is a set partitioning problem. The CA evaluates the possible coalition among the suppliers: since the number of variables of possible coalitions grows exponentially with the number of partners, here, the authors have considered coalitions with two or maximum three suppliers. Moreover, in the considered case, the set of partners combination S does not represent a partition of N; indeed, indicating with $S_{N,2}$ and with $S_{N,3}$ the set of possible suppliers combination with two and three elements respectively, it will be $\mathbf{S} = \mathbf{S}_{N,2} \cup \mathbf{S}_{N,3}$. Let us indicate with *(i, j)* -or with *(i, j, k)* in case of three players- the generic set s_l belonging to S; $s_l \in S$ can compete for the order acquisition if:

$$V_l \leq V^* \tag{10}$$

being

- $V_l = \sum_{z=i,j/z=i,j,k} V_z$ the volume that can be offered by the considered coalition, and
- V^* the volume required by the customer.

Equation (10) expresses that for each combination of suppliers, the coalition l is created if and only if the offered volume (V_l) is smaller minor than the volume required by the customer; each single supplier is also allowed to compete for the order as a particular case of coalition. In the subsequent step the CA computes the coalition counter proposal through the following steps:

the coalition due date (dd_l) is the maximum due date among those proposed by the suppliers participating at the coalition:

$$dd_l = \max_{z=i,j/z=i,j,k} \{dd_z\} \tag{11}$$

2. the coalition volume is the sum given by equation (10);

the coalition offered price is computed as follows:

first a weighted price (pr_mp_l) is computed through the following expression:

$$pr\_mp_l = \frac{\sum_{z=i,j/z=i,j,k} p_z \cdot V_z}{\sum_{z=i,j/z=i,j,k} V_z} \tag{12}$$

then, CA computes an index (d_l) measuring the distance between the proposed counteroffer and the customer request:

$$d_z = \frac{V^* - V_z}{V^*} + \frac{p_z - p^*}{p^*} + \frac{dd_z - dd^*}{dd^* - t_{arr}^*} \tag{13}$$

afterwards, an indifference price pr_ind_l, representing the price that with dd_l and V_l guarantee the customer with an offer as good as the best one among those generated by suppliers *i, j* and *k*, is computed as the price satisfying the following equation:

$$d_l = \frac{V^* - V_l}{V^*} + \frac{pr\_ind_l - p^*}{p^*} + \frac{dd_l - dd^*}{dd^* - t_{arr}^*} = \min_{z=i,j/z=i,j,k} (d_z) \tag{14}$$

Finally a coalition price $pr\_coa^*_l$ is computed as the price satisfying the following expression:

$$d_l \cdot f_s = \frac{V^* - V_l}{V^*} + \frac{pr\_coa^*_l - p^*}{p^*} + \frac{dd_l - dd^*}{dd^* - t^*_{err}} = \min_{z=i,j/z=i,j,k}\left(d_z\right) \text{, where } f_s < 1. \quad (15)$$

$pr\_coa^*_l$ represents a price that with dd_l and V_l will guarantee to the customer an offer better than the best alternative offer among those generated by supplier i, j and k. Therefore, it represents the added value the coalition l provides the customer with. The coalition price pr_coa_l is computed by the following expression:

$$pr\_coa_l = \begin{bmatrix} if\ pr\_mp_l > pr\_coa^*_l; \\ \max\left(pr\_mp_l; pr\_ind_l\right); pr\_coa^*_l \end{bmatrix} \quad (16)$$

pr_coa_l, as computed in equation (16), assures all the coalition participants that at least gainthe same profit they would have achieved by competing alone; moreover, whether possible, they gain an extra profit ($pr\_coa=pr\_indl$) and, when the best alternative is considered, also the customer gains a benefit from the coalition formation ($pr\_coa = pr\_coa^*_l$).

4. The CA collects the coalition and the single supplier proposals. Moreover, it evaluates the index d of equation (13) for each proposal (coalitions and single supplier too).
5. The CA submits to the customer the proposal with minimum value of d.
6. The customer evaluates the proposal and, as explained in the above paragraph, it can accept the counter-proposal and signs the agreement with the supplier whether the related utility is greater than a threshold value; afterwards it updates its database with the agreement data. Conversely, if the utility associated with the counter-proposal is lower than the threshold value, the customer evaluates if a negotiation with the supplier can be activated; in particular, if more negotiation time is available, the customer asks for a new counter-proposal, otherwise -the negotiation time is over- the customer rejects the proposal and quits the negotiation. In case the contract is signed with a coalition, then two alternatives are possible:
   a. the price of the coalition is the same of the pr_mp; in this case each coalition supplier updates its database with the price proposed;
   the price of the coalition is more than the pr_mp; in this case the surplus of expression (17) will be shared among the coalition suppliers:

$$extra - profit_l = \left(pr\_coa_l - pr\_mp_l\right) \cdot V_l \quad (17)$$

A modified coalition strategy (SVA^*) has also been set up; in this case the supplier can compete, differently from the previous approach, only joining in a coalition or alone: therefore the algorithm does not explore all the possible combinations as previously showed. The decision to participate in a coalition is based on the capability of the supplier to provide the volume required by the customer.

Profit Sharing Mechanism

In case of surplus, the Shapley approach is utilised to split it among the coalition suppliers. As explained above, the characteristic function is one of the basic concepts in cooperative game theory: it is the key to the value based approach and in particular to the Shapley value. Therefore, the characteristic function has been utilised in this chapter to calculate this last value that could be interpreted as an average contribution measure that each seller brings to the coalition. For all *i, j, k*, the considered characteristic function is build as follows:

$v(i)$ = supplier *i* profit;

$v(i, j)$ = coalition extra profit;

$v(i, j, k)$ = coalition extra profit; (18)

Extra profit is computed as reported in equation (17). In case a coalition reaches an agreement with the buyer and in case an utility surplus to share among the winning coalition players exists, then the proposed mechanism shares this surplus proportionally to the Shapley value calculated, for each player *i*, as follows:

$$\Phi_i(\nu) = \frac{1}{n!} \sum_{k=1,2,3/k=1,2} (n-k)!(k-1)!\left[\nu(K) - \nu(K \setminus i)\right] \quad (19)$$

being *k* the magnitude order of coalition with seller *i* and *n* the seller number.

SIMULATION ENVIRONMENT

In order to test the proposed coalition approach a proper test environment of the e-marketplace context has been developed. It consists of a simulation environment that can be used to test the functionality of the proposed models and to understand the advantages of the added value services. In order to cut times and costs for the development of an actual e-marketplace environment, the simulation environment has been developed directly in open source architecture by using Java Development Kit (JDK) package. The modeling formalism in here adopted is a collection of independent objects interacting via messages. This formalism is quite suitable for Multi Agent Systems development. In particular, each object represents an agent and the system evolves through a message-sending engine managed by a discrete event scheduler. In particular, the following agents have been developed the *CNA*, the *SNA*, the *SCA*, the *CoNa* and the *Scheduler*. Moreover, the *CNA* and the *SNA* have been provided with a local database to manage supplier and customer data. A proper interface has been developed to connect the Java code to the database. Finally, the *SNA* has been linked with a mathematical interface to solve the supplier's production planning MILP, fully described in (Argoneto end Renna, 2009). The described simulation environment has been used to test the following test-case.

Test Case

An e-marketplace consisting of 9 customers and 9 suppliers has been considered. Each customer can submit an order for 10 different part-types. Table 1 reports the 48 orders data that have been submitted for the test case. For each order index, *o*, the arrival time, t_a, the due date, dd^*, the required price expressed in monetary units, p^*, the required volume, V^*, the customer identification number, C_{id}, and the part type are reported.

The parameters reported in Table 1 have been generated in the following way:

- the order arrival time, t_a^o, has been randomly generated to guarantee at least five orders within the same re-planning time bucket;
- the order due date, dd^*_o, has been randomly generated, for each order, following a uniform distribution with lower bound equal to t_a^o +3 and the upper bound equal to the value of the end of the re-planning time bucket;
- the volume of the order, V^*_o, has been randomly generated by using the following expression:

Table 1. Orders data

o	t_a	*dd**	*p**	*V**	C_{id}	*Part-type*
1	2	9	556.690	356	3	2
2	15	20	391.249	276	1	7
3	19	24	100.678	73	5	8
4	25	30	250.819	165	4	9
5	42	51	641.576	446	5	8
6	48	53	50.816	33	9	4
7	55	60	82.577	55	3	5
8	56	60	141.847	94	2	10
9	52	60	123.921	80	2	1
10	63	71	409.207	271	5	8
11	67	89	759.415	562	6	10
12	72	77	262.234	166	9	3
13	78	82	81.574	60	8	10
14	79	88	735.504	475	4	2
15	95	100	228.229	160	6	1
16	98	106	90.266	60	5	6
17	100	117	540.165	336	3	2
18	103	115	699.524	486	6	7
19	111	116	394.020	284	4	1
20	122	128	507.832	312	3	3
21	136	141	256.757	181	1	1
22	137	143	263.635	172	1	7
23	142	148	402.521	282	7	9
24	145	150	115.069	74	7	7
o	t_a	***dd****	***p****	***V****	C_{id}	***Part-type***
25	157	168	397.363	276	4	2
26	160	172	750.230	542	6	1
27	166	175	383.990	259	4	3
28	169	173	120.418	88	2	9
29	171	177	274.699	170	2	9
30	181	187	209.061	140	3	9
31	184	197	533.574	362	7	1
32	189	200	464.609	327	7	6
33	194	204	520.106	348	1	7
34	201	210	80.650	48	8	5
35	218	236	1.267.693	902	3	2
36	230	238	288.852	181	3	10
37	232	236	183.398	129	8	8
38	233	237	376.985	230	8	9

continued on following page

Table 1. continued

o	t_a	dd^*	p^*	V^*	C_{id}	*Part-type*
39	235	240	177.906	108	2	6
40	244	251	316.362	206	7	7
41	246	253	323.239	206	8	7
42	263	268	337.758	224	6	10
43	265	270	273.187	172	4	1
44	271	276	149.202	94	6	9
45	273	283	660.202	411	1	3
46	274	295	1.119.717	728	3	4
47	279	300	1.176.105	728	8	10
48	296	298	170.216	116	4	3

$$V^*_o = Unif\left[0.1, 1.1\right] \cdot \underset{j \in S}{Max}\left(Ord\_cap_j\right) \cdot (dd^*_o - t_a^{\,o} + 1) \tag{20}$$

being Ord_cap_j the ordinary production capacity of the *jth* supplier, as reported in Table 2.

The order price, p^*_o, has been computed according to the following expression:

$$p^*_o = mk\_up \cdot \underset{j \in S}{Min}\left(\frac{\underset{j}{Max}\left(CU_{o,j}\right) + \underset{j}{Min}\left(CU_{o,j}\right)}{2}\right) \cdot V^*_o \tag{21}$$

being:

- $CU_{o,j}$, the unit ordinary cost for manufacturing a single product of order o in the *jth* supplier's manufacturing system;
- *mk_up*, the mark up applied for computing the price; the mark-up has been obtained by a uniform distribution: Unif [1.1, 1.4].

As the reader can notice, the price is computed by applying a mark-up strategy to obtain an average ordinary cost over the supplier set. Supplier costs and capacity data are reported in Table 2, while Table 3 reports data used by the customer in equations (5)-(9) for computing its utility of supplier's counter-proposal.

SIMULATION RESULTS

The test case has been carried out under the following experimental conditions:

- *No Coalitions*, in this case a Contemporary Multi Negotiation policy is considered as benchmark with no possibility to make a coalition (Argoneto et al., 2004);
- *50%*, in this case a Contemporary Multi Negotiation policy is considered with the possibility to make a coalition composed by two suppliers that subdivide the requested volume in equal part. This approach is considered as benchmark for all the other coalition policies.
- *SVA*; in this case a Contemporary Multi Negotiation policy is chosen together with the coalitional approach based on the Shapley value. The supplier that veri-

Table 2. Suppliers' data

	Suppliers (s)								
	1	*2*	*3*	*4*	*5*	*6*	*7*	*8*	*9*
Process Plan fixed cost (*PP_cost*)	300	600	150	300	200	250	450	500	400
Ordinary cost (*Ord_cost*) per unit of time	30	10	45	15	20	15	20	15	20
Overtime cost (*Ov_cost*) per unit of time	60	20	70	35	40	50	30	30	35
Outsourcing cost (*Out_cost*) per unit of time	70	120	60	45	45	90	45	100	70
Ordinary capacity (*Ord_cap*)	96	288	96	64	48	96	120	144	96
Overtime capacity (*Ov_cap*)	24	12	36	12	12	32	12	48	24
Outsourcing capacity (*Out_cap*)	96	32	192	24	24	96	48	24	32

fies the equation (10) can operate in all the possible combinations (alone, with a set of two and three suppliers) to provide the volume required by the customer; therefore, the generic supplier can act alone, in a coalition or in both cases.

- *SVA**: the difference from the *SVA* approach lies in the supplier's possibility to participate alone at the negotiation. Differently from the previous case, whether the equation (10) is verified, it could participate in a coalition of two or three suppliers, but not alone. In a certain sense this approach is more realistic for a real application because in here at the generic supplier is not allowed the competition, during the negotiation process, with a coalition that involves himself.

Simulation experiment results have been reported in Table 4, where, for each experimental condition, the following performance have been reported:

- *Customer utility*; is the average utility the customer reports after having sequenced all the orders of Table 1; the utility is computed as reported in Section 3;
- *Supplier utility*; the suppliers' cumulative profit computed over all the orders has been assumed as a measure of the supplier's utility;
- *Refused orders*; this reports the number of customer orders refused by the suppliers;
- *Normalized customer utility*; this is the normalized customer utility computed over all the customers' utility reported in the first row of Table 4;
- *Normalized supplier utility*; this is the normalized supplier utility computed over all the suppliers' utility reported in the second row of Table 4;
- *Total normalized utility*; this is sum of the normalized customer and supplier utilities.

The normalized values are obtained by the ratio of the performance and the best value of this performance among the approaches, therefore the value of one identifies the best performance.

From the analysis of the simulation results reported in the previous Table 4, the following issues can be drawn:

Table 3. Data for the customer's counter-proposal evaluation

Utility	*Price*	*Volume*	*Due Date*	*Utility Function Slope*
$Thu_{min}=3$, $Thu_{max}=1.5$	$P_{max}=1,6\cdot p^*$	$V_{min}=0,3\cdot V^*$	$dd_{min}=dd^*-5$, $dd_{max}=dd^*+5$	$F=2.7$

Table 4. Simulation results

	No Coalitions	*50%*	**SVA**	**SVA***
Customer utility	2.48	2.45	2.51	2.43
Supplier utility	12,852,848	11,650,492	14,071,233	15,873,345
Refused Orders	5	10	6	2
Normalized Customer Utility	0.99	0.98	1	0.97
Normalized Supplier Utility	0.81	0.73	0.89	1
Total Normalized Utility	1.80	1.71	1.89	1.97

- the possibility to make a coalition among the suppliers, with any opportune strategy (*50%*) does not improve the considered performances. As the reader can notice, the performance evaluated in case of "50%" gets worse than the "no coalition" approach, for all the measures: the total normalized utility is the lower value among the investigated approaches;
- the Shapley value based approaches (both *SVA* and *SVA**) lead to an increase the total normalized utility thanks to the significant increment of the suppliers' profit. That means that these approaches could lead to a real value added particularly for the suppliers involved in an e-marketplace;
- the *SVA* approach leads to improve both customer and suppliers' utilities, but at the same time it increases the number of refused order (specifically, just one more than in case of "*No coalitions*"). Then, this approach leads to a very low difference if compared with the first case investigated, but allows the suppliers to gain more benefits with the same level of utility;
- The *SVA** leads to the better suppliers'performance: particularly the maximum value of profit is reached. The reason is the strong reduction of refused orders. The same reason leads to a slight reduction of the customer's utility.

In conclusion, the *SVA** approach leads to the better global performance (total normalized utility); moreover it reduces the number of refused orders that is easily considered as a customer's index of satisfaction.

SUMMARY AND CONCLUSION

This chapter deals with Value Added Services in linear neutral e-marketplace. In particular, the aim of the research was to deeply investigate advantages brought by coalition of suppliers in e-marketplace and to measure that advantage in order to quantify the "stay-together economies" approach by using the cooperative game theory. Specifically, the coalition formation matches with the following items:

- the suppliers that compose the coalition;
- the counter-proposal formulation of the coalition;
- how the suppliers of a coalition share the profit when the coalition wins the negotiation.

In this chapter the authors proposed two different approaches to manage this issue:

- The Shapley approach (*SVA*), in which the coalition is composed by suppliers that cannot completely satisfy the whole volume required by the customer. All the possible combinations of players are considered, but only the ones with at maximum three agents are allowed. The profit sharing is proportionally computed by using the Shapley value.

- The Modified Shapley approach (*SVA**); in this case, whether equation (10) is verified, the single supplier cannot participate as a single coalition or alone, but only in a coalition.

To deeply analyse this approaches, two benchmark models have been considered:

- A model with no possibility to make coalition among the suppliers: they can only participate as a single agent;
- A model with no strategy to make a coalition among the suppliers: the coalition is composed by two suppliers that share exactly 50% the volume required by the customer.

A proper simulation environment has been developed in open source architecture, in order to test the proposed coalition approaches. The simulation results showed that coalitions can be considered as real advantages for customer and suppliers because of their capacity to improve the satisfaction of all the involved agents and to reduce the number of refused order, generating higher profits. Moreover, a proper strategy to make coalition is a critical factor to improve the customer's and suppliers' performance. In fact, if coalitions are created in absence of any strategy (as in case of the "50%" approach), the performance get worse than in case of "No coalition". These important results can be summarized as follows:

- The Shapley value is proposed as a method to share the profit surplus: any specific policy regarding the composition of the coalitions, but the volume constraint, has been considered. This simple approach has lead us to significantly improve the suppliers' performance and to obtain a good compromise between the customer and suppliers' degree of satisfaction.
- The typology of coalition approaches (*SVA* or *SVA**) does not significantly improve the customer's utility, but in the *SVA** case the number of refused orders is drastically reduced. This means that the customer satisfaction is anyhow improved because of the increment of reached agreements.
- This research allows to understand which approach is better to be utilized in an e-marketplace in which the coalition formation is allowed. In particular, the Shapley policy shows its potentiality to be used in a seller-centric marketplace.

Further research will deeply investigate the following aspects:

- A proper decision making strategy could be provided to each supplier. The supplier will use a strategy based on its performance in order to make the decision to participate in a coalition. The performance could be: the profit gained in the past negotiations; the potential profit related to the orders required by the customer; the benefits that the supplier could obtain by the possible relations with other suppliers.
- The simulations should be extended; the benefits highlighted by this research will be investigated in different conditions. In particular, it will be analyzed the performance trend in case the number of suppliers is variable during the negotiation process, in case of stable or turbulent market environment (depending on the characteristics of the orders) and in case the characteristics of the suppliers are changing (risk attitude, and so on);
- An investigation should take place on how the information sharing (among the sup-

pliers involved in the e-marketplace) can change the evaluated performance. This study is expected to highlight the benefits that each supplier can gain when the quantity of the available information increases. Therefore, several levels of sharing will be investigated starting from the case in which any information is shared to the ones where no private information is allowed.

REFERENCES

Anderson, R. (1992). The Core in Perfectly Competitive Economics. In R. Aumann & S. Hart, (Eds.), *Handbook of Game Theory with Economic Applications* (pp.413-457). Amsterdam, North-Holland: Elsevier.

Argoneto, P., Bruccoleri, M., Lo Nigro, G., Noto La Diega, S., Perrone, G., & Renna, P. (2004). Evaluating multi-lateral negotiation policies in manufacturing e-marketplace. *The 37th CIRP International Seminar on Manufacturing Systems*, May 19-21, 2004, Budapest, Hungary.

Argoneto, P., & Renna, P. (2009). Production planning, negotiation and coalition integration: A new tool for an innovatie e-business model. *Robotics and Computer-integrated Manufacturing*. doi:. doi:10.1016/j.rcim.2009.01.001

Ash, C. G., & Burn, J. M. (2006). Evaluating benefits of e-procurement in a B2B marketplace: a case study of Quadrem. *Journal of Information Technology Case Application Research*, *8*(2), 5–23.

Barratt, M., & Rosdahl, K. (2002). Exploring business-to-business marketsites. *European Journal of Purchasing & Supply Management*, *8*, 111–122. doi:10.1016/S0969-7012(01)00010-7

Belenky, A. (2002). Cooperative Games of Choosing Partners and Forming Coalitions in the Marketplace. *Mathematical and Computer Modelling*, *36*, 1279–1291. doi:10.1016/S0895-7177(02)00276-5

Calvo, E., & Santos, J. C. (2000). Weighted weak semivalues. *International Journal of Game Theory*, *29*, 1–9. doi:10.1007/s001820050001

Dubey, P., Neyman, A., & Weber, R. J. (1981). Value theory without efficiency. *Mathematics of Operations Research*, *6*, 122–128. doi:10.1287/moor.6.1.122

Eng, T.-Y. (2004). The role of e-marketplaces in supply chain management. *Industrial Marketing Management*, *33*(2), 97–105. doi:10.1016/S0019-8501(03)00032-4

Gabszewicz, J. J., & Shitovitz, B. (1992). The Core in Imperfectly Competitive Economies. In R. Aumann & S. Hart, (Ed), *Handbook of Game Theory with Economic Applications*. Amsterdam, North-Holland: Elsevier.

Gillies, D. B. (1953). *Some Theorems on N-Person Games*. Ph.D. Dissertation Department of Mathematics, Princeton University, Princeton, N.J.

Greiger, M. (2003). Electronic marketplaces: A literature review and a call for supply chain management research. *European Journal of Operational Research*, *144*, 280–294. doi:10.1016/S0377-2217(02)00394-6

Hoffman, W., Keedy, J., & Roberts, K. (2002). The unexpected return of B2B. *The McKinsey Quarterly*, 3.

Kannai, Y. (1992). The Core and the Balancedness. In R. Aumann & S. Hart, (Ed), *Handbook of Game Theory with Economic Applications*. Amsterdam, North-Holland: Elsevier.

Khosrow-Pour, M. (2005). Advanced Topics in Electronic Commerce: *Vol. 1*. (*Advanced Topics in Electronic Commerce Series*). Hershey, PA: IGI Publishing.

Kurbel, K., & Loutchko, I. (2005). A model for multi-lateral negotiations on an agent-based job marketplace. *Electronic Commerce Research and Applications*, *4*(3), 187–203. doi:10.1016/j.elerap.2005.01.002

Laruelle, A., & Valenciano, F. (2008). Potential, value, and coalition formation. *TOP: An Official Journal of the Spanish Society of Statistics and Operations Research, 16*, 73–89.

Lerman, K., & Shehory, O. (2000). Coalition formation for large scale electronic markets. In *Proceedings of the 4th International Conference on Multi agent Systems ICMAS(2000),* July 2000.

Louta, M., Roussaki, I., & Pechlivanos, L. (2008). An intelligent agent negotiation strategy in the electronic marketplace environment. *European Journal of Operational Research, 187*(3), 1327–1345. doi:10.1016/j.ejor.2006.09.016

Min, H. (2009). Artificial intelligence in supply chain management: theory and applications. *International Journal of Logistics Research and Applications, 13*(1), 13–39. doi:10.1080/13675560902736537

Murillo, L. (2001). Supply chain management and the international dissemination of e-commerce. *Industrial Management & Data Systems, 101*(7), 370–377. doi:10.1108/EUM0000000005825

Osborne, M. J., & Rubinstein, A. (1994). *A Course in Game Theory*. Cambridge, MA: MIT Press.

Peleg, B. (1984). *Game Theoretic Analysis of Voting in Committees*. Cambridge University Press.

Peleg, B. (1992). Axiomatizations of the Core. In R. Aumann & S. Hart (Eds.), *Handbook of Game Theory with Economic Applications*. Amsterdam, North-Holland: Elsevier.

Rosenschein, J. S., & Zlotkin, G. (1994). *Rules of Encounter*. Cambridge, MA: MIT Press.

Sandholm, T., Larson, K., Andersson, M., Shehory, O., & Tohme, F. (1999). Coalition structure generation with worst case guarantees. *Artificial Intelligence Journal, 111*(1), 209–238. doi:10.1016/S0004-3702(99)00036-3

Shapley, L. S. (1953a). *Additive and non-additive set functions*. PhD thesis, Department of Mathematics, Princeton University.

Shapley, L. S. (1953b). A value for n-person games. *Annals of Mathematics Studies*, 28, 307-317. Reprint in A.E. Roth (Ed.) (1988), 31-40.

Tombuş, O., & Bilgiç, T. (2004). A column generation approach to the coalition formation problem in multi-agent systems. *Computers & Operations Research, 31*, 1635–1653. doi:10.1016/S0305-0548(03)00112-6

Tully, S. (2000). The B2B tool that really is changing the world. *Fortune Magazine, 141*(6), 132–145.

Turowski, K. (2002). Agent-based e-commerce in case of mass customization. *International Journal of Production Economics, 75*, 69–81. doi:10.1016/S0925-5273(01)00182-7

Wang, S., & Archer, N. (2007). Business-to-business collaboration through electronic marketplaces: An exploratory study. *Journal of Purchasing and Supply Management, 13*, 113–126. doi:10.1016/j.pursup.2007.05.004

Weber, R. J. (1979). Subjectivity in the valuation of games. In Moeschlin, O., & Pallaschke, D. (Eds.), *Game theory and related topics* (pp. 129–136). Amsterdam: North-Holland.

Weber, R. J. (1988). Probabilistic values for games. In Roth, A. E. (Ed.), *The Shapley Value: Essays in Honor of Lloyd S. Shapley* (pp. 101–119). Cambridge University Press. doi:10.1017/CBO9780511528446.008

Yamamoto, J., & Sycara, K. (2001). A Stable and Efficient Buyer Coalition Formation Scheme for E-Marketplaces. *International Conference on Autonomous Agents (Agents 2001),* Montreal Canada, May 28-June 1.

Yu, Y.-W., Yu, H.-C., Itoga, H., & Lin, T.-R. (2008). Decision-making factors for effective industrial e-procurement. *Technology in Society, 30*, 163–169. doi:10.1016/j.techsoc.2007.12.004

Chapter 3
Investing in Excess Capacity: Combining Real Options and Fuzzy Approaches in a Co-Opetitive Network

Pierluigi Argoneto
University of Basilicata, Italy

Paolo Renna
University of Basilicata, Italy

ABSTRACT

The cooperation among firms allows them to focus on their core products, improving efficiency and competiveness. The emerging paradigm of co-opetition, considering at the same time cooperative and competitive aspects, seems to be the most promising approach both in traditional and electronic network. This chapter investigates the excess capacity issue for independent plants operating in a co-opetitive network. Two models have been proposed: the first without any information exchange, based on classical real options approach, and the second characterized by a certain degree of information sharing: in here the real options methodology is combined with a fuzzy engine. A simulation environment based on Multi Agent Architecture has been developed in order to test the proposed models. The simulation results show that the innovative combined approach drastically reduces the investment, maintaining a high level of profit.

INTRODUCTION

Market globalization and aggressive economic competition have gained a manufacturing tendency toward the adoption of flexibility features in order to better react to changes related to customer needs, process technologies and government directives. Many research efforts have been made in order to really understand which of such flexibility features are critical in achieving the particular business tasks and how or when to implement them. This issue has great relevance from an entrepreneur point of view. Investments in manufacturing systems including flexibility features are perceived as high risk decisions in a very uncertain and complex environment. This perception is principally due to the following reasons: (a) flexible manufacturing systems require higher investment if compared with other manufacturing investments; (b) flexibility enlarges

DOI: 10.4018/978-1-61520-633-9.ch003

the investment scenario making the investment uncertainty higher; (c) the competitive scenario evolution needs to be also evaluated in order to carry out a correct investment planning and timing. Enormous research efforts have already been devoted to the analysis and valuation of investment projects (De Reyck et al., 2008). Traditional financial theory proposes the Net Present Value (NPV) concept, using a cost of capital based on the inherent project risk. The NPV framework has been criticized because it is claimed that it cannot cope with the potential flexibility that comes with investment projects, resulting in changes in the original cash flow pattern. Trigeorgis (1996) claims that traditional capital budgeting methods or discounted cash flow approaches cannot cope with the operation flexibility options and other strategic aspects of various projects but that the application of option techniques results in the correct solution. These critiques to the NPV methodology, see Brealey and Myers (2000), for valuing projects have led to the emergence of Real Options Analysis (ROA) for valuing managerial flexibility in projects. The contingent claims analysis approach to ROA uses market-priced securities to construct a portfolio that replicates the payoffs of the project and determines the project value using a no-arbitrage argument. Moreover, it is well known that entrepreneurial firms, characterized by a lack of internal resources and other start-up handicaps can use external resources through inter-firm networks to overcome these liabilities. In this context, inter-firm networks are considered an important model of organization development to enable an entrepreneurial firm to grow and survive. These strategic networks are composed of inter-organizational ties that are enduring and include strategic alliances, joint ventures, long-term buyer-supplier partnerships and a host of similar ties. When a rapport among firms includes elements of both cooperation and competition, i.e. these firms can compete and cooperate simultaneously, the relationship is called *co-opetition*. The rising question is: how ROA for valuing managerial flexibility, particularly considering investments in excess capacity, can be influenced by such kind of relationship among firms? In this chapter, we present an innovative approach to this issue: the added value for each firm, deriving from the co-opetitive network, is evaluated by a fuzzy engine and utilised to ponder the results obtained by the traditional ROA to overcome the weaknesses of the traditional approach. Specifically, the chapter is focused on planning the capacity of:

- a set of plants that do not share information and
- a set of plant that, differently, share information.

Specifically we highlight:

- the applications of the co-opetition paradigm at an electronic network of plants willing to exchange their productive capacity and, in a defined period (periodic review approach), able to evaluate the opportunity of expand their productive capacity;
- the estimation of the added value, for each firm, in re-modulating the ROA output considering the added value coming from the co-opetitive network (information sharing);
- the schematization and simulation of the proposed model by using a Multi Agent System.

The chapter is structured as follows. Section 2 presents the literature overview. Section 3 describes the research context. The benchmark model with a brief introduction to the real options approach is reported in Section 4. The proposed model is reported in Section 5, while the negotiation mechanism is presented in Section 6. The developed simulation environment and results are respectively presented in sections 7 and 8. Finally, summary and conclusions are withdrawn in section 9.

LITERATURE REVIEW

When dealing with investment decisions, the classical method is a simple NPV calculation of the different cash flows, in order to select the investment that has the highest positive NPV and discard the projects with negative NPV. In recent years, however, many researchers have shown that conventional economic analysis based on Discounted Cash Flow (DCF) is not able to capture the strategic impact of projects. In particular, DCF analysis ignores the "operating flexibility" that gives project managers options to revise decisions in response to changing exogenous economic conditions. The importance of such operating options becomes critical when the environment is highly volatile (extremely changing market demand and product prices) and the technology is flexible, thus allowing managerial intervention at a reasonable cost. Many methods have been explored to make optimal investment decisions, but none of them seems to be able to overcome the drawbacks of DCF analysis. Harrison and Van Mieghem (1999) have developed a theoretical model, solved with multi-dimensional newsvendor solution, to determine the optimal investment strategies for a manufacturing firm employing multiple resources to market several products to an uncertain demand. Jain and Nag (1996) propose a decision support tool that allows identifying successful new ventures, i.e. firms that are likely to provide superior long-run operating performance. The model integrates information from both quantitative and qualitative variables; it takes into account decision maker's judgments through an AHP model generator, and provides access to statistical models and evaluation tools. Mohamed and McCowan (2001) address the issue of combining both monetary and non-monetary aspects of an investment option; they propose a method that utilizes interval math and possibility theory to handle the uncertainty associated with investment parameters. The model is able to rank various options, but it's specifically developed for construction projects. It is now recognized by academics and entrepreneurs that DCF techniques often undervalue projects with real operating options and other strategic interactions (Miller and Park, 2002). Real Options approach, by explicitly capturing the flexibility and its effects on uncertainty, provide for a consistent treatment of risk in the valuation of investment in production systems (Schwarz, 2001). An option is the right, but not the obligation, to take an action in the future. Options are valuable when there is uncertainty; this is one of the most important shifts in thinking from the real options approach: uncertainty creates opportunities (Amram and Kulatilaka, 1999). However, ROA is not a new decision making technique: DCF and ROA are two complementary tools. The result from the application of both DCF and ROA is the Extended Net Present Value (ENPV), which is given by the traditional NPV plus the value of all the options embedded in the project.

Excess Capacity

Dedicated Manufacturing Lines (DML), Flexible Manufacturing Systems (FMS) and Reconfigurable Manufacturing Systems (RMS) are, nowadays, the three production paradigms representing three ways of thinking and implementing production systems. Surely, FMS and RMS are the two main research responses to the previous pointed out flexibility requirements. They represent the widely accepted comebacks to the DML. In effect, excess capacity would seem to be undesirable, since it implies non-utilization of valuable productive resources (Smith, 1969). Kim (1999) proposed various policies to reduce excess capacity, which suggests that it is undesirable; in addition, excess capacity seems to invite government intervention (Baden-Fuller, 1990) and has been blamed for losses or lower profits in certain industries. However, in spite of its seemingly negative aspects, persistent excess capacity is widely observed. It would seem natural to analyze excess capacity in a real options setting, since excess capacity is essentially a real option (to increase the output when market conditions improve). Thus, investing in excess capacity is equivalent to purchasing this implicit real option. The value of this option stems from the asymmetry in operational flexibility resulting from excess capacity, i.e. the firm has the ability to increase the output, but will only do so if market conditions improve. There have been a few explanations for excess capacity in the literature, e.g. demand growth (Aguerrevere, 2003) or rhythmic demand (with predictable highs and lows, where building peak-load capacity necessarily results in excess capacity during off-peak periods). However, in both these cases the firm expects to be operating at full capacity in the future and any excess capacity is expected to be short-lived; hence, they are unable to justify persistent excess capital. Another explanation for excess capacity relies on strategic/ game-theoretic considerations (to deter new entrants). Julka et al. (2007) discussed the state-of-the-art in multi-factor models for capacity expansion of manufacturing plants within a corporation. One of the weakness is that the solution strategy adopted by most authors is almost exclusively mathematical. Kogan et al. (2009) have focused on the co-investment problem in a supply chain infrastructure. Several applications and examples were presented and open-loop, as well as feedback solutions were found for non-cooperating firms, long- and short-run investment cooperation and non-simultaneous moves (Stackelberg) firms. Ahlert et al. (2009) investigated a production network that uses the capacity of network partners in order to fulfil network orders. The network partners are autonomous enterprises, therefore an iterative coordination algorithm has been designed aiming at balancing both the objectives of the network level as well as of the corporate level. The central problem of sizing the network capacity pool is solved iteratively by a decentralised planning process applying the top-down/bottom-up principle. But how this approach, tested quite exclusively for a single firm, could modify its impact on managerial decision when many firms, facing with this issue, are involved in a co-opetitive network?

Co-Opetition

The management literature generally considers industries to be collections of firms bound together by rivalry, therefore questioning the value of relationships with competitors (Dollinger, 1985). Firms can use competitors as subcontractors in times where the firm has temporarily reached full capacity. This cooperative behavior, especially with regional competitors, will increase the likelihood of the favor being returned. Overall, relationships with competitors can give access to temporarily needed resources or lead to the temporary pooling of resources, which should positively influence firm performance especially in the years after foundation, when sales tend to grow discontinuously (Lechner and Dowling, 2003). Entrepreneurial firms that view competitors not only as pure rivals but also as a potential resource should therefore be more successful. Building on the theoretical framework of co-opetition, according to which both cooperation and competition are needed in inter-organizational relationships to allow firms to obtain reciprocal advantages (Bengtsson and Kock, 2000), it could be useful to understand whether (and how) co-opetition could be applied in a decision making problem using ROA. Christie and Wu (2002) proposed an approach to manage the capacity planning in a multi-fabs environment. Each fab is modeled as a single resource with variable production level. Several discrete scenarios are considered in a multi-period, multistage and stochastic programming model. The goal is to minimize the expected mismatch between planned and actual capacity allocation as defined in the scenarios. Chen et al. (2008) proposed a model that enables a collaborative integration for resource and demand sharing. A negotiation algorithm is utilized to sharing capacity from factory that sells to factory that requires extra capacity. Each factory applies an economic resource planning model based on Genetic Algorithm to improve its local objectives. The model is tested only between two factories: one seller and one buyer. Renna and Argoneto (2008) proposed a distributed approach, for a network of independent enterprises, to facilitate the resources sharing process. The distributed architecture is based on Multi Agent Architecture paradigm and the coordination mechanism is performed by a negotiation protocol. In this work just two performance indices are considered: the total profit of the network and the total unsatisfied capacity. Anyway, co-opetition concepts from procurement, marketing and R&D can be also adapted to this area and, therefore, open many spaces for research. To use a sentence from Brandenburger and Nalebuff (1996), in any case, the goal of a firm is to do well for its self-interest, but, especially in a globalized context, to pursue an objective, such as new product development, procurement cost reduction as well as new market entrance, an ally might be necessary. Specifically, in our work co-opetition is meant to be utilized in resources procurement among competing firms. That is not the only form of co-opetition in procurement, but it is one of the most common in reality for SME.

Co-Opetiton: Real Cases

In the 90s GM and Ford, the major American carmakers, established an e-procurement platform for procuring basic components. The joint venture between Toyota and PSA Citroen-Peugeot, established in 2002, is another very relevant example of co-opetition in automobile industry. The two companies agreed in building a common plant in Czech Republic and using common components for the production of three new separately-owned city cars. In Italy, in 2002, the two biggest motorcycle companies, Aprilia and Piaggio made an alliance for joint-procurement, though competing in the final market. In ICT industry, the Simian joint-venture is among the main mobile wireless telephones manufacturers in the world, Nokia, Ericsson, Panasonic, Samsung, Siemens AG, and the leading company in the mobile digital computing, Psion, which, however, has sold its own shares in 2004. The phenomenon of co-opetition in R&D activities and co-promotion is also very common in pharmaceutical and biotechnology industry. So far the above examples from the industry world have concerned worldwide firms' strategies of co-opetition. To conclude this overview, which makes clearly understandable how relevant issue of co-opetition is and provides justifications to our work, we cannot miss to mention some examples of co-opetition in medium and small businesses. If, most of the time, for big worldwide firms co-opetition strategy is a way to get competitive advantages and succeed in the global arena, for medium and small firms it is a mean to survive to competition from big players by maintaining their independency. All around the world, industrial districts and both local and national consortia can be considered examples of co-opetition of medium and small businesses in several industries, such textile and clothing, agri-food, hardware and retailing. Also, in the automotive industry, web-based technology opens up opportunity of cooperation among small and medium firms. For instance, Supply On is a successful provider of supply and engineering services founded by suppliers competing in the same market (Meder, 2005). Finally, an interesting empirical research from Quintana-Garcia and Benavides-Velasco (2004) provides evidence of co-opetition in new product development among European small and medium firms in biotechnology industry. Through cooperation in one or more activities, small firms can get same advantages as big companies, however, because of proximity, they inevitably keep competing each others in other activities.

RESEARCH CONTEXT

The research contest consists of a set of independent plants that collaborate in a co-opetitive network. Each plant works in a market where the customers require products submitting an order and knows the following data:

$price_p^k$: the market price of the *kth* product, for the generic *pth* plant;

$cost_p^k$: the production cost of the *kth* product, for the generic *pth* plant. It is a function of productive and managerial costs. It also takes into account the efficiency of the plant and its relative geographical dispersion. It is obtained with by using a mark-up strategy;

C_p^k : the productive capacity of the *kth* product, for the generic *pth* plant;

R_p^k : the quantity of the *kth* product required by the market, for the generic *pth* plant.

Each plant at the same *periodic fixed time Tp* (e.g. twelve months), uses the moving average of the actual demand of the last *Tp* in order to obtain a forecast for the next period. Then, the plants apply the proposed approaches (explained in the following two paragraphs) to decide if and how much excess capacity it is convenient to acquire.

NO INFORMATION SHARING MODEL (NIS)

Traditional NPV, which was initially developed to value bonds or stocks, implicitly assumes that corporations hold a collection of real assets passively. The value of active management, i.e. the value of flexibility, is better captured using decision tree analysis. Here flexibility is modeled through decision nodes allowing future managerial decisions to be made after some uncertainty has been resolved and more information has been obtained, before proceeding to the next stage. The presence of flexibility, however, changes the payoff structure and therefore the risk characteristics of an actively managed asset in a way that invalidates the use of a constant discount rate.

Figure 1. Binomial tree with the cash flow of a project

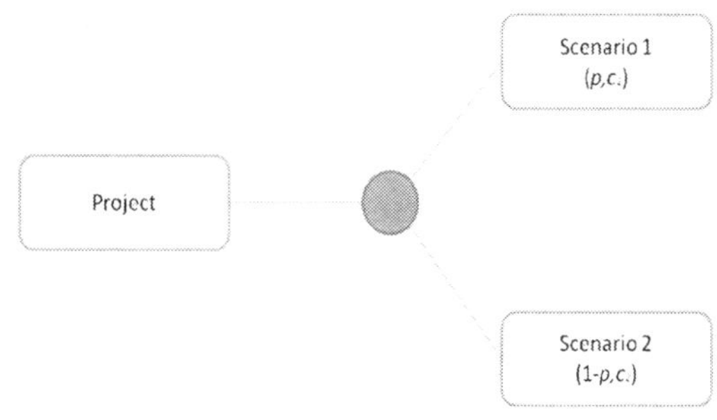

Binomial Trees and Real Options

The binomial tree in Figure 1 represents a one-period project resulting in cash flows $c=(c_1;c_2)$, with probabilities p and $1-p$. An investment I is required at the start of the project, r denotes the risk-free rate and the project is discounted using the project's specific cost of capital j, obtained through the market valuation of a security or project with exactly the same payoff pattern. The present value of the project is:

$$P(c) = \frac{E(c)}{1+j} = \frac{p \cdot c_1 + (1-p) \cdot c_2}{1+j} \quad (1)$$

where $E(c)$ denotes the expected value of the project's cash flows. Subtracting the investment costs gives the project's net present value:

$$NPV(c) = -I + P(c) \quad (2)$$

In the literature, various types of real options are defined: abandon, expand, contract, defer, switch, as well as compound options and rainbow options relying on multiple underlying projects. These real options result in different project cash flows, denoted by $o=(o_1; o_2)$. For instance, a deferral option, where the firm has a license granting it the exclusive right to defer undertaking the project for one period, will change the project's cash flows to:

$$o_s = \max(c_s - I', 0),\ s = 1,2 \tag{3}$$

with I' the investment cost next year. An expand option will change the project cash flows to:

$$o_s = \max(f \cdot c_s - e, 0),\ s = 1,2 \tag{4}$$

with f the expand factor and e the cost of the expansion or the option's exercise price. Therefore, the risk has changed, invalidating the use of the discount rate j to compute the NPV of the option's cash flows.

The Benchmark Model

The scenario is based on a production system, for each considered plant, able to manufacture k different products. The initial capacity $C^k_{p(0)}$ is based on the initial investment I_0, therefore we are able to produce $C^k_{p(0)}$ items per year of a single product and to sell them with a certain contribution margin (we assume that the contribution margin does not depend on the time). The approach is completely based on the traditional *ROA*: the plant computes the moving average demand on the last *Tp*, obtaining θ^k_{Tp}. At this point, the forecast is done considering the market uncertainty by the parameter u and d (i.e. it can either increase or decrease):

$$\theta^k_{Tp+1} \begin{cases} \nearrow \ \theta^{u,k}_{Tp+1} = \theta^k_{Tp} \cdot u \\ \searrow \ \theta^{d,k}_{Tp+1} = \theta^k_{Tp} \cdot d \end{cases} \quad \text{being } d < 1 < u; \tag{5}$$

The excess capacity to acquire (EC^k) for considered product k will be

$$EC^k = \begin{cases} \max(0; \theta^{u,k}_{Tp+1} - C^k_{p(0)}),\ if\ \theta^k_{Tp+1} = \theta^{u,k}_{Tp+1} \\ \max(0; \theta^{d,k}_{Tp+1} - C^k_{p(0)}),\ if\ \theta^k_{Tp+1} = \theta^{d,k}_{Tp+1} \end{cases} \tag{6}$$

The related investments I are computed by using the following function:

$$I = EC^k \cdot \alpha \tag{7}$$

being α the unitary cost of capacity (no scale economy is considered).

The related productive cost is given by:

$$C(EC^k) = \cos t^k_p \cdot EC^k \tag{8}$$

and, considering the market price ($price^k_p$) independent in respect of the produced quantity of *kth* product (perfect market), the gross profit (π) will be given by:

$$\pi_k = (price^k_p - \cos t^k_p) \cdot EC^k\,. \tag{9}$$

The NPV is computed as:

$$NPV = \frac{\pi}{j} - I\,, \tag{10}$$

being $j = \sum_{a=1}^{W} \frac{1}{(1+r)^a}$ (11)

r is the risk-less interest rate, by which each plant discount the future return and W is the length of the project (in years). To evaluate the results we used the backward induction model proposed by Cox, Ross and Rubinstein for the financial option:

$$NPV(t) = \frac{NPV(t+1,u) \cdot p + NPV(t+1,d) \cdot (1-p)}{1+r}$$

, being: (12) $NPV(t+1,u)$ the value of the optimal strategy in case the market demand will increase and $NPV(t+1,d)$ the value of the optimal strategy in case the market demand will decrease.

In formula (12) we find the neutral-risk probability *p* and *1-p*: in this research is considered a neutral risk strategy (i.e. *p* is fixed to 0.5). The effective value of $EC^{k}*$ the generic plant will buy is computed by the reverse formula obtained by (12).

INFORMATION SHARING MODEL (IS)

This case is concerning the situation in which each plant decides how much to invest in excess capacity considering the fact that it can interact with other plants of the network to exchange some productive capacity (see the Negotiation paragraph for more details). What is changing, in confront to what reported in the previous paragraph, is the "critical" evaluation of the *EC** value. Each plant, by using a fuzzy engine, computes a reductive factor (*RF*) that takes into account the added value coming from the network: the possibility to exchange with other plants the productive capacity. We use the fuzzy approach because many aspects of this interaction cannot be assessed in a quantitative form, but rather in a qualitative one (See Appendix for more information on Fuzzy Sets.). Whereas characteristics of the fuzziness and vagueness are inherent in various decision-making problems, a proper decision-making approach should be capable of dealing with vagueness or ambiguity (Yager, 1995). The fuzzy engine developed in this chapter is essentially represented in the following Figure 2.

The considered inputs, for each considered plant, are:

Figure 2. Fuzzy engine

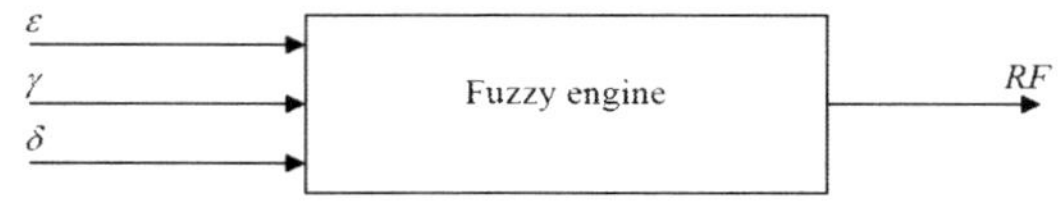

- ε: the percentage of unutilized capacity of the plant *pth*; this value is computed as average on the last *Tp*. It can assume values comprised between 0 and 1. The increasing of ε leads to the reduction of *EC** by increasing the *RF*;
- $\gamma = \sum_{k} (AC^{k} - SC^{k}) / C^{k}$, being *AC* the acquired and *SC* the sold capacity for the generic product *k* on the last *Tp*. Its value is comprised between -1 and 1; a value bigger than zero means that the plant satisfies its market requests by using a certain amount of capacity negotiated with other plants. In this case *RF* increases its value because it is convenient for the plant investing in excess capacity. Differently, if the value is lower than zero, the plant has satisfied the past request of the market by its own capacity, therefore could be not profitable to invest in excess capacity: *RF* assume a lower value in order to reduce the *EC**;
- the last parameter, δ, is computed considering the number the relations with other plants of the network. For example, considering *4* different plants (*p1, p2, p3* and *p4*), the generic plant *p2* computes how many links (transactions) it has activated in the last *Tp* with each other plant, obtaining the vector $\phi^{P2} = [\phi^{P2}_{P1}, \phi^{P2}_{P2}, \phi^{P2}_{P3}, \phi^{P2}_{P4}] = [\phi^{P2}_{P1}, 0, \phi^{P2}_{P3}, \phi^{P2}_{P4}]$

Supposing that *p1 and p3* have already activated the process to evaluate if to invest or not in excess capacity (this information is available to other plants of the network),

Figure 3. Membership function for the parameter ε

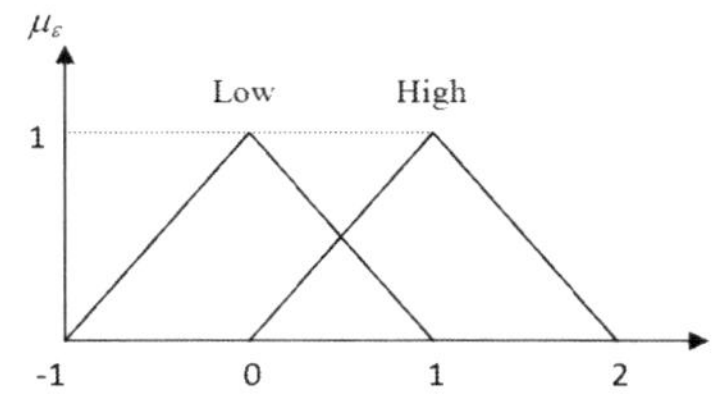

δ is computed as: $\delta = \frac{Nlink *_{P2}}{Nlinktot_{P2}}$, being: $Nlink *_{P2} = \phi_{P1}^{P2} + \phi_{P3}^{P2}$, a value that takes into account the amount of links with plants that could invest in excess capacity and $Nlinktot_{P2} = \phi_{P1}^{P2} + \phi_{P3}^{P2} + \phi_{P4}^{P2}$ the total amount of activated links by the *pth* plant. It can assume values comprised between 0 and 1: a high value means that in the past the considered plant reached several agreements with the plants that have decided to acquire excess capacity, therefore *RF* assumes a lower value. Differently, a lower value of δ means that the plant had difficulties to reach agreements with other plants in the past, therefore *RF* assumes a high value because it could be convenient to be more independent in the future.

Their membership functions are respectively showed in Figure 3, Figure 4 and Figure 5.

The rules of the engine are the following:

1. If ε is Low *then RF* is High
2. If ε is High *then RF* is Low

Figure 5. Membership function for the parameter δ

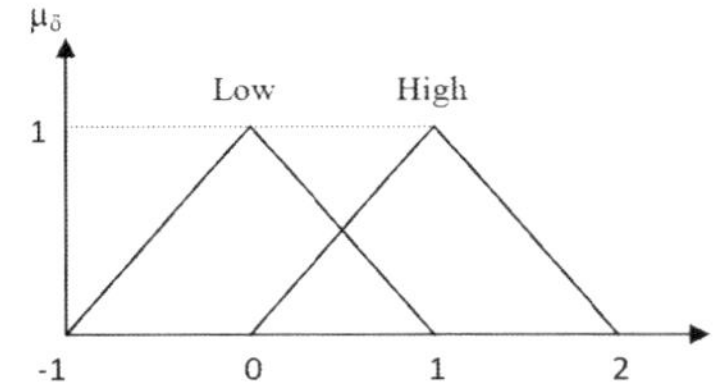

Figure 4. Membership function for the parameter γ

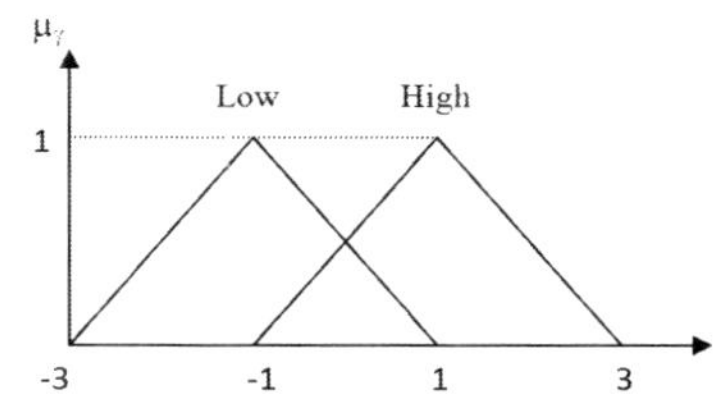

3. If γ is Low *then RF* is Low
4. If γ is High *then RF* is High
5. If δ is Low *then RF* is High
6. If δ is High *then RF* is Low

The fuzzy engine evaluates the above rules by a *max-min inferencing* method: the *RF* value is computed by the centroid defuzzification technique and the membership function of *RF* is showed in Figure 6.

Specifically, the IS decision making process is performed as follows:

1. a ranking of the plants is made considering the capacity they need: it is realized in decreasing order, considering the difference between the forecasted demand and the capacity they hold;
2. the first plant of the list is selected. Its *EC* value is computed as explained in the real option approach explained in the previous paragraph;
3. the reduction value *RF* it is computed by the fuzzy engine, as explained in the following. If the considered plant is the first one of the list, the fuzzy engine works with only

Figure 6. Membership function for RF

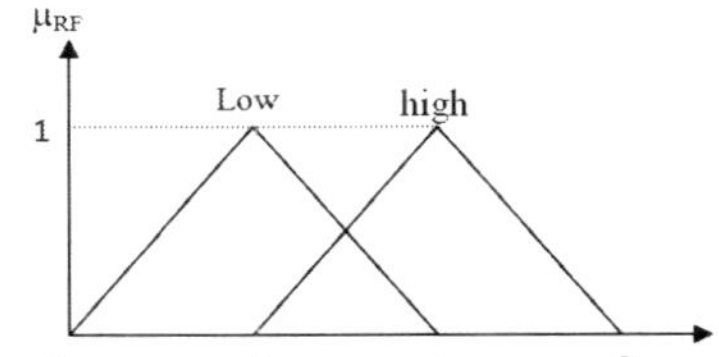

two inputs (ε and γ), because the input δ is evaluated on the plants that already made the capacity decision investment;

4. the plant computes the capacity investment EC^*;
5. the algorithm keeps running until when all the plants have made their decision about whether and how much invest in excess capacity.

NEGOTIATION

After the decision whether to invest or not in excess capacity is made by using one of the previous explained methods, each plant can negotiate with other plants a certain amount of capacity to supply overloaded periods. This is allowed in the period of time comprised between one *Tp* to another. The plants are classified in overloaded $OG = \{1,\ldots,i,\ldots,N\}$ and underloaded $UG = \{1,\ldots,j,\ldots,M\}$. Afterwards, each of them belonging to *OG* computes the capacity it needs to produce a given product *k* (i.e. RC_i^k) and compete with other plants to obtain it. At the same time the plants belonging to the *UG* set evaluate the capacity they can offer for the same product, (i.e. OC_j^k). The only variable all agents take into account in this phase is the price to pay to obtain /make over the capacity. Therefore, the plants compete among themselves, but at the same time collaborate to satisfy the customer requests. The agent architecture in here adopted is the following: each plant belonging to *OG* is represented by a *Capacity Offering Agent* (*COA*) who is in charge for negotiating the capacity with the *Requiring Capacity Agent* (RCA) representing the plants that require it, belonging to the *UG* set. Finally, there is a *Mediator Agent* (*MA*) who is in charge for allowing communication and coordination among *COAs* and *RCAs*. The coordination is obtained by a negotiation mechanism. The UML activity diagram of Figure 7 shows the agents' interaction workflow. As the reader can notice three swim lines, corresponding to the above described agents, have been located in the diagram.

Specifically, for the *COA* the following activities can be highlighted:

- **Wait**: the agent is in its initial state of waiting for a proposal (from *RCA*);

Evaluates proposal: the *COA* evaluates the proposal of the *RCA* in terms of required capacity and offered price. At the first round the *COA* communicates the amount of capacity it is willing to offer (the minimum value between the one requested by the *RCA* and its own unused capacity). Subsequently, the *COA* communicates to the *RCA* if it accepts or refuses the proposed price to exchange the promise amount of capacity. Then the *COA* evaluates the proposal of the *RCA* by a threshold function given by (13):

$$val_j^{k,r_l} = \left[price_j^k - (price_j^k - \cos t_j^k)\cdot\frac{r_l - 1}{r_{\max} - 1}\right]\cdot M_{ij}^k \quad (13)$$

being $M_{ij}^k = \min(RC_i^k, OC_j^k)$ (14)

Expression (13) is a threshold level starting from the market price of the good. During the negotiation time (i.e. the value of the round r_l increases) the threshold level is reduced: it stops when the related profit is null. At this point, the following expression is checked:

$$val_i^{k,r_l} \geq val_j^{k,r_l} \quad (15)$$

If (15) is verified, the *jth* plant supplies the *ith* plant with the required capacity: they reach an agreement and each ones can update their data.

Figure 7. UML Activity Diagram

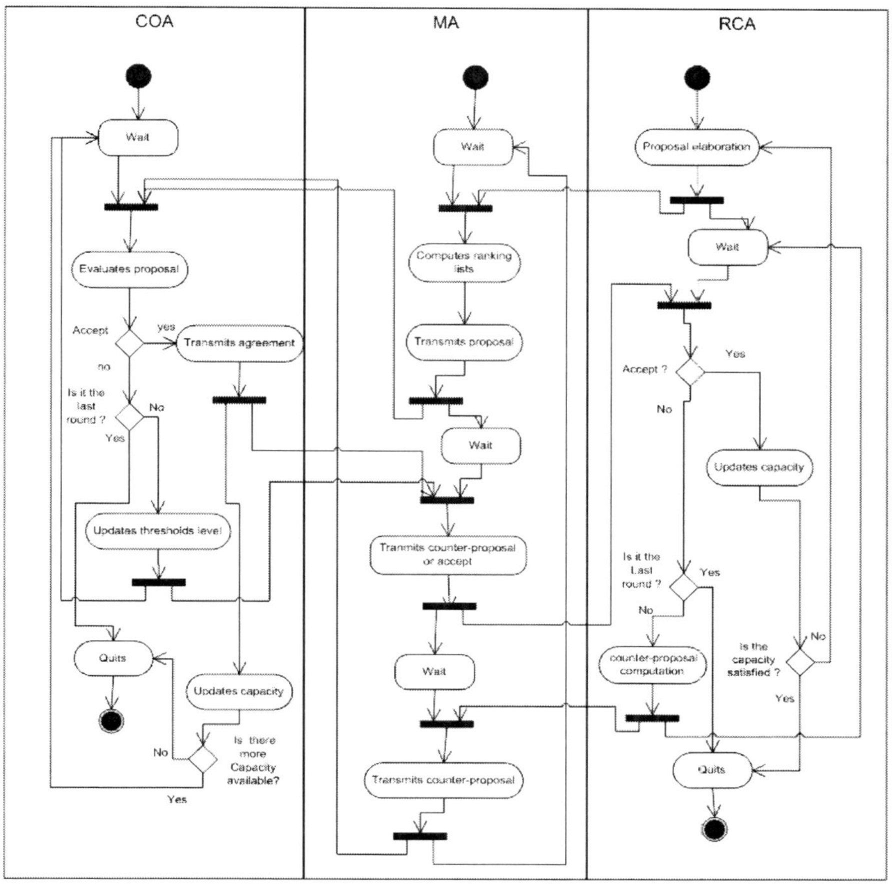

- **Updates threshold level**: if the *COA* refuses the price submitted by the *RCA*, it modifies the threshold level: the value of r_1 in expression (13) is increased. In case the algorithm reaches the last round, the *COA* simply quits the negotiation.
- **Updates capacity**: if the negotiation reaches an agreement, the *COA* updates the capacity it owns. In case no more capacity resources are available it quits, otherwise it goes in its Wait state.

The *RCA* performs the following activities:

Proposal elaboration: the *RCA* elaborates a proposal, in terms of price and amount of capacity to acquire, and transmits this information to the *MA*. The submitted price is obtained by the following expression:

$$val_i^{k,r_1} = \left[price_i^k - (price_i^k - \cos t_i^k) \cdot \frac{r_{\max} - r_1}{r_{\max} - 1} \right] \cdot M_{ij}^k \quad (16)$$

Expression (16) computed by the *RCA* starts with a value equal to the production costs: in this case the profit is the same obtainable when the product is produced by itself. This value is increased until its market price: in this case the obtainable profit is null.

- **Wait**: the *RCA* waits for counter-proposal by the *COAs*.
- **Counter-proposal computation**: if the *COA* refuses the proposal and the negotiation is still running, the *RCA* computes a new counter-proposal (the value of r_l in expression (16) is increased). Otherwise (i.e. we consider the last round of negotiation), the process ends with no agreement.
- **Updates capacity**: if the negotiation reaches an agreement, the *RCA* updates their data; if the acquired capacity is exactly the required one it quits, otherwise it computes a new proposal for the residual capacity it needs.

The *MA* performs the coordination activities between *COA* and *RCA*. In particular it:

- **Wait**: the *MA* is in its initial state of waiting for a proposal (from the *RCA*).
- **Computes raking list**: the *MA* computes a ranking list among all the plants that required capacity. The way it does it is depending on several variables; in this research the ranking is done favoring first plants with high need of capacity, allowing them to better satisfy the customers' requests.
- **Transmits proposal**: the *MA* transmits the proposal computed by *RCA*, at the ranking list of *COAs*.
  - **Wait**: the *MA* is in state of waiting for the counter-proposal by all the *COAs*.
  - **Transmits counter-proposal**: the *MA* transmits the counter-proposal of the *COA* to the *RCA*.

After having uploaded all the necessary data, for the generic *ith* plant that does not reach the entire capacity it needs is again inserted in the ranking list. At this point the negotiation starts again. To avoid a deadlock, the agent that does not reach any agreement at the end of the negotiation process is removed by the ranking list. The decision of capacity investment is done by using a periodic review methodology.

Figure 8 shows the sequence of the activities among the models NIS, IS and negotiation.

SIMULATION ENVIRONMENT

We had developed a distributed simulation environment based on the proposed Multi Agent Architecture to simulate the co-opetitive network represented in Figure 9.

Figure 8. Sequence of the activities

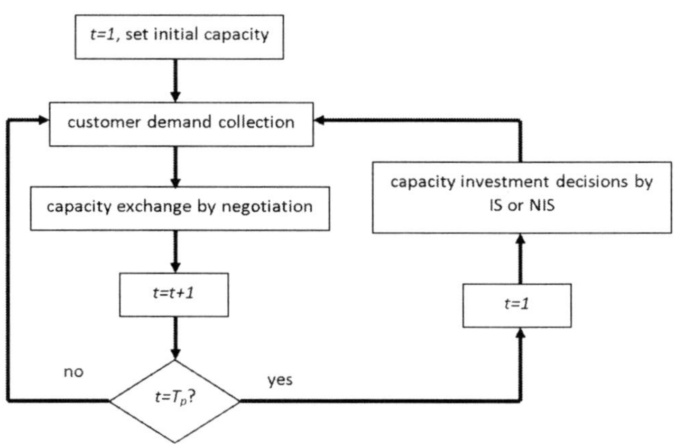

Figure 9. The co-opetitive network

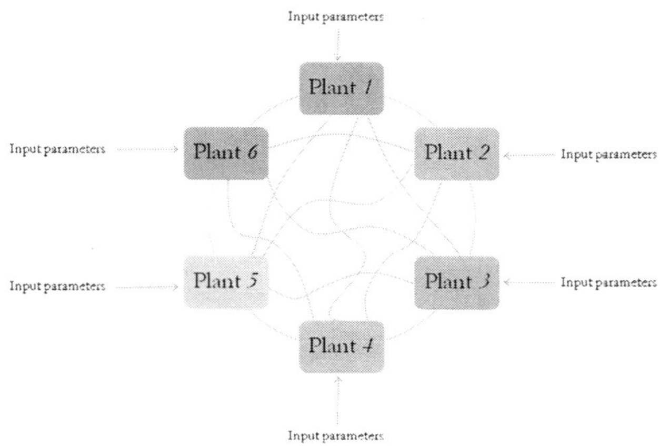

It consists of a simulation environment, developed by using Java development kit package, able to test the functionality of the proposed approaches and to understand the related advantages and/or limits. The modeling formalism in here adopted is a collection of independent agents interacting via messages. This formalism is quite suitable for MAS development. In particular, each object represents an agent and the system evolves through a message sending engine managed by a discrete event scheduler. Specifically, the following objects have been developed: the *COA*, the *RCA*, the *MA* – deeply described in the previous section-, the *Scheduler*, the *Model, option, fuzzy engine* and *co-option agents*. The *Scheduler* agent is in charge with the system evolution by managing the discrete events of the simulation engine. Differently, *Model* agent is in charge with the agents' interaction. The *option* agent is activated when the generic plant has to decide whether and, how much capacity to acquire; the *co-option* agent is activated when the generic plant has to decide whether and the amount of capacity to acquire, but in this case the decision is influenced by information sharing among plants. To do this the plant agent uses the *fuzzy engine (*described in Information sharing model Section). The simulative network supply 48 orders divided in four macro-periods; at the end of each macro-period the plants decide the amount of capacity to acquire. Each macro-period (*Tp*) consists of 12 orders. In order to reduce the computational time, just one product typology has been considered (*k=1*). In order to highlight the difference between the capacity investment decisions between *No sharing information* and *Sharing information*, for each plant is generated a fixed stream of demand over the 48 orders. The demand is generated by using a uniform distribution different for each plant and macro-period: Table 1 reports the distribution

Table 1. Distribution ranges

Macro period	Plant 1	Plant 2	Plant 3	Plant 4	Plant 5	Plant 6
1	[80-100]	[100-120]	[90-100]	[100-120]	[80-100]	[70-120]
2	[80-120]	[80-120]	[100-110]	[120-140]	[80-100]	[70-120]
3	[60-120]	[100-140]	[110-120]	[80-120]	[80-100]	[70-120]
4	[60-140]	[100-160]	[120-130]	[60-100]	[80-100]	[70-120]

ranges. These differences emulate all the possible behaviors of the customer's demand: for example the market of plant 1 is very unpredictable because of the large ranges, the market demand of plant 4 before increases (for two macro-periods) then decreases (for the last two periods) and so on.

The values obtained by the distributions (see Table 1) generate the input order streaming reported in Table 2.

Table 2. Input orders streaming

Order no.	Plant 1	Plant 2	Plant 3	Plant 4	Plant 5	Plant 6
1	88	105	97	101	87	75
2	92	118	99	100	93	78
3	98	102	97	104	89	107
4	87	101	90	104	94	101
5	92	114	95	118	93	90
6	84	118	93	109	82	76
7	96	111	91	115	95	115
8	95	109	97	112	81	84
9	81	102	93	105	87	80
10	93	109	96	105	98	93
11	99	111	96	107	82	88
12	80	115	97	112	80	108
13	89	90	103	120	93	99
14	116	95	108	124	80	114
15	114	119	109	122	99	76
16	118	95	101	122	97	116
17	107	93	104	127	80	97
18	89	98	104	131	99	95
19	98	97	108	127	89	104
20	111	97	108	136	91	108
21	109	100	101	133	97	103
22	111	99	104	123	93	72
23	101	117	106	126	88	105
24	91	97	104	131	93	110
25	105	120	110	83	84	118
26	105	109	115	84	99	103
27	95	111	119	90	92	78
28	99	121	119	98	90	94
29	64	117	118	80	86	100
30	87	129	119	93	87	81
31	99	133	116	81	98	81
32	97	121	114	92	92	95

continued on following page

Table 2. continued

Order no.	Plant 1	Plant 2	Plant 3	Plant 4	Plant 5	Plant 6
33	88	133	111	94	96	82
34	70	132	118	97	92	98
35	96	125	115	97	86	93
36	90	130	113	97	85	88
37	126	120	123	94	95	114
38	129	135	121	89	89	117
39	61	110	122	67	89	94
40	89	137	127	93	93	96
41	104	126	121	68	80	109
42	139	120	120	85	82	108
43	119	151	125	77	94	89
44	130	153	128	76	94	111
45	115	129	128	93	87	84
46	80	125	121	61	93	110
47	95	153	120	74	88	108
48	82	141	121	85	99	93

The focus of the simulation is to evaluate the differences among the two proposed approaches, therefore the following parameters are constant and equal for all the plants:

- initial capacity of the plants, C_p^k, at the beginning of the simulation;
- the unitary price of the market, $price_p^k$;
- the unitary capacity costs $\cos t_p^k$, as a mark-up of 20% of $price_p^k$;
- the unitary costs to acquire excess capacity, α;
- the parameters u and d;
- the parameter j to compute NPV (see expression 10).

The values of these parameters are reported in the following Table 3.

To compare the proposed strategies, the following performance measures have been considered:

- the *total profit* reached by the whole network; it has been computed as the sum of the single profit generated by all the plants belonging to the network;
- the *total unsatisfied demand:* it is the difference existing between the quantity of products required by the market and the

Table 3. Plants characteristics

Parameter	Values
C_p^k	100
$price_p^k$	8
$\cos t_p^k$	6.4
α	8
u	0.8
d	1.3
j	0.2

one the network has been able to satisfy. It could be considered as a customer's performance;

- the *total unutilized capacity*: it is the difference existing between the whole capacity of the network and the total unallocated capacity;
- the *number of activated links* among plants. This performance is an index explaining how much could be complicated the logistic management of the network;
- the *transactions value*. It is the quantity of money exchanged among plants, obtained as output of the negotiation approach.
- *Final capacity* of the plants. It is the capacity each plant holds at the end of the simulation.
- *Total acquired capacity*. It is the amount of capacity acquired by the network.
- *Investments costs*; It is the cost to acquire excess capacity by the network.

RESULTS

Table 4 reports the performance measures obtained by the simulations. The last column reports the percentage difference between the two proposed approaches.

The above results highlight the following considerations:

- The total profit of the network is the same for the two approaches, moreover the differences among each plant, from one approach to another, is very low.
- The NIS approach leads to reduce the unsatisfied demand of the customers. This

Table 4. Simulation results

Performance	IS	NIS	NIS *vs* IS (%)
Total profit	45,424	45,464	0.09
Unsatisfied demand	25	0	-100.00
Unallocated capacity	2,726	4,465	63.79
Plant 1 (profit)	7,502	7,524	0.30
Plant 2 (profit)	8,944	8,949	0.05
Plant 3 (profit)	8,410	8424	0.17
Plant 4 (profit)	7,760	7,792	0.25
Plant 5 (profit)	6,930	6,928	-0.02
Plant 6 (profit)	5,878	5,859	-0.33
Number of links	74	39	-47.30
Transaction of links	9,387	4,894	-47.86
Final capacity (plant 1)	112	128	14.29
Final capacity (plant 2)	133	156	17.29
Final capacity (plant 3)	137	147	7.30
Final capacity (plant 4)	132	140	6.06
Final capacity (plant 5)	100	115	15.00
Final capacity (plant 6)	100	102	2.00
Total acquired capacity	114	188	64.91
Investments costs	912	1504	64.91

reduction is considerable, but the network doesn't gain a real advantage in term of profit. This because the reduction regards the elevated peak of demand that the plants obtain by negotiating with other plants: the capacity obtained in this way has a low profit level.

- The above consideration is also confirmed by the number of links activated among the plants. In case of NIS, the number of activated links is reduced (47.30%): the collaboration among plants is reduced. This is true not only for the number of links, but also for the amount of transactions exchanged among the plants (reduced of 47.86%).
- The final capacity of the plants shows that the increment in capacity investments (in case of NIS) is prevalent for the plants that have a low average demand. In particular, this can be noticed for plant 5 that operates in a market with a demand always minor than the plant capacity.
- The NIS approach leads to an increment of amount of excess capacity of 64.91% that strongly reduces the real profit gained by the network. Moreover, this strong increment of investment increases the risk of the plant when a drastic reduction of the demand occurs.

SUMMARY AND CONCLUSIONS

The chapter deals with the capacity investment decision for plants that operate in a co-opetitive environment.

The methodology proposed allows to support a network of enterprises for the capacity investment decisions. The research suggests how to use the information of the network to decide the amount of capacity to acquire. The main benefits of the proposed methodology are the reduction of investment in capacity keeping the same level of profit of the network.

In particular, two approaches have been proposed:

- No information sharing: each plant make the decision whether invest or not in excess capacity with any information coming from the network;
- Information sharing: each plant use the information coming from the network, processed by a fuzzy engine, in order to decide whether invest or not.

A *ROA* is utilized for the proposed approaches.

The network is supported by Multi Agent architecture and the coordination among the plants is performed by a negotiation mechanism. Then, a simulation environment has been developed using a JAVA package in order to evaluate the performance of the proposed approaches. The results of this research can be summarized as follow:

- the simulation environment allows to investigate the capacity investment decision in a co-opetitive environment, in particular how the capacity decision investment influence the network over its life cycle;
- the IS approach in here proposed leads to good performances from the network point of view: investments in capacity are minor if compared with the NIS case, by keeping the same amount of profit. Moreover, the IS approach allows to keep an high level of collaboration among the plants;
- the IS lead to a disadvantage for the customers: there is a reduction of the satisfied demand in confront of the NIS case.

Further research will deeply investigate the following aspects:

- the proposed approaches will be tested in a different environmental condition. The performance will be evaluated when the customer behavior change: from steady to very dynamic demand;

- the number of plants that can cooperate in the network. The models will be investigated when the number of plants change during the network lifetime and their characteristics are all different from each other;
- the information processed by the fuzzy engine. It will be evaluated if other information can be used as input for the fuzzy engine and how these information can allow to improve the performance of both the plant and network.

REFERENCES

Aguerrevere, F. L. (2003). Equilibrium investment strategies and output price behavior: a real-options approach. *Review of Financial Studies, 16*, 1239–1272. doi:10.1093/rfs/hhg041

Ahlert, K.-H., Corsten, H., & Gossinger, R. (2009). Capacity management in order driven production networks - A flexibility-oriented approach to determine the size of a network capacity pool. *International Journal of Production Economics, 118*(2), 430–441. doi:10.1016/j.ijpe.2008.11.013

Amram, M., & Kulatilaka, N. (1999). *Real options: managing strategic investment in an uncertain world.* Harvard Business School Press.

Baden-Fuller, C. (1990). *Managing Excess Capacity*. New York: Basil Blackwell Publishers.

Bengtsson, J. (2001). Manufacturing flexibility and real options: A review. *International Journal of Production Economics, 74*, 213–224. doi:10.1016/S0925-5273(01)00128-1

Bengtsson, M., & Kock, S. (2000). Coopetition in business networks to cooperate and compete simultaneously. *Industrial Marketing Management, 29*(5), 411–426. doi:10.1016/S0019-8501(99)00067-X

Brandenburger, A., & Nalebuff, B. (1996). *Co-Opetition: A Revolution Mindset That Combines Competition and Cooperation*. New York: Harper Collins Business.

Brealey, R. A., & Myers, S. C. (2000). *Principles of Corporate Finance* (6th ed.). London: McGraw-Hill.

Chen, J. C., Wang, K. J., Wang, S. M., & Jang, S. J. (2008). Price negotiation for capacity sharing in two-factory environment using genetic algorithm. *International Journal of Production Research, 46*(7), 1847–1868. doi:10.1080/00207540601008440

Christie, R. M. E., & Wu, S. D. (2002). Semiconductor capacity planning: Stochastic modeling and computational studies. *IIE Transactions, 34*(2), 131–144. doi:10.1080/07408170208928856

Corrado, C., & Mattey, J. (1997). Capacity utilization. *The Journal of Economic Perspectives, 11*, 151–167.

Cox, J. C., Ross, S. A., & Rubenstein, M. (1979). Option Pricing: A Simplified Approach. *Journal of Financial Economics, 7*, 229–263. doi:10.1016/0304-405X(79)90015-1

De Reyck, B., Degraeve, Z., & Vandenborre, R. (2008). Project options valuation with net present value and decision tree analysis. *European Journal of Operational Research, 184*, 341–355. doi:10.1016/j.ejor.2006.07.047

Dixit, A. K., & Pindyck, R. S. (1995). *The options approach to capital investment. Harvard Business Review*. May-June.

Dollinger, M. (1985). Environmental contacts and financial performance of the small firm. *Journal of Small Business Management, 23*(1), 24–30.

Driver, C. (2000). Capacity utilization and excess capacity: theory, evidence, and policy. *Review of Industrial Organization, 16*, 69–87. doi:10.1023/A:1007864132477

Fagnart, J.-F., Licandro, O., & Sneessens, H. R. (1997). Capacity utilization and market power. *Journal of Economic Dynamics & Control, 22*, 123–140. doi:10.1016/S0165-1889(97)00050-X

Herrera-Viedma, E., & Peis, E. (2003). Evaluating the informative quality of documents in SGML format from judgments by means of fuzzy linguistic techniques based on computing with words. *Information Processing & Management, 39*(2), 233–249. doi:10.1016/S0306-4573(02)00049-3

Jain, B. A., & Nag, B. N. (1996). A decision-support model for investment decisions in new ventures. *European Journal of Operational Research, 90*, 473–486. doi:10.1016/0377-2217(95)00154-9

Julka, N., Baines, T., Tjahjonob, B., Lendermanna, P., & Vitanov, V. (2007). A review of multi-factor capacity expansion models for manufacturing plants: Searching for a holistic decision aid. *International Journal of Production Economics, 106*(2), 607–621. doi:10.1016/j.ijpe.2006.08.002

Karsak, E. E., & Tolga, E. (2001). Fuzzy multi-criteria decision-making procedure for evaluating advanced manufacturing system investments. *International Journal of Production Economics, 69*(1), 49–64. doi:10.1016/S0925-5273(00)00081-5

Kim, H. Y. (1999). Economic capacity utilization and its determinants: theory and evidence. *Review of Industrial Organization, 15*, 321–339. doi:10.1023/A:1007747813591

Kogan, K., Charles, S., & Tapiero, C. S. (2009). Optimal co-investment in supply chain infrastructure. *European Journal of Operational Research, 192*, 265–276. doi:10.1016/j.ejor.2007.08.038

Koren, Y. U., Heisel, J.F., Moriwaki, T., Pritschow, G., Ulsoy, G., & Van Brussel, H. (1999). Reconfigurable Manufacturing Systems. *Annals of the CIRP*, 48/2, Keynote Paper.

Lechner, C., & Dowling, M. (2003). Firm networks: external relationships as sources for the growth and competitiveness of entrepreneurial firms. *Entrepreneurship and Regional Development, 15*, 1–26. doi:10.1080/08985620210159220

Lin, C. T., & Chen, Y. T. (2004). Bid/no-bid decision-making – A fuzzy linguistic approach. *International Journal of Project Management, 22*(7), 585–593. doi:10.1016/j.ijproman.2004.01.005

Mehrabi, M. G., Ulsoy, A. G., & Koren, Y. (2000). Reconfigurable manufacturing systems: Key to future manufacturing. *Journal of Intelligent Manufacturing, 11*, 403–419. doi:10.1023/A:1008930403506

Miller, T. L., & Park, C. S. (2002). Decision Making Under Uncertainty-Real Options to the Rescue? *The Engineering Economist, 47*, 105–150. doi:10.1080/00137910208965029

Mohamed, S., & McCowan, A. K. (2001). Modelling project investment decisions under uncertainty using possibility theory. *International Journal of Project Management, 19*, 231–241. doi:10.1016/S0263-7863(99)00077-0

Perry, G. L. (1966). *Unemployment, Money Wage Rates, and Inflation*. Cambridge, MA: MIT Press.

Renna, P., & Argoneto, P. (2008). Capacity Allocation in Multi-Site Factory Environment: a Multi Agent Systems Approach. Intelligent Computation in Manufacturing Engineering Innovative and Cognitive Production Technology and Systems, 23-25 July, Naples, Italy.

Sarkar, S. (2009). A Real-option Rationale for Investing in Excess Capacity. *Managerial and Decision Economics, 30*, 119–133. doi:10.1002/mde.1446

Schwarz, E. S., & Trigeorgis, L. (Eds.). (2001). *Real options and investment under uncertainty: classical readings and recent contributions*. Cambridge, MA: MIT Press.

Smith, K. R. (1969). The effect of uncertainty on monopoly price, capital stock and utilization of capital. *Journal of Economic Theory*, *1*, 48–59. doi:10.1016/0022-0531(69)90011-8

Trigeorgis, L. (1996). *Real Options: Managerial Flexibility and Strategy in Resource Allocation*. Cambridge, MA: The MIT Press.

Wang, R. C., & Chuu, S. J. (2004). Group decision-making using a fuzzy linguistic approach for evaluating the flexibility in a manufacturing system. *European Journal of Operational Research*, *154*(3), 563–572. doi:10.1016/S0377-2217(02)00729-4

Wang, W. P. (2009). Toward developing agility evaluation of mass customization systems using 2-tuple linguistic computing. *Expert Systems with Applications*, *36*(2), 3439–3447. doi:10.1016/j.eswa.2008.02.015

Winston, G. C. (1974). The theory of capital utilization and idleness. *Journal of Economic Literature*, *74*, 1301–1320.

Yager, R. R. (1995). An approach to ordinal decision making. *International Journal of Approximate Reasoning*, *12*(3-4), 237–261. doi:10.1016/0888-613X(94)00035-2

Yeo, K. T., & Qiu, F. (2003). The value of management flexibility – a real option approach to investment evaluation. *International Journal of Project Management*, *21*, 243–250. doi:10.1016/S0263-7863(02)00025-X

Zadeh L. A. (1975). The concept of a linguistic variable and its application to approximate reasoning. *Information Science*, 8, 199–249 (pt. I), 301–357(pt. II)

Zadeh, L. A. (1985). Syllogistic reasoning in fuzzy logic and its application to usuality and reasoning with dispositions. *IEEE Transactions on Systems, Man, and Cybernetics*, *SMC-15*, 754–765.

Zimmermann, H.-J. (1991). *Fuzzy set theory and its applications* (2nd ed.). Dordrecht: Kluwer.

APPENDIX

FUZZY SETS

Fuzzy set theory is a very feasible method to handle the imprecise and uncertain information in a real world. Especially, it is more suitable for subjective judgment and qualitative assessment in the evaluation processes of decision making than other classical evaluation methods applying crisp values (Lin and Chen 2004; Wang and Chuu, 2004). Basic definitions and concepts of fuzzy sets, as fuzzy numbers and linguistic variables, are briefly reported. A positive triangular fuzzy number (PTFN) $\tilde{A}$ can be denoted as $\tilde{A} = (a, b, c)$, where $a \leq b \leq c$ and a > 0, which are illustrated in Figure 2. The membership function, $\mu_{\tilde{A}}(x)$, is defined as (Zimmermann, 1991):

$$\mu_{\tilde{A}}(x) = \begin{cases} (x-a)/(b-a), & a \leq x \leq b \\ (x-c)/(b-c), & b \leq x \leq c \\ 0, & otherwise \end{cases} \qquad (17)$$

where x takes its values on the real line. A larger $\mu_{\tilde{A}}(x)$ means a stronger degree of belongingness for x in X. Triangular fuzzy numbers appear as useful means of quantifying the uncertainty in decision making due to their intuitive appeal and computationally efficient representation (Karsak and Tolga, 2001; Wang, 2009). Another important concept is the one regarding the linguistic variables. A linguistic variable is a variable whose values are expressed in linguistic terms. In other words, variable whose values are not numbers but words or sentences in a nature or artificial language. For example, "important" is a linguistic term whose values are very low, low, medium, high, very high, etc. Linguistic values can also be represented by fuzzy numbers. It is suitable to represent the degree of subjective judgment in qualitative aspect than in crisp value. The concept of linguistic variable is very useful in dealing with situations which are too complex or too ill-defined to be reasonably described in conventional quantitative expressions. Many aggregation operators have been developed presently to aggregate information. The fuzzy linguistic approach represents qualitative aspects as linguistic values by means of linguistic variables (Herrera-Viedma and Peis, 2003; Zadeh,1975).

In the composition sub-process, all of the fuzzy subsets assigned to each output variable are combined together to form a single fuzzy subset for each output variable.

Let R be a fuzzy relation in $X \times Y$, and S be a fuzzy relation in $Y \times Z$. The Max-Min composition of R (first introduced by Zadeh, 1985) and S, R°S, is a fuzzy relation in $X \times Z$ such that

Figure 10. Triangular membership function

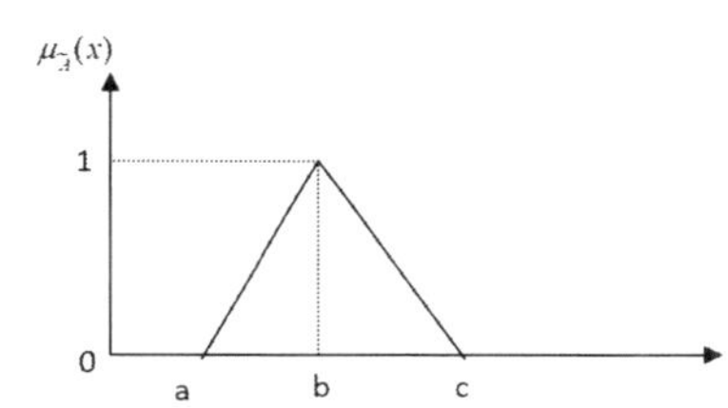

$R°S \leftrightarrow \mu_{RoS}(x,z) = \vee \{\mu_R(x,y) \wedge \mu_S(y,z)\} = \text{Max. } \{\text{Min. } \{\mu_R(x,y), \mu_S(y,z)\}\}/(x,z)$

The defuzzification can be performed by several heuristic methods; one of the most used method is to take the center gravity of the fuzzy set. Figure 11 shows an example of max-min inferencing and centroid defuzzification for a system with input variables "x" and"y", and an output variable "n".

Figure 11. Inferencing example

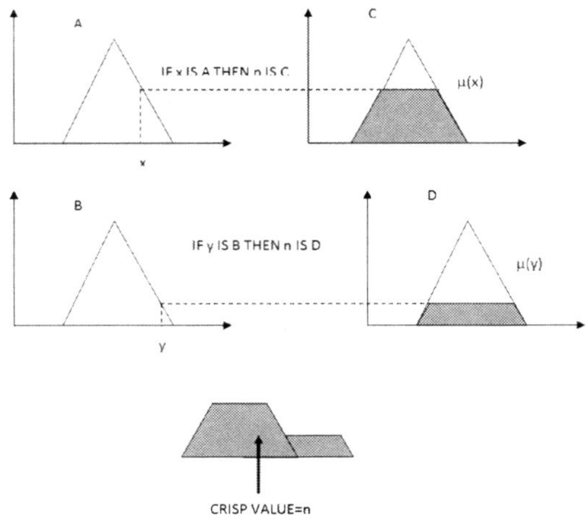

Chapter 4
Optimal Design and Operation of Supply Chain Networks under Demand Uncertainty

Michael C. Georgiadis
University of Western Macedonia, Greece

Pantelis Longinidis
University of Western Macedonia, Greece

ABSTRACT

This chapter considers a detailed mathematical formulation for the problem of designing supply chain networks comprising multiproduct production facilities with shared production resources, warehouses, distribution centers and customer zones and operating under time varying demand uncertainty. Uncertainty is captured in terms of a number of likely scenarios possible to materialize during the life time of the network. The problem is formulated as a mixed-integer linear programming problem and solved to global optimality using standard branch-and-bound techniques. A case study concerned with the establishment of Europe-wide supply chain is used to illustrate the applicability and efficiency of the proposed approach. The results obtained provide a good indication of the value of having a model that takes into account the complex interactions that exist in such networks and the effect of inventory levels to the design and operation.

INTRODUCTION

The "problem" of supply chain network design is very broad and means different things to different enterprises. It generally refers to a strategic activity that will take one or more of the following decisions (Shapiro, 1999):

DOI: 10.4018/978-1-61520-633-9.ch004

- Where to locate new facilities (be they production, storage, logistics, etc.).
- Significant changes to existing facilities, e.g. expansion, contraction or closure.
- Sourcing decisions – what suppliers and supply base to use for each facility
- Allocation decisions – e.g. what products should be produced at each production fa-

cility; which markets should be served by which warehouses, etc.

These decisions aim in some way to increase shareholder value. This means that models are employed to try to exploit potential trade-offs. These may include (Shapiro, 2003):

i. Differences in regional production costs.
ii. Distribution costs of raw materials, intermediates and products.
iii. Differences in regional taxation and duty structures.
iv. Exchange rate variations.
v. Manufacturing complexity and efficiency (related to the number of different products being produced at any one site).
vi. Network complexity (related to the number of different possible pathways from raw materials to ultimate consumers).

Most companies do not aim to quantify the latter two explicitly, but rather employ policies (e.g. single-sourcing of customer zones; exclusive product-plant allocation) to simplify operation to the desired degree.

A relatively rare instance of this class of problems is the "greenfield" design of a new supply chain where no significant assets exist at the time of the analysis (e.g. design of a future hydrogen infrastructure). A more common instance occurs when part of the infrastructure already exists, and a retrofit activity is being undertaken, where products may be re-allocated between sites, manufacturing resources may be restructured, the logistics network may be restructured, etc.

Models for the design and operation of supply chain networks may be steady-state or dynamic and may be deterministic or deal with uncertainties (particularly in product demands). Research in this field started very early on, with location-allocation problems forming part of the early set of "classical" operations research problems, see e.g. Geoffrion and Graves (1974) who consider the problem of distribution system layout and sizing and DC-customer allocation. It was recognised early on that systematic, optimisation-based approaches should be used, and that "common-sense" heuristics might lead to poor solutions (Geoffrion and van Roy, 1979). These early models tended to focus on the logistics aspects. Clearly, much more benefit could be achieved by simultaneously considering the production aspects and other issues related to integration of inventory, transportation, supplier selection, and investment budgeting decisions (Melo, Nickel and Saldanha da Gama, 2006).

Almost in the begging of 90's the concept of supply chain began to emerge as one of the most popular field of research and study until today. Chopra and Meindl (2004) describe the supply chain as a dynamic network of collaboration that consists of many parties such as suppliers, manufacturers, transporters, warehouses, distribution centers, retailers, customers etc. and its objective is to maximize the overall value generated for all the members of supply chain.

Since companies recognized the potential competitive advantages, gained through a holistic management of their supply chain, the academic community has been developing several models that describe their design and operation. Flexibility, supplier selection and coordination of supply chain members are the most popular current issues in the field.

The role of flexibility in supply design and modeling has been discussed in a special issue edited by Chandra and Crabis (2009). In this issue, flexibility was mainly assessed in terms of product flexibility aspects (Francas and Minner, 2009; Hallgren and Olhager, 2009; Hasuike and Ishii, 2009). Supplier selection in the supply chain context was discussed in the work of Cakravastia, Toha and Nakamura (2002) and Xu and Nozick (2009). Cakravastia et al. (2002) developed a model for the selection of suppliers during the design of a supply chain. Prices and lead times measured the performance of customers' dissatisfaction whereas the structure of the network was influenced from the special characteristics of product and orders size. In the same direction, Xu and Nozick (2009) presented a two-stage stochastic model for supplier selection that incorporated hedging against disruptions such as loss of production capability at supplier sites. Finally, there is a substantial literature contribution on coordination issues among suppliers and others members of the supply chain network (Petersen, Ragatz and Monczka, 2005). Competitive advantage requires the integration of all procedures and stages, even tactics with common shared information. It was concluded that the optimal function of a network depends on levels of trust developed among members and the quality of common shared information.

Design and Planning of Supply Chain Networks under Demand Uncertainty

Manufacturing industry companies operate a wide variety of assets, with widely varying ages and expected lifetimes. At any given time, the decisions relating to investment in infrastructure include how best to configure assets at existing sites and whether to establish new sites. These are tied in with production and inventory planning. The main issue associated with investment planning is that capacity-related decisions have impacts far beyond the time period over which confidence in data exists. Hence, decisions must be made in the face of significant uncertainty relating in particular to the economic circumstances that will prevail in the future. Uncertainty may be caused by external factors, such as demand, prices, availability of production resources etc. or internal ones like promotion of new products, improvement of product quality etc. Demand uncertainty has been early recognized in the supply chain management context as the essential cause of the "bullwhip effect", which is characterized by excess volatility in demand (Davis, 1993). In order to capture terms of uncertainty in design and operating supply chain networks, two mathematical formulations developed: a) scenarios or multi-period approaches and b) probabilistic approaches.

Tsiakis, Shah and Pantelides (2001) show how demand uncertainty can be introduced in a multiperiod steady-state model. They argue that future uncertainties can be captured well through a scenario tree, where each scenario represents a different discrete future outcome. These should correspond to significant future events rather than just minor variations in demand. They utilise a multipurpose production model where flexible production capacity is to be allocated between different products, and determine the optimal layout and flow allocations of the distribution network.

Guillèn, Mele, Bagajewicz, Espuña and Puigjaner (2005) proposed a multi-echelon stochastic model for the design of chemical supply chains under demand uncertainty. A clever combination of genetic algorithms and mathematical programming was employed for the solution of the underlying problems. Applequist, Penky and Reklaitis (2000) presented an approach for the design chemical supply chains under demand uncertainty. They mentioned that in such cases, risk appears and management issues become more complex and difficult.

Papageorgiou (2009) presents an excellent review of the supply chain optimization problem for the process industries. He emphasized that systematic consideration of uncertainty can facilitate calculation of expected return and evaluation of associated risks based on current status and future predictions.

The pharmaceuticals supply chains constitute an interesting area in which significant discrete uncertainty exist (related to success or failure of product tests and clinical trials). The problem of testing and capacity planning in this sector has been reviewed by Shah (2003).

Al-Othman, Lababidi, Alatiqi and Al-Shayji (2008) presented a multi-period optimization model framework for the optimal design of petroleum supply chains under uncertainty in both product demands and prices. They concluded that the design of supply chains in such uncertain and unstable economic environments is characterized by high levels of danger and risk, since many unpredictable factors can be appeared.

Pan and Nagi (2010) considered the design of a supply chain for a new market opportunity with uncertain customer demands. A robust optimization model was proposed where expected total costs, cost variability due to demand uncertainty, and expected penalty for demand unmet were the three components in the objective function. In this model uncertainty was captured via scenario approach while the objective was to choose one partner for each echelon and simultaneously decide for each partner the production plan, inventory level, and backorder amount.

Gupta, Maranas and McDonald (2000) presented a mathematical programming framework for the mid-term supply chain planning under demand uncertainty. Issues relevant to customer demand satisfaction and inventory management were considered in details. Results illustrated that significant improvement in customer services levels can be achieved with a small charge in total cost. This work was then extended by Gupta and Maranas (2003), who modeled the manufacturing decisions as "here-and-now" decisions and the logistics ones as "wait-and-see decisions".

You and Grossmann (2008) presented a mixed-integer optimization approach for the optimal design of responsive supply chains in the present of demand uncertainty. A multi-period mixed-integer nonlinear programming model was developed for the maximization of net present value and minimization of expected lead time. Hua, Li and Liang (2006) illustrated how coordination between manufactures and retailers can improve competitive advantage in supply chain networks. Two situations with different market conditions were examined. In the first case, wholesale prices and orders size were decisions, whereas in the second case retailer prices were also taken into account. It was concluded that an efficient coordination mechanism can benefit supply chains. Chen and Lee (2004) presented a mixed-integer non-linear programming problem for the design and operation of supply chain under multiple objectives and uncertain product demand. Mitra, Gudi, Patwardham and Sardar (2008) developed a chance constrained programming approach to consider uncertainty issues in the multisite multiproduct supply chain planning problem.

Sabri and Beamon (2000) developed a multi-objective supply chain model that facilitates simultaneous strategic and operational supply chain planning. Customer demand, production lead time, and supply lead times were sources of uncertainty in the proposed model which objective was the optimization of a supply chain performance vector consisted of total costs, volume flexibility, customer service level index, and delivery flexibility index. The model was comprised of a strategic submodel, which optimizes the supply chain configuration and flow, and a stochastic operational submodel, which optimizes production, distribution, and transportation costs.

Alonso-Ayuso, Escudero, Garín, Ortuño and Pérez (2003) introduced a two-stage stochastic 0-1 modeling and a related algorithmic approach aiming to formulate strategic and tactical supply chain decisions under uncertainty. The objective was the maximization of the product net profit over the time horizon minus the investment depreciation and operations costs. The strategic decisions were made in the first stage and concerned chain topology, product and vendor selection, and plant location, sizing and assignment. The tactical decisions were made in the second stage and were related to the better utilization of the supply chain along a time horizon with uncertainty in the product demand and price, and production and raw material costs.

Santoso, Ahmed, Goetschalckx and Shapiro (2005) proposed a stochastic programming model and a solution algorithm to solve large-scale global supply chain network design problems under uncertainty and with an extremely large number of scenarios. Uncertainty was captured in terms of randomness in costs, capacities, supplies and demands. The objective was the minimization of the total investment and operational costs. The supply chain configuration decisions were made in the first stage while at the second stage decisions concerned processing and transporting products from suppliers to customers in an optimal fashion based upon the configuration and the realized uncertain scenario.

An excellent review presenting quantitative-based approaches for supply chain planning under uncertainty is presented by Peidro, Mula, Poler and Lario (2009). Gümüs and Güneri (2007) provide a comprehensive review of the literature relevant to multi-echelon inventory management in supply chains with uncertain demand and lead times.

In this work we purpose a detailed, dynamic model for the problem of designing and operating supply chain network, comprising multiproduct production facilities with shared production resources, warehouses, distribution centers and customer zones, in which demands products are both uncertain and time-varying. Inventories can be kept in different nodes of the network over several time periods, whereas uncertainty is expressed with scenarios approach. The objective is the minimization of total annualized expected cost of the network, considered all structural and operating constraints.

Our model goes beyond the literature described above by considering a one-stage multiperiod multiscenario model that captures both design and operation decision of multi-echelon supply chain networks and allows product demands to be both uncertain and time varying. More specifically, product demand is allowed to change from one time period to another and in each period different demand patterns are realized. These innovative features allow a better representation of uncertainty and a better inventory management in each node of the supply chain.

The remainder of the chapter is organized as follow. Section 2 introduces the approach according to which demand uncertainty is tackled followed by a mathematical programming framework in section 3. The applicability of the developed model is illustrated in section 4 by using a large-scale case study, under different levels of safety stocks. Finally, concluding remarks are drawn in section 5.

REPRESENTATION OF UNCERTAINTY

The operation of a supply chain network does not normally occur at a steady state. Usually product demands vary with time as a result of fluctuations in consumption patterns and product life cycles. For this reason, companies are forced to predict demand variation and to be prepared to face possible increases or decreases. A dynamic model for supply chain operation and design in which demands can be both uncertain and time varying is presented in this work.

Steady state models are a justified approximation of the operation of supply chains when we are not interested in long term variability. This is because short-term fluctuations are captured implicitly, to a certain extent, by averaging the material flows in the network over a sufficiently long period of time. On the other hand, modelling of long term variations, such as systematic variation of demand with time (e.g. seasonality or growing declining markets), necessitates a time dependent approach.

Due to the long planning horizon intrinsic in these kinds of problems a high level of uncertainty is often encountered. The handling of this uncertainty raises many challenges from the choice of an appropriate modelling method to the solution method selected to attack the problem (Wets, 1996). In the case of supply chain networks as in any production and distribution system we are mainly interested in the uncertainty in product demands, prices and costs and availability of resources. Dynamic mathematical formulations approach uncertainty in two ways (Ierapetritou, Pistikopoulos and Floudas; 1996):

- scenario or multi period approaches often including discretization applied to a continuous uncertain parameter space;
- probabilistic approaches using two stage stochastic programming.

The scenario-based approach divides the planning horizon into a number of stages. The boundaries between successive stages reflect points in time where important uncertainties will be resolved. These often relate to important external events (economic or geopolitical etc.) or important internal events (launches of new products, patent losses on existing products etc.). Normally, the number of scenarios is kept small, the aim being to capture only the most important events. Schoemaker (1993) explains how to construct scenarios.

In the supply chain literature uncertainty in time varying demands has received attention in the context of the planning and control of inventories in multi-echelon networks. Some of the mathematical programming models tend to require substantial amounts of data and to make many restrictive assumptions which renders them impractical to some extent (Stenger, 1996). On the other hand, heuristic models fail to consider the interactions between echelons and frequently result in excessive inventories.

The scenario approach to modelling of uncertainty is particularly well suited to problems involving a combination of "wait-and-see" and "here-and-now" decisions. The nature of the scenarios that need to be postulated depends on the existence of "wait-and-see" decisions. If the problem under consideration involves no such decisions, then each scenario is a distinct profile of product demand(s) over time. In this case, all decisions are of the "here-and-now" type and are determined only on the basis of information available at the initial stage.

On the other hand in problems involving a combination of "wait-and-see" and "here-and-now" decisions the postulated scenarios are typically of the form shown in Figure 1. Here the information pertaining to product demands in a given period becomes available at the end of the preceding period and this results in each scenario branch breaking into multiple branches at these

Figure 1. Scenarios for problems involving both "here-and-now" and "wait-and-see" decisions

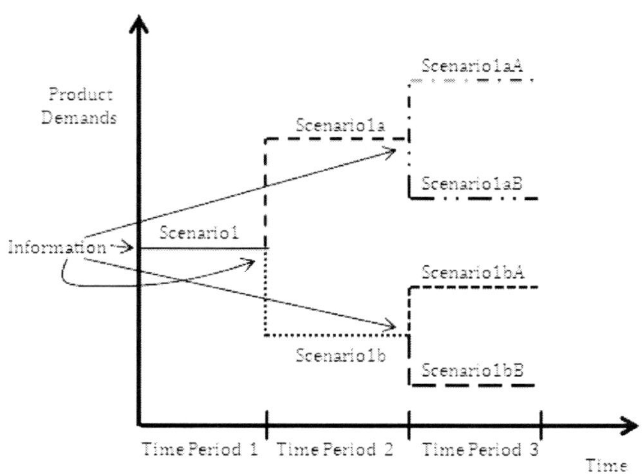

points (c.f. Figure 1). In many cases there is little or no uncertainty regarding the very first period this results in a single scenario branch over this period as shown in Figure 1.

There are now three important sets of decisions associated with each decision-making time period and each branch on the tree:

- whether to invest in new capacity and if so, how much;
- how much material to produce;
- how much inventory to carry over to the next period.

In some decision-making models, the amounts produced over each branch are assumed to be equal to demand; this effectively removes the inventory decisions and the additional flexibility of action that is available to the decision maker. If maintenance strategy is important, then maintenance decisions and their effect on equipment availability would be included.

From the mathematical point of view, the scenario-based approach results in a mathematical programming optimisation problem. The complexity of the latter depends primarily on:

- the complexity of the underlying process model; for example, nonlinear models are more complex than linear ones, and models involving discrete decisions (as is often the case with flexible multipurpose plants) are even more complex;
- the number of postulated scenarios.

The scenario-based approach determines simultaneously:

- the optimal capital investment in new capacity that must be put in place by the start of each planning stage under each and every scenario;
- the optimal operating policy (e.g. plant throughput) and sales volume throughout each planning stage of every scenario;
- the inventory amounts that should be carried over from one stage to the next in each branch of the scenario tree;
- where relevant, the maintenance strategies for different items of equipment.

Note that, while the (postulated) product demand during any particular stage provides an upper bound on the (optimal) sales volume, the two are not necessarily equal. Moreover, the sales volume during a certain stage is not necessarily equal to the production rate given the possibility of inventory carry-over from earlier stages.

MATHEMATICAL FRAMEWORK

We consider a four stage network of the type shown in Figure 2. The locations of the plants and customers are assumed to be fixed and known. A number of warehouses and distributions centres must be selected from a set of possible locations (see Figure 2). The notation that is used in the mathematical model is given in the end of the article.

Due to the importance of binary variables we give them in this point in order to be pointed out:

Binary Variables:

$$Y_m = \begin{Bmatrix} 1, \textit{if warehouse } m \textit{ is to be established} \\ 0, \textit{otherwise} \end{Bmatrix}$$

$$Y_k = \begin{Bmatrix} 1, \textit{if distribution center } k \textit{ is to be established} \\ 0, \textit{otherwise} \end{Bmatrix}$$

$$X_{mk} = \begin{Bmatrix} 1, \textit{if material is to be transported from} \\ \textit{warehouse to distribution center } k \\ 0, \textit{otherwise} \end{Bmatrix}$$

Figure 2. The supply chain network considered in this study

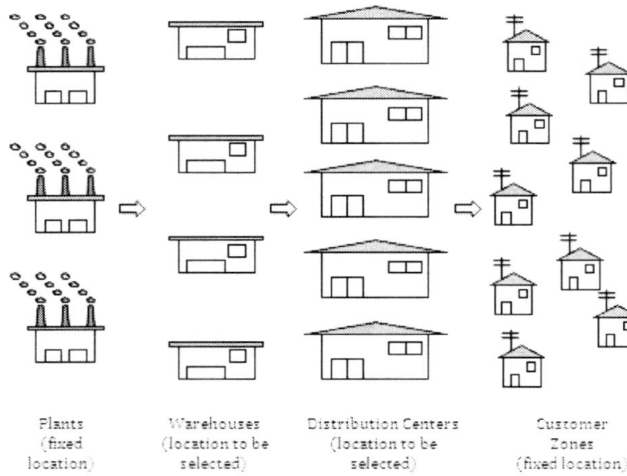

$$X_{kl} = \begin{Bmatrix} 1, \textit{if material is to be transported from} \\ \textit{distribution center k to customer zone l} \\ 0, \textit{otherwise} \end{Bmatrix}$$

Product demands are assumed to vary as piecewise constant functions of time defined over a number of time periods of given but not necessarily equal duration. The uncertainty in these demands is taken into account by postulating a number of scenarios s=1... NS, each with a potentially different set of piecewise constant demand functions. Our objective is to design a network that can handle any one of these scenarios, should it materialize at some point during the lifetime of the network, so as to minimise the combined operating and capital cost of the network.

In order to arrive at a meaningful objective function for the optimisation we assume that the probability of scenario s occurring in practice is known and is denoted by ψ_s. These probabilities will generally satisfy:

$$\sum_{s=1}^{NS} \psi_s = 1 \qquad (1)$$

Our aim is to minimise the expected value of the cost of the network taken over all the scenarios and during the operation of the network. The mathematical model proposed for this problem is an MILP as described below.

Constraints

Network Structure Constraints

The link between a warehouse m and a distribution center k can exist only if warehouse m is also established:

$$X_{mk} \leq Y_m, \forall m, k \qquad (2)$$

It is sometimes required that certain distribution centers be served by a single warehouse (single sourcing). This can be enforced via the constraints:

$$\sum_m X_{mk} = Y_k, \forall k \in K^{SS} \qquad (3)$$

If the distribution centre does not exist then its links with warehouses cannot exist either. This leads to the constraint:

$$X_{mk} \leq Y_k, \forall m, k \notin K^{SS} \quad (4)$$

The above is written only for the distribution centers that are not single sourced. For the rest of the distribution centers constraint (3) already suffices.

The link between a distribution centre k and a customer zone l will exist only if the distribution centre also exists:

$$X_{kl} \leq Y_k, \forall k, l \quad (5)$$

Some customer zones may be subject to a single sourcing constraint requiring that they be served by exactly one distribution center:

$$\sum_k X_{kl} = 1, \forall l \in L^{SS} \quad (6)$$

Logical Constrains for Transportation Flows

Flow of material i from plant j to warehouse m can take place only if warehouse m exists:

$$Q_{ijmt}^{[s]} \leq Q_{ijm}^{[s],max} Y_m, \forall i, j, m, t, s = 1, \cdots, NS \quad (7)$$

The above constraints are enforced over both each scenario s and each time period t. Flow of material i from warehouse m to distribution center k can take place only if the corresponding connection exists:

$$Q_{imkt}^{[s]} \leq Q_{imk}^{[s],max} X_{mk}, \forall i, m, k, t, s = 1, \cdots, NS \quad (8)$$

Flow of material i from distribution center k to customer zone l can take place only if the corresponding connection exists:

$$Q_{iklt}^{[s]} \leq Q_{ikl}^{[s],max} X_{kl}, \forall i, k, l, t, s = 1, \cdots, NS \quad (9)$$

Appropriate values for the upper bounds appearing on the right hand size of the above constraint can be obtained as described in Tsiakis et al. (2001).

There is usually a minimum total flow rate of material (of whatever type) that is needed to justify the establishment of a transportation link between two locations in the network. This consideration leads to the following constraints:

$$\sum_i Q_{imkt}^{[s]} \geq Q_{mk}^{min} X_{mk}, \forall m, k, t, s = 1, \cdots, NS \quad (10)$$

$$\sum_i Q_{iklt}^{[s]} \geq Q_{kl}^{min} X_{kl}, \forall k, l, t, s = 1, \cdots, NS \quad (11)$$

for the links between a warehouse m and a distribution center k, and between a distribution center k and a customer zone l, respectively.

Material Balances

The mathematical model supposes that inventory may be kept at different stages in the network. If no product inventories were held at the plants locations, the actual rate of production of product i by plant j would equal the total flow of this product from plant j to all warehouses m. However, if inventory of product i allowed to be held in plant j at time t, then the material balance on the plant over period t becomes:

$$I_{ijt}^{[s]} = I_{ij,t-1}^{[s]} + \left(P_{ijt}^{[s]} - \sum_m Q_{ijmt}^{[s]} \right) \quad (12)$$

$$" T_t, \forall i, j, t, s = 1, \cdots, NS$$

Constraint (12) states that the available inventory of product i held in plant j at the end of period t (left side of equation) is equal to the inventory held at the end of period t-1 plus any product accumulated in the plant due to the production during the period, minus any product transported from the plant to warehouses during the same period. Since both production and transportation are expressed as flows of material over time (e.g. te/wk), we calculate the total amount of material during period [t-1, t] by multiplying these rates by the duration ΔT_t of time period t. Typically, the durations ΔT_t range from a few weeks to several months depending on the actual planning procedures of the corporation.

Similarly, we can formulate the following constraints for the warehouses and distribution centers:

$$I_{imt}^{[s]} = I_{im,t-1}^{[s]} + \left(\sum_j Q_{ijmt}^{[s]} - \sum_k Q_{imkt}^{[s]} \right) \quad (13)$$
$$'' T_t, \forall i, m, t, s = 1, \cdots, NS$$

$$I_{ik}^{[s]} = I_{ik,t-1}^{[s]} + \left(\sum_m Q_{imkt}^{[s]} - \sum_l Q_{iklt}^{[s]} \right) \quad (14)$$
$$'' T_t, \forall i, k, t, s = 1, \cdots, NS$$

Customer zones do not normally hold significant amounts of inventory. Consequently, the total flow of each product i received by each customer zone l from the distribution centers is assumed to be equal to the corresponding market demand:

$$\sum_k Q_{iklt}^{[s]} = D_{ilt}^{[s]}, \forall i, l, t, s = 1, \cdots, NS \quad (15)$$

The initial inventories $I_{ij0}^{[s]}$, $I_{im0}^{[s]}$ and $I_{ik0}^{[s]}$, are assume to be given as part of the specification of each distinct scenario s.

Production Resources Constraints

An important issue in the operation of the distribution network is the ability of the manufacturing plants to cover the demands of the customers as expressed through the orders received from the warehouses. The rate of production of each product at any plant cannot exceed certain limits. Thus, there is always a minimum production capacity for any one product; moreover there is often a minimum production rate that must be maintained while the plant is operating: All the above are expressed through the following constraint which is enforced for each and every scenario s and each time period t:

$$P_{ijt}^{[s],min} \le P_{ijt}^{[s]} \le P_{ijt}^{[s],max}, \forall i, j, t, s = 1, \cdots, NS \quad (16)$$

It is common in many manufacturing sites for some resources (equipment, utilities, manpower, etc.) to be used by several production lines and at different stages of the production of each product. This share usage limits the availability of the resource that can be used for any one purpose as expressed by the following constraint:

$$\sum_i Á_{ije} P_{ijt}^{[s]} \le R_{je}, \forall j, e, t, s = 1, \cdots, NS \quad (17)$$

The coefficient ρ_{ije} express the amount of resource e used by plant j to produce a unit amount of product i, while R_{je} represents the total rate of availability of resource e at plant j.

Capacity of Warehouses and Distribution Centers

One of the most significant issues during the design and the life time of the network are the capacities of warehouses and distribution centers. These amounts specify the quantity of products, which can be stored there temporary, before their conveyance at the market.

The capacity of a warehouse m generally has to lie between given lower and upper bounds, W_m^{min} and W_m^{max}, provided, of course that the warehouse is actually established (i.e. $Y_m=1$):

$$W_m^{min} Y_m \leq W_m \leq W_m^{max} Y_m, \forall m \tag{18}$$

Similar constraints apply to the capacities of distribution centers k:

$$D_k^{min} Y_k \leq D_k \leq D_k^{max} Y_k, \forall k \tag{19}$$

The dynamic formulation of this chapter allows an arguably more precise characterization of these capacities in terms of the actual inventory being held. More specifically, the capacity of a warehouse or a distribution center cannot be less than the combined inventory to be held there at any time period under each scenario. This leads to constraints of the form:

$$W_m \geq \sum_i^3 {}_{im} I_{imt}^{[s]}, \forall m, t, s = 1, \cdots, NS \tag{20}$$

$$D_k \geq \sum_i^3 {}_{ik} I_{ikt}^{[s]}, \forall k, t, s = 1, \cdots, NS \tag{21}$$

where γ_{im} and γ_{ik} are given coefficients expressing the amount of warehousing capacity required to hold a unit amount of a particular product i at a warehouse m or a distribution center k respectively.

Safety Stock Constraints

Maintaining a safety stock (also known as "buffer inventory") is often desirable, providing a means of overcoming unforeseen production disturbances or unexpected product demands. In general, the higher the level of inventory, the better the customer service, with fewer stockouts. On the other hand, excess inventory causes higher operating costs. Consequently, safety stock is usually only as much as is necessary to keep the network functioning for a short period of time (e.g. from a few days to a week) in case of disruption at one or more of its nodes.

The need for safety stock can be expressed by the following constraints:

$$I_{ijt}^{[s]} \geq I_{ijt}^{[s],min}, \forall i, j, t, s = 1, \cdots, NS \tag{22}$$

$$I_{imt}^{[s]} \geq I_{imt}^{[s],min} Y_m, \forall i, m, t, s = 1, \cdots, NS \tag{23}$$

$$I_{ikt}^{[s]} \geq I_{ikt}^{[s],min} Y_k, \forall i, k, t, s = 1, \cdots, NS \tag{24}$$

The above constraints ensure that inventory is kept at warehouses or distribution centers only if these are established. We also note that the minimum inventory handling requirements may vary from scenario to scenario and from one time period to another. In fact they are often expressed as functions (e.g. constant multiples) of the corresponding material flows delivered by each plant, warehouse or distribution center node to all other nodes that are served by it.

Since we assume constant rates of production, transportation and demand over each time period, inventories vary linearly with time during a period. Consequently, it suffices to enforce constraints (22) to (24) at the time period boundaries for them to hold at all times during the planning time horizon.

As explained above the amount of safety stock to be held at each plant, warehouse or distribution centre node is usually expressed in terms of a given number of days' equivalent of material flow delivered by the node to all nodes supplied by it. Here we assume that this number of days is the same for all nodes of the same type (e.g.

plants, warehouses or distribution centres). Thus, the safety stock is given by:

$$I_{ijt}^{[s],min} = \frac{n^P}{7}\sum_m Q_{ijmt}^{[s]}, \forall i, j, t, s = 1, \cdots, NS \quad (25)$$

$$I_{imt}^{[s],min} = \frac{n^W}{7}\sum_k Q_{imkt}^{[s]}, \forall i, m, t, s = 1, \cdots, NS \quad (26)$$

$$I_{ikt}^{[s],min} = \frac{n^{DC}}{7}\sum_l Q_{iklt}^{[s]}, \forall i, j, k, s = 1, \cdots, NS \quad (27)$$

where n^P, n^W, n^{DC} are the numbers of days equivalent for plants, warehouses and distribution centers respectively and the division by 7 reflects the fact that all our material flows are expressed as tonnes per week. The right hand sides of equations (25)–(27) are used to replace the minimum inventory quantities appearing in the right hand sides of constraints (22)–(24) respectively. Initial inventories for each product and for each production plant are assumed to been known at a certain level.

Non-Negativity Constraints

All continuous variables must be non-negative:

$$P_{ijt}^{[s]} \geq 0, \forall i, j, t, s = 1, \cdots, NS \quad (28)$$

$$I_{ijt}^{[s]} \geq 0, \forall i, j, t, s = 1, \cdots, NS \quad (29)$$

$$I_{imt}^{[s]} \geq 0, \forall i, m, t, s = 1, \cdots, NS \quad (30)$$

$$I_{ikt}^{[s]} \geq 0, \forall i, k, t, s = 1, \cdots, NS \quad (31)$$

$$Q_{ijmt}^{[s]} \geq 0, \forall i, j, m, t, s = 1, \cdots, NS \quad (32)$$

$$Q_{imkt}^{[s]} \geq 0, \forall i, m, k, t, s = 1, \cdots, NS \quad (33)$$

$$Q_{iklt}^{[s]} \geq 0, \forall i, k, l, t, s = 1, \cdots, NS \quad (34)$$

Objective Function

The objective of the optimisation is to minimise the overall expected cost of the supply chain network over a planning time horizon. This includes both (annualised) capital costs and operating costs, and lead to an objective function which includes the following five terms.

Fixed Infrastructure Cost

The infrastructure costs considered by our formulation are related to the establishment of a warehouse or a distribution centre at a candidate location. These costs are represented by the following objective function terms:

$$\sum_m C_m^W Y_m + \sum_k C_k^D Y_k \quad (35)$$

The annualized fixed cost of establishing a warehouse at location m, denoted as C_m^W, is multiplied by the binary variable Y_m. Thus, only if the warehouse m is selected, the corresponding cost participates in the objective function. We assume that the manufacturing plants are already established. Therefore, we do not consider the capital cost associated with their design and construction. We also ignore any infrastructure cost associated with the customer zones.

Production Cost

The production cost is given by the product of the production rate $P_{ijt}^{[s]}$ of product i in plant j at time period t under scenario s, by the unit production cost C_{ij}^{P}. The corresponding term in the objective function is of the form:

$$\sum_{i,j} C_{ij}^{P} P_{ijt}^{[s]}, \forall t, s = 1, \cdots, NS \tag{36}$$

Material Handling Cost at Warehouses and Distribution Centers

Material handling costs such as wages, extra packing, insurance contracts, electricity, etc. can usually be approximated as linear functions of the total throughput. They can be expressed as follows:

$$\sum_{i,m} C_{im}^{WH} \left(\sum_{j} Q_{ijmt}^{[s]} \right) + \sum_{i,k} C_{ik}^{DH} \left(\sum_{m} Q_{imkt}^{[s]} \right), \quad \forall t, s = 1, \cdots, NS \tag{37}$$

Inventory Holding Cost at Different Nodes

Since inventory may be kept at different stages in the network, a cost is associated with their management. In general, the cost incurred over a given time period t is proportional to the average amount of inventory held over this period. The average inventory is expressed by the arithmetic mean of the starting and finishing inventories for this period, as inventories vary linearly over each time period.

$$\sum_{i,j} C_{ijt}^{I} \frac{I_{ijt}^{[s]} + I_{ij,t-1}^{[s]}}{2} + \sum_{i,m} C_{imt}^{I} \frac{I_{imt}^{[s]} + I_{im,t-1}^{[s]}}{2} + \sum_{i,k} C_{ikt}^{I} \frac{I_{ikt}^{[s]} + I_{ik,t-1}^{[s]}}{2}, \forall t, s = 1, \cdots, NS \tag{38}$$

Transportation Cost

The total transportation cost for product i during time period t under scenario s, is proportional to the amount of material transferred between echelons. Transportation costs that we include are those between production plant to distribution centres and distribution centres to customers. A more detailed modelling approach reflecting economies of scale can be found in Tsiakis et al. (2001).

$$\sum_{i,j,m} C_{ijm}^{TR} Q_{ijmt}^{[s]} + \sum_{i,m,k} C_{imk}^{TR} Q_{imkt}^{[s]} + \sum_{i,k,l} C_{ikl}^{TR} Q_{iklt}^{[s]}, \forall t, s = 1, \cdots, NS \tag{39}$$

Objective Function

The final form of the objective function is as follows:

$$\min \left(\sum_{m} C_{m}^{W} Y_{m} + \sum_{k} C_{k}^{D} Y_{k} \right) \sum_{t} \Delta T_{t}$$
$$+ \sum_{s=1}^{NS} \grave{E}_{S} \Bigg(\sum_{t}{}'' T_{t} \Bigg(\sum_{i,j} C_{ij}^{P} P_{ijt}^{[s]} + \sum_{i,m} C_{im}^{WH} \left(\sum_{j} Q_{ijmt}^{[s]} \right) + \sum_{i,k} C_{ik}^{DH} \left(\sum_{m} Q_{imkt}^{[s]} \right)$$
$$+ \sum_{i,j,m} C_{ijm}^{TR} \left(\sum Q_{ijmt}^{[s]} \right) + \sum_{i,m,k} C_{imk}^{TR} \left(\sum Q_{imkt}^{[s]} \right) + \sum_{i,k,l} C_{ikl}^{TR} \left(\sum Q_{iklt}^{[s]} \right)$$
$$+ \sum_{i,j} C_{ijt}^{I} \frac{I_{ijt}^{[s]} + I_{ij,t-1}^{[s]}}{2} + \sum_{i,m} C_{imt}^{I} \frac{I_{imt}^{[s]} + I_{im,t-1}^{[s]}}{2} + \sum_{i,k} C_{ikt}^{I} \frac{I_{ikt}^{[s]} + I_{ik,t-1}^{[s]}}{2} \Bigg) \Bigg)$$

It should be noted that

- The objective function reflects actual total costs incurred over the planning horizon rather than rate of expenditure (i.e. it is measured in rmu[1] instead of rmu/week)
- The annualized capital costs are multiplied by the total length of the time horizon under consideration $\sum_t^{NT} T_t$
- The rate of operating expenditure varies from one time period to the next. Consequently the operating cost in each period t is multiplied by the corresponding duration ΔT_t

The overall problem of considering the optimal design of multi-echelon supply chains under transient demand conditions is formulated as a Mixed-Integer Linear Programming (MILP) problem and solved to global optimality using the ILOG CPLEX 11.2.0 solver incorporated in the GAMS tool (Rosenthal, 2008). In all cases an integrality gap of 0% was imposed.

Scenario-Dependent Distribution Network Structure

The formulation presented above was based on the assumption that the structure of the distribution network (i.e. the transportation links between warehouses, distribution centers and customer zones) were independent of the scenario. In many cases, this is unnecessary since the costs associated with the establishment of a transportation link are relative small. This is especially the case when transportation is outsourced to third parties. In such cases, we could allow the network of transportation links to vary both over time and depending on the scenario instead of treating these decisions as "here-and-now" variables to be fixed once and for all at the design stage. This effectively allows for some reconfiguration of the supply chain network during operation.

The required changes in the mathematical model formulation are minimal. More, specifically, the binary variables X_{mk} and X_{kl} will now have a superscript [s] and a subscript [t]to denote that they can change for each possible scenario and during each time period of the operation of the network.

The constraints that need to change are:

$$X_{mkt}^{[s]} \le Y_m, \forall m, k, t, s = 1, \cdots, NS \quad (2')$$

$$\sum_m X_{mkt}^{[s]} = Y_k, \forall k \in K^{SS}, t, s = 1, \cdots, NS \quad (3')$$

$$X_{mkt}^{[s]} \le Y_k, \forall m, k \notin K^{SS}, t, s = 1, \cdots, NS \quad (4')$$

$$X_{klt}^{[s]} \le Y_k, \forall k, l, t, s = 1, \cdots, NS \quad (5')$$

$$\sum_k X_{klt}^{[s]} = 1, \forall l \in L^{SS}, t, s = 1, \cdots, NS \quad (6')$$

$$Q_{imkt}^{[s]} \le Q_{imk}^{[s],max} X_{mkt}^{[s]}, \forall i, m, k, t, s = 1, \cdots, NS \quad (8')$$

$$Q_{iklt}^{[s]} \le Q_{ikl}^{[s],max} X_{klt}^{[s]}, \forall i, k, l, t, s = 1, \cdots, NS \quad (9')$$

$$\sum_i Q_{imkt}^{[s]} \ge Q_{mk}^{min} X_{mkt}^{[s]}, \forall m, k, t, s = 1, \cdots, NS \quad (10')$$

$$\sum_i Q_{iklt}^{[s]} \ge Q_{kl}^{min} X_{klt}^{[s]}, \forall k, l, t, s = 1, \cdots, NS \quad (11')$$

This option gives the network an additional degree of flexibility. Only the locations of warehouses and distribution centers are constant through the operation of the system, while the links between nodes may be re-allocated in every time

Figure 3. The case study network

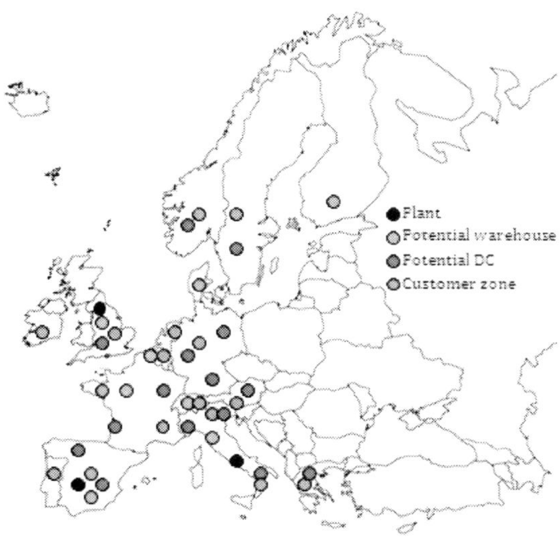

period and scenario in order to satisfy customer demand in the most coast-efficient manner.

CASE STUDY

Problem Description

To consider the applicability of the MILP model presented in the previous section we consider a European wide production and distribution network comprising of three manufacturing plants producing 14 different types of products and located in three different European countries, namely the United Kingdom, Spain and Italy (see Figure 3).

Product demands are such that Europe can be divided into 18 customer zones located in 16 different countries. We consider the establishment of a sufficient network of distribution centers (DCs) to cover the whole market. The distribution centers can be located anywhere in 15 countries, and are to be supplied by up to six warehouses, the location of which is also to be chosen among six candidate places.

Because of the fact that customer demand is both uncertain and time-varying, we work with a scenario-based approach. Last but not least inventories are held in different stages in the network in low or high levels, thus we examine two case studies. All data provided in the work of Tsiakis et al. (2001).

Manufacturing Plants and Production Procedure

The three manufacturing plants are already established in specified European countries and produce 14 types of different products. Each plant produces several products using a number of shared production resources. However, no single plant produces the entire range of products. Table 1 shows the maximum production rate $P_{ijt}^{[s],max}$ of each manufacturing plant, whereas the corresponding minimum production rate is assumed to be zero $\left(\text{i.e. } P_{ijt}^{[s],min} = 0, \forall i, j\right)$.

In Table 2 all columns give the values of the ρ_{ije} coefficient, while the last column represents the total availability of resource e in manufacturing plant j (R_{je}). The unit production cost is indicated in Table 3.

Table 1. Maximum production capacity of each manufacturing plant j for each product i

Plants	Products (ton/week)*													
	i_1	i_2	i_3	i_4	i_5	i_6	i_7	i_8	i_9	i_{10}	i_{11}	i_{12}	i_{13}	i_{14}
j_1	158	2268	1701	1512	0	812	642	482	320	504	0	661	441	221
j_2	0	1411	1058	1328	996	664	664	0	0	0	530	496	330	0
j_3	972	778	607	540	0	416	416	312	208	0	403	0	270	0

* There is no difference among several scenarios and time periods

Table 2. Utilization and availability data for each shared production resource e for each product i in each manufacturing plant j

Plants	Shared resource utilization coefficient ρ_{ije} (hours/ton)*														Total resource availability (hours/week)
	i_1	i_2	i_3	i_4	i_5	i_6	i_7	i_8	i_9	i_{10}	i_{11}	i_{12}	i_{13}	i_{14}	
$j_1 \cdot e_1$										0.2381					120
$j_1 \cdot e_2$		0.0463	0.0617	0.0694											105
$j_1 \cdot e_3$							0.1634	0.2178	0.3268						105
$j_1 \cdot e_4$												0.2267	0.3401	0.6802	150
$j_1 \cdot e_5$						0.1292									105
$j_1 \cdot e_6$	0.6667														105
$j_1 \cdot e_1$											0.1984	0.2118	0.3174		105
$j_2 \cdot e_2$				0.0793	0.1054	0.1582	0.1582								105
$j_3 \cdot e_3$		0.0740	0.1000												105
$j_1 \cdot e_1$			0.1976	0.2222											120
$j_2 \cdot e_2$						0.3968	0.3968	0.5291	0.7936						165
$j_3 \cdot e_3$	0.1200	0.1543													120
$j_4 \cdot e_4$											0.2976		0.4444		120

* There is no difference among several scenarios and time periods

Table 3. Unit production cost of each product i in each manufacturing plant j

Plants	Unit production cost (relative money units/ton)*													
	i_1	i_2	i_3	i_4	i_5	i_6	i_7	i_8	i_9	i_{10}	i_{11}	i_{12}	i_{13}	i_{14}
j_1	61.27	61.27	61.27	61.27	61.27	61.27	256.90	256.90	256.90	61.27	256.90	256.90	256.90	256.90
j_2	59.45	59.45	59.45	59.45	59.45	59.45	268.50	268.50	268.50	59.45	268.50	268.50	268.50	268.50
j_3	61.44	61.44	61.44	61.44	61.44	61.44	270.80	270.80	270.80	61.44	270.80	270.80	270.80	270.80

* There is no difference among several scenarios and time periods

Table 4. Fixed infrastructure and material handling costs for candidate warehouse m and distribution center k

Warehouses	Infrastructure cost (relative money units/week)*	Material handling cost (relative money units/ton)*
m_1	10,000	4.25
m_2	5,000	4.55
m_3	4,000	4.98
m_4	6,000	4.93
m_5	6,500	4.06
m_6	4,000	5.28
Distribution Centers	**Infrastructure cost (relative money units/week)***	**Material handling cost (relative money units/ton)***
k_1	10,000	4.25
k_2	5,000	4.55
k_3	4,000	4.98
k_4	6,000	4.93
k_5	6,500	4.85
k_6	4,000	3.90
k_7	6,000	4.06
k_8	4,000	3.08
k_9	5,000	6.00
k_{10}	3,000	4.85
k_{11}	4,500	4.12
k_{12}	7,000	5.66
k_{13}	9,000	5.28
k_{14}	5,500	4.95
k_{15}	8,500	4.83
* There is no difference among several scenarios and time periods		

Warehouses and Distribution Centers

All products after their production go to warehouses, where they will be stored and then placed at distribution centers. Warehouses will be selected among six candidate locations and distribution centers among fifteen possible locations. Each warehouse and distribution center cannot keep more than 14,000 ton/week (W_m^{max}) and 7,000 (D_k^{max}) ton/week, respectively. On the other hand, there are no requirements for minimum material handling capacities ($W_m^{min} = 0$ and $D_k^{min} = 0$). Despite the fact that capacities are the same, fixed infrastructure costs vary for each node, whereas material handling costs are the same for all products but may differ from place to place, as shown in Table 4. The coefficients γ_{im} and γ_{ik}, which show the capacity of each warehouse m or distribution center k that is required for the storage of a product i are equal to one.

Table 5. Demand for product i for customer zone l over the first time period

Customer Zone	Product demands (ton/week)*													
	i_1	i_2	i_3	i_4	i_5	i_6	i_7	i_8	i_9	i_{10}	i_{11}	i_{12}	i_{13}	i_{14}
l_1	18	0	0	506	0	452	0	0	43	0	0	0	120	34
l_2	0	499	155	203	76	0	30	0	0	0	20	0	0	0
l_3	0	155	0	166	0	66	17	0	0	0	0	0	15	0
l_4	15	0	126	0	0	0	5	27	0	0	0	25	0	0
l_5	0	0	92	0	0	0	0	0	21	0	0	0	50	0
l_6	0	0	0	0	0	68	0	0	20	0	0	0	10	10
l_7	0	14	0	40	0	0	0	0	34	0	0	0	68	0
l_8	0	0	0	45	0	23	0	0	5	0	0	0	0	0
l_9	0	0	0	0	0	0	52	0	7	0	0	0	0	0
l_{10}	0	0	0	17	0	0	0	0	5	0	0	0	16	0
l_{11}	0	0	0	31	0	0	0	0	0	0	0	0	15	0
l_{12}	0	31	0	0	0	0	13	0	0	38	0	0	0	0
l_{13}	0	21	0	0	0	0	15	0	0	0	0	0	0	0
l_{14}	0	0	0	0	0	0	0	7	0	0	0	0	0	0
l_{15}	0	0	0	0	0	0	10	0	0	0	15	0	0	0
l_{16}	15	0	68	0	0	0	5	20	0	0	0	20	0	0
l_{17}	0	103	0	110	0	44	12	0	0	0	0	0	13	0
l_{18}	0	0	0	0	0	0	0	0	0	266	0	0	0	0

* All scenarios

Product Demand

We consider a planning horizon comprising three four-week time periods ($\Delta T_1 = \Delta T_2 = \Delta T_3 = 4$ weeks). Product demands over the first period are assumed to be known with certainty, and are shown in Table 5.

However, there are two distinctly different predictions for demands over the second period, shown in tables 6 and 7, respectively. Moreover, each of these demand predictions for the second period leads to two distinct demand predictions for the third period (see Tables 8 to 11).

Overall we need to consider four distinct scenarios (i.e. s=1, …, 4) organized in a tree structure of the type shown in Figure 1. The formulation of the previous section is directly applicable to this situation, provided:

The operational variables of all four scenarios are treated as identical in the first time period, e.g.

$$P_{ijl}^{[1]} = P_{ijl}^{[2]} = P_{ijl}^{[3]} = P_{ijl}^{[4]}, \forall i, j$$

The operational variables of scenarios 1 and 2 are treated as identical in the second time period, e.g.

$$P_{ij2}^{[1]} = P_{ij2}^{[2]}, \forall i, j$$

The operational variables of scenarios 3 and 4 are treated as identical in the second time period, e.g.

Table 6. Demand for product i for customer zone l over the second time period

Customer Zone	Product demands (ton/week)*													
	i_1	i_2	i_3	i_4	i_5	i_6	i_7	i_8	i_9	i_{10}	i_{11}	i_{12}	i_{13}	i_{14}
l_1	14	0	0	547	0	412	0	0	46	0	0	0	94	30
l_2	0	612	144	248	83	0	33	0	0	0	24	0	0	0
l_3	0	117	0	202	0	70	21	0	0	0	0	0	12	0
l_4	17	0	157	0	0	0	6	25	0	0	0	27	0	0
l_5	0	0	97	0	0	0	0	0	19	0	0	0	56	0
l_6	0	0	0	0	0	65	0	0	16	0	0	0	10	11
l_7	0	14	0	40	0	0	0	0	42	0	0	0	63	0
l_8	0	0	0	51	0	25	0	0	5	0	0	0	0	0
l_9	0	0	0	0	0	0	49	0	8	0	0	0	0	0
l_{10}	0	0	0	17	0	0	0	0	5	0	0	0	13	0
l_{11}	0	0	0	33	0	0	0	0	0	0	0	0	11	0
l_{12}	0	26	0	0	0	0	14	0	0	38	0	0	0	0
l_{13}	0	21	0	0	0	0	11	0	0	0	0	0	0	0
l_{14}	0	0	0	0	0	0	0	8	0	0	0	0	0	0
l_{15}	0	0	0	0	0	0	11	0	0	0	14	0	0	0
l_{16}	11	0	51	0	0	0	5	24	0	0	0	20	0	0
l_{17}	0	124	0	135	0	36	14	0	0	0	0	0	20	0
l_{18}	0	0	0	0	0	0	0	0	0	327	0	0	0	0
* Scenarios 1 and 2														

$$P_{ij2}^{[3]} = P_{ij2}^{[4]}, \forall i, j$$

In practice the above inequalities are used to eliminate a priori a large proportion of the problem variables. All four scenarios are assumed to be equally probable ($\psi_1 = \psi_2 = \psi_3 = \psi_4 = 0.25$).

4.1.4 Transportation Procedure and Cost

The supply chain network cannot transfer between two nodes more than 100,000 products per each time period. Transportation costs are independent from economies of scale and are provided in Tables 12-14 and expressed in relative money units/ton.

Inventory

The inventory holding cost is shown in Table 15, and it is independent of the product being held, but varies from one location to another. Initial inventories for each product for the manufacturing plants are assumed to be known and at a certain level. This is equal to the maximum production capacity of the plants for a week. Warehouses and distribution centers are assume to hold zero initial inventories.

We examine two distinct cases with different levels of safety stock held in the system. This is ensured by the values of parameters n^P, n^W, n^{DC}, as provided in Table 16. In the first version there are low safety stock requirements, whereas in second version the needs of safety stock quantities are high.

Table 7. Demand for product i for customer zone l over the second time period

Customer Zone	Product demands (ton/week)*													
	i_1	i_2	i_3	i_4	i_5	i_6	i_7	i_8	i_9	i_{10}	i_{11}	i_{12}	i_{13}	i_{14}
l_1	18	0	0	436	0	568	0	0	54	0	0	0	149	31
l_2	0	633	154	195	62	0	25	0	0	0	26	0	0	0
l_3	0	172	0	189	0	58	16	0	0	0	0	0	15	0
l_4	14	0	159	0	0	0	6	33	0	0	0	29	0	0
l_5	0	0	74	0	0	0	0	0	17	0	0	0	57	0
l_6	0	0	0	0	0	57	0	0	18	0	0	0	11	12
l_7	0	16	0	41	0	0	0	0	44	0	0	0	67	0
l_8	0	0	0	46	0	19	0	0	6	0	0	0	0	0
l_9	0	0	0	0	0	0	54	0	6	0	0	0	0	0
l_{10}	0	0	0	22	0	0	0	0	4	0	0	0	20	0
l_{11}	0	0	0	28	0	0	0	0	0	0	0	0	14	0
l_{12}	0	29	0	0	0	0	12	0	0	45	0	0	0	0
l_{13}	0	20	0	0	0	0	15	0	0	0	0	0	0	0
l_{14}	0	0	0	0	0	0	0	8	0	0	0	0	0	0
l_{15}	0	0	0	0	0	0	10	0	0	0	19	0	0	0
l_{16}	13	0	62	0	0	0	4	19	0	0	0	21	0	0
l_{17}	0	97	0	122	0	51	13	0	0	0	0	0	16	0
l_{18}	0	0	0	0	0	0	0	0	0	327	0	0	0	0

* Scenarios 3 and 4

Figure 4. Optimal network configuration for low inventories case

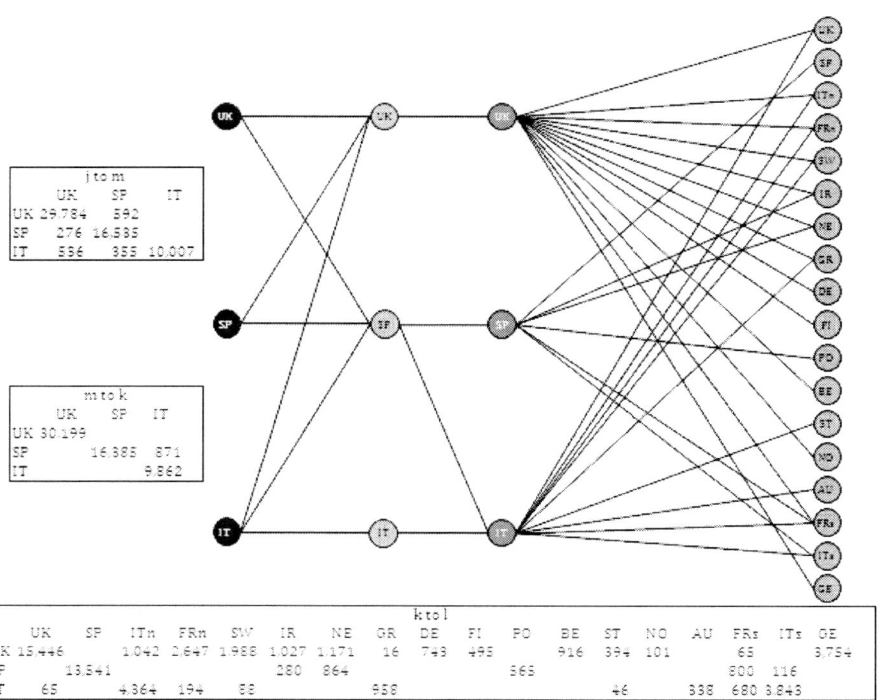

Table 8. Demand for product i for customer zone l over the third time period

Customer Zone	Product demands (ton/week)*													
	i_1	i_2	i_3	i_4	i_5	i_6	i_7	i_8	i_9	i_{10}	i_{11}	i_{12}	i_{13}	i_{14}
l_1	19	0	0	528	0	559	0	0	50	0	0	0	106	40
l_2	0	657	164	279	82	0	42	0	0	0	22	0	0	0
l_3	0	113	0	205	0	95	28	0	0	0	0	0	12	0
l_4	21	0	196	0	0	0	6	30	0	0	0	33	0	0
l_5	0	0	112	0	0	0	0	0	23	0	0	0	65	0
l_6	0	0	0	0	0	77	0	0	14	0	0	0	15	16
l_7	0	16	0	45	0	0	0	0	46	0	0	0	79	0
l_8	0	0	0	70	0	24	0	0	6	0	0	0	0	0
l_9	0	0	0	0	0	0	50	0	7	0	0	0	0	0
l_{10}	0	0	0	17	0	0	0	0	6	0	0	0	12	0
l_{11}	0	0	0	44	0	0	0	0	0	0	0	0	13	0
l_{12}	0	30	0	0	0	0	17	0	0	51	0	0	0	0
l_{13}	0	27	0	0	0	0	13	0	0	0	0	0	0	0
l_{14}	0	0	0	0	0	0	0	11	0	0	0	0	0	0
l_{15}	0	0	0	0	0	0	13	0	0	0	14	0	0	0
l_{16}	14	0	56	0	0	0	5	29	0	0	0	27	0	0
l_{17}	0	160	0	172	0	35	20	0	0	0	0	0	12	0
l_{18}	0	0	0	0	0	0	0	0	0	331	0	0	0	0

* Scenario 1

Results for Low Inventories Case

The model was solved using ILOG CPLEX 11.2.0 solver incorporated in GAMS 22.9 software and consisted of 181,104 single equations, 73,692 single variables, and 381 discrete variables. A Pentium M, with 1.6 GHz and 512 RAM, was employed for running the model and the solution was reached in 293 CPU seconds with 0% integrality gap.

The optimal network structure for this case is shown in Figure 4. The network consists of three warehouses, placed in United Kingdom, Spain and Italy and three distribution centers located in the same countries. The structure is primarily a result of the demand patterns considered since the three countries which host the manufacturing plants are also the biggest customers. However, since none of the plants can produce the whole range of products, and plant capacity is restricted due to production constraints, all plants provide

Figure 5. Inventory levels in plants, warehouses, and distribution centers in the low inventories case

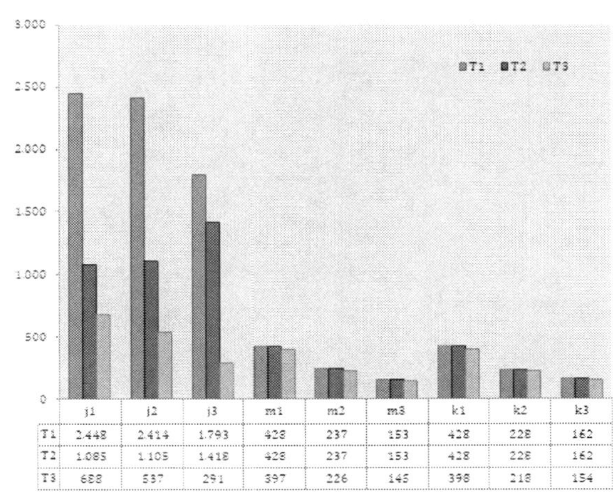

Table 9. Demand for product i for customer zone l over the third time period

Customer Zone	Product demands (ton/week)*													
	i_1	i_2	i_3	i_4	i_5	i_6	i_7	i_8	i_9	i_{10}	i_{11}	i_{12}	i_{13}	i_{14}
l_1	18	0	0	761	0	551	0	0	55	0	0	0	125	37
l_2	0	706	209	282	104	0	38	0	0	0	34	0	0	0
l_3	0	152	0	233	0	88	24	0	0	0	0	0	15	0
l_4	19	0	164	0	0	0	7	30	0	0	0	35	0	0
l_5	0	0	115	0	0	0	0	0	27	0	0	0	80	0
l_6	0	0	0	0	0	81	0	0	16	0	0	0	11	15
l_7	0	15	0	42	0	0	0	0	44	0	0	0	82	0
l_8	0	0	0	65	0	30	0	0	6	0	0	0	0	0
l_9	0	0	0	0	0	0	67	0	8	0	0	0	0	0
l_{10}	0	0	0	21	0	0	0	0	7	0	0	0	15	0
l_{11}	0	0	0	37	0	0	0	0	0	0	0	0	14	0
l_{12}	0	36	0	0	0	0	14	0	0	39	0	0	0	0
l_{13}	0	22	0	0	0	0	16	0	0	0	0	0	0	0
l_{14}	0	0	0	0	0	0	0	10	0	0	0	0	0	0
l_{15}	0	0	0	0	0	0	16	0	0	0	18	0	0	0
l_{16}	12	0	72	0	0	0	6	33	0	0	0	25	0	0
l_{17}	0	169	0	794	0	35	15	0	0	0	0	0	13	0
l_{18}	0	0	0	0	0	0	0	0	0	329	0	0	0	0

* Scenario 2

Figure 6. Optimal network configuration for the high inventories case

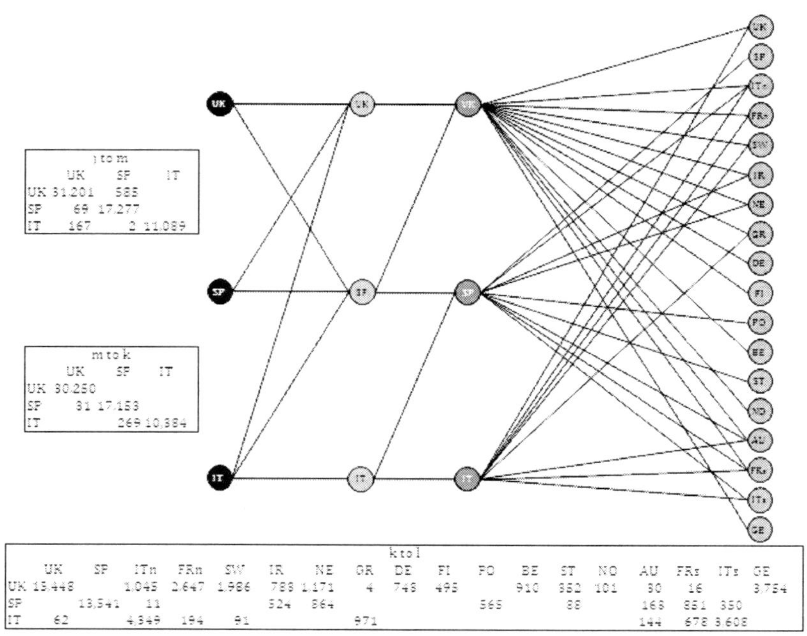

Table 10. Demand for product i for customer zone l over the third time period

Customer Zone	Product demands (ton/week)*													
	i_1	i_2	i_3	i_4	i_5	i_6	i_7	i_8	i_9	i_{10}	i_{11}	i_{12}	i_{13}	i_{14}
l_1	24	0	0	420	0	772	0	0	58	0	0	0	169	40
l_2	0	680	175	220	62	0	32	0	0	0	24	0	0	0
l_3	0	165	0	191	0	78	22	0	0	0	0	0	16	0
l_4	17	0	198	0	0	0	6	41	0	0	0	35	0	0
l_5	0	0	85	0	0	0	0	0	21	0	0	0	65	0
l_6	0	0	0	0	0	67	0	0	16	0	0	0	15	16
l_7	0	18	0	46	0	0	0	0	48	0	0	0	84	0
l_8	0	0	0	63	0	18	0	0	8	0	0	0	0	0
l_9	0	0	0	0	0	0	55	0	6	0	0	0	0	0
l_{10}	0	0	0	21	0	0	0	0	6	0	0	0	19	0
l_{11}	0	0	0	37	0	0	0	0	0	0	0	0	16	0
l_{12}	0	34	0	0	0	0	15	0	0	60	0	0	0	0
l_{13}	0	25	0	0	0	0	18	0	0	0	0	0	0	0
l_{14}	0	0	0	0	0	0	0	11	0	0	0	0	0	0
l_{15}	0	0	0	0	0	0	12	0	0	0	19	0	0	0
l_{16}	16	0	68	0	0	0	4	23	0	0	0	27	0	0
l_{17}	0	124	0	155	0	50	18	0	0	0	0	0	16	0
l_{18}	0	0	0	0	0	0	0	0	0	448	0	0	0	0

* Scenario 3

products to all warehouses. The total expected cost of the network comes to 6,031,650 relative money units and its breakdown is shown in Table 17. Inventories in plants, warehouses, and distribution centers are presented in Figure (5). It is noted that inventories reduce with the time periods.

Results for High Inventories Case

If we assume that the network needs to hold higher levels of inventories in order to minimize the probability of not satisfying product demands, the optimal structure changes as shown in Figure (6).

Some transportation links between warehouses and distribution centers and between distribution centers and customer zones are modified compared to the low inventories case. More specifically, the warehouse of Spain no longer supplies products to Italy's distribution center and begun to supply the U.K. distribution center. Furthermore, Italy's warehouse begun to provide products to Spain's distribution center. The changes occurred in transportation links between distribution centers and customer zones are mainly concern Spain's distribution center which started serving the customer zones of North Italy, Switzerland, and Austria. Moreover, the U.K. distribution center started serving Austria's customer zone whereas Italy's distribution center interrupted its service to Switzerland's customer zone.

The total cost increases to 6,874,790 relative money units. As expected all operating costs of the network are increased, as higher volumes of products and inventories have to be produced, transferred and stored (see Table 18). Regarding inventories it should be noted that the profile of

Table 11. Demand for product i for customer zone l over the third time period

Customer Zone	Product demands (ton/week)*													
	i_1	i_2	i_3	i_4	i_5	i_6	i_7	i_8	i_9	i_{10}	i_{11}	i_{12}	i_{13}	i_{14}
l_1	24	0	0	606	0	760	0	0	64	0	0	0	198	37
l_2	0	730	223	222	78	0	29	0	0	0	37	0	0	0
l_3	0	222	0	218	0	72	19	0	0	0	0	0	19	0
l_4	15	0	165	0	0	0	7	41	0	0	0	37	0	0
l_5	0	0	88	0	0	0	0	0	24	0	0	0	80	0
l_6	0	0	0	0	0	71	0	0	18	0	0	0	11	16
l_7	0	17	0	43	0	0	0	0	45	0	0	0	87	0
l_8	0	0	0	59	0	23	0	0	7	0	0	0	0	0
l_9	0	0	0	0	0	0	73	0	7	0	0	0	0	0
l_{10}	0	0	0	27	0	0	0	0	6	0	0	0	24	0
l_{11}	0	0	0	30	0	0	0	0	0	0	0	0	18	0
l_{12}	0	41	0	0	0	0	12	0	0	46	0	0	0	0
l_{13}	0	21	0	0	0	0	21	0	0	0	0	0	0	0
l_{14}	0	0	0	0	0	0	0	9	0	0	0	0	0	0
l_{15}	0	0	0	0	0	0	14	0	0	0	24	0	0	0
l_{16}	14	0	87	0	0	0	5	26	0	0	0	25	0	0
l_{17}	0	131	0	174	0	50	14	0	0	0	0	0	18	0
l_{18}	0	0	0	0	0	0	0	0	0	446	0	0	0	0

* Scenario 4

Table 12. Transportation cost between manufacturing plant j and warehouse m

Plants	Warehouse (relative money units/ton)*					
	m_1	m_2	m_3	m_4	m_5	m_6
For products i_1-i_6 and i_{10}						
j_1	1.24	58.56	62.30	26.16	17.44	36.13
j_2	60.82	1.68	70.96	43.93	70.96	55.76
j_3	76.16	79.21	1.52	54.83	68.54	41.12
For products i_7-i_9						
j_1	1.35	63.46	67.51	28.35	18.90	39.15
j_2	82.70	2.29	96.48	59.72	96.48	75.81
j_3	94.90	98.69	1.89	68.32	85.41	51.24
For products i_{11}-i_{14}						
j_1	1.46	68.88	73.28	30.77	20.51	42.50
j_2	79.69	2.21	92.97	57.55	92.97	73.05
j_3	92.82	96.53	1.85	66.83	83.54	50.12

* There is no difference among several scenarios and time periods

Table 13. Transportation cost between warehouse m and distribution center k

Warehouse	Distribution center (relative money units/ton)*														
	k_1	k_2	k_3	k_4	k_5	k_6	k_7	k_8	k_9	k_{10}	k_{11}	k_{12}	k_{13}	k_{14}	k_{15}
For products i_1-i_6 and i_{10}															
m_1	0	74.40	76.13	25.96	69.21	29.41	17.30	117.66	44.99	110.74	76.13	12.11	39.79	64.02	60.56
m_2	58.85	0	62.96	45.16	109.49	69.80	67.06	94.44	90.33	145.08	17.79	60.22	52.01	108.12	72.54
m_3	72.83	76.14	0	49.66	94.35	99.32	62.90	43.04	79.45	129.12	94.35	62.90	33.10	104.29	28.14
m_4	28.54	62.78	57.08	0	87.52	58.98	32.34	106.55	62.78	135.09	72.30	22.83	19.02	89.42	49.47
m_5	16.51	73.58	57.06	25.52	48.05	37.54	0	93.10	25.52	84.09	78.08	7.50	30.03	45.05	42.04
m_6	69.52	67.78	34.76	17.38	78.21	69.52	34.76	79.95	59.09	121.66	78.21	33.02	0	83.42	27.80
For products i_7-i_9															
m_1	0	75.28	77.03	26.26	70.02	29.76	17.50	119.04	45.51	112.04	77.03	12.25	40.26	64.77	61.27
m_2	60.87	0	65.12	46.71	113.25	72.20	69.36	97.68	93.43	150.06	18.40	62.29	53.79	111.84	75.03
m_3	90.75	94.88	0	61.88	117.57	123.76	78.38	53.63	99.00	160.89	117.57	78.38	41.25	129.95	35.06
m_4	28.88	63.54	57.77	0	88.58	59.58	32.73	107.83	63.54	136.72	73.17	23.10	19.25	90.50	50.06
m_5	17.90	79.77	61.86	27.67	52.09	40.70	0	100.93	27.67	91.16	84.65	8.14	32.56	48.84	45.58
m_6	86.62	84.46	43.31	21.65	97.45	86.62	43.31	99.62	73.63	151.59	97.45	41.14	0	103.95	34.65
For products i_{11}-i_{14}															
m_1	0	69.15	70.78	24.14	64.32	27.33	16.08	109.35	41.81	102.92	70.76	11.25	36.98	59.50	56.28
m_2	69.66	0	74.52	53.46	129.61	82.63	79.38	111.79	106.93	171.74	21.06	71.28	61.56	127.99	85.87
m_3	92.01	96.19	0	62.73	119.19	125.47	79.46	54.37	100.37	163.11	119.19	79.46	41.82	131.74	35.55
m_4	26.53	58.37	53.07	0	81.37	54.83	30.07	99.06	58.37	125.59	67.2	21.22	17.69	83.14	45.99
m_5	20.49	91.29	70.80	31.67	59.62	46.58	0	115.51	31.67	104.33	96.88	9.31	37.26	55.89	52.16
m_6	87.82	85.63	43.91	21.95	98.80	87.82	43.91	85.70	63.34	130.42	83.84	35.40	0	89.43	35.13

* There is no difference among several scenarios and time periods

Table 14. Transportation cost between distribution center k and customer zone l

Distribution Center	Customer Zone (relative money units/ton)*																	
	l_1	l_2	l_3	l_4	l_5	l_6	l_7	l_8	l_9	l_{10}	l_{11}	l_{12}	l_{13}	l_{14}	l_{15}	l_{16}	l_{17}	l_{18}
For products i_1-i_6 and i_{10}																		
k_1	0	75.61	54.51	12.30	70.34	29.89	17.58	119.57	45.72	112.54	77.37	12.30	40.44	65.06	61.54	45.72	100.23	38.68
k_2	73.55	0	78.68	73.55	136.84	87.23	83.81	118.02	112.89	181.31	22.23	75.26	64.99	135.12	90.65	34.21	71.84	94.07
k_3	73.28	76.61	21.65	49.96	94.93	99.93	63.28	43.30	79.94	129.90	94.93	63.28	33.31	104.92	28.31	51.63	21.65	58.29
k_4	26.58	58.47	53.16	14.17	81.51	54.93	30.12	99.23	58.47	125.81	67.33	21.26	17.72	83.28	46.07	54.93	17.72	40.75
k_5	77.16	154.33	109.96	84.88	0	90.67	59.80	136.97	27.00	48.23	160.12	69.45	86.81	21.22	77.16	106.10	131.18	50.15
k_6	27.08	84.65	79.57	38.93	79.57	0	42.32	143.90	57.56	118.51	77.87	38.93	67.72	67.72	88.03	67.72	126.97	64.33
k_7	19.97	88.99	67.19	25.42	58.11	45.40	0	112.60	30.87	101.70	94.44	9.08	36.32	54.48	50.58	45.40	94.44	21.79
k_8	118.02	121.49	64.22	109.34	123.23	147.53	107.61	0	116.29	149.27	142.32	109.34	79.84	137.12	60.74	86.78	27.77	93.72
k_9	42.02	106.72	61.44	48.51	22.63	54.98	27.49	108.34	0	64.68	109.96	35.57	54.98	24.25	53.36	67.91	85.70	24.25
k_{10}	107.82	178.57	116.24	117.92	42.11	117.92	94.34	144.88	67.38	0	181.94	104.45	117.92	50.54	104.45	134.77	144.88	84.23
k_{11}	75.72	22.37	87.77	67.12	142.85	79.17	89.49	141.13	117.03	185.87	0	79.17	79.17	137.68	104.98	60.23	115.31	103.26
k_{12}	11.91	74.91	44.26	13.62	61.29	39.15	8.51	107.26	37.45	105.56	78.31	0	30.64	61.29	49.37	39.15	88.53	25.53
k_{13}	69.11	67.38	13.82	29.37	77.75	69.11	34.55	79.47	58.74	120.94	77.75	32.82	0	82.93	27.64	19.00	58.74	34.55
k_{14}	63.10	134.74	88.69	71.63	18.76	68.22	51.16	134.74	25.58	51.16	136.44	61.40	81.86	0	80.16	95.51	127.92	51.16
k_{15}	56.62	85.60	17.76	50.06	64.60	83.98	45.22	56.52	53.29	100.13	98.52	46.83	25.84	75.90	0	41.99	45.22	30.68
For products i_7-i_9																		
k_1	0	73.12	52.71	11.90	68.02	28.90	17.00	115.63	44.21	108.83	74.82	11.90	39.11	62.91	59.51	44.21	96.92	37.41
k_2	73.20	0	78.31	73.20	136.20	86.82	83.42	117.47	12.36	180.46	22.13	74.91	64.69	134.49	90.23	34.05	71.50	93.63
k_3	81.65	85.36	24.12	55.67	105.78	111.34	70.52	48.25	89.07	144.75	105.78	70.52	37.11	116.91	31.54	57.52	24.12	64.95
k_4	24.76	54.48	49.53	13.20	75.95	51.18	28.06	92.46	54.48	117.22	62.74	19.81	16.51	77.60	42.92	51.18	16.51	37.97
k_5	77.52	155.04	110.47	85.27	0	91.09	60.08	137.60	27.13	48.45	160.86	69.77	87.21	21.31	77.52	106.59	131.79	50.39
k_6	32.65	102.06	95.93	46.94	95.93	0	51.03	173.50	69.40	142.88	93.89	46.94	81.64	81.64	106.14	81.64	153.09	77.56
k_7	19.54	87.05	65.73	24.87	56.85	44.41	0	110.15	30.20	99.49	92.38	8.88	35.53	53.30	49.74	44.41	92.38	21.32
k_8	127.18	130.92	69.20	117.83	132.79	158.98	115.96	0	125.31	160.85	153.37	117.83	86.03	147.76	65.46	93.52	29.92	101.00
k_9	48.45	123.01	70.82	55.91	26.09	63.36	31.68	124.87	0	74.55	126.73	41.00	63.36	27.95	61.50	78.27	98.78	27.95
k_{10}	111.91	185.36	120.66	122.40	43.71	122.40	97.92	150.38	69.94	0	188.85	108.41	122.40	52.46	108.41	139.89	150.38	87.43

Table 14. continued

Distribution Center	Customer Zone (relative money units/ton)*																	
	l_1	l_2	l_3	l_4	l_5	l_6	l_7	l_8	l_9	l_{10}	l_{11}	l_{12}	l_{13}	l_{14}	l_{15}	l_{16}	l_{17}	l_{18}
k_{11}	81.65	24.12	94.64	72.37	154.03	85.36	96.50	152.17	126.19	200.42	0	85.36	85.36	148.46	113.20	64.95	124.33	11.34
k_{12}	12.44	78.21	46.21	14.22	63.99	40.88	8.88	111.98	39.10	110.21	81.76	0	31.99	63.99	51.55	40.88	92.43	26.66
k_{13}	58.96	57.48	11.79	25.05	66.33	58.96	29.48	67.80	50.11	103.18	66.33	28.00	0	70.75	23.58	16.21	50.11	29.48
k_{14}	60.11	128.35	84.48	68.23	17.87	64.98	48.74	128.35	24.37	48.74	129.97	58.48	77.98	0	76.36	90.98	121.85	48.74
k_{15}	60.97	92.32	19.16	54.00	69.68	90.58	48.77	60.97	57.48	108.00	106.26	50.51	27.87	81.87	0	45.29	48.77	33.09
For products i_{11}-i_{14}																		
k_1	0	72.82	52.50	11.85	67.74	28.79	16.93	115.17	44.03	108.39	74.52	11.85	38.95	62.66	59.27	44.03	96.54	37.26
k_2	69.04	0	73.86	69.04	128.46	81.89	78.68	110.80	105.98	170.21	20.87	70.65	61.02	126.85	85.10	32.11	67.44	88.31
k_3	74.54	77.92	22.02	50.82	96.56	101.64	64.73	44.04	81.31	132.13	96.56	64.37	33.88	106.72	28.79	52.51	22.02	59.29
k_4	28.74	63.22	57.48	15.32	88.13	59.39	32.57	107.29	63.22	136.03	72.80	22.99	19.16	90.05	49.81	59.39	19.16	44.06
k_5	65.66	131.33	93.57	72.23	0	77.15	50.89	116.56	22.98	41.04	136.26	59.10	73.87	18.05	65.66	90.29	111.63	42.68
k_6	31.07	97.12	91.29	44.67	91.29	0	48.56	165.10	66.04	135.96	89.35	44.67	77.69	77.69	101.00	77.69	145.68	73.81
k_7	20.58	91.67	69.22	26.19	59.87	46.77	0	116.00	31.80	104.77	97.29	9.35	37.42	56.13	52.38	46.77	97.29	22.45
k_8	121.40	124.97	66.05	112.48	126.76	151.75	110.69	0	119.62	153.54	146.40	112.48	82.12	141.04	62.48	89.27	28.56	96.41
k_9	55.75	141.52	81.48	64.32	30.02	72.90	36.45	143.66	0	85.77	145.81	47.17	72.90	32.16	70.76	90.06	113.64	32.16
k_{10}	106.08	175.70	114.37	116.03	41.44	116.03	92.82	142.55	66.30	0	179.02	102.77	116.03	49.72	102.77	132.60	142.55	82.88
k_{11}	74.81	22.10	86.72	66.31	141.13	78.21	88.42	139.43	115.62	183.64	0	78.21	78.21	136.03	103.72	59.51	113.92	102.02
k_{12}	13.58	85.41	50.47	15.53	69.88	44.64	9.70	122.30	42.70	120.36	89.29	0	34.94	69.88	56.29	44.64	100.94	29.11
k_{13}	72.36	70.55	14.47	30.75	81.40	72.36	36.18	83.21	61.50	126.63	81.40	34.37	0	86.83	28.94	19.90	61.50	36.18
k_{14}	72.66	155.15	102.12	82.48	21.60	78.56	58.92	155.15	29.46	58.92	157.12	70.70	94.27	0	92.30	109.98	147.30	58.92
k_{15}	62.62	94.83	19.68	55.47	71.57	93.04	50.10	62.62	59.05	110.94	109.15	51.89	28.63	84.10	0	46.52	50.10	33.99

* There is no difference among several scenarios and time periods

Table 15. Inventory holding cost in plant j in warehouse m and in distribution center k

Plants	Inventory holding cost (relative money units/ton) *
j_1	8.25
j_2	8.55
j_3	8.98
Warehouses	**Inventory holding cost (relative money units/ton) ***
m_1	8.25
m_2	8.55
m_3	8.98
m_4	8.93
m_5	8.06
m_6	10.28
Distribution Centers	**Inventory holding cost (relative money units/ton)***
k_1	8.25
k_2	8.55
k_3	8.98
k_4	8.93
k_5	8.85
k_6	6.90
k_7	8.06
k_8	6.08
k_9	12.00
k_{10}	8.85
k_{11}	8.12
k_{12}	10.66
k_{13}	10.28
k_{14}	8.95
k_{15}	8.83

* There is no difference among several scenarios and time periods

Table 16. Minimum inventories requirements in plant j in warehouse m and in distribution center k

Case	Safety stock held (in number of days equivalent) *		
	n^P	n^W	n^{DC}
low inventories	1	1	1
high inventories	6	3	2

* There is no difference among several scenarios and time periods

Figure 7. Inventory levels in plants, warehouses, and distribution centers in the high inventories case

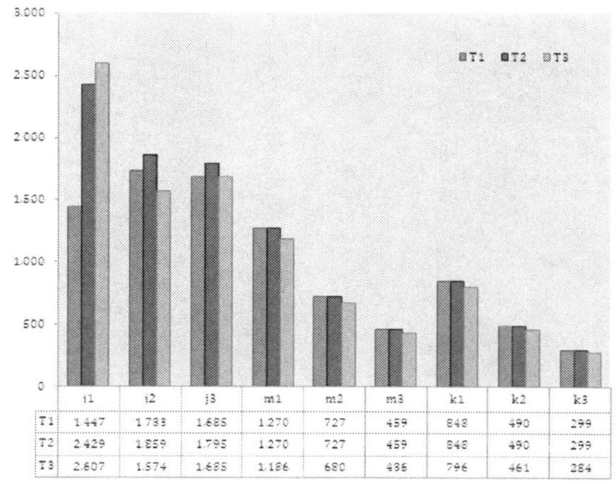

inventories held in the plants change and tend to increase with time as shown in Figure (7).

Parameter Sensitivity Analysis

In this part of our work we test the performance of the proposed model in several cases by changing some of the parameters, which express the production, distribution, and material handling conditions.

In many business occasions a production decrease is a frequent result of activities such as labor force strikes, equipment accidents and raw materials stock outs. At an aggregate level this potential condition could be expressed by decreasing the maximum production capacity of each plant ($P_{ijt}^{[s],max}$).

Figure (8) presents the optimal configuration and cost breakdown of the network after a 10% decrease in the maximum production capacity. The optimal network structure in this case results in an additional transportation link between the warehouse of Spain and the U.K. distribution center, comparing to the base case.

Another interesting business situation that requires further investigation is when the total transportation flow from one node to other must exceeds a minimum requirement in order to be placed. In this way fixed costs associated with the establishment of a transportation link (fleet management expenses, cargo handling equipment investments etc.) are covered by the revenues earned from this minimum flow. In our case study, the zero minimum transportation flow $Q_{mk}^{min} = 0$, $Q_{kl}^{min} = 0$, in many business cases is unrealistic.

Figure (9) illustrates the optimal configuration and cost breakdown of the network when the minimum total transportation flow between a warehouse and a distribution is set to 1,000 tones/week. The optimal network in this case, comparing to the base case, results in an additional transportation link between UK's plant and the warehouse of Italy and deleted the transportation link between the Spain's warehouse and the distribution center of Italy. Moreover, the distribution center of U.K. is now serving the customer zone of Austria while the distribution center of Spain is serving

Table 17. Optimal cost breakdown for low inventories case in relative money units

Fixed infrastructure cost	456,000
Production cost	3,359,600
Material handling cost	515,770
Transportation cost	1,170,700
Inventory cost	529,580
Total optimal cost	6,031,650

Table 18. Optimal cost breakdown for high inventories case in relative money units

Fixed infrastructure cost	456,000
Production cost	3,866,900
Material handling cost	529,800
Transportation cost	1,203,200
Inventory cost	818,890
Total optimal cost	6,874,790

Figure 8. Optimal network configuration with low inventories and for a 10% decrease in the maximum production capacity

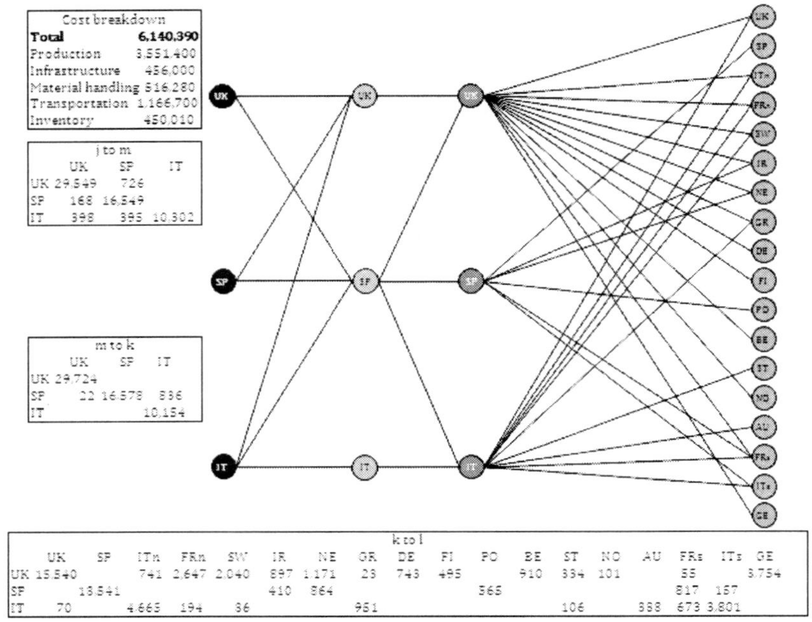

Figure 9. Optimal network configuration with low inventories and for a minimum total flow between warehouses and distribution centers equal to 100

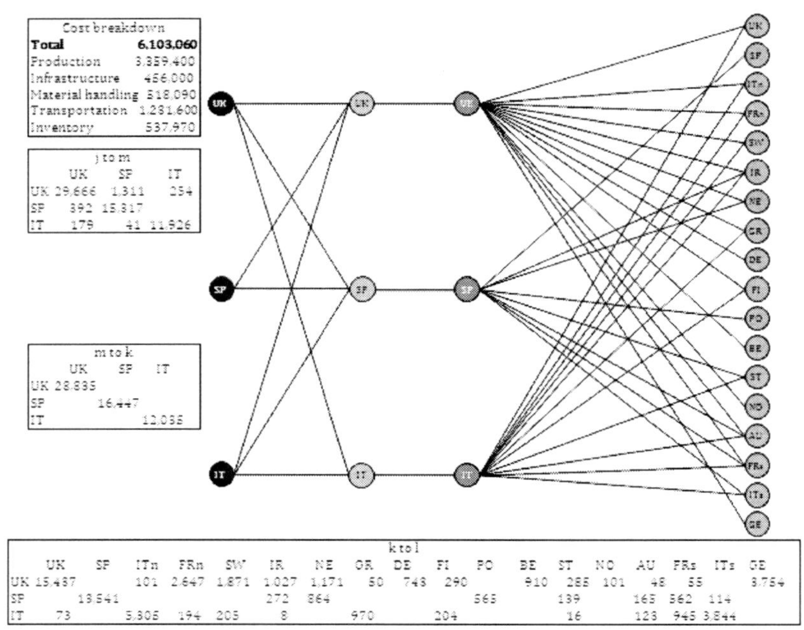

the customer zones of Switzerland, and Austria. Finally, the Italy's distribution center started serving Ireland's and Finland's customer zones.

CONCLUSION

This work presents a detailed mathematical formulation for the problem of designing supply chain networks comprising multiproduct production facilities with shared production resources, warehouses, distribution centers and customer zones and operating under demand uncertainty, while inventory may be kept at different stages in the network. Uncertainty is captured in terms of a number of likely scenarios possible to materialize during the life time of the network. The problem is formulated as a mixed-integer linear programming program (MILP) and solved to global optimality.

A large-scale European wide distribution network has been used to illustrate the applicability of the developed model. The results obtained provide a good indication of the value of having a model that takes into account the complex interactions that exist in such networks and the effect of inventory levels to the design and operation. The computational cost associated with the problems considered here has been found to be relatively low, thus making the overall model attractive for the solution of large-scale problems.

The proposed MILP model aims to assist senior operations management to take decisions about production allocation, production capacity per site, purchase of raw materials and network configuration taking into account transient demand conditions. The purpose of the model is to be used not as frequent as an Advanced Planning Scheduling (APS) system (daily, weekly or monthly) but for longer periods (such as quarterly, six months or yearly) to address strategic and tactical supply design aspects. Its allocation decisions are set as production targets for the APS systems to optimise production sequences.

The proposed mathematical programming approach can provide the basis for future research focusing on the following areas:

- The integration of financial statement analysis along with supply chain network design and operation decisions, to explore mutual interactions between financial aspects (e.g. leveraging and/or liquidity requirements) and supply chain design decisions.
- The incorporation of stochastic uncertainty in each time-varying scenario (e.g. by assuming that product demands follow a stochastic distribution function).
- The incorporation of stochastic inventory control in the overall framework.

REFERENCES

Al-Othman, W. B. E., Lababidi, H. M. S., Alatiqi, I. M., & Al-Shayji, K. (2008). Supply chain optimization of petroleum organization under uncertainty in market demands and prices. *European Journal of Operational Research, 189*(3), 822–840. doi:10.1016/j.ejor.2006.06.081

Alonso-Ayuso, A., Escudero, L. F., Garín, A., Ortuño, M. T., & Pérez, G. (2003). An approach for strategic supply chain planning under uncertainty based on stochastic 0–1 programming. *Journal of Global Optimization, 26*(1), 97–124. doi:10.1023/A:1023071216923

Applequist, G. E., Penky, J. F., & Reklaitis, G. (2000). Risk and uncertainty in managing chemical manufacturing supply chains. *Computers & Chemical Engineering, 24*(9-10), 2211–2222. doi:10.1016/S0098-1354(00)00585-8

Cakravastia, A., Toha, I., & Nakamura, N. (2002). A two-stage model for the design of supply chain networks. *International Journal of Production Economics, 80*(3), 231–248. doi:10.1016/S0925-5273(02)00260-8

Chandra, C., & Grabis, J. (2009). Role of flexibility in supply chain design and modeling-Introduction to the special issue. *Omega*, *37*(4), 743–745. doi:10.1016/j.omega.2008.07.003

Chen, C.-L., & Lee, W.-C. (2004). Multi-objective optimization of multi-echelon supply chain networks with uncertain product demand and prices. *Computers & Chemical Engineering*, *28*(6-7), 1131–1144. doi:10.1016/j.compchemeng.2003.09.014

Chopra, S., & Meindl, P. (2004). *Supply Chain Management: Strategy, Planning and Operations*. New Jersey: Prentice Hall.

Davis, T. (1993). Effective supply chain management. *Sloan Management Review*, *34*(4), 35–46.

Francas, D., & Minner, S. (2009). Manufacturing network configuration in supply chains with product recovery. *Omega*, *37*(4), 757–769. doi:10.1016/j.omega.2008.07.007

Geoffrion, A. M., & Graves, G. W. (1974). Multicommodity distribution system design by Benders decomposition. *Management Science*, *20*(5), 822–844. doi:10.1287/mnsc.20.5.822

Geoffrion, A. M., & van Roy, T. J. (1979). Caution: common sense planning methods can be hazardous to your corporate health. *Sloan Management Review*, *20*(4), 31–42.

Guillén, G., Mele, B., Bagajewicz, M. J., Espuña, A., & Puigjaner, L. (2005). Multi-objective supply chain design under uncertainty. *Chemical Engineering Science*, *60*(6), 1535–1553. doi:10.1016/j.ces.2004.10.023

Gümüs, A. T., & Güneri, A. F. (2007). Multi-echelon inventory management in supply chains with uncertain demand and lead times: literature review from an operational research perspective. *Journal Engineering Manufacture*, *221*(10), 1553–1570. doi:10.1243/09544054JEM889

Gupta, A., & Maranas, C. D. (2003). Managing demand uncertainty in supply chain planning. *Computers & Chemical Engineering*, *27*(8-9), 1219–1227. doi:10.1016/S0098-1354(03)00048-6

Gupta, A., Maranas, C. D., & McDonald, C. M. (2000). Mid-term supply chain planning under demand uncertainty: customer demand satisfaction and inventory management. *Computers & Chemical Engineering*, *24*(12), 2613–2621. doi:10.1016/S0098-1354(00)00617-7

Hallgren, M., & Olhager, J. (2009). Flexibility configurations: empirical analysis of volume and product mix flexibility. *Omega*, *37*(4), 746–756. doi:10.1016/j.omega.2008.07.004

Hasuike, T., & Ishii, H. (2009). On flexible product-mix decision problems under randomness and fuzziness. *Omega*, *37*(4), 770–787. doi:10.1016/j.omega.2008.07.005

Hua, Z., Li, S., & Liang, L. (2006). Impact of demand uncertainty on supply chain cooperation of single-period products. *International Journal of Production Economics*, *100*(2), 268–284. doi:10.1016/j.ijpe.2004.11.007

Ierapetritou, M. G., Pistikopoulos, E. N., & Floudas, C. A. (1996). Operational planning under uncertainty. *Computers & Chemical Engineering*, *20*(12), 1499–1516. doi:10.1016/0098-1354(95)00235-9

Melo, M. T., Nickel, S., & Saldanha da Gama, F. (2006). Dynamic multi-commodity capacitated facility location: a mathematical modeling framework for strategic supply chain planning. *Computers & Operations Research*, *33*(1), 181–208. doi:10.1016/j.cor.2004.07.005

Mitra, K., Gudi, R. D., Patwardham, S. C., & Sardar, G. (2008). Mid-term supply chain planning under uncertainty: a multi-objective chance constrained programming framework. *Industrial & Engineering Chemistry Research*, *47*(15), 5501–5511. doi:10.1021/ie0710364

Pan, F., & Nagi, R. (2010). Robust supply chain design under uncertain demand in agile manufacturing. *Computers & Operations Research, 37*(4), 668–683. doi:10.1016/j.cor.2009.06.017

Papageorgiou, L. G. (2009). Supply chain optimisation for the process industries: advances and opportunities. *Computers & Chemical Engineering, 33*(12), 1931–1938. doi:10.1016/j.compchemeng.2009.06.014

Peidro, D., Mula, J., Poler, R., & Lario, F.-C. (2009). Quantitative models for supply chain planning under uncertainty: a review. *International Journal of Advanced Manufacturing Technology, 43*(3-4), 400–420. doi:10.1007/s00170-008-1715-y

Petersen, K., Ragatz, G., & Monczka, R. (2005). An examination of collaborative planning effectiveness and supply chain performance. *The Journal of Supply Chain Management, 41*(2), 14–25. doi:10.1111/j.1055-6001.2005.04102002.x

Rosenthal, R. E. (2008). *GAMS: A User's Guide*. Washington, D.C.: GAMS Development Corporation.

Sabri, E. H., & Beamon, B. M. (2000). A multi-objective approach to simultaneous strategic and operational planning in supply chain design. *Omega, 28*(5), 581–598. doi:10.1016/S0305-0483(99)00080-8

Santoso, T., Ahmed, S., Goetschalckx, M., & Shapiro, A. (2005). A stochastic programming approach for supply chain network design under uncertainty. *European Journal of Operational Research, 167*(1), 96–115. doi:10.1016/j.ejor.2004.01.046

Schoemaker, P. J. H. (1993). Multiple scenario development: its conceptual and behavioral foundation. *Strategic Management Journal, 14*(3), 193–213. doi:10.1002/smj.4250140304

Shah, N. (2003). Pharmaceutical supply chains: key issues and strategies for optimisation. In *Proceedings of 4th international conference on foundations of computer-aided process operations* (pp. 73-85).

Shapiro, J. F. (1999). On the connections among activity-based costing, mathematical programming models for analyzing strategic decisions, and the resource-based view of the firm. *European Journal of Operational Research, 118*(2), 295–314. doi:10.1016/S0377-2217(99)00027-2

Shapiro, J. F. (2003). Challenges of strategic supply chain planning and modelling. In *Proceedings of 4th international conference on foundations of computer-aided process operations* (pp. 27-34).

Stenger, A. J. (1996). Reducing inventories in a multi-echelon manufacturing firm: a case study. *International Journal of Production Economics, 45*(1-3), 239–249. doi:10.1016/0925-5273(94)00146-4

Tsiakis, P., Shah, N., & Pantelides, C. C. (2001). Design of multi-echelon supply chain networks under demand uncertainty. *Industrial & Engineering Chemistry Research, 40*(16), 3585–3604. doi:10.1021/ie0100030

Wets, R. J.-B. (1996). Challenges in stochastic programming. *Mathematical Programming, 75*(2), 115–135. doi:10.1007/BF02592149

Xu, N., & Nozick, L. (2009). Modeling supplier selection and the use of options contracts for global supply chain design. *Computers & Operations Research, 36*(10), 2786–2800. doi:10.1016/j.cor.2008.12.013

You, F., & Grossmann, I. E. (2008). Design of responsive supply chains under demand uncertainty. *Computers & Chemical Engineering, 32*(12), 3090–3111. doi:10.1016/j.compchemeng.2008.05.004

ENDNOTE

1 rmu stands for relative money units

APPENDIX

Notation

Indices

- e production resources (equipment, manpower, utilities, etc.)
- i products
- j plants
- k possible distribution centers
- l customer zones
- m possible warehouses
- s product demand scenario
- t time period

Sets

- K^{SS} set of distribution centers that should be supplied by a single warehouse
- L^{SS} set of customer zones that should be supplied by a single distribution center

Parameters

- C_{im}^{WH} unit handling cost for product i at warehouse m
- C_{ik}^{DH} unit handling cost for product i at distribution center k
- C_{m}^{W} annualized fixed cost of establishing warehouse at location m
- C_{k}^{D} annualized fixed cost of establishing distribution center at location k
- C_{ij}^{P} unit production cost for product i at plant j
- C_{ijm}^{TR} unit transportation cost of product i transferred from plant j to warehouse m
- C_{imk}^{TR} unit transportation cost of product i transferred from warehouse m to distribution center k
- C_{ikl}^{TR} unit transportation cost of product i transferred from distribution center k to customer zone l
- C_{ijt}^{I} unit inventory cost of product i at plant j during time period t
- C_{imt}^{I} unit inventory cost of product i at warehouse m during time period t
- C_{ikt}^{I} unit inventory cost of product i at distribution center k during time period t
- D_{k}^{max} maximum capacity of distribution center k
- D_{k}^{min} minimum capacity of distribution center k
- $D_{ilt}^{[s]}$ demand for product i from customer zone l during time period t under scenario s
- $I_{ijt}^{[s],min}$ minimum inventory of product i held in plant j at the end of time period t under scenario s
- $I_{imt}^{[s],min}$ minimum inventory of product i held in warehouse m at the end of time period t under scenario s
- $I_{ikt}^{[s],min}$ minimum inventory of product i held in distribution center k at the end of time period t under scenario s

- n^{DC} minimum inventory held at distribution centers expressed in terms of number of days equivalent of materials handled
- n^{W} minimum inventory held at warehouses expressed in terms of number of days equivalent of materials handled
- n^{P} minimum inventory held at production plants expressed in terms of number of days equivalent of materials handled

NS number of product demand scenarios

- $P_{ijt}^{[s],max}$ maximum production capacity of plant j for product i during time period t under scenario s
- $P_{ijt}^{[s],min}$ minimum production capacity of plant j for product i during time period t under scenario s
- Q_{mk}^{min} minimum rate of flow of material that can practically and economically be transferred from warehouse m to distribution center k
- Q_{kl}^{min} minimum rate of flow of material that can practically and economically be transferred from distribution center k to customer zone l
- $Q_{ijm}^{[s],max}$ maximum rate of flow of product i that can be transferred from plant j to warehouse m under scenario s
- $Q_{imk}^{[s],max}$ maximum rate of flow of product i that can be transferred from warehouse m to distribution center k under scenario s
- $Q_{ikl}^{[s],max}$ maximum rate of flow of product i that can be transferred from distribution center k to customer zone l under scenario s
- R_{je} total rate of availability of resource e at plant j
- W_{m}^{max} maximum capacity of warehouse m
- W_{m}^{min} minimum capacity of warehouse m
- ” T_t duration of time period t

Continuous Variables

- D_k capacity of distribution center k
- $I_{ijt}^{[s]}$ inventory level of product i being held at plant j at the end of time period t under scenario s
- $I_{imt}^{[s]}$ inventory level of product i being held at warehouse m at the end of time period t under scenario s
- $I_{ikt}^{[s]}$ inventory level of product i being held at distribution center k at the end of time period t under scenario s
- $P_{ijt}^{[s]}$ production rate of product i in plant j during time period t under scenario s
- $Q_{ijmt}^{[s]}$ rate of flow of product i transferred from plant j to warehouse m during time period t under scenario s

- $Q^{[s]}_{imkt}$ rate of flow of product i transferred from warehouse m to distribution center k during time period t under scenario s
- $Q^{[s]}_{iklt}$ rate of flow of product i transferred from distribution center k to customer zone l during time period t under scenario s
- W_m capacity of warehouse m

Binary Variables

- Y_m 1 if warehouse m is to be established, 0 otherwise
- Y_k 1 if distribution center k is to be established, 0 otherwise
- X_{mk} 1 if material is to be transported from warehouse m to distribution center k, 0 otherwise
- X_{kl} 1 if material is to be transported from distribution center k to customer zone l, 0 otherwise
- $X^{[s]}_{mkt}$ 1 if material is to be transported from warehouse m to distribution center k during time period t under scenario s, 0 otherwise
- $X^{[s]}_{klt}$ 1 if material is to be transported from distribution center k to customer zone l during time period t under scenario s, 0 otherwise

Greek Symbols

- ${}^{3}{}_{im}$ coefficient relating capacity of warehouse m to inventory of product i held
- ${}^{3}{}_{ik}$ coefficient relating capacity of distribution center k to inventory of product i held
- $Á_{ije}$ coefficient of rate of utilization resource e in plant j to produce product i
- $È_s$ probability of product demand scenario s occurring during the lifetime of the network

Section 2
Planning in Large Supply Chains

Chapter 5
A Computational Intelligence Approach to Supply Chain Demand Forecasting

Nicholas Ampazis
University of the Aegean, Greece

ABSTRACT

Estimating customer demand in a multi-level supply chain structure is crucial for companies seeking to maintain their competitive advantage within an uncertain business environment. This work explores the potential of computational intelligence approaches as forecasting mechanisms for predicting customer demand at the first level of organization of a supply chain where products are presented and sold to customers. The computational intelligence approaches that we utilize are Artificial Neural Networks (ANNs), trained with the OLMAM algorithm (Optimized Levenberg-Marquardt with Adaptive Momentum), and Support Vector Machines (SVMs) for regression. The effectiveness of the proposed approach was evaluated using public data from the Netflix movie rental online DVD store in order to predict the demand for movie rentals during the critical, for sales, Christmas holiday season.

INTRODUCTION

The Supply Chain (SC) of both manufacturing and commercial enterprises comprises a highly distributed environment, in which complex processes evolve within a network of interacting companies. A typical SC includes different levels as shown in the diagram of Figure 1. As shown in this figure, and reading the diagram from right to left ("Customer Information Flow"), the first level of organization is "Sales" where products are sold to customers; the second level of organization is "Distribution" where products are delivered from in-house or 3PL (3rd Party Logistics) warehouses to retailers; the third organization level is "Storage" where products are stored in warehouses for future distribution; the fourth level of organization is "Production" where products are produced within plants according to determined production and inventory schedules; finally, the fifth organization level is "Supply" which comprises of the

DOI: 10.4018/978-1-61520-633-9.ch005

Figure 1. The multiple levels of a supply chain

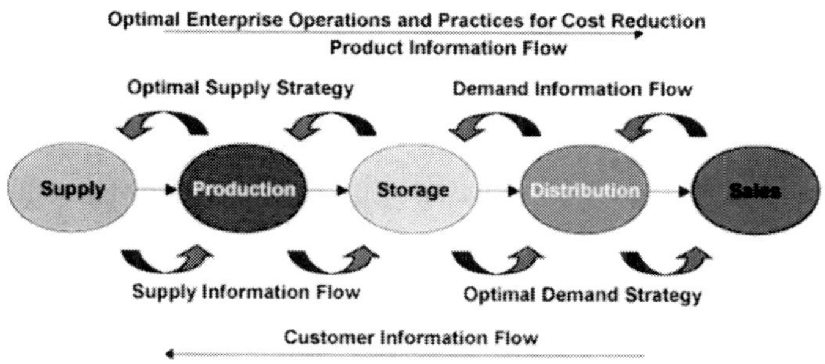

suppliers that provide raw materials transported to production plants.

The optimization of SC operational procedures is crucial for businesses since these operations directly affect customer service, inventory and distribution costs, and responsiveness to the ever changing markets. To this end, decision making in supply chain systems should consider intrinsic uncertainties, while coordinating the interests and goals of the multitude of processes involved. Since supply can rarely meet demand at any given period, the demand information is distorted as it is transmitted up the chain and this can misguide upstream members in their inventory and production decisions ("bullwhip" effect) (Lee, Padmanabhan, & Whang, 1997a), (Lee, Padmanabhan, & Whang, 1997b).

Computational intelligence approaches can offer effective tools for both modeling and managing operations in the uncertain environment of the supply chain, especially since the associated computational techniques are capable of handling complex interdependencies. As a result, these computational techniques may form the basis for the development of optimization methods and systems that optimize effectively the various objectives of the supply chain (Minis & Ampazis, 2006). This chapter presents the application of computational intelligence methods in supply chain demand forecasting. More specifically, we focus on the first level of SC which is directly related to customer side demand forecasting in an uncertain environment. Forecasting the expected demand for a certain period of time for one or more products is one of the most important targets in an enterprise since it directly affects revenue as well as customer satisfaction. To this end, we utilize Artificial Neural Networks (ANNs) and Support Vector Machines (SVMs) as an approach for forecasting demand in order to create a supply chain framework with dynamic characteristics.

The remainder of this chapter is structured as follows: In the next section we present a review of previous studies on demand forecasting in SC using computational intelligence techniques. After that we analytically describe the techniques used in the present work, that is, the theoretical principles behind ANNs, the OLMAM training algorithm, and SVMs. A real-world case study utilizing data for the Netflix online DVD rental store is presented in Section "Information Sources". The section immediately after that presents the results of the computational intelligence techniques. Finally in the last section we discuss the conclusions drawn from this study.

BACKGROUND

Computational intelligence methods have already been used in a variety of SC optimization tasks. Especially ANNs, as a new methodology, have been used for optimization of transportation management, resources allocation and scheduling, for modeling and simulation, and decision support (Minis & Ampazis, 2006).

For the task of forecasting SC demand, a variety of computational intelligence methods have been used as statistical forecasting models for smoothing and classifying noisy data to match the relationships between complicated SC operations. In general, statistical forecasting models fall into two broad categories, univariate and multivariate. Univariate methods (also referred to as time-series methods) work with the past history of the variable to be forecasted. They aim to capture patterns such as the level, trend, and seasonal patterns and extrapolate them forward (Gardner, 1985), (Armstrong, 2002). Examples of standard statistical time-series methods include exponential smoothing models, Box-Jenkins models (Box, Jenkins, & Reinsel, 1976), and Croston's demand model (Croston, 1972), (Marien, 1999), (Syntetos & Boylan, 2001).

A computational intelligence technique for univariate SC demand forecasting was investigated in (Liang & Huang, 2006). In this study the authors proposed a solution for forecasting orders in a multi-echelon supply chain using a genetic algorithm (GA). Their results showed that, under certain assumptions, their proposed methodology could globally optimize the total cost of the SC. (Aburto & Weber, 2007) proposed a hybrid intelligent system which combined Autoregressive Integrated Moving Average (ARIMA) univariate models and ANNs for demand forecasting in a replenishment system for a Chilean supermarket. In their study neural networks outperformed ARIMA models and the proposed additive hybrid approach gave the best results in terms of prediction accuracy. In the study of (Gutierrez, Solis, & Mukhopadhyay, 2008), neural networks were applied as univariate models for forecasting lumpy demand, and was found that they generally perform better than traditional methods, for a variety of performance measures. The applicability of more advanced computational intelligence techniques as univariate models was investigated also by (Carbonneau, Laframboise, & Vahidov, 2008). In their study they included neural networks, recurrent neural networks, and support vector machines, to forecast distorted demand at the end of a supply chain (bullwhip effect). They compared these methods with other, more traditional ones, including naïve forecasting, trend, moving average, and linear regression in two data sets (one obtained from a simulated supply chain, and another from actual Canadian Foundries orders). Their results indicated that while recurrent neural networks and support vector machines showed the best performance, their forecasting accuracy was not statistically significantly better than that of the regression model. (Kimbrough, Wu, & Zhong, 2002) used artificial agents in order to investigate whether they could mitigate the bullwhip effect or discover good and effective business strategies (in the face of deterministic demand with fixed lead-time), and also to examine the potential of artificial agents to cooperate across the supply chain. A genetic algorithm was also employed by (O'donnell, Maguire, McIvor, & Humphreys, 2006) in order to reduce the bullwhip effect and cost, and to determine the optimal ordering policy for members of the SC.

Multivariate approaches combine time-series approaches with the ability to include additional explanatory variables, for example, promotional schedules, price information, economic indicators, etc. Multivariate methods usually include dynamic regression models, event models, as well as computational intelligence methods, such as ANNs. Even though ANNs as multivariate forecast approaches have been employed in the task of SC demand forecasting, there is still a limited number of publications exploring their potential. In (Rabelo, Helal, & Lertpattarapong, 2004), 17 explanatory variables, namely, minimum order processing time, time to perceive present demand, time to update channel orders, competitors' attractiveness, and others, were identified as independent and used as inputs to a neural network. Due to the increasing market complexity and ambiguity, SC demand forecasting has been studied with collaborative techniques in order to produce more satisfactory results. Combinations of neural networks and fuzzy systems are an example of such techniques. In (Efendigil, Önüt, & Kahraman, 2009) a comparative analysis on the use of ANNs and neuro-fuzzy models to forecast demand was presented. The effectiveness of their approach was demonstrated using real-world data from a consumer goods industry in Turkey.

Apart from the few applications of ANNs as multivariate SC forecasting models there is no evidence that there are any studies applying more advanced computational intelligence techniques as multivariate SC forecasting models. In addition, the training of ANNs in the existing studies is usually accomplished using very basic variations of the backpropagation algorithm (see next section) which is known to produce sub-optimal solutions in many cases. Thus, this study is a first attempt to develop a multivariate forecasting methodology using more advanced training methods in ANNs as well as exploring the potential of the powerful SVMs theory as multivariate SC forecasting mechanism. The proposed methodology including ANNs trained with the OLMAM (Optimized Levenberg-Marquardt with Adaptive Momentum) algorithm as well as the SVM regression techniques are explained in the following sections.

ARTIFICIAL NEURAL NETWORKS

Artificial Neural Networks (ANNs) are computational systems whose architecture and operation are inspired from our knowledge about biological neural cells (neurons) in the brain. ANNs can be described either as mathematical and computational models for non-linear function approximation, data classification, clustering and non-parametric regression or as simulations of the behavior of collections of model biological neurons (Bishop, 1995). These are not simulations of real neurons in the sense that they do not model the biology, chemistry, or physics of a real neuron. They do, however, model several aspects of the information combining and pattern recognition behavior of real neurons in a simple yet meaningful way. Neural modeling has shown considerable capability for emulation, analysis, prediction, and association. ANNs can be used in a variety of powerful ways: to learn and reproduce rules or operations from given examples; to analyze and generalize from sample facts and make predictions from these; or to memorize characteristics and features of given data and to match or make associations from new data to the old data.

ANNs are able to solve difficult problems in a way that resembles human intelligence. What is unique about neural networks is their ability to learn by example. Traditional artificial intelligence (AI) solutions rely on symbolic processing of the data, an approach which requires *a priori* human knowledge about the problem. Also neural networks techniques have an advantage over statistical methods of data classification and regression because they are distribution-free and require no a priori knowledge about the statistical distributions of the data sources. Unlike the statistical approaches, ANNs are able to solve problems without any a priori assumptions. As long as sufficient data is available, a neural network will extract any regularities and form a solution.

The main operations that can be performed by ANNs are the following:

- *Classification*: An input pattern is presented to the network, and the network produces the representative class at its output
- *Comparison-Pattern Matching*: An input pattern is presented to the network, and the network generates the corresponding output pattern
- *Pattern Completion*: An incomplete pattern is presented to the network, and the network produces an output pattern with all the missing characteristics of the input pattern

- *Noise Cancellation*: A noise distorted pattern is presented to the network, and the network removes part of the noise (or even all the noise) and produces a clean version of the input pattern
- *Optimization*: An input pattern representing the initial values for an optimization problem is presented to the network, and the network produces a set of variables that represents a solution to the problem
- *Control*: An input pattern represents the current state of a controller and its desired response and the output is a suitable command sequence that will induce the desired response
- *Function Approximation*: The network can practically simulate any function within an arbitrary degree of accuracy

As ANNs are models of biological neural structures, the starting point for any kind of neural network analysis is a model neuron whose behavior follows closely our understanding of how real neurons work. This model neuron is shown in Figure 2.

The neuron has N input lines and a single output. Each input signal is weighted, that is, it is multiplied with the weight value of the corresponding input line (by analogy to the synaptic strength of the connections of real neurons). The neuron will combine these weighted inputs by forming their sum and, with reference to a threshold value and activation function, it will determine its output. In mathematical terms, we may describe the neuron by writing the following pair of equations:

$$u = \sum_{i=1}^{N} w_i x_i \tag{1}$$

$$y = f(u - \theta) \tag{2}$$

where $x_1, x_2, \ldots x_N$ are the input signals, $w_1, w_2, \ldots w_N$ are the synaptic weights, u is the net neuron input, θ is the threshold, y is the output signal of the neuron, and $f()$ is the activation function.

For notational convenience, the above equations may be reformulated by letting $w_0 = \theta$ and setting $x_0 = -1$. Then

$$\sum_{i=1}^{N} w_i x_i - \theta = \sum_{i=0}^{N} w_i x_i \tag{3}$$

and

$$y = f\left(\sum_{i=0}^{N} w_i x_i\right) \tag{4}$$

Figure 2. Neuron Model

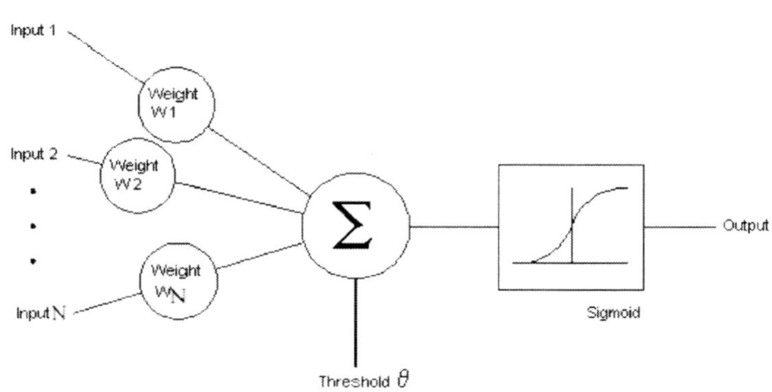

The combination of a fixed input and of an extra input weight accounts for what is known as a *bias* input. Note that the new notation has augmented any input vector $X \epsilon R^N$ to the vector $(-1,X) \epsilon R^{N+1}$ and also the weight vector $W \epsilon R^N$ of the neuron to the vector $(w_0,W) \epsilon R^{N+1}$.

The activation function, denoted by $f()$, defines the output of the neuron in terms of the activity level at its input. The most common form of activation function used in the construction of ANNs is the *sigmoid* function. An example of the sigmoid is the logistic function, defined by

$$f\left(u\right) = \frac{1}{1+\exp\left(-\alpha u\right)} \tag{5}$$

where α is the slope parameter of the sigmoid function. By varying the parameter α we can obtain sigmoid functions of different slopes. In the limit, as the slope parameter approaches infinity, the sigmoid function becomes simply a threshold function. The threshold function however, can take only the values 0 or 1, whereas a sigmoid function assumes a continuous range of values from 0 to 1. Also the sigmoid function is differentiable, whereas the threshold function is not. Differentiability is an important feature of neural network theory since it has a fundamental role in the learning process in ANNs.

Learning in ANNs is based on the selection of a suitable error function or cost function, whose values are determined by the actual and desired outputs of the network and which is also dependent on the network parameters such as the weights and the thresholds. The basic idea is that the cost function has a particular surface over the weight space and therefore an iterative process such as the gradient descent method can be used for its minimization.

For a feedforward ANN, such as the one shown in Figure 3 (in which signals from neurons propagate in a forward way from the input layer to the output layer), with K output units and a set of P training patterns, the Mean Square Error (MSE) cost function is defined as

Figure 3. Feedforward Artificial Neural Network

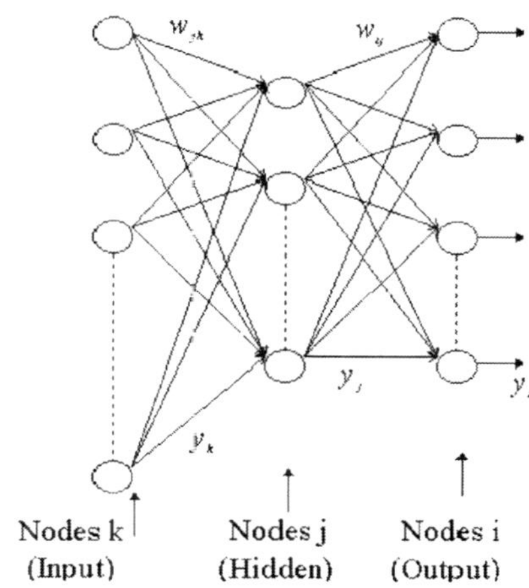

$$E\left(w\right) = \frac{1}{2}\sum_{p=1}^{P}\sum_{i=1}^{K}\left(d_i^{(p)} - y_i^{(p)}\right)^2 \tag{6}$$

where $y_i^{(p)}$ and $d_i^{(p)}$ denote the output activations and desired responses respectively, and w is the column vector containing all the weights and thresholds of the network.

The method of *gradient descent* is based on the fact that, since the gradient of a function always points in the direction of maximum increase of the function then, by moving to the direction of the negative gradient induces a maximal "downhill" movement that will eventually reach the minimum of the function surface over its parameter space. This is a rigorous and well established technique for minimization of functions and has probably been the main factor behind the success of the *backpropagation* algorithm (Rumelhart, Hinton, & Williams, 1986). However this simple method does not guarantee that it will always converge to the minimum of the error surface as the network can be trapped in various types of minima and thus will produce an inferior solution to the learning problem.

THE OLMAM ALGORITHM

The Optimized Levenberg Marquardt with Adaptive Momentum (OLMAM) algorithm is a very efficient second-order algorithm for training feedforward neural networks and, in some cases, it has been shown to achieve the best training results on standard benchmark datasets reported in the neural networks literature (Ampazis & Perantonis, 2002).

The main idea in the formulation of the algorithm is that while trying to minimize the neural network's cost function of equation (6), a one-dimensional minimization in the direction dw_{t-1} followed by a second minimization in the direction dw_t does not guarantee that the cost function has been minimized on the subspace spanned by both of these directions.

This can be achieved by the selection of *conjugate* directions which form the basis of the CG method (Gilbert & Nocedal, 1992). Two vectors dw_t and dw_{t-1} are non-interfering or mutually conjugate with respect to $\nabla^2 E(w_t)$ when

$$dw_t^T \nabla^2 E\left(w_t\right) dw_{t-1} = 0 \tag{7}$$

Therefore, the objective is to reach a minimum of the cost function of equation (6) with respect to the synaptic weights, and to simultaneously maximize the quantity $\Phi_t = dw_t^T \nabla^2 E\left(w_t\right) dw_{t-1}$ without compromising the need for a decrease in the cost function.

The strategy which we adopt for the solution of this constrained optimization problem follows the methodology for incorporating additional knowledge in the form of constraints in neural network training originaly proposed in (Perantonis & Karras, 1995). This strategy yields the following weight update rule for the neural network

$$dw_t = -\frac{\lambda}{2\lambda_2}\left[J_t^T J_t + \mu_t I\right]^{-1} \nabla E\left(w_t\right) + \frac{1}{2\lambda_2} dw_{t-1} \tag{8}$$

where J_t is the Jacobian matrix of first derivatives at step t and λ_1 and λ_2 can be evaluated in terms of known quantities. Equation (8) is similar to the Levenberg-Marquard (LM) weight update rule with the important differences that in equation (8) there is an additional adaptive momentum term and that the LM step is multiplied with an adaptive factor which controls its size. The quantity μt can be selected as in (Hagan & Menhaj, 1994). Further details on the OLMAM algorithm can be found in (Ampazis & Perantonis, 2002).

SUPPORT VECTOR MACHINES

Support Vector Machines (SVM) were first introduced as a new class of machine learning techniques by Vapnik (Vapnik, 1998), (Cortes & Vapnik, 1995) and are based on the structural risk minimization principle (Cristianini, Nello, Shawe-Taylor John, 2000). An SVM seeks a decision surface to separate the training data points into two classes and makes decisions based on the *support vectors* that are selected as the only effective elements from the training set (Wang, 2005). The goal of SVM learning is to find the optimal separating hyper-plane (OSH) that has the maximal margin to both sides of the data classes (Boser, Guyon, & Vapnik, 1992). This can be formulated as:

$$\text{Minimize } \frac{1}{2} w^T w$$

$$\text{subject to } y_i\left(wx_i + b\right) \geq 1 \tag{9}$$

where $y_i \in [-1\ +1]$ is the decision of SVM for pattern x_i and b is the bias of the separating hyperplane. After the OSH has been determined, the SVM makes decisions based on the globally optimized separating hyperplane by finding out on which side of the OSH the pattern is located, as shown in Figure 4 for a two-dimensional example. This property makes SVM highly competitive with other traditional pattern recognition methods in terms of predictive accuracy and efficiency.

Support Vector Machines may also be used for regression problems with the following simple modification (Vapnik, Golowich, & Smola, 1996):

$$\text{Minimize } \frac{1}{2} w^T w C \sum_{i=1}^{n} \left(\xi_i + \xi_i\right)$$

$$\text{subject to } \left(wx_i + b\right) - y_i \leq \varepsilon + \xi_i$$

$$\text{and } \ y_i - \left(wx_i + b\right) \leq \varepsilon + \xi_i \qquad (10)$$

where ξ_i is a slack variable introduced for exceeding the target value by more than ε and ξ_i a slack variable for being more than ε below the target value (Webb, 2002).

The idea of the Support Vector Machine is to find a model which guarantees the lowest classification or regression error by controlling the model complexity (VC-dimension) based on the structural risk minimization principle. This avoids over-fitting, which is the main problem for other learning algorithms.

INFORMATION SOURCES

Our approach was evaluated using public data provided by the Netflix movie rental online DVD store, namely "Netflix's Facebook Notes" webpages[1]. In these webpages Netflix reports the most rented movies for each period between note updates. We used data covering a period from March 4, 2009 until December 1st, 2009 and the task was to predict the demand for movie rentals during the critical, for sales, Christmas holiday season (December 2009), as shown in Figure 5.

Figure 4. Optimal Separating Hyperplane and bias

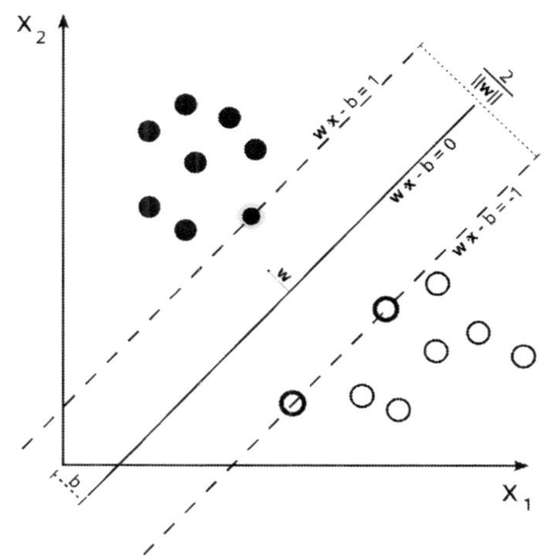

In our multivariate approach to forecasting SC demand, we utilized the following variables as important factors that can affect demand, in the light of the papers of (Aburto & Weber, 2007) and (Efendigil et al.., 2009):

- *Past unit sales*: Past unit sales is a competitive unit factor indicating customer behavior. In this work past unit sales was processed as quantitative information by taking into account the number of times each movie made it into a "Most Rented" list during the period under consideration. Figure 6 shows the top-10 movie titles that appeared most times in "Most Rented" lists during this period.
- *Product quality*: Product quality involves the evaluation about product quality according to customers' opinions. Even though product quality is a subjective qualitative measure, in this study we utilize this factor as quantitative information similarly

Figure 5. Netflix's Facebook Notes for most rented movies in 2009. The first entry ("25 Most Rented Movies from Netflix for the Month of December 2009") was used as the testing dataset to be predicted from all the other notes appearing in this figure (source:Facebook)

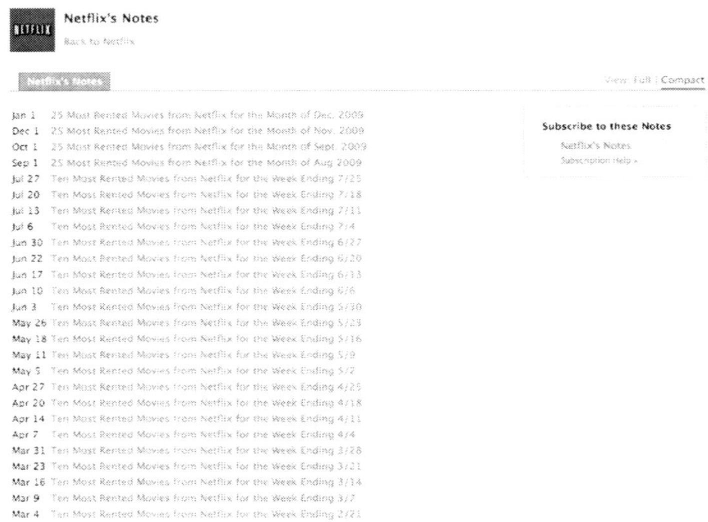

to the methodology proposed in (Lathia, Amatriain, & Pujol, 2009). We crawled two different sources of movie reviews and ratings: Rotten Tomatoes[2] and Flixster[3]. Based on how ratings are input into each of these systems, these sources are labeled by (Lathia et al.., 2009) as *"Experts"* and *"Enthusiasts"* respectively:

a. *Experts*: The Rotten Tomatoes website is an aggregator for a number of movie reviews utilizing a variety of web sources, including newspapers, specialized websites, and magazines. The critics use different rating scales; some range from 1-10 stars, others 1-5, and some use a 100-point scale. In this work we normalized all ratings in a 1-5 scale by adopting a simple linear transformation to reinterpret ratings from one scale to another.
b. *Enthusiasts*: Flixster is one of the largest movie oriented social networks, and contains ratings given by the site's movie-enthusiast subscribers. We followed public review profiles of some Flixster's top-users discussing movies within our training set. The Flixster users rate movies on a 1-5 star scale, but there are also two further options available: "Want to See" (WS), and "Not Interested" (NI). In fact, the majority of ratings in the data fall into one of these two latter categories. WS ratings were given a value of 5, whereas NI were assigned the value 1.

- *Customer interest decay indicator*: In addition to the above explanatory variables, we introduced this third parameter in order to encapsulate the fact that the interest for previous movie releases declines with time as new releases appear. In order to quantify this information we gave to customer interest decay indicator its maximum value whenever a title appeared for the first time in a "Most Rented" list and we allowed it to diminish exponentially with time.

As a final note in this section, we should mention that we did not take into account the effect of any promotions appearing in the Netflix web site during the period spanned by the test set, i.e. the impact in demand due to promotions or special days (such as Christmas, new year's day, etc.).

RESULTS

In our experiments we compared the demand forecasting performance of ANNs trained with the OLMAM algorithm and the SVM for regression. For all models the training dataset was randomly divided 10 times into train and test data using 60% and 40% of the samples respectively each time. For each feedforward neural network configuration trained with OLMAM (i.e. for each different selection of hidden nodes) we performed a total of 100 training trials resulting from training the network 10 times for each of the 10 random splits of the dataset. Each different training trial was performed by initializing the network's weights in the range [-0.1, 0.1]. In each trial the maximum number of epochs was set to 500 and training was considered successful whenever the training MSE of equation (6) was $\varepsilon \leq 0.01$. All inputs and targets were normalized in the range [0, +1] in order to avoid saturation of the sigmoid. The best performance was achieved with a network configuration of a single hidden layer with four hidden nodes. All experiments were carried in MATLAB using the LMAM/OLMAM Neural Network Toolbox (Ampazis, 2002).

For training the SVM we used the SVM^{light} package (Joachims, 2002) compiled with the Intel C/C++ Compiler Professional Edition for Linux. Training of the SVM was run on a 2.5GHz Quad Core Pentium CPU with 4G RAM running Ubuntu 9.10 desktop x86_64 (Karmic Koala) operating system. In our experiments we linearly scaled each feature to the range [-1, +1]. Scaling training data before applying SVM is very important. The main advantage is to avoid attributes in greater numeric ranges to dominate those in smaller numeric ranges. Another advantage is to avoid numerical difficulties during the calculation. Because kernel values usually depend on the inner products of feature vectors, large attribute values might cause numerical problems (Chang & Lin, 2001). With the same method, testing data features were scaled to the training data ranges before testing. The training target outputs were also scaled to [0, +1] and the output of the SVM was then transformed back from the [0, +1] range to its original target value in order to calculate the MSE.

We also evaluated the Mean Absolute Percentage Error (MAPE) of the test data set at each training trial defined as (Makridakis, Wheelwright, & Hyndman, 2008):

Figure 6. 10 most rented movie titles within the period covered in the training set (in parentheses the number of times each title appeared in a "Most Rented" list)

Table 1. MSE and MAPE averaged over all the training/test splits, for OLMAM and SVM

	OLMAM	SVM
MSE	0.007 ± 0.003	0.005 ± 0.002
MAPE	12.16 ± 1.1	11.70 ± 0.8

$$MAPE = \frac{1}{P}\sum_{p=1}^{P}\left|\left(\frac{d^{(p)} - y^{(p)}}{d^{(p)}}\right)\right| * 100 \qquad (11)$$

where as in equation (6), $d^{(p)}$ and $y^{(p)}$ denote the actual observation and the forecast respectively.

In Table 1 we report the average MSE and MAPE values over all 10 random splits of the dataset for the OLMAM and SVM regressors, as well as the standard deviation over the 10 trials. From this table we can observe that in all cases the performance of the best OLMAM trained neural network with 4 hidden nodes is directly

Figure 7. 25 most rented movie titles from Netflix for the month of December 2009 (source:Facebook)

Figure 8. ANN results for the demand forecasting for the 15 common movie titles appearing both in the training set and the December 2009 test set (in parentheses the actual rankings)

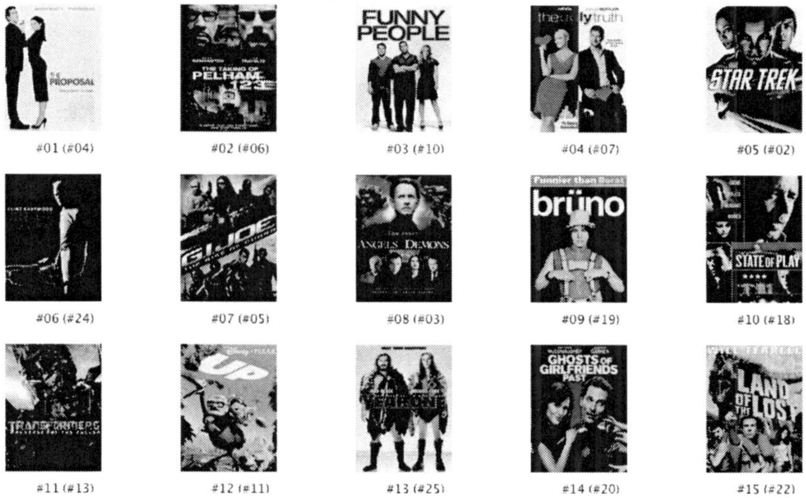

comparable to that of the SVM regressor. In order to obtain a more qualitative feeling of the results, Figure 7 shows the actual list reported by Netflix for the 25 most rented movie titles for the month of December 2009. Among these titles there were only 15 common movies appearing both in the training set and in this list. Figure 8 shows the demand predictions for these 15 titles made by the best OLMAM trained ANN, while Figure 9 shows the results obtained by the SVM. From these figures we can see that the predictions made by both algorithms for the demand of the most rented movies are quite accurate since the top places are dominated by titles that were indeed in the top places of the list reported by Netflix. It is interesting to note that within the top predictions

Figure 9. SVM results for the demand forecasting for the 15 common movie titles appearing both in the training set and the December 2009 test set (in parentheses the actual rankings)

of both algorithms there is only one title ("Gran Torino") that appeared most of the times within the period covered in the training set, as was shown in Figure 6. This indicates that the results are based on a balanced combination of the input explanatory variables, and are not heavily affected from the past unit sales quantity alone, as would most probably have been the case with a linear or nonlinear univariate (time-series) approach.

CONCLUSION

In this chapter, a supply chain risk demand forecasting approach based on neural networks and support vector machines was presented. Our first aim was to explore the potential of more advanced computational intelligence algorithms for predicting demand in a SC than those already explored in the relevant literature. For this purpose, several ANN architectures trained with the OLMAM algorithm were tried in a real world SC demand forecasting problem, namely predicting the demand for movie rentals during the critical, for sales, Christmas holiday season for the Netflix movie rental online DVD store. All the OLMAM trained ANNs performed quite well, and the winner was an ANN with a single hidden layer and 4 hidden neurons, which exhibited reasonable prediction capability. Its performance was comparable to the SVM for regression algorithm which is well known for its ability to avoid over-fitting. The results obtained also provide a good indication of the value of having advanced multivariate models that take into account the complex interactions that exist among factors that can influence SC demand in an uncertain environment. The computational intelligence approach presented in this chapter was intended to optimally combine the integration of data from various sources of information and the power of advanced algorithms for lowering the uncertainty barrier.

REFERENCES

Aburto, L., & Weber, R. (2007). Improved supply chain management based on hybrid demand forecasts. *Applied Soft Computing*, *7*(1), 136–144. doi:10.1016/j.asoc.2005.06.001

Ampazis, N. (2002). LMAM/OLMAM neural network toolbox []. (Software available at http://authorid.fme.aegean.gr/OLMAM/toolbox)

Ampazis, N., & Perantonis, S. J. (2002). Two highly efficient second order algorithms for training feedforward networks. *IEEE Transactions on Neural Networks*, *13*(5), 1064–1074. doi:10.1109/TNN.2002.1031939

Armstrong, J. (2002). *Principles of forecasting: a handbook for researchers and practitioners*. Kluwer.

Bishop, C. M. (1995). *Neural Networks for Pattern Recognition*. Oxford: Oxford University Press.

Boser, B. E., Guyon, I. M., & Vapnik, V. N. (1992). A training algorithm for optimal margin classifiers. In *Colt '92: Proceedings of the fifth annual workshop on computational learning theory* (pp. 144–152). New York: ACM.

Box, G., Jenkins, G., & Reinsel, G. (1976). *Time series analysis: forecasting and control*. Holden-day San Francisco.

Carbonneau, R., Laframboise, K., & Vahidov, R. M. (2008). Application of machine learning techniques for supply chain demand forecasting. *European Journal of Operational Research*, *184*(3), 1140–1154. doi:10.1016/j.ejor.2006.12.004

Chang, C. C., & Lin, C. J. (2001). LIBSVM: a library for support vector machines. (Software available at http://www.csie.ntu.edu.tw/~cjlin/libsvm)

Cortes, C., & Vapnik, V. (1995). Support-vector networks. *Machine Learning*, *20*(3), 273–297. doi:10.1007/BF00994018

Cristianini, N., & John, S.-T. (2000). *An Introduction to Support Vector Machines and other kernel-based learning methods*. Cambridge: Cambridge University Press.

Croston, J. (1972). Forecasting and stock control for intermittent demands. *Operational Research Quarterly (1970-1977), 23*(3), 289–303.

Efendigil, T., Önüt, S., & Kahraman, C. (2009, Apr). A decision support system for demand forecasting with artificial neural networks and neuro-fuzzy models: A comparative analysis. *Expert Systems with Applications, 36*(P2), 6697–6707. doi:10.1016/j.eswa.2008.08.058

Gardner, E. (1985). Exponential smoothing: The state of the art. *Journal of Forecasting, 4*(1), 1–38. doi:10.1002/for.3980040103

Gilbert, J. C., & Nocedal, J. (1992). Global convergence properties of conjugate gradient methods for optimization. *SIAM Journal on Optimization, 2*(1), 21–42. doi:10.1137/0802003

Gutierrez, R. S., Solis, A. O., & Mukhopadhyay, S. (2008, February). Lumpy demand forecasting using neural networks. *International Journal of Production Economics, 111*(2), 409–420. doi:10.1016/j.ijpe.2007.01.007

Hagan, M. T., & Menhaj, M. (1994). Training feedforward networks with the Marquardt algorithm. *IEEE Transactions on Neural Networks, 5*(6), 989–993. doi:10.1109/72.329697

Joachims, T. (2002). *SVM light,* http://svmlight.joachims.org. An implementation of Support Vector Machines (SVMs) in C. http://svmlight.joachims. org.

Kimbrough, S., Wu, D., & Zhong, F. (2002). Computers play the beer game: can artificial agents manage supply chains? *Decision Support Systems, 33*(3), 323–333. doi:10.1016/S0167-9236(02)00019-2

Lathia, N., Amatriain, X., & Pujol, J. (2009, July). Collaborative Filtering With Adaptive Information Sources. In *Ijcai workshop on intelligent techniques for web personalisation and recommender systems.* Pasadena.

Lee, H., Padmanabhan, V., & Whang, S. (1997a). The bullwhip effect in supply chains. *Sloan Management Review, 38*, 93–102.

Lee, H., Padmanabhan, V., & Whang, S. (1997b). Information distortion in a supply chain: the bullwhip effect. *Management Science, 43*(4), 546–558. doi:10.1287/mnsc.43.4.546

Liang, W., & Huang, C. (2006). Agent-based demand forecast in multi-echelon supply chain. *Decision Support Systems, 42*(1), 390–407. doi:10.1016/j.dss.2005.01.009

Makridakis, S., Wheelwright, S., & Hyndman, R. (2008). *Forecasting methods and applications*. Wiley India Pvt. Ltd.

Marien, E. (1999, Jan). Demand planning and sales forecasting: A supply chain essential. *Supply Chain Management Review*.

Minis, I., & Ampazis, N. (2006). Applications of neural networks in supply chain management. In Rennard, J. P. (Ed.), *Handbook of research on nature inspired computing for economics and management* - (*Vol. 2*). Hershey, PA: Idea Group Reference.

O'donnell, T., Maguire, L., McIvor, R., & Humphreys, P. (2006). Minimizing the bullwhip effect in a supply chain using genetic algorithms. *International Journal of Production Research, 44*(8), 1523–1543. doi:10.1080/00207540500431347

Perantonis, S. J., & Karras, D. A. (1995). An efficient constrained learning algorithm with momentum acceleration. *Neural Networks, 8*(2), 237–239. doi:10.1016/0893-6080(94)00067-V

Rabelo, L., Helal, M., & Lertpattarapong, C. (2004, Jan). Analysis of supply chains using system dynamics, neural nets, and eigenvalues. In J. S. S. R.G. Ingalls M. D. Rossetti & B. A. Peters (Eds.), *Proceedings of the 36th winter simulation conference.*

Rumelhart, D. E., Hinton, G. E., & Williams, R. J. (1986). Learning internal representations by error propagation. *Parallel distributed processing: explorations in the microstructure of cognition* (Vol. 1. *Foundations*, 318–362.

Syntetos, A., & Boylan, J. (2001). On the bias of intermittent demand estimates. *International Journal of Production Economics, 71*(1-3), 457–466. doi:10.1016/S0925-5273(00)00143-2

Vapnik, V. (1998). *The nature of statistical learning theory*. New York: Wiley.

Vapnik, V., Golowich, S. E., & Smola, A. J. (1996). *Support vector method for function approximation, regression estimation and signal processing* (pp. 281–287). Nips.

Wang, L. (2005). *Support vector machines: Theory and applications (studies in fuzziness and soft computing)*. Secaucus, NJ, USA: Springer-Verlag New York, Inc.

Webb, A. R. (2002). *Statistical pattern recognition* (2nd ed.). Wiley. doi:10.1002/0470854774

ENDNOTES

1 http://www.facebook.com/netflix

2 http://www.rottentomatoes.com

3 http://www.flixster.com

Chapter 6
Generating Supply Chain Ordering Policies using Quantum Inspired Genetic Algorithms and Grammatical Evolution

Seán McGarraghy
University College Dublin, Ireland

Michael Phelan
University College Dublin, Ireland

ABSTRACT

Contributions to a supply chain's overall cost function (such as the bullwhip effect) are sensitive to the different players' ordering policies. This chapter addresses the problem of developing ordering policies which minimise the overall supply chain cost. Evolutionary Algorithms have been used to evolve such ordering policies. The authors of this chapter extend existing research in a number of ways. They apply two more recent evolutionary algorithms to the problem: Grammatical Evolution (GE), using a standard Genetic Algorithm (GA) search engine; and Quantum Inspired Genetic Algorithm (QIGA), used both as a standalone algorithm, and as an alternative search engine for GE. The authors benchmark these against previous work on the linear Beer Game supply chain, and extend our approaches to arborescent supply chains (without gaming), and capacitated inventory. The ordering-policy-generating grammars investigated range from simple — only using the demand presented at that point — to complex — which may incorporate lagged demands, forecasting approaches such as Moving Average or Simple Exponential Smoothing, conditional statements and other operators. The different grammars and search engines are compared for deterministic demand, and various stochastic demand distributions. Overall,

DOI: 10.4018/978-1-61520-633-9.ch006

GE outperforms other approaches by discovering more efficient ordering policies. However, its performance is sensitive to the choice of grammar: simple grammars do best on deterministic demand, while grammars using conditionals, information sharing and forecasting do better on stochastic demand. GE with a QIGA search engine has similar performance overall to GE with a standard GA search engine: typically QIGA is better if demand follows a Poisson distribution, with GA better for Normal demand.

INTRODUCTION

Supply chains may be linear, with only one player at each tier, or arborescent (tree-like), with multiple players at each tier. The well-known Beer Game (see below) is a linear 4-tier supply chain. Supply chains exhibit the bullwhip effect, where demand variance at the customer end is amplified along the chain upstream. This effect, and the total supply chain cost, are sensitive to the players' ordering policies.

An example of an ordering policy is the "one for one" policy: the order received from the immediate downstream customer is passed on to the immediate upstream supplier.

The problem this research addresses is to develop ordering policies which minimise the overall cost in the supply chain, and implicitly mitigate the bullwhip effect. For supply chains of very simple stucture, e.g., two tiers, there exist analytical solutions to the optimal order quantity problem, such as the Box-Jenkins ARMA/ARIMA approach Box & Jenkins (1970). However, for more complex supply chains, with multiple tiers, branching, capacitation, or other enrichments, such approaches may fail or simply not exist. Furthermore, such approaches are mathematically involved, and not always understood or adopted by practitioners. There is a need for an approach which is flexible enough to be applicable to a wide range of real situations, while being tunable with a few parameters (and so lending itself to use by practitioners), yet still being accurate enough to perform at least as well as current approaches.

The rise in popularity of Evolutionary Algorithms (EAs) has led researchers to investigate models of the Beer Game incorporating evolution — such as the Genetic Algorithm (GA) and Genetic Programming (GP) — and simulation. These models evolve ordering policies that minimise total supply chain cost. For the supply chain problems so far investigated, EAs appear to be at least competitive with previous approaches.

Our research extends this existing work in several ways. We apply two recent EAs:

- Quantum Inspired Genetic Algorithm (QIGA) (the first supply chain use we know of); and
- Grammatical Evolution (GE), using as search engine either a standard GA (denoted GE-GA) or QIGA (denoted GE-QIGA). GE (O'Neill & Ryan, 2001, 2003; Brabazon & O'Neill, 2006) is an EA, more specifically, a form of GP using linear genomes. It can evolve complete programs (in our case, ordering policies) in an arbitrary language using a variable-length binary string (genome). The binary string determines which production rules in a Backus-Naur Form (BNF) grammar definition are used in a genotype-to-phenotype mapping process to generate a program.

GE is an intelligent metaheuristic, newly introduced to the supply chain domain. A major motivation for its use here is the capability of encoding the particular supply chain structure in the grammar, so meeting the flexibility requirement above; it is also tunable; and it holds out the hope of being competitive with existing approaches in terms of accuracy, as well as being attractive to practitioners. By hybridising GE with GA and

QIGA, we hope to extend recent promising results of hybrid algorithms.

We benchmark QIGA, GE-GA and GE-QIGA against previous work on the Beer Game, and extend our approaches to arborescent supply chains. We investigate stochastic demand distributions, and the effects of capacitated inventory (with resulting additional cost of stockouts).

Our model is sufficiently general for any supply chain configuration that does not involve gaming effects among the players (e.g., in the automotive industry). We apply it not only to the standard Beer Game supply chain (Figure 1) but also to an arborescent supply chain with four players (Figure 2). In each, the manufacturer is merely a source of inventory, and places no orders.

The high-level approach is as follows. The GA and QIGA use a simple "one for one" ordering policy for each player; in the GE setup, each individual in a population of bit-strings is mapped by a grammar to a set of agent ordering policies (a policy for each player in the chain). A bespoke-developed agent-based simulation model of the supply chain (with variable agent behaviour and awareness of environment) produces a cost which measures the individual's fitness. Fitter individuals are given preference in the next generation, whether by having a higher probability of reproduction (in the standalone GA and GE-GA) or by seeding the next generation of a quantum population with the best observed from this population (in the standalone QIGA and GE-QIGA). Over multiple generations, the best individual is found. Minimum and mean cost, and other performance measures, are recorded.

Figure 1. Beer Game supply chain configuration

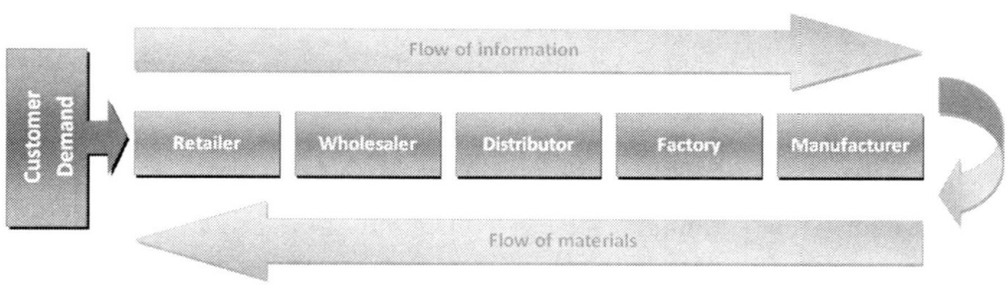

Figure 2. Example Arborescent supply chain configuration

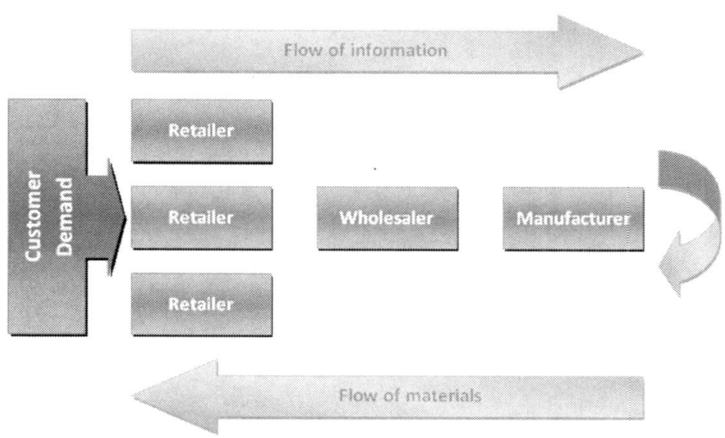

The grammar approach's flexibility is highlighted by the fact that we can investigate the effect of allowing agents to develop their ordering policies by using, for example, the demand presented to them, the demand at other points in the chain (information sharing), lagged demands, forecasting approaches (e.g., Moving Average, Simple Exponential Smoothing), conditional (**if**) statements and other operators.

The different grammars and search engines are tested in the settings of (*a*) deterministic demand (the classical Beer Game); and (*b*) stochastic demand. The results are compared to exact results from an Integer Program (where feasible/appropriate).

Results compare favourably with existing research on generating ordering policies using a GA (Kimbrough et al., 2001, 2002; O'Donnell et al., 2006): we find the same (optimal) policies as the GA in all experimental setups used by these authors. In some cases when demand and/or lead times are stochastic, GE outperforms other approaches by discovering more efficient ordering policies (in cost reduction terms) for agents in the supply chain. However, its performance is sensitive to the choice of grammar: simple grammars do best on deterministic data, while grammars using conditionals, information sharing and forecasting do better on stochastic data. This is evidence of the vital rôle grammar selection has in GE's results. GE-QIGA has similar performance overall to GE-GA, but performs better in certain settings.

The supply chain simulation model is further enriched by current research in order to examine more complex supply chain networks, incorporating service level agreements and capacitated shipments; along with grammar structures (incorporating agent memory) leading to more efficient ordering policies.

BACKGROUND

The Beer Game

Researchers and practitioners have used the MIT Beer Distribution Game (Jarmain & Fey, 1963; Mosekilde & Larsen, 1988; Sterman, 1989) to simulate a supply chain with four tiers: Retailer, Wholesaler, Distributor and Factory. Its basic setup and weekly operation are as in Figure 3.

Shipments arrive from upstream players; orders arrive from downstream players; orders are filled and shipped where possible, affecting the inventory and backorders of a player; each player decides how much to order to replenish inventory; and, finally, inventory holding costs and backorder costs are calculated for each player every week. The only decision a player makes is how much to order from his/her upstream supplier.

The Beer Game is used world-wide in academia and business to demonstrate a simplified supply chain and the difficulty of keeping costs low. A

Figure 3. The Beer Game

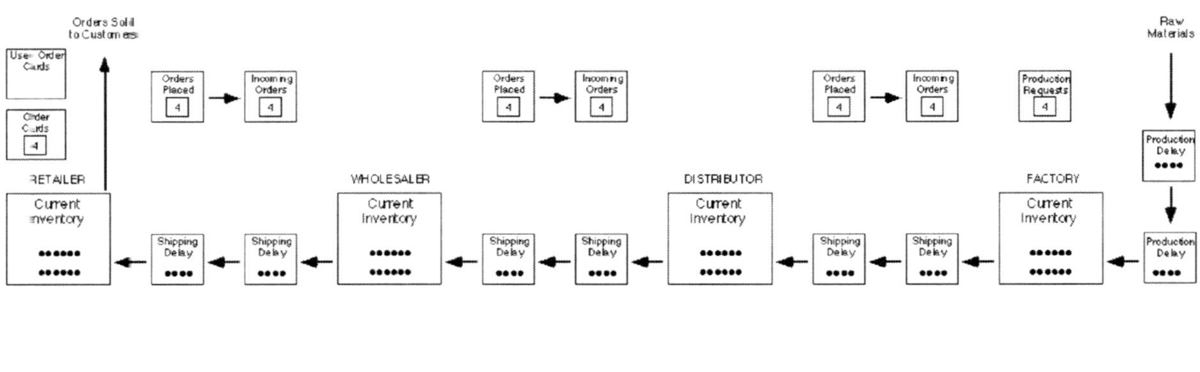

Figure 4. The Bullwhip Effect - Increasing variability of orders up the supply chain

major contributor to these costs is the *Bullwhip effect* or *Forrester effect* (see Figure 4).

Forrester (1958, 1961) showed that small changes (e.g., in input demand, stockouts in supply chain execution, etc.) to this naturally oscillating system can have serious impacts on its operation. This variance may be minor for any one customer, but when it propagates back through the supply chain can result in large and costly fluctuations at the supplier end. Often, these demand oscillations will lead to a period of overproduction (with the need to acquire more raw materials). This can cause vast sums of money to be caught up in the supply chain (Cooke, 1993), with dramatic inefficiencies affecting all echelons. Problems such as excess inventories, quality issues, and higher costs of raw material, overtime and shipping are common. In the worst case, customer service declines, lead-times increase, sales are lost, costs increase and capacity must be adjusted. The four main causes of the bullwhip effect as identified by Lee et al. (1997a,b) are: demand forecast updating; order batching; rationing and shortage gaming; and price variations; leading to players' overreaction to orders.

The Beer Game is complex enough (being an intractable 23rd order non-linear difference equation (Sterman, 1989)) to be used for simulations, and employed for research into bullwhip mitigation techniques. For its use as an active learning teaching aid, see (Sparling, 2002; Goodwin & S.G. Franklin, 1994; Sterman, 1992; Meadows, 2007; Coakley et al., 1998; Nienhaus et al., 2006; Jacobs, 2000; Chen & Samroengraja, 2000; Teixeira et al., 2004). Because of the literature's close study of the Beer Game (as a "laboratory" supply chain), we use it as one test bed for our approaches.

In Sterman (1989), irrationality in ordering patterns is reduced by using a stock management heuristic employing the widely used forecasting technique, Simple Exponential Smoothing (SES) (Gardner, 1985a,b). Kimbrough et al. (2001, 2002) suggest that this irrationality while playing the Beer Game may be due to lack of incentives for information sharing, bounded rationality, or the consequence of individually rational behaviour that works against the interests of the group. Chen (1999) showed that the bullwhip effect can be reduced using a base-stock installation policy, assuming all players in the supply chain work as a team. Base-stock is optimal when facing stochastic demand; but a "one for one" (1—1) policy is optimal when facing deterministic demand (Kimbrough et al., 2001, 2002). This has led to research on artificial agents replacing humans in the Beer Game. We will see that, using GAs and GE, the overreaction identified by Lee et al. (1997a,b) is ameliorated, giving reduced costs throughout the supply chain, and more efficient ordering and stocking policies.

Evolutionary Algorithms in Supply Chain Management

The last decade has seen much interest in the application of biologically inspired algorithms to supply chain research, including GAs, GP, Artificial Neural Networks and Ant Colony Optimisation. A recent special issue of the International Journal of Computer Applications in Technology (2008) — "Intelligent Techniques to Solve Complex Problems in Logistics and Supply Chains" — investigates the effectiveness of Differential Evolution (Falcone et al., 2008) and Particle Swarm Optimisation (Yadav et al., 2008). Evolutionary algorithms (EA) are a subset of biologically inspired algorithms which mimic the process of natural selection to evolve solutions for a given problem. They borrow terms from Biology such as: *genotype* for the genetic code of an organism; and *phenotype* for the realisation of that code in the world, namely, a living creature.

Kimbrough et al. (2001, 2002) and O'Donnell et al. (2006) successfully use a GA to evolve an "$x + y$" order quantity for each agent in the Beer Game, where x is the demand requested from an agent's immediate downstream customer and y is an increment determined by the GA. They experiment with various demand and lead time values. Here, the genotype is the encoding scheme (typically as a bit string) of the ordering policy, while the phenotype is the actual policy (or set of policies). The fitness of a policy is estimated by running a Beer Game simulation using that policy, typically for 35—100 time periods. Chan et al. (2006) adopt a similar approach to Kimbrough et al. (2001, 2002), except that each agent chooses an inventory policy from a set of candidate policies and determines its ordering quantity for each period according to the chosen policy. Strozzi et al. (2007) employ GAs to evolve parameters used in Sterman's stock management heuristic (Sterman, 1989). Moore & DeMaagd (2004) use GP to evolve ordering policies while Kleinau & Thonemann (2004) evolve both inventory control policy structures and parameters using GP. Chaharsooghi et al. (2008) use an agent-based model and reinforcement learning to find effective ordering policies for the Beer Game. Phelan & McGarraghy (2007) introduce Grammatical Evolution to supply chain dynamics and bullwhip mitigation.

Quantum Inspired Genetic Algorithms

Quantum-inspired genetic algorithms (QIGA) aim to improve the performance of genetic algorithms by emulating properties of Quantum Mechanics, such as the *quantum bit* and *superposition of states* (Han & Kim, 2002, 2004; Narayanan & Moore, 1996; Yang et al., 2004a,b). These algorithms run on classical computers; they are not quantum algorithms, which run on quantum computers. They cannot simulate certain quantum effects such as the non-local *entanglement* effect: when the wave function (or quantum state) of a many-particle system cannot be separated into independent wave functions, one for each particle. The application of quantum concepts to optimisation and business problems is an area of active research interest. For example, Fan et al. (2008) give a Finance application.

In Quantum Mechanics, a *two-state system* is one where the quantum state ψ is a linear superposition of just two eigenstates, say $|0\rangle$ and $|1\rangle$ in the standard Dirac bra-ket notation; that is,

$$\psi = \alpha|0\rangle + \beta|1\rangle.$$

Here, $|0\rangle$ and $|1\rangle$ are orthogonal basis vectors for a 2-dimensional complex Hilbert space, and $\alpha,\beta \in C$, with $|\alpha|^2 + |\beta|^2 = 1$ for ψ normalised. A two-state system where the states are normalised and orthogonal, as here, is called a *quantum bit* or *qubit* and written as a pair $(\alpha,\beta) \in C^2$. A system of m qubits may be written as a $2 \times m$ matrix of complex numbers,

$$\begin{pmatrix} \alpha_1, \alpha_2, \ldots, \alpha_m \\ \beta_1, \beta_2, \ldots, \beta_m \end{pmatrix}$$

where, for each i, $\alpha_i^2 + \beta_i^2 = 1$.

Quantum systems can compactly convey information on many possible system states. In classical bit strings, a string of length m can represent 2^m possible states; but a quantum system of m qubits can simultaneously represent *all* possible bit strings of length 2^m, e.g., an 8 qubit system can simultaneously encode 256 distinct strings. This suggests the possibility of modifying standard EAs to work with very few quantum individuals, or even just one, rather than a large population.

In EA language, an m-qubit system may be called a *quantum chromosome*. When used in a QIGA (Han & Kim, 2002; Narayanan & Moore, 1996), α and β are usually real numbers, so we may view a qubit (also called a Q-bit in QIGAs) as lying on the unit circle in R^2 (Figure 5).

Algorithm 1 provides an example of a canonical binary QIGA; see (Han & Kim, 2002).

Figure 5. A QIGA qubit (ai,bi) on the unit circle of R2, rotated by an angle Dθi to (a¢i,b¢i)

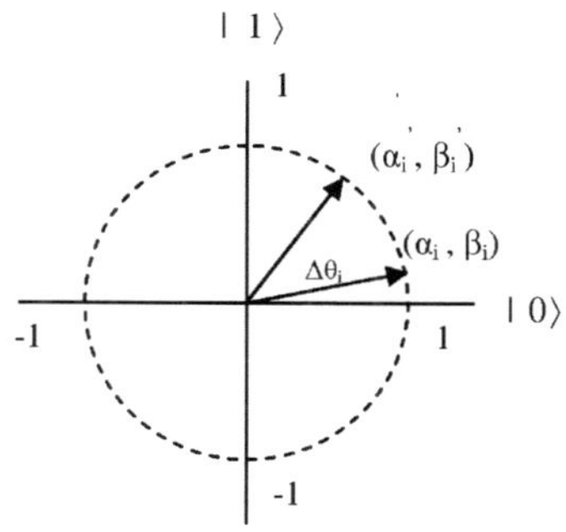

Initially, the population of n quantum chromosomes (n could be 1) is created as

$$Q(t) = \{q^1(t), q^2(t), \ldots, q^n(t)\},$$

where each member $q^i(t) = (q_1^{\,i}(t), \ldots, q_m^{\,i}(t))$ of the population consists of a qubit string of length m. The α and β values for each qubit are initialised to $1/\sqrt{2}$, so the states $|0\rangle$ and $|1\rangle$ are equally likely. Domain knowledge, e.g, that some states are likely to lead to better results, can be used to seed

Algorithm 1. Binary Quantum-inspired Genetic Algorithm

```
Set t:= 0;
Initalise Q(t) (the quantum chromosomes);
fori:= 1 to ndo
        Create P_i(t) by undertaking an observation (sample) of Q(t);
end
Evaluate P(t) and select the best solution from this population;
Store the best solution in B(t);
whilet < t_max do
        t:= t + 1;
        Create P*(t) by undertaking observations of Q(t - 1);
        Evaluate the population of solutions P*(t);
        Compare best solution in P*(t) with that of B(t - 1) and store best
solution in B(t);
        Update Q(t) using B(t);
end
```

Figure 6. GE process (left) and modular structure (right)

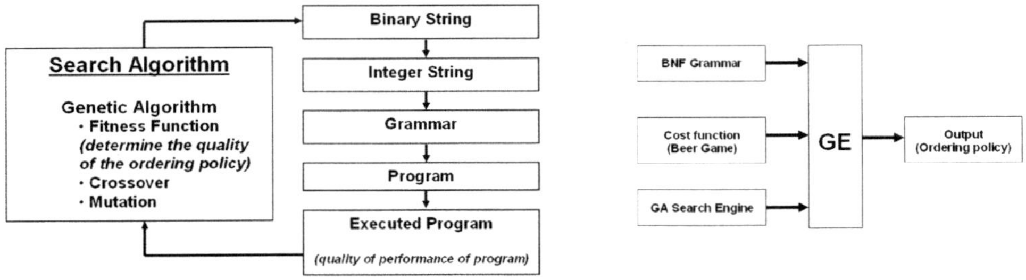

the initial quantum chromosome(s). Once $Q(t)$ is created, it can be used to create a population $P(t) = \{p^1(t), p^2(t), \ldots, p^n(t)\}$ of binary (solution encoding) strings by performing 'observations' on the quantum chromosome(s).

Because the observation step is stochastic, the QIGA could be implemented using a few (or just one) quantum chromosome(s), with each chromosome observed (sampled) multiple times in order to generate the population $P(t)$.

In the **while** loop, an update step is performed on $Q(t)$, e.g., using rotations (Figure 5). Its purpose is to adjust the quantum chromosome(s) so as to increase the chance of generating the best solution found so far in the next iteration. As the QIGA system approaches an optimum, each coefficient of the quantum chromosome will tend towards either 0 or 1, corresponding to a high probability that the quantum chromosome will generate a specific solution vector $p = (p_1, \ldots, p_m)$ when observed.

Grammatical Evolution

Grammatical Evolution (GE) is an EA developed by O'Neill & Ryan (2001, 2003) that can evolve computer programs, sentences in any language or, for the purposes of this research, ordering policies. Unlike Koza's GP, where solutions are represented as syntax trees, GE uses a linear genome representation together with a grammar. Each individual (genotype) is a variable length binary string comprising codons (8-bit strings) used to select production rules from the grammar (O'Neill & Ryan, 2001, 2003; Brabazon & O'Neill, 2006). See Figure 6 (left).

Any search engine that can operate on binary or integer strings could employ GE's mapping process to generate a program or policy (Figure 6 (right)).For example, particle swarm and differential evolution engines have been used in grammatical swarm and grammatical differential evolution algorithms respectively (Brabazon & O'Neill, 2006).

The language to be generated is described using a Backus-Naur Form (BNF) grammar definition. BNF is a notation for expressing the grammar of a language (in our case, a set of ordering policies) in the form of production rules. BNF grammars consist of: terminals, which are fully determined elements that can exist in the language, e.g., constants; and non-terminals, which can be expanded using the production rules into one or more terminals or non-terminals. When using GE on a problem, a suitable BNF grammar must first be defined. The selection of an appropriate grammar is essential for finding efficient solutions (here, ordering policies) in GE (Brabazon & O'Neill, 2006). An example grammar tailored to the Beer Game is given later.

METHODOLOGY & IMPLEMENTATION

This section describes the application of GE and QIGA to discover optimal ordering policies for artificial agents, in both the Beer Game and an arborescent supply chain. The simulations used to generate the agents' ordering policies and fitness functions are similar to those of Kimbrough et al. (2001, 2002) and O'Donnell et al. (2006), with the key difference being the EA employed to generate the ordering policies. Kimbrough et al. (2001, 2002) use a fixed-length binary string and a GA. Our GE method uses various grammar definitions representing ordering policy rules, a fitness function similar to those of Kimbrough et al. (2001, 2002) and O'Donnell et al. (2006), and a GA or QIGA search engine. Results show how, depending on a chosen grammar, the GE can discover more complex ordering policies that reduce the agents' total cost.

Performance Comparison

Traditional analysis of algorithms (involving worst-case run times in terms of input-problem size) has limited applicability to stochastic search/optimisation algorithms (or *metaheuristics*) of the type considered here, since the stochastic nature of the algorithms is central. Average computational effort taken to reach an adequate solution is one possible metric, while another that has been used is the quality of the best-of-run solution achieved. In this work, we use the quality-of-solution metric (as recommended for EAs by Luke & Panait (2002) and Christensen & Oppacher (2002)), while also remarking on computational effort.

Supply Chain Configurations

Three configurations were used, as in Table 1.

Table 1. Configurations used in experiments

Name	Description	Capacitated?
Config. A	4 tier linear supply chain	No
Config. B	2 tier tree	No
Config. C	2 tier tree	Yes

Configuration A is the standard Beer Game (Figure 1) while Configurations B and C are arborescent with four players (Figure 2). Only Configuration C has inventory capacity constraints. All four approaches, GA, QIGA, GE-GA and GE-QIGA, are applied to each configuration.

Encoding and Fitness Function

As in Kimbrough et al. (2001, 2002) and O'Donnell et al. (2006), each human player is replaced by an artificial agent (in Configuration A, these are Retailer, Wholesaler, Distributor and Factory; in Configurations B and C they are three Retailers and one Wholesaler). Each agent's rule is represented by a 6-bit binary string. The leftmost bit represents the sign ('+' or '-') and the next five bits represent (in base 2) how much to order this time period, denoted by y. Let x denote the agent's incoming demand this time period. Each agent's ordering policy is understood to mean $\max\{0, x + y\}$ each time period. For example, rule 101001 can be interpreted as "$x + 9$": if the customer demand is x, then the agent will place an order $x + 9$ with his/her supplier.

The fitness of an individual is defined as the negative of the total supply chain cost C, where

$$C = \sum_{A=1}^{4} \sum_{T=1}^{N} Inv_{AT} \times HC\ Back_{AT} \times BC \qquad 1$$

with all costs measured in the appropriate currency unit, and notation:

- A Agent identifier (four in each model used)
- T Current time period
- N Total number of time periods
- Inv_{AT} Amount of inventory on hand for agent A in time period T
- HC Cost of holding 1 unit of inventory per time period

Example 1.

```
(A)    <agent>    ::=    <policy><policy><policy><poli
cy>    (0)
(B)    <policy>   ::=    <var>    (0)
           |    <var><op><int>    (1)
           |    <policy><op>(<var><op><int>)    (2)
(C)    <op>    ::=    +    (0)
           |    -    (1)
(D)    <int>   ::=    0    (0)
           |    1    (1)
           |    2    (2)
           :    :    :
           :    :    :
           |    19    (19)
           |    20    (20)
(E)    <var>   ::=    x    (0)
```

$Back_{AT}$ Amount of backorders for agent A in time period T

BC Backorder cost for 1 unit of inventory per time period

The best ordering policies (phenotypes) after playing the game for a number of time periods (35—100) are retained for evolving better policies in future generations.

Use of Grammars

To apply GE, a BNF grammar is defined, representing ordering policy choices that an agent can have. A grammar can be represented by the 4-tuple (N, T, P, S), where N is the set of non-terminals, T is the set of terminals, P is a set of production rules and S is a start symbol which is a member of N. When there are multiple productions that can be applied to an element of N, the choices are delimited with the '|' symbol. An example of a BNF grammar used in finding optimal ordering policies is:

```
N    =    {<agent>, <policy>,
<op>, <int>, <var>},
T    =    {x, +, -, 0, 1, 2, 3,
4, 5, 6, 7, 8, 9, 10, 11, 12, 13, 14,
15, 16, 17, 18, 19, 20},
S    =    {<agent>},
```

and P can be represented as:

```
<agent>    ::= <policy><policy><pol
icy><policy>
<policy>    ::= <var>|<var><op><int>
|<policy><op>(<var><op><int>)
```

Table 2. Summary of production rules and number of choices available for each rule. e.g., production rule B has 3 possible choices (1) <var>, (2) <var><op><int> and (3) <policy><op>(<var><op><int>)

Rule	*Number of Choices*
A	1
B	3
C	2
D	21
E	1

```
<op>            ::=          +|-
<int>           ::= 0|1|2|3|4|5|6|7|8|9|
    10|11|12|13|14|15|16|17|18|19|20
<var>           ::= x
```

which can be rewritten as in Example 1.

Table 2 shows the production rules and choices available for each rule.

S is mapped onto terminals by sequentially reading an 8-bit codon from the genotype and converting this to an integer value *c*, from which an appropriate production rule is selected by the mapping:

Rule:= $c \pmod{r}$.

Here, *r* is the number of rule choices for the current non-terminal symbol.

During the genotype to phenotype mapping process, individuals may run out of codons; in this case the *wrap* operator is applied which re-uses the codon string, starting with the leftmost codon to determine the next rule to be selected. Each time the same codon is expressed, the same integer value is given; however, depending on the current non-terminal to which it is applied, it may result in a different production rule. Each time a given individual is mapped from its genotype to its phenotype, the same output is generated, since the same choices are made each time. An incomplete mapping can occur even after several wrappings; thus, an upper bound is placed on the number of wrappings allowed.

Mapping Process Example: Beer Game Ordering Policy

Consider the binary string (genotype):

```
11111000 11110111 00100111 00101111
10110101 10000101 00010010 (DNA)
```

Converting this bitstring into an integer codon string, where each codon is 8 bits, gives:

```
248 247 39 47 181 133 18 (RNA)
```

As there is only one production rule for the start symbol <agent>, it is automatically replaced and no codons are used. The ordering policy becomes:

```
<policy><policy><policy><policy>
```

Taking the leftmost non-terminal <policy> (representing the ordering policy for the Retailer agent) there are 3 possible replacements:

```
<var> | <var><op><int> |
<policy><op>(<var><op><int>)
```

The codon being read is 248. Now 248 $\equiv 2 \pmod 3$ so 2 is selected from rule B, and applying the mapping function gives <policy><op>(<var><op><int>). The ordering policy becomes:

```
<policy><op>(<var><op><int>)<policy><
policy><policy>
```

Again, reading the leftmost non-terminal <policy> and reading the next codon to the right, 247, we have 247 $\equiv 1 \pmod 3$ so 1 is selected from rule B. Applying the mapping function gives <var><op><int>. The ordering policy becomes:

```
<var><op><int><op>(<var><op><int>)<po
licy><policy><policy>
```

The next leftmost non-terminal <var> has only one possible choice, x, giving:

```
x<op><int><op>(<var><op><int>)<policy
><policy><policy>
```

The next leftmost non-terminal <op> has 2 possible choices "+", "-". The next available codon value, 39 $\equiv 1 \pmod 2$ selects 1 from rule C, giving "-". The ordering policy becomes:

```
x-<int><op>(<var><op><int>)<policy><p
olicy><policy>
```

The next leftmost non-terminal <int> has 21 possible choices 0, 1, …, 20. The next available codon value, 47 $\equiv 5 \pmod{21}$ selects 5 from rule D, so the ordering policy becomes:

Table 3. This ordering policy (phenotype) recommends that 13 units are ordered each time period by each agent. This example is not the best policy discovered by GE

Agent	*Ordering Policy*
Retailer	x-5-(x-18)
Wholesaler	x-5-(x-18)
Distributor	x-5-(x-18)
Factory	x-5-(x-18)

```
x-5<op>(<var><op><int>)<policy><polic
y><policy>
```

The next leftmost non-terminal, <op>, has 2 possible choices "+", "-". The next available codon value, 181 ≡ 1 (mod 2) selects 1 from rule C, giving "-". The ordering policy becomes:

```
x-5-(<var><op><int>)<policy><policy>
<policy>
```

Continuing thus, the next (<var><op><int>) evaluates to (x-18), giving

```
x-5-(x-18)<policy><policy><policy>
```

At this stage, the mapping process has generated an ordering policy for the Retailer agent; all other agents' policies are generated similarly, resulting in the complete phenotype (set of ordering policies) in Table 3. By coincidence, all of the codon values were used in generating the Retailer policy. The wrap operator is applied and the next codon used (to start the Wholesaler policy) is the leftmost codon, 248.

Once all agents' policies have been generated, the fitness of this individual's phenotype is estimated, by running a Beer Game simulation with these policies (100 times for statistical significance) and using Equation (1).

Demand Distributions

Standard demand distributions are used (Chen, 1999; Chen & Samroengraja, 2000; Kimbrough et al., 2002; Sparling, 2002; Kleinau & Thonemann, 2004):

- Uniform on [0,15]
- Poisson, mean 10 (slow demand)
- Normal, mean 50, standard deviation 10 (strong demand)

To better deal with stochastic demand, some grammars used provide agents with forecasting techniques and the ability to use their own historical demand data when generating ordering policies.

Grammars

A significant potential advantage of GE is that (in contrast to GA) the structure of the ordering policy does not have to be known a priori for encoding purposes.

Four grammars, of increasing complexity, were used (see Appendix for full Backus-Naur forms):

Grammar 1

$x + y$ rule

Grammar 2

more complex, e.g., $x + y - (x + z)$, etc.

Grammar 3

allows use of

- H(l), historical demand from time periods $t-l, \ldots, t$ (current time): the parameter l is the time lag
- M(s), Moving Average (MA), with one parameter s, the smoother
- S(α), Simple Exponential Smoothing (SES) with one smoothing parameter, α

Grammar 4

uses **if** … **else** statement & selection from Grammars 1—3.

Results

Five experiments (0, 1, 2, 3, 4) were conducted to determine the efficiency of GE's ordering policies in minimising total supply chain cost. All costs are given per unit per time period. Because of lack of space, some other experiments conducted are not described. Experimental results are compared with an Integer Programming (IP) approach using branch and bound, where meaningful.

Experiment 0 (split into three parts, 0a, 0b and 0c) is used to validate the GE approach by comparing GE-GA results with the Beer Game results of Kimbrough et al. (2001, 2002); O'Donnell et al. (2006).

Table 4. Beer Game benchmarking: experimental parameters

Beer Game parameters	
Number of time periods played	35
Inventory holding cost	1
Backorder cost	2
GE and GA parameters	
Number of generations	30
Population size	500
Crossover rate	0.87
Mutation rate	0.03
GE-specific parameters	
Pruning rate	0.01
Duplication rate	0.01
Generation gap	0.9
Codon size (bits)	8
Min codons	5
Max codons	10
Max wrappings	10

Experiments 1—4 compare GA, QIGA, GE-GA and GE-QIGA on normally and Poisson distributed customer demand and constant lead times. The variables over these four experiments are the supply chain configuration and/or inventory capacity, and — to an extent — the choice of GE grammars used.

Experiment 0a—c Parameter Values

Parameter values are as used by Kimbrough et al. (2001, 2002) unless otherwise stated; the exception is the population size: Kimbrough et al. (2001, 2002) used a population of 1000 whereas the experiments presented in this section use a population size of 500 unless otherwise stated. A summary of the parameters for the Beer Game and the evolutionary algorithms are given in Table 4.

The initial values for inventory, units on order, and units in the pipeline are the same as in the Beer Game board game setup (Sterman, 1989); see Figure 3. Results are presented in tables with headings as in Table 5.

Experiment 0a

Experiment 0a tests if GE-GA can discover the optimal "1—1" ordering policy as discovered by both the IP and GA, using the classic deterministic Beer Game setup (customer demand of 4 units

Table 5. Experimental result table headings

Heading	*Meaning*
Method	Algorithm name (e.g., IP, GA, GE-GA)
Grammar	Grammar used (where applicable)
Min	Best solution (lowest cost) over all generations
Max	Worst solution (highest cost) over all generations
Mean	Mean of the best solutions over all generations
Std Dev	Standard deviation of the best solutions over all generations
Rate	Occurrence rate of the best solution over all generations

for the first 4 time periods followed by 8 units from time period 5 onwards). The GA found the optimal "1—1" policy 60% of the time resulting in a total supply chain cost of 312.

GE-GA with Grammar 1 is capable of discovering the "*x* + *y*" ordering policies described by Kimbrough et al. (2001, 2002) and O'Donnell et al. (2006). Using Grammar 1, GE-GA found the optimal solution in all generations. Table 6 indicates that GE-GA is a more efficient algorithm than GA when facing deterministic demand and lead times.

The optimal policy discovered by all algorithms was an "*x* − 0" (i.e., "1—1") policy.

Experiment 0b

In Experiment 0b, customer demand comes from a uniform distribution on [0, 15], identical in setup and initial conditions to that of Kimbrough et al. (2001, 2002) and O'Donnell et al. (2006). The best solution found using IP gave an overall supply chain cost of 2,816. The GA found a better solution of 1,814 in 50% of generations using an ordering policy "*x* + 1" for each agent, i.e., each time period, the order placed with the immediate (upstream) supplier is got by adding 1 to the order received from the immediate (downstream) customer. See Table 7.

Using Grammar 1, GE-GA was also able to find the "*x* + 1" policy in all generations, indicating that GE-GA is a more efficient algorithm than GA even when demand is stochastic. Using Grammar 2, GE-GA found a more efficient ordering policy "*x* + 9 - (*x* - 1)" for each agent in 93% of the generations with a total cost of 480. This policy states that each agent orders 10 units per time period regardless of orders received from his/her immediate customers. Given that the demand distribution is uniform (stationary data), the mean demand is a good predictor of future demand (Makridakis et al., 1998). The mean customer demand is 8.74 (the nearest integer is 9). If GE-GA used the mean customer demand of 9 for all agents, the resulting total cost would be 900, as opposed to using an order of 10 units each time period giving a total of 480: thus GE was able to find a better solution.

Experiment 0c

In this experiment, stochastic lead times are also used, from a uniform distribution on [0, 4], identical to that of Kimbrough et al. (2001, 2002).

Table 6. Experiment 0a results

Method	*Grammar*	*Min*	*Max*	*Mean*	*Std Dev*	*Rate*
IP		312				
GA		312	5607	1590.87	1908.96	60.00%
GE-GA	1	312	312	312.00	0.00	100.00%

Table 7. Experiment 0b results

Method	*Grammar*	*Min*	*Max*	*Mean*	*Std Dev*	*Rate*
IP		2816				
GA		1814	9011	3177.43	2027.68	50.00%
GE-GA	1	1814	1814	1814.00	0.00	100.00%
GE-GA	2	480	1377	523.90	178.42	93.33%

Table 8. Experiment 0c results

Method	*Grammar*	*Min*	*Max*	*Mean*	*Std Dev*	*Rate*
IP		2555				
GA		2555	7818	3772.17	1516.19	36.67%
GE-GA	1	2555	3024	2648.93	74.19	6.67%
GE-GA	2	3060	3071	3069.90	3.36	10.00%
GE-GA	3	5560	5945	5641.30	150.69	76.67%

The best solution found using IP, an overall cost of 2,555, was also discovered by GA (37% of the time) resulting from an ordering policy of "$x + 1$" for the Retailer, Wholesaler and Factory while the Distributor uses an "$x + 2$" rule. Using Grammar 1, GE-GA found the same solution as GA and IP in 7% of the generations; however, GE using Grammars 2 and 3 with the parameters in Table 4 was unable to find a comparable or better solution. See Table 8.

Figure 7. Experiment 1. Poisson: Fixed (top left), Tuned (top right); Normal: Fixed (bottom left), Tuned (bottom right)

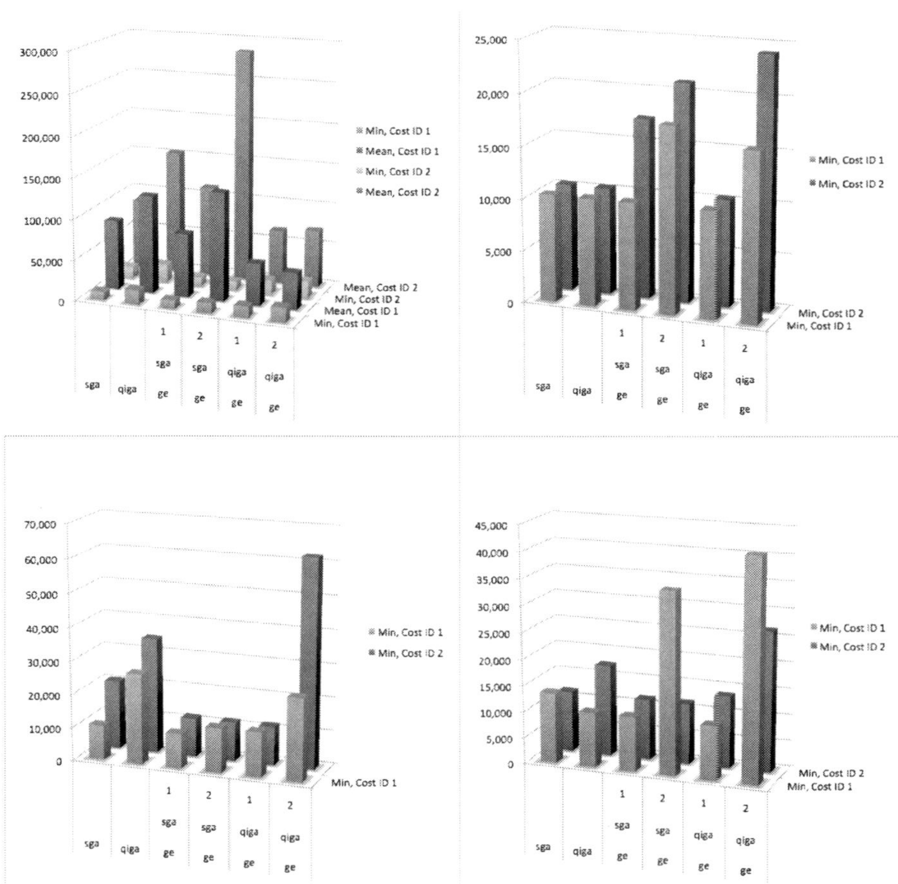

Experiments 1—4 Setup and Parameter Values

Each experiment is run with customer demand drawn from (*a*) Normal(50, 10) and (*b*) Poisson(10) distribution, rounded to the nearest integer. If negative demand occurs, we re-sample to ensure positive integer demand. In each experiment, GA, QIGA, GE-GA (two grammars) and GE-QIGA (two grammars) are compared. Results are given in Figures 7—11; in these, sga denotes (Standard) GA, and each run of GE gives the search engine (sga or qiga) and grammar (1—4) used.

Cost Values Used

Each experiment is run for two choices of sets of cost values comprising

- Holding cost (*HC*);
- Holding cost excess (*HC* excess), meaningful only in the capacitated inventory case (Configuration C) where the need arises to use extra more expensive inventory storage; and
- Backorder cost (*BC*), used in all experiments

with values as in Table 9. The sets are referred to as Cost IDs 1 and 2.

Table 9. Sets of cost values

Cost ID	*HC*	*HC excess*	*BC*
1	1	2	5
2	1	5	10

Parameter Selection

'Good' parameter values are selected by cyclic coordinate search on a 5-dimensional grid with coordinates as in Table 10.

(No more than 50 generations were allowed, to keep computational effort to a reasonable level.) We optimise along dimensions in the order Population size, No. Generations, Crossover probability, Mutation probability, No. Time Periods. This is done separately for each algorithm, on each of Configurations A and B, to give the best chance of finding good solutions (we use the "quality of solution" measure of algorithm performance). These runs are called "Tuned" below.

To aid comparison, runs were also done with the same values for each algorithm (called "Fixed" below): 30 generations with population size 100.

Layouts

Experimental setups are in Table 11.

Each of the four experiments is run for:

- both "Fixed" and "Tuned" parameter values;
- two Cost IDs, 1 and 2;
- two demand distributions, Poisson(10) and Normal(50,10); and
- six combinations of EA and/or grammar, namely, GA, QIGA, GE-GA, and GE-QIGA (these last two with the same two

Table 10. Configurations used in experiments

Generations	*Pop. size*	*Crossover Prob.*	*Mutation Prob.*	*Time Periods*
30	100	0.7	0.005	100
50	500	0.8	0.010	150
	1000	0.9	0.100	200

grammars; standalone GA and QIGA do not use grammars).

This gives 4 × 2 × 2 × 2 × 6 = 192 runs, each producing up to 50 generations of populations of policies. Each policy's performance is tested on 100 supply chain simulations for statistical significance.

Parameter Values

The parameters used are given in Table 12.

Experiment 1

Figure 7 (top left) shows Experiment 1 minimum and mean costs found for Poisson demand (fixed parameters), for CostIDs 1 and 2.

For each CostID, GA and GE-GA have the best min; but GE-QIGA has best mean. For each algorithm, the min costs found are approximately the same for both Cost IDs; whereas, the mean costs for Cost ID 2 are somewhat higher (substantially higher in the case of GE-GA) than those for Cost ID 1. The large difference between min and mean is typical of all experiments; thus, means are omitted in all subsequent diagrams (bar Experiment 2 for Poisson demand). Also, all subsequent diagrams show CostIDs 1 and 2 together, for comparison.

Figure 7 (top right) shows minimum costs found for Poisson demand (tuned parameters). All approaches, bar GE with grammar 2, perform more or less equally well. (For CostID 2, GE-GA with Grammar 1 also has worse performance.)

Figure 7 (bottom) shows minimum costs found for Normal demand.

With fixed parameters: for each CostID, all approaches, bar QIGA and GE-QIGA with Grammar 2, perform about equally well (GA on CostID 2 is also worse than other approaches). With tuned parameters, results are more mixed: most approaches do equally well, except for GA, GE (Grammar 2) on CostID 1; and QIGA, GE-QIGA (Grammar 2) on CostID 2.

Overall, GE with Grammar 1 always outperforms Grammar 2.

Experiment 2

Figure 8 shows Experiment 2 minimum costs found for Poisson and Normal demand, both fixed and tuned parameters. Means for the Poisson fixed parameter case are also shown.

For Poisson demand: as with Experiment 1, GE-QIGA (both Grammars 1 and 2) has much lower mean values than any other approach. We find two instances where Grammar 2 outperforms Grammar 1 on min cost (Fixed, GE-QIGA on CostID 1; and Tuned, GE-GA on CostID 2) but in all other cases, Grammar 1 is superior. For tuned parameters, in most cases QIGA and GE-QIGA are somewhat (5—20%) better than GA and GE-GA, respectively.

For Normal demand: performance of all approaches for all CostIDs is roughly comparable, except that for GE, Grammar 1 outperforms Grammar 2 in all cases (usually by a large margin). QIGA and GE-QIGA are somewhat (5—20%) worse than GA and GE-GA, respectively.

Table 11. Layouts of Experiments 1—4

Expt.	*Config*	*Layout*	*Capacitated?*	*Cost ID*	*Demand*	*Grammars*
1	A	Beer Game: Figure 1	No	1 and 2	Poisson, Normal	1 and 2
2	B	Tree: Figure 2	No	1 and 2	Poisson, Normal	1 and 2
3	C	Tree: Figure 2	Yes: dmd×2	1 and 2	Poisson, Normal	2 and 3
4	C	Tree: Figure 2	Yes: dmd×4	1 and 2	Poisson, Normal	3 and 4

Table 12. Experimental parameters ad values

Configuration	
Number Of Time Periods	100
Initialisation Period	50
Test Period	50
Initial Goods In Pipeline	0
Initial Inventory	0
Lead time	2
Number Of Agents	4 (arranged differently according to config)
Initial Rand Num Gen Seed	System time
EA Global: common to GA and QIGA	
Number Of Generations	30 or 50
Population Size	100 or 500
Genome Length	24 bits (6 bits per agent)
Crossover Rate	0.8
Mutation Rate	0.01
EA Specific: GA Only	
Selection Method	Roulette
Genome Type	Fixed
EA Specific: QIGA Only	
Initial α	$1/\sqrt{2}$
Initial β	$1/\sqrt{2}$
EA Specific: GE Only	
Grammar	Grammars 1—4
Engine	GA, QIGA
Pruning Rate	0
Duplication Rate	0
Codon Size	8
Min no. of Codons	20
Max no. of Codons	30
Max no. of Wrappings	10

Overall, GE with Grammar 1 outperforms Grammar 2, except in the two instances noted above; in other respects, all approaches have roughly similar performance.

Experiment 3

This had noticeable differences between the Poisson and Normal demand cases.

Figure 9 shows minimum costs found for Poisson and Normal demands (both fixed and tuned parameters).

For Poisson demand: other than the somewhat worse performance of QIGA in (Fixed, CostID 1) and (Tuned, CostID 2), all approaches give roughly equal quality solutions.

For Normal demand: GE with Grammar 3 in all cases gives a quality of solution between 3 and 10 times worse than GE with Grammar 2, regardless of search engine used, or CostID. Other than this, all approaches are of similar quality (bar QIGA and GE-QIGA in the Fixed setting).

Experiment 4

The main finding here is an enormous difference between the performances of Grammars 3 and 4: the ability to use a conditional statement in the grammar leads to an order of magnitude improvement in solution quality.

Figure 10 shows minimum costs found for Poisson and Normal demand (both fixed and tuned parameters).

For Poisson demand: all approaches have roughly equal performance, except for GE with Grammar 4 (both GA and QIGA search engines), which is between 2.5 and 5 times *better* than all the others.

For Normal demand: all approaches have roughly equal performance, except for GE with Grammar 3 (both GA and QIGA search engines), which is between 10 and 17 times *worse* than all the others.

Overall, GE-GA (Grammar 4) was best in all Fixed cases, and in Tuned Normal CostID 1; GE-QIGA (Grammar 4) was best for Tuned parameters and Poisson demand; QIGA was best in Tuned Normal CostID 2.

Figure 8. Experiment 2. Poisson: Fixed (top left), Tuned (top right); Normal: Fixed (bottom left), Tuned (bottom right)

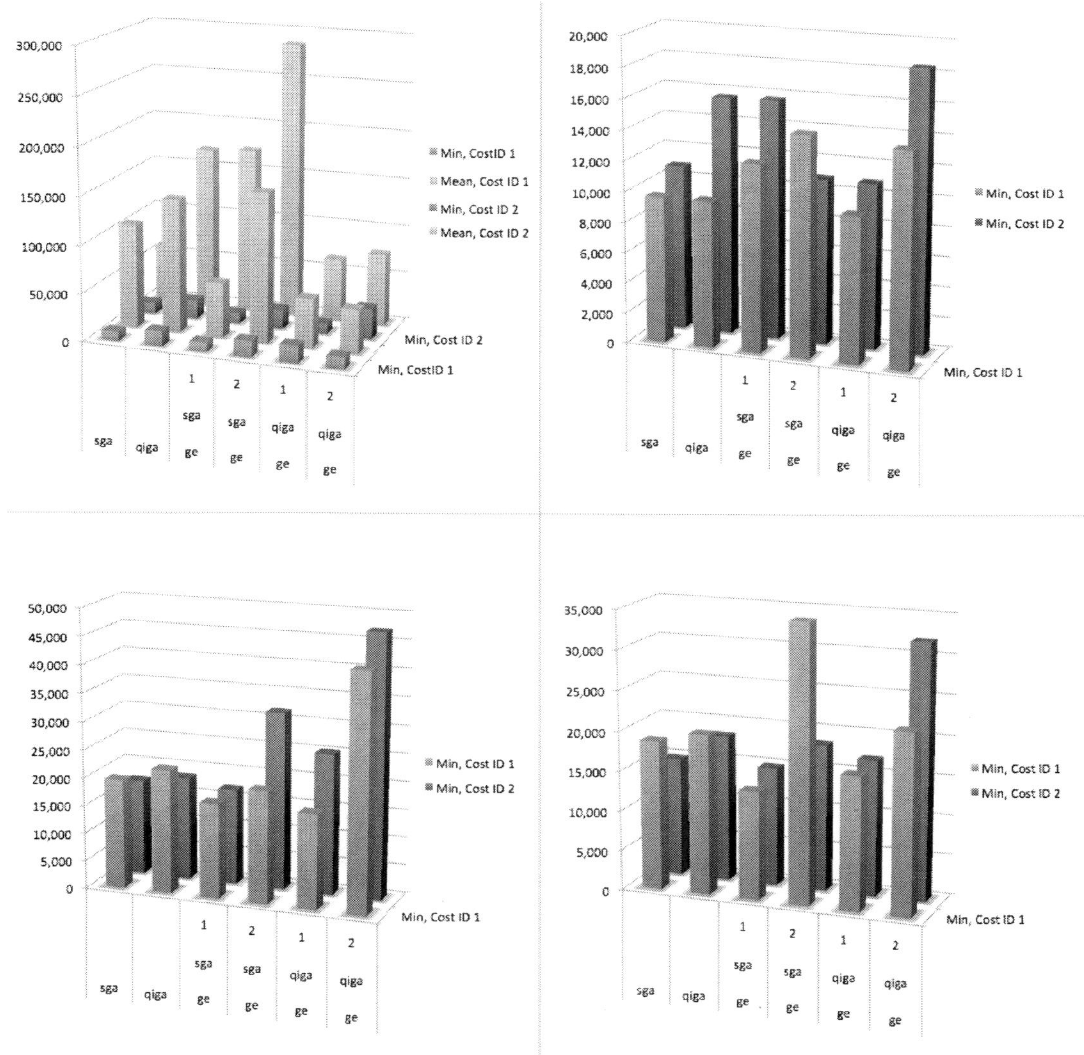

DISCUSSION

Experiment 0

For purposes of benchmarking, Experiment 0 is identical in setup to those of Kimbrough et al. (2001, 2002) and O'Donnell et al. (2006) on ordering policy generation in the Beer Game. It shows that GE with GA as search engine is capable of matching or improving on existing GA results for deterministic or uniformly distributed demand, and even with uniformly distributed lead times; however, in the last case, the choice of grammar is very important.

This experiment gives some evidence that we should use the simplest possible grammar that can find good/best solutions. Experiment 0a, using the simplest Grammar 1, always finds the optimal 1—1 policy for deterministic demand. In Experiment 0b a slightly more complex gram-

Figure 9. Experiment 3. Poisson: Fixed (top left), Tuned (top right); Normal: Fixed (bottom left), Tuned (bottom right)

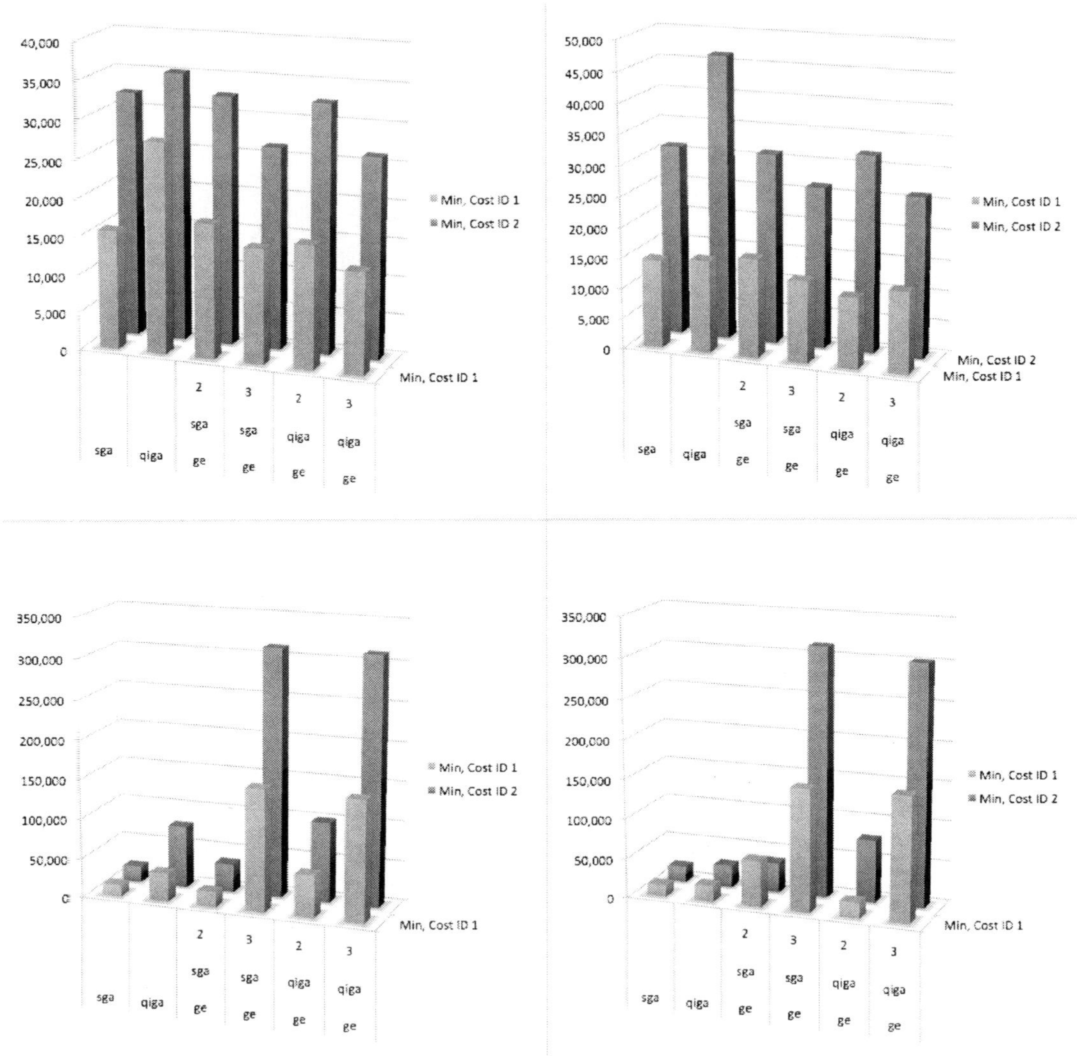

mar, capable of evolving constants, was able to evolve a policy of ordering slightly more than mean demand, which had least cost over a finite time horizon. In Experiment 0c, even though three grammars of varying complexity were tested, the simplest (Grammar 1) performed best. The effect of stochastic lead times is unclear, and is being investigated further.

QIGA and GE-QIGA were also benchmarked against existing results, and found to perform satisfactorally, but details are not included here for reasons of space.

Experiments 1—4

These experiments go beyond benchmarking and extend EA approaches to supply chain topologies and properties not previously considered, namely, arborescent supply chains and capacitated inventory.

Figure 10. Experiment 4. Poisson: Fixed (top left), Tuned (top right); Normal: Fixed (bottom left), Tuned (bottom right)

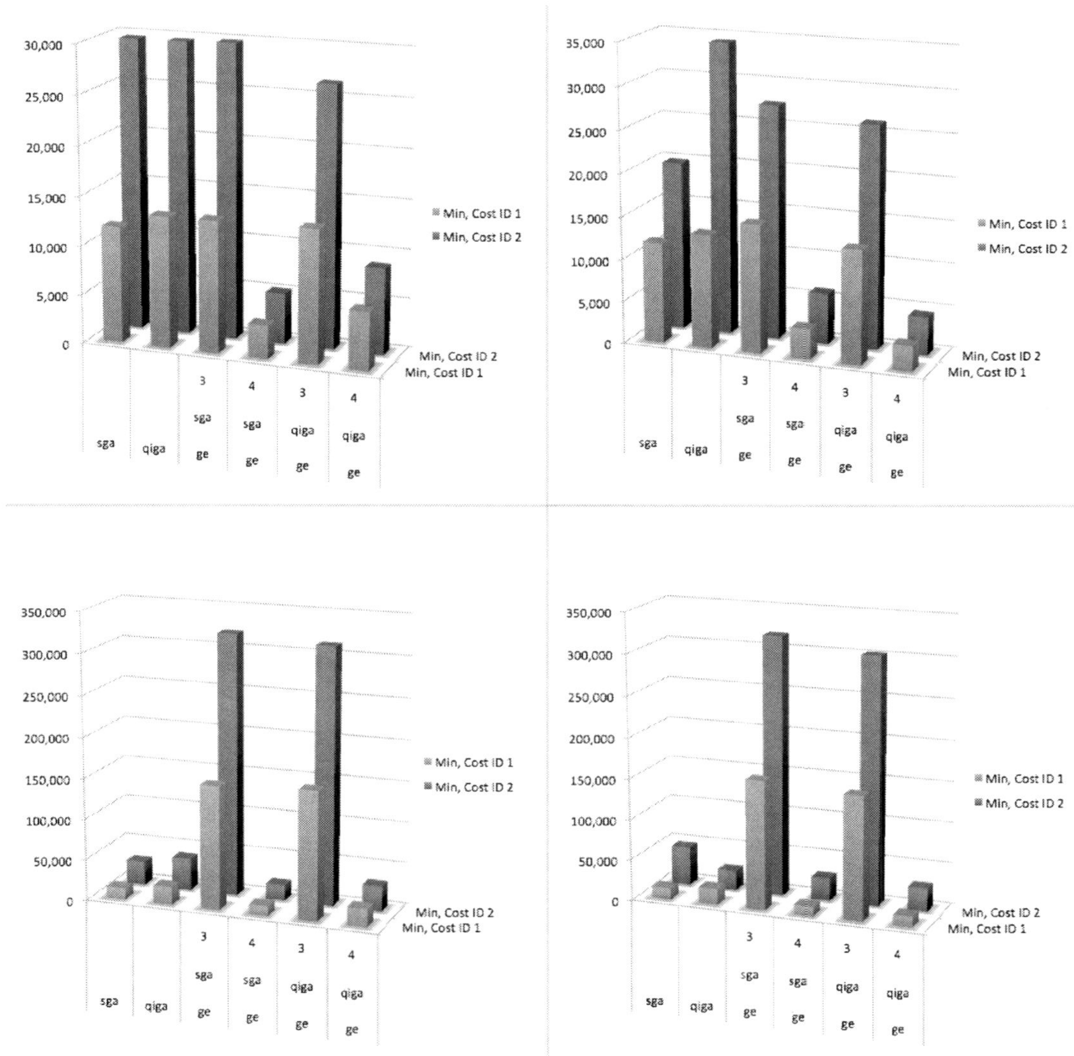

Fixed vs. Tuned Parameters

Some results were the same in both these settings and lead to certain conclusions, of varying strength.

- On *mean* cost, GE-QIGA consistently outperforms other approaches, by a factor of 2 to 12 (we have only shown this on some charts but it holds throughout). Given the large dispersion of costs in all approaches and that GE-QIGA is competitive or sometimes best (provided parameters are tuned), it appears that GE-QIGA gives faster convergence of the population as a whole, while not suffering from premature convergence. Thus GE-GIGA may require fewer generations to achieve adequate convergence. Further investigation is required.
- Throughout Experiment 1, and in 14 of 16 cases in Experiment 2, GE with Grammar

1 outperforms Grammar 2. This indicates that more complexity in a grammar may not lead to better performance, and highlights the importance of using a grammar suited to the problem.

- There do not seem to be significant differences between Experiments 1 and 2 in performance pattern of approaches; thus, we find no evidence that supply network topology has an impact (both networks considered have four players). Further investigation is required on a wider range of topologies and other variables, before any stronger conclusions can be reached on the effect of network configuration.
- In Experiment 3, apart from two isolated cases of QIGA, all approaches give about equal quality solutions for Poisson demand. However, for Normal demand, GE with Grammar 3 in all cases gives a quality of solution about an order of magnitude *worse*, even though Grammar 3 allows use of historical data and forecasting approaches. This is distinct from the potential extra computation effort associated with Grammar 3, and — as with Experiments 1 and 2 above — indicates that more complexity in a grammar may actually be detrimental to solution quality.
- Experiment 3's noticeable differences, between the Poisson and Normal demand cases, indicate that demand distribution should be taken into account when designing an EA approach to order policy generation.
- In Experiment 4, the inclusion of conditional tests in Grammar 4 compared to Grammar 3 seems to be a crucial ability, given the large difference in solution quality (a factor of between 2.5 and 17) of GE using these two grammars (Figures 11—11).
- Comparison of Grammar 3 to Grammar 2 (in Experiment 3) and to Grammar 4 (in Experiment 4) leads us *not* to recommend Grammar 3 (allowing use of Historical Information, SES, and Moving Averages), as it may be significantly worse than both a simpler grammar (2) and a grammar with conditionals (4).
- In Experiments 2—4, we would expect the best policies generated for agents 1, 2 and 3 to be the same, as there is a symmetry among these three agents in tier 2 of the supply network in Figure 2. However, in Experiment 4 (and, to a lesser extent, 2 and 3), we notice some policy variation: see Tables 13 and 14.

A tentative explanation is that possibly many policies have approximately equal fitness (the fitness check, being a mean over 100 simulation runs, is necessarily stochastic). This may indicate wide global optima in the search landscape, and many acceptable solutions. Also, agents may have identical demand distributions, yet experience different demand in different samples. (We would not, a priori, expect similar policies in Beer Game layouts, as each agent in a linear supply chain experiences qualitatively different inputs.)

However, some results were different and are discussed in more detail in the following two subsections. Table 13 summarises results for fixed parameter values, while Table 14 does the same for where GA and QIGA are allowed to use (tuned) optimal parameter values. In both tables some column headings are shrunk to fit, namely, *E*: *Experiment*; *D*: *Demand*; *ID*: *CostID*. The *Best Policy* column gives the (semicolon-separated) policies evolved for the four agents, in order left-right then by top-bottom. If the *Best EA* is a type of GE, then the number(s) after it indicate which grammar performed best.

Fixed Parameters

In Experiments 1 and 2, GE-GA (Grammar 1) is always (at least joint) best. GA also does well in

Table 13. Best policies found and EAs: Fixed parameters

E	*D*	*ID*	*Min*	*Best Policy*	*Best EA(s)*
1	P	1	10332	x+1;x+1;x+1;x+1;	ga, ge-ga 1
	N	1	10487	x+2;x+2;x+2;x+2;	ga, ge-ga 1
	P	2	10332	x+1;x+1;x+1;x+1;	ge-ga 1&2
	N	2	11597	x+2;x+2;x+2;x+2;	ge-ga 1&2, ge-qiga 1
2	P	1	9608	x+1;x+1;x+1;x+1;	ga, ge-ga 1
	N	1	16964	x+1;x+2;x+2;x+5;	ge-ga/qiga 1
	P	2	10878	x+1;x+1;x+1;x+1;	ga, ge-ga&qiga 1
	N	2	17062	x+1;x+2;x+2;x+5;	ga, ge-ga 1
3	P	1	13426	M(3);M(5);M(5);M(5);	ge-qiga 3
	N	1	14270	+2;x+2;x+2;x+5;	ga
	P	2	26276	M(3);M(5);M(5);M(5);	ge-qiga 3
	N	2	19834	x+2;x+2;x+2;x+5;	ga
4	P	1	3444	if (M(5)≥x) {return M(3)} else {return M(3)};	ge-ga 4
				if (M(3)≥S(0.8)) {return H(9)} else {return S(0.4)};	
				if (M(5)≤M(3)) {return M(3)} else {return H(9)};	
				if (M(4)≥H(1)) {return M(2)} else {return H(1)};	
	N	1	11967	if (S(0.4)≤x) {return M(2)} else {return M(5)};	ga, gega 4
				if (M(3)<x) {return x} else {return M(2)};	
				if (x<H(8)) {return S(0.7)} else {return x};	
				if (x≥M(4)) {return x} else {return H(4)};	
	P	2	5143	if (S(0.9)≤M(3)) {return x} else {return H(5)};	ge-ga
				if (M(3)=M(2)) {return H(6)} else {return S(0.7)};	
				if (H(8)<M(3)) {return x} else {return M(4)};	
				if (H(3)≥x) {return H(9)} else {return x};	
	N	2	18675	if (x≤M(4)) {return S(0.2)} else {return x};	ga, ge-ga 4
				if (S(0.9)<H(9)) {return x} else {return S(0.9)};	
				if (S(0.3)>M(2)) {return H(1)} else {return x};	
				if (S(0.2)≥x) {return S(0.6)} else {return x};	

many cases. In Experiment 3, GE-QIGA (Grammar 3) wins on Poisson demand, while GA wins on Normal demand. In Experiment 4, GE-GA (Grammar 4) is always best, with GA equally good on Normal demand. See Table 13.

On average, with parameters not tuned to best performance, QIGA takes about twice as much computational effort as GA to reach a solution of equal quality, particularly when used in conjunction with GE. We posit that the QIGA code implementation is not as efficient or as tightly integrated with GE as is the standard GA search engine. Work is underway to streamline the QIGA code and GE interface.

Tuned Parameters

Here, QIGA and GE-QIGA perform more strongly (particularly on Poisson demand), apparently sensitive to parameter choice. The only Poisson

Table 14. Best policies found and EAs: Tuned parameters

E	*D*	*ID*	*Min*	*Best Policy*	*Best EA(s)*
1	P	1	10332	x+1;x+1;x+1;x+1;	ga, qiga,
					ge-ga 1, ge-qiga 1
	N	1	10487	x+2;x+2;x+2;x+2;	qiga, ge-ga, ge-qiga
	P	2	10332	x+1;x+1;x+1;x+1;	ga, qiga, ge-qiga 1
	N	2	11597	x+2;x+2;x+2;x+2;	ga, ge-ga 1&2
2	P	1	9608	x+1;x+1;x+1;x+1;	ga, qiga, ge-qiga 1
	N	1	13577	x+2;x+2;x+2;x+5;	ge-ga 1
	P	2	10878	x+1;x+1;x+1;x+1;	ga, ge-ga 1
	N	2	14904	x+2;x+2;x+2;x+6;	ga, ge-ga 1
3	P	1	11586	x+4-(x-6);x+(x-9);x;x+1;	ge-qiga 2
	N	1	14270	x+2;x+2;x+2;x+5;	ga
	P	2	26276	M(3);M(5);M(5);M(5);	ge-qiga 3
	N	2	19834	x+2;x+2;x+2;x+5;	ga
4	P	1	2985	if (M(4)<H(6)) {return H(5)} else {return M(4)};	ge-qiga 4
				if (S(0.7)=H(2)) {return H(8)} else {return M(3)};	
				if (M(5)=S(0.4)) {return H(9)} else {return M(4)};	
				if (S(0.8)>S(0.3)) {return x} else {return H(5)};	
	N	1	11554	if (S(0.6)<x) {return x} else {return H(7)};	ge-ga 4
				if (H(7)≤S(0.8)) {return S(0.5)} else {return H(5)};	
				if (H(3)>S(0.6)) {return H(7)} else {return M(2)};	
				if (H(6)≤x) {return x} else {return H(3)};	
	P	2	4519	if (x≤S(0.3)) {return H(4)} else {return M(3)};	ge-qiga 4
				if (S(0.3)=S(0.7)) {return M(5)} else {return M(4)};	
				if (M(3)≤M(2)) {return M(5)} else {return M(4)};	
				if (M(2)≤S(0.3)) {return H(4)} else {return M(3)};	
	N	2	23376	x+2;x+3;x+3;x+6;	qiga

case where neither QIGA nor GE-QIGA is the best approach is Experiment 2, CostID 2. QIGA also is best on Experiment 4, CostID 2, Normal. GA and GE-GA also perform strongly, particularly on Normal demand. See Table 14.

A pattern here is that, by the "quality of solution" metric, GA & GE-GA combinations perform better with fast moving (Normal) demand, whereas QIGA & GE-QIGA work better with slow moving (Poisson) demand. However, QIGA is 3—9 times slower than GA (including when used with GE), due to larger population size chosen during initial parameter search. A possible contributory factor to this is inefficiency of the QIGA implementation and GE-QIGA interface, as mentioned above.

CONCLUSIONS AND FUTURE RESEARCH DIRECTIONS

This research addresses the problem of developing efficient supply chain ordering policies and extends the Grammatical Evolution work of Phelan & McGarraghy (2007) to the contexts of stochastic demand and lead times, arborescence and capacitated inventory. GE is benchmarked against existing GA results (Kimbrough et al., 2001, 2002; O'Donnell et al., 2006) on the Beer Game.

Our results give evidence that GE, with an appropriate grammar, can outperform other EA approaches over a range of supply network topologies and constraints such as capacitation. In all experiments conducted, except Experiment 3 with normal demand, GE discovers equal or more efficient ordering policies (in cost reduction terms). In some configurations, e.g., Experiment 4, the improvement is almost an order of magnitude. The findings also highlight a significant advantage of GE over GA: the ability of GE to construct solutions based on a set of building blocks or rules that govern the solutions produced. As noted earlier, for purposes of adequate encoding of solutions, GE requires from the user less knowledge of the solution structure than does a GA.

In summary, the results confirm the high efficiency of the GE intelligent metaheuristic. However, this is qualified by the observation that GE's ability to produce more efficient policies depends on the grammar definition; this dependency underlines the vital rôle grammar selection (O'Neill & Ryan, 2003; Brabazon & O'Neill, 2006) has on the algorithm's results. An interesting finding is that in simple cases, such as the Beer Game with deterministic demand where a 1—1 policy is provably optimal, a grammar that is rich enough to capture that policy *but no richer* is to be preferred (Experiment 0). This indicates the value of building domain knowledge into the grammar, where such knowledge is available.

The relative simplicity and generic nature of GE, combined with the possibility of a user being able to (at least partially) define a grammar based on domain knowledge and available tools, augurs well for GE's ability to support a decision support system for ordering.

QIGA and GE-QIGA yield some insightful results; notably on Poisson demand when allowed to use parameter values optimised for it; but also in some situations of fixed parameters and/or Normal demand. However, overall QIGA performance is relatively unimpressive compared to standard GA. It is hypothesised that this may be due to implementation issues, in particular its interface with GE: it is clear that this needs overhauling, and will be the subject of future work. Nevertheless, for mean cost, GE with a QIGA search engine consistently outperforms other approaches, sometimes by a factor of 10 or more. Though not the main focus of our work, this gives an interesting angle: the combination of these two new approaches seems to give faster convergence of the population as a whole, while maintaining enough diversity to avoid premature convergence. Future research will investigate this more closely.

Capacitation of inventory does not — on this evidence — greatly affect any approach's ability to generate useful policies; it seems to affect all equally, with some increase in total cost (as expected). No approach seems to outperform any other in Experiments 3—4 compared to 1—2. More work is needed here.

We have also investigated approaches not discussed here because of lack of space. Information sharing is a known mitigating factor of the Bullwhip effect (Lee et al., 1997a,b), and grammars incorporating this — where each agent has access to other agents' historical demand as well as its own — have been implemented and tested. Also, a recent real-valued QIGA (Cruz et al., 2006) and modifications thereof have been investigated.The effects of stochastic lead times have been studied too.

The supply chain structure examined in this chapter, while an improvement on existing models in that it incorporates tree structures, capacitated inventory and resulting cost, stockout cost and other enrichments, is still not truly reflective of complex supply chains. The research described here is being extended in a number of directions. Further enrichment of the supply chain simulation model in order to examine more complex supply networks — with stochastic lead times and additional constraints such as capacitated shipping, additional ordering costs, and service level agreements — is currently under investigation.

GE is ideally suited to examine these problems, given its grammar based approach. Current research includes ongoing development of new grammars to allow agents to use existing inventory policy models (e.g., periodic and continuous replenishment policies) similar to those of (Chan et al., 2006), with the exception that GE determines all the model parameters that can be compared with deterministic inventory policies. Grammars incorporating agent memory are being examined. Grammars are also being developed to determine what incentives (Chen, 1999) can be given to agents in a decentralised supply chain in order to minimise the total cost of the supply chain.

Conceivably, any search engine (e.g., particle swarm, as in Grammatical Swarm) that can operate on binary or integer strings could employ the GE mapping process to generate a program or policy; this is the subject of ongoing research.

Finally, the flexibility of GE gives hope that it may also be useful not only in determining inventory policy, but also in developing other policies, both strategic and operational, for location, production, and distribution. It is intended to also investigate these in this research programme.

ACKNOWLEDGMENT

The authors wish to thank the referees for their helpful comments which enhanced this chapter.

REFERENCES

Box, G., & Jenkins, G. (1970). *Time series analysis: Forecasting and control*. San Francisco: Holden-Day.

Brabazon, A., & O'Neill, M. (2006). *Biologically inspired algorithms for financial modelling*. Berlin, Heidelberg, Tokyo, New York: Springer-Verlag.

Chaharsooghi, S. K., Heydari, J., & Zegordi, S. H. (2008). A reinforcement learning model for supply chain ordering management: An application to the beer game. *Decision Support Systems*, *45*(4), 949–959. doi:10.1016/j.dss.2008.03.007

Chan, C.-C. H., Cheng, C.-B., & Huang, S.-W. (2006). Formulating ordering policies in a supply chain by genetic algorithm. *Int. J. Model. Simul.*, *26*(2), 129–136.

Chen, F. (1999). Decentralized supply chains subject to information delays. *Management Science*, *45*(9), 1076–1090. doi:10.1287/mnsc.45.8.1076

Chen, F., & Samroengraja, R. (2000). The stationary beer game. *Production and Operations Management*, *9*(1), 19–30. doi:10.1111/j.1937-5956.2000.tb00320.x

Christensen, S., & Oppacher, F. (2002). An analysis of Koza's computational effort statistic for genetic programming. In Foster, J. A., Lutton, E., Miller, J. F., Ryan, C., & Tettamanzi, A. (Eds.), *EuroGP* (*Vol. 2278*, pp. 182–191). Springer.

Coakley, J., & Drexler, J.A., J., Larson, E., & Kircher, A. (1998). Using a computer-based version of the beer game: Lessons learned. *Journal of Management Education*, *22*(3), 416. doi:10.1177/105256299802200311

Cooke, J. (1993). The $30 billion promise. *Traffic Management*, *32*, 57–59.

da Cruz, A., Vellasco, M., & Pacheco, M. (2006, 16-21 July). Quantum-inspired evolutionary algorithm for numerical optimization. In *Proceedings of the 2006 IEEE Congress on Evolutionary Computation (CEC 2006)* (pp. 9180-9187). Vancouver, Canada: IEEE Press.

Falcone, M. A., Lopes, H. S., & Coelho, L. D. S. (2008). Supply chain optimisation using evolutionary algorithms. *Int. J. Comput. Appl. Technol.*, *31*(3/4), 158–167. doi:10.1504/IJCAT.2008.018154

Fan, K., O'Sullivan, C., Brabazon, A., O'Neill, M., & McGarraghy, S. (2008). Calibration of the VGSSD Option Pricing Model using a Quantum-inspired Evolutionary Algorithm. In N. Nedjah, L. dos Santos Coelho, & L. de Macedo Mourelle (Eds.), Quantum inspired intelligent systems (pp. 133–153). Berlin, Heidelberg, Tokyo, New York: Springer-Verlag. doi:10.1007/978-3-540-78532-3_7doi:10.1007/978-3-540-78532-3_7

Forrester, J. W. (1958). Industrial dynamics: a major break though for decision-makers. *Harvard Business Review*, *36*(4), 37–66.

Forrester, J. W. (1961). *Industrial dynamics*. Cambridge, Mass.: Productivity Press, Wiley.

Gardner, E. S. (1985a). Exponential smoothing: The state of the art. *Journal of Forecasting*, *4*(1), 1–28. doi:10.1002/for.3980040103

Gardner, E. S. (1985b). Exponential smoothing: The state of the art — response. *Journal of Forecasting*, *4*(1), 37–38. doi:10.1002/for.3980040108

Goodwin, J., & Franklin, S.G., S. (1994). The beer distribution game: Using simulation to teach systems thinking. *Journal of Management Development*, *13*(8), 7–15. doi:10.1108/02621719410071937

Han, K.-H., & Kim, J.-H. (2002). Quantum-inspired evolutionary algorithm for a class of combinatorial optimization. *IEEE Transactions on Evolutionary Computation*, *6*(6), 580–593. doi:10.1109/TEVC.2002.804320

Han, K.-H., & Kim, J.-H. (2004). Quantum-inspired evolutionary algorithms with a new termination criterion, H_ε gate and two-phase scheme. *IEEE Transactions on Evolutionary Computation*, *8*(3), 156–169. doi:10.1109/TEVC.2004.823467

Jacobs, F. (2000). Playing the beer distribution game over the internet. *Production and Operations Management*, *9*(1), 31–39. doi:10.1111/j.1937-5956.2000.tb00321.x

Jarmain, W., & Fey, W. (1963). *Problems in industrial dynamics*. Cambridge, MA: The MIT Press.

Kimbrough, S. O., Wu, D. J., & Zhong, F. (2001). Computers play the beer game — can artificial agents manage supply chains? In *HICSS '01: Proceedings of the 34th Annual Hawaii International Conference on System Sciences (HICSS-34), volume 7* (pp. 2303-2312). Washington, DC, USA: IEEE Computer Society.

Kimbrough, S. O., Wu, D. J., & Zhong, F. (2002). Computers play the beer game: can artificial agents manage supply chains? *Decision Support Systems*, *33*(3), 323–333. doi:10.1016/S0167-9236(02)00019-2

Kleinau, P., & Thonemann, U. (2004, October). Deriving inventory-control policies with genetic programming. *OR-Spektrum*, *26*(4), 521–546. Retrieved from http://dx.doi.org/10.1007/s00291-004-0159-5. doi:10.1007/s00291-004-0159-5

Lee, H. L., Padmanabhan, V., & Whang, S. (1997a). The bullwhip effect in supply chains. *Sloan Management Review*, *38*(3), 93–102.

Lee, H. L., Padmanabhan, V., & Whang, S. (1997b). Information distortion in a supply chain: The bullwhip effect. *Management Science*, *43*(4), 546–558. Retrieved from http://dx.doi.org/10.2307/2634565. doi:10.1287/mnsc.43.4.546

Luke, S., & Panait, L. (2002). Is the perfect the enemy of the good? In Langdon, W. B. (Eds.), *GECCO* (pp. 820–828). New York: Morgan Kaufmann.

Makridakis, S., Wheelwright, S. C., & Hyndman, R. J. (1998). *Forecasting: Methods and applications* (3rd ed.). Chichester, UK-Hoboken, NJ: John Wiley & Sons.

Meadows, D. (2007). A brief and incomplete history of operational gaming in system dynamics. *System Dynamics Review*, *23*(2), 199–203. doi:10.1002/sdr.372

Moore, S., & DeMaagd, K. (2004). *Using a genetic program to search for supply chain reordering*. Berlin, Heidelberg, Tokyo, New York: Springer-Verlag.

Mosekilde, E., & Larsen, E. (1988). Deterministic chaos in the beer production-distribution model. *System Dynamics Review*, *4*(1-2), 131–147. doi:10.1002/sdr.4260040108

Narayanan, A., & Moore, M. (1996, May). Quantum-inspired genetic algorithms. In *Proceedings of IEEE International Conference on Evolutionary Computation* (pp. 61-66). IEEE Press.

Nienhaus, J., Ziegenbein, A., & Schoensleben, P. (2006). How human behaviour amplifies the bullwhip effect. a study based on the beer distribution game online. *Production Planning and Control*, *17*(6), 547–557. doi:10.1080/09537280600866587

O'Donnell, T., Maguire, L., McIvor, R., & Humphreys, P. (2006). Minimizing the bullwhip effect in a supply chain using genetic algorithms. *International Journal of Production Research*, *44*(8), 1523–1543. doi:10.1080/00207540500431347

O'Neill, M., & Ryan, C. (2001). Grammatical evolution. *IEEE Transactions on Evolutionary Computation*, *5*(4), 349–358. doi:10.1109/4235.942529

O'Neill, M., & Ryan, C. (2003). *Grammatical evolution: Evolutionary automatic programming in an arbitrary language*. Norwell, MA, USA: Kluwer Academic Publishers. Available from http://portal.acm.org/ citation.cfm?id=862025

Phelan, M., & McGarraghy, S. (2007, 29 July-2 August). Mitigating the bullwhip effect in supply chains using grammatical evolution. In *Proceedings of the System Dynamics Society Conference*. Boston, MA, USA: System Dynamics Society. (See also http://systemdynamics.org/conferences/ 2007/ proceed/index.htm)

Sparling, D. (2002). Simulations and supply chains: strategies for teaching supply chain management. *Supply Chain Management: An International Journal*, *7*(5), 334–342. doi:10.1108/13598540210447782

Sterman, J. D. (1989). Modeling managerial behavior: Misperceptions of feedback in a dynamic decision making experiment. *Management Science*, *35*(3), 321–339. doi:10.1287/mnsc.35.3.321

Sterman, J. D. (1992). Teaching takes off: flight simulators for management education. *OR/MS Today*, *19*(5), 40-44.

Strozzi, F., Bosch, J., & Zaldívar, J. M. (2007). Beer game order policy optimization under changing customer demand. *Decision Support Systems*, *42*(4), 2153–2163. doi:10.1016/j.dss.2006.06.001

Teixeira, J. F., Brito, A. C., & Saw, R. (2004, 7-9 June). Distributed application for supply chain management training. In J. Marin & V. Koncar (Eds.), *Proceedings of International Simulation Conference* (p. 335). University of Malaga, Malaga, Spain: EUROSIS.

Yadav, S. R., Dashora, Y., Shankar, R., Chan, F. T. S., & Tiwari, M. K. (2008). An interactive particle swarm optimisation for selecting a product family and designing its supply chain. *Int. J. Comput. Appl. Technol.*, *31*(3/4), 168–186. doi:10.1504/IJCAT.2008.018155

Yang, S., Wang, M., & Jiao, L. (2004b, 19-23 June). A novel quantum evolutionary algorithm and its application. In *Proceedings of IEEE Congress on Evolutionary Computation 2004 (CEC 2004)* (Vol. 1, pp. 820-826). IEEE Press, New Jersey.

Yang, S., Wang, M., & Jiao, L. (2004a, 31 August—4 September). A genetic algorithm based on quantum chromosome. In *Proceedings of IEEE International Conference on Signal Processing (ICSP 04)* (pp. 1622-1625). IEEE Press.

KEY TERMS AND DEFINITIONS

Supply Chain: An interconnected network of organisations, people and processes which together deliver a solution (product, service, or combination of these, including any raw materials and intermediate steps) to the end customer. It may involve the flow through the network of any or all of material, information, money and other resources.

Supply Chain Cost: The total cost for all players in the supply chain, covering all processes.

Ordering Policy: (of an Agent/Player): The approach taken by a given player in the supply chain to determining what quantity to order from his/her immediate upstream suppliers. This policy may be a formula, rule of thumb, or more complex program, as used in this work.

Evolutionary Algorithm: (EA): Search and/or optimisation approach inspired by the biological process of evolution by natural selection; they work on successive generations of a population and include operators such as selection based on fitness, reproduction, mutation and replacement. Strictly speaking, they are not algorithms but stochastic approaches or *metaheuristics*.

Genetic Algorithm: (GA): One of the first EAs, where individuals in the population are represented by linear genomes of fixed length.

Genetic Programming: (GP): An EA where the objects being evolved are programs or other rule based approaches to solving a problem. Most GP approaches, but not all, represent programs as trees. A fitness value is assigned to a program according to how well it performs on a task.

Grammatical Evolution: (GE): A version of GP where the genome is linear and is converted to a (derivation) tree using rules encoded in a grammar. It can thus use GA (or any other approach that works on linear genomes) as an optimisation module, rather than applying reproduction or mutation operators directly to trees, as standard GP approaches do.

Grammar: In this context, a Backus-Naur Form description of the syntactically legal ways in which a node in a derivation tree may be expanded, given its form and inputs.

Quantum Inspired Genetic Algorithm: (QIGA): An EA inspired by the physical process of collapse of a quantum state upon observation. A population (possibly very small) of quantum individuals is observed (sampled) to produce a standard population: the fitter individuals of this are used to influence the form of the quantum population at the next generation.

APPENDIX: GRAMMARS USED

Grammar 1

```
<agent>    ::= <policy>;<policy>;<policy>;<policy>;    <policy>    ::=
<var><op><int>    <op>       ::= +|-    <int>       ::= 0|1|2|3|4|5|6|7|8|9    <va
r>       ::= x
```

Grammar 2

```
<agent>    ::= <policy>;<policy>;<policy>;<policy>;    <policy>    ::= <var> |
<var><op><int> | <policy><op>(<var><op><int>)    <op>       ::= +|-    <int>
::= 0|1|2|3|4|5|6|7|8|9    <var>       ::= x
```

Grammar 3

```
<agent>    ::= <policy>;<policy>;<policy>;<policy>;    <policy>    ::=
<var>    <var>       ::= x | H(<time>) | M(<smoother>) | S(<alpha>)    <time>
::= 1|2|3|4|5|6|7|8|9    <smoother> ::= 2|3|4|5    <alpha>     ::= 0.1|0.2|0.3|0.
4|0.5|0.6|0.7|0.8|0.9
```

Grammar 4

```
<agent>    ::= <policy>;<policy>;<policy>;<policy>;    <policy>    ::=
<expr>    <var>       ::= x | H(<time>) | M(<smoother>) | S(<alpha>)    <expr>
::= if (<condition>) { return (<statement>); }                    else {
return (<statement>); }    <condition>::= <var><boolop><var>    <state-
ment>::= <var>    <boolop>    ::= >|>=|<|<=|==    <time>      ::=
1|2|3|4|5|6|7|8|9    <smoother> ::= 2|3|4|5    <alpha>     ::= 0.1|0.2|0.3|0.4|0.
5|0.6|0.7|0.8|0.9
```

Chapter 7
Quantitative Risk Management Models for Newsvendor Supply Chains

Dimitrios Vlachos
Aristotle University of Thessaloniki, Greece

ABSTRACT

As the practices of offshoring and outsourcing force the supply chain networks to keep on expanding geographically in the globalised environment, the logistics processes are becoming more exposed to risk and disruptions. Thus, modern supply chains seem to be more vulnerable than ever. It is clear that efficient logistics risk and security management emerges as an issue of pivotal importance in such competitive, demanding and stochastic environment and is thus vital for the viability and profitability of a company. In this context, this chapter focuses on a set of stochastic quantitative models that study the impact of one or more supply chain disruptions on optimal determination of single period inventory control policies. The purpose of this research is to provide a critical review of state-of-the-art methodologies to be used as a starting point for further research efforts.

INTRODUCTION

During the last decade globalization has provided new challenges for supply chain management and the logistics industry. As the practices of offshoring and outsourcing force the supply chain networks to keep on expanding geographically in the globalized environment, the logistics processes are becoming more exposed to risk and are ever more prone to disruption. Almost all industries strive for making their business processes and supply chains either more efficient or more responsive by outsourcing many core business activities, like transportation, warehousing, research and development (R&D), etc. Although these initiatives have great potential to make operations agile, leaner and more efficient in a low risk and variability environment, at the same time they tend to increase the vulnerability of supply chains to disruptions. However, the traditional decision-making processes and software tools used most often by industry and the methodological models

DOI: 10.4018/978-1-61520-633-9.ch007

and the paradigms covered by academia, in many cases, have been proven quite incapable of addressing satisfactorily many relevant practical real-world risk management supply chain and logistics issues.

Thus, it is clear that efficient logistics risk and security management emerges as an issue of pivotal importance in such competitive, demanding and stochastic environment and is thus vital for the viability and profitability of a company. The explosion in long distance sourcing and supply is exposing supply chains and shareholder value at ever increasing risks. The development of new methodologies that would attempt to combine acceptable logistics security protection with acceptable efficiency, while attaining an acceptable economic value added would be of great merit. Moreover, it is important to consider the entire supply chain, across all countries, when selecting and implementing risk-management strategies, as it is highly possible that an event affecting one supply chain entity or process may interrupt the operations of other supply chain partners.

Recent trends in managing global supply chain risks focus on the development of robust (effective performance for a range of operations risks) and resilient (quick to recover from disruption) supply chain systems. However, there is still a clear lack of contingency strategic policies and the appropriate analytical methodologies for the determination of their optimal parameters, when considering the different modes of disruptions in a supply chain. Definitely, risk management is a decision making process that needs extensive decision analysis in order to reach effective and applicable results. In fact, sometimes the process is so complicated, that not only a single technique but a set of quantitative methods is needed for selecting the best course of action among several alternatives. Several of these methods are widely used and an extensive classification according to the type of application, industry, problem formulation, desired output, perspective, disruption, information, etc. is beyond the purposes of this chapter.

In this context, this chapter examines supply chain management methodologies that quantify the impact of supply disruption on optimal determination of inventory control policies for stochastic environments; thus capturing the trade-off between inventory policies and disruption risks for supply networks with unreliable sourcing. Specifically, this chapter first provides a review and a new classification of related literature, combining the traditional inventory control policies with the new research field of methodologies based on game theory. Then, the chapter focuses on single period (newsvendor-type) problems and analyzes specific typical methodologies for systems with multiple unreliable suppliers due to production or distribution disruptions. The reason for narrowing down the chapter scope is on one hand that single period models can be used for inventory decision-making for a wide range of SKUs ranging from high tech items (with limited shelf life due to obsolescence) to fashion items of limited life ("one shot deals" in the retailing business) and on the other that is not possible a single chapter to cover typical methodologies for all the paper appear in the literature review.

Thus, the contribution of this research is two-fold: first to provide a critical review of general state-of-the-art quantitative methodologies in the research area under study and then, to demonstrate typical models for single period systems that can be used as a starting point for further research efforts. Moreover, the discussion of the most popular methods for supply chain risk management can be a practical guide to mitigate risks.

The chapter content is organized as follows: the following Section presents the current environment of supply chain risk management, the types of interventions for reducing vulnerability of supply chains and improving their resilience and a review and taxonomy of the up-to-date literature. Selected single period supply chain risk management problems are discussed in Section 3 together with their solution methodologies. Finally, the last Section summarizes the content of this work and provides future research directions.

LITERATURE REVIEW AND TAXONOMY

Although risk management issues are a constant and diachronic problem for the logistics service industry and companies have been aware of the need for contingency planning, especially after the terrorist attacks of September 11 of 2001, risk and security issues have moved up in the corporate agenda of logistics managers. Supply risks can have a significant impact on business results, including lost revenues, increased costs, lost assets, and decreased market value. While awareness of the need for risk management continues to rise, the majority of companies are still in the planning phase when it comes to supply risk management (Khemani, 2007). A survey of 800 supply chain executives worldwide (Aberdeen Group, 2007) reports that 82% of companies are concerned about supply chain resiliency, while the percentage of companies that were actively managing this risk is only 30% although it has been increased from 11% the previous year. Moreover, best-in-class companies are two times more likely than all others to have a formalized supply chain risk management initiative.

Business risks originate from a variety of sources. Iakovou (2007) presents a classification of business risks into four major categories: financial, hazard, strategic, and tactical risks. Similarly, Sheffi et al. (2003) have identified six basic supply chain disruption modes: disruptions in supply, transportation, at facilities, freight breaches, disruptions in communications and disruptions in demand.

Supply chain risk management actions aim at reducing a company's vulnerability to disruption and they can be partitioned into two categories; the first class includes interventions aiming at increasing security and thus reducing the likelihood of intentional disruptions, while the second class includes actions aiming at increasing the resilience of the supply chain, thus building in capabilities for "bouncing back" promptly (Sheffi, 2005). More specifically:

- Security interventions aim at improving security and encompass initiatives for preventing security breaches, inspections, information protection, and compliance to international standards, etc.
- Resilience is the ability to resume and restore the logistics operations promptly after a disruption (Cranfield University, 2003). Interventions aiming at increasing resilience include both the straightforward ones that build redundancy (including among others additional inventory, capacity and multiple supplies), along with interventions aiming at increasing flexibility that can be used to "bounce back" following a disruption.

Supply chain disruptions are shown to have both short-term and long-term erosion in corporate profitability and shareholder value (Hendricks and Singhal, 2005). As every enterprise is exposed to disruption risks, firms need first to analyze and understand these risks and then find solutions to limit their effect. According to a study conducted by LCP Consulting and the Centre for Logistics and Supply Chain Management of Cranfield University (2003), supply chain risk and security management should seek opportunities and design solutions enabling exploiting these opportunities at minimum risk. It is clear that the design and execution of appropriate methodological approaches can play a critical role in handling risks and disruptions for various operational settings. However, only in the last decade the literature body dealing with the joint tackling of inventory and risk/disruption management appears to grow. While the literature on disruption supply chain management is still rather limited, it is already quite clear that designing and implementing appropriate methodological approaches may play a pivotal role in handling disruptions in various operational settings.

Supply chain risk management issues concern both business and financial academic journals. Moreover, a few books and several book chapters discuss related topics. One of the main goals of this work is to systematically identify and present the major quantitative model contributions that appear in the literature. To this end, the following two major classes of quantitative models have been identified:

- Extensions of inventory control models to incorporate risk or disruption issues. This class of models concerns mostly researchers with an industrial management background. Since there are numerous researchers, all over the world, working on inventory control and supply chain management, most of proposed models belong to this class. These research efforts are presented in the following subsection.
- Models based on game theory principles. A background in economics usually characterizes the authors of this second class of problems. Although many researchers work on game or utility theory, only few papers on supply chain risk management have been published so far. These research efforts are presented just after the following subsection.

Inventory Control Models

There is a variety of research methodological approaches on risk and disruption management. These research papers can be classified in two major categories. The first one addresses inventory and production systems where the supply or production rate varies. In these systems the quantities delivered or produced differ from the replenishment or production orders (random yield). A second category includes methodologies that model the disruption mechanisms. We refer to this research area as disruption modeling. In both categories we can distinguish methodologies for single sourcing or for dual/multiple sources. Table 1 depicts a classification of the research papers that we have included in this review. The literature in random yield models is extensive and a comprehensive literature review on lot-sizing problems with yield uncertainty is not in the scope of this chapter. Instead, the reader can find comprehensive literature reviews on quantitatively-oriented approaches for determining lot sizes when the production or supply yields are random in Yano and Lee (1995), Khouja (1999), Tang (2006), and Minner (2003).

Production **random yield** problems with a **single supplier** or production facility have been studied by several authors in various forms. Comprehensive literature reviews on stochastic manufacturing flow control and lot sizing with random yields or unreliable manufacturers can be found in Haurie (1995), as well as Yano and Lee (1995). In addition, Wang and Gerchak (2000)

Table 1. Classification of inventory control models

Methodology	Single sourcing	Dual/multiple sourcing
Random Yield	(Haurie, 1995), (Yano and Lee, 1995), (Wang and Gerchak, 2000), (Henig and Gerchak, 1990)	(Agrawal and Nahmias, 1998), (Tomlin and Wang, 2005), (Tomlin, 2006), (Federgruen and Yang, 2009), (Dada et al., 2007)
Disruption Management	(Moinzadeh and Aggarwal, 1997), (Parlar, 1997), (Arreola-Risa and DeCroix, 1998), (Xia et al., 2004), (Xiao and Qi, 2008), (Iakovou et al., 2007)	(Parlar and Perry, 1996), (Gurler and Parlar, 1997), (Golany et al., 2002), (Snyder et al., 2006), (Wu et al., 2007), (Wilson (2007), (Tang, 2006)

consider make-to-order batch manufacturing with random yield. In this paper it is proven that the optimal policy is of the threshold control type—stop if and only if the stock is larger than some critical value. This critical value is studied for different production cases. Moreover, Henig and Gerchak (1990) developed a periodic review production/inventory model with random supply yield.

Agrawal and Nahmias (1998) developed a **multiple-sourcing** deterministic demand model to determine the optimal lot sizes and number of suppliers, when the supply yield from each supplier is random. The authors consider also the fixed costs associated with each supplier. Later on, Tomlin and Wang (2005) developed a single period dual-sourcing model with yield uncertainty (i.e. uncertainty at the time of order placement as to the fraction of the order that will be delivered). By considering one unreliable and one reliable (and thus more expensive) supplier the focus of this paper is on inventory and sourcing mitigation. In the same context, Tomlin (2006) developed a Markov chain single-product model by considering capacity constraints for both suppliers and order quantity flexibility for the reliable vendor (extra capacity is available in case of a disruption). It is shown that contingent rerouting may constitute a basic element of the optimal disruption management strategy by reducing a firm's system-wide costs. Furthermore, Federgruen and Yang (2009) and Dada et al. (2007) examined the multiple sourcing random yield problem and proposed interesting analytical and heuristic solutions based on type I service level-related constraints.

As far as supply chain **disruptions modeling** in a **single-sourcing** setting is concerned, Moinzadeh and Aggarwal (1997) considered the an (s,S) inventory policy for a constant production and demand rate system with random disruptions in a bottleneck production facility, in which supply could be randomly disrupted and the disruption lasts a random period. Near optimal production policies are derived via a heuristic procedure. Parlar (1997) considered random supply disruptions with stochastic demand and lead-time in a continuous review inventory system, while supplier availability is modeled as a semi-Markov process. Next, Arreola-Risa and DeCroix (1998) considered a stochastic (s,S) inventory system in which supply could be randomly disrupted for a random period. This paper considers partial backorders – that is scenarios in which some customer orders may wait as backorders, while others lead to lost sales. Xia et al. (2004) developed a deterministic EOQ-type inventory model for a two-stage supply chain that is susceptible to several types of production- and demand-related disruptions. In this work, two classes of problems are defined: one with fixed setup epochs and another with flexible setup epochs. More recently, Xiao and Qi (2008) investigated a supply chain with one supplier and two competing retailers that experiences a disruption in production cost during a single period. Appropriate quantitative conditions are derived that indicate when the maximum profit can be achieved once a disruption in the original production plan occurs. Finally, Iakovou et al. (2007) present a risk management policy for a single period supply chain with known disruption probabilities.

Two significant research works in the field of joint disruption inventory management and dual-sourcing are those of Parlar and Perry (1996) and Gurler and Parlar (1997). Both papers consider a firm that faces constant demand and sources from two identical-cost infinite-capacity suppliers. The firm faces a fixed cost of ordering, which is only incurred once even if the order is split between suppliers. Interfailure and repair times are exponentially distributed for both suppliers in Parlar and Perry. The authors propose a suboptimal ordering policy that is solved numerically. Gurler and Parlar extended the work of Parlar and Perry by considering the case of Erlang interfailure times and general repair times.

Investigating other disruption inventory management approaches, Golany et al. (2002) proposed a general approach, based on a three-level lexicographical goal-programming formulation, to address various types of disruptions. A penalty cost for deviations from the original production and inventory plan is accommodated and the concept of a disruption recovery time window is addressed. Snyder et al. (2006) developed a broad range of facility location models for designing supply chain networks that are resilient to disruptions. Furthermore, Wu et al. (2007) presented a Petri network-based methodology approach to determine how disruptions disseminate in supply chains (similar to the well-known bullwhip effect) and the attributes of their impact. Wilson (2007) developed a system dynamics simulation model, in order to investigate the impact of a transportation disruption between two echelons, on supply chain performance by comparing a simple supply chain with a vendor managed inventory system.

In a noteworthy work, Tang (2006) attempted to classify the relevant supply chain risk and disruption inventory management models. The research works that model supply risks are divided into those considering disruptions caused by uncertain: i) demand, ii) supply yields, iii) lead times, iv) supply capacity, and v) supply cost.

Game Theory Models

The growth and realignment of corporate entities into strategic, global and market sensitive, supply chains are altering the conception of operations modeling. The system complexity and the interdependence of decision-makers lead to a multi-decision-making framework. The success of decisions on supplier selection, ordering or outsourcing is based on the supplier or the subcontractor self-interest. Even when collaboration and coordination of the supply chain activities lead to increased total benefits, these collaboration benefits should be appropriately split among the supply chain partners.

Game theory involves decision-making between two or more parties in which an individual's success in making choices depends on the choices of others. Economists have long used game theory to analyze a wide array of economic phenomena, including auctions, bargaining, duopolies, fair division, oligopolies, social network formation, and voting systems. Although there are several research efforts especially in supply chain contracts, publications on game theory modeling for supply chain risk management appear only the very last years. Xiao and Yu (2006) introduced an indirect evolutionary game model with two-vertically integrated channels to study stable strategies in the duopoly situation. Their model captures the impact of raw material supply disruptions on the retailers' strategies and on the average channels' profits. Tomlin (2009) evaluates twelve alternative disruption management strategies for a two-product newsvendor problem. The paper investigates the influence of nine attributes that include supplier reliability, supplier failure correlation, payment responsibility in the event of a supply failure, product contribution margin, product substitutability, demand uncertainties and correlation, and the decision maker's risk aversion. The risk-averse decision maker is modeled through a specific utility function. VanMighem (2007) examines through jointed operational and financial perspective newsvendor networks and how resource allocation can mitigate risk exposure. The paper focuses on how risk attitude affects that strategic placement of operational resources to reduce financial risks. Chen et al. (2009) consider a risk-averse newsvendor with stochastic price-dependent demand. They employ Conditional Value at Risk (CVaR) as the decision criterion to find optimal pricing and ordering policies. Finally, Kogan and Tapiero (2007) provide an extended review on supply chain games that also includes risk management problems.

PROBLEMS AND SOLUTION METHODOLOGIES

As discussed in the literature review section there are two main categories of problems that combine inventory and risk management. The first category assumes random order yield where the disruption risk is incorporated in the yield distribution function. The second category examines systems operating in two states, a state where disruptions have occurred and the regular state characterized by no disruptions. In this section, two selected problems (one from each category) and their solution methodologies are presented. Both problems refer to multiple sourcing supply chains examined for a single demand period (newsvendor setting).

Random Yield

Following a setting similar to the approach of Yang et al. (2007), we consider a single period inventory system consisting of one retailer facing random demand X and n suppliers. Let y_iQ be the random yield of supplier i when Q items are ordered from her/him, where y_i is a random variable between 0 and 1. Also let $c_i(Q_i, y_i) = c_i'Q_i + c_i''y_iQ_i$ be the cost owed to supplier i when Q_i items are ordered while y_iQ_i items are actually delivered. Yang et al. (2007) provide possible interpretations for such a cost structure. The first one is that the retailer besides having to pay c_i'' for each unit it gets, it has also have to pay upfront c_i' for each unit it orders. The unit selling price is denoted by s and it is assumed that $s > c_i$, and the unit salvage value by r; it is assumed that $r < c_i$. Moreover, k indicates the unit shortage cost.

The retailer's goal is to maximize her/his expected profit. The vector of order quantities $\boldsymbol{Q} = (Q_1, \ldots, Q_n)$ placed before the realization of the random demand constitutes the retailer's decision variables. The problem is to find the $\boldsymbol{Q}$ that maximizes the total profit of the retailer:

(R): max G(**Q**)

with

$$G(\mathrm{Q}) = \mathrm{s} \cdot \mathrm{E}\left[X - \left(X - \sum_{i=1}^{n} y_i Q_i\right)^{+}\right] + r \cdot \mathrm{E}\left[\left(\sum_{i=1}^{n} y_i Q_i - X\right)^{+}\right] - \sum_{i=1}^{n} E\left[c_i' Q_i + c_i'' y_i Q_i\right] - k \cdot \mathrm{E}\left[\left(X - \sum_{i=1}^{n} y_i Q_i\right)^{+}\right] \quad (1)$$

where the four terms of $G(\boldsymbol{Q})$ correspond, in the order that they appear in equation (1), to the revenues from selling items, to the income from salvaging the unsold items, to the payment to the suppliers and to the shortage cost. Since, the function $G(\boldsymbol{Q})$ is easily proven jointly concave, the optimal solution is obtained by Karush-Kuhn-Tucker local optimality conditions using the appropriate mathematical software. Yang et al. (2007) propose the Active Set Method algorithm to reduce the calculation time and provides extensive numerical results and managerial insights for variation of the above problem.

The above newsvendor setting can be expanded for examining newsvendor supply networks. Keren (2009) studies a two-tier supply chain (producer-distributor-end user) with known end user demand and stochastic yield of orders placed to the distributor and the producer. The paper examines both a multiplicative and an additive yield effect to model the effect of the random yield variable on the order quantities. The problem is formulated as a mathematical programming problem where the optimal solution of the producer is a constraint, and it can be solved using any available mathematical software.

Stochastic Disruption Management

Iakovou et al. (2010) consider a supply chain of one manufacturer and two competing, potentially unreliable, suppliers which are both susceptible to supply chain disruptions, such as production- transportation- and security-related disruptions. They propose a single period inventory system where a single ordering decision is to be made before the sales period begins (thus, emergency replenishment is not allowed), so as to maximize expected total profit. Figure 1 presents a typical dual sourcing unreliable supply network.

Demand X is assumed to be a positive stochastic random variable with probability density function $f(x)$ and cumulative distribution function $F(x)$. The unit purchase cost paid to supplier i ($i = 1, 2$) is denoted by c_i. The unit selling price is denoted by s and it is assumed that $s > c_i$ ($i = 1, 2$) The surplus stock that remains unsold at the end of the period can be sold to a secondary market at a unit salvage value r; it is assumed that $r < c_i$ ($i = 1, 2$). Moreover, k indicates the 'loss of goodwill' cost due to the shortage in products/parts; thus the total lost sales cost is the sum of the opportunity cost ($s - c_i$) plus k.

Disruptions may occur only once for each of the two suppliers, during the selling period with probability p_i ($i = 1, 2$). Moreover, when a disruption occurs a constant percentage of the order quantity Q_i, denoted by y_i ($i = 1, 2$), will be available in time to satisfy the demand during the selling period (the remaining quantity will not be delivered or it will be delivered after the end of the selling period). As a result, in case of a disruption the available quantity will be y_iQ_i (see Figure 1), with y_i capturing the 'severity' of the impact of the supply disruptions. Vlachos and Dekker (2003) discuss how y_i can be modeled in an inventory system with commercial returns. The y_i variables could model either the case of a limited production rate in a previous supply chain echelon (disruption in production) or the case of delayed delivery (disruption in transportation). In the first case, y_i models the effective production capacity as a result of a production failure, while in the second y_i corresponds to the part of the order quantity that may be utilized, since a specific part of the demand of the selling period might be lost in the case of late delivery.

Initially, when none of the supply channels face a disruption, that occurs with probability $(1-p_1)(1-p_2)$, the expected single period profit $G_0(Q_1,Q_2)$ is obtained by the classical newsvendor problem analysis:

Figure 1. The dual sourcing unreliable supply chain network under study

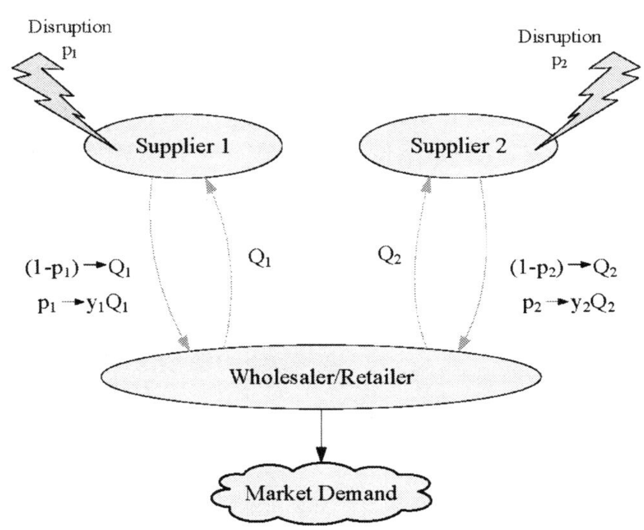

$$G_0(Q_1,Q_2)=\int_0^{Q_1+Q_2}\left[sx-c_1Q_1-c_2Q_2+r(Q_1+Q_2-x)\right]f(x)dx + \int_{Q_1+Q_2}^{\infty}\left[s(Q_1+Q_2)-c_1Q_1-c_2Q_2-k(x-Q_1-Q_2)\right]f(x)dx \quad (2)$$

When a disruption occurs only to the first supplier (probability $(1-p_2)p_1$) only a fraction of Q_1, initially ordered to the first supplier (y_1Q_1), can be now used to fill demand along with the order from the second supplier. The expected profit $G_1(Q_1,Q_2)$ is then expressed by the following equation:

$$G_1(Q_1,Q_2)=\int_0^{y_1Q_1+Q_2}\left[sx-c_1y_1Q_1-c_2Q_2+r(y_1Q_1+Q_2-x)\right]f(x)dx + \int_{y_1Q_1+Q_2}^{\infty}\left[s(y_1Q_1+Q_2)-c_1y_1Q_1-c_2Q_2-k(x-y_1Q_1-Q_2)\right]f(x)dx \quad (3)$$

Similarly, when a disruption occurs to the second supplier (probability $(1-p_1)p_2$), the expected profit $G_2(Q_1,Q_2)$ is expressed by:

$$G_2(Q_1,Q_2)=\int_0^{Q_1+y_2Q_2}\left[sx-c_1Q_1-c_2y_2Q_2+r(Q_1+y_2Q_2-x)\right]f(x)dx + \int_{Q_1+y_2Q_2}^{\infty}\left[s(Q_1+y_2Q_2)-c_1Q_1-c_2y_2Q_2-k(x-Q_1-y_2Q_2)\right]f(x)dx \quad (4)$$

Moreover, when disruptions occur at the same time to both suppliers (probability p1p2), the total available quantity to satisfy demand is $y_1Q_1+y_2Q_2$, and the expected profit $G_{12}(Q_1,Q_2)$ is provided by:

$$G_{12}(Q_1,Q_2)=\int_0^{y_1Q_1+y_2Q_2}\left[sx-c_1y_1Q_1-c_2y_2Q_2+r(y_1Q_1+y_2Q_2-x)\right]f(x)dx + \int_{y_1Q_1+y_2Q_2}^{\infty}\left[s(y_1Q_1+y_2Q_2)-c_1y_1Q_1-c_2y_2Q_2-k(x-y_1Q_1-y_2Q_2)\right]f(x)dx \quad (5)$$

Finally, the objective function of the optimization model *(P)* is the total expected profit $G(Q_1,Q_2)$ obtained as the weighted sum of the expected profits given in (2), (3), (4) and (5) taking into account the probabilities of disruptions on none, on the first, on the second and on both supply channels respectively.

(P): max $G(Q_1,Q_2)$

with

$$G(Q_1,Q_2)=(1-p_1)(1-p_2)G_0(Q_1,Q_2)+p_1(1-p_2)G_1(Q_1,Q_2) + (1-p_1)p_2G_2(Q_1,Q_2)+p_1p_2G_{12}(Q_1,Q_2) \quad (6)$$

For model *(P)* Proposition 1 applies. The proof of proposition is provided in (Iakovou et al., 2010).

Proposition 1:

a) The total expected profit $G(Q_1,Q_2)$ is concave in Q_1 and Q_2.

The maximum value of $G(Q_1,Q_2)$ is attained for Q_1* and Q_2* (optimal order lot sizes), by solving the system of equations of the first order conditions:

$$(1-p_1)(1-p_2)F(Q_1+Q_2)-p_1(1-p_2)y_1F(y_1Q_1+Q_2) + (1-p_1)p_2F(Q_1+y_2Q_2)+p_1p_2y_1F(y_1Q_1+y_2Q_2)=\left[1-p_1(1-y_1)\right]U_1 \quad (7)$$

$$(1-p_1)(1-p_2)F(Q_1+Q_2)+p_1(1-p_2)F(y_1Q_1+Q_2) + (1-p_1)p_2y_2F(Q_1+y_2Q_2)+p_1p_2y_2F(y_1Q_1+y_2Q_2)=\left[1-p_2(1-y_2)\right]U_2 \quad (8)$$

where the parameters $U_1=\dfrac{s-c_1+k}{s-r+k}$ and $U_2=\dfrac{s-c_2+k}{s-r+k}$ are the critical ratios of the classical single sourcing newsvendor problem.

The above model *(P)* corresponds to risk-neutral decision-makers. Model *(P)* can be extended through the consideration of a fill rate (Type II service level) constraint, so as to take also into account risk-aversion. Fill rate β measures the part of the season demand that is satisfied from the delivered quantity. Risk-averse decision-makers would prefer higher service levels than risk-neutral ones, but with a lower expected pay-off. The resulting optimization model, which represents the maximization of the total weighted expected profit subject to a fill rate constraint, is:

(P_β): max $G(Q_1,Q_2)$

subject to *Fill Rate* $> \beta_0$

with

$$Fill\ \text{Rate} = 1\text{-}\frac{Expected\ Shortage}{Mean\ Demand} = 1\text{-}\frac{\mathrm{E}\left(n\left(Q_1,Q_2\right)\right)}{\mu}$$

where

$$\mathrm{E}\left(n\left(Q_1,Q_2\right)\right) = \left(1\text{-p}_1\right)\left(1\text{-p}_2\right)\int_{Q_1+Q_2}^{\infty}\left(x\text{-}Q_1\text{-}Q_2\right)f\left(x\right)dx + p_1\left(1\text{-p}_2\right)\int_{y_1Q_1+Q_2}^{\infty}\left(x\text{-y}_1Q_1\text{-}Q_2\right)f\left(x\right)dx$$
$$+\left(1\text{-p}_1\right)\text{p}_2\int_{Q_1+y_2Q_2}^{\infty}\left(x\text{-}Q_1\text{-y}_2Q_2\right)f\left(x\right)dx + p_1p_2\int_{y_1Q_1+y_2Q_2}^{\infty}\left(x\text{-y}_1Q_1\text{-y}_2Q_2\right)f\left(x\right)dx$$

For model (P_β) Proposition 2 applies. The proof of proposition is given in (Xanthopoulos et al., 2010).

Proposition 2:

a) Model (P_β) is a convex programming problem in Q_1 and Q_2.

The global maximum value for problem (P_β) is attained for Q_1* and Q_2* (optimal order lot sizes) and λ_β* (optimal value of the Lagrangian multiplier corresponding to the Type II service level constraint), by solving the system of equations of the following first order conditions:

$$\left(1\text{-p}_1\right)\left(1\text{-p}_2\right)F\left(Q_1 - Q_2\right)+p_1\left(1\text{-p}_2\right)y_1F\left(y_1Q_1+Q_2\right)$$
$$+\left(1\text{-p}_1\right)\text{p}_2F\left(Q_1+y_2Q_2\right)+p_1p_2y_1F\left(y_1Q_1+y_2Q_2\right)=\left[1\text{-p}_1\left(1\text{-}y_1\right)\right]\frac{\left(s\text{-}c_1+k\right)+\frac{\lambda_\beta}{\mu}}{\left(s\text{-}r+k\right)+\frac{\lambda_\beta}{\mu}} \tag{9}$$

$$\left(1\text{-p}_1\right)\left(1\text{-p}_2\right)F\left(Q_1+Q_2\right)+p_1\left(1\text{-p}_2\right)F\left(y_1Q_1+Q_2\right)$$
$$+\left(1\text{-p}_1\right)\text{p}_2y_2F\left(Q_1+y_2Q_2\right)+p_1p_2y_2F\left(y_1Q_1+y_2Q_2\right)=\left[1\text{-p}_2\left(1\text{-}y_2\right)\right]\frac{\left(s\text{-}c_2+k\right)+\frac{\lambda_\beta}{\mu}}{\left(s\text{-}r+k\right)+\frac{\lambda_\beta}{\mu}} \tag{10}$$

$$1\text{-}\frac{1}{\mu}\begin{bmatrix}\left(1\text{-p}_1\right)\left(1\text{-p}_2\right)\int_{Q_1+Q_2}^{\infty}\left(x\text{-}Q_1\text{-}Q_2\right)f\left(x\right)dx + p_1\left(1\text{-p}_2\right)\int_{y_1Q_1+Q_2}^{\infty}\left(x\text{-y}_1Q_1\text{-}Q_2\right)f\left(x\right)dx + \\ \left(1\text{-p}_1\right)\text{p}_2\int_{Q_1+y_2Q_2}^{\infty}\left(x\text{-}Q_1\text{-y}_2Q_2\right)f\left(x\right)dx + p_1p_2\int_{y_1Q_1+y_2Q_2}^{\infty}\left(x\text{-y}_1Q_1\text{-y}_2Q_2\right)f\left(x\right)dx\end{bmatrix} = \beta \tag{11}$$

Gradient search algorithms or any of the commercially available mathematics problem-solving software packages can be used for solving the system of equations (9) to (11).

Xanthopoulos et al. (2010) present another extension of the basic model (P) towards risk-averse decision-makers considering a Type I service level constraint, also discussed by Federgruen and Yang (2009) and Dada et al. (2007). Type I service level represents the probability α that the random demand during the season is no greater than the delivered quantity.

Based on the closed form analytical solution presented above it is interesting to explore (i) the shape of the objective function and the form of the optimal solution in the case of unconstrained optimization problem *(P)*, and (ii) how a risk-averse manager change her ordering decisions and what is the impact on system's total expected profit.

Figure 2 illustrates, indicatively, the effect of various combinations of Q_1 and Q_2 on the total weighted expected profit (via contour graphs), for various levels of the impact of a potential disruption. Specifically, Figures 2(a), 2(b) and 2(c) are obtained by altering only the level of parameter y_1, while keeping all the other parameters constant. In Figure 2(a) a level of $y_1 = 0.9$ is employed, while in 2(b) a level of *0.6*, and at 2(c) a level of *0.1*. Analogous figures are obtained, when altering only the supply cost (c_i), or the probability that a disruption occurs (p_i).

Figure 2. Impact of Q_1 and Q_2 on the total profit for various levels of y_1: (a) 0.9; (b) 0.6; (c) 0.1

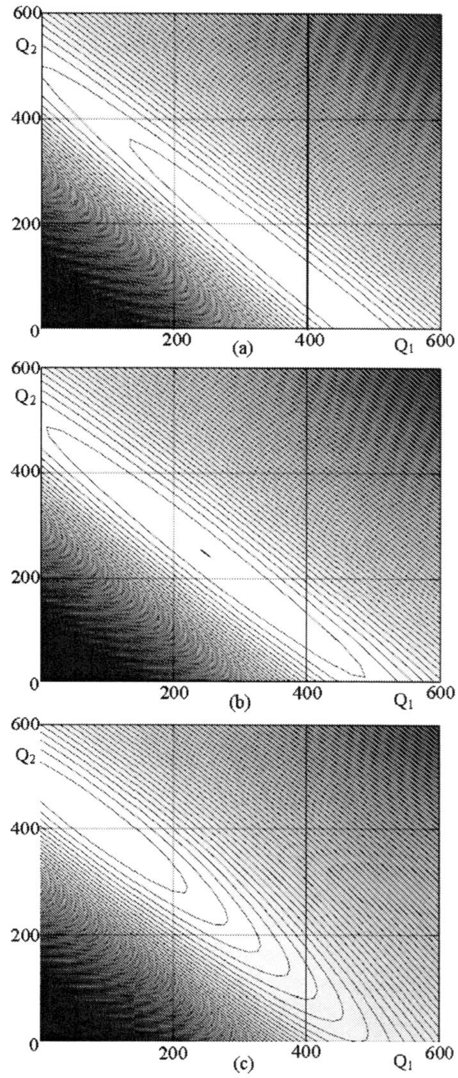

We observe that the profit function $G(Q_1,Q_2)$ is relatively flat for several combinations of the decision variables Q_1 and Q_2 with a close to optimal performance. In other words, the proposed ordering policy seems to be robust and economically insensitive to minor changes on the optimal values of the decision variables. It is also observed that as the impact of a disruption on the first supplier increases, the optimal solution moves from a solution that mainly utilizes the first supplier to a solution that mainly utilizes the second one. In the case of Figure 2(b) both suppliers are equally attractive and thus the final decision, on the mix of orders from them, could be based on other significant business-related issues (e.g. alternative ways of sourcing with almost identical profit could result in different customer service levels). Similar findings also result when keeping constant all the parameters and altering only the purchase costs (c_i) or the probabilities (p_i) of a supply disruption.

Depending on the values of the purchase costs (c_i), the disruption probabilities (p_i), and the effect of a disruption (y_i), one of the suppliers may dominate over the other one, and thus it will be optimal to order only from him/her. Generally, all else being equal the source with the smaller purchase cost or disruption probability or with the higher yield rate will get more orders.

Nevertheless for certain combinations of the values of c_i, p_i, and y_i ($i=1, 2$), a dual policy outperforms single sourcing and it is optimal to order from both channels (a similar conclusion results in the recent work of Veeraraghavan and Scheller-Wolf (2008)). In such cases, it is optimal to place the larger part of the total order to the dominant supplier and its lesser part to the second one, so as to hedge/mitigate the disruption risks. The risk is generally greater when ordering only from one unreliable source than ordering from two unreliable sources, because in case of a disruption to the one supplier, at least a part of the total order will be available through the other one. Moreover, when placing orders to both channels and when the possibility of a disruption and/or the impact of a disruption increases (lower yield rates), then the total ordering quantity increases as well, while the total profit decreases.

Considering now the numerical analysis conducted to the service level-constrained problem ($P\beta$), Figure 3 depicts some illustrative problem instances. All the given charts present how the ordering policy (Q_1 and Q_2) and the total profit

$G(Q_1,Q_2)$ change as β_0 increases. In all cases for values of β_0 from *0%* to up to a case-specific percent (that exceeds the *85%* limit in all instances) the ordering policy remains unchanged. This limit corresponds to the fill rate of the optimal policy of the unconstrained problem *(P)*. As we can see in all problem instances the total profit is a decreasing function of β_0, when β_0 reaches the aforementioned case-specific critical value. Furthermore, the upper effective bound of β_0 is the percent that leads to zero profit. This percent is certainly lower than the *100%* and values of β_0 greater than this bound does not make any sense, since they lead to a negative profit.

From Figures 3(a) and 3(b) we observe that as fill rate increases, the optimal solution moves from a solution that mainly utilizes the cheaper but less reliable supplier to a solution that mainly utilizes the more reliable and more expensive one. A risk-averse decision-maker will certainly select the 'safety' of higher service levels by further utilizing the more reliable supplier, irrespectively of the lower expected pay-off. Moreover, for service levels close to 100%, large orders should be placed to both suppliers. Similarly, it is observed from Figure 3(c) that even if one supplier dominates over the other one (the only activated source) but he/she is the more unreliable from the two, then as β_0 increases it will be optimal for risk-averse decision-makers to place an additional order to the second supplier, in order to reduce/hedge the disruption risks; the order to the second source increases with β_0. Of course, the less the "reliability gap" is between the dominant supplier and the second one, the higher the service level will be at which the second more reliable supplier will become active. Furthermore, Figure 3(d) depicts the case in which the first supplier is the dominant one as well as the more reliable from the two. In such a case, no matter

Figure 3. Impact of fill rate on optimal ordering policy

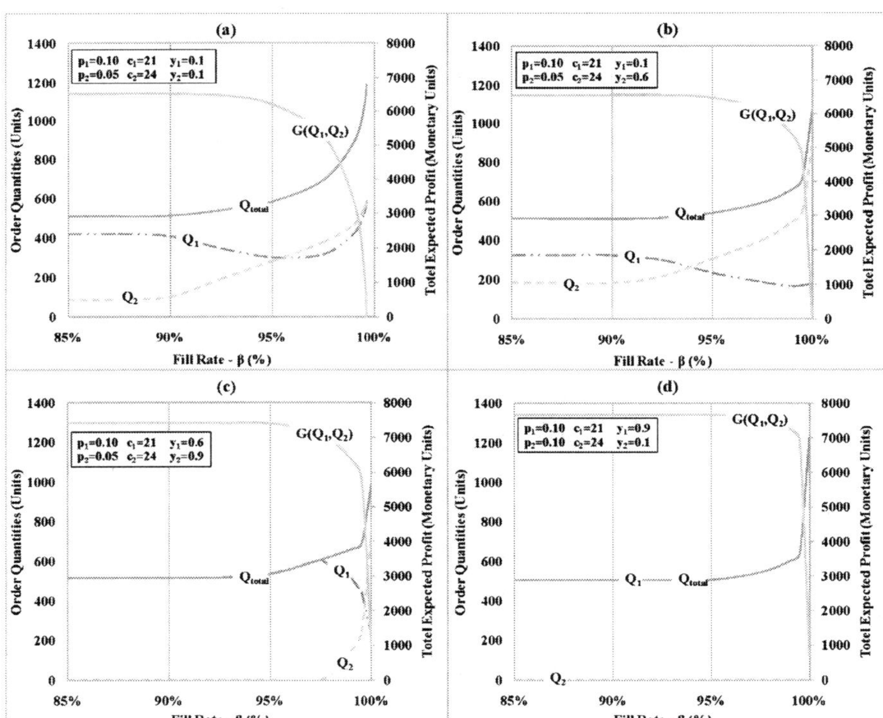

how high the fill rate will be, orders should be placed only to the first supplier and the second one should not be activated at all.

CONCLUSION AND FUTURE RESEARCH

Risk management has emerged as an issue of critical importance for supply chain management and corporate profitability. An effective disruption-management strategy that enhances supply chain resilience is a necessary component of a firm's overall hedging strategy. Firms that passively accept the risk of disruptions are susceptible to the risk of severe financial and market-share loss. In this context, the related literature includes several papers that are based either on appropriate modifications or extensions of inventory control policies that incorporate risk issues or on new approaches that usually employ methodological tools from other disciplines, such as game theory. The most significant research works are thoroughly presented in the literature review section. The paper also includes two selected models for multiple sourcing newsvendor-type supply chains, which outline potential ways to model and analyze such systems.

Several promising avenues for future research in this field have emerged. For instance, the extensions of the current research efforts for multiple types of products, for more than two suppliers or for supply chains with more than two echelons, as well as the consideration of the correlation among orders' yield and disruptions, and the explicit inclusion of service level concerns are some directions that appear worthwhile to be pursued. The development of such models will enhance the richness, variety, and applicability of the inventory management methodologies for the design of resilient supply chains. Furthermore for the newsvendor supply chains, it would be interesting a detailed study of how delayed deliveries that result from disruptions affect the part of demand that may be served. Furthermore, the decision-maker risk attitude should be incorporated in already existing models by employing either service level constraints such as in the second model of the third section, or using other modeling approaches including game theory.

REFERENCES

Aberdeen Group. (2007). *The Supply Chain Executive's Strategic Agenda 2008: Managing Global Supply Chain Transformation*. Retrieved April 8, 2010 from http://www-304.ibm.com/jct03004c/tools/ cpeportal/fileserve/download0/143747/AberdeenSCMStrategicAgenda08.pdf?contentid=143747

Agrawal, N., & Nahmias, S. (1998). Rationalization of the supplier base in the presence of yield uncertainty. *Production and Operations Management*, *6*(3), 291–308. doi:10.1111/j.1937-5956.1997.tb00432.x

Arreola-Risa, A., & DeCroix, G. A. (1998). Inventory Management under Random Supply Disruptions and Partial Backorders. *Naval Research Logistics*, *45*, 687–703. doi:10.1002/(SICI)1520-6750(199810)45:7<687::AID-NAV3>3.0.CO;2-7

Chen, Y.(F.), Xu. M., & Zhang, Z.G. (2009). A Risk-Averse Newsvendor Model under the CVaR Criterion. *Operations Research*, *57*(4), 1040–1044. doi:10.1287/opre.1080.0603

LCP Consulting, Centre for Logistics and Supply Chain Management (2003). *Understanding Supply Chain Risk: a Self-Assessment Workbook*. Cranfield University: School of Management, Department for Transport.

Cranfield University (2003). Creating Resilient Supply Chains: A Practical Guide. Cranfield University, Department for Transport.

Dada, M., Petruzzi, N. C., & Schwarz, L. B. (2007). A Newsvendor's Procurement Problem when Suppliers are Unreliable. *Manufacturing & Service Operations Management*, *9*(1), 9–32. doi:10.1287/msom.1060.0128

Federgruen, A., & Yang, N. (2009). Optimal Supply Diversification under General Supply Risks. *Operations Research*, *57*(6), 1451–1468. doi:10.1287/opre.1080.0667

Golany, B., Xia, Y., Yang, J., & Yu, G. (2002). An Interactive Goal-Programming Procedure for Operational Recovery Problems. *Optimization and Engineering*, *40*, 959–971.

Gordon, B. H. (2003). The Changing Face of 3rd Party Logistics. *Supply Chain Management Review*, *7*(2), 50–57.

Gurler, U., & Parlar, M. (1997). An Inventory Problem with Two Randomly Available Suppliers. *Operations Research*, *45*, 904–918. doi:10.1287/opre.45.6.904

Haurie, A. (1995). Time Scale Decomposition in Production Planning for Unreliable Flexible Manufacturing System. *European Journal of Operational Research*, *82*, 339–358. doi:10.1016/0377-2217(94)00268-H

Hendricks, K. B., & Singhal, V. R. (2005). Association between Supply Chain Glitches and Operating Performance. *Management Science*, *51*(5), 695–711. doi:10.1287/mnsc.1040.0353

Henig, M., & Gerchak, Y. (1990). The structure of periodic review policies in the presence of variable yield. *Operations Research*, *38*, 634–643. doi:10.1287/opre.38.4.634

Iakovou, E., Vlachos, D., & Xanthopoulos, A. (2007). An Analytical Methodological Framework for the Optimal Design of Resilient Supply Chains. *International Journal of Logistics Economics and Globalisation*, *1*, 1–20. doi:10.1504/IJLEG.2007.014498

Iakovou, I., Vlachos, D., & Xanthopoulos, A. (2010). A stochastic inventory management model for a dual sourcing supply chain with disruptions. *International Journal of Systems Science*, *41*(3), 315–324. doi:10.1080/00207720903326894

Keren, B. (2009). The single-period Inventory Problem: Extension to Random Yield from the Perspective of the Supply Chain. *Omega: The International Journal of Management Science*, *37*(4), 801–810. doi:10.1016/j.omega.2008.07.006

Khemani, K. (2007). Bringing Rigor to Risk Management. *Supply Chain Management Review*, *11*(2), 67–80.

Khouja, M. (1999). The Single Period (News-vendor) Problem: Literature Review and Suggestions for Future Research. *Omega: The International Journal of Management Science*, *27*, 537–553. doi:10.1016/S0305-0483(99)00017-1

Knight, P. (2003). *Supply Chain Security Guidelines*, IBM Corporation, Import Compliance Office.

Kogan, K., & Tapiero, C.S. (2007). *Supply Chain Games: Operations Management and Risk Valuation*. Springer.

Minner, S. (2003). Multiple-supplier Inventory Models in Supply Chain Management: a Review. *International Journal of Production Economics*, *81-82*, 265–279. doi:10.1016/S0925-5273(02)00288-8

Moinzadeh, K., & Aggarwal, P. K. (1997). Analysis of a Production/Inventory System subject to Random Disruptions. *Management Science*, *43*, 1577–1588. doi:10.1287/mnsc.43.11.1577

Parlar, M. (1997). Continuous-Review Inventory Problem with Random Supply Interruptions. *European Journal of Operational Research*, *99*, 366–385. doi:10.1016/S0377-2217(96)00165-8

Parlar, M., & Perry, D. (1996). Inventory Models of Future Supply Uncertainty with Single and Multiple Suppliers. *Naval Research Logistics*, *43*, 191–210. doi:10.1002/(SICI)1520-6750(199603)43:2<191::AID-NAV3>3.0.CO;2-5

Sheffi, Y. (2005). *The Resilient Enterprise: Overcoming Vulnerability for Competitive Advantage*. Cambridge, MA: MIT Press.

Sheffi, Y., Rice Jr, J.B., Caniato, F., Fleck, J., Disraelly, D., Lowtan, D., Lensing, R. & Pickett, C. (2003). *Supply Chain Response to Terrorism: Creating Resilient and Secure Supply Chains*. Supply Chain Response to Terrorism Project – Interim Report, MIT Center for Transportation and Logistics.

Snyder, L.V., Scaparra, P.M., Daskin, M.S., & Church, R.L. (2006). Planning for Disruptions in Supply Chain Networks. *Tutorials in Operations Research*, 234-256.

Tang, C. S. (2006). Perspectives in Supply Chain Risk Management. *International Journal of Production Economics*, *103*, 451–488. doi:10.1016/j.ijpe.2005.12.006

Tomlin, B. (2006). On the Value of Mitigation and Contingency Strategies for Managing Supply Chain Disruption Risks. *Management Science*, *52*(5), 639–657. doi:10.1287/mnsc.1060.0515

Tomlin, B. (2009). Disruption Management Strategies for Short Life-Cycle Products. *Naval Research Logistics*, *56*(4), 318–347. doi:10.1002/nav.20344

Tomlin, B., & Wang, Y. (2005). On the Value of Mix Flexibility and Dual Sourcing in Unreliable Newsvendor Networks. *Manufacturing & Service Operations Management*, *7*(1), 37–57. doi:10.1287/msom.1040.0063

Van Mieghem, J. (2007). Risk Mitigation in Newsvendor Networks: Resource Diversification, Flexibility, Sharing, and Hedging. *Management Science*, *53*(8), 1269–1288. doi:10.1287/mnsc.1070.0700

Veeraraghavan, S., & Scheller-Wolf, A. (2008). Now or Later: a Simple Policy for Effective Dual Sourcing in Capacitated Systems. *Operations Research*, *56*(4), 850–864. doi:10.1287/opre.1080.0552

Vlachos, D., & Dekker, R. (2003). Return Handling Options and Order Quantities for Single Period Products. *European Journal of Operational Research*, *151*, 38–52. doi:10.1016/S0377-2217(02)00596-9

Wang, Y., & Gerchak, Y. (2000). Input Control in a Batch Production System with Lead Times, Due Dates and Random Yields. *European Journal of Operational Research*, *126*, 371–385. doi:10.1016/S0377-2217(99)00295-7

Wilson, M. C. (2007). The Impact of Transportation Disruptions on Supply Chain Performance. *Transportation Research Part E, Logistics and Transportation Review*, *43*(4), 295–320. doi:10.1016/j.tre.2005.09.008

Wu, T., Blackhurst, J., & O'Grady, P. (2007). Methodology for supply chain disruption analysis. *International Journal of Production Research*, *45*(7), 1665–1682. doi:10.1080/00207540500362138

Xanthopoulos, A., Vlachos, D., & Iakovou, E. (2010). Newsvendor Disruption Management Policies for a Two-Echelon Supply Chain. Working paper, Aristotle University of Thessaloniki.

Xia, Y., Yang, M. H., Golany, B., Gilbert, S. M., & Yu, G. (2004). Real-Time Disruption Management in a Two-Stage Production and Inventory System. *IIE Transactions*, *36*, 111–125. doi:10.1080/07408170490245379

Xiao, T., & Qi, X. (2008). Price Competition, Cost and Demand Disruptions and Coordination of a Supply Chain with one Manufacturer and Two Competing Retailers. *Omega: The International Journal of Management Science*, *36*(5), 741–753. doi:10.1016/j.omega.2006.02.008

Xiao, T., & Yu, G. (2006). Supply Chain Disruption Management and Evolutionarily Stable Strategies of Retailers in the Quantity-Setting Duopoly Situation with Homogeneous Goods. *European Journal of Operational Research*, *173*, 648–668. doi:10.1016/j.ejor.2005.02.076

Yang, S., Yang, J., & Abdel-Malek, L. (2007). Sourcing with Random Yields and Stochastic Demand: A Newsvendor Approach. *Computers & Operations Research*, *34*, 3682–3690. doi:10.1016/j.cor.2006.01.015

Yano, C., & Lee, H. L. (1995). Lot Sizing with Random Yields: a Review. *Operations Research*, *43*(2), 311–334. doi:10.1287/opre.43.2.311

Chapter 8
Relief Distribution Networks:
Design and Operations

Soumia Ichoua
Johnson C. Smith University, USA

ABSTRACT

Logistics area is often recognized as one of the key elements in achieving effective disaster preparedness and response efforts. This chapter presents modeling and solution approaches for both the problem of prepositioning emergency supplies prior to a disaster as well as the problem of their distribution after the disaster onset. Depending on whether uncertainty is taken into account or not, work in these areas will be classified into two major categories: stochastic or deterministic. A distinction will also be made between exact methods and heuristics. In addition, the advantages and limitations of each of these two classes of approaches will be discussed. An emphasis will be put on the particularities and characteristics of relief distribution networks. More advanced issues in the design and operations of these networks will also be discussed as interesting research avenues.

INTRODUCTION

In the past few years, there has been an increased interest in the design and operations of relief distribution networks. This attention is mainly motivated by a worldwide increasing trend in natural disaster numbers (see Figure 1) as well as the alarming and devastating impacts of these disasters on human lives and global economy.

DOI: 10.4018/978-1-61520-633-9.ch008

According to the Center for Research on the Epidemiology of Disasters (CRED), the number of disasters resulting in 100,000 to 999,999 victims around the globe doubled during 1987-2006 (CRED 2006). In 2007, 414 natural disasters were reported worldwide killing 16847 persons, affecting more than 211 million others and causing over 74.9 US$ billion in economic damages (CRED 2007). On its part, the United States was affected by many costly disasters that year. These disasters caused more than US$ 9 billion in damage (CRED 2007). However, with almost US$ 129 billion,

Figure 1. Natural disasters reported 1900-2008. Source: EM-DAT DATABASE

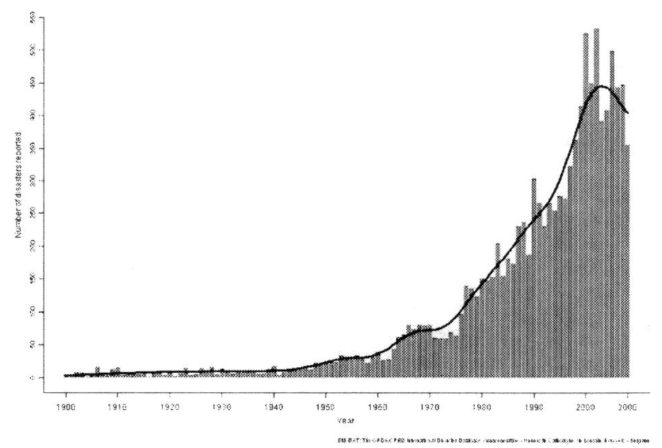

hurricane Katrina 2005 remains the hydro meteorological disaster responsible for the highest damages ever reported (CRED 2006). The severity of disaster impacts is often aggravated by the worldwide economy connectivity that helps spreading disaster effects far-away from the region where they actually occur (Akkihal 2006). This was the case of hurricane Katrina in 2005 and hurricane Ike in September 2008. Both disasters stroked the Gulf region which is a source of fuel supply, causing fuel price increases in distant regions. Figure 2 illustrates the importance of natural disasters economical impacts for the last few years.

Despite the importance of disasters economical effects, mitigating their impacts on human lives remains the major concern. This can be achieved through an adequate and timely delivery of emergency supplies such as tents and medical products to affected populations. However, efforts dedicated to provide these kinds of supplies after a disaster onset are often criticized (GPO 2007, OIG-08-11). In fact, disaster preparedness has been widely identified as an important strategy to ensure an effective disaster response. Logistics area is indeed often recognized as one of the key elements in achieving effective disaster preparedness and response efforts (OIG-08-11, Jenkins 2007, CRID 2006, OIG-06-32, Kemball-Cook and Stephenson 1984, Ardekani and Hobeika 1988, Larson et al. 2005).

This chapter is aimed at addressing both pre-disaster preparedness and post-disaster responsiveness in a distribution network operated by a humanitarian relief organization. In this context, different types of emergency supplies must be delivered quickly to disaster-affected populations in order to mitigate their sufferings. Emergency supplies may generally be classified into two categories: consumable items such as clothing and food; and non-consumable items such as shelters and electricity devices. As noticed in Akkihal (2006), non-consumable items are critical to a timely disaster-response and must therefore be delivered in the early stages of the disaster. We are interested in a relief distribution network where emergency supplies are first received and stored in permanent facilities (logistics centers) generally located in large cities. These supplies are then shipped to temporary supply units (local distribution centers) in theater where they are pre-positioned for distribution to people in need. Since disasters are generally low probability high impact events, demand arrival, size and location

Figure 2. Estimated damage (US$ billion) caused by reported natural disasters 1975-2008. Source: EM-DAT DATABASE

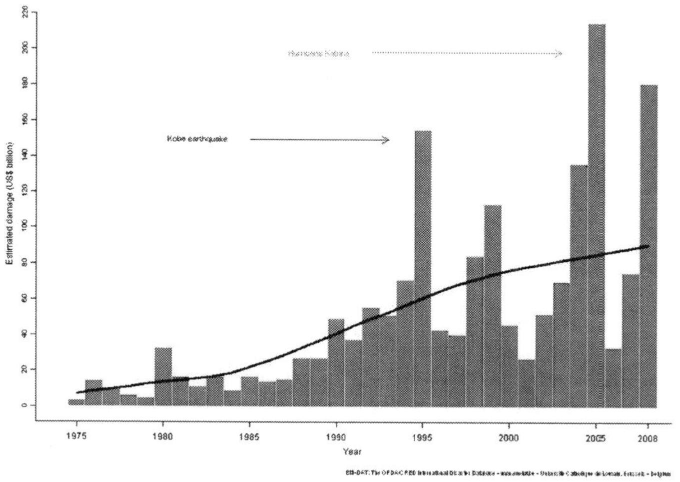

are random factors that are hard to forecast. Moreover, demand of each type is characterized by its degree of urgency and its targeted response time.

Prior to the disaster onset, design decisions including the number and location of local distribution centers needed as well as their inventory levels for each type of emergency supply are made. This activity is commonly called Pre-positioning of emergency supplies and is part of pre-disaster preparedness. It intends to enhance the response when a disaster strikes (i.e., delivering enough supplies to affected populations in a timely manner). Design decisions are typically constrained by budget limitations that restrict the number of local supply units to establish as well as their storage capacity (Balcik and Beamon 2008). Moreover, solution quality is typically assessed through service-based objective functions that often prioritize demand satisfaction and /or risk reduction (e.g. maximizing the expected total demand covered).

After the disaster onset, the organization will use the designed network to conduct daily distribution of emergency supplies to affected populations over a planning time horizon that covers the disaster duration. This activity is part of post-disaster responsiveness and is conducted under various operational constraints at the pre-established distribution centers (e.g. limited fleet size and limited vehicle capacity). The goal is to determine visit schedule at each demand point, the quantity of supplies of each type to be delivered at each visit and the vehicle route to be used for each visit over the planning horizon. Given that an emergency scene is a highly dynamic environment, these decisions must be made based on real-time information about the emergency scene (e.g. demand, state of the physical network, inventory levels at distribution centers, etc…). Though solution quality typically prioritizes demand satisfaction, it may incorporate operational costs such as the total inventory costs and/or the total distance traveled by the vehicles.

Several researchers have compared humanitarian relief chains to their commercial counterparts (Oloruntoba and Gray 2006, Thomas 2003, Thomas and Kopczak 2005, Van Wassebhove 2006). An important distinction between these two types of distribution chains is the objective function. While commercial chains typically focus on minimizing costs, humanitarian relief chains are more concerned about satisfying demand for emergency supplies and saving lives. This task is particularly challenging given that emergency managers must operate under strict budget restrictions. Moreover, humanitarian relief chains take place in a highly dynamic disruption-prone environment where a timely response is vital and resources are scarce. Furthermore, disasters are generally low probability high impact events. Therefore there is typically not enough historic data that can be used to estimate their probabilistic distributions in order to better prepare for their fatal strikes.

In this chapter, we are interested in modeling and solution approaches for both the problem of prepositioning emergency supplies prior to a disaster as well as the problem of their distribution after the disaster onset. The reminder of the chapter is as follows. Section 2 discusses some of the key aspects that are critical to the design and operations of effective relief distribution networks. Section 3 reviews different algorithmic approaches reported in the literature of pre-disaster prepositioning of emergency supplies. This section also presents a non-exhaustive survey of solution approaches for the post-disaster distribution of supplies. Depending on whether uncertainty is taken into account or no, work in these two areas will be classified into two major categories: stochastic or deterministic. A distinction will also be made between exact methods and heuristics. In addition, the advantages and limitations of each of these two classes of approaches will be discussed. Section 4 discusses a methodological framework for addressing the design and operation of relief distribution networks. Finally, section 5 concludes and proposes some interesting research avenues.

HANDLING THE PARTICULARITIES OF RELIEF DISTRIBUTION NETWORKS

As stated before, because of their particularities and characteristics, humanitarian relief chains are more complex and more challenging than their commercial counterparts. Thus, a better understanding of the characteristics and processes that govern a real-world disaster scene is the first step towards the design and operations of effective relief distribution networks. In fact, the elaboration of suitable modeling and solution approaches for the problem is inherent to a judicious integration of these particularities and characteristics. In the following, we roughly discuss some aspects to consider in achieving this goal.

Assessing System Performance

Contrary to commercial distribution chains that are more interested in maximizing profit and minimizing operating costs, their humanitarian counterparts primarily focus on saving lives and mitigating population sufferings. However these goals are unlikely to be fully met due to the strict budget and resource restrictions under which humanitarian relief chains typically operate. Thus, spreading unsatisfied demand fairly among affected populations is an important issue that must be addressed. Therefore, service-based objective functions that incorporate equity seem to be more appropriate to assess the system performance and to achieve a better tradeoff between efficiency and fairness. An Example of these objective functions can be found in Balcik et al. (2008) where the total penalty costs for unsatisfied and late-satisfied demand are minimized. The authors associate a penalty cost factor to each item type at each location to help allocating supplies equitably among the demand locations. Other examples include the minimization of the maximum arrival time (minmax) and the minimization of the average arrival time (minavg) as proposed in Campbell et al. (2008). Equity issues are also discussed in Ogryczak (2000) for the location of public facilities.

Modeling Uncertainly

Humanitarian relief chains take place in a highly dynamic disruption-prone environment where parameters such as travel times, demand arrivals and volumes are random variables that are subject to frequent unpredictable changes. Because disasters are generally low probability events, there is typically not enough historic data that can be used to estimate the probabilistic distribution of these parameters. Hence, scenario-based approaches are often used. In these approaches, a set of probabilistic scenarios are generated to represent different realizations of the random variables. The solution quality increases with the number of scenarios used and greatly depends on the accuracy of these scenarios. An example of scenario-based approaches, namely the Sample Average Approximation method (SAA) is discussed in Ahmed and Shapiro (2002).

Modeling Demand Coverage

Prepositioning emergency supplies is a covering type problem where the objective function typically accounts for total demand covered given that each type of emergency supplies is characterized by its priority and its response time. Covering models have been widely reported in the literature of facility location. The interested reader is referred to Daskin (1995) for a review of these models. A basic covering model assumes that a demand is either fully covered if the service occurs within its response time, or lost otherwise. This assumption does not reflect what is actually observed in a real-disaster scene where demand of some items may be partially covered within a pre-specified coverage interval. An example is the demand for non-consumable items such as equipments or tents. Satisfying this kind of demand fully when it occurs at the beginning of the disaster is highly desirable since this leads to a total benefit. However, receiving partial deliveries of these items later can still be somewhat beneficial as compared to not receiving them at all. Berman et al. (2003) introduces the gradual covering model which is more suitable in this case. In this model, demand is characterized by a covering interval. The model assumes a gradual coverage decreasing from full coverage at the lower bound of the covering interval to no coverage at the upper bound of this interval. A similar model is proposed in Balcik et al. (2008) for the design of a humanitarian relief chain.

Storage and Replenishment Strategy

In the distribution of emergency supplies, routing and inventory decisions are made concurrently over the planning horizon that covers the disaster duration. Inventory decisions include visit schedule for each demand point and the quantity of supplies of each type to be delivered to each demand point at each visit. These decisions must take into account the particularities of different types of supplies (i.e. fully filled vs. backordered demand, various storage requirements, etc…). As stated in Baclik et al. (2008) demand for non-consumable items occurs only in the first period of the planning horizon and may be backordered with a penalty while demand for daily consumable items such as food or medication is considered lost if not fully filled on time. Moreover, non-consumable items are distributed as they are received and therefore do not require storage. Conversely, surplus of delivered quantities of consumable items may be stored for future use with no or some storage limitation. Clearly, these diverse characteristics and requirements must be addressed with caution to elaborate an appropriate replenishment strategy.

LITERATURE REVIEW

This section reviews different algorithmic approaches found in the literature of pre-disaster prepositioning of emergency supplies. It also presents a non-exhaustive survey of solution approaches that have been proposed for the post-disaster distribution of these supplies. Depending on whether uncertainty is taken into account or no, work in each of these two areas will be classified into two major categories: stochastic or deterministic.

The Prepositioning Problem in Humanitarian Supply Chains

Deterministic Prepositioning

Papers that belong to this category assume that all the problem inputs like demand quantities and demand locations are known in advance with certainty. These papers are reviewed in the following.

Iakovou et al. (1996) consider the problem of locating clean-up equipments for oil spill response. The authors propose a mixed-integer linear programming model to determine the locations and quantities of equipments to store as well as their allocation to affected regions. A relaxation of the problem is solved and numerical results are presented for two real-world problem instances. Akkihal (2006) also presents an integer programming model that identifies optimal locations for non-consumable inventories while minimizing the average distance from the nearest warehouse to a demand point. The model also determines the assignment of opened warehouses to demand regions. The author uses historical information on mean annual homeless resulting from natural disasters to estimate demand for non-consumable material requirements.

Tzeng et al. (2007) address the design of a relief delivery system where a set of transfer depots serve as a bridge between collection points and demand points. The authors present a fuzzy multi-objective programming method to locate transfer depots and to determine the amounts of commodities to be transferred to and from these depots. Three objectives are considered: minimizing the total cost, minimizing the total travel time, and maximizing the minimal satisfaction during the planning period. Clark and Culkin (2007) propose a mathematical transshipment multi-commodity model for a similar problem. The model is validated using a small real-life problem instance.

Ghanmi and Shaw (2007) focus on analyzing and assessing the effectiveness of a variety of pre-positioning options. The authors develop a Monte Carlo simulation framework to this end. In these simulations, historical data drawn from previous Canadian Forces deployments provide a baseline performance measure against which different pre-positioning alternatives are compared.

Stochastic Prepositioning

Since disasters are generally low probability events, uncertainty is an inherent characteristic to the pre-disaster pre-positioning problem. Therefore, pre-positioning decisions that are derived from deterministic approaches are likely to be inaccurate in a real-life disaster setting. To overcome this problem, efforts have been made to develop modeling and solution approaches where problem inputs such as demand size and/or location are prone to random variations over time. In the following, we briefly review some of the work that belongs to this category.

Jia et al. (2007) propose a general facility location model to establish facilities for emergency supplies in large-scale emergencies. This general model uses a subset of discrete scenarios from a set of possible emergency settings to represent the likelihood that a certain emergency situation affects a given demand point. However, the model does not account for inventory decisions. To accommodate the characteristics of each large-scale emergency, different models are derived from the proposed general formulation (i.e., set covering, *P*-median or *P*-center models). A review of stochastic facility location models can be found in Snyder (2006).

Ukkusuri and Yushimoto (2008) model the pre-positioning of supplies for disasters as a location-transportation problem. The authors do not consider capacity constraints associated to the facilities or to the vehicles. Moreover, the only source of uncertainty considered is disruption in the transportation network where some pre-selected links have a probability of failure. The authors propose an Integer Programming formulation that determines the pre-positioning of facilities after evaluating the most reliable paths in the network.

Other researchers consider the problem of locating emergency supplies under stochastic demand and capacity constraints on facilities (Baclik and Beamon 2008, Chang et al. 2007, Mete and Zabinsky 2009, Duran et al. 2009). In these papers, decision variables include facility locations, the amount of supplies to hold as well as their allocation to demand points. In Chang et al. (2007), the location of demand points is also stochastic. The authors propose two stochastic programming models to formulate the problem of flood emergency logistics preparation. The objective is to minimize the expected shipping distance of rescue equipment under a set of possible flood scenarios. The proposed models are solved using a sample average approximation scheme. Mete and Zabinsky (2009) use a similar approach for the location and distribution of medical supplies where the objective is to minimize the expected sum of location costs, transportation costs and a penalty of unsatisfied demand. The proposed approach is tested on a small problem based on two earthquake scenarios in the Seattle area. Balcik and Beamon (2008) address a related problem and assume that demand for relief supplies can be met from suppliers and warehouses. The authors propose a variant of the maximal covering location model where the objective is to maximize covered demand under pre-disaster and post-disaster budget constraints. However, in their mixed-integer linear programming model a scenario consists of a single event (i.e., a single demand location and amount). Thus, it is assumed that shortage never occur at distribution centers. This assumption is not realistic since replenishment time is typically not negligible.

Duran et al. (2009) address a similar problem in collaboration with CARE International (one of the largest humanitarian organizations). However, their model account for multiple demand points and assume that demand for relief supplies can be fully satisfied from both pre-established warehouses and suppliers. They propose a mixed integer programming model that minimizes the expected average response time assuming a maximal number of warehouses to open. The authors also assume a maximal total inventory allocated to all warehouses and require that demand at each region is fully satisfied. Since humanitarian organizations typically have restricted budgets, satisfying all demand is not realistic. Moreover, an aggregate capacity constraint over all distribution centers does not reflect real-life conditions.

To the best of our knowledge, all papers found in the literature of pre-disaster prepositioning of emergency supplies propose exact methods. Unfortunately, these methods are unable to handle the large scale computing issues that are inherent to the problem. Thus, they are typically tested on small sized instances only.

Post-Disaster Distribution of Emergency Supplies

This problem generally aims at effectively using a fleet of vehicles to distribute different types of emergency supplies stored in pre-established warehouses to a set of demand points. An objective function that accounts for minimizing disaster impacts is typically optimized under a set of capacity and operational constraints. Different variants have been addressed in the literature to reflect different emergency situations. These variants account for different constraints and objective functions.

It is worth noticing that the problem of distributing emergency supplies can be viewed as a variant of the Inventory Routing Problem (IRP).

In this problem, a fleet of vehicles is used to deliver various items to a set of customers over a finite planning time horizon. Decisions include visit schedule of each customer, the quantity of supplies of each type to be delivered at each visit and the vehicle route to be used for each visit. While demand satisfaction and equitable service are prioritized in the distribution of emergency supplies, the objective function in the IRP typically minimizes total transportation and inventory costs. A review of the IRP can be found in Baita et al. (1998) and Campbell et al. (2001).

Deterministic Post-Disaster Distribution of Emergency Supplies

Solution approaches reported in the literature of this problem can be classified into two major categories. They are reported in the following.

i. Exact Methods

These methods are based on mathematical formulations of the problem that are solved using some commercial optimization software like Cplex. Ray (1987) presents one of the earliest works in this category. The author addresses the distribution of food-aid. He proposes a single-commodity multi-modal network flow model on a capacitated network over a multi-period planning horizon. The objective is to minimize the sum of total transportation and inventory costs incurred during the planning horizon.

Knott (1987) develops a linear programming model for food delivery from a single distribution center to a set of camps using a homogonous fleet of vehicles. Two objective functions are considered: maximizing the total quantity to deliver and minimizing total transportation while satisfying demand. However, routing is not addressed since the model assumes that loads cannot be consolidated. Angelis et al. (2007) also address an emergency food distribution problem where routing is not considered. Multiple depots are used and planes are required to deliver full load to a visited demand point. The authors develop a linear integer programming model that maximizes the total satisfied demand. Computational results are reported for small real-world problem instances.

Balcik et al. (2008) address the problem of delivering consumable and non-consumable emergency supplies from a local distribution center to disaster-affected populations. The authors propose a mixed integer programming model that accounts for capacity and delivery time restrictions. The objective is to minimize the sum of routing costs and penalty costs for lost and backordered demand. Mete and Zabinsky (2009) also propose a mixed integer programming model for delivering medical supplies after a disaster onset. The proposed model is tested on a small real-world problem instance based on two earthquake scenarios in the Seattle area.

Other researchers focus on equity and fairness in humanitarian supply chains. For example, Desai et al. (2004) address these issues in the dispatch of emergency response resources to mitigate risks attributable to natural or man-made disasters. The authors develop a non-convex program which determines the number of emergency responders to allocate to each of the affected regions while assuring risk equity across these regions. A linear programming relaxation is derived for the proposed model which is solved using a branch and bound procedure. A hypothetical case scenario is used to assess the effectiveness of the proposed solution approach.

ii. Heuristics and Other Approaches

Since comprehensive mathematical formulations are hard to derive for real-life emergency situations, heuristics and simulation based approaches have been proposed in the literature. Knott (1988) proposes heuristics inspired from artificial intelligence to vehicle scheduling for supplying bulk relief of food to a disaster area. Brown and Vassiliou (1993) develop a real-time decision support system which uses optimization methods, simulation, and the decision maker's judgment for operational assignment of units to tasks and for tactical allocation of units to task requirements. The proposed decision system is tested on a hypothetical scenario where major damages to public works are repaired following a major earthquake.

Other researchers model the problem of emergency logistics as a multi-period multi-commodity network flow where routing is also considered (Haghani and Oh 1996, Oh and Haghani 1997, Ozdamar et al. 2004, Ozdamar and Yi 2008). Haghani and Oh (1996) and Oh and Haghani (1997) develop a large-scale mixed-integer linear programming that minimizes total operational costs. The proposed formulation is based on the concept of a time-space network where time-varying movements of commodities and personnel are represented by three types of links, including routing, transfer, and supply/demand carry-over links. Two heuristics are proposed. One is based on Lagrangian relaxation and the other is an interactive fix-and-run procedure. Ozdamar et al. (2004) consider a dynamic version of the problem with pick-up and delivery where new plans are generated to account for new events such as new demand requests and new supplies. The objective is to minimize the total unsatisfied demand. The authors propose a greedy heuristic and a lagrangian relaxation algorithm. Ozdamar and Yi (2008) propose a constructive greedy heuristic for a similar problem where the objective is to minimize total service delay. The devised heuristic is based on a greedy *l*-neighborhood search technique that extends the definition of neighborhood to account for the problem special needs.

Barbarosoglu et al. (2002) develop a multi-objective mathematical model for helicopter mission planning during a disaster. The authors propose a bi-level hierarchical decomposition approach and an iterative coordination heuristic to solve the proposed model. The top-level of this mathematical model deals with tactical decisions such as crew missions and the assignment of helicopters from the air force bases to the operation base. The base-level of the model tackles the corresponding operational decisions such as routing, rescue plans and re-fueling schedules.

Campbell et al (2008) address equity issues in the distribution of emergency supplies. The authors discuss two alternatives to the use of operating cost-based objective functions typically found in commercial TSP and VRP. The first one minimizes the maximum arrival time (minmax) while the second one minimizes the average arrival time (minavg). The authors argue that these objective functions represent equity in relief distribution networks. Solution approaches that are based on local search techniques and simple insertion procedures are presented for these new variants. Worst case performance analysis is also conducted for optimal TSP and VRP solutions that account for these alternate objectives. Computational results are reported on randomly generated problem instances where 31 to 79 customers are uniformly distributed and where the depot is not necessarily in the center.

Stochastic Post-Disaster Distribution of Emergency Supplies

The stochastic distribution of emergency supplies has been seldom addressed. In the following, we review the few papers that we found in the literature of this problem.

Barbarosoglu and Arda (2004) propose a two-stage stochastic programming model to plan the distribution of first-aid commodities. The model is a multi-commodity multi-model network flow formulation where demand, arc capacities and supply amounts at nodes are represented as random variables. The objective is to minimize the expected sum of total costs and the penalty of unsatisfied demand. The authors propose a scenario-based exact approach which is tested on small real-case problems.

Shen et al. (2005) address a stochastic vehicle routing problem in response to large-scale emergencies. The problem is decomposed into two stages where pre-planned routes are designed in the first stage and adjustments to these routes are made in the second stage. A chance constrained model is proposed for the planning stage and is solved using a tabu search heuristic. On the other hand, three different recourse strategies are developed for the operational stage and are solved using exact and heuristic methods. Simulations are conducted to assess the effectiveness of the proposed modeling and solution approaches.

The literature discussed in this section on the prepositioning problem in humanitarian Supply Chains and the post-disaster distribution of emergency supplies is summarized in Table 1.

Table 1. Summary of previous and current research

Author(s)	Pre-Disaster Prepositioning Problem	Post-Disaster Distribution Problem	Deterministic	Stochastic
Iakovou et al. (1996)	✓		✓	
Akkihal (2006)	✓		✓	
Tzeng et al. (2007)	✓		✓	
Clark and Culkin (2007)	✓		✓	
Ghanmi and Shaw (2007)	✓		✓	
Jia et al. (2007)	✓			✓
Snyder (2006)	✓			✓
Ukkusuri and Yushimoto (2008)	✓			✓
Balcik and Beamon (2008)	✓			✓
Chang et al. (2007)	✓			✓
Mete and Zabinsky (2009)	✓	✓	✓	✓
Duran et al. 2009	✓			✓
Chang et al. (2007)	✓			✓
Knott (1987)		✓	✓	
Knott (1988)		✓	✓	
Angelis et al. (2007)		✓	✓	
Balcik et al. (2008)		✓	✓	
Desai et al. (2004)		✓	✓	
Brown and Vassiliou (1993)		✓	✓	
Haghani and Oh (1996)		✓	✓	
Oh and Haghani (1997)		✓	✓	
Ozdamar et al. (2004)		✓	✓	
Ozdamar and Yi (2008)		✓	✓	
Barbarosoglu et al. (2002)		✓	✓	
Campbell et al. (2008)		✓	✓	
Barbarosoglu and Arda (2004)		✓		✓
Shen et al. (2005)		✓		✓

METHODOLOGICAL FRAMEWORK

Prepositioning emergency supplies is a strategic decision aimed at designing the relief distribution network away before the disaster strikes. The designed distribution network is used latter to conduct daily operations aimed at delivering emergency supplies to disaster-affected populations. Thus, pre-positioning of emergency supplies and their distribution is a typical decision time hierarchy situation as defined in Schneeweiss (2003). In the following, we discuss a methodological framework for the design and operations of relief distribution networks using the conceptual approach proposed in Schneeweiss (2003). A similar framework has been used to tackle the Stochastic Multi-Period Location-Routing Problem (Klibi et al. 2009).

Design decisions including the number of local distribution centers, their locations and quantities of supplies to hold in them are made at the strategic-level at an instant t_0. The designed distribution network is used afterward at the operational-level starting at some instant $t_1 > t_0$, for the disaster duration, to daily determine when and how much to deliver to each demand point and which route to use. Clearly, design decisions and daily operational decisions have a significant mutual impact on each other. Thus, a judicious integration of these two decision processes is essential to enhance the relief network performance. A major issue in achieving this integration is that the two decision processes take place at different points of time relying on different information status. Strategic decisions are made at instant t_0 based on vague information available at that time (e.g. estimate demand of each type over the disaster duration, estimate traveling costs, etc…). Operational decisions on the other hand rely on more recent and precise information (e.g. actual demand of each type per period, explicit available routes, more accurate traveling times, etc...). To overcome this problem, strategic and operational decisions can be integrated using a distributed decision process as proposed in Schneeweiss (2003). At the strategic level, design decisions are made based on information available at instant t_0 such as feasible locations for the distribution centers and the matrix of distances between these locations. These strategic decisions minimize the expected cost of establishing the distribution centers while taking into account an anticipation of the operational level. The latter represents operational decisions that optimize an estimate of some operational criterion under approximate operational information available at instant t_0. For example, the operational level anticipation may minimize total transportation and inventory costs and/or maximize total satisfied demand based on forecasted demand of each type at each time period, estimate resources available at each time period, etc…

It is worth noticing that the operational-level anticipation used in the distributed decision process described above is an approximate way of taking into account the effect of the network design on its future use. Thus the accuracy of the resulting design is inherent to the precision of models used to accomplish this approximation. Clearly, the more details we include in the approximation models, the better the anticipation is. A possible anticipation can be obtained using an estimate unit cost of transporting an item type from a distribution center to a demand point instead of actual routing costs. Demand of each type can also be aggregated over the disaster duration. These estimated parameters can be obtained using a set of probabilistic scenarios. A better anticipation would consider the actual traveling costs which depend on the explicit routes used. The resulting problem would be a Stochastic Multi-Period Location-Inventory-Routing Problem. Klibi et al. (2009) propose a similar approach for the Stochastic Multi-Period Location-Routing Problem. This problem naturally leads to complex models that are hard to solve. The integration of inventory decisions brings additional concerns that must be addressed with caution. Section 2 discusses some of these issues.

Having anticipated the operational-level, the strategic-level selects the best design decisions to implement. The implemented design will be used later for the distribution of emergency supplies during a disaster of duration T. Hence, at each time period $t \in T$ actual operational information is used to determine the schedule of visits for each demand point, quantities to deliver of each product type and vehicle routes.

CONCLUSION

In the past few years, there has been an increased interest in the design and operations of relief distribution networks. This attention is mainly motivated by a worldwide increasing trend in natural and man-made disaster numbers as well as the alarming and devastating impacts of these disasters on human lives and global economy. Researchers have focused on developing effective modeling and solution approaches to enhance the performance of relief distribution networks. However, this research line has not reached maturity yet and many related challenging issues still need to be investigated. Some of these new research directions are presented in the following.

- Modeling approaches for the Prepositioning Problem in Humanitarian Supply Chains typically lead to large-scale mixed integer programs. These models are commonly tackled in the literature using exact methods. Unfortunately, these methods require an extensive computing time and can therefore be applied to small sized instances only. Thus, the elaboration of heuristic approaches that can tackle realistic relief distribution networks must be investigated. In addition to large-scale computing issues, these heuristics should handle the complexity and particularities of humanitarian supply chains accurately. A key element to the success of these efforts is to account for uncertainty while integrating long-term and tactical decisions. To address these issues, innovative ways need to be devised.
- Recent advances in communication and information technologies now afford opportunities for using real-time information in the distribution of emergency supplies after a disaster onset. However there is still a lack of solution approaches that integrate real-time information while effectively coping with time pressure which is inherent to a disaster scene. An interesting avenue to explore would be the elaboration of meta-heuristics that effectively combine fast on-line strategies and neighborhood search procedures. Fast on-line strategies would handle dynamic changes while neighborhood search procedures would be used to improve the solution quality. In this process, the integration of routing and inventory decisions under the particular storage and replenishment requirements of relief distribution networks should be addressed with caution.
- The distribution of emergency supplies after a disaster onset takes place in a highly dynamic stochastic setting. In this environment, decision makers are faced with the urgency of making vital decisions in limited time based on limited a priori information. To cope with these challenging issues, novel solution approaches need to be developed.
- In the literature, uncertainty is often associated with predictable events for which probability distributions can be derived from historical data (e.g. changes in travel times during peak hours, demand arrival and quantity in stable markets, etc…). However an emergency scene is characterized by a high disruption level where unpredictable events often arise. Examples

of these events include sudden changes in travel times due to severe damages in the transportation network, unavailability of supplies due to unexpected shutdown of some affected distribution centers, etc... Since these events are associated with scarce and low quality a priori information, planning in advance for solution approaches that account for them seems to be challenging. At the best, one can only hope being able to mitigate their impacts when they happen. This can be achieved through the elaboration of judicious recourse strategies that allow a quick and effective restoration of the pre-planned solution whenever an unpredictable event occurs. Taxonomy of such events need to be developed to help identifying appropriate responses.

- Time pressure is a major challenge in humanitarian distribution networks because of the urgency to supply affected populations with what is needed when it is exactly needed. Thus the elaboration of fast solution approaches that lead to quick decision making is essential to the system effectiveness. Recent developments in parallel computing techniques offer a powerful tool that can be used to this end. However, as pointed out in Ichoua et al. (2007), the literature of parallel optimization algorithms for dynamic distribution networks is very limited.
- Major natural or man-made disasters typically require the involvement of different organizations including local, state and federal agencies. In such distributed settings, managing the coordination of all these parties effectively is essential to a successful emergency response. Specific distributed algorithms for the dispatch and management of resources must be developed. A successful implementation of these algorithms is inherent to a judicious management of the flow of real-time information that unfolds in this complex environment. Issues related to effectively communicating and sharing information as well as rapidly integrating and processing the shared information need to be addressed carefully.

ACKNOWLEDGMENT

This material is based upon work supported by the National Science Foundation under Grant No. 0927129. This support is gratefully acknowledged.

REFERENCES

Ahmed, S., & Shapiro, A. (2002). The Sample Average Approximation Method for Stochastic Programs with Integer Recourse. *SIAM Journal on Optimization*, *12*, 479–502.

Akkihal, A. R. (2006). Inventory pre-positioning for humanitarian operations. Master's thesis, MIT.

Angelis, V. D., Mecoli, M., Nikoi, C., & Storchi, G. (2007). Multiperiod integrated routing and scheduling of World Food Programme cargo planes in Angola. *Computers & Operations Research*, *34*, 1601–1615. doi:10.1016/j.cor.2005.07.012

Ardekani, S. A., & Hobeika, A. (1988). Logistics problems in the aftermath of the 1985 Mexico City earthquake. *Transportation Quarterly*, *42*, 1077124.

Baita, F., Ukovich, W., Pesenti, R., & Favaretto, D. (1998). Dynamic routing-and-inventory problems: A review. *Transportation Research*, *32*(8), 585–598.

Balcik, B., & Beamon, B. M. (2008). Facility location in humanitarian relief. *International Journal of Logistics: Research and Applications*, *11*(2), 101–121. doi:10.1080/13675560701561789

Balcik, B., Beamon, B. M., & Smilowitz, K. (2008). Last Mile Distribution in Humanitarian Relief. *Journal of Intelligent Transportation Systems*, *12*(2), 51–63. doi:10.1080/15472450802023329

Barbarosoglu, G., & Arda, Y. (2004). A two-stage stochastic programming framework for transportation planning in disaster response. *The Journal of the Operational Research Society*, *55*(1), 43–53. doi:10.1057/palgrave.jors.2601652

Barbarosoglu, G., Ozdamar, L., & Cevik, A. (2002). An interactive approach for hierarchical analysis of helicopter logistics in disaster relief operations. *European Journal of Operational Research*, *140*(1), 118–133. doi:10.1016/S0377-2217(01)00222-3

Berman, O., Krass, D., & Drezner, Z. (2003). The gradual covering decay location problem on a network. *European Journal of Operational Research*, *151*(3), 447–674. doi:10.1016/S0377-2217(02)00604-5

Brown, G. G., & Vassiliou, A. L. (1993). Optimizing disaster relief: real-time operational and tactical decision support. *Nav. Res. Logist.*, *40*, 1-23. doi:10.1002/1520-6750(199302)40:1<1::AID-NAV3220400102>3.0.CO;2-S

Campbell, A. M., Clarke, L. W., & Savelsbergh, M. W. P. (2001). Inventory routing in practice. In *Inventory routing in practice* (pp. 309–330). Philadelphia, PA: Society for Industrial and Applied Mathematics.

Campbell, A. M., Vandenbussche, D., & Hermann, W. (2008). Routing for Relief Efforts. *Transportation Science*, *42*(2), 127–145. doi:10.1287/trsc.1070.0209

Chang, M. S., Tseng, Y. L., & Chen, J. W. (2007). A scenario planning approach for the flood emergency logistics preparation problem under uncertainty. *Transportation Research Part E, Logistics and Transportation Review*, *43*, 737–754. doi:10.1016/j.tre.2006.10.013

Church, R.L. & ReVelle, C. (1974). The maximal covering location problem, Papers Region. *Sci. Assoc.*, *32*(1), 101–118. doi:10.1007/BF01942293

Clark, A., & Culkin, B. (2007). *A Network Transshipment Model for Planning Humanitarian Relief Operations after a Natural Disaster*. Paper presented at EURO XXII - 22nd European Conference on Operational Research, Prague.

CRID. The Federal Response to Hurricane Katrina: Lessons Learned (2006, February 23) White House Homeland Security Council. Retrieved February 10, 2009 from http://www.crid.or.cr/digitalizacion/pdf/eng/doc17272/doc17272-0.pdf

Daskin, M. S. (1995). *Network and discrete location: Models, algorithms and applications*. New York: Wiley.

Desai, J., Sherali, H. D., & Glickman, T. S. (2004). Allocating emergency response resources to minimize risk under equity considerations. *American Journal of Mathematical and Management Sciences*, *24*(3/4), 367–410.

Duran, S., Gutierrez, M. A., & Keskinocak, P. (2009). Pre-Positioning of Emergency Items Worldwide for CARE International. Retrieved January 28, 2009 from http://www.scl.gatech.edu/research/humanitarian/files/CAREPrepositioningofInventorypaper.pdf

EM-DAT. (n.d.). The OFDA/CRED International Disaster Database, Université Catholique de Louvain- Brussels – Belgium, UR. Retrieved January 20, 2009 from http://www.em-dat.net

Ghanmi, A., & Shaw, R. (2007). Modeling and analysis of Canadian Forces strategic lift and pre-positioning options. *The Journal of the Operational Research Society*, 1–12.

GPO. (n.d.). Hurricane Katrina: A Nation Still Unprepared, U.S. Senate Report 109-322. Retrieved July 24, 2007 from http://www.gpoaccess.gov/serialset/creports/pdf/sr109-322/ch24.pdf

Haghani, A., & Oh, S. C. (1996). Formulation and solution of a multi-commodity, multi-modal network flow model for disaster relief operations. *Transportation Research Part A, Policy and Practice*, *30*(3), 231–250. doi:10.1016/0965-8564(95)00020-8

Iakovou, E., Ip, C. M., Douligeris, C., & Korde, A. (1996). Optimal location and capacity of emergency cleanup equipment for oil spill response. *European Journal of Operational Research*, *96*(1), 72–80. doi:10.1016/S0377-2217(96)00106-3

Ichoua, S., Gendreau, M., & Potvin, J. Y. (2007). Planned Routes Approaches for Real-Time Vehicle Routing. In *Dynamic Fleet Management: Concepts, Systems, Algorithms & Case Studies*. New York: Springer-Verlag.

Jenkins, W. O., Jr. (2007, March 9). Homeland Security: Preparing for and Responding to Disasters, homeland security and justice issues, before the Subcommittee on Homeland Security, House Committee on Appropriations. GAO-07-395T. Retrieved February 10, 2009 from http://www.gao.gov/cgi-bin/getrpt?GAO-07-395T

Jia, H., Ordonez, F. & Dessouky, M. (2007). A modeling framework for facility location of medical services for large-scale emergencies. *IIE Transactions*, *39*(1), 41-55(15).

Kemball-Cook, D., & Stephenson, R. (1984). Lessons in logistics from Somalia. *Disasters*, *8*, 57–66. doi:10.1111/j.1467-7717.1984.tb00853.x

Klibi, W., Lasalle, F., Martel, A., & Ichoua, S. (2010). The Stochastic Multi-Period Location Transportation Problem. *Transportation Science*, *44*, 221–237. doi:10.1287/trsc.1090.0307

Knott, R. (1987). The logistics of bulk relief supplies. *Disasters*, *11*, 113–115. doi:10.1111/j.1467-7717.1987.tb00624.x

Knott, R. (1988). Vehicle scheduling for emergency relief management: A knowledge-based approach. *Disasters*, *12*, 285–293. doi:10.1111/j.1467-7717.1988.tb00678.x

Larson, R. C., Metzger, M. D., & Cahn, M. F. (2005). Emergency Response for Homeland Security: Lessons Learned and the Need for Analysis. Retrieved June 2, 2008 from http://www.sdcorp.net/public/Pub_Emergency_Response_Homeland_Security.pdf

Mete, H. O., & Zabinsky, Z. B. (2009). Preparing for Disasters: Medical Supply Location and Distribution. Retrieved January 25, 2009 from http://parvac.washington.edu/papers/downloadpaper.php/id=13/parvac_13.pdf

Ogryczak, W. (2000). Inequality measures and equitable approaches to location problems. *European Journal of Operational Research*, *122*, 374–391. doi:10.1016/S0377-2217(99)00240-4

Oh, S. C., & Haghani, A. (1997). Testing and evaluation of a multi-commodity multi-modal network flow model for disaster relief management. *Journal of Advanced Transportation*, *31*(3), 249–282. doi:10.1002/atr.5670310304

OIG-06-32 (2006, March). Office of Inspector General, Department of Homeland Security: "A Performance Review of FEMA Disaster Management Activities in Response to Hurricane Katrina. Retrieved April 29, 2006 from http://www.dhs.gov/xoig/assets/mgmtrpts/OIG_06-32_Mar06.pdf

OIG-08-11 (2008, January). Department of Homeland Security Inspector General, Major Management Challenges Facing the Department of Homeland Security. Retrieved February 10, 2009 from http://www.dhs.gov/xoig/assets/mgmtrpts/OIG_08-11_Jan08.pdf

Oloruntoba, R., & Gray, R. (2006). Humanitarian aid: an agile supply chain. *Supply Chain Management: an International Journal, 11*(2), 115–120. doi:10.1108/13598540610652492

Ozdamar, L., Ekinci, E., & Kucukyazici, B. (2004). Emergency logistics planning in natural disasters. *Annals of Operations Research, 129*, 217–245. doi:10.1023/B:ANOR.0000030690.27939.39

Ozdamar, L., & Yi, W. (2008). Greedy Neighborhood Search for Disaster Relief and Evacuation Logistics. *IEEE Intelligent Systems, 23*(1), 14–23. doi:10.1109/MIS.2008.7

Ray, J. (1987). *A multi-period linear programming model for optimally scheduling the distribution of food-aid in West Africa*. MS Thesis, University of Tennessee, Knoxville, TN.

Schneeweiss, C. (2003). *Distributed Decision Making* (2nd ed.). Berlin: Springer-Verlag.

Shapiro, A. (2003). Monte Carlo Sampling Methods. In Raszczynski & Shapiro (Eds.), *Stochastic Programming, Handbooks in OR-MS 10*. Amsterdam: Elsevier.

Shen, Z., Dessouky, M., & Ordonez, F. (2005). Stochastic vehicle routing problem for large-scale emergencies (Technical Report 2005-06). Department of Industrial and Systems Engineering, University of Southern California.

Snyder, L. V. (2006). Facility location under uncertainty: a review. *IIE Transactions, 38*, 537–554. doi:10.1080/07408170500216480

Thomas, A. S. (2003). *Humanitarian Logistics: Enabling Disaster Response*. Fritz Institute. Retrieved July 4, 2008 from http://www.fritzinstitute.org/PDFs/WhitePaper/EnablingDisasterResponse.pdf

Thomas, A. S., & Kopczak, L. R. (2005). *From Logistics to Supply Chain Management: The Path Forward in the Humanitarian Sector*. Fritz Institute. Retrieved July 4, 2008 from http://www.fritzinstitute.org/PDFs/WhitePaper/FromLogisticsto.pdf

Tzeng, G. H., Cheng, H. J., & Huang, T. D. (2007). Multi-objective optimal planning for designing relief delivery systems. *Transportation Research Part E, Logistics and Transportation Review, 43*, 673–686. doi:10.1016/j.tre.2006.10.012

Ukkusuri, S. V., & Yushimoto, W.F. (2008). Location Routing Approach for the Humanitarian Prepositioning Problem. *Journal of Transportation Research Record*, 18-25.

Van Wassenhove, L. N. (2006). Blackett memorial lecture - humanitarian aid logistics: supply chain management in high gear. *The Journal of the Operational Research Society, 57*(5), 475–489. doi:10.1057/palgrave.jors.2602125

Section 3
Supply Chain Operations

Chapter 9

An Analytical Model to Estimate the Optimum Production Rate of Picking Processes in a Modular Warehouse Environment

Dimitrios M. Emiris
University of Piraeus, Greece

Athanasios Skarlatos
University of Piraeus, Greece

ABSTRACT

One of the most important, complicated and expensive processes in a warehouse is order-picking. The cost associated with order preparation and picking typically varies between 40% and 60% of the total cost of all the processes in a warehouse; therefore, improving the productivity in order picking would result directly in cost reduction. In any attempt to reduce costs in order picking, one has to take into account: (i) the design of the warehouse so that the pickers' work may be controlled at all instances, (ii) the existence of standards on the pickers' work so that performance measurements may be compared and contrasted reliably, and (iii) the analysis of the phases of the picking process so that the pickers' productivity may be measured and maximized. Such a series of concerns and parameters leads to the necessity of developing a mathematical parametric model which may serve as a useful tool for the warehouse manager in his efforts to not only measure productivity but also to intervene in the process and proceed to improvements. The present work deals with the development of such an analytical parametric model for the order picking process in a modular warehouse. The research attempts to address and solve three distinct, yet relevant, areas of focus: (i) to produce a generic and analytical framework to model the order picking process, (ii) to define practical and easy to adopt performance measures for

DOI: 10.4018/978-1-61520-633-9.ch009

the order picking process, and (iii) to provide the tools for a warehouse manager to set goals, measure performance and identify areas of improvement in his areas of responsibility. In addition to these, the research sets the foundations to further expand on other warehouse processes, such as loading/unloading, products receipt, etc., that supersede the boundaries of order picking. The analysis is corroborated by a real case study, among the many monitored in a pragmatic setup, accompanied by ABC analysis of the warehouse operation and a presentation of a fair frame to measure workers' performance.

INTRODUCTION

The increased competition among 3PL firms has led them to make efforts to provide the highest service level and, at the same time, to decrease the cost. The latter may be achieved in several ways, among which is the improvement in the personnel productivity and the increase in the correctness of order execution.

One of the most important, complicate and expensive processes in a warehouse is *order-picking*, and is a key process for cost reduction. The cost associated with order preparation and picking typically varies between 40% and 60% of the total cost of all the processes in a warehouse; therefore, improving the productivity in order picking would result directly in cost reduction. Some common immediate concerns that arise when trying to achieve this goal are: How can we improve the order-picking productivity? How can we set realistic goals and monitor everyday performance? How can personnel and resources utilization be maximized? How can the productivity of each picker be tracked? How can we define the warehouse capacity with respect to order execution?

At the same time, one has to take into account the following parameters: (i) the design of the warehouse so that the pickers' work may be controlled at all instances, (ii) the existence of standards on the pickers' work so that performance measurements may be compared and contrasted reliably, and (iii) the analysis of the phases of the picking process so that the pickers' productivity may be measured and maximized. Such a series of concerns and parameters leads to the necessity of developing a mathematical parametric model, aiming to monitor accurately the order-picking process and improve productivity. This model may serve as a useful tool for the warehouse manager in his efforts to not only measure productivity but also to intervene in the process and proceed to improvements.

The present work deals with the development of an analytical parametric model for the order picking process in a modular warehouse. The modules of the warehouse are considered to be the distinct sections where operations reside; typically, each operation corresponds to one customer. This research attempts to address and solve three distinct, yet relevant, areas of focus: (i) to produce a generic and analytical framework to model the order picking process, (ii) to define practical and easy to adopt performance measures for the order picking process, and (iii) to provide the tools for a warehouse manager to set goals, measure performance and identify areas of improvement in his areas of responsibility. In addition to these, the research sets the foundations to further expand on other warehouse processes, such as loading/unloading, products receipt, etc., that supersede the boundaries of order picking.

This article is structure as follows. We provide a brief literature review on performance measurement in the supply chain and in order picking, in particular. Then, we describe the parameters that compose the model and overview the steps towards the model development. We also record and classify the elementary movements involved in any picking process, we provide the definitions for basic, normal and standard times for picking movements, and explain how these result from observation and sampling. In the next section, we study the issue of performance measurements and show how these can be extracted in a modular warehouse environment; then, we illustrate how the parametric model is implemented, by first calculating the total standard times per profile, then by setting the targets per profile and finally, by setting the total target for the operation (warehouse module). Our analysis is enriched with a real case study, among the many we have monitored in a pragmatic setup. Then, we present the results of our analysis and demonstrate our findings on the ABC analysis of the warehouse operation; furthermore, we indicate how performance can be improved and we set a fair frame to measure workers' performance. Finally, we summarize our contributions and set the guidelines for future research.

BRIEF LITERATURE REVIEW

The problem of determining supply chain costs has been recognized since the 1930s (Heckert, 1940).The analysis of distribution costs appears to have paralleled the evolution of the integrated logistics management concept. Distribution costs remained largely a "dark continent" through the early 1960s. Mentzer and Konrad (1991) first presented a set of indices to measure the logistics performance using an analytical approach. They divided the logistics operation into the areas of transportation, warehousing, inventory control, order processing and logistics administration and proposed a set of performance criteria for each of these areas. The criteria were, in turn, classified in terms of their areas of measurement into labor, cost, time, utilization, equipment, energy, and transit time measures and in each class a set of distinct measures was attributed. Issues in supply chain costing with respect to supply chain performance have been investigated by Lalonde and Pohlen (1996). They examined the available tools for effectively costing an extended supply chain and evaluated the methods in terms of their cost-effectiveness; they also investigated how these cost measures apply to profitability and performance over time. One of the methods to measure performance is ABC analysis, which emerged during the 80s as a means to assign costs within an organization (Cooper, (1989)). Over the years, ABC has gained considerable attention as a potential tool for evaluating supply chain performance. General concerns and characteristics of supply chain performance measurements were investigated by Lapide and Happen (2000). They addressed questions, such as, why is performance measurement important, what approaches exist to measure supply chains, what methods exist for setting performance targets, etc.

In this context, several literature reviews about supply chain modeling as a whole have been presented, which gathered the knowledge presented at that time on models and methods. Beamon (1998) focused on the literature review in multi-stage supply chain modeling and in particular, in the performance, design and analysis of the supply chain as a whole. Min and Zhou (2002) synthesized past supply chain modeling efforts and identified key challenges and opportunities associated with supply chain modeling; furthermore, they provided various guidelines for the successful development and implementation of supply chain models. Meixell and Gargeya (2005) reviewed decision support models for the design of global supply chains and assessed the fit between the research literature in the area and the practical issues of global supply chain design. Their classification scheme included four review dimensions, among which was that of the performance metrics including works for order picking. Most recently, Gu et al. (2007) performed an extensive review on warehouse operation planning problems and classified them according to the basic warehouse functions, i.e., receiving, storage, order picking, and shipping. The literature in each category was summarized with an emphasis on the characteristics of various decision support models and solution algorithms. At the same time, de Koster et al. (2007) gave a literature overview (140 papers) on typical decision problems in design and control of manual order-picking processes and focus on the optimal (internal) layout design, storage assignment methods, routing methods, order batching and zoning. They recommended promising research directions among which is the performance measurement and the order picking objectives.

Parallel to the general research on supply chain modeling, extensive research efforts have been targeted to the development of metrics for the performance measurement in various aspects of a warehouse operation. Performance measurement in distribution centers has been addressed, among others, by Kuo et al. (1999). They selected five distribution centers in the Pacific Northwest and discussed their characteristics and their measurement systems. One of the processes they examined was order-picking, where they identified the performance measurements used which were expressed either in volume processed per time unit, or percent of orders completed daily, or as hours worked over hours planned. They did not proceed into further detail and examined order picking as a whole rather as aggregation of primitive movements. Holmberg (2000) used IKEA as an example to introduce a performance model, used to reflect the systemic structure of the underlying supply chain and a potential integrator. He emphasized the importance of his systemic approach as an adequate one to reveal relationships not only among operations in a warehouse but also among processes and performance indices.

During the last decade, Lambert and Pohlen (2001) provided a framework for developing supply chain metrics which translated performance into shareholder value. The framework focused on managing the interfacing customer relationship management and supplier relationship management processes at each link in the supply chain. Gunasekaran et al. (2001) developed a framework for measuring the strategic, tactical and operational level performance in a supply chain and presented a list of key performance metrics. In developing these metrics, they made an effort to align and relate them to customer satisfaction. Faber et al. (2002) focused on warehouse operations and, among other observations, they concluded that the number of order lines to be processed per day and the number of stock-keeping units are the two main observable aspects of warehouse complexity. Although this is a valid statement, it reveals the lack of insight that many firms have into the inner mechanisms and factors that affect performance and should be measured. Chan and Qi (2003), proposed a process-based approach to mapping and analyzing the particularly complex supply chain network. Through this approach, they proposed a performance measurement system, in which a method called performance of activity was used to identify the performance measures and metrics. Dekker et al. (2004) experimented on a warehouse of a wholesaler of tools and garden equipment and aimed in determining a good combination of policies for storage assignment and routing. They adapted existing solution techniques and managed to reduce the average route length in the order-picking operation by 31% and the number of order pickers by 25%. Hwang and Cho (2006) studied the problem of developing a performance evaluation model for the order picking facility in a supply center by reducing the travel distance of transporters. They incorporated important aspects of warehouse design and operational parameters such as, warehouse size, rack size, number of transporters, etc., and developed both mathematical and simulation modes considering probabilistic demand and picking frequency. Finally, Manzini et al. (2007) introduced an analytical model and a multi-parametric dynamic model to quickly estimate the traveled distance during a picking cycle and performed a factorial analysis of several what-if scenarios that revealed which factors and combinations of factors are the most critical in affecting the picking system's response.

Apart of performance metrics and performance evaluation, special interest has been targeted on picking processes and warehouse layout design to optimize order picking. One such study was presented by Brynzer at al. (1994). They adapted a methodology previously applied for assembly production systems and enumerated the elementary processes involved in order-picking. They further classified the latter into direct supporting activities, related activities and disturbances. A distinct contribution of their work was that they identified the loss-generating processes during order-picking. Van der Vorst (2006) investigated performance measurement in agri-food supply-chain networks. He also recognized that operations are composed of processes which are further broken down into a directed and connected network of (sub-)processes/ activities. The latter should be measured and their individual performance affects the entire supply-chain performance. A systemic and technical solution for the measurement of performance in order picking was presented by Chow et al. (2006). They designed a RFID-based Resource Management System (RFID-RMS) to help users select the most suitable resource usage packages for handling warehouse operation orders by retrieving and analyzing useful knowledge from a case-based data warehouse for solutions in both time saving and cost effective manner. They incorporated a customized route optimizing programming model, using real-time data of an RFID tag to solve the order picking problems of material handling equipment.

Most recently, Hsich and Tsai (2006) considered the effects on the order picking system for factors such as quantity and layout type of cross aisles in a warehouse system, storage assignment policy, picking route, average picking density inside an aisle, and order combination type. Le-Duc and de Koster (2007) investigated the order batching problem (OBP), that is, the problem of determining the number of orders to be picked together in one picking tour, by setting as objective the minimization of the average throughput time of a random order. Following this work, Nieuwenhuyse and de Koster (2009) studied the impact of order batching policy, the capacity of picking and sorting operations, and the picking policy used, on the average customer order throughput time, and extended the results of the previous research to warehouses with time window batching and separate picking and sorting functions. Almost at the same time, Roodbergen et al. (2008) presented a model that minimizes travel distances in the picking area by identifying an appropriate layout structure consisting of one or more blocks on parallel aisles. The model was developed for one commonly used routing policy, but was shown to be fairly accurate for other routing policies.

ANALYSIS OF THE PARAMETRIC MODEL

In this section, we present the methodology that was followed for the production of the parametric model. The basic variables that affect the model, are: (i) the nature of the product, (ii) the characteristics of the order (boxes - codes), (iii) the spatial characteristics of storage, and (iv) the methods and strategies of order preparation and picking. Each of these variables corresponds to a discrete step of the model development.

The Nature of the Product

Products are characterized subject to their nature with respect to three main criteria that formulate respective categories. The first category classifies the products based on their particular storage conditions (normal, cool and frost). Storage conditions affect a picker's work, productivity and quality of picking. Picking in frost conditions, for example, typically exhibits lower productivity than picking in room temperature conditions. The second category classifies the products based on their logistics data, that is, the weight and volume of the product. These characteristics affect product collection and handling and are related to the time needed for order preparation. Handling of products with large volume or weight is more difficult and often involves use of special equipment, thus increasing the duration of order preparation. The third category classifies the products based on their value and texture. Products of higher value typically require more complex and demanding picking processes, to ensure proper handling and minimization of failures and errors. Figure 1 illustrates how the order picking process is affected subject to the above characteristics.

The Characteristics of the Order

This second stage classifies orders based on their characteristics, which are the *number of codes (lines)* that it includes, the respective *quantities* and the *number of boxes (cubes) prepared.* The aim of this stage is to create standardized order profiles that will be used to measure productivity.

Figure 1. Relationship between difficulty of picking process and the product characteristics

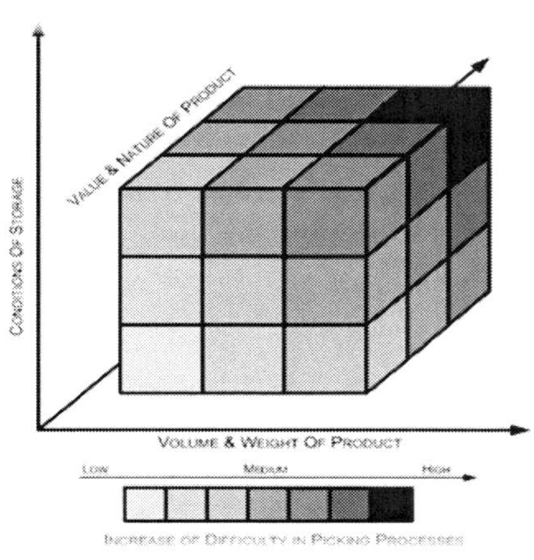

The standardized order profiles require the use of a large number of data over a long period of time, so as to calculate the average number of codes, quantities and boxes prepared per order. Order profiles may change quite often subject to market demand or seasonality; even in the same warehouse sector several different order profiles may exist. As a result, it is essential to update such profiles quite frequently. An example of categorization based on characteristics of the order is shown in Figure 2 (adapted from Frazelle (2002)).

The Spatial Characteristics of Storage

The third stage of the model development deals with mapping the space within which the picker moves, since a large (if not, the largest) portion of time consumed by a picker corresponds to traveling to and from the picking positions, the place where picking lists exit, the packing space, or the loading area; therefore, decreasing distances is a direct, efficient and rather simple way to increase productivity. This stage also deals with the way products are stored, that is, whether products are in pallets, boxes, carousels, drawers or simple bins, and whether they are on the ground or at a higher level (thus requiring a lifting machine or a clark). Obviously, the way products are stored affects the picking time.

Figure 2. Lines and cubes per order and percentage of order profiles for a product

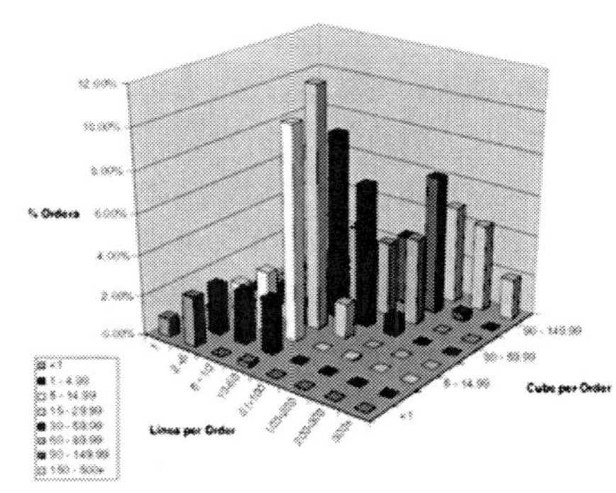

The Methods and Strategies of Order Preparation and Picking

The fourth stage deals with the methods and strategies of order preparation and picking. The four most common methods for order preparation are:

- **Pick by list**, where the order is placed in a list describing in order the positions that the picker has to visit, the codes that must be picked along with their description, the expiration date of the product, and the quantities for each code. The main advantage of this method is its low computer support cost and the low risk, while the main disadvantage is the large preparation time.
- **Pick by light**, where microcomputers with a light indicator are attached in picking positions. The picker collects the quantity referred in the computer of each lighted position. Only one order may be executed at a time. The main advantage of this method is the high rate of order execution, while the main disadvantage is the high cost of the equipment.
- **Voice picking**, where the picker performs his work under guidance by voice commands. The main advantages are the freedom of motion of the picker, the acceptable level of accuracy and the satisfactory productivity level, while the main disadvantage is the rather high cost of equipment.
- **RF picking**, where the picker performs his work using a Jenny (handheld computer-scanner). The picker proceeds to the picking place instructed by his computer and confirms the picking quantity using the barcode scanner. This method is most suitable for products where product traceability is required. The main advantages are the high level of accuracy and the ability to collect products using their serial numbers, while the main disadvantage is often the low rate of order execution.

The order picking strategies aim primarily in the minimization of moves by assigning the order execution to more than one pickers, however increasing the time and effort needed to verify the order integrity and completeness. The most common order picking strategies are:

- **Single order picking**, where each picker is assigned only one order at a time and undertakes the execution of the entire order and the collection of the entire quantity. The main advantage of this strategy is that it ensures order integrity; however, the picker may be obliged to travel long distances, especially for small orders. This strategy is therefore more suitable for large orders with several codes, so that the time of travel per code is decreased.
- **Batch picking**, where each picker is assigned a group (batch) of orders and collects all the quantities for all the orders in a single travel. The main advantage of this strategy is that distances traveled are minimized, and so does the average time per code; however, the time required to place products correctly per order is increased and the risk of wrong order execution is higher. This strategy is recommended for order profiles with less than five codes.
- **Zone picking**, where the picker collects only products in the zone that has been assigned to him, either per order or per batch. The main advantages are the minimization of travel time and the acquaintance of the picker with his area; however, same as in batch picking, the time required to place products correctly per order is increased and the risk of wrong order execution is higher.

CLASSIFICATION OF MOVEMENTS IN THE ORDER PICKING PROCESS

This section examines all the movements that are encountered during order picking, for each order type and for each method and strategy of order picking. These movements have been observed and analyzed for a large number of different pickers and for a long period of time. A typical example of the moves recorded for a simple picking operation using hand-held scanner is described as: "*The picker moves to the area where the picking lists and the carton labels lie. After obtaining these, logs in the scanner with the order data and moves to the empty cartons area where he/she selects and prepares the cartons to be used based on the order data. Subsequently, he/she moves to the first picking place and picks the first code at the appropriate quantity and scans the barcodes of the collected objects. Before moving to the next place, he/she verifies the collection and scans the final position which is the carton label. Once all the quantities are picked, he/she closes the cartons and moves to the wrap machine area and seals them. The order picking is completed by placing the boxes (cartons) in the loading area*".

The movements that generally occur at least once during order picking for different storage conditions, warehouse layout, picking strategy, order preparation method, type of product, etc., are classified in the following categories:

- **Set up management**, which includes movements that set up the picking process, such as, placing the pallet in the truck, logging in the scanner, etc.
- **Traveling management**, which includes movements that occur during order preparation, such as, moving from the area of picking lists to the area of empty pallets, moving from the area of stretch wrap to the area of prepared orders, etc.
- **Searching and documentation management**, which includes the movements needed for finding the order and handling the documentation, such as, scanning the serial number of each picking unit, scanning the weight of the picking unit, etc.
- **Reaching and handling management**, which includes the movements needed to collect the items in the picking list, such as, putting the picking unit in the pallet, using the stairs to reach the second level, etc.
- **Marking and labeling management**, which includes the movements needed to identify the collected units, such as, writing the loading series, sticking the order label on the carton, etc.
- **Packaging and palletization management**, which includes the movements that are needed to handle the packaging equipment, such as, creating an empty carton, loading the pallet, etc.
- **Missing and re-handling management**, which includes the movements not supposed to occur, but occur because of missing products or failures (e.g., create a new carton, wait replenishments, etc.)

Table 1 summarizes these categories and the respective movements.

ELEMENTS OF SPECIAL MODELS

The movements described above constitute the so-called *General Model*, which does not take into account any parameterization. This model will then be used to generate *Special Models* that will be adapted to the parameters that affect the order-picking process, namely, the picking methods, the picking strategies, the orders' classification and the warehouse operations (layout, storage conditions, families of products, work requirements, etc.). The elements of the Special Model are presented in Figure 3.

BASIC, NORMAL AND STANDARD TIMES

The finalization of the parametric mathematical model requires measuring the durations for each movement. These measurements have to be statistically robust; therefore, a large number of samples

Table 1. General model of movements

Picking System Mgmt. (PSM)	Group of Movements
Set up Management	Take picking lists
	Find the essential equipment (e.x. handle truck pallet)
	Log in to Scanner
	Log in to Order
Travelling Management	Move from area of picking lists to the area of empty pallets
	Move from the area of empty pallets to the start of picking circuit
	Move from the area of empty pallets to the area of empty cartons
	Move from the area of empty cartons to the start of picking circuit
	Move along picking circuit
	Move from the end of picking circuit to the area of shrink wrap machine
	Move from the area of shrink wrap machine to stretch wrap machine
	Move from the end of picking circuit to the area of stretch wrap machine
	Move from the area of stretch wrap machine to the area of prepared orders
	Stand in / out of electric powered pallet
	Ride on /off electric powered pallet
Searching & Documentation Management	Search of position
	Recognition of code
	Documentation of movement on picking list
	Scan the postion
	Scan the barcode of picking unit
	Scan the serial number of each picking unit
	Scan the weight of picking unit
	Scan the sscc of pallet
	Scan the label of carton
	Manual input of data in scanner
	Count of quantity
Reaching & Handling Management	Reach in the 2nd level of rack
	Pick up units
	Put picking unit in carton
	Put picking unit on pallet
	Open a carton to take the picking unit
	Open and close drawer
	Use of stair to reach the 2nd level
	Use of high lift pallet truck
Marking & Labeling Management	Write the series of loading
	Write the number of order
	Stick the label of order on carton
	Stick the packing list on carton

continued on following page

Table 1. continued

Packaging & Palletization Management	Creat an empty carton
	Close the picked carton
	Shrink the carton
	Band the carton
	Load pallet
	Unload pallet
	Wrap pallet
	Unwrap pallet
	Block stack pallet
Missing & Re-Handling Management	Move to the area of replenishments and back to picking circuit
	Wrong Case Selection move back to area of empty cartons
	Create a new empty carton
	Re-Handling picking units
	Re-Handling cases of pallet
	Waiting for replenishments

is needed. In our approach, we have measured the duration of each movement as performed by different pickers, in various times of the day, in different instances of the picker's shift, since productivity is higher at the beginning of the shift and drops as the shift progresses. The sampling has been performed in a percentage of 80% of the personnel, in random days of the week, and has included experienced and novice employees, in days of varying workload and working with or without supervision. The sampling period was six months and over forty-five thousand samples have

Figure 3. Elements of special models for order picking

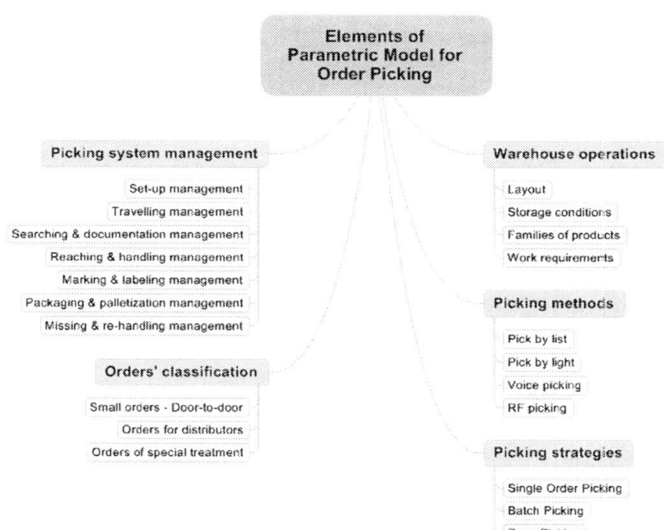

Figure 4. The database of the parametric model

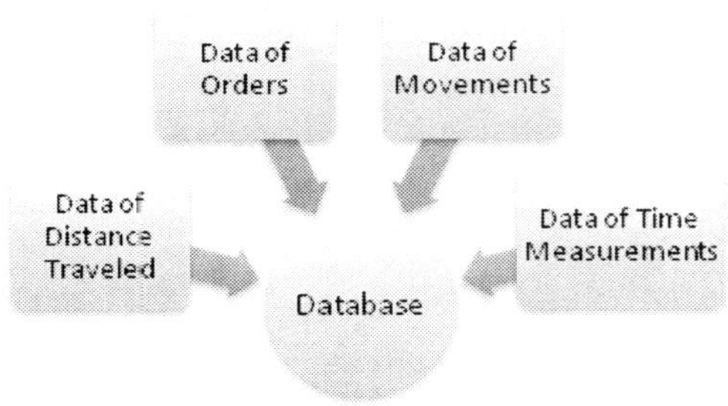

been gathered and processed. Once the measurements have been completed, we have extracted the basic, normal and standard times for each movement. In particular:

The **basic time** is the direct outcome of measurements performed with visual inspection. It is the average of the measurements t_i (i=1,...,N) for N repetitions of the movement:

$$T_B = \frac{1}{N}\sum_{i=1}^{N} t_i$$

The **normal time** is attributed to a specific picker and is equal to the basic time divided by the performance ratio r of the picker. It expresses the deviation between the basic time for the specific movement and the average of times for the specific picker for the specific movement. If, for example, the basic time for a movement is 1,5 secs but a picker executes this movement in 1,2 secs, then his performance ratio is 1,5/1,2=1,25 or 125%. The normal time is thus given by:

$$T_N = \frac{T_B}{r}$$

The **standard time** is equal to the normal time augmented by the non-productive time that corresponds to general conditions and particularities of the work and the needs of each picker:

$$T_S = T_N\left(1 + \lambda\right)$$

where λ expresses the ratio of non-productive time compared to the normal time, and is also referred to as *relaxation allowance*.

PERFORMANCE MEASUREMENTS

The parametric model aims in extracting a feasible target, which can be interpreted in several forms,

Figure 5. Warehouse layout

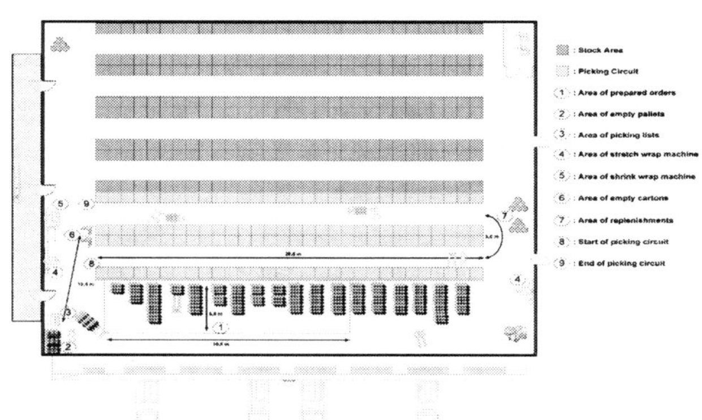

such as, cartons/hr, scans/hr, codes/day, pallets/hr, etc. This target corresponds to the performance measurement index for each operation. This model may also be used to measure performance in the entire spectrum of picking system management (PSM) processes, for any order type of an operation. The synthesis of the parametric model follows three steps, which are: (i) the database development, (ii) the processing mechanisms, and (iii) the results.

Data Collection and Database Development

The database of the parametric model contains data for distance traveled, orders, movements and time measurements (Figure 4). In the sequel, each of these types is addressed in turn. To better understand the methodology, the present section is corroborated by a real example for a sector of the warehouse (Figure 5) with three order profiles. The products are simple and belong to the same family, the storage conditions are normal and the weight and volume of the products are of average difficulty.

Data of Distance Traveled

The movements that a picker performs during order picking are separated into those within the picking circuit and those out of it. The distance covered within the picking circuit, can be calculated either practically or theoretically. Practical calculation requires the actual measurement of the distance. The theoretical calculation of the distance results from the following formula:

$$D = \left(\frac{\alpha}{l}\right) \cdot w \cdot \left(\frac{x}{2}\right) + \left(n - 1\right) \cdot d$$

where α is the number of picking positions, l is the number of levels of the picking circuit, w is the mixed width of the picking position, n is the number of corridors, d is the distance between corridors and x is equal to 1 for picking only in one direction and 2 for picking in two directions. In our example, the operation in Figure 5 consists of α=120 picking positions, all at the same level (l=1), the mixed width of each position is w=0,95m, there are two corridors distanced at d=5,80m, and the picker travels each corridor twice and picks

Table 2. Calculation of distances for positions outside the picking circuit

From / To	Area of prepared orders	Area of empty pallets	Area of picking lists	Area of stretch wrap machine	Area of shrink wrap machine	Area of empty cartons	Area of replenishments	Start of picking circuit	End of picking circuit
Area of prepared orders		15,6	16,2	20,4	24,2	22,4	31,3	20,8	24,7
Area of empty pallets	15,6		2,4	7,5	11,3	9,8	40,8	8,6	12,6
Area of picking lists	16,2	2,4		5,1	8,9	7,8	38,4	6,2	10,5
Area of stretch wrap machine	20,4	7,5	5,1		3,8	3,3	34,9	2,7	5,6
Area of shrink wrap machine	24,2	11,3	8,9	3,8		2,8	36,6	4,4	3,3
Area of empty cartons	22,4	9,8	7,8	3,3	2,8		33,8	1,6	3,1
Area of replenishments	31,3	40,8	38,4	34,9	36,6	33,8		32,2	32,2
Start of picking circuit	20,8	8,6	6,2	2,7	4,4	1,6	32,2		5,8
End of picking circuit	24,7	12,9	10,5	5,6	3,3	3,1	32,2	5,8	

products only from the right hand side (therefore, x=2). Using these data, the theoretical distance D traveled is 119,8m. The distance covered for movements outside the picking circuit requires the recording of the potential points visited and physical measurement of the distances between them. These data for the warehouse layout in Figure 5 are tabulated in Table 2.

Data of Orders

In this step, the number of different order profiles is determined and subsequently, the following data are extracted for each order profile:

- Average lines/order
- Average of total units/line (the term units may refer to cartons, items, pallets, etc.)
- Average of total units/order
- Average of cartons/order
- Average of pallets/order
- Average of pallets/platform (that corresponds to the floor area that an order occupies)

Once the above data are recorded for each order profile, the same data are recorded for different products only in the case that there exist different products with the same order profile. An example of a common difference in this case is the number of scans. In our example, we deal with three different order profiles for the same product. The first profile refers to small orders where the collected unit is one item and serves door-to-door customers. The second profile refers to large orders where the collected unit is a box, while the third

Table 3. Data of orders

Orders Cluster	*%*	*Products Cluster*	*Lines/Order*	*Units / Line*	*Units / Order*	*Cartons/ Order*	*Pallets / Order*	*Pallets / Platform*
Type 1	83%	A	10,66	3,23	34,43	7,35	0,95	0,95
Type 2	6%	A	9,90	20,60	203,94		9,90	3,30
Type 3	11%	A	7,68	12,40	95,23		1,65	1,65
Total	100%		28,24	36,23	333,60	7,35	12,50	5,90

Table 4. Data of times for different equipment types

Equipment \ Action	**Speed (sec /m)**	**Load Pallet (sec)**	**Unload Pallet (sec)**	**Ride on /off (sec)**	**Stand in / out (sec)**
E1_Hand small trolley	0,96	0,00	0,00	0,00	0,00
E2_Hand stock trolley	1,65	0,00	0,00	0,00	0,00
E3_Hand low lifting pallet truck	1,42	18,00	5,00	0,00	0,00
E4_Hand high lifting pallet truck	1,42	18,00	5,00	0,00	0,00
E5_Walk - with electric pallet truck	0,85	9,00	4,00	0,00	0,00
E6_Ride - on electric pallet truck	0,60	7,00	4,00	3,00	0,00
E7_Stand - in electric pallet truck	0,45	7,00	4,00	0,00	4,00
E8_Walk - with powered pallet stackers	0,75	9,00	4,00	0,00	0,00
E9_Ride - on electric powered pallet stackers	0,60	7,00	4,00	3,00	0,00
E10_Standin electric powered pallet stackers	0,45	7,00	4,00	0,00	4,00
E11_Pedestrian (On foot)	0,85	0,00	0,00	0,00	0,00

profile refers to large orders where the collected unit is a box but serves door-to-door customers. The respective data are shown in Table 3. It is noticed that for types 2 and 3 the cartons/order data is null, since the picking unit is the carton.

Data of Time Measurements

The third element to complete the database concerns the data of basic times. These data should take into account those factors apart of the human-related ones that affect the execution times. Such factors are mostly related to equipment, such as small or stock trolley, pallet trucks, etc., or even handheld or wrist attached scanners. Table 4 presents a collection of times recorded over a large number of samples, for movements where mechanical equipment is used. These data will be used in calculating the expected performance for the picking process.

Data of Movements

At this stage, for each order profile, we record the specific movements that are needed to perform the entire picking process. In other words, we derive the special model of movements for each order profile. A large number of movements is common in all profiles; nevertheless, there also exist movements that are order-specific. Apart of the necessary movements, we also record the movements that may delay the picker, thus adding extra time in the order execution. The method and strategy of order preparation may also seriously affect the movements and the performance. The typical movements for our case study are shown in Table 5.

Model Mechanisms

The model mechanism aims to extract the final result and provide the optimum target for an operation or a set of operations in a warehouse. This is performed in three steps (Figure 6).

The first step calculates the total standard times for each order profile. This calculation passes through the determination of basic and normal times. The total basic time for a movement is:

Total basic time = (*Total number of units*) x (*basic time per unit*) x (*frequency of movement*)

For example, if the basic time for the movement "Pick up units" is 3 seconds per unit and the frequency of movement is 100% (that is, the movement is performed for every picking unit of the order), then the total basic time for this movement to execute an order of 25 units is 25x3x100%=75 secs. For any order profile, of the parametric model, the total basic time is given by the equation:

$$T_{Bj} = \sum_{o=1}^{x}\sum_{m=1}^{y}\sum_{s=1}^{z}\sum_{i=1}^{w} u_{j,omsi}\, t_{Bj,omsi}\, f_{j,omsi}$$

Where:

T_{Bj}: the total basic time for the order profile j

o: the parameter of the operation, $o=1,\ldots,x$

m: the parameter of the picking method, $m=1,\ldots,y$

s: the parameter of the picking strategy, $s=1,\ldots,z$

i: the parameter of the movements, $i=1,\ldots,w$

$u_{j,omsi}$: the units of movement *omsi* for order profile j with $u_{j,omsi} \geq 1$

$t_{Bj,omsi}$: the basic time for movement *omsi* for order profile j

$f_{j,omsi}$: the frequency of movement *omsi* for order profile j

The total T_{Nj} normal time for the order profile j for a picker with performance ratio r results as:

Table 5. Data of movements

Warehouse - OPERATION 1				
Picking Methods: Pick by List - Picking Strategies: Single Order Picking				
PSM	*Orders' Classification* *Group of Movements*	***Type 1***	***Type 2***	***Type 3***
SUM	Take picking lists	√	√	√
	Find the essential equipment	√	√	√
TM	Move from area of picking lists to the area of empty pallets	√	√	√
	Move from the area of prepared orders to the area of empty pallets		√	√
	Move from the area of empty pallets to the start of picking circuit		√	√
	Move from the area of empty pallets to the area of empty cartons	√		
	Move from the area of empty cartons to the start of picking circuit	√		
	Move along picking circuit	√	√	√
	Move from the end of picking circuit to the area of shrink wrap machine	√		
	Move from the area of shrink wrap machine to stretch wrap machine	√		
	Move from the end of picking circuit to the area of stretch wrap machine		√	√
	Move from the area of stretch wrap machine to the area of prepared orders	√	√	√
	Stand in / out of electric powered pallet	√	√	√
	Ride on /off electric powered pallet	√	√	√
SDM	Search of position	√	√	√
	Recognition of code	√	√	√
	Documentation of movement on picking list	√	√	√
	Count of quantity	√	√	√
RHM	Pick up units	√	√	√
	Put picking unit in carton	√		
	Put picking unit on pallet		√	√
	Open a carton to take the picking unit	√		
MLM	Write the series of loading	√	√	√
	Write the number of order	√	√	√
	Stick the label of order on carton	√		
	Stick the label of order on pallet	√	√	√
PPM	Create an empty carton	√		
	Close the picked carton	√		
	Load pallet	√	√	√
	Unload pallet	√	√	√
	Band the carton	√		
	Wrap pallet	√	√	√
	Unwrap pallet	√	√	√
	Block stack pallet		√	

continued on following page

Table 5. continued

MRM	Move to the area of replenishments and back to picking circuit	√	√	√
	Wrong Case Selection move back to area of empty cartons	√		
	Create a new empty carton	√		
	Re-Handling of picking units	√		
	Re-Handling cases	√	√	√
	Waiting for replenishments	√	√	√

$$T_{Nj} = T_{Bj} \,/\, r$$

Taking into account a relaxation factor λ, the total standard time T_{Sj} for order profile j is:

$$T_{Sj} = T_{Nj}(1 + \lambda)$$

For the case study we examine in this article, the above time are shown in Table 6.

Figure 6. The steps of the model mechanism

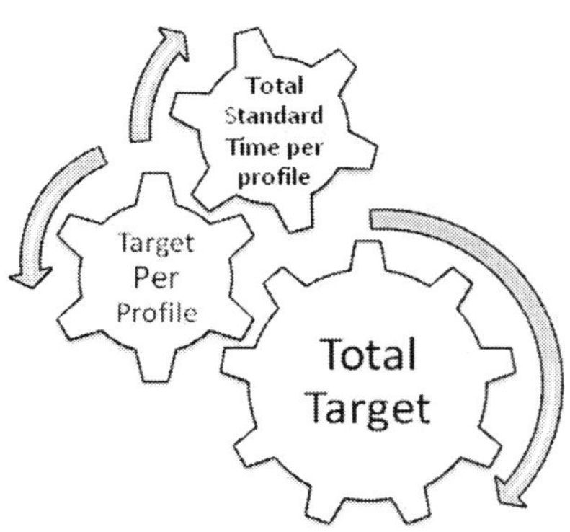

The targets for each order profile, result in the second step of the model mechanism, and depend on the unit for measurement of the target (e.g, lines/hour, cases/hour, pallets/hour, etc.). The target Q_j for order profile j with U_j units is then given by:

$$Q_j = \frac{U_j}{T_{Sj}}$$

In the case study examined, the respective targets are shown in Table 7.

In the final step of the model mechanism, we calculate the total time Q_{Total} of the operation (warehouse section) or the entire warehouse. This is calculated as:

$$Q_{Total} = \sum_{j=1}^{P} p_j Q_j$$

Where:

P: the total number of order profiles

Table 6. Total times (in secs) for the case study

Profile 1			**Profile 2**	**Profile 3**
Total T_B per profile		993,21	1756,98	969,28
r = 100%	**Total T_N per profile**	1045,48	1849,46	1020,29
λ = 10%	**Total T_S per profile**	1092,53	1932,68	1066,21

Table 7. Targets for order profiles of the case study

	Profile 1	Profile 2	Profile 3
Total Picking Units	34,43	203,94	95,23
Total T_S	1.092,53	1.932,68	1.066,21
Q: Target Per Profile (picking units/hr)	**113,46**	**379,88**	**321,55**

j: the number of order profile, $j=1,..,P$

p_j: the percentage of the order profile *j* in the operation

Q_j: the target for order profile *j*

For the case examined, these results are summarized in Table 8.

It should be emphasized that the above results are based on order data for three months, while the percentages were based on order data of one month; furthermore, the pickers that were involved were asked to record the delays they confronted during the picking process, so that the movements of the MRM group and their frequency could be calculated.

RESULTS AND DISCUSSION

The results of the parametric model are of importance to warehouse managers, as they enable them to:

- Monitor and plan the order picking process
- Manage and evaluate the pickers
- Improve the order picking performance
- Decide on the equipment which is most suitable for picking
- Estimate the cost of picking
- Obtain an insight and calculate the times of the Picking System Management (PSM)
- Decide on the method and strategy for order picking

In the sequel, some of the most critical aspects of usability of the parametric model are discussed.

ABC Analysis of the PSM

The parametric model enables the categorization of movements in the PSM based on their total time so as to extract their contribution on the performance and the cost of the picking process. The use of ABC analysis, allows us to:

- Calculate more accurately and rationally the time needed for each movement and group of movements
- Compare and contrast the total times for each PSM group of movements
- Monitor and focus on the most time-consuming and expensive groups of the PSM
- Support the decision-making on how to execute orders

Table 8. Total target for the operation

	Profile 1	Profile 2	Profile 3
Q: Target Per Profile (picking units/hr)	113,46	379,88	321,55
Percentage	83%	6%	11%
Q_{Total}	**152 (picking units / hr)**		

Table 9. ABC analysis for all the movements per order profile and for the entire operation

Orders' Classification	Profile 1		83%	Profile 2		6%	Profile 3		11%	Total		
Group of Movements	Total Time	Per-cent-age	Clus-ter	Total Time	Per-cent-age	Clus-ter	Total Time	Per-cent-age	Clus-ter	Total Time	Per-centage	Clus-ter
Close the picked carton	28,1	2,9%	A	0,0	0,0%	C	0,0	0,0%	C	23,3	2,3%	A
Wrap pallet	20,8	2,1%	B	75,9	4,3%	A	38,0	3,8%	B	26,0	2,5%	A
Put picking unit on pallet	0,0	0,0%	C	216,7	12,3%	A	119,0	12,0%	A	26,1	2,5%	A
Count of quantity	24,1	2,4%	B	107,1	6,1%	A	56,7	5,7%	A	32,7	3,2%	A
Recognition of code	34,1	3,5%	A	31,7	1,8%	B	24,6	2,5%	B	32,9	3,2%	A
Open a carton to take the picking unit	42,3	4,3%	A	0,0	0,0%	C	0,0	0,0%	C	35,1	3,4%	A
Find the essential equipment	40,0	4,1%	A	40,0	2,3%	B	40,0	4,0%	A	40,0	3,9%	A
Move along picking circuit	39,4	4,0%	A	51,2	2,9%	B	48,0	4,8%	A	41,0	4,0%	A
Band the carton	51,3	5,2%	A	0,0	0,0%	C	0,0	0,0%	C	42,6	4,1%	A
Unwrap pallet	50,4	5,1%	A	120,3	6,8%	A	88,1	8,9%	A	58,7	5,7%	A
Put picking unit in carton	82,6	8,4%	A	0,0	0,0%	C	0,0	0,0%	C	68,6	6,6%	A
Pick up units	51,6	5,2%	A	260,0	14,7%	A	142,8	14,4%	A	74,2	7,2%	A
Create an empty carton	118,7	12,1%	A	0,0	0,0%	C	0,0	0,0%	C	98,5	9,5%	A
Stand in / out of electric powered pallet	99,3	10,1%	A	163,4	9,2%	A	94,0	9,5%	A	102,5	9,9%	A
Waiting for replenishments	115,1	11,7%	A	249,5	14,1%	A	152,1	15,3%	A	127,3	12,3%	A
Move from the area of shrink wrap/band machine to stretch wrap machine	1,6	0,2%	C	0,0	0,0%	C	0,0	0,0%	C	1,3	0,1%	B
Move from the area of empty pallets to the start of picking circuit	0,0	0,0%	C	12,8	0,7%	B	6,4	0,6%	C	1,5	0,1%	B
Move from the area of prepared orders to the area of empty pallets	0,0	0,0%	C	16,1	0,9%	B	4,6	0,5%	C	1,5	0,1%	B
Wrong Case Selection move back to area of empty cartons	2,5	0,3%	C	0,0	0,0%	C	0,0	0,0%	C	2,1	0,2%	B
Move from the area of empty pallets to the area of empty cartons	4,2	0,4%	C	0,0	0,0%	C	0,0	0,0%	C	3,5	0,3%	B
Unload pallet	3,6	0,4%	C	13,2	0,7%	B	6,6	0,7%	B	4,5	0,4%	B
Block stack pallet	0,0	0,0%	C	99,0	5,6%	A	0,0	0,0%	C	5,9	0,6%	B
Write the number of order	8,1	0,8%	B	0,0	0,0%	C	0,0	0,0%	C	6,7	0,7%	B
Write the series of loading	10,5	1,1%	B	0,0	0,0%	C	0,0	0,0%	C	8,7	0,8%	B
Move to the area of replenishments and back to picking circuit	3,3	0,3%	C	51,6	2,9%	B	27,8	2,8%	B	8,9	0,9%	B
Stick the label of order on carton	11,2	1,1%	B	0,0	0,0%	C	0,0	0,0%	C	9,3	0,9%	B

continued on following page

Table 9. continued

Take picking lists	10,0	1,0%	B	10,0	0,6%	B	10,0	1,0%	B	10,0	1,0%	B
Load pallet	6,3	0,6%	B	69,3	3,9%	A	11,6	1,2%	B	10,7	1,0%	B
Move from the area of stretch wrap machine to the area of prepared orders	8,7	0,9%	B	30,3	1,7%	B	15,1	1,5%	B	10,7	1,0%	B
Re-Handling cases	5,1	0,5%	B	40,0	2,3%	B	42,7	4,3%	A	11,4	1,1%	B
Create a new empty carton	20,9	2,1%	B	0,0	0,0%	C	0,0	0,0%	C	17,4	1,7%	B
Search of position	21,3	2,2%	B	19,8	1,1%	B	15,4	1,5%	B	20,6	2,0%	B
Documentation of movement on picking list	21,3	2,2%	B	19,8	1,1%	B	15,4	1,5%	B	20,6	2,0%	B
Stick the label of order on pallet	17,1	1,7%	B	59,4	3,4%	A	29,7	3,0%	B	21,0	2,0%	B
Re-Handling of picking units	27,5	2,8%	A	0,0	0,0%	C	0,0	0,0%	C	22,8	2,2%	B
Ride on /off electric powered pallet	0,0	0,0%	C	0,0	0,0%	C	0,0	0,0%	C	0,0	0,0%	C
Move from the area of empty cartons to the start of picking circuit	0,7	0,1%	C	0,0	0,0%	C	0,0	0,0%	C	0,6	0,1%	C
Move from the end of picking circuit to the area of stretch wrap machine	0,0	0,0%	C	8,3	0,5%	B	4,2	0,4%	C	1,0	0,1%	C
Move from area of picking lists to the area of empty pallets	1,0	0,1%	C	1,1	0,1%	B	1,1	0,1%	C	1,0	0,1%	C
Move from the end of picking circuit to the area of shrink wrap/band machine	1,4	0,1%	C	0,0	0,0%	C	0,0	0,0%	C	1,2	0,1%	C
Total	984,27	100%		1766,41	100%		993,60	100%		1032,2	100,0%	

The movements are first categorized in three groups for each order profile, as follows:

- Group A contains movements that correspond to approximately 80% of the total time
- Group B contains movements that correspond to approximately 19% of the total time
- Group C contains movements that correspond to approximately 1% of the total time

The categorization of movements is different for each order profile. Out of forty (40) movements in total, only four (4) of them belong to all three order profiles. In order to categorize the movements for the entire operation, that is, for all order profiles jointly, one has to take into account the weight (i.e., the percentage) of each order profile. The total time for a movement n is thus obtained as:

$$T_{Bn} = \sum_{o=1}^{x}\sum_{m=1}^{y}\sum_{s=1}^{z}\sum_{j=1}^{P} p_{n,omsj} u_{n,omsj} t_{Bn,omsj} f_{n,omsj}$$

Where:

T_{Bj}: the total basic time for the order profile j

Table 10. ABC analysis for each group of movements per order profile and entire operation

	Profile 1		*Profile 2*		*Profile 3*		*Total*	
PSM	T_b	%	T_b	%	T_b	%	T_b	%
SUM	*50,00*	*5%*	*50,00*	*3%*	*50,00*	*5%*	*50,0*	*5%*
TM	*156,28*	*16%*	*283,17*	*16%*	*173,27*	*17%*	*165,8*	*16%*
SDM	*100,85*	*10%*	*178,35*	*10%*	*111,96*	*11%*	*106,7*	*10%*
RHM	*176,55*	*18%*	*476,71*	*27%*	*261,89*	*26%*	*203,9*	*20%*
MLM	*46,94*	*5%*	*59,40*	*3%*	*29,70*	*3%*	*45,8*	*4%*
PPM	*279,14*	*28%*	*377,69*	*21%*	*144,23*	*15%*	*270,2*	*26%*
MRM	*174,51*	*18%*	*341,09*	*19%*	*222,55*	*22%*	*189,8*	*18%*
Total	***984,27***	***100%***	***1766,41***	***100%***	***993,60***	***100%***	***1032,23***	***100%***

$p_{n,omsj}$: the frequency of movement n for order *omsj*

$u_{n,omsj}$: the units of movement n for order *omsj* with $u_{n,omsj} \geq 1$

$t_{Bn,omsj}$: the basic time of movement n for order *omsj*

$f_{n,omsj}$: the frequency of movement n for order *omsj*

Based on the above equation and the results of the parametric model, the ABC analysis for the case study we examine is summarized in Table 9. Similarly, we can calculate the respective percentage for each group of movements in the PSM. These results are tabulated in Table 10 and depicted as charts in Figure 7.

Performance Optimization

The parametric model also serves the purpose of helping improve the order picking performance. The model is compliant to the time compression philosophy expressed by Gregory and Rawling (1997) which states that: "*Time compression is not about making **people** faster; it is about making a **product** move faster through a factory or office, or making new design move faster through the new product process*". The parametric model aims to improve the order picking performance by watching current system failures and missing and trying to correct or delete them. The amount of necessary improvement could be calculated as the quantified desirable performance minus the current performance.

The first step towards performance improvement is thus to categorize movements and respective times into *value adding* and *non-value adding*. The first category contains the required movements to complete an order picking process, while the second category covers the movements that should not exist in a perfect system without failures. The value adding movements are all the movements of the PSM except of those belonging in the Missing & Re-Handling Management (MRM) category, which are non-value adding movements. Minimizing the MRM movements would thus lead to performance improvement. Table 11 summarizes the effect of MRM minimization to the overall performance.

For the case study we examine, it is noted that a 30% decrease in the non-value adding MRM time, would improve overall performance by 6%, while for a 100% decrease of MRM time (as in a perfect system), the overall performance would be improved by 24%. Apart of the relative percentages that can be observed, the crisp numbers for total productivity provide the range between actual, feasible and optimum targets. As can be observed in Table 11, the optimum picking performance could be as much as 188 picking units/

Figure 7. Charted results of ABC analysis for each group of movements per order profile and the entire operation

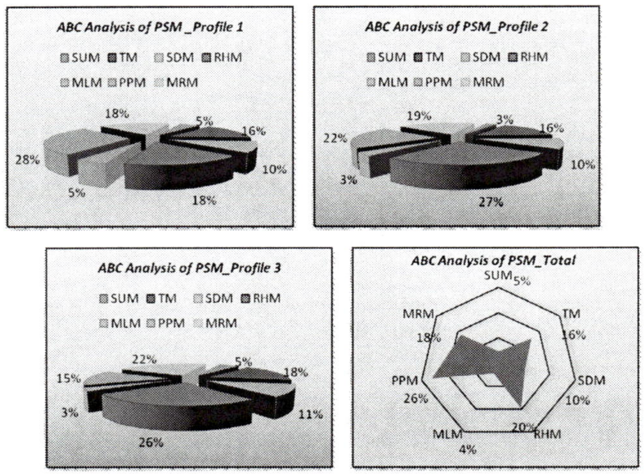

hour, for the specific order profiles and percentages, methods and strategies for picking and equipment used.

Workers' Monitoring and Evaluation

A final contribution of the parametric model is that it enables the fair and in-depth evaluation of pickers. This is because the model provides the feasible targets of performance, based on long-term data and evaluates pickers not based on units picked but rather compared to a target depending on the order mix, order profile characteristics, equipment, etc. Assume, for example, that in our case study, there exist two pickers, A and B. Picker A has managed to pick 735 picking units in 7,5 hours (or 98 pick-

Table 11. Effect of decrease of non-value adding times to the overall picking productivity

Percentage of MRM Decrease	Profile 1			Profile 2			Profile 3			Total		
	MRM	Target (Q_1)	% of Q_1 Increase	MRM	Target (Q_2)	% of Q_2 Increase	MRM	Target (Q_3)	% of Q_3 Increase	MRM	Target (Q_{Total})	% of Q_{Total} Increase
0%	174,51	114,49	0%	341,1	377,9	0%	222,5	313,7	0%	189,8	152	0%
10%	157,06	116,55	2%	307,0	385,3	2%	200,3	320,9	2%	170,8	155	2%
20%	139,61	118,70	4%	272,9	393,0	4%	178,0	328,4	5%	151,8	158	4%
30%	122,16	120,92	6%	238,8	401,1	6%	155,8	336,3	7%	132,9	161	6%
40%	104,71	123,23	8%	204,7	409,5	8%	133,5	344,5	10%	113,9	165	8%
50%	87,25	125,62	10%	170,5	418,2	11%	111,3	353,2	13%	94,9	168	11%
60%	69,80	128,12	12%	136,4	427,4	13%	89,0	362,4	16%	75,9	172	13%
70%	52,35	130,71	14%	102,3	436,9	16%	66,8	372,0	19%	56,9	176	15%
80%	34,90	133,41	17%	68,2	446,9	18%	44,5	382,2	22%	38,0	180	18%
90%	17,45	136,22	19%	34,1	457,3	21%	22,3	392,9	25%	19,0	184	21%
100%	0,00	139,16	22%	0,0	468,3	24%	0,0	404,2	29%	0,0	**188**	**24%**

ing units/hour), while picker B has managed to pick 1.155 picking units in the same time (or 154 picking unit/hour). The examination of these two numbers only, would lead to the result that picker B is far more productive than A; however, if we take into account that picker A deals with orders of Profile 1 and picker B with orders of Profile 2 (see Table 3), then a more correct measure of picking performance would be the one described by the following formula:

$$P = \frac{Q_{Actual}}{Q_P}$$

Where:

P: it the performance quotient or productivity

Q_{Actual}: the actual productivity per working hour

Q_P: the target for performance for order profile P

Table 12 summarizes the results for the two pickers. It is noted that the performance quotient (or relative performance) of picker A is 86%, while for picker B it is only 75%! The parametric model, therefore, provides the true productivity for each picker based on the picking conditions, and is significantly more objective than the picking rate itself.

CONCLUSION

The present work has dealt with the development of an analytical parametric model for the order picking process in a modular warehouse. In Section 2, we have described the parameters that compose the model and overviewed the steps towards the model development. We have also recorded the elementary movements involved in any picking process and classified them in seven major categories. Following that, we have provided the definitions for basic, normal and standard times for picking movements, and explained how these result from observation and sampling. In Section 3, we have studied the issue of performance measurements and showed how these can be extracted in a modular warehouse environment; then, we have illustrated how the parametric model is implemented, by first calculating the total standard times per profile, then by setting the targets per profile and finally, by setting the total target for the operation (warehouse module). We have corroborated our analysis with a real case study, among the many we have monitored in a pragmatic setup. In Section 4, we have presented the results of our analysis and demonstrated our findings on the ABC analysis of the warehouse operation. We have, furthermore, indicated how performance can be improved and we set a fair frame to measure workers' performance.

The contributions of our approach are threefold: (i) we have produced a generic and analytical framework to model the order picking process in a modular warehouse, (ii) we have defined practical and easy to adopt performance measures, and (iii) we have provided the tools for a warehouse manager to set goals, measure performance and identify areas of improvement in his areas of responsibility. In the future, our approach can be expanded to include other warehouse processes, such as loading/unloading, products receipt, etc.,

Table 12. Performance ratios for different pickers

Picker	Q_{Actual}	Q_P	P
A	98 units/hr	114,5 units/hr	**86%**
B	154 units/hr	204 units/hr	**75%**

and to set global performance targets that supersede the boundaries of order picking.

REFERENCES

Beamon, B. M. (1998). Supply Chain Design and Analysis: Models and Methods. *International Journal of Production Economics*, *55*(3), 281–294. doi:10.1016/S0925-5273(98)00079-6

Brynzer, H., Johansson, M. I., & Medbo, L. (1994). A Methodology for Order Picking Systems as a Base for System Design and Managerial Decisions. *International Journal of Operations & Production Management*, *14*(3), 126–139. doi:10.1108/01443579410058595

Chan, F. T. S., & Qi, H. J. (2003). Feasibility of Performance Measurement System for Supply Chain: A Process-Based Approach and Measures. *Integrated Manufacturing Systems*, *14*(3), 179–190. doi:10.1108/09576060310463145

Chow, H. K. H., Choy, K. L., Lee, W. B., & Lau, K. C. (2006). Design of a RFID Case-Based Resource Management System for Warehouse Operations. *Expert Systems with Applications*, *30*, 561–576. doi:10.1016/j.eswa.2005.07.023

Cooper, R. (1989). The Rise of Activity-Based Costing – Part Three: How Many Cost Drivers Do You Need and How Do You Select Them? *Journal of Cost Management*, 34-46.

De Koster, R., Le-Duc, T., & Roodbergen, K. J. (2007). Design and Control of Warehouse Order Picking: A Literature Review. *European Journal of Operational Research*, *182*(2), 481–501. doi:10.1016/j.ejor.2006.07.009

Dekker, R., de Koster, M. B. M., Roodbergen, K. J., & van Kalleveen, H. (2004). Improving Order-Picking Response Time at Ankor's Warehouse. *Interfaces*, *34*(4), 303–313. doi:10.1287/inte.1040.0083

Faber, N., de Koster, R., & Van de Velde, S. (2002). Linking Warehouse Complexity to Warehouse Planning and Control Structure. *International Journal of Physical Distribution and Logistics Management*, *32*(5), 381–395. doi:10.1108/09600030210434161

Frazelle, E. H. (2002). *World- Class Warehousing & Material Handling*. New York: McGraw Hill.

Gu, J., Goetschakckx, M., & McGinnis, L. F. (2007). Research on Warehouse Operation: A Comprehensive Review. *European Journal of Operational Research*, *177*, 1–121. doi:10.1016/j.ejor.2006.02.025

Gunasekaran, A., Patel, C., & Tirtiroglu, E. (2001). Performance Measures and Metrics in a Supply Chain Environment. *International Journal of Operations & Production Management*, *21*(1/2), 71–87. doi:10.1108/01443570110358468

Heckert, J. B. (1940). *The Analysis and Control of Distribution Costs*. New York: Ronald Press Company.

Holmberg, S. (2000). A Systems Perspective on Supply Chain Measurements. *International Journal of Physical Distribution and Logistics Management*, *30*(10), 847–868. doi:10.1108/09600030010351246

Hsich, L.-F., & Tsai, L. (2006). The Optimum Design of a Warehouse System on Order Picking Efficiency. *International Journal of Advanced Manufacturing Technology*, *28*, 626–637. doi:10.1007/s00170-004-2404-0

Hwang, H. S., & Cho, G. S. (2006). A Performance Evaluation Model for Order Picking Warehouse Design. *Computers & Industrial Engineering*, *51*, 335–342. doi:10.1016/j.cie.2005.10.002

Kuo, C.-H., Dunn, K. D., & Randhawa, S. U. (1999). A Case Study Assessment of Performance Measurement in Distribution Centers. *Industrial Management & Data Systems*, *99*(2), 54–63. doi:10.1108/02635579910261068

LaLonde, B. J., & Pohlen, T. L. (1996). Issues in Supply Chain Costing. *The International Journal of Logistics Management*, *7*(1), 1–12. doi:10.1108/09574099610805395

Lambert, D. M., & Pohlen, T. L. (2001). Supply Chain Metrics. *The International Journal of Logistics Management*, *12*(1), 1–19. doi:10.1108/09574090110806190

Lapide, L., & Happen, I. (2000). What About Measuring Supply Chain Performance? *Achieving Supply Chain Excellence Through Technology*. Retrieved from http://lapide.ASCET.com

Le-Duc, T., & de Koster, R. M. B. M. (2007). Travel Time Estimation and Order Batching in a 2-Block Warehouse. *European Journal of Operational Research*, *176*, 374–388. doi:10.1016/j.ejor.2005.03.052

Manzini, R., Gamberi, M., Persona, A., & Regattieri, A. (2007). Design of a Class Based Storage Picker to Product Order Picking System. *International Journal of Advanced Manufacturing Technology*, *32*, 811–821. doi:10.1007/s00170-005-0377-2

Meixell, M. J., & Gargeya, V. B. (2005). Global Supply Chain Design: A Literature Review and Critique. *Transportation Research Part E, Logistics and Transportation Review*, *41*, 531–550. doi:10.1016/j.tre.2005.06.003

Mentzer, J. T., & Konrad, B. P. (1991). An Efficiency/Effectiveness Approach to Logistics Performance Analysis. *Journal of Business Logistics*, *12*(1), 33–61.

Min, H., & Zhou, G. (2002). Supply Chain Modeling: Past, Present and Future. *Computers & Industrial Engineering*, *43*, 231–249. doi:10.1016/S0360-8352(02)00066-9

Nieuwenhuyse, I. V., & de Koster, R. B. M. (2009). Evaluating Order Throughput Time in 2-Block Warehouses with Time Window Batching. *International Journal of Production Economics*, *121*, 654–664. doi:10.1016/j.ijpe.2009.01.013

Roodbergen, K. J., Sharp, G. P., & Vis, I. F. A. (2008). Designing the Layout Structure of Manual Order Picking Areas in Warehouse. *IIE Transactions*, *40*(11), 1032–1045. doi:10.1080/07408170802167639

Van der Vorst, J. G. A. J. (2006). Performance Measurement in Agri-Food Supply Chain Networks. In Ondersteijn, C. J. M. (Eds.), *Quantifying the Agrifood Supply Chain* (pp. 15–26). The Netherlands: Springer. doi:10.1007/1-4020-4693-6_2

Chapter 10
Constrained Optimization of JIT Manufacturing Systems with Hybrid Genetic Algorithm

Alexandros Xanthopoulos
Democritus University of Thrace, Greece

Dimitrios E. Koulouriotis
Democritus University of Thrace, Greece

ABSTRACT

This research explores the use of a hybrid genetic algorithm in a constrained optimization problem with stochastic objective function. The underlying problem is the optimization of a class of JIT manufacturing systems. The approach investigated here is to interface a simulation model of the system with a hybrid optimization technique which combines a genetic algorithm with a local search procedure. As a constraint handling technique we use penalty functions, namely a "death penalty" function and an exponential penalty function. The performance of the proposed optimization scheme is illustrated via a simulation scenario involving a stochastic demand process satisfied by a five–stage production/ inventory system with unreliable workstations and stochastic service times. The chapter concludes with a discussion on the sensitivity of the objective function in respect of the arrival rate, the service rates and the decision variable vector.

INTRODUCTION

This chapter addresses the problem of production coordination in serial manufacturing lines which consist of a number of unreliable machines linked with intermediate buffers. Production coordination in systems of this type is essentially the control of the material flow that takes place within the system in order to resolve the trade-off between minimizing the holding costs and maintaining a high service rate. A time-honored approach to modeling serial manufacturing lines is to treat them as Markov Processes (Gershwin, 1994, Veatch and Wein, 1992) and then solve the related MarkovDecisionProblem, (MDP), by using standard iterative algorithms such as policy iteration, (Howard, 1960), value iteration, (Bellman, 1957) etc. However the classic dynamic programming, (DP), approach entails two major drawbacks: Bellman's curse of dimensionality, i.e. the com-

DOI: 10.4018/978-1-61520-633-9.ch010

putational explosion that takes place with the increase of the system state space, and the need for a complete mathematical model of the underlying problem. The limitations of the DP approach gave rise to the development of sub-optimal yet efficient production control mechanisms.

A class of production control mechanisms that implement the JIT (JustInTime) manufacturing philosophy known as *pull type* control policies/mechanisms has come to be widely recognized as capable of achieving quite satisfactory results in serial manufacturing line management. Pull type control policies coordinate the production activities in a serial line based only on actual occurrences of demand rather than demand forecasts and production plans as is the case in MRP-based systems. In this chapter, six important pull control policies are examined, namely Kanban and Base Stock (Buzacott and Shanthikumar, 1993), Generalised Kanban (see Buzacott and Shanthikumar (1992), for example), Extended Kanban (Dallery and Liberopoulos, 2000), CONWIP (Spearman *et al.*, 1990) and CONWIP/Kanban Hybrid (Paternina-Arboleda and Das, 2001). Pull production control policies are heuristics characterised by a small number of control parameters that assume integer values. Parameter selection significantly affects the performance of a system operating under a certain pull control policy and is therefore a fundamental issue in the design of a pull-type manufacturing system. In this chapter the performance of JIT manufacturing systems is evaluated by means of discrete-event simulation (Law and Kelton, 1991). In order to optimize the control parameters of the system the simulation model is interfaced with a hybrid optimization technique which combines a genetic algorithm with a local search procedure.

The application of simulation together with optimization meta-heuristics for the modeling and design of manufacturing systems is an approach that has attracted considerable attention over the past years. In Dengiz and Alabas (2000) simulation is used in conjunction with tabu search in order to determine the optimum parameters of a manufacturing system while Bowden *et al.* (1996) utilize evolutionary programming techniques for the same task. Alabas *et al.* (2002) develop the simulation model of a Kanban system and explore the use of genetic algorithm, simulated annealing and tabu search to determine the number of kanbans. Simulated annealing for optimizing the simulation model of a manufacturing system controlled with kanbans is applied in Shahabudeen *et al.* (2002), whereas Hurrion (1997) constructs a neural network meta-model of a Kanban system using data provided by simulation. Koulouriotis *et al.* (2008) apply Reinforcement Learning methods to derive near-optimal production control policies in a serial manufacturing system and compare the proposed approach to existing pull type policies. Some indicative applications of genetic algorithms (GAs) in manufacturing problems can be found in Yang *et al.* (2007), Yamamoto *et al* (2008), Smith and Smith (2002), Shahabudeen and Krishnaiah (1999) and Koulouriotis *et al.* (2010). Panayiotou and Cassandrass (1999) develop a simulation-based algorithm for optimizing the number of kanbans and carry out a sensitivity investigation by using finite perturbation analysis. It has been suggested in the literature that the results of a genetic algorithm can be enhanced by conducting a local search around the best solutions found by the GA, (for related work see Yuan, He and Leng, 2008 and Vivo-Truyols, Torres-Lapasio and Garcıa-Alvarez-Coque, 2001). On that basis, this hybrid optimization scheme has been adopted in the present study.

The main contributions of this work are the following. The performance of six important pull production control policies in a hypothetical scenario is investigated using discrete event simulation. In order to determine the control parameters of each policy the proposed hybrid GA is employed. The objective function to be optimized is a weighted sum of the mean WorkInProcess, (WIP), inventories subject to the constraint of maintaining the service level, (*SL*), above a specified target. Due to the fact that the objective function is stochastic we use resampling, i.e., performing multiple evaluations of the same parameter vector and using the mean of these evaluations as the fitness measurement of this individual, a practice discussed by Fitzpatrick and Grefenstette, (1988) and Hammel and Bäck, (1994). As a constraint handling technique two types of penalty functions are explored; a "death penalty" function and an exponential penalty function. The exponential penalty function is designed according to an empirical method which is based on locating points which lie on the boundaries between feasible and infeasible region from the output of the genetic algorithm with the "death penalty" function. Our numerical results support the intuitive perception that the "death penalty" approach most of the times will yield worse results than the exponential penalty function which penalizes solutions according to the level of the constraint violation. The chapter concludes with a discussion on how the objective function behaves for different levels of arrival rate and service rates as well as on its sensitivity to the decision variable vector.

The remaining material of this chapter is structured as follows. Sections "Base Stock Control Policy" to "CONWIP/Kanban Hybrid Control Policy" give a brief description of six important pull production control policies for serial manufacturing lines. In sections "Optimization Problem: Objective Function" and "Hybrid Genetic Algorithm" we discuss the main aspects of the simulation optimization methodology that we followed and namely, the formal definition of the parameter optimization problem and issues concerning the genetic algorithm and local search procedure that was used. We report our findings from the simulation experiments that we conducted for one serial line starting from section "Experimental Results: Simulation Case" and thereafter. Finally, in the last section we state our concluding remarks and point to possible directions for future research.

SYSTEM DESCRIPTION: JIT PRODUCTION CONTROL POLICIES

We examined manufacturing serial lines that produce a single product type and consist of a number of workstations/machines with intermediate buffers. We assume that the first machine is never starved. Customer demands arrive at random time intervals and request the release of one finished part from the finished goods buffer. Demands are satisfied immediately from the finished parts inventory while in the case where there are no parts available in the last buffer the demand is backordered. We do not consider customer impatience in our model, so no demand is ultimately lost to the system. Manufacturing facilities have the ability to work on only one part at a time during a manufacturing cycle. All machines have random production time, time between failures and repair time. As soon as a stage *i* part is manufactured, it is placed in the output buffer of that station. A control policy coordinates the release of parts from the output buffer of that station to the next machine. The unreliability of the manufacturing operations along with the stochastic demand for final products dictates the use of safety buffers of intermediate and finished parts in order to attain the target service rate. However the use of safety stocks incurs significant holding costs that could bring the manufacturer to a position of competitive disadvantage, and therefore, it is essential to balance the trade-off between minimizing WIP inventories and maintaining a high service level. Figure 1 shows a manufacturing system with three stations in tandem.

Figure 1. A three station manufacturing line

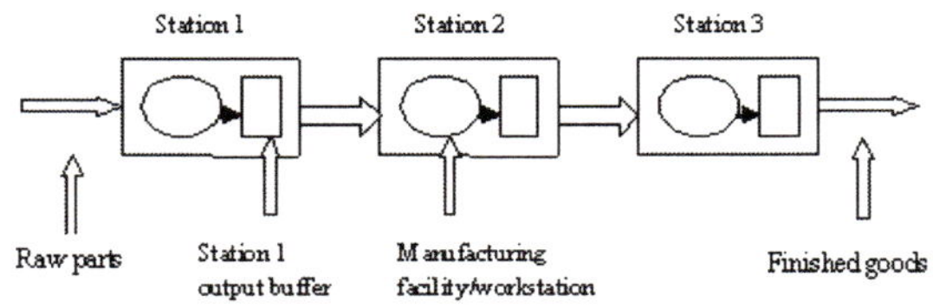

The following sections briefly explain the way that the Kanban, Base Stock, CONWIP, CONWIP/Kanban Hybrid, Extended Kanban and Generalized Kanban control policies for serial lines operate.

BASE STOCK CONTROL POLICY

A Base Stock, (see Buzacott and Shanthikumar, 1993), manufacturing line is completely described by N parameters, the base stock levels S_i of each production station, $i = 1, 2, \ldots, N$ where N is the number of the system's workstations. The S_i parameters correspond to the number of parts that exist in the system's buffers at the time the system is in its initial state that is before any demands have arrived to the system. This control policy operates as follows. When a demand arrives to the system it is immediately transmitted to every manufacturing station, authorizing it to start working on a new station i part. Base Stock has the advantage of reacting rapidly to incoming demand, with the drawback of providing no control at all on the system's inventories.

KANBAN CONTROL POLICY

The Kanban control policy that was originally developed by the Toyota Motor industry and became the topic of considerable research thereafter, (Sugimori et al, 1977, Buzacott and Shanthikumar, 1993, Berkley, 1992, Karaesmen and Dallery, 2000). A Kanban manufacturing line's control parameters are the production authorizations K_i of each station, $i = 1, 2, \ldots, N$. The K_i parameter corresponds to the maximum number of parts that are allowed in station i (manufacturing facility – output buffer). Workstation i is authorized to start working on a new part as soon as a finished station i part is released from its output buffer. The information of a demand arrival is transmitted from the last manufacturing station to the first one station – by – station. If there is a buffer with no parts in it then this transmission is interrupted. The Kanban policy offers very tight synchronization between the various production stations of the system at the expense of the relatively slow response to demand fluctuations.

CONWIP CONTROL POLICY

CONWIP is an abbreviation for CONstand Work In Process (Spearman et al, 1990). According to this policy the total number of parts that exist in the system, (Work In Process), can never exceed a certain level, which is the C control parameter of the policy. Parameter C is equal to the sum of the system's base stocks S_i, $i = 1, 2, \ldots, N$. All machines in a CONWIP line are authorized to produce whenever they have this ability, (they are operational and have a raw part to work on), except the first one. The first machine of the system is authorized to start working on a new part as soon as a unit from the finished parts buffer is released to a customer.

GENERALIZED KANBAN AND EXTENDED KANBAN CONTROL POLICIES

These two control policies combine the merits of Base Stock and Kanban as they react rapidly to the arrival of demands and effectively control the WIP at the same time. They are described by two parameters per station, the base stocks S_i and the production authorizations K_i,($K_i \geq S_i$), which are borrowed from the Base Stock and Kanban policies respectively. The finite number of production authorizations guarantees that the system's inventories will not exceed the pre – defined levels, but the station coordination here is not as tight as in Kanban. A station can be granted a production authorization even if a part is not released from its output buffer. For a detailed description of the way Generalized Kanban and

Extended Kanban operate the reader is referred to Liberopoulos and Dallery (2000) and Buzacott and Shanthikumar (1992).

CONWIP/KANBAN HYBRID CONTROL POLICY

A CONWIP/Kanban Hybrid system (see Paternina – Arboleda and Das (2001) for example), as implied, operates under a combination of the CONWIP and Kanban control policies. Departure of a finished part from the system authorizes the first station to allow a new raw part to enter the system. All workstations except the last one have a finite number of production authorizations K_i, $i = 1, 2, \ldots, N-1$. Station production authorizations K_i, the base stock S_N of the last workstation and the total WIP, (parameter C), that is allowed in the system are CONWIP/Kanban Hybrid's control parameters.

OPTIMIZATION PROBLEM: OBJECTIVE FUNCTION

The mathematical formulation of the parameter optimization problem for serial lines controlled by pull production control policies is given below. Let $\mathbf{x} = [x_1\ x_2\ \ldots.\ x_n]$, $x_i \in \mathbf{Z}$, be the control parameter vector of some pull production control policy, i.e. the station i production authorizations (kanbans) in a Kanban system, or the initial buffer levels in a Base Stock system etc. The objective is to find the control parameter values $\mathbf{x}$ that maximize the expected value of the stochastic objective function $f(\mathbf{x}, \omega)$, subject to the constraint of maintaining the service level (SL) equal to or above a specified target t.

$$\text{maximize: } E\left[f\left(\mathbf{x}, \omega\right)\right],\ x_i \in \mathbf{Z},\ i = 1, 2, \ldots., n \tag{1}$$

$$\text{subject to: } E\left[SL\left(\mathbf{x}, \omega\right)\right] \geq t \tag{2}$$

ω is used to denote the stochastic nature of f, and SL. SL is an unknown function of $\mathbf{x}$ and $t \in \Re^+$. The evaluation of functions f and SL is the result of a simulation experiment. The value of SL is the number of demands satisfied by on-hand inventory divided by the number of total demands which arrived to the system. The value of f is a weighted sum of the mean WorkInProcess inventories and is calculated according to 3.

$$f = -\sum_{i=1}^{N} h_i \bar{H}_i \tag{3}$$

where h_i stands for the cost of storing one item in output buffer i per time unit, and $\bar{H}_i$ is the average inventory level in buffer i We know that the optimal solution in this type of problems is located very close to the boundaries between feasible and infeasible region. Additional difficulty in obtaining the optimal solution emanates from the fact that fitness measurements contain random "noise" caused by the simulation model.

HYBRID GENETIC ALGORITHM

In order to solve the optimization problem stated in the previous section we propose a hybrid optimization technique which combines a genetic algorithm with a local search procedure. The genetic algorithm evolves a population of candidate solutions (individuals), where each solution is evaluated with the use of a simulation model, and the individual with the highest fitness value found by the GA is used to initialize the local search procedure. The fitness $v(\mathbf{x})$ of each individual is represented by Equation (4).

$$v(\mathbf{x}) = \frac{1}{m}\sum_{i=1}^{m}\left[f(\mathbf{x},\omega) + p\left(SL(\mathbf{x},\omega)\right)\right] \quad (4)$$

where $f(\mathbf{x},\omega)$ is calculated according to (3), $p(\mathbf{x})$ is a properly defined penalty function of the service level, and *m* is a positive integer (sample size). The parameters of the GA are the chromosome length *l*, the population size *s*, the sample size m, a positive integer *e* called elite count, the crossover probability P_{cross}, the mutation probability P_{mut} and the max number of generations *g*. The individuals which constitute the genetic algorithm population are encoded as binary bit-strings, therefore parameter *l* controls the size of the search space. Parameter *e* determines the number of individuals that pass deterministically to the next generation. The local search procedure is characterized by a single parameter $\delta \in \Re^+$. Let $\mathbf{x}_{cur}$ be the current solution of the local search algorithm, v_{cur} its fitness value and v_{best} the best fitness value found so far. If we denote the search space by S and a distance function, (e.g. Euclidean distance), by *dist()*, then the neighborhood of $\mathbf{x}_{cur}$ is written as $N(\mathbf{x}_{cur}) = \{\mathbf{y} \in S : dist(\mathbf{x},\mathbf{y}) \le \delta\}$. The pseudo-code of the hybrid genetic algorithm is presented below.

1. Input GA parameters: chromosome length *l*, population size *s*, sample size m, elite count *e*, crossover probability P_{cross}, mutation probability P_{mut}, max number of generations *g*
2. Initialize population randomly, set $generation\_counter \leftarrow 0$
3. WHILE($generation\_counter < g$)
   a. Evaluate population. set $generation\_counter \leftarrow generation\_counter + 1$
   b. Scale fitness values proportionally to raw fitness measurements
   c. Apply selection operator
      - Select *e* individuals with highest fitness values
      - Select the remaining $s - e$ individuals using stochastic uniform selection
   d. Apply crossover operator
   e. Apply mutation operator
4. Return individual $\mathbf{x}_{best}$ with highest fitness
5. Initialize local search algorithm: $\mathbf{x}_{cur} \leftarrow \mathbf{x}_{best}$, define neighborhood parameter δ
6. Evaluate $\mathbf{x}_{cur}$. Set $v_{best} \leftarrow v_{cur}$, $flag \leftarrow TRUE$
7. WHILE($flag = TRUE$)
   a. Evaluate all points in $N(\mathbf{x}_{cur})$
   b. Select $\mathbf{x}_{new} \in N(\mathbf{x}_{cur})$ with best fitness value v_{new}
   c. IF($v_{new} > v_{best}$) THEN set $v_{best} \leftarrow v_{new}$, $\mathbf{x}_{cur} \leftarrow \mathbf{x}_{new}$ ELSE THEN $flag \leftarrow FALSE$
8. Return $\mathbf{x}_{cur}$. Terminate

The selection operator (Step 3.c) determines which individuals will be chosen to create the next generation. The first e individuals in terms of fitness value pass to the next generation by default. The remaining *s* - *e* individuals are selected with the use of a stochastic uniform selection routine. This technique can be visualized as a line in which each individual corresponds to a section of the line of length proportional to its scaled fitness value. The algorithm moves along the line in equal-sized steps. At each step, the algorithm selects an individual from the corresponding section it finds itself on. In the crossover stage (Step 3.d), pairs of individuals are selected at random with probability $P_{cross} \in (0,1)$ in order to be recombined. In the implementations of the GA for the one-parameter-per-workstation manufacturing systems we used the single-point crossover method. For the remaining systems, (Extended and Generalized Kanban) uniform crossover was used. According to this technique, two individuals exchange bits on the basis of a randomly generated binary vector of equal length called crossover mask. The mutation operator (Step 3.e) modifies the value of a bit in the population with probability $P_{mut} \in (0,1)$. The genetic algorithm terminates when it completes a predefined number of iterations g and returns the individual with the highest fitness value which is used to initialize the local search algorithm. The complexity of the hill-climbing procedure is $O(t \times k)$, where t is the number of iterations and k the neighborhood size. The complexity of the genetic algorithm depends on the number of generations, the size of the population and the genetic operators/parameters used.

EXPERIMENTAL RESULTS: SIMULATION CASE

We examined a five-machine manufacturing line with equal operation times. The base simulation scenario consists of the following parameters: Machines operate with service rates which are normally distributed random variables with mean 1.1 parts/time unit and st.d. 0.01. Repair to failure times are exponentially distributed with mean 1000 time units. Failures are operation dependent. Repair times are also assumed exponential with a MeanTimeToRepair of 10 time units. Times between two successive customer arrivals are exponential random variables with mean 1.11 time units, i.e. the arrival rate is $R_a = 0.9$. Since the service rates are all equal to 1.1 parts/ time unit and the machines are failure-prone, the maximum attainable throughput rate under any control policy will be $T_{\max} < 1.1$. Consequently, the arrival rate set to 0.9 parts/time unit corresponds to a heavy loading conditions simulation case. The inventory costs for storing one part per time unit in buffer i are $\mathbf{h} = [h_1\ h_2\ ....\ h_5] = [1.0\ 1.2\ 1.44\ 1.73\ 2.07]$. Note that the holding costs increase at a rate of 20% when moving downstream from buffer to buffer. This increase is due to the value which is added to a part as it is progressively converted into a final product. The system operates under a complete backordering policy, which means that no customer demand is ultimately lost to the system. The justification for selecting the aforementioned probability distributions in order to model the arrival process, the service rates etc. can be found in queueing theory and in manufacturing systems literature. Some indicative references, among others, are the influential works of Law and Kelton (2000) and Bhat (2008). The input parameters of the simulation model were selected in a manner to mimic a situation where the system is under heavy loading conditions. This is a case of primary interest since the differences in performance between the various pull type control policies are most clearly illustrated when the manufacturing line is pushed towards its maximum throughput rate. In order to investigate the sensitivity of the production/ inventory system under examination for different levels of arrival rates and service rates as well as the robustness of the solutions obtained by the proposed optimization methodology, four variants of the base simulation scenario are also considered. In the first two variants, all inputs to the simulation model are kept constant except for the arrival rates which are set to $R_a = 1.0$ and $R_a = 0.8$ respectively, i.e. we examine the system's behaviour for increased/decreased demand for final products. In the remaining two variants of the base simulation case we vary the standard deviation of the service rates. In one case the system's performance is evaluated for service rates that vary significantly around the mean (st.d. = 0.1) and in the other case we examine what would happen if the "randomness" of the service rates decreased (st.d. = 0.001). The system configura-

Table 1. Simulation scenarios parameters

	R_a	R_p	*st.d.*	*MTBF*	*MTTR*	*inventory costs*
base case	0.9	1.1	0.01	1000	10	**h**
variant 1	1.0	1.1	0.01	1000	10	**h**
variant 2	0.8	1.1	0.01	1000	10	**h**
variant 3	0.9	1.1	0.1	1000	10	**h**
variant 4	0.9	1.1	0.001	1000	10	**h**

tion for the five simulation cases is presented in Table 1.

The goal is to maximize the expected value of the weighted sum of the mean WorkInProcess inventories $f = -\sum_{i=1}^{N} h_i \overline{H}_i$, $i = 1,2,..,5$, subject to the constraint of $E\left[SL(\mathbf{x})\right] \geq 90.0\%$.

HYBRID GENETIC ALGORITHM PARAMETERS

The dimensions of the related optimization problem for the Kanban, Base Stock, CONWIP and Kanban/CONWIP Hybrid systems are *dim* = 5. For the Extended and Generalized Kanban systems the dimensionality of the problem rises to *dim'* = 10. The authors conducted a series of pilot experiments in order to come up with the most suitable hybrid genetic algorithm parameters for this particular problem. An important issue was to resolve the trade-off between quality of final solution and computational cost as the evaluation of the fitness value of the candidate solutions is computationally expensive. We experimented with population sizes in the range $\left[20, 50\right]$, crossover probabilities in the range $\left[0.3, 0.8\right]$ and mutation probabilities in the range $\left[0.001, 0.1\right]$. For the one-parameter-per stage policies the single-point crossover operator was implemented whereas for the two-parameter-per-stage policies we applied uniform crossover. The reason for making this distinction is that offspring produced with the latter crossover technique are generally more diverse compared to their parents than offspring generated by single-point crossover. This is a desirable property due to the fact that the search space for the two-parameter-per-stage policies is by orders of magnitude larger that the search space for the one-parameter-per-stage policies and therefore an intense exploration strategy is required. The neighborhood of the local search algorithm was set to include all data points around the current point **x** with Euclidean distance equal to or less than 1: $N\left(\mathbf{x}\right) = \left\{\mathbf{y} \in S : \sqrt{\sum_{i=1}^{n}\left(x_i - y_i\right)^2} \leq 1\right\}$. Given that the decision variables are integers this is obviously the minimum neighborhood size one could select but since the major part of the search is carried out by the genetic algorithm and the local search procedure is used merely to fine-tune the already obtained solutions, it is acceptable to use a small neighborhood. Admittedly, the parameters of the optimization algorithm were initialized heuristically and one cannot discard the possibility that different values for the parameters could yield better results but a full factorial experiment for the design of the optimization scheme would fall beyond the scope of this chapter. The genetic algorithm's parameters that were ultimately selected are: population size = 30, crossover and mutation probabilities, $P_{cross} = 0.5$ and $P_{mut} = 0.05$ respectively. The individual which scored the highest fitness value passes to the next generation with probability 1, i.e. the elite count parameter was set to 1. Each individual was evaluated 50 times, $m = 50$, where each replicate was executed for 80,000 time units. The GA produced 100 generations for the problems with dimensionality $dim = 5$, (optimizing Kanban, Base Stock, CONWIP, CONWIP/Kanban Hybrid systems). For the problems with dimensionality $dim' = 10$, (optimization of Extended Kanban and Generalized Kanban systems) the GA produced 240 generations of individuals.

COMPUTATIONAL COST

The simulators for the six pull type manufacturing systems as well as the proposed optimization algorithm were coded in C++ and the experiments were conducted on a PC with AMD Athlon processor at 1.8 GHz and 512 MB RAM. The factor that primarily affects the execution time of the hybrid GA is the control parameter evaluation, i.e. the computational cost of the simulation model. Every solution evaluation, that is 50 independently seeded executions of the simulation model, lasts approximately 5 seconds and therefore the evaluation of a generation of candidate solutions (30 individuals) takes about 2.5 minutes to complete. The execution of the hybrid GA for a one-parameter-per-stage policy (100 generations) lasts approximately 4.7 hours, of which 4.2 hours are consumed by the simulation model. On the other hand, the execution of the hybrid GA for a two-parameter-per-stage policy (240 generations) lasts approximately 11 hours, where 10 hours are devoted to the solution evaluation phase.

DEATH PENALTY RESULTS

For the implementation of the hybrid genetic algorithm with "death" penalty we used the following penalty function.

$$p(\mathbf{x}) = \begin{cases} 0.0, & if \quad E\left[SL(\mathbf{x})\right] \geq 90.0\% \\ -1000.0, & if \quad E\left[SL(\mathbf{x})\right] < 90.0\% \end{cases} \tag{5}$$

We reiterate that the expected value $E\left[SL(\mathbf{x})\right]$ is the arithmetic mean of m measurements of SL. This is a very straight-forward implementation. Every individual that does not satisfy the service level constraint is penalized heavily and will be probably discarded in the next iteration of the algorithm. The results from the hybrid genetic algorithm runs for each control policy are displayed in Table 2. The rows containing the results of the standard genetic algorithm, (without the local search component), are labeled with the initials GA followed by the control policy's name, while the results of the hybrid algorithm are labeled with the initials GAL and the control policy's name. We made this distinction in order to clarify whether the local search offers some significant improvement or not. The last column of Table 2 contains the fitness values calculated according to Equation (4) of the corresponding parameter sets.

The CONWIP system scored the highest fitness value $v_b = -25.29$ followed by the Generalized Kanban, the Extended Kanban, the Hybrid CONWIP/Kanban, the Kanban and the Base Stock systems in decreasing fitness value order. With the exception of the CONWIP system, the local search algorithm enhanced the best fitness values found by the standard genetic algorithm in a range from 1.35% to 9.34%. It is important to stress here that this improvement refers to the fitness values and not the actual objective function values of the optimization problem. In the case of the Generalized Kanban system the local search algorithm appears to have "repaired" the infeasible solution found by the standard genetic algorithm. The average percentage of infeasible solutions in the final generations of the genetic algorithm runs was equal to 7.2%. Table 3 contains the objective function values $E\left[f(\mathbf{x})\right]^*$ and service levels $E\left[SL(\mathbf{x})\right]^*$ % with 95% confidence bounds of the best parameters found by both the standard

Table 2. Best parameter sets and fitness values for "death" penalty function (n.i. stands for "no improvement")

Policies	$x_1(/x_1')$	$x_2(/x_2')$	$x_3(/x_3')$	$X_4(/x_4')$	$x_5(/x_5')$	*C*	*v(x)*
GA_Kanban (K_i)	2	2	1	8	13	-	-32.11
GAL_Kanban (K_i)	1	2	1	8	12	-	-29.12
GA_BaseStock (S_i)	2	7	2	0	14	-	-31.70
GAL_BaseStock (S_i)	1	6	2	0	14	-	-29.49
GA_CONWIP (S_i, C)	0	5	3	5	6	19	-25.29
GAL_CONWIP (S_i, C)	n.i.	n.i.	n.i.	n.i.	n.i.	n.i.	n.i.
GA_Hybrid (K_i, i=1,2,3,4, B_5, C)	1	1	3	7	10	22	-28.75
GAL_Hybrid(K_i,i=1,2,3,4, S_5, C)	1	1	2	7	10	21	-26.71
GA_E. Kanban (K_i/S_i)	10/0	11/2	9/1	2/2	23/15	-	-26.54
GAL_E. Kanban (K_i/S_i)	6/0	11/2	6/1	2/2	23/15	-	-26.18
GA_G. Kanban (K_i/S_i)	8/4	2/0	15/3	16/2	14/14	-	-1028.14
GAL_G.Kanban (K_i/S_i)	6/2	2/0	15/3	15/2	14/14	-	-26.15

genetic algorithm and the hybrid genetic algorithm with the "death" penalty function.

These data were produced by running 50 replicates of each of the six simulation models for $t_{sim} = 1,500,000.0$ time units and then averaging the corresponding variables. This is a 18.75 times longer simulation than that used to evaluate the fitness of the individuals in the genetic algorithm. By using exhaustively long simulation times we can compute far more accurate estimators, (indi-

Table 3. Objective function values $E\left[f(\mathbf{x})\right]*$ and % service levels $E\left[SL(\mathbf{x})\right]*\%$ for best parameter sets found by standard GA and hybrid GA with "death penalty" (95% confidence). (K stands for Kanban, BS for Base Stock etc. n.i. stands for "no improvement")

GA results			**Hybrid GA (with local search)**		
Policies	$E\left[SL(\mathbf{x})\right]*\%$	$E\left[f(\mathbf{x})\right]*$	Policies	$E\left[SL(\mathbf{x})\right]*\%$	$E\left[f(\mathbf{x})\right]*$
K	91.17 ± 0.09	-32.07 ± 0.04	K	90.08 ± 0.09	-29.13 ± 0.03
BS	90.37 ± 0.09	-31.73 ± 0.02	BS	90.03 ± 0.11	-29.53 ± 0.02
C	89.87 ± 0.08	-25.26 ± 0.01	C	n.i.	n.i.
C/K H	91.34 ± 0.08	-28.83 ± 0.03	C/K H	90.43 ± 0.11	-26.79 ± 0.04
EK	90.29 ± 0.07	-26.57 ± 0.0	EK	90.21 ± 0.09	-26.23 ± 0.03
GK	90.23 ± 0.09	-28.18 ± 0.02	GK	89.91 ± 0.01	-26.12 ± 0.02

cated by the superscript *), which can be considered to approximate the true expected values of these performance measures. This way, relatively safe conclusions can be drawn regarding both the quality of the solutions found by the hybrid genetic algorithms and the performance of each of the competing pull type control policies. Of course, by increasing the simulation time and/or the resampling, the optimization algorithm is less likely to be mislead by "lucky" candidate solutions which score well once by chance but the consequent computational cost is prohibitive of doing so. Apart from that, we are interested in establishing whether the algorithm is capable of locating good and hopefully optimal solutions in the presence of a relatively low signal-to-"noise" ratio. By observing the data in Table 3 we see that the local search algorithm produced actual improvements in the objective function values while preserving the feasibility of the solutions in all cases except the CONWIP and Generalized Kanban systems. The results regarding the Generalized Kanban system are somehow contradicting. In Table 2 the local search algorithm appears to have repaired the infeasible solution, while in Table 3 the original solution is now found to be actually feasible and the local search solution is the one which violates the constraint. Actually, these results merely demonstrate an inherent weakness of search algorithms that generate a single point per iteration when compared to genetic algorithms in "noisy" environments. A hill-climbing method, like the one used here, compares candidate solutions in each iteration only with best solution found so far, and therefore, it is easy to be mislead by a "lucky" solution. In genetic algorithms, on the contrary, for a solution to be maintained it must outweigh an entire collection of solutions and not just a previously best one. As an overall assessment, we could argue that the results presented in this section support the conclusion that even with this simple static penalty function a genetic algorithm can produce quite good solutions. Two typical plots of the best solution found by the genetic algorithm with the "death" penalty function versus the number of generations can be found in Figure 2.

These two plots exhibit a somehow similar pattern. For illustration purposes we use a time window of 140 generations and divide the plot areas in two regions with a perpendicular dotted line. Notice that in the left side of the plots, if we disregard random fluctuations caused by the simulation model, the two curves are increasing almost monotonically. In this area, the best solution found by the algorithm is not lying somewhere

Figure 2. Typical plots of best fitness value found by GA with "death" penalty function versus number of iterations (140 iterations window)

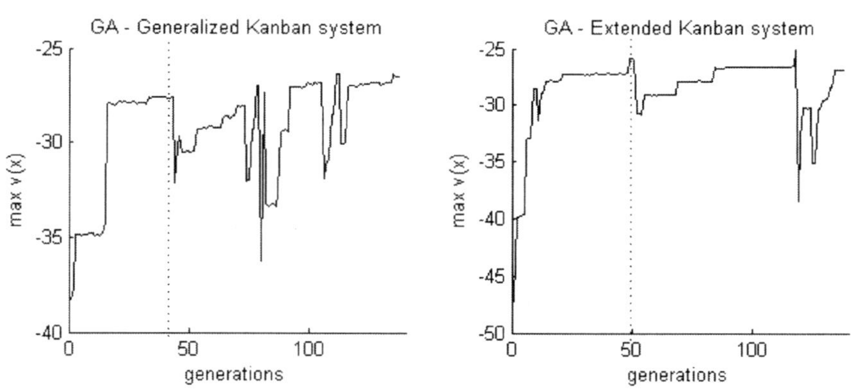

near the boundaries between feasible and infeasible region. In the intersection point of the curve with the dotted perpendicular line the curve suddenly "dives". This is indicative that the currently best individual is marginally feasible, (or infeasible), and that it failed to satisfy the constraint in this evaluation. As a consequence, it was penalized heavily and substituted by another individual which happened to have a lower fitness value. From this point on, the curve displays similar abrupt fluctuations, indicating that the population evolves towards the boundaries between feasible and infeasible region and the optimal solution.

DESIGNING EXPONENTIAL PENALTY FUNCTION

Intuitively, the "death" penalty approach, as attractive as it can be due to its simplicity, does not seem to be the best approach to handle constraints. Even the slightest violation of the imposed constraints results in penalizing heavily a good solution. This way an individual which scores excellently for a series of consecutive generations may be discarded by the algorithm. This is an undesired property in the kind of optimization problem that we are dealing with, where fitness measurements are distorted by random fluctuations caused by the stochasticity of the simulation model. Another weakness of this approach is that it damages the diversity of the population, as the majority of the individuals are crowded in the feasible region. Given that the optimal solution lies on the feasibility boundaries, the search would probably be more efficient if the population evolved towards the boundaries from both feasible and infeasible regions. For example, it is unclear why a slightly infeasible individual which is located very close to the optimal solution should be assigned a worse fitness value than a feasible individual that scores poorly. For all of the above mentioned reasons, the idea of penalizing infeasible solutions according to the level of the constraint violation seems more appealing, (see Venkatraman and Yen (2005) for guidelines on designing penalty functions). The problem that needs to be addressed now is how to design such a "soft-limit" penalty function. A reasonable choice is to use an exponential penalty function $p(\mathbf{x}) = c^u$, where $c = const \in \Re$ and $u = t - SL$ is the difference between the target service level and $E\left[SL(\mathbf{x})\right]$ the measured expected service level. The intuitive, *minimal penalty rule*, (Le Riche *et al.* 1995), suggests that the penalty for infeasible individuals should be just above the threshold below which infeasible solutions score better than their feasible, possibly optimal, neighbors. In practice, however, it is quite difficult to achieve this. The procedure we followed in order to implement, at least to some extent, this intuition, is the following. Using the output of the executions of the genetic algorithm with the "death" penalty function we created plots like the ones in Figure 2. By examining these plots it was easy to locate solutions that were very close to the feasibility boundaries, (these points are indicated by the characteristic "dive" of the curve). The next step was to examine the neighborhood of such a point in order to determine how a small change in parameters affected the service level *SL* as well as the objective function $f(\mathbf{x})$. The value of *SL* is affected primarily by the control parameters of the last three machines so we could limit ourselves to a relatively small neighborhood. Having collected this data, we were able to select the parameter c of the penalty function $p(\mathbf{x}) = c^u$, in the spirit of the "minimal penalty rule". This is an empirical technique that may not be easy or even possible to apply to other problems, nevertheless it provides the means to design a penalty function that will work well and outperform most of the times the "death" penalty approach as supported by our experimental results presented in the following section.

EXPONENTIAL PENALTY FUNCTION RESULTS

After following the procedure outlined in the previous section we were able to construct the following penalty function (6).

$$p(\mathbf{x}) = \begin{cases} 0.0, & u \leq 0.0 \\ 9.0^{u}, & 0.0 < u < 3.0 \\ 9.0^{3}, & 3.0 \leq u \end{cases} \quad (6)$$

where $u = t - E\left[SL(\mathbf{x})\right]$ is the difference between the target service level t = 90.0% and the measured service level $E\left[SL(\mathbf{x})\right]$. Note that for service levels equal to or lower than 87.0% we ground the penalty to a constant value. The reason we do this is that we want the raw fitness values $v(\mathbf{x})$ to be within a range for the selection operator of the genetic algorithm to work properly. We reiterate that in our implementation the values of the individuals are scaled proportionally to their raw fitness measurements prior to selection.

The results from the hybrid genetic algorithm runs for each control policy are displayed in Table 4. The rows containing the results of the standard genetic algorithm, (without the local search component), are labeled with the initials GA followed by the control policy's name, while the results of the hybrid algorithm are labeled with the initials GAL and the control policy's name. The last column of Table 4 contains the fitness values of the corresponding parameter sets. The CONWIP system scored the highest fitness value $v_b = -25.31$ followed by the Extended Kanban, the Hybrid CONWIP/Kanban, the Generalized Kanban, the Base Stock and the Kanban systems in decreasing fitness value order. The hybrid optimization algorithm outperformed the standard genetic algorithm in the cases of the Base Stock, the Extended Kanban and the Generalized Kanban systems. For the three remaining systems the local search failed to offer an improvement in minimizing $v(\mathbf{x})$. Table 5 contains the objective function values $E\left[f(\mathbf{x})\right]$* and service levels

Table 4. Best parameter sets and fitness values for exponential penalty function (n.i. stands for "no improvement")

Policies	$x_1(/x_1')$	$x_2(/x_2')$	$x_3(/x_3')$	$x_4(/x_4')$	$x_5(/x_5')$	C	v(x)
GA_Kanban (Ki)	1	1	1	7	13	-	-28.05
GAL_Kanban (Ki)	n.i.	n.i.	n.i.	n.i.	n.i.	-	n.i.
GA_BaseStock (Si)	0	3	0	0	17	-	-27.19
GAL_BaseStock (Si)	0	2	0	0	17	-	-25.95
GA_CONWIP (Si, C)	0	6	1	6	6	19	-25.31
GAL_CONWIP (Si, C)	n.i.	n.i.	n.i.	n.i.	n.i.	n.i.	n.i.
GA_Hybrid (Ki, i=1,2,3,4, S5, C)	1	4	5	9	1	20	-25.92
GAL_Hybrid(Ki,i=1,2,3,4, S5, C)	n.i.	n.i.	n.i.	n.i.	n.i.	n.i.	n.i.
GA_E. Kanban (Ki/Si)	4/1	10/0	2/2	4/2	22/15	-	-25.82
GAL_E. Kanban (Ki/Si)	3 /1	10/0	2/2	4/2	22/15	-	-25.72
GA_G. Kanban (Ki/Si)	12/5	7/0	14/4	13/1	16/14	-	-29.34
GAL_G.Kanban (Ki/Si)	9/2	3/0	13/4	13/1	15/14	-	-25.95

Table 5. Objective function values $E\left[f(\mathbf{x})\right]*$ and % service levels $E\left[SL(\mathbf{x})\right]*$ % for best parameter sets found by standard GA and hybrid GA with "exponential penalty" (95% confidence). (K stands for Kanban, BS for Base Stock etc. n.i. stands for "no improvement")

GA results			Hybrid GA (with local search)		
Policies	$E\left[SL(\mathbf{x})\right]*$ %	$E\left[f(\mathbf{x})\right]*$	Policies	$E\left[SL(\mathbf{x})\right]*$ %	$E\left[f(\mathbf{x})\right]*$
K	90.10 ± 0.08	-28.01 ± 0.03	K	n.i.	n.i.
BS	90.34 ± 0.12	-27.20 ± 0.03	BS	89.95 ± 0.13	-25.97 ± 0.03
C	89.94 ± 0.10	-25.27 ± 0.02	C	n.i.	n.i.
C/K H	90.21 ± 0.09	-25.87 ± 0.02	C/K H	n.i.	n.i.
EK	90.07 ± 0.11	-25.84 ± 0.02	EK	89.98 ± 0.10	-25.71 ± 0.02
GK	90.31 ± 0.09	-29.34 ± 0.02	GK	89.73 ± 0.09	-25.89 ± 0.02

$E\left[SL(\mathbf{x})\right]*$ % with 95% confidence bounds of the best parameters found by both the standard genetic algorithm and the hybrid genetic algorithm with the exponential penalty function. These data were produced by running 50 replicates of each of the six simulation models for $t_{sim} = 1,500,000.0$ time units and then averaging the corresponding variables.

All three solutions found by the local search algorithm when initialized with the solutions of the genetic algorithm were marginally infeasible. The local search algorithm falsely interpreted the effect of random noise as an actual improvement and thus substituted the feasible solutions by infeasible ones. Of course, we cannot rule out that this was caused in part by the penalty function itself. However, we must mention that the amount of the constraint violation was rather trivial. The average percentage of infeasible solutions in the final generations of the genetic algorithm runs with the exponential penalty function was equal to 8.5%.

DISCUSSION ON THE PERFORMANCE OF THE TWO PENALTY FUNCTIONS

By comparing the data in Tables 3 and 5 we notice that the standard genetic algorithm with the exponential penalty function outperforms both the standard genetic algorithm and the hybrid algorithm with the "death penalty" function for all systems except the CONWIP and the Generalized Kanban. In terms of objective function value, the use of the exponential penalty function rather than the "death penalty" improved the solution by 3.84% for the Kanban system, by 7.89% for the Base Stock system and by 3.43% for the CONWIP/Kanban Hybrid system. For the Extended Kanban system we monitored a 1.5% lower value of $E\left[f(\mathbf{x})\right]*$, while for the CONWIP system the results were practically the same. Only for the Generalized Kanban system the "death" penalty approach succeeded in producing a 4% better solution than the exponential penalty approach. The superiority of the exponential penalty function over the "death" penalty function can be explained

Figure 3. Typical plots of best fitness value found by GA with "death" and exponential penalty functions versus number of iterations

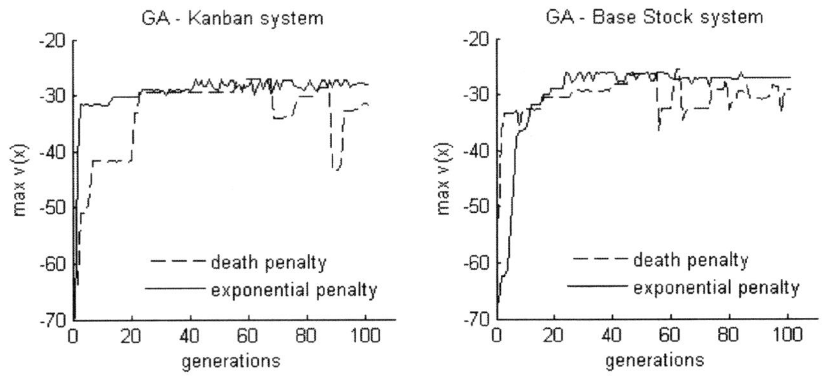

qualitatively as follows: Figure 3 shows typical plots of the genetic algorithm's convergence with the "death" penalty and the exponential penalty function. Notice that at some point near the 60th generation both curves have approximately the same height. The best solutions found by the two implementations of the algorithm in these points probably belong to the same level set and are lying somewhere close to the feasibility boundaries. In some subsequent iteration of the algorithm with the "death" penalty, this solution apparently violates the constraint and is therefore discarded. The height of the curve shows that the individual which replaced it has a significantly lower fitness value. This is not the case in the algorithm with the exponential penalty where the properly designed penalty function prevents the good solution to be discarded, at least not from a much worse candidate solution. Concluding the discussion on the performance of the hybrid GA we state summarize our major findings: i) the incorporation of a local search element can enhance the genetic algorithm's performance with the disadvantage of that the local search algorithm is more susceptible to falsely interpreting random noise as actual objective function improvements than the genetic algorithm, ii) the "death penalty" approach most of the times will yield worse results than a function which penalizes solutions according to the level of the constraint violation like the exponential penalty function used here.

COMPARISON OF PULL TYPE PRODUCTION CONTROL POLICIES-SENSITIVITY ANALYSIS

Table 6 presents the objective function values and the corresponding service levels for the six JIT control policies with the best parameters found by the proposed optimization strategy. Note that the Base stock, CONWIP and Extended Kanban solutions attain a service level below 90% but since the constraint is within the 95% confidence halfwidth we consider them to be feasible. The CONWIP policy ranks first followed in close distance by the Extended Kanban, Hybrid and Base Stock policies. The Kanban and Generalized Kanban policies occupy the last two positions of the objective function value ranking. Since in this simulation scenario the demand process pushes the manufacturing system towards its maximum throughput rate, the poor performance of the Kanban mechanism is anticipated since this policy offers tight coordination between the manufacturing stages but does not respond rapidly to incoming orders. On the other hand the performance of the Generalized Kanban system is somewhat unexpected since it is supposed to be an enhancement

Table 6. Objective function values – service levels of pull control policies with best parameters for base simulation case

	Kanban	Base Stock	CONWIP	CONWIP/Kanban Hybrid	Extended Kanban	Generalized Kanban
$E\left[f(\mathbf{x})\right]^*$	-28.01 $\pm$ 0.03	-25.97 $\pm$ 0.03	-25.27 $\pm$ 0.02	-25.87 $\pm$ 0.02	-25.71 $\pm$ 0.02	-28.18 $\pm$ 0.02
$E\left[SL(\mathbf{x})\right]^*$	90.10 $\pm$ 0.08	89.95 $\pm$ 0.13	89.94 $\pm$ 0.10	90.21 $\pm$ 0.09	89.98 $\pm$ 0.10	90.23 $\pm$ 0.09

of the original Kanban policy. However, this is not the case for the control policy that is mostly related to Generalized Kanban, the Extended Kanban mechanism, which ranks second. The main characteristic of the Base Stock policy, that is fast reaction to demand, is supported by the experimental output. Finally, the fact that in a CONWIP or CONWIP/Kanban Hybrid system the WIP tends to accumulate to the last buffer allows this two policies to achieve a high service level while operating a lean manufacturing mode.

Table 7 shows the statistics of the system's performance measures for the four variants of the basic simulation case. In the case where the demand rate increases (first column of Table 7) we notice that the service level as well as the average WIP decreases for all policies, but some control mechanisms are more sensitive to this change than others. Specifically, the service rate in the Kanban and Hybrid systems decreases dramatically, whereas the Base Stock and Generalized Kanban policies seem to be more robust regarding the increase of the demand rate. In the second variant (decreased arrival rate) of the basic simulation case one can see that all six control policies practically achieve the same service level. This is an indication that when the demand can be easily satisfied by the manufacturing system the role of the production control policy diminishes. In this case the distribution of the objective function values over the control mechanisms also tends to level out.

The increase of the standard deviation of the processing times (variant 3) has an effect similar

Table 7. Objective function values – service levels of pull control policies with best parameters for variants of base simulation case

	R_a=1.0		R_a=0.8		st.d.=0.1		st.d.=0.001	
	$E\left[f(\mathbf{x})\right]^*$	$E\left[SL(\mathbf{x})\right]^*$	$E\left[f(\mathbf{x})\right]^*$	$E\left[SL(\mathbf{x})\right]^*$	$E\left[f(\mathbf{x})\right]^*$	$E\left[SL(\mathbf{x})\right]^*$	$E\left[f(\mathbf{x})\right]^*$	$E\left[SL(\mathbf{x})\right]^*$
K	-15.21	55.61	-32.77	96.52	-20.92	76.2	-28.32	90.43
BS	-23.75	64.2	-28.57	96.05	-25.48	88	-26.01	90.07
C	-19.15	62.89	-28.68	96.18	-24.54	87.91	-25.33	90.12
H	-14.71	57.91	-30.06	96.38	-21.23	79.43	-26.03	90.42
EK	-18.05	61.89	-29.33	96.21	-24.96	88.05	-25.74	90.07
GK	-20.57	62.92	-31.74	96.29	-27.56	88.72	-28.17	90.27

to that of the increase of the demand rate. The reasons for that can be attributed to the resulting decreased coordination among the various production stages which increases the frequency with which machine starvation or blockage events occur. Again, the Kanban mechanism is mostly affected by this parameter due to its tight production coordination scheme, while the Generalized Kanban mechanism seems to react rather robustly. Finally, the decrease of the standard deviation of the processing times (variant 4) seems to have a negligible effect on the system's behavior as indicated by the experimental data presented in the last column of Table 7. Tables 8 and 9 contain data regarding the sensitivity of the system's behavior in respect to the parameters of the controlling policy. For example, in Table 8, the cells in the *i*-th row that belong to the columns labeled as "Base Stock" show the objective function value and service level that result when the *i*-th component (parameter S_i) of the corresponding decision variable vector is increased by the minimum possible value, i.e. by one. In general, the service level (objective function) is an increasing (decreasing) function of the control parameters. However, the rate with which the service level/objective function changes depends on the type of the control policy and the index (position) of the parameter in the parameter vector. For instance, in the five-station Kanban system, adding an additional kanban in the last stage will result in a larger decrease of the objective function value than adding an extra kanban in any of the upstream stages. It is interesting to observe the cases of the CONWIP and CONWIP/Kanban Hybrid systems where the unitary increase of a control parameter in any of the stages 2,3,4,5 seems to have the same effect. This can be explained by the fact that since the last workstation is authorized to produce whenever it has this ability all parts in upstream buffers are continuously "pushed" towards the finished goods buffer, and therefore WIP in intermediate stages is scarce. By increasing the initial stock in the first buffer the average WIP in intermediate stages increases and thus this change has greater impact to the objective value and service level. Generalized Kanban and Extended Kanban are characterized by two parameters per stage and therefore the sensitivity analysis must consider both of these parameters. The systems' performance for a unitary change in the base stock of the *i*-th stage is shown in the columns labeled as "base stocks" whereas the cells under the label "free kanbans" contain system performance information when the total number of kanbans of the *i*-th stage is increased by one but the base stock remains unaltered.

Table 8. Objective function value – service level sensitivity to parameter vector (Kanban, Base Stock, CONWIP, Hybrid)

	Kanban		Base Stock		CONWIP		CONWIP/Kanban Hybrid	
	$E[f(\mathbf{x})]^*$	$E[SL(\mathbf{x})]^*$	$E[f(\mathbf{x})]^*$	$E[SL(\mathbf{x})]^*$	$E[f(\mathbf{x})]^*$	$E[SL(\mathbf{x})]^*$	$E[f(\mathbf{x})]^*$	$E[SL(\mathbf{x})]^*$
1	-29.1	90.32	-27.15	90.35	-27.53	90.92	-28.03	91.13
2	-29.34	90.51	-27.19	90.26	-27.24	90.82	-27.84	91.02
3	-29.52	90.65	-27.77	90.80	-27.24	90.77	-27.83	91.02
4	-29.61	90.51	-27.83	90.74	-27.24	90.81	-27.79	91.0
5	-29.86	90.94	-27.86	90.78	-27.24	90.83	-27.76	90.99

Table 9. Objective function value – service level sensitivity to parameter vector (Extended Kanban, Generalized Kanban)

	Extended Kanban				Generalized Kanban			
	base stocks (S_i)		**free kanbans (K_i-S_i)**		**base stocks (S_i)**		**free kanbans (K_i-S_i)**	
	$E[f(\mathbf{x})]^*$	$E[SL(\mathbf{x})]^*$	$E[f(\mathbf{x})]^*$	$E[SL(\mathbf{x})]^*$	$E[f(\mathbf{x})]^*$	$E[SL(\mathbf{x})]^*$	$E[f(\mathbf{x})]^*$	$E[SL(\mathbf{x})]^*$
1	-26.75	90.21	-25.83	90.07	-29.18	90.35	-28.20	90.27
2	-27.12	90.47	-25.79	90.01	-29.65	90.63	-28.27	90.29
3	-27.16	90.55	-25.8	90.1	-29.58	90.69	-28.29	90.24
4	-27.38	90.66	-25.77	90.06	-29.81	90.78	-28.26	90.28
5	-27.61	90.86	-25.73	90.06	-30.08	91.13	-28.21	90.32

The effect of adding an extra base stock to a stage of a Generalized/Extended Kanban system is similar to that of adding a kanban to a stage of a Kanban system. The mean WIP is also an increasing function of the control parameters (K_i - S_i) but as one can see from Table 9 rather large changes in the number of free kanbans are needed for a significant change in the objective function value to occur.

CONCLUSION AND FUTURE RESEARCH

We implemented a hybrid optimization technique which combines a genetic algorithm with a local search procedure to find optimal decision variables for a family of JIT manufacturing systems. The goal was to maximize a weighted sum of the mean WorkInProcess inventories subject to the constraint of maintaining a target service level. Our numerical results indicate that the performance of a genetic algorithm can be easily enhanced by incorporating a local search component, however, the local search algorithm is more susceptible to falsely interpreting random noise as actual objective function improvements than the genetic algorithm. Moreover, our results support the intuitive perception that penalizing candidate solutions according to the level of constraint violation will yield better results than the "death penalty" approach most of the times. The performance of the JIT control policies with optimized parameters is presented analytically and commented upon. Finally, we conduct a sensitivity analysis in respect to the variation of the demand rate, the standard deviation of the service rates and the control parameter vector. The results of the analysis offer considerable insight to the underlying mechanics of the JIT control policies under consideration. Constraint handling and "noisy" or dynamic environments in the context of genetic optimization of manufacturing systems are currently active research fields. Indicatively, a relatively recent and interesting direction is to use evolutionary multi-objective techniques to handle constraints as additional objectives.

REFERENCES

Alabas, C., Altiparmak, F., & Dengiz, B. (2002). A comparison of the performance of artificial intelligence techniques for optimizing the number of kanbans. *The Journal of the Operational Research Society*, *53*(8), 907–914. doi:10.1057/palgrave.jors.2601395

Bellman, R. E. (1957). *Dynamic Programming*. Princeton: Princeton University Press.

Berkley, B. J. (1992). A review of the kanban production control research literature. *Production and Operations Management*, *1*(4), 393–411. doi:10.1111/j.1937-5956.1992.tb00004.x

Bhat, U. N. (2008). *An Introduction to Queueing Theory: Modelling and Analysis in Applications*. Boston: Birkhauser.

Bowden, R. O., Hall, J. D., & Usher, J. M. (1996). Integration of evolutionary programming and simulation to optimize a pull production system. *Computers & Industrial Engineering*, *31*(1&2), 217–220. doi:10.1016/0360-8352(96)00115-5

Buzacott, J. A., & Shanthikumar, J. G. (1992). A general approach for coordinating production in multiple cell manufacturing systems. *Production and Operations Management*, *1*(1), 34–52. doi:10.1111/j.1937-5956.1992.tb00338.x

Buzacott, J. A., & Shanthikumar, J. G. (1993). *Stochastic Models of Manufacturing Systems*. New York: Prentice Hall.

Dallery, Y., & Liberopoulos, G. (2000). Extended kanban control system: combining kanban and base stock. *IIE Transactions*, *32*(4), 369–386. doi:10.1080/07408170008963914

Fitzpatrick, J. M. & Grefenstette, J. J. (1988) Genetic algorithms in noisy environments. *Machine Learning: Special issue on genetic algorithms, 3*, 101-120.

Gershwin, S. B. (1994). *Manufacturing Systems Engineering*. New York: Prentice Hall.

Hammel, U., & Bäck, T. (1994). Evolution strategies on noisy functions. How to improve convergence properties. *Parallel Problem Solving from Nature*, *3*, 159–168.

Howard, R. (1960). *Dynamic Programming and Markov Processes. Massachussets*. MIT Press.

Hurrion, R. D. (1997). An example of simulation optimization using a neural network metamodel: finding the optimum number of kanbans in a manufacturing system. *The Journal of the Operational Research Society*, *48*(11), 1105–1112.

Karaesmen, F., & Dallery, Y. (2000). A performance comparison of pull type control mechanisms for multi-stage manufacturing. *International Journal of Production Economics*, *68*, 59–71. doi:10.1016/S0925-5273(98)00246-1

Koulouriotis, D. E., Xanthopoulos, A. S., & Gasteratos, A. (2008). A Reinforcement Learning Approach for Production Control in Manufacturing Systems. In *1st International Workshop on Evolutionary and Reinforcement Learning for Autonomous Robot Systems*, (pp. 24-31). Patra, Greece.

Koulouriotis, D. E., Xanthopoulos, A. S., & Tourassis, V. D. (2010). Simulation optimisation of pull control policies for serial manufacturing lines and assembly manufacturing systems using genetic algorithms. *International Journal of Production Research*, *48*(10), 2887–2912. doi:10.1080/00207540802603759

Law, A., & Kelton, D. (2000). *Simulation Modelling and Analysis*. New York: McGraw Hill.

Le Riche, R., Knopf-Lenoir, C., & Haftka, R. T. (1995). A Segregated Genetic Algorithm for Constrained Structural Optimization. In *Sixth International Conference on Genetic Algorithms* (pp. 558-565).

Liberopoulos, G., & Dallery, Y. (2000). A unified framework for pull control mechanisms in multi-stage manufacturing systems. *Annals of Operations Research*, *93*, 325–355. doi:10.1023/A:1018980024795

Panayiotou, C. G., & Cassandras, C. G. (1999). Optimization of kanban - based manufacturing systems. *Automatica*, *35*(3), 1521–1533. doi:10.1016/S0005-1098(99)00074-6

Paternina – Arboleda, C. D, & Das, T. K. (2001). Intelligent dynamic control policies for serial production lines. *IIE Transactions*, *33*, 65–77. doi:10.1080/07408170108936807

Shahabudeen, P., Gopinath, R., & Krishnaiah, K. (2002). Design of bi-criteria kanban system using simulated annealing technique. *Computers & Industrial Engineering*, *41*(4), 355–370. doi:10.1016/S0360-8352(01)00060-2

Shahabudeen, P., & Krishnaiah, K. (1999). Design of a Bi-Criteria kanban system using Genetic Algorithm. *International Journal of Management and System*, *15*(3), 257–274.

Smith, G. C., & Smith, S. S. F. (2002). An enhanced genetic algorithm for automated assembly planning. *Robotics and Computer-integrated Manufacturing*, *18*(5-6), 355–364. doi:10.1016/S0736-5845(02)00029-7

Spearman, M. L., Woodruff, D. L., & Hopp, W. J. (1990). CONWIP: a pull alternative to kanban. *International Journal of Production Research*, *28*, 879–894. doi:10.1080/00207549008942761

Sugimori, Y., Kusunoki, K., Cho, F., & Uchikawa, S. (1977). Toyota production system and kanban system materialization of just-in-time and respect-for-humans systems. *International Journal of Production Research*, *15*(6), 553–564. doi:10.1080/00207547708943149

Veatch, M. H., & Wein, L. M. (1992). Monotone control of queueing networks. *Queueing Systems*, *12*, 391–408. doi:10.1007/BF01158810

Venkatraman, S., & Yen, G. G. (2005). A generic framework for constrained optimization using genetic algorithms. *IEEE Transactions on Evolutionary Computation*, *9*(4), 424–435. doi:10.1109/TEVC.2005.846817

Vivo-Truyols, G., Torres-Lapasio, J. R., & Garcıa-Alvarez-Coque, M. C. (2001). A hybrid genetic algorithm with local search: I. Discrete variables: optimisation of complementary mobile phases. *Chemometrics and Intelligent Laboratory Systems*, *59*, 89–106. doi:10.1016/S0169-7439(01)00148-4

Yamamoto, H., Qudeiri, J. A., & Marui, E. (2008). Definition of FTL with bypass lines and its simulator for buffer size decision. *International Journal of Production Economics*, *112*(1), 18–25. doi:10.1016/j.ijpe.2007.03.007

Yang, T., Kuo, Y., & Cho, C. (2007). A genetic algorithms simulation approach for the multi-attribute combinatorial dispatching decision problem. *European Journal of Operational Research*, *176*(3), 1859–1873. doi:10.1016/j.ejor.2005.10.048

Yuan, Q., He, Z., & Leng, H. (2008). A hybrid genetic algorithm for a class of global optimization problems with box constraints. *Applied Mathematics and Computation*, *197*, 924–929. doi:10.1016/j.amc.2007.08.081

Chapter 11
Multi-Period Routing in Hybrid Courier Operations

Theodore Athanasopoulos
University of the Aegean, Greece

Ioannis Minis
University of the Aegean, Greece

ABSTRACT

Appointment-based logistics systems, such as special courier services, or repair / maintenance services, face ever increasing competitive pressures for efficiency and on-time performance. For example, in addition to typical (core) operations, courier service providers lately deal with micrologistics activities, such as bulk product deliveries. The promise dates of such deliveries have some flexibility within a pre-specified service level. In this hybrid environment, bulk deliveries are typically planned on an ad hoc basis, without taking explicitly into account the workload for core operations, a practice that may lead to inefficiencies. This chapter proposes a new method to perform assignment of service requests (calls) with some flexibility taking into account expected routes in a multi-period horizon. The problem is solved on a rolling horizon basis in order to address the dynamics of arriving calls. The method is tested through several theoretical examples, as well as in an extensive industrial case, and appears to be superior to current methods used in practice.

INTRODUCTION

The problem addressed in this chapter is related to environments in which a fleet of vehicles serves a set of customers using a hybrid service policy that includes (a) mandatory and (b) flexible requests (calls). The mandatory requests must be served strictly within the current period of service (period 1) and the flexible requests must be served within a certain number of subsequent periods (e.g. periods 1, 2, ..., P).

This is a practical planning problem that may be encountered in many supply chains, and is, at the same time, of significant theoretical interest. In particular, the multi-period nature of the problem has not been given much attention, by the vehicle routing literature. However, addressing this characteristic properly may lead to significant

DOI: 10.4018/978-1-61520-633-9.ch011

enhancements both in efficiency and service quality. To this effect intelligent computational methods may be used to allocate the flexible service requirements (calls) within the multi-period horizon in a way that minimizes overall routing costs, respecting all service level requirements.

Typical operational environments that feature these characteristics are, among others, courier services as well as on-site (home or other) maintenance and repair services. The courier environment has been the application area of this work. A typical courier network consists of several service centers, which are responsible for the distribution and collection of parcels and letters using a dedicated fleet. The main tasks of a service center can be summarized in (a) deliveries, (b) pickups, and (c) bulk product deliveries. Tasks (a) and (b) are the mandatory tasks, the requests of which arrive usually during the night or early morning prior to the beginning of the service period. Tasks (c) are flexible, arrive daily but should be served within the next P periods (days) after arrival. For these tasks, the customers to be served should be informed at least one period prior to the actual service delivery. A mixture of 80% mandatory calls and 20% flexible calls is typical in many courier operations.

Note that there is no flexibility in planning the "mandatory" calls, since they must be served within the designated period. However, there is flexibility in planning the "flexible" calls, i.e. in selecting the most convenient period within the designated horizon of P periods to serve these calls. A significant issue in allocating the flexible calls, i.e. selecting those to serve during each period of operations, is that their assignment depends on the attributes of the mandatory calls.

Another operational environment of relevance to the service call allocation problem is maintenance/ repair services that are delivered on-site. In this environment, a group of repair persons provide services on location (e.g. appliance, or home equipment, maintenance). Mandatory calls typically are the repair tasks that need immediate attention (e.g. breakdowns), while flexible calls are the ones that concern preventive maintenance. In this case, customer service is typically problematic, forcing customers to wait for unspecified time within the promise day of service delivery. The main reason for this difficulty is that service planners have no prior knowledge of the total picture of the pending tasks, as well as of the dependencies among them (priorities, adjoined requests, etc.). The decisions are mostly based on experience and typically each day is taken as independent from the others, without taking into account the characteristics of the demand.

The overall problem addressed in this chapter falls into the category of vehicle routing problems (VRPs). A comprehensive survey is presented by Toth & Vigo (2002), while the latest advances regarding the most known VRP variations are presented in Golden *et al.* (2008). Below we focus on the literature related to the two major parts of the problem under consideration: (a) the creation of expected routes and (b) the allocation of flexible service calls. The former part concerns the development of expected (typical) routes the vehicles follow to serve the mandatory calls. These typical routes are used by the second part to allocate the flexible calls throughout the (multiple) periods of the planning horizon (part b).

Creation of Expected Routes

Several researchers have utilized historical data to determine periodical patterns of customer requests (location, demand, etc) in a VRP setting. Christofides (1971) and Beasley (1984) investigated the Fixed Routes Problem, in which routes remain unchanged for several periods within a certain time horizon. These authors proposed the use of historical data or a sample distribution of the customer demands. Additionally, Beasley & Christofides (1997) emphasize the value of historical data for estimating the expected number of customers and the workload of the vehicles in certain geographical regions of the area under investigation. Furthermore, in environments in which customers are characterized by dynamism, future events regarding the expected location of customers or the expected time of service within a day can be "predicted" by using historical data. Ichoua *et al.* (2006) discuss the "*exploitation of knowledge about future customer requests*" in a dynamic vehicle routing case, in which customers are characterized by known probabilistic distributions.

Allocation of Flexible Calls

The allocation of flexible calls in a multi-period environment is related to periodic routing problems. The most common periodic problems in the literature include: (a) the Inventory Routing Problem (IRP), in which each customer consumes a product/ commodity at a certain rate, and the fleet has to serve all customers efficiently without allowing stock outs; and (b) the Periodic Vehicle Routing Problem (PVRP), in which customers require a certain service frequency and can be served in predefined periodical patterns. IRP (Dror *et al.*, 1985; Campbell & Savelsbergh, 2004) combines inventory management with vehicle routing in a multi-period environment. Extended reviews can be found in Campbell *et al.* (1998) and Bertazzi *et al.* (2008). PVRP was introduced by Beltrami & Bodin (1974). Francis *et al.* (2008) provide a comprehensive review on the problem, its variations, the solution methods and future research opportunities.

Another area of periodic routing concerns multi-period routing problems. Generally, these problems do not share the characteristics of the IRP or PVRP but feature a dynamic arrival of customer requests, and thus, they are related to the present problem more closely.

Teng *et al.* (2006) solved a single-vehicle multi-period routing problem that is based on the travelling salesman subset-tour problem (Mittenhal & Noon, 1992). In this case, customers are to be serviced within certain predefined time periods. An additional profit is associated if service occurs within this time period. A column generation procedure is proposed and its efficiency is compared against heuristic methods. Andreatta & Lulli (2008) also considered a single-vehicle multi-period routing problem, in which the customer demand is random and service is provided either the next day after the arrival of the request (urgent service) or the following day (regular service). The problem was formulated as a Markov decision process. The authors suggest the solution using the method proposed by Howard (1960) for Markov processes using rewards and an aggregate Markov model. Angelelli *et al.* (2005; 2007) present a similar single-vehicle multi-period problem and minimize the cumulative distance (cost). In their setting, customer requests arrive at the beginning of each period, and can be serviced in the next two consecutive periods. Different strategies for the allocation of customers (i.e., as soon as possible, as late as possible and more intelligent combinations) are proposed and benchmarked.

Angelelli *et al.* (2009) and Wen *et al.* (2010) expanded their research in multiple-vehicle multi-period routing problems. Since customer requests arrive during route execution, Angelelli *et al.* (2009) used re-optimization while en-route. Several different objective functions were presented, including distance minimization, customer satisfaction and/ or workload balancing. Both, Angelelli et al. (2009) and Wen et al. (2010) have based their solutions on variable neighborhood search techniques (Mladenovic & Hansen, 1997).

Tricoire (2006; 2007) and Bostel (2008) have studied a special multi-period vehicle routing problem, in which customer requests are served over a certain horizon of *P* periods. Each customer requests service within a certain period-window (in the following *P*-period horizon). The requests are served by a limited fleet of vehicles using multiple depots. Vehicle capacity has not been considered, but several operational constraints have (break intervals, maximum route length). The problem is addressed both with a metaheuristic (memetic) algorithm and an exact approach (column generation).

The current chapter investigates an interesting practical case that is partially related with the general multi-period routing problem, but, to our knowledge, has yet to be addressed by the literature; the multi-period routing problem with predefined fixed routes. A novel approach is proposed to address this problem. As mentioned earlier, typical (expected) routes are initially created to form the basis for serving the expected mandatory calls. Subsequently, the flexible calls are allocated using these expected routes and respecting the service level requirements.

The remainder of this Chapter is organized as follows. Section "*Main Concept*" defines the call assignment problem. Section "*Model for Allocating Flexible Service Calls to Expected Routes*" presents the proposed mathematical model. Section "*Proposed Methods*" presents the proposed solution methods. Section "*Test Results – Allocation of Flexible Calls*" compares the proposed methods with empirical methods typically employed in practice, in various test instances. Section "*Case Study*" presents a case study in the courier sector. Finally, Section "Conclusions" summarizes our key findings and results.

MAIN CONCEPT

There are significant operational parameters to be considered in the environment under investigation, which make the problem both interesting and complex. These include the following:

- **Assignment of flexible calls:** According to the service level norms, flexible calls should be assigned in such a way that the customer is notified one period (day) in advance of the service visit. This operational constraint implies that the flexible calls are assigned without prior knowledge of the actual mandatory calls to be serviced. Note that the demand of the latter becomes known a few hours prior to the start of daily operations, and, thus, after the customers of the flexible calls have been notified.
- **Process of arriving requests for flexible calls:** A flexible call that arrives in the current period, say p_c, may be served in the interval $[p_c - 1, p_c + P]$ where P is the length of the planning horizon. This implies that not all flexible calls that may be served in period p: $[p_c - 1 < p \leq P]$ are known in the current period p_c. However, all calls to be served in the period p_c - 1 are known in period p_c.

The main concept of our proposed approach is illustrated in Figure 1, and it is outlined below.

Determination of expected (typical) routes

In an environment as the one previously discussed, many vehicles serve and operate in

Figure 1. Solution approach and implementation timings

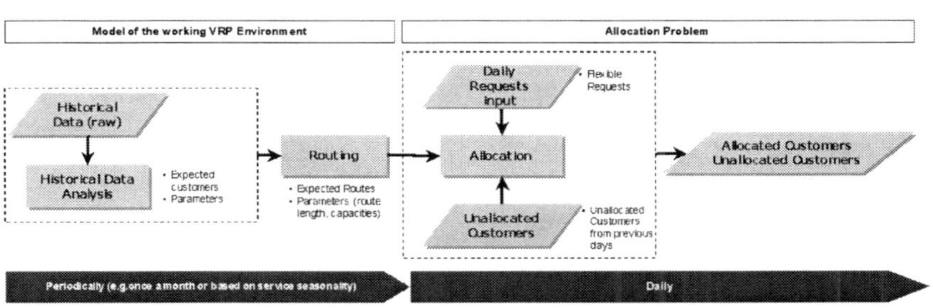

specific geographical areas with high customer density (e.g. business centres, residential areas multi-unit apartment buildings). Although the customers to be served each day may change, vehicles are typically required to visit/ pass by the same high density areas. Thus, the vehicle routes to be implemented each day are oftentimes similar with limited alterations that reflect the specific customer sites.

This observation allows us to determine "expected" customer locations (in the high density areas) and design "expected" vehicle routes that are likely to be implemented each day. In order to obtain these expected customer locations, to be visited in a daily routine, as well as their characteristics, information regarding customers (location, service time, etc.) is collected for adequately long time horizon.

Such typical routes may vary within e.g. a week, reflecting each workday's different characteristics.

Assignment of flexible calls

Using the expected routes, calls are assigned over the next **P** periods $[p_c - 1, p_c + P]$. Note that this assignment is performed without taking into account the actual mandatory calls, which are not known at this time.

The objective of the process is to assign the flexible calls in the most cost effective manner. A significant constraint is to assign in period $p_c - 1$ (at least) all flexible calls, for which period $p_c - 1$ is the last allowable period (expiration period). All other flexible calls with expiration period $p > p_c - 1$ should be assigned in periods in the interval $[p_c - 1, p]$. An additional constraint is the maximum number of flexible service calls to be served per day.

Having assigned all known flexible calls within the planning horizon $[p_c - 1, p_c + P]$, the calls in the first period in this horizon, $p_c - 1$, are selected for service. These calls, together with the mandatory calls for period $p_c - 1$ which arrive by the end of the current period **P** are provided as inputs to a commercial routing software in order to develop the integrated routes for the (next) period $p_c - 1$.

MODEL FOR ALLOCATING FLEXIBLE SERVICE CALLS TO EXPECTED ROUTES

In this formulation, for simplicity but without loss of generality, the expected (typical) routes are assumed to be the same for each day in the planning horizon. This is not unreasonable in cases where certain dense urban areas are served repeatedly every day.

Let's define the current period $p_c = 0$ and let us consider a planning horizon of **P** periods. Then, following the discussion in the previous Section, flexible calls that arrive within period 0 should be served in periods 1, |, P. Based on this remark, the notation and the mathematical formulation of the problem are presented in Table 1.

Objective Function

$$\min(z) = \sum_{p=1}^{P} \sum_{k \in K_p} \sum_{\{i,j\} \in W} c_{ijpk} x_{ijpk} \qquad (1)$$

Constraints

As shown in Table 2, the objective function (1) expresses the total routing cost over the entire planning horizon. Constraint (2) specifies that each flexible customer will be visited by only one route and during a period within the corresponding allowable interval for that customer. Constraint (3) specifies that each typical customer should be serviced once per period (day) of the time horizon; this is because we have assumed invariant typical routes within the time horizon. Constraints (4-6) are the flow conservation constraints for every route. Constraint (7) is the well known subtour elimination constraint. Constraint (8) respects capacity for flexible customers per period of the

Table 1.

$p = 1,\dots, P$	Periods of planning horizon of length $\|P\|$
$N = \{n_1,\dots n_N\}$	Set of known flexible nodes – customers; i.e., the related requests have arrived prior to period 0, but the last allowable period of service is in the horizon [1, $P - 1$]
$F = \{f_1,\dots,f_N\}$	Set of expected mandatory nodes-customers. These nodes belong to the typical routes
Node 0	Node representing the depot
$W = N \cup F \cup \{0\}$	Set of all customers (incl. depot)
$W = N \cup F$	Set of all customers (excl. depot)
$A = \{(i, j):i, j \in W\}$	Set of arcs connecting all nodes in W
c_{ij}	Cost or travel time to traverse arc (i, j), $\{i, j \in W\}$
K_p	Set of available routes per each period. Initially, these routes include all the mandatory customers.
S^{n_i} S^{n_i}	State of node n_i, (remaining periods to service node n_i)
C_p	Maximum number of flexible customers to be served in period p
$x_{ijpk} = \begin{Bmatrix} 1 \\ 0 \end{Bmatrix}$	If route k of period p traverses arc (i, j) Otherwise

time horizon (i.e. not more than C_p flexible calls can be assigned in period p). In order to adhere to the service level, Constraint (9) forces any flexible call (n_i) to be scheduled no later than its expiring period. For example, consider customer **a** that must be served by period 3 (at the latest), that is $S^a = 3$. If customer **a** is considered for route 2 in period 4 (i.e. $x_{aj42} = 1$) and given that $S^a = 3 < p = 4$, then constraint (9) will not allow this assignment since $\sum_{p=1}^{P}\sum_{k\in K_p}\sum_{j\in W}(x_{ajpk} \times p) = 4$ which is greater than. Finally, constraint (10) forces the flow variables to binary values (0,1).

PROPOSED METHODS

In this Section the proposed method for solving the overall problem is presented. Initially, the first phase of the solution process is described (Subsection "*Definition of Expected Routes for Mandatory Customers*"), in which the expected routes are defined. In Subsection "*Allocation of Flexible Calls in a Multi-Period Horizon Framework*", the solution methods for solving the problem of allocating the flexible calls to the expected routes are presented.

Definition of Expected Routes for Mandatory Customers

Historical data are collected over a time horizon of **P** periods (H>>P) taking into account the demand characteristics, including seasonality. The necessary information per served customer comprises (a) spatial coordinates, (b) date of service, (c) start time of service, (d) end time of service, (e) type of service and (f) demand (in an

Table 2.

$\sum_{p=1}^{P}\sum_{k\in K_p}\sum_{\{i,j\}\in W} x_{ijpk} = 1$	$\forall n_i \in N$	(2)
$\sum_{k\in K_p}\sum_{j\in W} x_{ijpk} = 1$	$\forall f_i \in F, \forall p \in P$	(3)
$\sum_{j\in W} x_{0jpk} = 1$	$\forall p \in P, \forall k \in K_p$	(4)
$\sum_{i\in W} x_{ijpk} - \sum_{i'\in W} x_{i'jpk} = 0$	$\forall p \in P, \forall k \in K_p, \forall j \in W'$	(5)
$\sum_{j\in W'} x_{j0pk} = 1$	$\forall p \in P, \forall k \in K_p$	(6)
$\sum_{i\in S}\sum_{j\in S} x_{ijpk} \leq \lvert S \rvert -1$	$\forall S \subseteq W', \lvert S \rvert \geq 2, \forall p \in P, \forall k \in K_p$	(7)
$\sum^{P}_{k\in K_p}\sum_{i\in N}\sum_{j\in W} x_{ijpk} \leq C_p$	$\forall p \in P$	(8)
$\sum_{p=1}^{P}\sum_{k\in K_p}\sum_{j\in W} (x_{ijpk} \times p) \leq S^{n_i}$	$\forall n_i \in N$	(9)
$x_{ijpk} \in \{0,1\}$	$\forall p \in P, \forall k \in K_p, (i,j) \in A$	(10)

appropriate unit of measure). Note that much of the data required for this stage can be collected through commercial fleet management systems (based on GPS/ GPRS technology). The analysis of the historical data is as follows.

Firstly, the total geographical area is divided by imposing a grid that comprises of rectangular or square cells of appropriate refinement, based on the characteristics of the area considered and on the customer distribution within this area. All customers (throughout the macro horizon H) that fall in the same cell are treated as a group and are analyzed together.

Subsequently, the analysis of the customer data per grid cell is performed. Let's consider cell Z_i (i^{th} geographical grid) and subset A_i of historical customers, where A_i are all customers that fall within cell Z_i. Let represent the total number of customers collected over the H-period horizon that belong to cell Z_i. The operational characteristics of each element of A_i are: The related spatial co-ordinates, (service time), and (demand), where. Based on this notation we define the following parameters for each cell Z_i:

Expected number of mandatory calls per period:

$$\overline{A}_i = M_i / H \tag{11}$$

Expected service time per call:

$$\overline{S_i} = \sum_{m=1}^{M_i} S_i^m \Big/ M_i \qquad (12)$$

Expected demand per call:

$$\overline{D_i} = \sum_{m=1}^{M_i} D_i^m \Big/ M_i \qquad (13)$$

In order to obtain the expected (mandatory) customers, a clustering procedure is used, as follows: For each cell Z_i the cluster centers belonging to this cell are calculated based on the k-means clustering algorithm (Kaufman & Rousseeuw, 1990) and are defined as the expected customers. Thus, the number of clusters to be created in cell Z_i is set equal to, which is the expected (average) number of customers per period. Each expected customer is characterized by the expected service time and the expected parameters defined above.

Figure 2 illustrates the results of this procedure based on data collected for the industrial case of Section "*Case Study*". The nodes shown in Figure 2(a) are the historical customers. Figure 2(b) zeroes-in a specific cell of the grid around the depot (green square). The nodes shown are the historical customers, while the red crosses show the expected (mandatory) customers.

Having obtained the expected (mandatory) customers, expected routes are defined. The required routing procedure can be performed by any efficient routing software or any routing algorithm, by respecting all necessary operational constraints.

Allocation of Flexible Calls in a Multi-Period Horizon Framework

Allocation is a periodic task that is implemented each period (day) of operations. Previous (unallocated) flexible customers are combined with newly arrived customers and are all allocated to the expected routes over the multi-period horizon. Then, the flexible customers allocated in the first period of the multi-period horizon are selected for service for this period, while the rest become the unallocated customers for the next scheduling period. This procedure is illustrated in Figure 3.

The heuristic described here is based on the idea of seeding the typical routes with selected flexible service calls. This mechanism resembles

Figure 2. Historical data analysis: Definition of expected (or typical) customers. (a) Historical customers, (b) Typical customers (+)

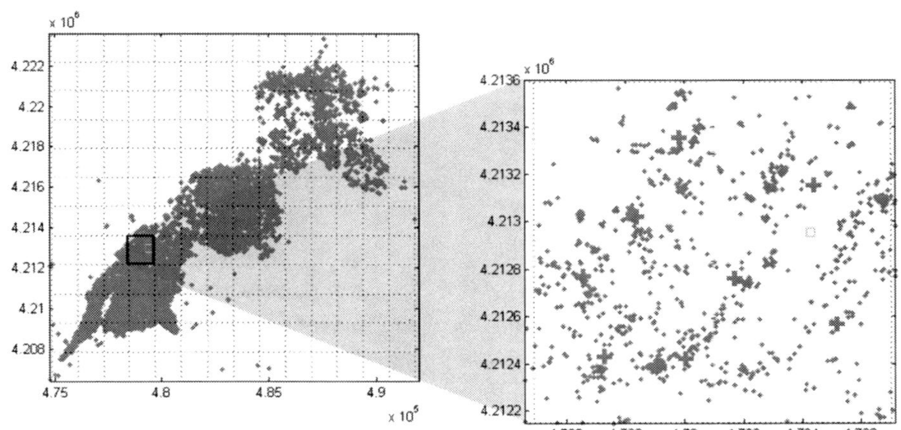

Figure 3. Rolling horizon scheme

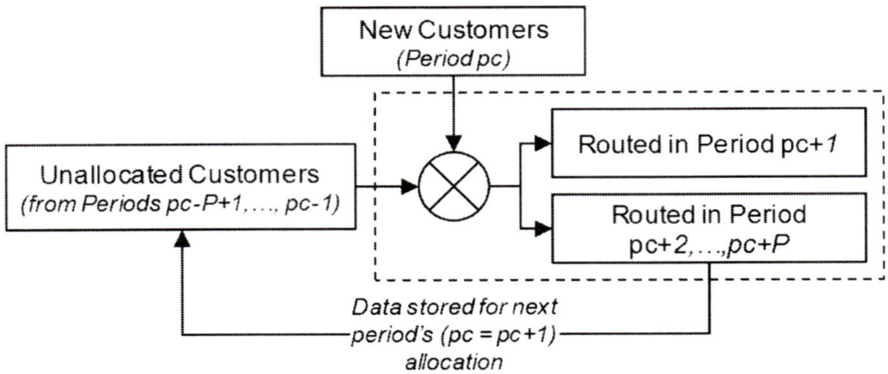

production planning methods where selected tasks (typically with long processing times) are scheduled first in the available work-center time, and are used to attract other tasks.

The approach comprises three main phases. The first two phases of the method produce the initial solution allocating the service calls to the **P** periods of the time horizon, while the third phase improves this initial solution.

Phase 1. Flexible calls expiring during period 1 are treated with priority due to the related constraints (state of customers). These expiring flexible calls ($S^i = 1, i \in N$) are allocated to the routes of the first period using a classic insertion technique (Toth & Vigo, 2002); that is, initially the call that is furthest from the depot is selected, along with the minimum cost insertion position (route, arc), and is inserted in the corresponding route and arc. The method proceeds to the next expiring flexible call until all calls have been inserted. It is clear that this is a greedy insertion procedure, which deals with the allocation of all the expiring flexible calls before considering all the remaining flexible calls.

Phase 2 addresses the allocation of the remaining flexible calls in the P-period horizon and comprises 3 main steps: (2a) selection of seeds, (2b) allocation of seeds, and (2c) allocation of calls.

Step 2a: For each remaining flexible call (excluding the expiring calls already routed in period 1) the following are computed, for the best insertion point: Cost, relevant arc, route and period, considering every arc of all routes in every permissible period of the horizon **P**. This information is stored in a list of descending cost. Note that the first period's calls have already been allocated and, thus, they are not included in the list.

Step 2b concerns the allocation of the seeds in the relevant routes. Starting from the top of the list (largest cost), flexible calls are selected as seeds and allocated to the relevant arc, route and appropriate day. Three alternative methods (**M1**, **M2** and **M3**) are used to determine the appropriate seeding pattern (see Table 3). After each insertion, each route that has been altered is characterized as not available for further insertion of seeds. Additionally, for all other periods in the horizon **P** the routes that correspond to the altered one also become not available (since, in our case the initial routes are identical for all periods).

Step 2c concerns the allocation of the remaining flexible calls. Initially, the original routes are altered to include the seeds, as appropriate, and the insertion costs are updated. Subsequently, the remaining flexible calls are allocated in the result-

Table 3. Alternative methods for allocating seeds

Method	Description
M1	Allocation of seeds is performed by inserting the seeds in the first available route starting from period 2, i.e. a seed that expires in period 3 can be inserted in any available route of period 2 to 3.
M2	Allocation of seeds is allowed considering only the routes belonging to the expiring period of each seed, i.e. a seed that expires in period 3 can be inserted as a seed only in third period's routes.
M3	Method M3 differentiates from the M1 and M2 methods by allocating all available flexible customers in their respective expiration periods. Thus, steps 2a, 2b and 2c are not relevant in this case, but the procedure of Phase 1 is used for periods 2,…,*P*.

ing routes one-by-one with a best insertion first technique, i.e. the customer that results to the lowest increase of the total routing cost is inserted in the relevant route and the procedure repeats for the other remaining customers. It is clear that this is a greedy procedure that leads to a suboptimal solution.

Phase 3 attempts to address the greedy aspect of steps 1 and 2c by improving the initial solution. This is performed by service call permutation between routes (including movements among the same and different periods) based on total cost improvement. The procedure moves first the customer resulting in the maximum cost reduction; that is, the maximum value of the difference between the total routing costs before and after moving the customer. The procedure continues until no more customer moves can be performed, and by respecting the capacity of the allowed flexible calls per period.

With the termination of the third phase, each flexible customer has been allocated to a period. As mentioned above, only flexible customers allocated in period $p = p_c - 1$ will be selected for routing. Flexible customers routed in $p \in [p_c - 2, p_c + P]$ are re-evaluated in the next scheduling period, along with the new customers to arrive in $p_c - 1$.

TEST RESULTS: ALLOCATION OF FLEXIBLE CALLS

In order to test the effectiveness of the flexible call allocation method, we compared it against a simple scheduling procedure (**S1**) used in actual operations of courier companies. Typically, such procedures focus on one period at a time and allocate the flexible calls in the most effective manner, while ensuring that all expiring calls are allocated. Thus, S1 examines the routes of the upcoming period without considering the other $P-1$ periods. All flexible calls that have not yet been serviced are considered for allocation: Initially, expiring flexible calls are allocated using the procedure of Phase 1 (see Section "*Proposed Methods*"). Subsequently, the other remaining flexible calls are considered for allocation using the same procedure. Note that, in this fashion, not all flexible calls are scheduled for service. The unallocated flexible calls are stored and considered in the next period.

The tests were constructed as follows: The number of periods (P) in the planning horizon was set equal to 5; thus, all flexible service calls had to be serviced within 5 periods (days) from their receipt. A rolling horizon framework of 40 consecutive days has been employed to compare all multi period heuristic alternatives (M1 to M3) against the single period (S1) method.

As the basis of the tests, 35 typical customers were considered. Their locations were uniformly distributed at random in a $[0, 1000]^2$ square and the depot was set to the center of the square. Four typi-

Table 4. Expected route characteristics

# of expected customers	# of routes	Cost
35	4	6,602.24

cal routes were constructed (see Table 4) through an insertion algorithm and were improved through well-known techniques of node exchange, 2-opt and crossover (Toth & Vigo, 2002).

Furthermore, three sets of flexible customer were created with random (R), clustered (C) and mixed (RC) geographical distribution. The first set includes customers that are uniformly distributed in the $[0, 1000]^2$ square; the second includes customers distributed uniformly in four clusters as shown in Figure 4. The RC customer set includes customers from the two previous sets.

For each customer set, three different arrival patterns were considered over the horizon of periods -4 to 40 (see Table 5). Periods -4 to 0 are the warm-up periods. Customers to be included

Figure 4. Indicative allocation of clustered (C) flexible customers

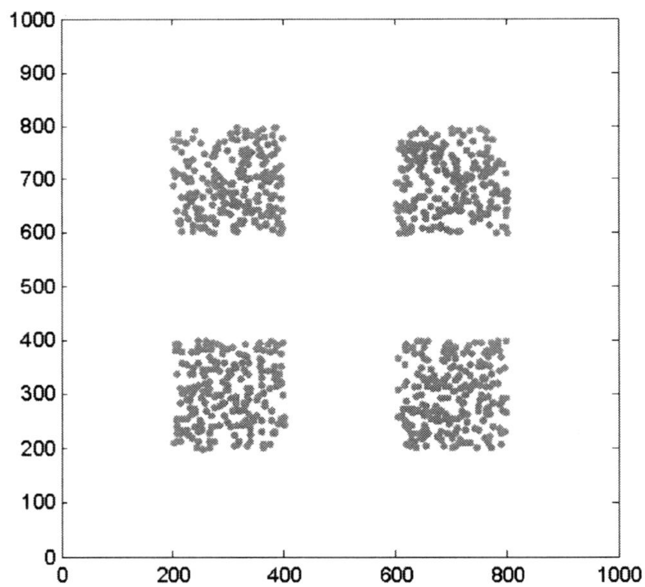

Table 5. Number of service calls per period (day): Small, medium and large case

		Warm-up Period					Period
	Test Instance	**-4**	**-3**	**-2**	**-1**	**0**	**1 to 40**
# of Service calls / period	Small (S)	1	2	3	4	**5**	5
	Medium (M)	6	7	8	9	**10**	10
	Large (L)	12	14	16	18	**20**	20

in each period were randomly selected by the pool of random, clustered and mixed customers.

Note that for scheduling period i the subset of expiring service calls derive from the service calls of period $i{-}P$; e.g., for the medium pattern, the six service calls received in period -4 comprise the expiring service calls of period 1. For all other planning periods, the number of expiring flexible service calls is derived based on the allocations of the previous periods. The maximum allowable number of flexible customers per route equals 6, 12 and 20 customers for the small, medium and large test instances, respectively.

The warm-up horizon of 5 periods was used as transition time in order to allow the system to reach a steady state. In this warm-up horizon, the number of unallocated service calls increase as shown in Table 3.

The performance measure used to evaluate all methods is defined as follows: Let C_i be the differential routing cost, derived by inserting the flexible service calls of period i and Π_i be the number of flexible service calls allocated in period i. Then, the performance measure is the average cumulative excess cost per service call, up to period t.

$$\overline{E}_t = \sum_{i=1}^{t} C_i \Big/ \sum_{i=1}^{t} \Pi_i \tag{14}$$

Figures 5 to 13 show the evolution of $\overline{E}_t$ within the time horizon (1, …, 40), for test cases R, C and RC and for the three instances [small (S), medium (M) and large (L)] per case, respectively. The methods were tested on a 1,83GHz PC system running Windows® XP and using the Matlab® 7 software.

Table 6 summarizes the results obtained. The last two columns of Table 6 list: (a) the % improvement between the single period method and the average performance of the three multi-period heuristic alternatives, and (b) the performance of the best multi-period alternative (M3) vs. the single period method.

From these results, it is clear that all multi-period methods result in overall cost reduction. Furthermore, M3 yields consistently the best results. As far as the geographical dispersion of customers is concerned, multi-period methods appear to be more efficient in cases, in which the flexible customers are clustered (C) or semi-clustered (RC). Additionally, in the medium and large instances the reduction compared to the single method reached 59% (M3 method for C-Large case).

Figure 5. Rolling horizon results (Problem R-S)

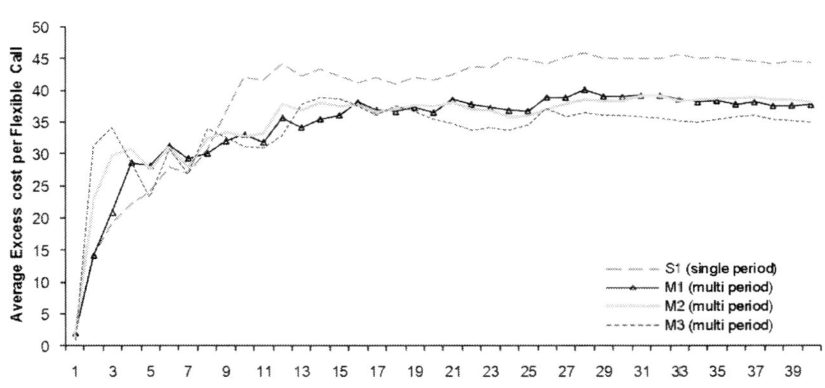

Figure 6. Rolling horizon results (Problem C-S)

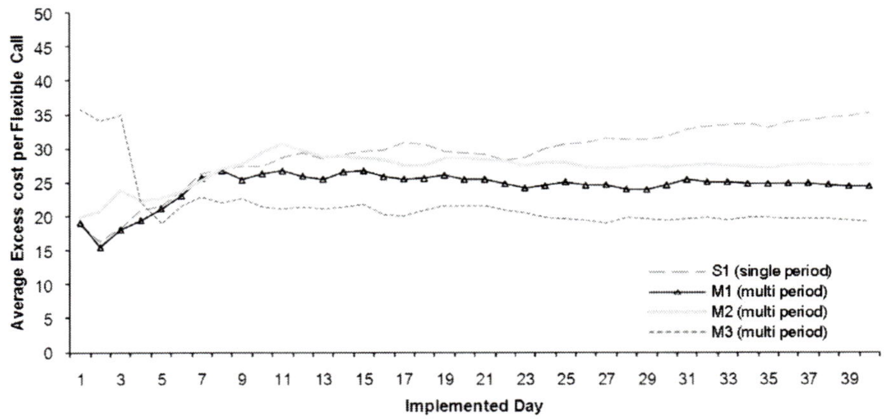

Figure 7. Rolling horizon results (Problem RC-S)

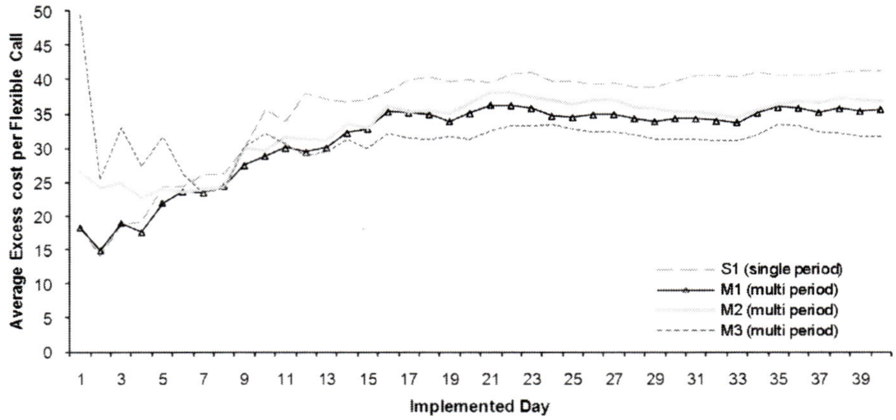

Figure 8. Rolling horizon results (Problem R-M)

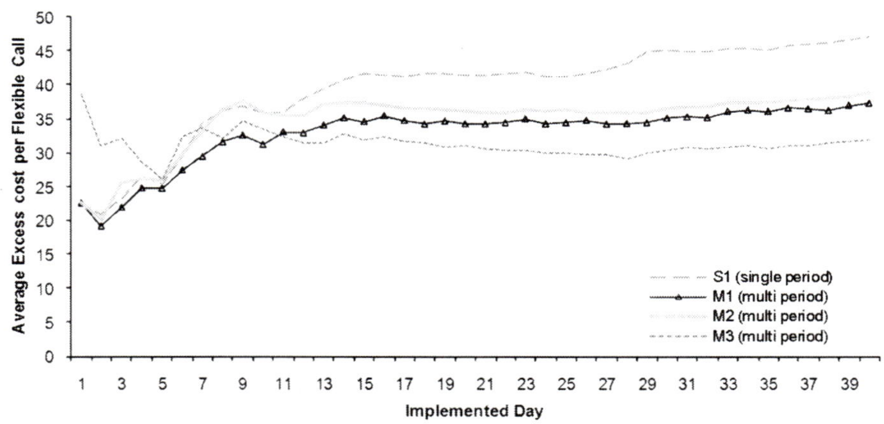

Figure 9. Rolling horizon results (Problem C-M)

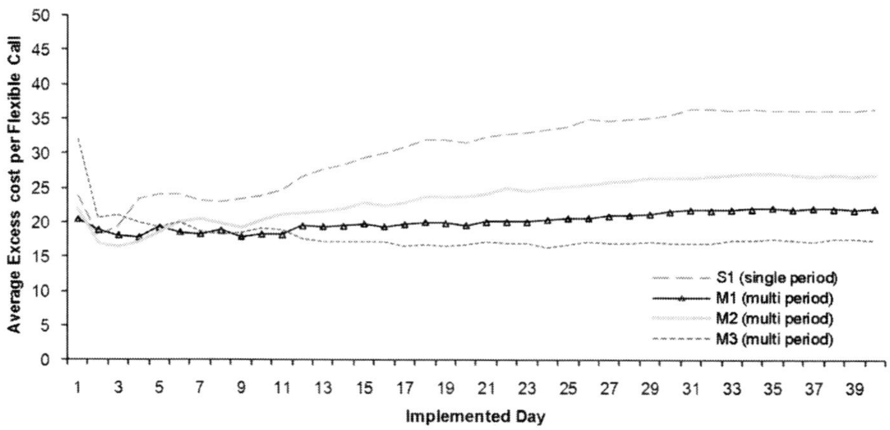

Figure 10. Rolling horizon results (Problem RC-M)

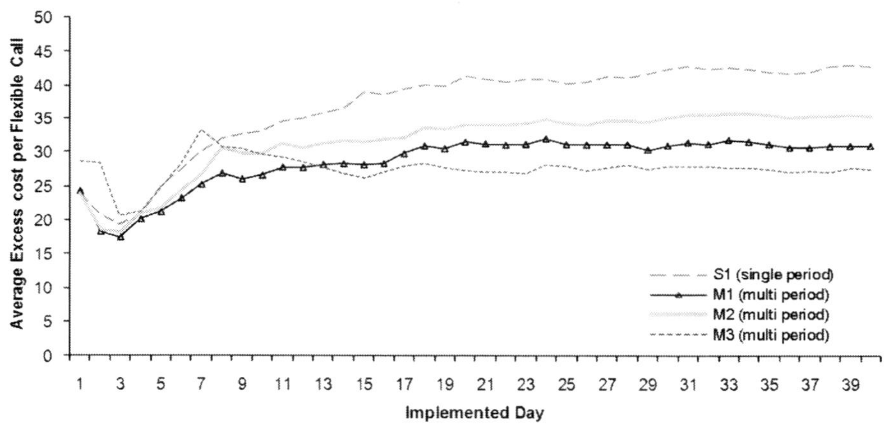

Figure 11. Rolling horizon results (Problem R-L)

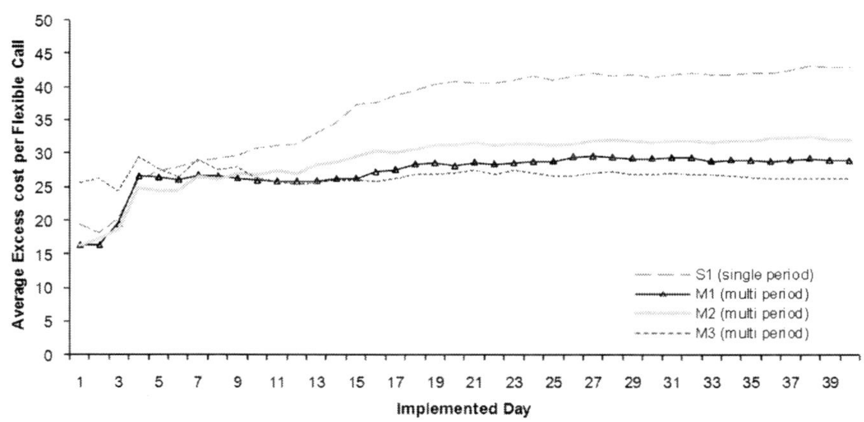

Figure 12. Rolling horizon results (Problem C-L)

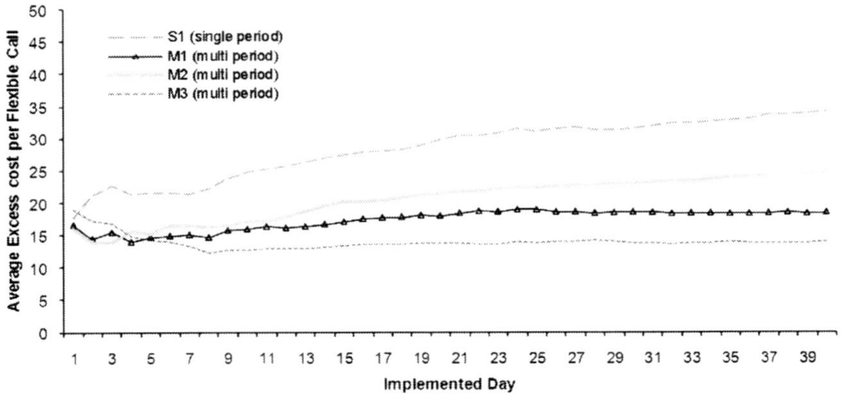

Figure 13. Rolling horizon results (Problem RC-L)

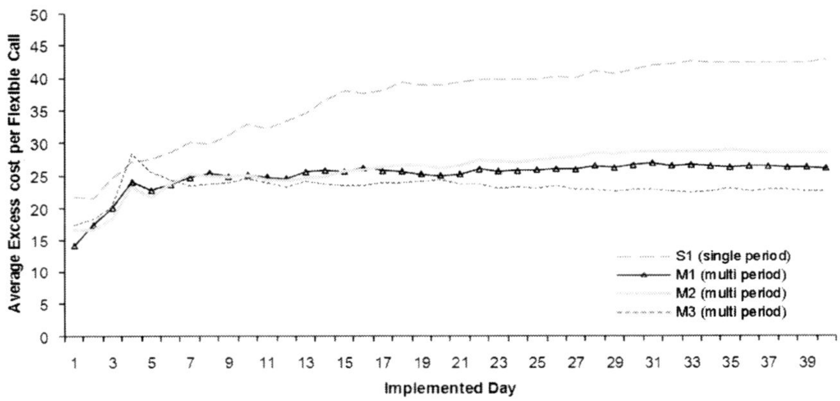

Table 6. Average excess cost per service call over the 40-day horizon (for $\overline{E_{40}}$)

Problem		Single Period	Multi Period				Improvement (%)	
		S1	M1	M2	M3	Average (M1, M2 & M3)	Average (M1, M2 & M3)	M3
Small	R	44.35	37.80	38.19	34.97	36.99	*17%*	*21%*
	C	35.05	24.40	27.61	19.20	23.74	*32%*	*45%*
	RC	41.21	35.60	36.86	31.62	34.69	*16%*	*23%*
Medium	R	47.05	37.28	38.87	31.82	35.99	*24%*	*32%*
	C	36.42	22.15	26.90	17.51	22.19	*39%*	*52%*
	RC	42.99	30.97	35.36	27.51	31.28	*27%*	*36%*
Large	R	42.88	28.93	32.18	26.24	29.12	*32%*	*39%*
	C	33.95	18.39	24.58	13.90	18.95	*44%*	*59%*
	RC	42.68	26.10	28.48	22.55	25.71	*40%*	*47%*

CASE STUDY

The proposed approach has been tested using actual data obtained from ELTA Courier, a subsidiary of the Greek Postal Service (ELTA), which serves the third largest market share among all couriers operating in Greece. In addition to its own network, ELTA Courier uses the extended distribution network of the Greek Postal Service. The case study focused in a major distribution centre serving the Northern Athens area.

Generation of Typical Routes

Historical data were collected from a 36-day period of operation in a total geographical area of 696.25 km^2. This area was divided in a 20x20 grid. The clustering procedure resulted in 120 expected customers (nodes). The relatively low number of nodes was due to the fact that some of the areas served by this center were not densely populated. The initial dispersion of the historical data along with the typical customers can be seen in Figure 2.

A well-known algorithm [sweep procedure (Gillett & Miller, 1974)] was used for the construction of the typical routes. The total allowable length of each route was set to 480 min and the maximum number of typical customers per route was set to 30. Euclidean distances were used, and an average speed of 10 km/h was assumed in order to approximate realistic travel conditions. Table 7 presents the expected customers per route along with the relevant route cost in minutes. Note that these are the expected routes to be implemented daily and constitute the basis for the allocation of flexible calls. Note also that the expected customers represent poles of demand and, thus, their number is much smaller with respect to the typical number of daily customers.

Allocation of Flexible Service Calls

Service calls were randomly generated following the spatial pattern of the historical data customers as follows: First, a number of service calls was uniformly generated around each typical customer. Subsequently, from this set of customers the required number of service calls was selected randomly. The numbers of flexible calls per period, including the warm-up period, follow the arrival pattern of Table 8. A 40-period horizon was used augmented by a 5-period warm-up horizon. The maximum allowable number of flexible customers per route set equal to 15 customers.

Figure 14 shows the average excess cost per service call (Equation 14). Table 9 summarizes the results obtained. The last two columns of

Table 7. Expected Routes of Case Study

	Route								
	1	**2**	**3**	**4**	**5**	**6**	**7**	**8**	**9**
Customers	16	16	14	17	11	9	11	14	12
Cost (min)	432.32	400.78	414.12	415.32	358.55	323.80	429.71	361.32	272.72

Table 8. Number of service calls per period (day)

	Start-up Period					**Period**
	-4	**-3**	**-2**	**-1**	**0**	**1 to 40**
# of service calls / period	8	9	10	11	**12**	12

Figure 14. Rolling horizon results (Case Study)

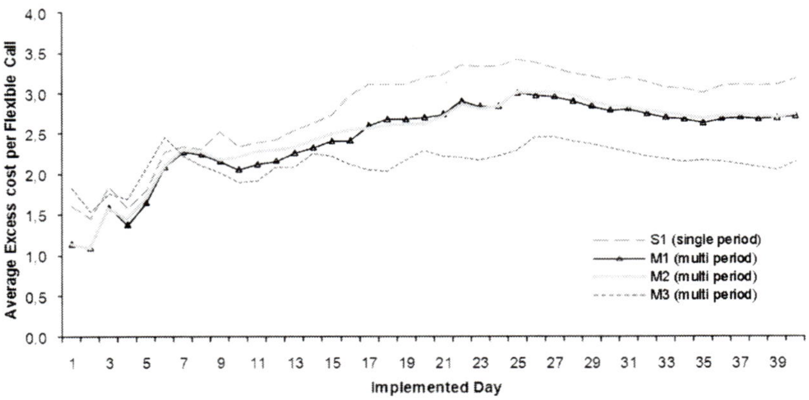

Table 7 list (a) the % improvement between the average performance of all three multi-period methods vs. the single period method; and (b) the performance of the best multi-period method (M3) vs. the single period method. M3 exhibits again the most efficient results. Also, while the multi period heuristics succeed in better overall cost reduction, the improvement resulting from M1 and M2 is somehow limited. On the other hand, M3 results in a total improvement of 32% and the difference is evident after period 14.

Table 10 presents the average run time of the algorithms per period (in sec), in which M3 presents the longest computational times. This is due to the extensive improvements that are necessary in Phase 3.

CONCLUSION

In order to plan operations in a hybrid courier environment we have proposed the decomposition of the problem in two stages: (a) Initially, we define expected (or typical) routes by using historical demand data; and (b) based on these typical routes, we perform allocation of flexible service calls on a rolling horizon basis in order to deal with the dynamics of arriving calls. The proposed

Table 9. Average excess cost per flexible call over the 40-day horizon (for)

Problem	Single Period	Multi Period				Improvement (%)	
	S1	M1	M2	M3	Average (M1, M2 & M3)	Average (M1, M2 & M3)	M3
	3.16	2.71	2.74	2.16	2.53	*20%*	*32%*

Table 10. Average running time of algorithms per period (in sec)

Single Period	Multi Period		
S1	M1	M2	M3
0.31	179.03	209.54	712.04

method targets improved overall performance, since service calls are allocated considering the overall multi-period horizon, and not following a myopic period-by-period way. Assuming the first period of the horizon, the allocated flexible service calls combined with the actual mandatory customers of this period form the input to any commercial routing software to determine the precise plan for that particular period.

The effectiveness of the approach in comparison to typical single-period approaches used in practice was tested by solving various test cases in a rolling horizon environment. The test results indicate a significant improvement (from 16% to 59%) of the average cost per flexible customer. Similar results were obtained from a case study involving a courier company in Greece. It has been observed that the single-period approach exhibits a steady increase of the average excess cost per flexible customer. This can be justified due to the greedy and myopic nature of the single-period method, which does not group together adjacent customer calls which arrive art different periods. Instead, it greedily tries to fit as many customers in the routes of a period. Additionally, the efficiency of M3 against M1 and M2 can be justified by the fact that although M3 starts from a worst initial solution, it improves this solution significantly by the employed improvement techniques. In comparison, M1 and M2 may start from a better initial solution but it appears that they are quickly trapped in local minima. This observation can be further supported by the significant difference in computational time among the methods. Finally, multi-period methods are more efficient in clustered and/ or semi-clustered (mixed) flexible customer patterns since more effective customer grouping can be performed.

Classical deliveries and service requests, both mandatory and flexible, may have time windows within which the service should be provided; i.e., a flexible call may be serviced only within a pre-specified time interval (time window) of each period and / or within a subhorizon (period window) of the P-period horizon. In this case the proposed model should be further enhanced by including time windows for each customer and by including various levels of service quality.

ACKNOWLEDGMENT

This chapter is part of the 03ED067 research project, implemented within the framework of the "Reinforcement Programme of Human Research Manpower" (PENED) and co-financed by National and Community Funds (20% from the Greek Ministry of Development-General Secretariat of Research and Technology and 80% from E.U.-European Social Fund).

REFERENCES

Andreatta, G., & Lulli, G. (2008). A multi-period TSP with stochastic regular and urgent demands. *European Journal of Operational Research, 185*, 122–132. doi:10.1016/j.ejor.2006.12.040

Angelelli, E., Bianchessi, N., Mansini, R., & Speranza, M. G. (2009). Short Term Strategies for a Dynamic Multi-Period Routing Problem. *Transportation Research Part C, Emerging Technologies, 17*(2), 106–119. doi:10.1016/j.trc.2008.02.001

Angelelli, E., Savelsbergh, M. W. P., & Speranza, M. G. (2007). Competitive analysis of a dispatch policy for a dynamic multi-period routing problem. *Operations Research Letters, 35*(6), 713–721. doi:10.1016/j.orl.2007.02.006

Angelelli, E., Speranza, M. G., & Savelsbergh, M. W. P. (2005). *A Dynamic Multi-Period Routing Problem*. Presented at the International Workshop on Vehicle Routing and Intermodal Transportation (ROUTE 2005), Italy.

Beasley, J. E. (1984). Fixed Routes. *The Journal of the Operational Research Society, 35*(1), 49–55.

Beasley, J. E., & Christofides, N. (1997). Vehicle routing with a sparse feasibility graph. *European Journal of Operational Research, 98*, 499–511. doi:10.1016/S0377-2217(96)00048-3

Beltrami, E. J., & Bodin, L. D. (1974). Networks and vehicle routing for municipal waste collection. *Networks, 4*(1), 65–94. doi:10.1002/net.3230040106

Bertazzi, L., Savelsbergh, M. W. P., & Speranza, M. G. (2008). Inventory Routing. In Golden, B., Raghavan, S., & Wasil, E. (Eds.), *The Vehicle Routing Problem: Latest Advances and New Challenges* (pp. 49–72). Springer. doi:10.1007/978-0-387-77778-8_3

Bostel, N., Dejax, P., Guez, P., & Tricoire, F. (2008). Multiperiod Planning and Routing on a Rolling Horizon for Field Force Optimization Logistics. In Golden, B., Raghavan, S., & Wasil, E. (Eds.), *The Vehicle Routing Problem: Latest Advances and New Challenges* (pp. 503–525). Springer. doi:10.1007/978-0-387-77778-8_23

Campbell, A., Clarke, L., Kleywegt, A., & Savelsbergh, M. W. P. (1998). Inventory routing. In Crainic, T., & Laporte, G. (Eds.), *Fleet Management and Logistics*, 95-112, Kluwer Academic Publishers, Boston.

Campbell, A. M., & Savelsbergh, M. W. P. (2004). A decomposition approach for the Inventory-Routing Problem. *Transportation Science, 38*(4), 488–502. doi:10.1287/trsc.1030.0054

Christofides, N. (1971). Fixed Routes and Areas for Delivery. *International Journal of Physical Distribution, 1*, 87–92. doi:10.1108/eb038829

Dror, M., Ball, M., & Golden, B. (1985). Computational comparison of algorithms for the inventory routing problem. *Annals of Operations Research, 4*, 3–23. doi:10.1007/BF02022035

Francis, P. M., Smilowitz, K. R., & Tzur, M. (2008). The Period Vehicle Routing Problem and its Extensions. In Golden, B., Raghavan, S., & Wasil, E. (Eds.), *The Vehicle Routing Problem: Latest Advances and New Challenges* (pp. 73–102). Springer. doi:10.1007/978-0-387-77778-8_4

Gillett, B. E., & Miller, L. R. (1974). A heuristic algorithm for the vehicle dispatch program. *Operations Research, 22*(2), 340–349. doi:10.1287/opre.22.2.340

Golden, B., Raghavan, S., & Wasil, E. (Eds.). (2008). *The Vehicle Routing Problem: Latest Advances and New Challenges. Operations Research/Computer Science Interfaces Series*. Springer. doi:10.1007/978-0-387-77778-8

Howard, R. A. (1960). *Dynamic Programming and Markov Processes*. Cambridge, MA: MIT.

Ichoua, S., Gendreau, M., & Potvin, J. Y. (2006). Exploiting Knowledge about Future Demands for Real-Time Vehicle Dispatching. *Transportation Science, 40*(2), 211–225. doi:10.1287/trsc.1050.0114

Kaufman, L., & Rousseeuw, P. (1990). *Finding Groups in Data: an Introduction to Cluster Analysis*. New York: John Wiley & Sons.

Mittenhal, J., & Noon, C. E. (1992). An insert/delete heuristic for the traveling salesman subset-tour problem with one additional constraint. *The Journal of the Operational Research Society, 43*(3), 277–283.

Mladenovic, N., & Hansen, P. (1997). Variable neighbourhood search. *Computers & Operations Research, 24*, 1097–1100. doi:10.1016/S0305-0548(97)00031-2

Teng, S. Y., Ong, H. L., & Huang, H. C. (2006). Heuristic algorithms for visiting the customers in a rolling schedule environment. *OR-Spektrum, 28*(2), 241–266. doi:10.1007/s00291-005-0002-7

Toth, P., & Vigo, D. (2002). *The vehicle routing problem*. USA: SIAM Monographs on Discrete Mathematics and Applications.

Tricoire, F. (2006). *Optimisation Des Tournées De Véhicules Et De Personnels De Maintenance: Application A La Distribution Et Au Traitement Des Eaux*. PhD Thesis, Université de Nantes

Tricoire, F. (2007). Vehicle and personnel routing optimization in the service sector: application to water distribution and treatment. *4OR*, 5, 165-168

Wen, M., Cordeau, J.-F., Laporte, G., & Larsen, J. (in press). The Dynamic Multi-Period Vehicle Routing Problem. *Computers & Operations Research*.

Chapter 12
Dynamic Travel Time Estimation Techniques for Urban Freight Transportation Networks Using Historical and Real-Time Data

Vasileios Zeimpekis
University of the Aegean, Greece

ABSTRACT

Effective travel time prediction is of great importance for efficient real-time management of freight deliveries, especially in urban networks. This is due to the need for dynamic handling of unexpected events, which is an important factor for successful completion of a delivery schedule in a predefined time period. This chapter discusses the prediction results generated by two travel time estimation methods that use historical and real-time data respectively. The first method follows the k-nn model, which relies on the non-parametric regression method, whereas the second one relies on an interpolation scheme which is employed during the transmission of real-time traffic data in fixed intervals. The study focuses on exploring the interaction of factors that affect prediction accuracy by modelling both prediction methods. The data employed are provided by real-life scenarios of a freight carrier and the experiments follow a 2-level full factorial design approach.

INTRODUCTION

Distribution arguably accounts for a significant percentage of the total logistics execution cost (Ballou, 2004). Urban freight distribution in particular is more susceptible to unexpected costs and delays that arise *during* the execution of the delivery plans due to unforeseen adverse delivery conditions, such as vehicle breakdown, traffic delays, road works, customer depot overload, and so on (Rego and Roucairol, 1995; Savelsbergh and Sol, 1998; Psaraftis, 1995).

Techniques to minimize distribution costs typically focus on the creation of a near-optimal *a priori* distribution plan. Lately, freight carriers have adopted the use of automated vehicle routing systems in order to create such plans. However, the use of an initial distribution plan, although necessary, is by no means sufficient to address events that are likely to occur during delivery

DOI: 10.4018/978-1-61520-633-9.ch012

execution and may have adverse effects on delivery performance. In such cases, typical in an urban distribution setting, a priori solutions may no longer be relevant and the distribution plan needs to be adjusted in real-time as a function of the dynamic system state.

Latest technologies such as real-time fleet management systems, give the ability to freight carriers to monitor the execution of the daily delivery schedules and handle some of the aforementioned issues. However, in order to cope with unforeseen events and manage possible deviations from the initial plan, there is a need for accurate travel time prediction. Indeed, estimation of arrival is critical in urban freight distributions in order to predict in advance possible delays and time window violations in the remaining customers.

The ability to accurately predict future link travel times in transportation networks is a critical component for many intelligent transportation systems (ITS) applications, such as fleet management systems (FMS), in-vehicle route guidance systems (RGS) and advanced traffic management systems (ATMS). Travel time in an urban traffic environment is highly stochastic and time-dependant due to random fluctuations in travel demands, interruptions caused by traffic control devices, incidents, and weather conditions. It has been increasingly recognized that for many transportation applications, estimates of the mean and variance of travel times significantly affect the accuracy of prediction (Chien & Kuchipudi, 2003).

To this end, this chapter presents and evaluates two travel time estimation techniques for urban freight transportation networks using historical and real-time data. The first method follows the *k-nn* model, which relies on the non-parametric regression method, whereas the second one relies on an interpolation scheme which is employed during the transmission of real-time traffic data in fixed intervals. The study focuses on exploring the interaction of factors that affect prediction accuracy by modelling both prediction methods. The data employed are provided by real-life scenarios of a freight carrier and the experiments follow a 2-level full factorial design approach.

The chapter is organized as follows. Section 2 reviews current techniques and methods for travel time prediction and traffic forecasting models. Section 3 describes the characteristics of the two proposed methods whereas Section 4 presents the evaluation of both techniques. Section 5 discusses the experimental results and the chapter concludes with Section 6 where important ascertainments are outlined together with a future research agenda.

BACKGROUND

Travel time can be defined as the total time required for a vehicle to travel from one point to another over a specified route under prevailing conditions. Its calculation depends on vehicle speed, traffic flow and occupancy, which are highly sensitive to weather conditions and traffic incidents (Park et al., 1998). Nonetheless, daily, weekly and seasonal patterns can be still observed at large scale. For instance, daily patterns distinguish rush hour and late night traffic, weekly patterns distinguish weekday and weekend traffic, while seasonal patterns distinguish winter and summer traffic. It has been increasingly recognized (Smith and Demetsky, 1996; Park et al., 1998; Chien & Kuchipudi, 2003; Stathopoulos & Karlaftis 2003) that for many transportation applications, estimates of the mean and variance of travel times affect the accuracy of prediction significantly.

Travel time data can be obtained through various surveillance devices, such as loop detectors, microwave detectors, and radars, though it is not realistic to have the road network completely covered by detectors. With the development of mobile and positioning technologies, the data can be more reliably collected and transmitted. More importantly, these devices can be set up on vehicles with minimal hardware using non-sophisticated communication and installation. However, travel time estimation is not so straightforward because

Figure 1. Basic components for travel time estimation

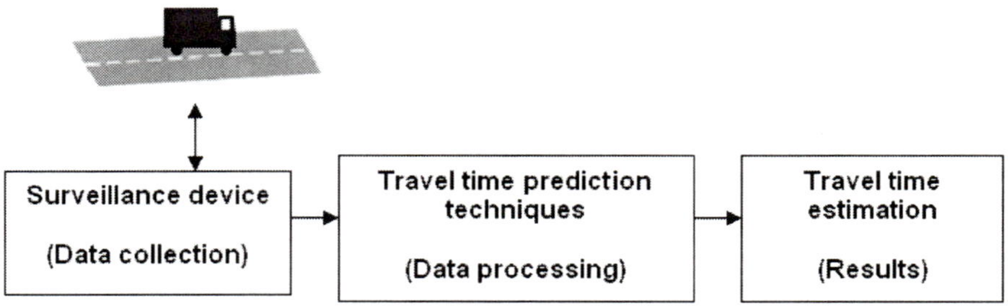

it depends not only from the surveillance devices, but also on the prediction technique that is being used for data processing. Figure 1, presents the basic components for travel time estimation.

Indeed, one of the major issues in travel time prediction and traffic forecasting is the selection of the appropriate modeling approach. Current practice involves two separate modeling approaches: parametric and non-parametric techniques (Vlahogianni et al., 2004). In the vast category of statistical parametric techniques, several forms of algorithms have been applied with greater weight to historical average algorithms (Smith and Demetsky, 1996) and smoothing techniques (Smith and Demetsky, 1997; Williams et al., 1998). In the early 1990s, autoregressive linear processes, such as the auto-regressive integrated moving average (ARIMA) family of models, which were first introduced in traffic forecasting by Ahmed and Cook (1979) and Levin and Tsao (1980), provided an alternative approach based on the stochastic nature of traffic. Davis et al. (1991) applied a single auto-regressive integrated moving average (ARIMA) model to forecast the bottleneck formulation in a freeway. Later, Hamed et al. (1995) applied an ARIMA model to forecast urban traffic volume.

Research has also used state-space models that belong to the multivariate family of time series models. The main reason is that they provide a good basis for modeling transportation data, due both to their multivariate nature and also to their ability of modeling simpler univariate time series. Generally, the term 'state-space' refers to the model and the term 'Kalman filter' refers to the estimation of the state. The advantage of the Kalman filter algorithm is that it allows the selected state variable to be updated continuously. The potential of this was first demonstrated by Okutani and Stephanedes (1984) who used Kalman filtering in urban traffic volume prediction and then developed an extended Kalman filter to predict traffic diversion in freeway entrance ramp areas. Whittaker et al. (1997) demonstrated the potential of this method in a multivariate setting. Both Chen and Chien (2001) and Chien and Kuchipudi (2003) then used Kalman filtering for travel time prediction. Stathopoulos and Karlaftis (2003) demonstrated its superiority over a simple ARIMA formulation when modelling traffic data from different periods of the day.

Recent advances in object-oriented programming, as well as, in real-time collecting, storing and managing large databases from several points of an extended transportation network, have given the opportunity to explore the robustness of non-parametric techniques in traffic and travel time forecasting. Non-parametric techniques do not assume any specific functional form for the dependent and independent variables. Frequently, these models are data driven, implying that their successful implementation is strongly related to the quality of the available data. The general idea behind these techniques is that they analyze the characteristic of interest of, say, a time series by allowing it to have a general form which is gradually approximated with a certain precision using a growing data set. Two distinct forms of non-parametric techniques, namely non-parametric regression and neural networks, have gained a great portion of short-term traffic forecasting research interest over the last decade.

Non-parametric regression is based on the principles of pattern recognition (Smith et al., 2002). Smith et al. (2002) suggested that traffic conditions near congestion can be modeled by non-parametric regression. The main purpose is to identify clusters of data with behavior similar to current traffic state at a certain forecasting interval. Non-parametric regression possesses a number of advantages such as its intuitive formulation, the lack of a need for assumption on the transition of traffic states from one period to another, and, finally, the simplicity in modeling multivariate settings (Clark, 2003).

In general, the literature shows promising results when using non-parametric regression. First, Smith and Demetsky (1996) tested the performance of nearest neighbor non-parametric regression compared with neural networks, a historical average and the ARIMA model and concluded that the first was superior in the field of transferability and robustness compared with different data sets. Smith et al. (2000) used kernel neighborhoods and suggested that the method produced predictions with an accuracy comparable with that of the seasonal version of an ARIMA model. Finally, Smith et al. (2002) tested the performance of non-parametric regression based on heuristically improved forecast generation methods and found that this approach did not produce better predictions than seasonal ARIMA. Nevertheless, they supported the fact that a combined model could be used in cases where the requirements of the seasonal ARIMA could not be met. More recently, Clark (2003) found that non-parametric regression was more accurate when predicting flow in motorways than speed.

Neural network applications to short-term traffic forecasting extend from the simple multilayer perceptrons (MLP) (Clark et al., 1993; Kwon and Stephanedes, 1994; Smith and Demetsky, 1994; Zhang, 2000) to more complex structures such as time-delayed recurrent neural networks (Yun et al., 1998; Abdulhai et al., 1999; Lingras and Mountford, 2001), finite impulse response networks (Yun et al., 1998), multirecurrent neural networks (Ulbricht, 1994), a spectral basis neural network (Park et al., 1999), and dynamic neural networks (Ishak and Alescandru, 2003).

The merit of neural networks is not only their proven ability to provide good predictions, but also their overall performance and robustness in modeling traffic data sets. Some of their advantages can be summarized as follows: a) they can produce accurate multiple step-ahead forecasts with less effort, b) they have been tested with significant success in modeling the complex temporal and spatial relationships lying in many transportation data sets, and c) they are capable of modelling highly non-linear relationships in a multivariate setting (Zhang et al., 1998).

Vlachogiani et al., (2004) has summarized various characteristics in modeling using parametric and non-parametric methods. This classification is shown in Table 1. These characteristics concern the data requirements in terms of quantity, the results regarding the difficulty or the straightforward nature in extracting qualitative results, and the nature of predictions provided (recursive, static or dynamic). Finally, the last two rows give a short description of the main advantages and disadvantages of the method regarding the efforts made in modeling traffic data.

In general, the estimation and prediction of travel times in an urban road network are critical for many Intelligent Transportation System applications (ITS), such as Route Guidance Systems (RGSs), Advanced Traveller Information Systems (ATIS), Fleet Management Systems (FMSs) and Advanced Traffic Management Systems (ATMSs). The common objective of these systems is to provide information necessary to help individual drivers or control centers to identify optimal routes

Table 1. Characteristics of travel time prediction and traffic forecasting methods (Vlachogianni et al., 2004)

Characteristics	Parametric modeling			Non-parametric modeling	
	Smoothing	**ARIMA**	**Kalman Filtering**	**Non-parametric regression**	**Neural networks**
Quantity of data	short series	extensive	extensive	extensive	extensive
Accuracy	low	low but acceptable	medium	high	high
Nature of predictions	static	recursive	static	dynamic	dynamic
Main advantages	short series needed	well-established theoretical back-ground	multivariate nature	simple model structure	wide mapping capabilities
Main disadvantages	relatively low ac-curacy	low accuracy, relative slow data processing	Gaussian hypoth-esis	intensive data	intensive data, complex internal structure

based on real-time information on current traffic conditions or handle unexpected incidents that take place.

According to the literature, travel time forecasting is strongly connected to the availability of appropriate data. In the case where the available traffic surveillance network supports advanced sensing as well as vehicle identification techniques that provide a way of direct travel time data collection, travel time forecasting is made directly from these travel time measurements (Park et al., 1998, Chien and Kuchipudi, 2003).

There exists a clear relation between the traffic parameter to predict (i.e. flow, speed) and the type of implementation to develop (traffic control, incident handling), as well as the area of implementation (i.e. urban arterial, highway). Predicting travel time or speed is conceptually more useful in ATIS and FMS applications, whereas traffic flow and occupancy predictions could be more valuable in traffic control applications.

Both parametric and non-parametric methods are used for travel time prediction. Nevertheless, a number of researchers (Smith and Demetsky, 1997; Clark et al. 1993) argue that the use of non-parametric techniques in urban networks is more efficient due to their ability to cope with the fluctuating nature of the observed traffic parameters such as flow, occupancy, speed and so on. Based on these findings, one of the proposed methods follows the non-parametric approach for travel time prediction.

However, as discussed previously, non parametric methods embrace two distinct methods namely non-parametric regression and neural networks. In order to reveal which method is the most suitable for real-time travel time prediction, another important factor of freight distributions must be taken into account, namely the manner in which urban delivery schedules are planned. Usually, freight carriers and operators use predefined schedules with a specific number of customers that each truck must visit and which are repeated usually in a weekly manner. This means that historical data of travel times between theses customers could be used as a basis for more accurate travel time predictions.

The non-parametric regression method relies on historical data. More specifically, the basic approach of non-parametric regression is heavily influenced by its roots in pattern recognition (Karlsson and Yakowitz, 1987). In essence, the approach locates the state of the system in a "neighborhood" of past or similar states. Once this neighborhood has been established, the past cases in the neighborhood are used to estimate the remaining travel time. Clearly, this approach assumes that the bulk of the knowledge about the relationship lies in the data rather than the person developing the model (Eubank, 1988). Of course, the quality of the database, particularly in storing past cases that represent the breath of all possible future conditions, dictates the effectiveness of a non-parametric regression model. To put it simply, if similar cases are not presented in the database, an accurate forecast is difficult to be generated (Smith et al., 2002). However, the use of AVL systems gives the opportunity to create a rich database with historical data.

The choice of non-parametric regression method is also supported by Smith and Demetsky (1996), which tested the performance of nearest neighbor non-parametric regression compared with neural networks and concluded that the first was superior in the field of transferability and robustness compared with different data sets. Indeed, the non-parametric methods have been proven (Yun et al., 1998; Vlahogiani et al., 2003; Clark, 2003) to give accurate predictions due to their ability to cope with time-dependent parameters such as speed and flow. The aforementioned authors have used mainly AVI or loop detectors for data collection. By taking into account that AVL provides more accurate data, the non-parametric regression method has been adopted so as to have the best possible travel time estimation.

TRAVEL TIME PREDICTION METHODS

This section discusses the prediction results generated by two travel time estimation methods that use historical and real-time data respectively. The first method follows the *k-nn* model, which relies on the non-parametric regression method, whereas the second one relies on an interpolation scheme which is employed during the transmission of real-time traffic data in fixed intervals.

Travel Time Prediction Using Historical Data

The proposed travel time estimation method uses historical data in order to predict the arrival time of a delivery vehicle to a customer. This historical data is retrieved from a database that stores information concerning the time that takes to a vehicle to travel from one point to another and provides mean travel times from any point of interest to any other.

Let us assume a route between two points of interest A and B and a vehicle travelling towards point B (Figure 2). The distance between these points is noted as D_{AB}. The vehicle has already travelled a certain distance, say D_{AC}. When the vehicle is travelling towards point B, the travelling time (t_{CB}) from point C to point B is estimated by:

$$t_{CB} = \frac{D_{AB} - D_{AC}}{D_{AB}} \times T_{AB} \quad (1)$$

,where D_{AB} and D_{AC} are the total and travelled distance respectively and T_{AB} is the mean historical travel time between these two customers which is revealed from the database that stores data for each delivery schedule.

As it can be seen, the predictions made by this method depend on how accurate the calculation of T_{AB} and on the homogeneity of the historical data.

As mentioned above, T_{AB} is derived from previous travel times between points A and B that the vehicle has carried out. However, the main problem is that when historical data concerning travel times between these two points are extracted, the latter include not only one arc which is direct from point A to point B but a sequence of arcs where other points are inserted between points A and B (Figure 3).

The latter causes inaccuracies to travel time prediction as the mean travel time T_{AB} is increased. In order to determine which historical travel times

Figure 2. Travel time prediction using historical data

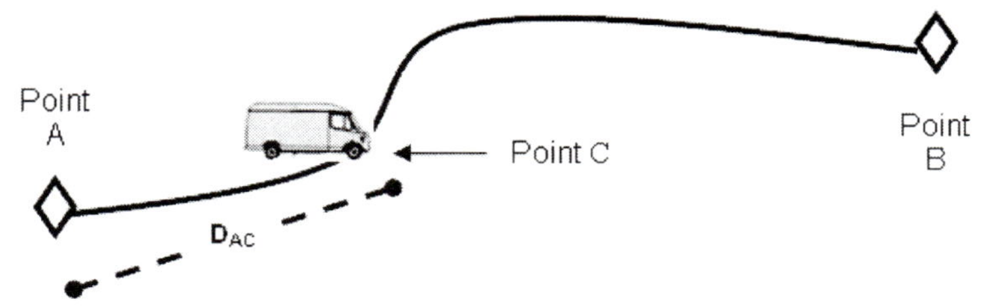

Figure 3. Three different links of getting from point A to point B

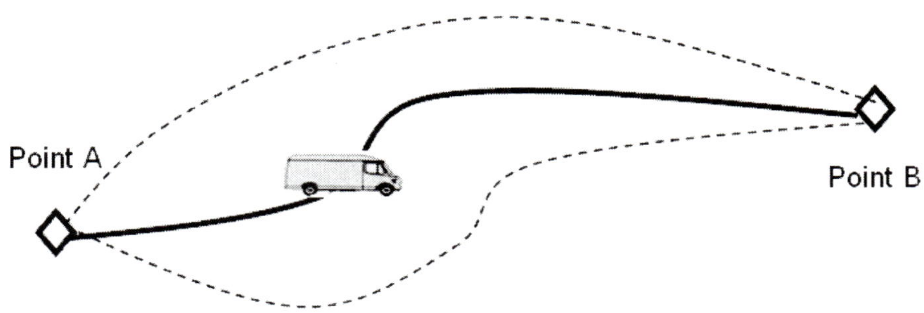

should be considered for deriving the mean time T_{AB}, we apply an outlier removal method (1st stage) where a selection of historical data is made based on time and the k-*nn* algorithm (2nd stage) where a refinement a data is made based on distance. Here is a step by step technique on how to identify from the database the routes with certain travel times:

1. Determine from the database the link that the vehicle has followed in order to travel from point A to point B with minimum travel time.
2. Identify whether the vehicle has used the same link previously more than once.
   a. If there is no such case, use only the specific data (i.e. historical travel times retrieved from this single trip) in order to estimate the arrival in the following customer
   b. If other delivery schedules are identified where the vehicle has used more than once the specific link, then:
      i. Identify these travel times
      ii. Remove outliers (i.e. travel times that are more than a certain percentage of the minimum travel time)
3. Determine parameter K (i.e. number of nearest neighbours)
4. Calculate the distance between the query-instance and all the training samples
5. Sort the distance and determine nearest neighbours based on the K-th minimum distance
6. Use their arithmetic mean in order to calculate T_{AB}

It must be mentioned though that we have assumed that the minimum historical travel time represents a direct route between the two customers (i.e. not including any intermediate stops). The probability of this being the case is dependent on the availability of historical data between the two customers in our database. In other words, the more historical data we have the more likely it is that the minimum travel time contained in this data will represent a direct link between any two customers. In our tests, we have chosen customer pairs that represent consecutive customers in the route and we have visually inspected the resulting route in the map to verify that no intermediate stops are included. Further to the aforementioned tests, we have chosen randomly, 100 cases from the database in order to investigate the percentage of cases where the minimum historical travel times represented a direct route between two customers. The results were very encouraging as in 97 cases out of 100 a direct route was observed.

Travel Time Prediction Using Real-Time Data

The first method can give very accurate results when traffic patterns at the moment of travel time prediction are similar to the historical ones retrieved from the database. However, the difficulty is that in urban environments the speed varies over time and depend on when a vehicle is traversing a particular segment. Indeed, according to Chung et al. (2004), patterns of travel time prediction in urban environments are not easy to quantify because:

- Travel demand changes everyday due to different activities and different departure times, and this result to travel time fluctuations and road congestion.
- Trip time is affected by incidents, traffic conditions and the weather.
- Urban road networks are complex and an adjacent congested route can affect the subject route.

In order to cope with such cases, we propose a second travel prediction method that uses real-time data to compute the network travel time in a dynamic manner. As the vehicle is travelling towards its destination, travel time is predicted sequentially by summing the travel time derived from speed measurements at different sections of the road.

Let us assume the same example used previously. A vehicle is travelling towards point B and in this case a data collection mechanism that records the actual velocity and the geographical position of the vehicle, is used in consecutive time slots (Figure 4).

When the vehicle is in point C and is travelling towards point B, the remaining travelling time (t_{CB}) can be calculated by subtracting the distance between client A and B (D_{AB}), which is known from historical data, from the distance travelled by the vehicle from client A until the point of data collection (D_{AC}), over the actual mean velocity (V_m) of the vehicle.

Figure 4. Travel time prediction with real-time data

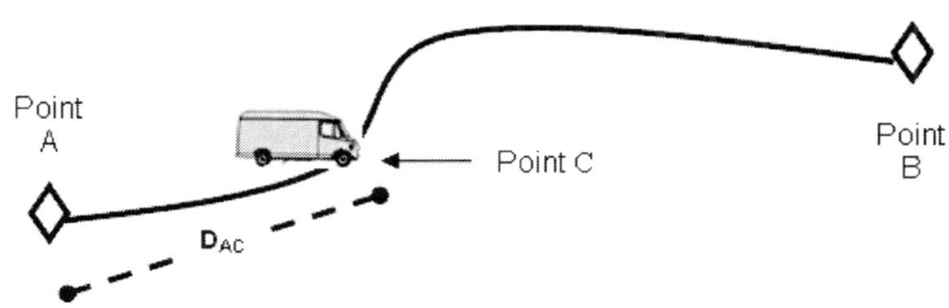

$$t_{CB} = \frac{D_{AB} - D_{AC}}{V_n} \quad (2)$$

where,

$D_{AC} = \sum_i d_{j\,j+1}$ where j is the time recorded by the system between A and B and

$d_{j\,j+1}$ is the Euclidian distance between two consecutive vehicle positions

EVALUATION OF TRAVEL TIME PREDICTION METHODS

The aforementioned travel time prediction methods use different techniques for predicting the arrival time to a point of interest (e.g. customer). The main aim is to evaluate both methods and identify which method gives the best accuracy according to traffic conditions or unexpected events that may occur during delivery execution.

In order to test and comparatively evaluate the prediction methods presented above, real-life travel time data were collected from a distribution company that makes use of a fleet of trucks for urban freight distributions. The following sections present the methodology followed to collect and process the data.

Data Collection

Data collection has been organized in two steps: a) raw data collection (i.e. information concerning a large number of data from past delivery trips) have been collected for a period of five months to create a database with historical information and b) cluster data collection (i.e. information from certain executed delivery schedules), which are a subset of the above raw information, were used to assess the accuracy of the two travel time prediction methods.

Raw Data Collection

Data were collected by using the fleet management system of a third party logistics (3PL) company. The system embraced three main modules: a) a back-end module (client-server architecture), which consisted of a fleet monitoring application with vector maps, b) a front-end module that included the telematic equipment that was responsible for acquiring, processing and transmitting various field information to the back-end, and c) a wireless communication module that allowed a two-way connection between the back-end and the front-end module.

The trucks that were equipped with this system were conducting deliveries in various points of interest (e.g. supermarkets, warehouses) that were located in Athens, Piraeus and in local suburbs. The data were captured and processed in the micro-controller of the telematic equipment and then transmitted via a modem wirelessly (in a consecutive time manner) to the back-end module through a terrestrial mobile network. Typical information transmitted included truck coordinates, its travelling time, arrival time to customers and field data (such as load temperature). This data was coupled with further information (i.e. customer coordinates, date of delivery) so as to

Figure 5. Vehicle track player of a vehicle

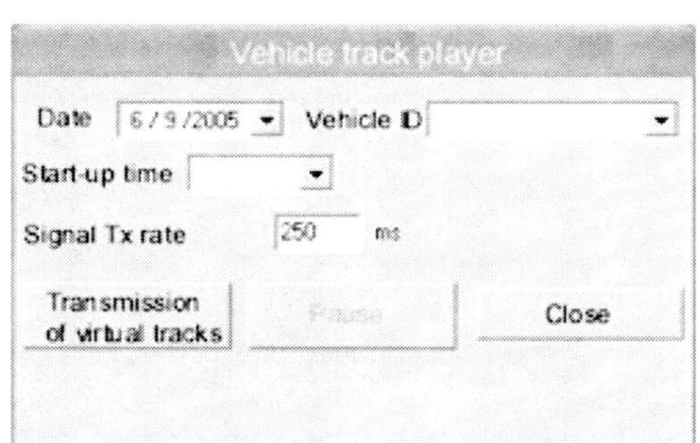

create a rich database, which was a prerequisite for the effectiveness of the proposed travel time prediction methods.

Cluster Data Collection

Having obtained historical data for a period of six months, so as to support the travel prediction methods effectively, a vehicle track player (Figure 5) was built to retrieve in detail all the information that was acquired during the execution of past deliveries (i.e. the route followed by each truck) and measure the performance of the travel time prediction methods.

For each test scenario (i.e. historical delivery schedule) a number of customers were chosen. As the actual arrival time in each client was known, it was possible to monitor the estimated arrival time in every client and thus calculate the prediction error as a step function (i.e. every time data were transmitted from the truck). A snapshot of this procedure is depicted in Figure 6.

All the data concerning prediction errors were stored in a log file that also included the information shown in Table 2. The first column of the table identifies the customer ID whereas the second and the third column show the geographical coordinates of the customer. The fourth and the fifth column show the vehicle's geographical coordinates in each data collection step. Then, the date where the delivery trip conducted is depicted, followed by the actual and the estimated arrival time of the vehicle. The last two columns provide details concerning the remaining distance to the customer and the velocity of the vehicle in each step.

Data Processing and Filtering of Biased Data

Each log file that was created from the vehicle track player was processed to be able to assess the travel time prediction methods. It must be mentioned that in each setting both methods (i.e. using historical or real-time data) were tested. A typical processing of data is presented in table 3. In this case the use of the prediction method with historical data gives more accurate estimation.

Figure 6. Actual versus predicted travel time

Customers	Actual	Predicted
Customer ID1	08:45	08:41
Customer ID2	09:15	09:10
Customer ID3	09:18	09:21

Table 2. Format of collected data for vehicle's trip towards customer A2

Customer ID	Customer X coordinate	Customer Y coordinate	Truck X coord.	Truck Y coord.	Date	Actual arrival time	Estimated arrival time	Distance left (m)	Instant velocity (Km)
A2	481980	4215740	478710	4213070	2/2/2005	15:45:00	15:44:20	1437	20
A2	481980	4215740	478740	4213130	2/2/2005	15:45:00	15:44:30	1320	18
A2	481980	4215740	478830	4213170	2/2/2005	15:45:00	15:44:55	1218	21
A2	481980	4215740	478840	4213200	2/2/2005	15:45:00	15:45:20	1211	23
A2	481980	4215740	478870	4213240	2/2/2005	15:45:00	15:45:05	1109	19

Table 3. Processing of data

Customer ID	Truck X coord.	Truck Y coord.	Actual arrival time	Estimated arrival time *(Method with historical data)*	Estimated arrival time *(Method with real time data)*	Time Divergence (sec) *(historical data)*	Time Divergence (sec) *(real time data)*	Distance left (m)
A2	478710	4213070	15:45:00	15:44:20	15:48:15	- 40	+ 195	1437
A2	478740	4213130	15:45:00	15:44:30	15:49:34	- 30	+ 274	1320
A2	478830	4213170	15:45:00	15:44:55	15:47:29	- 05	+ 149	1218
A2	478840	4213200	15:45:00	15:45:20	15:50:12	+ 20	+ 312	1211
A2	478870	4213240	15:45:00	15:45:05	15:49:23	+ 05	+ 263	1109

As it can be seen in the time divergence column, measurements can either show that a vehicle is delayed (-) or is going ahead schedule (+).

A range of conventional metrics were used to evaluate the comparative accuracy of the proposed travel time prediction methods. Defining the absolute error as $e_i = T_a - T_p$ where T_a is the actual travel time and T_p is the estimated travel time, and n as the number of samples, three measures were used:

$$\text{Mean absolute error (MAE)} = \frac{\sum_{i=1}^{n} |e_i|}{n} \quad (3)$$

$$\text{Root mean square error (RMSE)} = \sqrt{\frac{1}{n}\sum_{i=1}^{n} e_i^2} \quad (4)$$

$$\text{Mean absolute relative error (MARE)} = \frac{1}{n}\sum_{i=i}^{n} \frac{|e_i|}{T_a} \quad (5)$$

A typical graph that shows the performance of the proposed methods (normalized results) by using either historical or real-time data is presented in Figure 7. For comparison reasons, the graph also includes a method that uses a constant velocity of 20 Km/h throughout the route for travel time prediction. This value has been chosen as most researchers that design routing algorithms or systems for freight deliveries use the specific velocity when they assume constant travel times throughout the day (Ichoua, 2003).

Both proposed methods (either by using historical or real-time) data outperform the prediction mechanism that uses a steady velocity. This issue has also been mentioned by other researchers (Malandraki & Daskin, 1992; Ichoua, 2003; Fleischmann, 2004), who argued that time dependent information is critical for accurate predictions in dynamic incident handling.

However, both approaches (historical and real-time) experience a relatively high error (almost 15%-20%) at the starting point of the route, which becomes lower as the truck is approaching the delivery point. This initial error is very crucial as it may result in wrong decision making; that is, a false violation of a time window that can lead to an undesirable truck rerouting. For that reason, it was decided to filter a number of biased predictions until the system reached its steady-state.

In order to reach the steady-state condition, a number of different filtering methods can be implemented (Law & Kelton, 1991). For the purpose of travel-time prediction, the moving average method has been selected in order to act as a low-pass filter. Studying the convergence of a moving average of output data to determine a possible end of the initial transient period is attributable according to Gordon (1969) and Em-

Figure 7. Error of travel time prediction methods

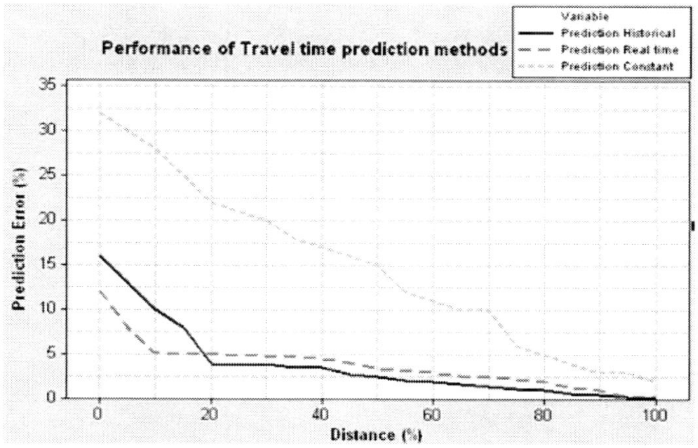

shoff & Sisson (1970). A typical way is to find an instant of time at which the running mean $\overline{X}(n)$ approaches a constant level with a given accuracy δ, $\delta > 0$.

The latter is given by:

$$\overline{X}(n) = \sum_{i=1}^{n} \frac{x_i}{n} \tag{6}$$

Thus, according to Pawlikowski (1990) we can assume that in a time series of observations $x_1, x_2, \ldots, x_i, \ldots$ the initial transient period is over after n_0 observations if k consecutive values of the running mean $\overline{X}(i)$ recorded after the observation n_0 differ less than $100\delta\%$ from $\overline{X}(n_0 + k)$; that is, for all i, $n_0 < i < n_0 + k$,

$$\frac{\left|\overline{X}(n_0 + k) - \overline{X}(i)\right|}{\left|\overline{X}(n_0 + k)\right|} < \delta \tag{7}$$

In our case δ was 0.95 (i.e. 95% accuracy) and we had a time series of 10 observations. Every prediction generated by the proposed methods was ignored prior to the average reaching a steady state. A typical output of a log file that shows the filtering session of the first predicted results is shown in Table 4.

The estimations show that at the beginning of the route, there is a high fluctuation in the estimated arrival time and for that reason each prediction result is ignored. A graphical representation of that case is also depicted in Figure 8. In this case, the biased prediction results are filtered (filtered area) and only the remaining values (after the system reaches its steady-state) are taken into account.

DESIGN OF EXPERIMENTS

The objective of this study was to investigate under what circumstances the use of real-time and historical data result in the minimum travel time estimation error. In order to do that, a series of experiments are performed by varying a number of factors. Lorenzen & Anderson (1993) define an experiment as a test or series of tests in which purposeful changes are made to the input factors of a process or system so that we may observe and identify the reasons for changes that may be observed in the output response. The basic aim in this case is to develop a robust process; that is

Table 4. Processing of data (with low-pass filtering)

Customer ID	Truck X coord.	Truck Y coord.	Customer X coordinate	Customer Y coordinate	Actual arrival time	Estimated arrival time	Prediction
A2	465710	4362070	466980	4375740	15:45:00	15:25:20	IGNORE
A2	465740	4362130	466980	4375740	15:45:00	15:18:30	IGNORE
A2	465830	4362170	466980	4375740	15:45:00	15:35:55	IGNORE
A2	465840	4362200	466980	4375740	15:45:00	15:55:20	IGNORE
A2	465870	4362240	466980	4375740	15:45:00	15:40:05	IGNORE
A2	.....	.....	.....	.....	.....	.....	.....
A2	.....	.....	.....	.....	.....	.....	.....
A2	465980	4362350	466980	4375740	15:45:00	15:43:15	ACCEPT
A2	466020	4362390	466980	4375740	15:45:00	15:44:20	ACCEPT
A2	466080	4362450	466980	4375740	15:45:00	15:44:55	ACCEPT
A2	466110	4362480	466980	4375740	15:45:00	15:43:25	ACCEPT

a process affected minimally by external sources of variability through a factorial experiment.

In order to choose, which method gives the best possible accuracy, a number of factors have been used for conducting a series of experiments. According to Chien & Kuchipudi (2003), the factors that can act as inputs to the experiment are (see also Figure 9):

- The method that is used for travel time prediction, (i.e. the travel prediction method can use either historical data or real-time data),
- The mean velocity variance ($\sigma^2 \overline{V}$) of a vehicle in a route that connects two points of interest (customers) and,
- The difference ($\Delta \overline{V}$) between the actual mean velocity of the vehicle (calculated in each route) and the mean velocity for the same route that has been calculated with historical data from the database.

Figure 8. Error of travel time prediction methods (with low-pass filtering)

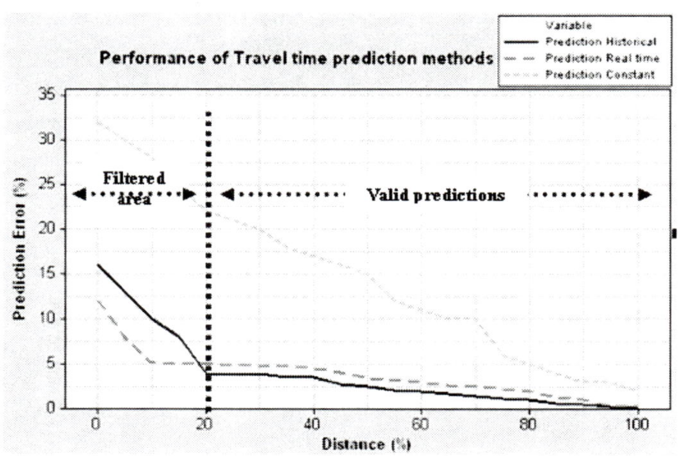

Figure 9. Model for travel-time prediction

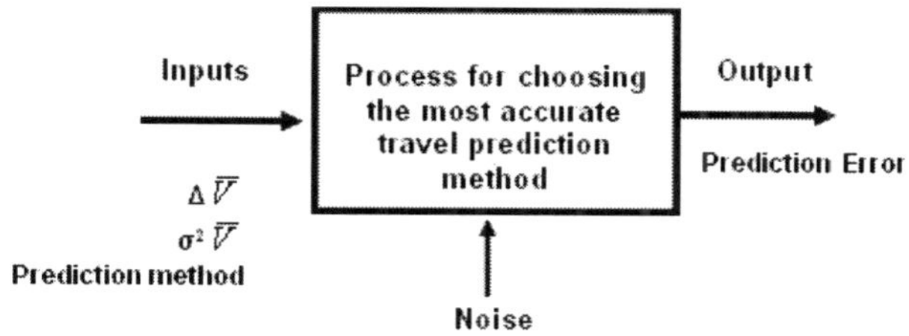

The output of the experiment is the estimation error that is produced by each travel prediction method and comprises the main element to evaluate their performance.

As mentioned above, the historical data are retrieved from identical routes (i.e. trips where the vehicle has traveled towards the same customers) that the vehicle has followed in previous delivery executions. That means that in order for a previous route to be considered in the historical data pool, it is assumed that the vehicle was departed from the same point, travelling towards the same customer, having the same time constraints.

Having that information in mind, we can classify which method can be used in each case according to: a) the type of area (city centre or suburbs), b) the day (weekends, normal days) as well as c) the time of travel (peak or off-peak hours). In that way, we will be able to use a certain travel-time prediction method as a default, when the movement of the vehicle follows the predefined patterns, or change to the other method in case of unexpected traffic patterns (e.g. congestion). For instance, if the experimental results show that in a certain scenario (suburbs, weekends, off-peak hours) the best accuracy is given by the method that uses historical data, and the moment of delivery execution a traffic accident takes place that changes the traffic flow, then we would use the prediction method that makes use of real-time data.

The model presented in Figure 10, is a factorial design that has three factors at two levels (High and Low) (Montgomery, 2001) and all possible combinations of the three factors across their levels are used in the design. The assumptions that are taken into considerations according to Anderson & McLean (1974) are:

1. **The factors are fixed:** A factor is fixed if its levels are purposely designed (or set) by the experimenter and not selected at random. In our case there are 3 factors (*ΔV, $\sigma^2 V$, and the prediction method)* with two levels (High & Low)
2. **The designs are completely randomized:** This assumption is required as the experiment must be performed in random order so that the environment in which the treatments are applied is as uniform as possible. In our case randomization has been ensured through our Design of Experiments and the statistical processing of data in MiniTAB.
3. **The normality assumptions are satisfied:** If we want to calculate confidence intervals for our predictions we need to know the probability distribution of the errors – in other words, how likely is it that errors will be big or small. For simplicity it is usually assumed that errors have a Normal distribution with mean zero and variance s^2. This means that if repeat measurements of y are taken for a particular value of x then most of them are expected to fall close to the regression line and very few to fall a long way from the line. In our case we have checked the normality assumption through the Kolmogorov-Smirnov test.

Figure 10. Geometric view

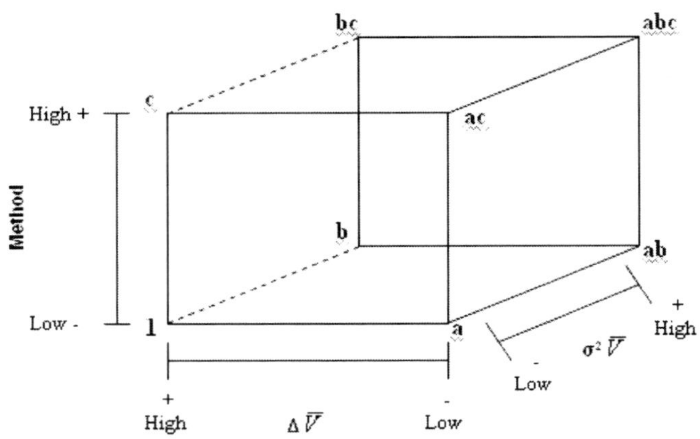

The design that will be used is called a 2^3 full factorial design and the eight treatment combinations can be displayed geometrically as a cube as shown in Figure 10.

Using the "+" and "-"notation to represent the low and high levels of the factors, the eight runs in the 2^3 design may be listed as in Table 5. This is called the design matrix. The treatment combinations can be written in standard order as *(1), a, b, ab, c, ac, bc* and, *abc*. These symbols also represent the total of all *n* observations taken at that particular treatment combination.

There are seven degrees of freedom between eight treatment combinations in the 2^3 design. Three degrees of freedom are associated with the main effects of *a, b,* and *c*. Four degrees of freedom are associated with interactions, one each with *ab, ac* and *bc* and one with *abc*.

In order to define the Low & High levels of each factor we collected data concerning ΔV and $\sigma^2 V$ from 100 different delivery trips retrieved from a database with real-life delivery schedules. According to Montgomery (2001), we identified two representative values from the dataset that were not close, so as to be able to group all data

Table 5. The design matrix

Run	$\Delta \overline{V}$	$\sigma^2 \overline{V}$	Method
1	Low	Low	Low
2	High	Low	Low
3	Low	High	Low
4	High	High	Low
5	Low	Low	High
6	High	Low	High
7	Low	High	High
8	High	High	High

Table 6. Definition of Low & High levels

	Low	*High*
ΔV	8	17
$\sigma^2 V$	1.5	4.5
Method	Method with historical data	Method with real-time data

in two levels (Low & High). The values that we used are presented in Table 6.

Based on the design matrix above we can distinguish 8 scenarios according to the area, day and hour of each case, (Table 7) that can be used in order to define which could be the proposed travel prediction method that would be used by the incident handling mechanism.

As mentioned above the three main factors are: a) the travel time prediction method, b) the mean velocity variance ($\sigma^2 \bar{V}$) and c) the difference ($\Delta \bar{V}$) between the actual mean velocity of the vehicle (calculated in each route) and the mean velocity for the same route that has been calculated with historical data from the database.

In order to analyze the velocity characteristics of each scenario, and identify the "Low" and "High" levels of each factor (i.e. $\Delta \bar{V}$ and $\sigma^2 \bar{V}$), we have performed the following test. Initially we identified from a database with historical data

Table 7. Scenarios

Scenario	Area	Day	Hour
I	City centre	Busy	Peak
II	City centre	Busy	Off-Peak
III	City centre	Non-busy	Peak
IV	City centre	Non-busy	Off-Peak
V	Suburbs	Busy	Peak
VI	Suburbs	Busy	Off-Peak
VII	Suburbs	Non-busy	Peak
VIII	Suburbs	Non-busy	Off-Peak

Table 8. Experimental scenarios

Scenario	Area	Day	Hour	$\Delta \bar{V}$	$\sigma^2 \bar{V}$
I	City centre	Busy	Peak	17	1.69
II	City centre	Busy	Off-Peak	15.4	4.92
III	City centre	Non-busy	Peak	16.7	4.67
IV	City centre	Non-busy	Off-Peak	18.1	1.72
V	Suburbs	Busy	Peak	8.7	4.12
VI	Suburbs	Busy	Off-Peak	7.9	1.52
VII	Suburbs	Non-busy	Peak	9.3	4.37
VIII	Suburbs	Non-busy	Off-Peak	8.1	1.44

Figure 11. Main effects plot

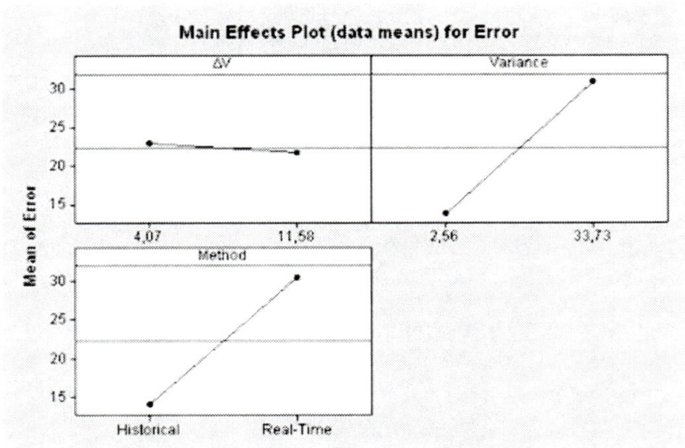

of urban freight deliveries, 10 delivery trips for each scenario. Then we calculated $\Delta\bar{V}$ and $\sigma^2\bar{V}$ for each case and lastly we find out the mean value for each factor. Table 8 presents the results from the aforementioned test.

EXPERIMENTAL RESULTS

Figures 11 and 12 present plots of the three main effects and their interactions. The main effect plots are graphs of the marginal response averages at the levels of the three factors. Notice that in Figure 11 the "Variance" and the "Method", have positive main effects; that is, increasing the factor increases the mean of error. On the contrary the "$\Delta\bar{V}$" factor has a negative effect as when is increased it moves the mean of error downward.

The performance of travel prediction methods can be determined accurately in the interaction plot depicted in Figure 12. Indeed, the interaction between "$\Delta\bar{V}$" and the method shows that when the actual mean velocity of a vehicle is "Low" (i.e. near the mean historical one), the approach

Figure 12. Interaction plot

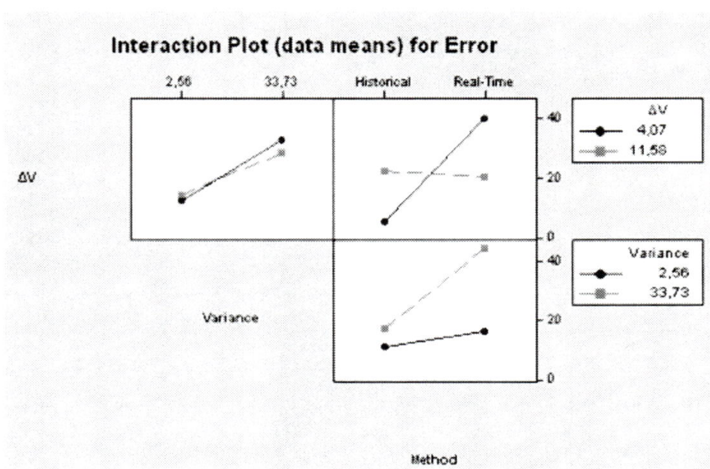

that uses historic data provides more accurate travel time predictions. On the contrary, in cases where the actual mean velocity of a vehicle is "High" (i.e. has a significant difference from the mean historical one), the approach that uses real-time data provides more accurate travel time predictions. As far as the interaction between "$\Delta \bar{V}$" and "Variance" is concerned, it is shown than the minimum error is achieved in both cases when there is a small variance of the velocity of a vehicle. Last but not least, there is no interaction between Variance and Method as shown by the similar shape of the two curves in Figure 12.

From the statistical analysis of data it is concluded that when the actual mean velocity of a vehicle is near the mean historical one (i.e. $\Delta \bar{V}$ is small), the approach that uses historic data provides more accurate travel time predictions due to smaller travel-time variance and larger sample size. If we consider the three main parameters "Area", "Day" and "Hour", this case is met usually when the vehicle is travelling in suburbs, in non-busy days and off-peak hours.

In cases where the actual mean velocity of a vehicle has a significant difference from the mean historical one (i.e. $\Delta \bar{V}$ is high), the approach that uses real-time data provides more accurate travel time predictions. This is usually the case of city centre environments, in busy-days and peak hours where a number of unpredicted events (usually traffic congestion) may occur, thus leading in large deviations from the mean historical velocity of a road link.

In order to confirm the results of the statistical analysis of the data, a range of conventional measures (Mean Absolute Error, Root Mean Square Error and Mean Absolute Relative Error) were used for each scenario and are presented in Table 9.

A t-test has been performed for identifying statistical difference (* $p<0.05$, ** $p<0.01$)

According to the aforementioned results the method that gave the best travel-time estimation for each scenario is presented in Table 10. Travel time prediction with historical data is reliable only when uniform traffic conditions prevail through the road network. Congestion or an accident would

Table 9. Prediction Errors for the eight scenarios (in seconds)

Scenarios	Method	MAE	RMSE	MARE
I	**Real-time data**	**43,143****	**161,425****	**0,242***
	Historical data	65,929	246,682	0,366
II	Real-time data	63,000	178,190	0,131
	Historical data	**54,000***	**152,735***	**0,109***
III	**Real-time data**	**52,043****	**249,591****	**0,070***
	Historical data	81,460	390,672	0,113
IV	Real-time data	115,776	1009,314	0,047
	Historical data	**71,743****	**625,444****	**0,029****
V	**Real-time data**	**35,333****	**86,548****	**0,084****
	Historical data	79,833	195,550	0,190
VI	Real-time data	107,620	854,212	0.051
	Historical data	**97,226***	**771,700****	**0,046***
VII	Real-time data	157,535	833,632	0,238
	Historical data	**113,607****	**601,152****	**0,172***
VIII	Real-time data	161,600	808,000	0.207
	Historical data	**106,160***	**530,800****	**0,136***

Table 10. Proposed method for each scenario

Scenario	Area	Day	Hour	Prediction method
I	City centre	Busy	Peak	Real-time data
II	City centre	Busy	Off-Peak	Historical data
III	City centre	Non-busy	Peak	Real-time data
IV	City centre	Non-busy	Off-Peak	Historical data
V	Suburbs	Busy	Peak	Real-time data
VI	Suburbs	Busy	Off-Peak	Historical data
VII	Suburbs	Non-busy	Peak	Historical data
VIII	Suburbs	Non-busy	Off-Peak	Historical data

affect the accuracy of the travel-time estimation using historical data, as it takes longer time for a vehicle to complete its trip. Thus, the sample size of the historical-based travel times is reduced depending on the degree of the congestion. On the other hand, travel time estimation using real-time data is more sensitive to respond to travel time spikes of a link with congestion or an accident.

Based on the results presented above, the real-time fleet management system may use the proposed methods of each scenario, however if an unexpected event occurs then the incident handling mechanism should incorporate the method that gives the best possible accuracy in the current moment.

CONCLUSION

The basic aim of this chapter was the design and evaluation of two travel time prediction methods that may be used by a real-time fleet management system in order to predict the arrival time to the remaining customers. These methods used historical and real-time data respectively for travel time estimation. The study focuses on exploring the interaction of factors that affect prediction accuracy by modeling both approaches. The employed real-time and historical data are provided by real-life scenarios of a freight carrier and the experiment follows a 2-level full factorial design approach. Results revealed that when the actual mean velocity of a vehicle is near the mean historical one, the approach that uses historic data provides more accurate travel time predictions due to smaller travel-time variance and larger sample size. In cases where the actual mean velocity of a vehicle has a significant difference from the mean historical one, the approach that uses real-time data provides more accurate travel time predictions. These results together with conventional measures have been taken into consideration in order to propose the best method for eight scenarios that reflect typical cases of a vehicle's travel between two points of interest. The results obtained are very encouraging showing that these methods can give a pretty good travel time prediction when applied in a real-time fleet management system.

ACKNOWLEDGMENT

The author gratefully acknowledge the Hellenic General Secretariat of Research & Development for partially funding this research under the project entitled Mobile Real-Time Supply Chain Execution (MORSE), as well as the project partners: Planning S.A, Athens University of Economics & Business, Emphasis Telematics, Nikas S.A, and Diakinisis S.A

REFERENCES

Abdulhai, B., Porwal, H., & Recker, W. (1999). *Short-term Freeway Traffic Flow Prediction Using Genetically-optimized Time-delay-based Neural Networks. UCB, UCB-ITS-PWP–99-1. Berkeley, CA: Institute of Transportation Studies*. Berkeley: University of California.

Ahmed, M. S., & Cook, A. R. (1979). Analysis of freeway traffic time-series data by using Box–Jenkins techniques. *Transportation Research Board, 722*, 1–9.

Anderson, V. L., & McLean, R. A. (1974). *Design of Experiments. Statistics Series: textbooks and Monographs* (*Vol. 5*). Dekker Press.

Ballou, R. H. (2004). *Business Logistics Management* (4th International Edition). Upper Saddle River, New Jersey: Prentice-Hall International Inc.

Chen, M., & Chien, S. I. J. (2001). Dynamic freeway travel time prediction using probe vehicle data: link-based vs. path-based. In *Proceedings of the Transportation Research Board 80th Annual Meeting*, Washington, DC

Chien, S. I. J., & Kuchipudi, C. M. (2003). Dynamic travel time prediction with real-time and historical data. In *Proceedings of the Transportation Research Board 81st Annual Meeting*, Washington, DC

Chung, E. Warita, H., Bajwa, S., & Kuwahara, M. (2004). Travel Time Prediction: Issues and Benefits. In *Proceedings of the 10th World Conference on Transport Research* (CD-ROM), Istanbul, Turkey

Clark, S. (2003). Traffic prediction using multivariate nonparametric regression. *Journal of Transportation Engineering, 129*(2), 161–168. doi:10.1061/(ASCE)0733-947X(2003)129:2(161)

Clark, S. D., Dougherty, M. S., & Kirby, H. R. (1993). The use of neural networks and time series models for short-term traffic forecasting: a comparative study. In *Proceedings of the PTRC 21st Summer Annual Meeting.*

Davis, G. A., Niham, N. L., Hamed, M. M., & Jacobson, L. N. (1991). Adaptive forecasting of freeway traffic congestion. *Transportation Research Record, 1287*, 29–33.

Emshoff, J. R., & Sisson, R. L. (1970). *Design and Use of Computer Simulation Models*. New York: Macmillan.

Eubank, R. L. (1988). *Spline Smoothing and Nonparametric Regression*. New York: Marcel Dekker Inc.

Fleischmann, B., Gietz, M., & Grutzmann, S. (2004). Time-varying Travel Times in Vehicle Routing. *Transportation Science, 38*(2), 160–174. doi:10.1287/trsc.1030.0062

Gordon, G. (1969). *System Simulation*. Englewood Cliffs, NJ: Prentice Hall.

Hamed, M. M., Al-Masaeid, H. R., & Bani Said, Z. M. (1995). Short-term prediction of traffic volume in urban arterials. *Journal of Transportation Engineering, 121*(3), 249–254. doi:10.1061/(ASCE)0733-947X(1995)121:3(249)

Ichoua, S., Gendreau, M., & Potvin, J. Y. (2003). Vehicle dispatching with time-dependent travel times. *European Journal of Operational Research, 144*, 379–396. doi:10.1016/S0377-2217(02)00147-9

Ishak, S., & Alecsandru, C. (2003). Optimizing traffic prediction performance of Neural networks under various topological, input and traffic condition settings. In *Proceedings of the Transportation Research Board 82nd Annual Meeting*, Washington, DC

Karlsson, M., & Yakowitz, S. (1987). Rainfall runoff forecasting methods old and new. *Stochastic Hydrology and Hydraulics, 1*, 303–318. doi:10.1007/BF01543102

Kwon, E., & Stephanedes, Y. J. (1994). Comparative evaluation of adaptive and neural-network exit demand prediction for freeway control. *Transportation Research Record, 1446*, 66–76.

Law, A., & Kelton, D. (1991). *Simulation Modelling and Analysis*. New York: McGraw-Hill.

Levin, M., & Tsao, Y.-D. (1980). On forecasting freeway occupancies and volumes. *Transportation Research Record, 773*, 47–49.

Lingras, P., & Mountford, P. (2001). Time delay neural networks designed using genetic algorithms for short-term inter-city traffic forecasting, IEA/AIE 2001 (LNAI 2070, pp. 290–299).

Lorenzen, T. J., & Anderson, V. (1993). *Design of Experiments. Statistics Series: textbooks and Monographs* (*Vol. 139*). CRC Press.

Maladraki, C., & Daskin, M. S. (1992). Time dependent vehicle routing problems: Formulations, properties and heuristic algorithms. *Transportation Science, 26*, 185–200. doi:10.1287/trsc.26.3.185

Montemanni, R. Gambardella, L.M., Rizzoli, A.E., & Donati, A.E. (2002). A new algorithm for a Dynamic Vehicle Routing Problem based on Ant Colony System (Technical Report IDSIA-23-02). IDSIA. Retrieved December 2009 from ftp://ftp.idsia.ch/pub/techrep/IDSIA-23-02.pdf.gz

Okutani, I., & Stephanedes, Y. J. (1984). Dynamic prediction of traffic volume through Kalman filtering theory. *Transportation Research Part B: Methodological, 18*(1), 1–11. doi:10.1016/0191-2615(84)90002-X

Park, D., Messer, C. J., & Urbanik, T. (1998). Short-term freeway traffic volume forecasting using radial basis function neural networks. *Transportation Research Record, 1651*, 39–47. doi:10.3141/1651-06

Park, D., Rilett, L. R., & Han, G. (1999). Spectral basis neural networks for real-time travel time forecasting. *Journal of Transportation Engineering, 125*(6), 515–523. doi:10.1061/(ASCE)0733-947X(1999)125:6(515)

Pawlikowski, K. (1990). Steady state simulation of Queuing Processes. *ACM Computing Surveys, 22*(2), 123–170. doi:10.1145/78919.78921

Psaraftis, H. N. (1995). Dynamic Vehicle Routing: Status and Prospects. *Annals of Operations Research, 611*, 143–164. doi:10.1007/BF02098286

Rego, C., & Rucairol, C. (1995). Using tabu search for solving a dynamic multi-terminal truck dispatching problem. *European Journal of Operational Research, 83*, 411–429. doi:10.1016/0377-2217(95)00016-J

Savelsbergh, M. W. P., & Sol, M. (1998). Drive: Dynamic routing of independent vehicles. *Operations Research, 46*, 474–490. doi:10.1287/opre.46.4.474

Smith, B. L., & Demetsky, M. J. (1994). Short-term traffic flow prediction: neural network approach. *Transportation Research Board, 1453*, 98–104.

Smith, B. L., & Demetsky, M. J. (1996). Multiple-interval freeway traffic flow forecasting. *Transportation Research Record, 1554*, 136–141. doi:10.3141/1554-17

Smith, B. L., & Demetsky, M. J. (1997). Traffic flow forecasting: comparison of modelling approaches. *Journal of Transportation Engineering, 123*(4), 261–266. doi:10.1061/(ASCE)0733-947X(1997)123:4(261)

Smith, B. L., Williams, B. M., & Oswald, K. R. (2000). Parametric and nonparametric traffic volume forecasting. In *Proceedings of the 80th TRB Annual Meeting*, Washington, DC

Smith, B. L., Williams, B. M., & Oswald, R. K. (2002). Comparison of parametric and nonparametric models for traffic flow forecasting. *Transportation Research Part C, Emerging Technologies*, *10*, 303–321. doi:10.1016/S0968-090X(02)00009-8

Stathopoulos, A., & Karlaftis, M. G. (2003). A multivariate state-space approach for urban traffic flow modelling and prediction. *Transportation Research Part C, Emerging Technologies*, *11*(2), 121–135. doi:10.1016/S0968-090X(03)00004-4

Vlachogianni, E. I., Colias, J. C., & Karlaftis, M. G. (2004). Short-term Traffic Forecasting: Overview of Objectives and Methods. *Transport Reviews*, *24*(5), 533–557. doi:10.1080/0144164042000195072

Whittaker, J., Garside, S., & Lindeveld, K. (1997). Tracking and predicting network traffic process. *International Journal of Forecasting*, *13*, 51–61. doi:10.1016/S0169-2070(96)00700-5

Williams, B. M., Durvasula, P. K., & Brown, D. E. (1998). Urban traffic flow prediction: application of seasonal autoregressive integrated moving average and exponential smoothing models. *Transportation Research Record*, *1644*, 132–144. doi:10.3141/1644-14

Yun, S.-Y., Namkoong, S., Rho, J.-H., Shin, S.-W., & Choi, J.-U. (1998). A performance evaluation of neural network models in traffic volume forecasting. *Mathematical and Computer Modelling*, *27*(9–11), 293–310. doi:10.1016/S0895-7177(98)00065-X

Zhang, G., Patuwo, B. E., & Hu, M. Y. (1998). Forecasting with artificial neural networks: the state of art. *International Journal of Forecasting*, *14*, 35–62. doi:10.1016/S0169-2070(97)00044-7

Zhang, H. M. (2000). Recursive prediction of traffic conditions with neural networks. *Journal of Transportation Engineering*, *126*(6), 472–481. doi:10.1061/(ASCE)0733-947X(2000)126:6(472)

Compilation of References

Abdelmaguid, T. F., & Dessouky, M. M. (2006). A genetic algorithm approach to the integrated inventory-distribution problem. *International Journal of Production Research*, *44*(21), 4445–4464. doi:10.1080/00207540600597138

Abdulhai, B., Porwal, H., & Recker, W. (1999). *Short-term Freeway Traffic Flow Prediction Using Genetically-optimized Time-delay-based Neural Networks. UCB, UCB-ITS-PWP–99-1. Berkeley, CA: Institute of Transportation Studies*. Berkeley: University of California.

Aberdeen Group. (2007). *The Supply Chain Executive's Strategic Agenda 2008: Managing Global Supply Chain Transformation*. Retrieved April 8, 2010 from http://www-304.ibm.com/jct03004c/tools/ cpeportal/fileserve/download0/143747/AberdeenSCMStrategicAgenda08.pdf?contentid=143747

Aburto, L., & Weber, R. (2007). Improved supply chain management based on hybrid demand forecasts. *Applied Soft Computing*, *7*(1), 136–144. doi:10.1016/j.asoc.2005.06.001

Adachi, N., & Matsuo, K. (2006). Ecological dynamics under different selection rules in distributed and iterated prisoner's dilemma game. In *Parallel Problem Solving from Nature* (*Vol. 496*, pp. 387–394). Berlin, Heidelberg: Springer. doi:10.1007/BFb0029780

Adleman, L. M. (1994). Molecular computation of solutions to combinatorial problems. *Journal of Science*, *265*(5187), 1021–1024. doi:10.1126/science.7973651

Agapitos, A., Dyson, M., Kovalchuk, J., & Lucas, S. M. (2008). On the genetic programming of time-series predictors for supply chain management. In *Proceedings of the 10th annual conference on Genetic and evolutionary computation* (pp. 1163-1170).

Agrawal, N., & Nahmias, S. (1998). Rationalization of the supplier base in the presence of yield uncertainty. *Production and Operations Management*, *6*(3), 291–308. doi:10.1111/j.1937-5956.1997.tb00432.x

Aguerrevere, F. L. (2003). Equilibrium investment strategies and output price behavior: a real-options approach. *Review of Financial Studies*, *16*, 1239–1272. doi:10.1093/rfs/hhg041

Ahlert, K.-H., Corsten, H., & Gossinger, R. (2009). Capacity management in order driven production networks - A flexibility-oriented approach to determine the size of a network capacity pool. *International Journal of Production Economics*, *118*(2), 430–441. doi:10.1016/j.ijpe.2008.11.013

Ahmed, S., & Shapiro, A. (2002). The Sample Average Approximation Method for Stochastic Programs with Integer Recourse. *SIAM Journal on Optimization*, *12*, 479–502.

Ahmed, M. S., & Cook, A. R. (1979). Analysis of freeway traffic time-series data by using Box–Jenkins techniques. *Transportation Research Board*, *722*, 1–9.

Ai, T. J., & Kachitvichyanukul, V. (2009). A particle swarm optimization for the vehicle routing problem with simultaneous pickup and delivery. *Computers & Operations Research*, *36*, 1693–1702. doi:10.1016/j.cor.2008.04.003

Ai, T. J., & Kachitvichyanukul, V. (2009). Particle swarm optimization and two solution representations for solving the capacitated vehicle routing problem. *Computers & Operations Research*, *56*, 380–387.

Akkihal, A. R. (2006). Inventory pre-positioning for humanitarian operations. Master's thesis, MIT.

Alabas, C., Altiparmak, F., & Dengiz, B. (2002). A comparison of the performance of artificial intelligence techniques for optimizing the number of kanbans. *The Journal of the Operational Research Society*, *53*(8), 907–914. doi:10.1057/palgrave.jors.2601395

Alba, E., & Dorronsoro, B. (2008). A hybrid cellular genetic algorithm for the capacitated vehicle routing problem. In *Engineering Evolutionary Intelligent Systems* (pp. 379–422). Berlin, Heidelberg: Springer. doi:10.1007/978-3-540-75396-4_14

Aliev, R. A., Fazlollahi, B., Guirimov, B. G., & Alien, R. R. (2007). Fuzzy-genetic approach to aggregate production-distribution planning in supply chain management. *Information Sciences*, *177*(20), 4241–4255. doi:10.1016/j.ins.2007.04.012

Alonso-Ayuso, A., Escudero, L. F., Garín, A., Ortuño, M. T., & Pérez, G. (2003). An approach for strategic supply chain planning under uncertainty based on stochastic 0–1 programming. *Journal of Global Optimization*, *26*(1), 97–124. doi:10.1023/A:1023071216923

Al-Othman, W. B. E., Lababidi, H. M. S., Alatiqi, I. M., & Al-Shayji, K. (2008). Supply chain optimization of petroleum organization under uncertainty in market demands and prices. *European Journal of Operational Research*, *189*(3), 822–840. doi:10.1016/j.ejor.2006.06.081

Altiparmak, F., Gen, M., Lin, L., & Karaoglan, I. (2009). A steady-state genetic algorithm for multi-product supply chain network design. *Computers & Industrial Engineering*, *56*(2), 521–537. doi:10.1016/j.cie.2007.05.012

Altiparmak, F., Gen, M., Lin, L., & Paksoy, T. (2006). A genetic algorithm approach for multi-objective optimization of supply chain networks. *Computers & Industrial Engineering*, *51*(1), 196–215. doi:10.1016/j.cie.2006.07.011

Amodeo, L., Prins, C., & Sanchez, D. R. (2009). Comparison of metaheuristic approaches for multi – objective simulation – based optimization in supply chain inventory management. In *Applications of Evolutionary Computing* (Vol. 5484, pp. 798-807).

Ampazis, N., & Perantonis, S. J. (2002). Two highly efficient second order algorithms for training feedforward networks. *IEEE Transactions on Neural Networks*, *13*(5), 1064–1074. doi:10.1109/TNN.2002.1031939

Ampazis, N. (2002). LMAM/OLMAM neural network toolbox []. (Software available at http://authorid.fme.aegean.gr/OLMAM/toolbox)

Amram, M., & Kulatilaka, N. (1999). *Real options: managing strategic investment in an uncertain world.* Harvard Business School Press.

Anderson, V. L., & McLean, R. A. (1974). *Design of Experiments. Statistics Series: textbooks and Monographs* (*Vol. 5*). Dekker Press.

Anderson, R. (1992). The Core in Perfectly Competitive Economics. In R. Aumann & S. Hart, (Eds.), *Handbook of Game Theory with Economic Applications* (pp.413-457). Amsterdam, North-Holland: Elsevier.

Andreatta, G., & Lulli, G. (2008). A multi-period TSP with stochastic regular and urgent demands. *European Journal of Operational Research*, *185*, 122–132. doi:10.1016/j.ejor.2006.12.040

Angelelli, E., Bianchessi, N., Mansini, R., & Speranza, M. G. (2009). Short Term Strategies for a Dynamic Multi-Period Routing Problem. *Transportation Research Part C, Emerging Technologies*, *17*(2), 106–119. doi:10.1016/j.trc.2008.02.001

Angelelli, E., Savelsbergh, M. W. P., & Speranza, M. G. (2007). Competitive analysis of a dispatch policy for a dynamic multi-period routing problem. *Operations Research Letters*, *35*(6), 713–721. doi:10.1016/j.orl.2007.02.006

Angelelli, E., Speranza, M. G., & Savelsbergh, M. W. P. (2005). *A Dynamic Multi-Period Routing Problem*. Presented at the International Workshop on Vehicle Routing and Intermodal Transportation (ROUTE 2005), Italy.

Angelis, V. D., Mecoli, M., Nikoi, C., & Storchi, G. (2007). Multiperiod integrated routing and scheduling of World Food Programme cargo planes in Angola. *Computers & Operations Research*, *34*, 1601–1615. doi:10.1016/j.cor.2005.07.012

Applequist, G. E., Penky, J. F., & Reklaitis, G. (2000). Risk and uncertainty in managing chemical manufacturing supply chains. *Computers & Chemical Engineering*, *24*(9-10), 2211–2222. doi:10.1016/S0098-1354(00)00585-8

Ardekani, S. A., & Hobeika, A. (1988). Logistics problems in the aftermath of the 1985 Mexico City earthquake. *Transportation Quarterly*, *42*, 1077124.

Argoneto, P., & Renna, P. (2009). Production planning, negotiation and coalition integration: A new tool for an innovative e-business model. *Robotics and Computer-integrated Manufacturing*. doi:.doi:10.1016/j.rcim.2009.01.001

Argoneto, P., Bruccoleri, M., Lo Nigro, G., Noto La Diega, S., Perrone, G., & Renna, P. (2004). Evaluating multi-lateral negotiation policies in manufacturing e-marketplace. *The 37th CIRP International Seminar on Manufacturing Systems*, May 19-21, 2004, Budapest, Hungary.

Armstrong, J. (2002). *Principles of forecasting: a handbook for researchers and practitioners*. Kluwer.

Arora, V., Chan, F. T. S. & Tiwari, M. K. (2009). An integrated approach for logistic and vendor managed inventory in supply chain. *Expert Systems with Applications*.

Arreola-Risa, A., & DeCroix, G. A. (1998). Inventory Management under Random Supply Disruptions and Partial Backorders. *Naval Research Logistics*, *45*, 687–703. doi:10.1002/(SICI)1520-6750(199810)45:7<687::AID-NAV3>3.0.CO;2-7

Ash, C. G., & Burn, J. M. (2006). Evaluating benefits of e-procurement in a B2B marketplace: a case study of Quadrem. *Journal of Information Technology Case Application Research*, *8*(2), 5–23.

Bachlaus, M., Pandey, M. K., Mahajan, C., Shankar, R., & Tiwari, M. K. (2008). Designing an integrated multi – echelon agile supply chain network: a hybrid tagushi – particle swarm optimization approach. *Journal of Intelligent Manufacturing*, *19*, 747–761. doi:10.1007/s10845-008-0125-1

Baden-Fuller, C. (1990). *Managing Excess Capacity*. New York: Basil Blackwell Publishers.

Baita, F., Ukovich, W., Pesenti, R., & Favaretto, D. (1998). Dynamic routing-and-inventory problems: A review. *Transportation Research*, *32*(8), 585–598.

Baker, B. M., & Ayechew, M. A. (2003). A genetic algorithm for the vehicle routing problem. *Computers & Operations Research*, *30*, 787–800. doi:10.1016/S0305-0548(02)00051-5

Balcik, B., & Beamon, B. M. (2008). Facility location in humanitarian relief. *International Journal of Logistics: Research and Applications*, *11*(2), 101–121. doi:10.1080/13675560701561789

Balcik, B., Beamon, B. M., & Smilowitz, K. (2008). Last Mile Distribution in Humanitarian Relief. *Journal of Intelligent Transportation Systems*, *12*(2), 51–63. doi:10.1080/15472450802023329

Ballou, R. H. (2004). *Business Logistics Management* (4th International Edition). Upper Saddle River, New Jersey: Prentice-Hall International Inc.

Banerjee, S., Dangayach, G. S., Mukherjee, S. K., & Mohanti, P. K. (2008). Modeling Process and Supply Chain Scheduling Using Hybrid Meta – heuristics. In *Metaheuristics for Scheduling in Industrial and Manufacturing Applications* (pp. 277–300). Berlin, Heidelberg: Springer. doi:10.1007/978-3-540-78985-7_11

Baraglia, R., Hidalgo, J. I., & Perego, R. (2001). A parallel hybrid heuristic for the TSP. In *Applications of Evolutionary Computing* (*Vol. 2037*, pp. 193–202). Berlin, Heidelberg: Springer. doi:10.1007/3-540-45365-2_20

Barbarosoglu, G., & Arda, Y. (2004). A two-stage stochastic programming framework for transportation planning in disaster response. *The Journal of the Operational Research Society*, *55*(1), 43–53. doi:10.1057/palgrave.jors.2601652

Barbarosoglu, G., Ozdamar, L., & Cevik, A. (2002). An interactive approach for hierarchical analysis of helicopter logistics in disaster relief operations. *European Journal of Operational Research*, *140*(1), 118–133. doi:10.1016/S0377-2217(01)00222-3

Barratt, M., & Rosdahl, K. (2002). Exploring business-to-business marketsites. *European Journal of Purchasing & Supply Management*, *8*, 111–122. doi:10.1016/S0969-7012(01)00010-7

Bashiri, M. & Tabrizi, M. M. (2009). Supply chain design: a holistic approach. *Expert Systems with Applications*.

Baykasoglu, A., Dereli, T., & Sabuncu, I. (2006). An ant colony algorithm for solving budget constrained and unconstrained dynamic facility layout problems. *Omega: the International Journal of Management Science*, *34*, 385–396. doi:10.1016/j.omega.2004.12.001

Beamon, B. M. (1998). Supply Chain Design and Analysis: Models and Methods. *International Journal of Production Economics*, *55*(3), 281–294. doi:10.1016/S0925-5273(98)00079-6

Beasley, J. E. (1984). Fixed Routes. *The Journal of the Operational Research Society*, *35*(1), 49–55.

Beasley, J. E., & Christofides, N. (1997). Vehicle routing with a sparse feasibility graph. *European Journal of Operational Research*, *98*, 499–511. doi:10.1016/S0377-2217(96)00048-3

Belenky, A. (2002). Cooperative Games of Choosing Partners and Forming Coalitions in the Marketplace. *Mathematical and Computer Modelling*, *36*, 1279–1291. doi:10.1016/S0895-7177(02)00276-5

Bell, J. E., & McMullen, P. R. (2004). Ant colony optimization techniques for the vehicle routing problem. *Advanced Engineering Informatics*, *18*, 41–48. doi:10.1016/j.aei.2004.07.001

Bellman, R. E. (1957). *Dynamic Programming*. Princeton: Princeton University Press.

Beltrami, E. J., & Bodin, L. D. (1974). Networks and vehicle routing for municipal waste collection. *Networks*, *4*(1), 65–94. doi:10.1002/net.3230040106

Bengtsson, J. (2001). Manufacturing flexibility and real options: A review. *International Journal of Production Economics*, *74*, 213–224. doi:10.1016/S0925-5273(01)00128-1

Bengtsson, M., & Kock, S. (2000). Coopetition in business networks to cooperate and compete simultaneously. *Industrial Marketing Management*, *29*(5), 411–426. doi:10.1016/S0019-8501(99)00067-X

Berkley, B. J. (1992). A review of the kanban production control research literature. *Production and Operations Management*, *1*(4), 393–411. doi:10.1111/j.1937-5956.1992.tb00004.x

Berman, O., Krass, D., & Drezner, Z. (2003). The gradual covering decay location problem on a network. *European Journal of Operational Research*, *151*(3), 447–674. doi:10.1016/S0377-2217(02)00604-5

Bertazzi, L., Savelsbergh, M. W. P., & Speranza, M. G. (2008). Inventory Routing. In Golden, B., Raghavan, S., & Wasil, E. (Eds.), *The Vehicle Routing Problem: Latest Advances and New Challenges* (pp. 49–72). Springer. doi:10.1007/978-0-387-77778-8_3

Bhat, U. N. (2008). *An Introduction to Queueing Theory: Modelling and Analysis in Applications*. Boston: Birkhauser.

Bianchi, L., Gambardella, L. M., & Dorigo, M. (2002). An ant colony optimization approach to the probabilistic traveling salesman problem. In *Proceedings of the PPSN – VII, 7th International Conference on Parallel Problem Solving from Nature* (pp. 883-892).

Bishop, C. M. (1995). *Neural Networks for Pattern Recognition*. Oxford: Oxford University Press.

Bontoux, B., Artigues, C. & Feillet, D. 2009, 'A memetic algorithm with a large neighborhood crossover operator for the generalized traveling salesman problem', *Computers & Operations Research*.

Boser, B. E., Guyon, I. M., & Vapnik, V. N. (1992). A training algorithm for optimal margin classifiers. In *Colt '92: Proceedings of the fifth annual workshop on computational learning theory* (pp. 144–152). New York: ACM.

Bostel, N., Dejax, P., Guez, P., & Tricoire, F. (2008). Multiperiod Planning and Routing on a Rolling Horizon for Field Force Optimization Logistics. In Golden, B., Raghavan, S., & Wasil, E. (Eds.), *The Vehicle Routing Problem: Latest Advances and New Challenges* (pp. 503–525). Springer. doi:10.1007/978-0-387-77778-8_23

Boudia, M., Prins, C., & Reghioui, M. (2007). An effective memetic algorithm with population management for the split delivery vehicle routing problem. In *Hybrid Metaheuristics* (*Vol. 4771*, pp. 16–30). Berlin, Heidelberg: Springer. doi:10.1007/978-3-540-75514-2_2

Bouhafs, L., Hajjam, A., & Koukam, A. (2006). A combination of simulated annealing and ant colony system for the capacitated location – routing problem. In *Knowledge-Based Intelligent Information and Engineering Systems* (pp. 409–416). Berlin, Heidelberg: Springer. doi:10.1007/11892960_50

Boukerche, A., Juca, K. R. L., Sobral, J. B., & Notare, M. S. M. A. (2004). An artificial immune based intrusion detection model for computer and telecommunication systems. *Parallel Computing*, *30*, 629–646. doi:10.1016/j.parco.2003.12.008

Bowden, R. O., Hall, J. D., & Usher, J. M. (1996). Integration of evolutionary programming and simulation to optimize a pull production system. *Computers & Industrial Engineering*, *31*(1&2), 217–220. doi:10.1016/0360-8352(96)00115-5

Box, G., & Jenkins, G. (1970). *Time series analysis: Forecasting and control*. San Francisco: Holden-Day.

Boysen, N., Fliender, M., & Scholl, A. (2007). Sequencing mixed-model assembly lines to minimize part inventory cost', in *OR Spectrum, 30*(3), 611-633.

Brabazon, A., & O'Neill, M. (2006). *Biologically inspired algorithms for financial modelling*. Berlin, Heidelberg, Tokyo, New York: Springer-Verlag.

Brandenburger, A., & Nalebuff, B. (1996). *Co-Opetition: A Revolution Mindset That Combines Competition and Cooperation*. New York: Harper Collins Business.

Branke, J., & Guntsch, M. (2003). New ideas for applying ant colony optimization to the probabilistic TSP. In *Applications of Evolutionary Computing* (*Vol. 2611*, pp. 127–134). Berlin, Heidelberg: Springer. doi:10.1007/3-540-36605-9_16

Branke, J., & Guntsch, M. (2004). Solving the probabilistic TSP with ant colony optimization. *Journal of Mathematical Modelling and Algorithms*, *3*, 403–425. doi:10.1023/B:JMMA.0000049380.86987.d4

Braysy, O., Dullaert, W., & Gendreau, M. (2004). Evolutionary algorithms for the vehicle routing problem with time windows. *Journal of Heuristics*, *10*, 587–611. doi:10.1007/s10732-005-5431-6

Brealey, R. A., & Myers, S. C. (2000). *Principles of Corporate Finance* (6th ed.). London: McGraw-Hill.

Brown, G. G., & Vassiliou, A. L. (1993). Optimizing disaster relief: real-time operational and tactical decision support. *Nav. Res. Logist.*, *40*, 1-23. doi:10.1002/1520-6750(199302)40:1<1::AID-NAV3220400102>3.0.CO;2-S

Brynzer, H., Johansson, M. I., & Medbo, L. (1994). A Methodology for Order Picking Systems as a Base for System Design and Managerial Decisions. *International Journal of Operations & Production Management*, *14*(3), 126–139. doi:10.1108/01443579410058595

Bullnheimer, B., Hartl, R. F., & Strauss, C. (1999). An improved ant system algorithm for the vehicle routing problem. *Annals of Operations Research*, *89*, 319–328. doi:10.1023/A:1018940026670

Buriol, L., & Franca, P. M. (2004). A new memetic algorithm for the asymmetric traveling salesman problem. *Journal of Heuristics*, *10*, 483–506. doi:10.1023/B:HEUR.0000045321.59202.52

Buzacott, J. A., & Shanthikumar, J. G. (1992). A general approach for coordinating production in multiple cell manufacturing systems. *Production and Operations Management*, *1*(1), 34–52. doi:10.1111/j.1937-5956.1992.tb00338.x

Buzacott, J. A., & Shanthikumar, J. G. (1993). *Stochastic Models of Manufacturing Systems*. New York: Prentice Hall.

Cakravastia, A., Toha, I., & Nakamura, N. (2002). A two-stage model for the design of supply chain networks. *International Journal of Production Economics*, *80*(3), 231–248. doi:10.1016/S0925-5273(02)00260-8

Caldeira, J., Azevedo, R., Silva, C. A., & Sousa, M. C. (2007). Beam – ACO Distributed Optimization Applied to Supply – Chain Management. In *Foundations of Fuzzy Logic and Soft Computing* (*Vol. 4529*, pp. 799–809). Berlin, Heidelberg: Springer. doi:10.1007/978-3-540-72950-1_78

Calvo, E., & Santos, J. C. (2000). Weighted weak semivalues. *International Journal of Game Theory*, *29*, 1–9. doi:10.1007/s001820050001

Campbell, A. M., Clarke, L. W., & Savelsbergh, M. W. P. (2001). Inventory routing in practice. In *Inventory routing in practice* (pp. 309–330). Philadelphia, PA: Society for Industrial and Applied Mathematics.

Campbell, A. M., Vandenbussche, D., & Hermann, W. (2008). Routing for Relief Efforts. *Transportation Science*, *42*(2), 127–145. doi:10.1287/trsc.1070.0209

Campbell, A. M., & Savelsbergh, M. W. P. (2004). A decomposition approach for the Inventory-Routing Problem. *Transportation Science*, *38*(4), 488–502. doi:10.1287/trsc.1030.0054

Campbell, A., Clarke, L., Kleywegt, A., & Savelsbergh, M. W. P. (1998). Inventory routing. In Crainic, T., & Laporte, G. (Eds.), *Fleet Management and Logistics*, 95-112, Kluwer Academic Publishers, Boston.

Cao, Q., & Leggio, K. B. (2008). Alleviating the bullwhip effect in supply chain management using the multi-agent approach: an empirical study. *International Journal of Computer Applications in Technology*, *31*(3-4), 225–237. doi:10.1504/IJCAT.2008.018159

Carbonneau, R., Laframboise, K., & Vahidov, R. M. (2008). Application of machine learning techniques for supply chain demand forecasting. *European Journal of Operational Research*, *184*(3), 1140–1154. doi:10.1016/j.ejor.2006.12.004

Carter, A. E., & Ragsdale, C. T. (2006). A new approach to solving the multiple traveling salesperson problem using genetic algorithms. *European Journal of Operational Research*, *175*, 246–257. doi:10.1016/j.ejor.2005.04.027

Chaharsooghi, S. K., Heydari, J., & Zegordi, S. H. (2008). A reinforcement learning model for supply chain ordering management: An application to the beer game. *Decision Support Systems*, *45*(4), 949–959. doi:10.1016/j.dss.2008.03.007

Chan, C. C. H., Cheng, C. B., & Huang, S. W. (2006). Formulating ordering policies in a supply chain by genetic algorithm. *International Journal of Modelling and Simulation*, *26*(2), 129–136. doi:10.2316/Journal.205.2006.2.205-4158

Chan, C. K., Cheung, B. K. S., & Langevin, A. (2003). Solving the multi-buyer joint replenishment problem with a modified genetic algorithm. *Transportation Research Part B: Methodological*, *37*(3), 291–299. doi:10.1016/S0191-2615(02)00015-2

Chan, F. T. S., Kumar, V., & Mishra, N. (2007). A CMPSO algorithm based approach to solve the multi – plant supply chain problem. In *Focus on Ant and Particle Swarm Optimization* (p. 532). Australia: Itech Education and Publishing.

Chan, F. T. S., & Qi, H. J. (2003). Feasibility of Performance Measurement System for Supply Chain: A Process-Based Approach and Measures. *Integrated Manufacturing Systems*, *14*(3), 179–190. doi:10.1108/09576060310463145

Chandra, C., & Grabis, J. (2009). Role of flexibility in supply chain design and modeling-Introduction to the special issue. *Omega*, *37*(4), 743–745. doi:10.1016/j.omega.2008.07.003

Chandrasekaran, C., Chandrasekharan, R., Krishnaian, O. V. C., & Hanumanna, D. (2007). Metaheuristics for solving economic lot scheduling problems (ELSP) using time-varying lot-sizes approach. *European Journal of Industrial Engineering*, *1*(2), 152–181. doi:10.1504/EJIE.2007.014107

Chang, Y. H. (in press). Adopting co-evolution and constraint-satisfaction concept on genetic algorithms to solve supply chain network design problems. *Expert Systems with Applications*.

Chang, M. S., Tseng, Y. L., & Chen, J. W. (2007). A scenario planning approach for the flood emergency logistics preparation problem under uncertainty. *Transportation Research Part E, Logistics and Transportation Review*, *43*, 737–754. doi:10.1016/j.tre.2006.10.013

Chang, C. C., & Lin, C. J. (2001). LIBSVM: a library for support vector machines. (Software available at http://www.csie.ntu edu.tw/~cjlin/libsvm)

Chang, P. C., Huang, W. H. & Ting, C. J. (2009). Dynamic diversity control in genetic algorithm for mining unsearched solution space in TSP problems. *Expert Systems with Applications*

Chatterjee, S., Carrera, C., & Lynch, L. A. (1996). Genetic algorithms and traveling salesman problems. *European Journal of Operational Research*, *93*, 490–510. doi:10.1016/C377-2217(95)00077-1

Chen, C. H., Ting, C. J., & Chang, P. C. (2005). Applying a hybrid ant colony system to the vehicle routing problem. In *Computational Science and Its Applications-ICCSA 2005* (*Vol. 3483*, pp. 417–426). Berlin, Heidelberg: Springer.

Chen, J. C., Wang, K. J., Wang, S. M., & Jang, S. J. (2008). Price negotiation for capacity sharing in two-factory environment using genetic algorithm. *International Journal of Production Research*, *46*(7), 1847–1868. doi:10.1080/00207540601008440

Chen, C.-L., & Lee, W.-C. (2004). Multi-objective optimization of multi-echelon supply chain networks with uncertain product demand and prices. *Computers & Chemical Engineering*, *28*(6-7), 1131–1144. doi:10.1016/j.compchemeng.2003.09.014

Chen, F. (1999). Decentralized supply chains subject to information delays. *Management Science*, *45*(9), 1076–1090. doi:10.1287/mnsc.45.8.1076

Chen, F., & Samroengraja, R. (2000). The stationary beer game. *Production and Operations Management*, *9*(1), 19–30. doi:10.1111/j.1937-5956.2000.tb00320.x

Chen, Y.(F.), Xu. M., & Zhang, Z.G. (2009). A Risk-Averse Newsvendor Model under the CVaR Criterion. *Operations Research*, *57*(4), 1040–1044. doi:10.1287/opre.1080.0603

Chen, M., & Chien, S. I. J. (2001). Dynamic freeway travel time prediction using probe vehicle data: link-based vs. path-based. In *Proceedings of the Transportation Research Board 80th Annual Meeting*, Washington, DC

Chen, S. H., & Ni, C. C. (1999). Using Genetic Algorithms to Simulate the Evolution of an Oligopoly Game. In *Simulated Evolution and Learning* (Vol. 1585, pp. 293-300).

Cheng, C. B., & Mao, C. P. (2007). A modified ant colony system for solving the traveling salesman problem with time windows. *Mathematical and Computer Modelling*, *46*, 1225–1235. doi:10.1016/j.mcm.2006.11.035

Chien, S. I. J., & Kuchipudi, C. M. (2003). Dynamic travel time prediction with real-time and historical data. In *Proceedings of the Transportation Research Board 81st Annual Meeting*, Washington, DC

Chitty, D. M., & Hernandez, M. L. (2004). A hybrid ant colony optimization technique for dynamic vehicle routing. In *Genetic and Evolutionary Computation-GECCO 2004* (*Vol. 3102*, pp. 48–59). Berlin, Heidelberg: Springer. doi:10.1007/978-3-540-24854-5_5

Chopra, S., & Meindl, P. (2004). *Supply Chain Management: Strategy, Planning and Operations*. New Jersey: Prentice Hall.

Chow, H. K. H., Choy, K. L., Lee, W. B., & Lau, K. C. (2006). Design of a RFID Case-Based Resource Management System for Warehouse Operations. *Expert Systems with Applications*, *30*, 561–576. doi:10.1016/j.eswa.2005.07.023

Christensen, S., & Oppacher, F. (2002). An analysis of Koza's computational effort statistic for genetic programming. In Foster, J. A., Lutton, E., Miller, J. F., Ryan, C., & Tettamanzi, A. (Eds.), *EuroGP* (*Vol. 2278*, pp. 182–191). Springer.

Christie, R. M. E., & Wu, S. D. (2002). Semiconductor capacity planning: Stochastic modeling and computational studies. *IIE Transactions*, *34*(2), 131–144. doi:10.1080/07408170208928856

Christofides, N. (1971). Fixed Routes and Areas for Delivery. *International Journal of Physical Distribution*, *1*, 87–92. doi:10.1108/eb038829

Chung, E. Warita, H., Bajwa, S., & Kuwahara, M. (2004). Travel Time Prediction: Issues and Benefits. In *Proceedings of the 10th World Conference on Transport Research* (CD-ROM), Istanbul, Turkey

Church, R.L. & ReVelle, C. (1974). The maximal covering location problem, Papers Region. *Sci. Assoc.*, *32*(1), 101–118. doi:10.1007/BF01942293

Clark, S. (2003). Traffic prediction using multivariate nonparametric regression. *Journal of Transportation Engineering*, *129*(2), 161–168. doi:10.1061/(ASCE)0733-947X(2003)129:2(161)

Clark, A., & Culkin, B. (2007). *A Network Transshipment Model for Planning Humanitarian Relief Operations after a Natural Disaster*. Paper presented at EURO XXII - 22nd European Conference on Operational Research, Prague.

Clark, S. D., Dougherty, M. S., & Kirby, H. R. (1993). The use of neural networks and time series models for short-term traffic forecasting: a comparative study. In *Proceedings of the PTRC 21st Summer Annual Meeting*.

Coakley, J., & Drexler, J.A., J., Larson, E., & Kircher, A. (1998). Using a computer-based version of the beer game: Lessons learned. *Journal of Management Education*, *22*(3), 416. doi:10.1177/105256299802200311

Cooke, J. (1993). The $30 billion promise. *Traffic Management*, *32*, 57–59.

Cooper, R. (1989). The Rise of Activity-Based Costing – Part Three: How Many Cost Drivers Do You Need and How Do You Select Them? *Journal of Cost Management*, 34-46.

Corrado, C., & Mattey, J. (1997). Capacity utilization. *The Journal of Economic Perspectives*, *11*, 151–167.

Cortes, C., & Vapnik, V. (1995). Support-vector networks. *Machine Learning*, *20*(3), 273–297. doi:10.1007/BF00994018

Cox, J. C., Ross, S. A., & Rubenstein, M. (1979). Option Pricing: A Simplified Approach. *Journal of Financial Economics*, *7*, 229–263. doi:10.1016/0304-405X(79)90015-1

Cranfield University (2003). Creating Resilient Supply Chains: A Practical Guide. Cranfield University, Department for Transport.

CRID. The Federal Response to Hurricane Katrina: Lessons Learned (2006, February 23) White House Homeland Security Council. Retrieved February 10, 2009 from http://www.crid.or.cr/digitalizacion/pdf/eng/doc17272/doc17272-0.pdf

Cristianini, N., & John, S.-T. (2000). *An Introduction to Support Vector Machines and other kernel-based learning methods*. Cambridge: Cambridge University Press.

Croom, S., Romano, P., & Giannakis, M. (2000). Supply chain management: an analytical framework for critical literature review. *European Journal of Purchasing & Supply Management*, *6*, 67–83. doi:10.1016/S0969-7012(99)00030-1

Croston, J. (1972). Forecasting and stock control for intermittent demands. *Operational Research Quarterly (1970-1977)*, *23*(3), 289–303.

da Cruz, A., Vellasco, M., & Pacheco, M. (2006, 16-21 July). Quantum-inspired evolutionary algorithm for numerical optimization. In *Proceedings of the 2006 IEEE Congress on Evolutionary Computation (CEC 2006)* (pp. 9180-9187). Vancouver, Canada: IEEE Press.

Dada, M., Petruzzi, N. C., & Schwarz, L. B. (2007). A Newsvendor's Procurement Problem when Suppliers are Unreliable. *Manufacturing & Service Operations Management, 9*(1), 9–32. doi:10.1287/msom.1060.0128

Dallery, Y., & Liberopoulos, G. (2000). Extended kanban control system: combining kanban and base stock. *IIE Transactions, 32*(4), 369–386. doi 10.1080/07408170008963914

Daniel, J. S. R., & Rajendran, C. (2005). A simulation-based genetic algorithm for inventory optimization in a serial supply chain. *International Journal in Operational Research, 12*(1), 101–127. doi:10.1111/j.1475-3995.2005.00492.x

Daskin, M. S. (1995). *Network and discrete location: Models, algorithms and applications*. New York: Wiley.

Davis, T. (1993). Effective supply chain management. *Sloan Management Review, 34*(4), 35–46.

Davis, G. A., Niham, N. L., Hamed, M. M., & Jacobson, L. N. (1991). Adaptive forecasting of freeway traffic congestion. *Transportation Research Record, 1287*, 29–33.

De Koster, R., Le-Duc, T., & Roodbergen, K. J. (2007). Design and Control of Warehouse Order Picking: A Literature Review. *European Journal of Operational Research, 182*(2), 481–501. doi:10.1016/j.ejor.2006.07.009

De Reyck, B., Degraeve, Z., & Vandenborre, R. (2008). Project options valuation with net present value and decision tree analysis. *European Journal of Operational Research, 184*, 341–355. doi:10.1016/j.ejor.2006.07.047

Dekker, R., de Koster, M. B. M., Roodbergen, K. J., & van Kalleveen, H. (2004). Improving Order-Picking Response Time at Ankor's Warehouse. *Interfaces, 34*(4), 303–313. doi:10.1287/inte.1040.0083

Dellaert, N., Jeunet, J., & Jonard, N. (2000). A genetic algorithm to solve the general multi-level lot-sizing problem with time-varying costs. *International Journal of Production Economics, 668*(3), 241–257. doi:10.1016/S0925-5273(00)00084-0

Desai, J., Sherali, H. D., & Glickman, T. S. (2004). Allocating emergency response resources to minimize risk under equity considerations. *American Journal of Mathematical and Management Sciences, 24*(3/4), 367–410.

Dimopoulos, C., & Mort, N. (2001). A hierarchical clustering methodology based on genetic programming for the solution of simple cell-formation problems. *International Journal of Production Research, 39*(1), 1–19. doi:10.1080/00207540150208835

Ding, C., Cheng, Y., & He, M. (2007). Two – level genetic algorithm for clustered traveling salesman problem with application in large – scale TSPs. *Tsinghua Science and Technology, 12*(4), 459–465. doi:10.1016/S1007-0214(07)70068-8

Disney, S. M., Naim, M. M., & Towill, D. R. (2000). Genetic algorithm optimization of a class of inventory control systems. *International Journal of Production Economics, 68*(3), 259–278. doi:10.1016/S0925-5273(99)00101-2

Dixit, A. K., & Pindyck, R. S. (1995). *The options approach to capital investment. Harvard Business Review*. May-June.

Doerner, K. F., Gutjahr, W. J., Hartl, R. F., & Lulli, G. (2008). Stochastic local search procedures for the probabilistic two – day vehicle routing problem. In *Advances in Computational Intelligence in Transport, Logistics, and Supply Chain Management* (*Vol. 144*, pp. 153–168). Berlin, Heidelberg: Springer. doi:10.1007/978-3-540-69390-1_8

Doerner, K. F., Hartl, R. F., Kiechle, G., Lucka, M., & Reimann, M. (2004). Parallel ant systems for the capacitated vehicle routing problem. In *Evolutionary Computation in Combinatorial Optimization* (*Vol. 3004*, pp. 72–83). Berlin, Heidelberg: Springer. doi:10.1007/978-3-540-24652-7_8

Dollinger, M. (1985). Environmental contacts and financial performance of the small firm. *Journal of Small Business Management*, *23*(1), 24–30.

Domoto, E., Okuhara, K., Ueno, N., & Ishii, H. (2007). Production Planning System with Multi-Stages for Controlling Bullwhip Effect by Using Particle Swarm Optimization. *Journal of Advanced Mechanical Design, Systems and Manufacturing*, *1*(3), 319–327. doi:10.1299/jamdsm.1.319

Donati, A. V., Montemanni, R., Casagrande, N., Rizzoli, A. E., & Gambardella, L. M. (2008). Time dependent vehicle routing problem with a multi ant colony system. *European Journal of Operational Research*, *185*, 1174–1191. doi:10.1016/j.ejor.2006.06.047

Donati, A. V., Darley, V., & Ramachandran, B. (2007). An Ant – bidding Algorithm for Multistage Flowshop Scheduling Problem: Optimization and Phase Transitions. *Advances in Metaheuristic for Hard optimization* (pp. 111- 136).

Dorigo, M., & Gambardella, L. M. (1997). Ant colonies for the travelling salesman problem. *Bio Systems*, *43*, 73–81. doi:10.1016/S0303-2647(97)01708-5

Dorigo, M., Maniezzo, V., & Colorni, A. (1996). Ant system: optimization by a colony of cooperating agents. *IEEE Transactions on Systems, Man, and Cybernetics*, *26*(1), 29–41. doi:10.1109/3477.484436

Driver, C. (2000). Capacity utilization and excess capacity: theory, evidence, and policy. *Review of Industrial Organization*, *16*, 69–87. doi:10.1023/A:1007864132477

Dror, M., Ball, M., & Golden, B. (1985). Computational comparison of algorithms for the inventory routing problem. *Annals of Operations Research*, *4*, 3–23. doi:10.1007/BF02022035

Dubey, P., Neyman, A., & Weber, R. J. (1981). Value theory without efficiency. *Mathematics of Operations Research*, *6*, 122–128. doi:10.1287/moor.6.1.122

Duran, S., Gutierrez, M. A., & Keskinocak, P. (2009). Pre-Positioning of Emergency Items Worldwide for CARE International. Retrieved January 28, 2009 from http://www.scl.gatech.edu/research/humanitarian/files/CAREPrepositioningofInventorypaper.pdf

Efendigil, T., Önüt, S., & Kahraman, C. (2009, Apr). A decision support system for demand forecasting with artificial neural networks and neuro-fuzzy models: A comparative analysis. *Expert Systems with Applications*, *36*(P2), 6697–6707. doi:10.1016/j.eswa.2008.08.058

EM-DAT. (n.d.). The OFDA/CRED International Disaster Database, Université Catholique de Louvain- Brussels – Belgium, UR. Retrieved January 20, 2009 from http://www.em-dat.net

Emshoff, J. R., & Sisson, R. L. (1970). *Design and Use of Computer Simulation Models*. New York: Macmillan.

Eng, T.-Y. (2004). The role of e-marketplaces in supply chain management. *Industrial Marketing Management*, *33*(2), 97–105. doi:10.1016/S0019-8501(03)00032-4

Eriksson, R., & Olsson, B. (1997). Cooperative coevolution in inventory control optimization. In *Proceedings of the Third International Conference on Artificial Neural Networks and Genetic Algorithms*.

Eubank, R. L. (1988). *Spline Smoothing and Nonparametric Regression*. New York: Marcel Dekker Inc.

Ezziane, Z. (2007). Artificial Intelligence and DNA Computing. In *Intelligent Computing Everywhere* (pp. 195–209). London: Springer. doi:10.1007/978-1-84628-943-9_10

Faber, N., de Koster, R., & Van de Velde, S. (2002). Linking Warehouse Complexity to Warehouse Planning and Control Structure. *International Journal of Physical Distribution and Logistics Management*, *32*(5), 381–395. doi:10.1108/09600030210434161

Fagnart, J.-F., Licandro, O., & Sneessens, H. R. (1997). Capacity utilization and market power. *Journal of Economic Dynamics & Control*, *22*, 123–140. doi:10.1016/S0165-1889(97)00050-X

Falcone, M. A., Lopes, H. S., & Coelho, L. D. S. (2008). Supply chain optimisation using evolutionary algorithms. *Int. J. Comput. Appl. Technol.*, *31*(3/4), 158–167. doi:10.1504/IJCAT.2008.018154

Fan K., O'Sullivan, C., Brabazon, A., O'Neill, M., & McGarraghy, S. (2008). Calibration of the VGSSD Option Pricing Model using a Quantum-inspired Evolutionary Algorithm. In Nedjah, N., dos Santos Coelho, L., & de Macedo Mourelle, L. (Eds.), *Quantum inspired intelligent systems* (pp. 133–153). Berlin, Heidelberg, Tokyo, New York: Springer-Verlag. doi:10.1007/978-3-540-78532-3_7

Fang, L., Chen, P., & Liu, S. (2007). Particle swarm optimization with simulated annealing for TSP. In *Proceedings of the 6th WSEAS International Conference on Artificial Intelligence* (pp. 206-210).

Farahani, R. Z., & Elahipanah, M. (2008). A genetic algorithm to optimize the total cost and service level for just-in-time distribution in a supply chain. *International Journal of Production Economics*, *111*(2), 229–243. doi:10.1016/j.ijpe.2006.11.028

Farmer, J. D., Packard, N. H., & Perelson, A. S. (1986). The immune system, adaptation, and machine learning. *Physica D. Nonlinear Phenomena*, *22*(1-3), 187–204. doi:10.1016/0167-2789(86)90240-X

Federgruen, A., & Yang, N. (2009). Optimal Supply Diversification under General Supply Risks. *Operations Research*, *57*(6), 1451–1468. doi:10.1287/opre.1080.0667

Ferretti, I., Zanoni, S., & Zavanella, L. (2006). Production – inventory scheduling using ant system metaheuristic. *International Journal of Production Economics*, *104*, 317–326. doi:10.1016/j.ijpe.2005.01.008

Fitzpatrick, J. M. & Grefenstette, J. J. (1988) Genetic algorithms in noisy environments. *Machine Learning: Special issue on genetic algorithms, 3*, 101-120.

Fleischmann, B., Gietz, M., & Grutzmann, S. (2004). Time-varying Travel Times in Vehicle Routing. *Transportation Science*, *38*(2), 160–174. doi:10.1287/trsc.1030.0062

Fogel, D. B. (1993). Applying evolutionary programming to selected traveling salesman problems. *Cybernetics and Systems*, *24*(1), 27–36. doi:10.1080/01969729308961697

Forrester, J. W. (1958). Industrial dynamics: a major break though for decision-makers. *Harvard Business Review*, *36*(4), 37–66.

Forrester, J. W. (1961). *Industrial dynamics*. Cambridge, Mass.: Productivity Press, Wiley.

Francas, D., & Minner, S. (2009). Manufacturing network configuration in supply chains with product recovery. *Omega*, *37*(4), 757–769. doi:10.1016/j.omega.2008.07.007

Francis, P. M., Smilowitz, K. R., & Tzur, M. (2008). The Period Vehicle Routing Problem and its Extensions. In Golden, B., Raghavan, S., & Wasil, E. (Eds.), *The Vehicle Routing Problem: Latest Advances and New Challenges* (pp. 73–102). Springer. doi:10.1007/978-0-387-77778-8_4

Frazelle, E. H. (2002). *World- Class Warehousing & Material Handling*. New York: McGraw Hill.

Fuellerer, G., Doerner, k. F., Hartl, R. F. & Iori, M. (2009). Metaheuristics for vehicle routing problems with three – dimensional loading constraints. *European Journal of Operational Research.*

Fuente, De La D. & Lozano, J. (2007). Application of distributed intelligence to reduce the bullwhip effect. *International Journal of Production Research, 45*(8), 1815-1833.

Gabszewicz, J. J., & Shitovitz, B. (1992). The Core in Imperfectly Competitive Economies. In R. Aumann & S. Hart, (Ed), *Handbook of Game Theory with Economic Applications*. Amsterdam, North-Holland: Elsevier.

Gajpal, Y., & Abad, P. L. (2009). Multi – ant colony system (MACS) for a vehicle routing problem with backhauls. *European Journal of Operational Research*, *196*, 102–117. doi:10.1016/j.ejor.2008.02.025

Gambardella, L. M., Rizzoli, A. E., Oliverio, F., Casagrande, N., Donati, A. V., Montemanni, R., & Lubicello, E. (2003). Ant Colony Optimization for vehicle routing in advanced logistics systems. In *Proceedings of the International Workshop on Modelling and Applied Simulation (MAS 2003)* (pp. 3-9).

Gardner, E. (1985). Exponential smoothing: The state of the art. *Journal of Forecasting*, *4*(1), 1–38. doi:10.1002/for.3980040103

Gardner, E. S. (1985b). Exponential smoothing: The state of the art — response. *Journal of Forecasting*, *4*(1), 37–38. doi:10.1002/for.3980040108

Geoffrion, A. M., & Graves, G. W. (1974). Multicommodity distribution system design by Benders decomposition. *Management Science*, *20*(5), 822–844. doi:10.1287/mnsc.20.5.822

Geoffrion, A. M., & van Roy, T. J. (1979). Caution: common sense planning methods can be hazardous to your corporate health. *Sloan Management Review*, *20*(4), 31–42.

Gershwin, S. B. (1994). *Manufacturing Systems Engineering*. New York: Prentice Hall.

Ghanmi, A., & Shaw, R. (2007). Modeling and analysis of Canadian Forces strategic lift and pre-positioning options. *The Journal of the Operational Research Society*, 1–12.

Ghariani, S., & Furnon, V. (2006). Constraint programming and ant colonies applied to vehicle routing problems. In *Metaheuristics for Hard Optimization* (pp. 307–326). Berlin, Heidelberg: Springer. doi:10.1007/3-540-30966-7_11

Gilbert, J. C., & Nocedal, J. (1992). Global convergence properties of conjugate gradient methods for optimization. *SIAM Journal on Optimization*, *2*(1), 21–42. doi:10.1137/0802003

Gillett, B. E., & Miller, L. R. (1974). A heuristic algorithm for the vehicle dispatch program. *Operations Research*, *22*(2), 340–349. doi:10.1287/opre.22.2.340

Gillies, D. B. (1953). *Some Theorems on N-Person Games*. Ph.D. Dissertation Department of Mathematics, Princeton University, Princeton, N.J.

Golany, B., Xia, Y., Yang, J., & Yu, G. (2002). An Interactive Goal-Programming Procedure for Operational Recovery Problems. *Optimization and Engineering*, *40*, 959–971.

Goldbarg, E. F. G., Sousa, G. R., & Goldbarg, M. C. (2006). Particle swarm for the traveling salesman problem. In *Evolutionary Computation in Combinatorial Optimization* (*Vol. 3906*, pp. 99–110). Berlin, Heidelberg: Springer. doi:10.1007/11730095_9

Golden, B., Raghavan, S., & Wasil, E. (Eds.). (2008). *The Vehicle Routing Problem: Latest Advances and New Challenges. Operations Research/Computer Science Interfaces Series*. Springer. doi:10.1007/978-0-387-77778-8

Gong, M., Jiao, L., & Zhang, L. (2006). Solving traveling salesman problems by artificial immune response. In *Simulated Evolution and Learning* (*Vol. 4247*, pp. 64–71). Berlin, Heidelberg: Springer. doi:10.1007/11903697_9

Gonsalves, T., & Itoh, K. (2008). Cost Minimization in Service Systems Using Particle Swarm Optimization. In *Software Engineering, Artificial Intelligence, Networking and Parallel* [). Berlin Heidelberg: Springer.]. *Distributed Computing*, *149*, 151–161.

Goodwin, J., & Franklin, S.G., S. (1994). The beer distribution game: Using simulation to teach systems thinking. *Journal of Management Development*, *13*(8), 7–15. doi:10.1108/02621719410071937

Gordon, B. H. (2003). The Changing Face of 3rd Party Logistics. *Supply Chain Management Review*, *7*(2), 50–57.

Gordon, G. (1969). *System Simulation*. Englewood Cliffs, NJ: Prentice Hall.

GPO. (n.d.). Hurricane Katrina: A Nation Still Unprepared, U.S. Senate Report 109-322. Retrieved July 24, 2007 from http://www.gpoaccess.gov/serialset/creports/pdf/sr109-322/ch24.pdf

Greiger, M. (2003). Electronic marketplaces: A literature review and a call for supply chain management research. *European Journal of Operational Research*, *144*, 280–294. doi:10.1016/S0377-2217(02)00394-6

Gu, J., Goetschakckx, M., & McGinnis, L. F. (2007). Research on Warehouse Operation: A Comprehensive Review. *European Journal of Operational Research*, *177*, 1–121. doi:10.1016/j.ejor.2006.02.025

Guillén, G., Mele, B., Bagajewicz, M. J., Espuña, A., & Puigjaner, L. (2005). Multi-objective supply chain design under uncertainty. *Chemical Engineering Science*, *60*(6), 1535–1553. doi:10.1016/j.ces.2004.10.023

Gümüs, A. T., & Güneri, A. F. (2007). Multi-echelon inventory management in supply chains with uncertain demand and lead times: literature review from an operational research perspective. *Journal Engineering Manufacture*, *221*(10), 1553–1570. doi:10.1243/09544054JEM889

Gunasekaran, A., Patel, C., & Tirtiroglu, E. (2001). Performance Measures and Metrics in a Supply Chain Environment. *International Journal of Operations & Production Management*, *21*(1/2), 71–87. doi 10.1108/01443570110358468

Guner, A. R. & Sevkli, M. (2008). A discrete particle swarm optimization algorithm for uncapacitated facility location problem. *Journal of Artificial Evolution and Applications*.

Guo, Y. W., Li, W. D., Mileham, A. R., & Owen, G. W. (2009). Applications of particle swarm optimization in integrated process planning and scheduling. *Robotics and Computer-integrated Manufacturing*, *25*, 280–288. doi:10.1016/j.rcim.2007.12.002

Gupta, R. K., Bhunia, A. K., & Goyal, S. K. (2009). An application of genetic algorithm in solving an inventory model with advance payment and interval valued inventory costs. *Mathematical and Computer Modelling*, *49*(5-6), 893–905. doi:10.1016/j.mcm.2008.09.015

Gupta, A., & Maranas, C. D. (2003). Managing demand uncertainty in supply chain planning. *Computers & Chemical Engineering*, *27*(8-9), 1219–1227. doi:10.1016/S0098-1354(03)00048-6

Gupta, A., Maranas, C. D., & McDonald, C. M. (2000). Mid-term supply chain planning under demand uncertainty: customer demand satisfaction and inventory management. *Computers & Chemical Engineering*, *24*(12), 2613–2621. doi:10.1016/S0098-1354(00)00617-7

Gurler, U., & Parlar, M. (1997). An Inventory Problem with Two Randomly Available Suppliers. *Operations Research*, *45*, 904–918. doi:10.1287/opre.45.6.904

Gutierrez, R. S., Solis, A. O., & Mukhopadhyay, S. (2008, February). Lumpy demand forecasting using neural networks. *International Journal of Production Economics*, *111*(2), 409–420. doi:10.1016/j.ijpe.2007.01.007

Guvenir, H. A., & Erel, E. (1998). Multicriteria inventory classification using a genetic algorithm. *European Journal of Operational Research*, *105*(1), 29–37. doi:10.1016/S0377-2217(97)00039-8

Hagan, M. T., & Menhaj, M. (1994). Training feedforward networks with the Marquardt algorithm. *IEEE Transactions on Neural Networks*, *5*(6), 989–993. doi:10.1109/72.329697

Haghani, A., & Oh, S. C. (1996). Formulation and solution of a multi-commodity, multi-modal network flow model for disaster relief operations. *Transportation Research Part A, Policy and Practice*, *30*(3), 231–250. doi:10.1016/0965-8564(95)00020-8

Hallgren, M., & Olhager, J. (2009). Flexibility configurations: empirical analysis of volume and product mix flexibility. *Omega*, *37*(4), 746–756. doi:10.1016/j.omega.2008.07.004

Hamed, M. M., Al-Masaeid, H. R., & Bani Said, Z. M. (1995). Short-term prediction of traffic volume in urban arterials. *Journal of Transportation Engineering*, *121*(3), 249–254. doi:10.1061/(ASCE)0733-947X(1995)121:3(249)

Hammel, U., & Bäck, T. (1994). Evolution strategies on noisy functions. How to improve convergence properties. *Parallel Problem Solving from Nature*, *3*, 159–168.

Han, C., & Damrongwongsiri, M. (2005). Stochastic modeling of a two-echelon multiple sourcing supply chain system with genetic algorithm. *Journal of Manufacturing Technology Management*, *16*(1), 87–108. doi:10.1108/17410380510574103

Han, Y., Tang, J., Kaku, I., & Mu, L. (2009). Solving uncapacitated multilevel lot-sizing problems using a particle swarm optimization with flexible inertial weight. *Computers & Mathematics with Applications (Oxford, England)*, *57*(11-12), 1748–1755. doi:10.1016/j.camwa.2008.10.024

Han, K.-H., & Kim, J.-H. (2002). Quantum-inspired evolutionary algorithm for a class of combinatorial optimization. *IEEE Transactions on Evolutionary Computation*, *6*(6), 580–593. doi:10.1109/TEVC.2002.804320

Han, K.-H., & Kim, J.-H. (2004). Quantum-inspired evolutionary algorithms with a new termination criterion, H_ε gate and two-phase scheme. *IEEE Transactions on Evolutionary Computation*, *8*(3), 156–169. doi:10.1109/TEVC.2004.823467

Hanshar, F. T., & Berman, B. M. O. (2007). Dynamic vehicle routing using genetic algorithms. *Applied Intelligence*, *27*, 89–99. doi:10.1007/s10489-006-0033-z

Hasuike, T., & Ishii, H. (2009). On flexible product-mix decision problems under randomness and fuzziness. *Omega*, *37*(4), 770–787. doi:10.1016/j.omega.2008.07.005

Haurie, A. (1995). Time Scale Decomposition in Production Planning for Unreliable Flexible Manufacturing System. *European Journal of Operational Research*, *82*, 339–358. doi:10.1016/0377-2217(94)00268-H

Heckert, J. B. (1940). *The Analysis and Control of Distribution Costs*. New York: Ronald Press Company.

Hendricks, K. B., & Singhal, V. R. (2005). Association between Supply Chain Glitches and Operating Performance. *Management Science*, *51*(5), 695–711. doi:10.1287/mnsc.1040.0353

Henig, M., & Gerchak, Y. (1990). The structure of periodic review policies in the presence of variable yield. *Operations Research*, *38*, 634–643. doi:10.1287/opre.38.4.634

Herrera-Viedma, E., & Peis, E. (2003). Evaluating the informative quality of documents in SGML format from judgments by means of fuzzy linguistic techniques based on computing with words. *Information Processing & Management*, *39*(2), 233–249. doi:10.1016/S0306-4573(02)00049-3

Ho, W., Ho, G. T. S., & Lau, H. C. W. (2008). A hybrid genetic algorithm for the multi – depot vehicle routing problem. *Engineering Applications of Artificial Intelligence*, *21*, 548–557. doi:10.1016/j.engappai.2007.06.001

Hoffman, W., Keedy, J., & Roberts, K. (2002). The unexpected return of B2B. *The McKinsey Quarterly*, 3.

Holland, J. (1975). *Adaptation in natural and artificial systems*. Ann Arbor, MI: University of Michigan Press.

Holmberg, S. (2000). A Systems Perspective on Supply Chain Measurements. *International Journal of Physical Distribution and Logistics Management*, *30*(10), 847–868. doi:10.1108/09600030010351246

Hong, S. P., & Kim, Y. H. (2009). A genetic algorithm for joint replenishment based on the exact inventory cost. *Computers & Operations Research*, *34*(1), 167–175. doi:10.1016/j.cor.2007.08.006

Hou, C., Du, H., & Jiao, L. (2005). An algorithm based on antibody immunodominance for TSP. In *Advances in Natural Computation* (*Vol. 3611*, pp. 876–879). Berlin, Heidelberg: Springer. doi:10.1007/11539117_123

Howard, R. (1960). *Dynamic Programming and Markov Processes. Massachussets*. MIT Press.

Howard, R. A. (1960). *Dynamic Programming and Markov Processes*. Cambridge, MA: MIT.

Hsich, L.-F., & Tsai, L. (2006). The Optimum Design of a Warehouse System on Order Picking Efficiency. *International Journal of Advanced Manufacturing Technology*, *28*, 626–637. doi:10.1007/s00170-004-2404-0

Hsu, C. M., Chen, K. Y., & Chen, M. C. (2005). Batching orders in warehouses by minimizing travel distance with genetic algorithms. *Computers in Industry*, *56*(2), 169–178. doi:10.1016/j.compind.2004.06.001

Hua, Z., Li, S., & Liang, L. (2006). Impact of demand uncertainty on supply chain cooperation of single-period products. *International Journal of Production Economics*, *100*(2), 268–284. doi:10.1016/j.ijpe.2004.11.007

Huang, S. H. & Lin, P. C. (2010). A modified ant colony optimization algorithm for multi-item inventory routing problems with demand uncertainty. *Transportation Research Part E: Logistics and Transportation Review*.

Hurrion, R. D. (1997). An example of simulation optimization using a neural network metamodel: finding the optimum number of kanbans in a manufacturing system. *The Journal of the Operational Research Society*, *48*(11), 1105–1112.

Hwang, H., Choi, B., & Lee, M. J. (2005). A model for shelf space allocation and inventory control considering location and inventory level effects on demand. *International Journal of Production Economics*, *97*(2), 185–195. doi 10.1016/j.ijpe.2004.07.003

Hwang, H. S. (2002). An improved model for vehicle routing problem with time constraint based on genetic algorithms. *Computers & Industrial Engineering*, *42*, 361–369. doi:10.1016/S0360-8352(02)00033-5

Hwang, H. S. (2002). Design of supply-chain logistics system considering service level. *Computers & Industrial Engineering*, *43*(1-2), 283–297. doi:10.1016/S0360-8352(02)00075-X

Hwang, H. S., & Cho, G. S. (2006). A Performance Evaluation Model for Order Picking Warehouse Design. *Computers & Industrial Engineering*, *51*, 335–342. doi:10.1016/j.cie.2005.10.002

Iakovou, E., Vlachos, D., & Xanthopoulos, A. (2007). An Analytical Methodological Framework for the Optimal Design of Resilient Supply Chains. *International Journal of Logistics Economics and Globalisation*, *1*, 1–20. doi:10.1504/IJLEG.2007.014498

Iakovou, I., Vlachos, D., & Xanthopoulos, A. (2010). A stochastic inventory management model for a dual sourcing supply chain with disruptions. *International Journal of Systems Science*, *41*(3), 315–324. doi:10.1080/00207720903326894

Iakovou, E., Ip, C. M., Douligeris, C., & Korde, A. (1996). Optimal location and capacity of emergency cleanup equipment for oil spill response. *European Journal of Operational Research*, *96*(1), 72–80. doi:10.1016/S0377-2217(96)00106-3

Ichoua, S., Gendreau, M., & Potvin, J. Y. (2007). Planned Routes Approaches for Real-Time Vehicle Routing. In *Dynamic Fleet Management: Concepts, Systems, Algorithms & Case Studies*. New York: Springer-Verlag.

Ichoua, S., Gendreau, M., & Potvin, J. Y. (2006). Exploiting Knowledge about Future Demands for Real-Time Vehicle Dispatching. *Transportation Science*, *40*(2), 211–225. doi:10.1287/trsc.1050.0114

Ichoua, S., Gendreau, M., & Potvin, J. Y. (2003). Vehicle dispatching with time-dependent travel times. *European Journal of Operational Research*, *144*, 379–396. doi:10.1016/S0377-2217(02)00147-9

Ierapetritou, M. G., Pistikopoulos, E. N., & Floudas, C. A. (1996). Operational planning under uncertainty. *Computers & Chemical Engineering*, *20*(12), 1499–1516. doi:10.1016/0098-1354(95)00235-9

Ip, W. H., Huang, M., Yung, K. L., & Wang, D. (2003). Genetic algorithm solution for a risk-based partner selection problem in a virtual enterprise. *Computers & Operations Research*, *30*(2), 213–231. doi:10.1016/S0305-0548(01)00092-2

Ishak, S., & Alecsandru, C. (2003). Optimizing traffic prediction performance of Neural networks under various topological, input and traffic condition settings. In *Proceedings of the Transportation Research Board 82nd Annual Meeting*, Washington, DC

Izquierdo, J., Minciardi, R., Montalvo, I., Robba, M., & Tavera, M. (2008). Particle swarm optimization for the biomass supply chain strategic planning. In *Proceedings of the International Congress on Environmental Modeling and Software* (pp. 1272 – 1280).

Jacobs, F. (2000). Playing the beer distribution game over the internet. *Production and Operations Management*, *9*(1), 31–39. doi:10.1111/j.1937-5956.2000.tb00321.x

Jain, B. A., & Nag, B. N. (1996). A decision-support model for investment decisions in new ventures. *European Journal of Operational Research*, *90*, 473–486. doi:10.1016/0377-2217(95)00154-9

Jarmain, W., & Fey, W. (1963). *Problems in industrial dynamics*. Cambridge, MA: The MIT Press.

Jenkins, W. O., Jr. (2007, March 9). Homeland Security: Preparing for and Responding to Disasters, homeland security and justice issues, before the Subcommittee on Homeland Security, House Committee on Appropriations. GAO-07-395T. Retrieved February 10, 2009 from http://www.gao.gov/cgi-bin/getrpt?GAO-07-395T

Jeon, G., Leep, H. R., & Shim, J. Y. (2007). A vehicle routing problem solved by using a hybrid genetic algorithm. *Computers & Industrial Engineering*, *53*, 680–692. doi:10.1016/j.cie.2007.06.031

Jeong, B., Jung, H. S., & Park, N. K. (2002). A computerized causal forecasting system using genetic algorithms in supply chain management. *Journal of Systems and Software*, *60*(3), 223–237. doi:10.1016/S0164-1212(01)00094-2

Jia, H., Ordonez, F. & Dessouky, M. (2007). A modeling framework for facility location of medical services for large-scale emergencies. *IIE Transactions, 39*(1), 41-55(15).

Joachims, T. (2002). *SVM light,* http://svmlight.joachims.org. An implementation of Support Vector Machines (SVMs) in C. http://svmlight. joachims. org.

Julka, N., Baines, T., Tjahjonob, B., Lendermanna, P., & Vitanov, V. (2007). A review of multi-factor capacity expansion models for manufacturing plants: Searching for a holistic decision aid. *International Journal of Production Economics*, *106*(2), 607–621. doi:10.1016/j.ijpe.2006.08.002

Kannai, Y. (1992). The Core and the Balancedness. In R. Aumann & S. Hart, (Ed), *Handbook of Game Theory with Economic Applications*. Amsterdam, North-Holland: Elsevier.

Karaesmen, F., & Dallery, Y. (2000). A performance comparison of pull type control mechanisms for multi-stage manufacturing. *International Journal of Production Economics*, *68*, 59–71. doi:10.1016/S0925-5273(98)00246-1

Karlsson, M., & Yakowitz, S. (1987). Rainfall runoff forecasting methods old and new. *Stochastic Hydrology and Hydraulics*, *1*, 303–318. doi:10.1007/BF01543102

Karsak, E. E., & Tolga, E. (2001). Fuzzy multi-criteria decision-making procedure for evaluating advanced manufacturing system investments. *International Journal of Production Economics*, *69*(1), 49–64. doi:10.1016/S0925-5273(00)00081-5

Katayama, K., Sakamoto, H., & Narihisa, H. (2000). The efficiency of hybrid mutation genetic algorithm for the traveling salesman problem. *Mathematical and Computer Modelling*, *31*, 197–203. doi:10.1016/S0895-7177(00)00088-1

Kaufman, L., & Rousseeuw, P. (1990). *Finding Groups in Data: an Introduction to Cluster Analysis*. New York: John Wiley & Sons.

Kemball-Cook, D., & Stephenson, R. (1984). Lessons in logistics from Somalia. *Disasters*, *8*, 57–66. doi:10.1111/j.1467-7717.1984.tb00853.x

Kennedy, J., & Eberhart, R. (1995). Particle Swarm Optimization. In *Proceedings of the IEEE international conference on neural networks* (Vol. 4, pp. 1942 -1948).

Keren, B. (2009). The single-period Inventory Problem: Extension to Random Yield from the Perspective of the Supply Chain. *Omega: The International Journal of Management Science*, *37*(4), 801–810. doi:10.1016/j.omega.2008.07.006

Khemani, K. (2007). Bringing Rigor to Risk Management. *Supply Chain Management Review*, *11*(2), 67–80.

Khosrow-Pour, M. (2005). Advanced Topics in Electronic Commerce: *Vol. 1*. (*Advanced Topics in Electronic Commerce Series*). Hershey, PA: IGI Publishing.

Khouja, M., Michalewicz, Z., & Wilmot, M. (1998). The use of genetic algorithms to solve the economic lot size scheduling problem. *European Journal of Operational Research*, *110*(3), 509–524. doi:10.1016/S0377-2217(97)00270-1

Khouja, M. (1999). The Single Period (News-vendor) Problem: Literature Review and Suggestions for Future Research. *Omega: The International Journal of Management Science*, *27*, 537–553. doi:10.1016/S0305-0483(99)00017-1

Kim, M. C., Kim, C. O., Hong, S. R., & Kwon, I. H. (2008). Forward-backward analysis of RFID-enabled supply chain using fuzzy cognitive map and genetic algorithm. *Expert Systems with Applications*, *35*(3), 1166–1176. doi:10.1016/j.eswa.2007.08.015

Kim, H. Y. (1999). Economic capacity utilization and its determinants: theory and evidence. *Review of Industrial Organization*, *15*, 321–339. doi:10.1023/A:1007747813591

Kimbrough, S. O., Wu, D. J., & Zhong, F. (2002). Computers play the beer game: can artificial agents manage supply chains? *Decision Support Systems*, *33*(3), 323–333. doi:10.1016/S0167-9236(02)00019-2

Kleinau, P., & Thonemann, U. W. (2004). Deriving inventory-control policies with genetic programming. *OR-Spektrum*, *26*(4), 521–546. doi:10.1007/s00291-004-0159-5

Klibi, W., Lasalle, F., Martel, A., & Ichoua, S. (2010). The Stochastic Multi-Period Location Transportation Problem. *Transportation Science*, *44*, 221–237. doi:10.1287/trsc.1090.0307

Knight, P. (2003). *Supply Chain Security Guidelines*, IBM Corporation, Import Compliance Office.

Knott, R. (1987). The logistics of bulk relief supplies. *Disasters*, *11*, 113–115. doi:10.1111/j.1467-7717.1987.tb00624.x

Knott, R. (1988). Vehicle scheduling for emergency relief management: A knowledge-based approach. *Disasters*, *12*, 285–293. doi:10.1111/j.1467-7717.1988.tb00678.x

Kochel, P., & Nielander, U. (2005). Simulation-based optimization of multi-echelon inventory systems. *International Journal of Production Economics*, *93-94*, 505–513. doi:10.1016/j.ijpe.2004.06.046

Kochel, P., & Theim, S. (in press). Search for good policies in a single-warehouse, multi-retailer system by particle swarm optimization. *International Journal of Production Economics*.

Kogan, K., Charles, S., & Tapiero, C. S. (2009). Optimal co-investment in supply chain infrastructure. *European Journal of Operational Research*, *192*, 265–276. doi:10.1016/j.ejor.2007.08.038

Kogan, K., & Tapiero, C.S. (2007). *Supply Chain Games: Operations Management and Risk Valuation*. Springer.

Koren, Y. U., Heisel, J.F., Moriwaki, T., Pritschow, G., Ulsoy, G., & Van Brussel, H. (1999). Reconfigurable Manufacturing Systems. *Annals of the CIRP*, 48/2, Keynote Paper.

Koulouriotis, D. E., Xanthopoulos, A. S., & Tourassis, V. D. (2010). Simulation optimisation of pull control policies for serial manufacturing lines and assembly manufacturing systems using genetic algorithms. *International Journal of Production Research*, *48*(10), 2887–2912. doi:10.1080/00207540802603759

Koulouriotis, D. E., Xanthopoulos, A. S., & Gasteratos, A. (2008). A Reinforcement Learning Approach for Production Control in Manufacturing Systems. In *1st International Workshop on Evolutionary and Reinforcement Learning for Autonomous Robot Systems*, (pp. 24-31). Patra, Greece.

Koza, R. J. (1992). *Genetic Programming: On the Programming of Computers by means of Natural Selection*. Cambridge, MA: MIT Press.

Kubiak, M., & Wesolek, P. (2007). Accelerating local search in a memetic algorithm for the capacitated vehicle routing problem. In *Evolutionary Computation in Combinatorial Optimization* (*Vol. 4446*, pp. 96–107). Berlin, Heidelberg: Springer. doi:10.1007/978-3-540-71615-0_9

Kumar, R., & Singh, P. K. (2007). Pareto evolutionary algorithm hybridized with local search for biobjective TSP. In *Hybrid Evolutionary Algorithms* (*Vol. 75*, pp. 361–398). Berlin, Heidelberg: Springer. doi:10.1007/978-3-540-73297-6_14

Kumar, V., Prakash, Tiwari, M. K. & Chan, F. T. S. (2006). Stochastic make-to-stock inventory deployment problem: an endosymbiotic psychoclonal algorithm based approach. *International Journal of Production Research*, *44*(11), 2245–2263. doi:10.1080/00207540500459678

Kuo, C.-H., Dunn, K. D., & Randhawa, S. U. (1999). A Case Study Assessment of Performance Measurement in Distribution Centers. *Industrial Management & Data Systems*, *99*(2), 54–63. doi:10.1108/02635579910261068

Kurbel, K., & Loutchko, I. (2005). A model for multilateral negotiations on an agent-based job marketplace. *Electronic Commerce Research and Applications*, *4*(3), 187–203. doi:10.1016/j.elerap.2005.01.002

Kwon, E., & Stephanedes, Y. J. (1994). Comparative evaluation of adaptive and neural-network exitdemand prediction for freeway control. *Transportation Research Record*, *1446*, 66–76.

Labadi, N., Prins, C., & Reghioui, M. (2008). An evolutionary algorithm with distance measure for the split delivery capacitated arc routing problem. In *Recent Advances in Evolutionary Computation for Combinatorial Optimization* (*Vol. 153*, pp. 275–294). Berlin, Heidelberg: Springer. doi:10.1007/978-3-540-70807-0_17

Lacomme, P., Prins, C., & Cherif, W. R. (2004). Cooperative memetic algorithms for arc routing problems. *Annals of Operations Research*, *131*, 159–185. doi:10.1023/B:ANOR.0000039517.35989.6d

LaLonde, B. J., & Pohlen, T. L. (1996). Issues in Supply Chain Costing. *The International Journal of Logistics Management*, *7*(1), 1–12. doi:10.1108/09574099610805395

Lambert, D. M., & Pohlen, T. L. (2001). Supply Chain Metrics. *The International Journal of Logistics Management*, *12*(1), 1–19. doi:10.1108/09574090110806190

Lan, Y. F., Liu, Y. K., & Sun, G. J. (2009). Modeling fuzzy multi – period production planning and sourcing problem with credibility service levels. *Journal of Computational and Applied Mathematics*, *231*, 208–221. doi:10.1016/j.cam.2009.02.009

Lapide, L., & Happen, I. (2000). What About Measuring Supply Chain Performance? *Achieving Supply Chain Excellence Through Technology*. Retrieved from http://lapide.ASCET.com

Larson, R. C., Metzger, M. D., & Cahn, M. F. (2005). Emergency Response for Homeland Security: Lessons Learned and the Need for Analysis. Retrieved June 2, 2008 from http://www.sdcorp.net/public/Pub_Emergency_Response_Homeland_Security.pdf

Laruelle, A., & Valenciano, F. (2008). Potential, value, and coalition formation. *TOP: An Official Journal of the Spanish Society of Statistics and Operations Research*, *16*, 73–89.

Lathia, N., Amatriain, X., & Pujol, J. (2009, July). Collaborative Filtering With Adaptive Information Sources. In *Ijcai workshop on intelligent techniques for web personalisation and recommender systems.* Pasadena.

Law A., & Kelton, D. (2000). *Simulation Modelling and Analysis*. New York: McGraw Hill.

LCP Consulting, Centre for Logistics and Supply Chain Management (2003). *Understanding Supply Chain Risk: a Self-Assessment Workbook*. Cranfield University: School of Management, Department for Transport.

Le Riche, R., Knopf-Lenoir, C., & Haftka, R. T. (1995). A Segregated Genetic Algorithm for Constrained Structural Optimization. In *Sixth International Conference on Genetic Algorithms* (pp. 558-565).

Lechner, C., & Dowling, M. (2003). Firm networks: external relationships as sources for the growth and competitiveness of entrepreneurial firms. *Entrepreneurship and Regional Development, 15*, 1–26. doi:10.1080/08985620210159220

Le-Duc, T., & de Koster, R. M. B. M. (2007). Travel Time Estimation and Order Batching in a 2-Block Warehouse. *European Journal of Operational Research, 176*, 374–388. doi:10.1016/j.ejor.2005.03.052

Lee, C. Y., Lee, Z. J., Lin, S. W., & Ying, K. C. (2008). An enhanced ant colony optimization (EACO) applied to capacitated vehicle routing problem. *Applied Intelligence, 32*(1), 88–95. doi:10.1007/s10489-008-0136-9

Lee, H. L., Padmanabhan, V., & Whang, S. (1997). Information distortion in a supply chain: The bullwhip effect. *Management Science, 43*(4), 546–558. doi:10.1287/mnsc.43.4.546

Lee, J. Y., Shin, S. Y., Park, T. H., & Zhang, B. T. (2004). Solving traveling salesman problems with DNA molecules encoding numerical values. *Bio Systems, 78*, 39–47. doi:10.1016/j.biosystems.2004.06.005

Lee, Y. H., Jeong, C. S., & Moon, C. (2002). Advanced planning and scheduling with outsourcing in manufacturing supply chain. *Computers & Industrial Engineering, 43*(1-2), 351–374. doi:10.1016/S0360-8352(02)00079-7

Lee, H., Padmanabhan, V., & Whang, S. (1997b). Information distortion in a supply chain: the bullwhip effect. *Management Science, 43*(4), 546–558. doi:10.1287/mnsc.43.4.546

Lee, H. L., Padmanabhan, V., & Whang, S. (1997a). The bullwhip effect in supply chains. *Sloan Management Review, 38*(3), 93–102.

Lerman, K., & Shehory, O. (2000). Coalition formation for large scale electronic markets. In *Proceedings of the 4th International Conference on Multi agent Systems ICMAS(2000),* July 2000.

Levin, M., & Tsao, Y.-D. (1980). On forecasting freeway occupancies and volumes. *Transportation Research Record, 773*, 47–49.

Li, L., & Zhang, Y. (2007). An improved genetic algorithm for the traveling salesman problem. In *Advanced Intelligent Computing Theories and Applications. With Aspects of Contemporary Intelligent Computing Techniques* (*Vol. 2*, pp. 208–216). Berlin, Heidelberg: Springer. doi:10.1007/978-3-540-74282-1_24

Li, S. G., & Kuo, X. (2008). The inventory management system for automobile spare parts in a central warehouse. *Expert Systems with Applications, 34*(2), 1144–1153. doi:10.1016/j.eswa.2006.12.003

Li, S. G., & Rong, Y. L. (2009). The reliable design of one – piece flow production system using fuzzy ant colony optimization. *Computers & Operations Research, 36*, 1656–1663. doi:10.1016/j.cor.2008.03.010

Li, X., & Tian, P. (2006). An ant colony system for the open vehicle routing problem. In *Ant Colony Optimization and Swarm Intelligence* (*Vol. 4150*, pp. 356–363). Berlin, Heidelberg: Springer. doi:10.1007/11839088_33

Li, Y., & Gong, S. (2003). Dynamic ant colony optimization for TSP. *International Journal of Advanced Manufacturing Technology, 22*, 528–533. doi:10.1007/s00170-002-1478-9

Liang, W. Y., & Huang, C. C. (2006). Agent-based demand forecast in multi-echelon supply chain. *Decision Support Systems, 42*(1), 390–407. doi:10.1016/j.dss.2005.01.009

Liberopoulos, G., & Dallery, Y. (2000). A unified framework for pull control mechanisms in multi-stage manufacturing systems. *Annals of Operations Research, 93*, 325–355. doi:10.1023/A:1018980024795

Lin, C. T., & Chen, Y. T. (2004). Bid/no-bid decision-making – A fuzzy linguistic approach. *International Journal of Project Management*, *22*(7), 585–593. doi:10.1016/j.ijproman.2004.01.005

Lingras, P., & Mountford, P. (2001). Time delay neural networks designed using genetic algorithms for short-term inter-city traffic forecasting, IEA/AIE 2001 (LNAI 2070, pp. 290–299).

Liu, B., Wang, L., & Jin, Y. H. (2007). An effective hybrid particle swarm optimization for no – wait flow shop scheduling. *International Journal of Advanced Manufacturing Technology*, *31*, 1001–1011. doi:10.1007/s00170-005-0277-5

Liu, F., & Zeng, G. (2009). Study of genetic algorithm with reinforcement learning to solve the TSP. *Expert Systems with Applications*, *36*, 6995–7001. doi:10.1016/j.eswa.2008.08.026

Liu, H., & Abraham, A. (2007). An hybrid fuzzy variable neighborhood particle swarm optimization algorithm for solving quadratic assignment problems. *Journal of Universal Computer Science*, *13*(9), 1309–1331.

Liu, S., Huang, W., & Ma, H. (2009). An effective genetic algorithm for the fleet size and mix vehicle routing problems. *Transportation Research Part E, Logistics and Transportation Review*, *45*, 434–445. doi:10.1016/j.tre.2008.10.003

Liu, X., Qi, H., & Chen, Y. (2006). Optimization of special vehicle routing problem based on ant colony system. [). Berlin Heidelberg: Springer.]. *Computational Intelligence*, *4114*, 1228–1233. doi:10.1007/978-3-540-37275-2_153

Liu, A., Deng, G. & Shan, S. (2006). Mean contribution ant system: an improved version of ant colony optimization for travelling salesman problem (Vol. 4247, pp. 489 – 496).

Lorenzen, T. J., & Anderson, V. (1993). *Design of Experiments. Statistics Series: textbooks and Monographs* (*Vol. 139*). CRC Press.

Loreto, T., & Martinelli, G. (2007). Novel pheromone updating strategy for speeding up ACO applied to VRP. In *Biological and Artificial Intelligence Environments* (pp. 175–182). The Netherlands: Springer.

Louta, M., Roussaki, I., & Pechlivanos, L. (2008). An intelligent agent negotiation strategy in the electronic marketplace environment. *European Journal of Operational Research*, *187*(3), 1327–1345. doi:10.1016/j.ejor.2006.09.016

Lu, J., Humphreys, P., McIvor, R., & Maguire, L. (2007). Emplying genetic algorithms to minimize the bullwhip effect in a supply chain. In *Proceedings of the IEEE International Conference on Industrial Engineering and Engineering Management* (pp. 1527-1531).

Luke, S., & Panait, L. (2002). Is the perfect the enemy of the good? In Langdon, W. B. (Eds.), *GECCO* (pp. 820–828). New York: Morgan Kaufmann.

Mahnam, M., Yadollahpour, M. R., Dasdashti, V. F., & Hejazi, S. R. (2009). Supply chain modeling in uncertain environment with bi – objective approach. *Computers & Industrial Engineering*, *56*, 1535–1544. doi:10.1016/j.cie.2008.09.038

Maiti, A. K., Bhunia, A. K., & Maiti, M. (2006). An application of real-coded genetic algorithm (RCGA) for mixed integer non-linear programming in two-storage multi-item inventory model with discount policy. *Applied Mathematics and Computation*, *183*(2), 903–915. doi:10.1016/j.amc.2006.05.141

Maiti, M. K., & Maiti, M. (2007). Two-storage inventory model with lot-size dependent fuzzy lead-time under possibility constraints via genetic algorithm. *European Journal of Operational Research*, *179*(2), 352–371. doi:10.1016/j.ejor.2006.03.029

Makridakis, S., Wheelwright, S. C., & Hyndman, R. J. (1998). *Forecasting: Methods and applications* (3rd ed.). Chichester, UK-Hoboken, NJ: John Wiley & Sons.

Maladraki, C., & Daskin, M. S. (1992). Time dependent vehicle routing problems: Formulations, properties and heuristic algorithms. *Transportation Science, 26*, 185–200. doi:10.1287/trsc.26.3.185

Malmborg, C. J. (1996). A genetic algorithm for service level based vehicle scheduling. *European Journal of Operational Research, 93*, 121–134. doi:10.1016/0377-2217(95)00185-9

Manfrin, M., Birattari, M., Stultze, T., & Dorigo, M. (2006). Parallel ant colony optimization for the traveling salesman problem. In *Ant Colony Optimization and Swarm Intelligence* (*Vol. 4150*, pp. 224–234). Berlin, Heidelberg: Springer. doi:10.1007/11839088_20

Mansouri, S. A. (2005). Coordination of set-ups between two stages of a supply chain using multi-objective genetic algorithms. *International Journal of Production Research, 43*(15), 3163–3180. doi:10.1080/00207540500103821

Manzini, R., Gamberi, M., Persona, A., & Regattieri, A. (2007). Design of a Class Based Storage Picker to Product Order Picking System. *International Journal of Advanced Manufacturing Technology, 32*, 811–821. doi:10.1007/s00170-005-0377-2

Marien, E. (1999, Jan). Demand planning and sales forecasting: A supply chain essential. *Supply Chain Management Review*.

Marinakis, Y., & Marinaki, M. (2008). A particle swarm optimization algorithm with path relinking for the location routing problem. *Journal of Mathematical Modelling and Algorithms, 7*, 59–78. doi:10.1007/s10852-007-9073-6

Marinakis, Y., & Marinaki, M. (2009). A hybrid multi – swarm particle swarm optimization algorithm for the probabilistic traveling salesman problem. *Computers & Operations Research, 37*, 432–442. doi:10.1016/j.cor.2009.03.004

Marinakis, Y., Migdalas, A., & Pardalos, P. M. (2007). A new bilevel formulation for the vehicle routing problem and a solution method using a genetic algorithm. *Journal of Global Optimization, 38*, 555–580. doi:10.1007/s10898-006-9094-0

Marinakis, Y. & Marinaki, M. (2009). A hybrid genetic – particle swarm optimization algorithm for the vehicle routing problem. *Expert Systems with Applications*.

Marinakis, Y., Marinaki, M., & Dounias, G. (2008). Honey bees mating optimization algorithm for the vehicle routing problem. In *Nature Inspired Cooperative Strategies for Optimization (NISCO 2007)* (Vol. 129, pp. 139 – 148). Berlin Heidelberg: Springer.

Martinez, C. G., Gordon, O., & Herrera, F. (2007). A taxonomy and an empirical analysis of multiple objective ant colony optimization algorithms for the bi – criteria TSP. *European Journal of Operational Research, 180*, 116–148. doi:10.1016/j.ejor.2006.03.041

Massim, Y., Yalaoui, F., Amodeo, L., Chatelet, E., & Zeblah, A. (2010). Efficient combined immune-decomposition algorithm for optimal buffer allocation in production lines for throughput and profit maximization. *Computers & Operations Research, 37*(4), 611–620. doi:10.1016/j.cor.2009.06.016

Masutti, T. A. S., & Castro, L. N. (2008). A neuro – immune algorithm to solve the capacitated vehicle routing problem. In *Artificial Immune Systems* (*Vol. 5132*, pp. 210–219). Berlin, Heidelberg: Springer. doi:10.1007/978-3-540-85072-4_19

Matos, A. C., & Oliveira, R. C. (2004). An experimental study of the ant colony system for the period vehicle routing problem. In *Ant Colony, Optimization and Swarm Intelligence* (*Vol. 3172*, pp. 286–293). Berlin, Heidelberg: Springer. doi:10.1007/978-3-540-28646-2_26

Meadows, D. (2007). A brief and incomplete history of operational gaming in system dynamics. *System Dynamics Review, 23*(2), 199–203. doi:10.1002/sdr.372

Mehrabi, M. G., Ulsoy, A. G., & Koren, Y. (2000). Reconfigurable manufacturing systems: Key to future manufacturing. *Journal of Intelligent Manufacturing, 11*, 403–419. doi:10.1023/A:1008930403506

Meixell, M. J., & Gargeya, V. B. (2005). Global Supply Chain Design: A Literature Review and Critique. *Transportation Research Part E, Logistics and Transportation Review*, *41*, 531–550. doi:10.1016/j.tre.2005.06.003

Melo, M. T., Nickel, S., & Saldanha da Gama, F. (2006). Dynamic multi-commodity capacitated facility location: a mathematical modeling framework for strategic supply chain planning. *Computers & Operations Research*, *33*(1), 181–208. doi:10.1016/j.cor.2004.07.005

Mentzer, J. T., & Konrad, B. P. (1991). An Efficiency/Effectiveness Approach to Logistics Performance Analysis. *Journal of Business Logistics*, *12*(1), 33–61.

Mete, H. O., & Zabinsky, Z. B. (2009). Preparing for Disasters: Medical Supply Location and Distribution. Retrieved January 25, 2009 from http://parvac.washington.edu/papers/downloadpaper.php/id=13/parvac_13.pdf

Miller, T. L., & Park, C. S. (2002). Decision Making Under Uncertainty-Real Options to the Rescue? *The Engineering Economist*, *47*, 105–150. doi:10.1080/00137910208965029

Min, H., Ko, H. J., & Ko, C. S. (2006). A genetic algorithm approach to developing the multi-echelon reverse logistics network for product returns. *Omega*, *34*(1), 56–69. doi:10.1016/j.omega.2004.07.025

Min, H. (2009). Artificial intelligence in supply chain management: theory and applications. *International Journal of Logistics Research and Applications*, *13*(1), 13–39. doi:10.1080/13675560902736537

Min, H., & Zhou, G. (2002). Supply Chain Modeling: Past, Present and Future. *Computers & Industrial Engineering*, *43*, 231–249. doi:10.1016/S0360-8352(02)00066-9

Minis, I., & Ampazis, N. (2006). Applications of neural networks in supply chain management. In Rennard, J. P. (Ed.), *Handbook of research on nature inspired computing for economics and management* - (*Vol. 2*). Hershey, PA: Idea Group Reference.

Minner, S. (2003). Multiple-supplier Inventory Models in Supply Chain Management: a Review. *International Journal of Production Economics*, *81-82*, 265–279. doi:10.1016/S0925-5273(02)00288-8

Mitra, K., Gudi, R. D., Patwardham, S. C., & Sardar, G. (2008). Mid-term supply chain planning under uncertainty: a multi-objective chance constrained programming framework. *Industrial & Engineering Chemistry Research*, *47*(15), 5501–5511. doi:10.1021/ie0710364

Mittenhal, J., & Noon, C. E. (1992). An insert/delete heuristic for the traveling salesman subset-tour problem with one additional constraint. *The Journal of the Operational Research Society*, *43*(3), 277–283.

Mladenovic, N., & Hansen, P. (1997). Variable neighbourhood search. *Computers & Operations Research*, *24*, 1097–1100. doi:10.1016/S0305-0548(97)00031-2

Moghadam, M. R. S., Afsar, A., & Sohrabi, B. (2008). Inventory lot-sizing with supplier selection using hybrid intelligent algorithm. *Applied Soft Computing*, *8*(4), 1523–1529. doi:10.1016/j.asoc.2007.11.001

Mohamed, S., & McCowan, A. K. (2001). Modelling project investment decisions under uncertainty using possibility theory. *International Journal of Project Management*, *19*, 231–241. doi:10.1016/S0263-7863(99)00077-0

Moinzadeh, K., & Aggarwal, P. K. (1997). Analysis of a Production/Inventory System subject to Random Disruptions. *Management Science*, *43*, 1577–1588. doi:10.1287/mnsc.43.11.1577

Montemanni, R., Gambardella, L. M., Rizzoli, A. E., & Donati, A. V. (2005). Ant colony system for a dynamic vehicle routing problem. *Journal of Combinatorial Optimization*, *10*, 327–343. doi:10.1007/s10878-005-4922-6

Montemanni, R. Gambardella, L.M., Rizzoli, A.E., & Donati, A.E. (2002). A new algorithm for a Dynamic Vehicle Routing Problem based on Ant Colony System (Technical Report IDSIA-23-02). IDSIA. Retrieved December 2009 from ftp://ftp.idsia.ch/pub/techrep/IDSIA-23-02.pdf.gz

Moon, C., Kim, J., Choi, G., & Seo, Y. (2002). An efficient genetic algorithm for the traveling salesman problem with precedence constraints. *European Journal of Operational Research*, *140*, 606–617. doi:10.1016/S0377-2217(01)00227-2

Moon, C., Kim, J., & Hur, S. (2002). Integrated process planning and scheduling with minimizing total tardiness in multi-plants supply chain. *Computers & Industrial Engineering*, *43*(1-2), 331–349. doi:10.1016/S0360-8352(02)00078-5

Moon, I., Silver, E. A., & Choi, S. (2002). Hybrid genetic algorithm for the economic lot-scheduling problem. *International Journal of Production Research*, *40*(4), 809–824. doi:10.1080/00207540110095222

Moore, S. A., & DeMaagd, K. (2006). Using genetic programming to search for supply chain reordering policies. In *Genetic Programming Theory and Practice II* (*Vol. 8*, pp. 207–223). Springer. doi:10.1007/0-387-23254-0_13

Moore, S., & DeMaagd, K. (2004). *Using a genetic program to search for supply chain reordering*. Berlin, Heidelberg, Tokyo, New York: Springer-Verlag.

Mosekilde, E., & Larsen, E. (1988). Deterministic chaos in the beer production-distribution model. *System Dynamics Review*, *4*(1-2), 131–147. doi:10.1002/sdr.4260040108

Murata, T., & Itai, R. (2007). Local search in two – fold EMO algorithm to enhance solution similarity for multi – objective vehicle routing problems. In *Evolutionary Multi-Criterion Optimization* (*Vol. 4403*, pp. 201–215). Berlin, Heidelberg: Springer. doi:10.1007/978-3-540-70928-2_18

Murillo, L. (2001). Supply chain management and the international dissemination of e-commerce. *Industrial Management & Data Systems*, *101*(7), 370–377. doi:10.1108/EUM0000000005825

Narayanan, A., & Moore, M. (1996, May). Quantum-inspired genetic algorithms. In *Proceedings of IEEE International Conference on Evolutionary Computation* (pp. 61-66). IEEE Press.

Naso, D., Surico, M., Turchiano, B., & Kaymak, U. (2007). Genetic algorithms for supply-chain scheduling: A case study in the distribution of ready-mixed concrete. *European Journal of Operational Research*, *177*(3), 2069–2099. doi:10.1016/j.ejor.2005.12.019

Nienhaus, J., Ziegenbein, A., & Schoensleben, P. (2006). How human behaviour amplifies the bullwhip effect. a study based on the beer distribution game online. *Production Planning and Control*, *17*(6), 547–557. doi:10.1080/09537280600866587

Nieuwenhuyse, I. V., & de Koster, R. B. M. (2009). Evaluating Order Throughput Time in 2-Block Warehouses with Time Window Batching. *International Journal of Production Economics*, *121*, 654–664. doi:10.1016/j.ijpe.2009.01.013

Noorul, H. A., & Kannan, G. (2006). Effect of forecasting on the multi-echelon distribution inventory supply chain cost using neural networks, genetic algorithm and particle swarm optimization. *International Journal of Services Operations and Informatics*, *1*(1-2), 1–22.

O'donnell, T., Maguire, L., McIvor, R., & Humphreys, P. (2006). Minimizing the bullwhip effect in a supply chain using genetic algorithms. *International Journal of Production Research*, *44*(8), 1523–1543. doi:10.1080/00207540500431347

O'Neill, M., & Ryan, C. (2001). Grammatical evolution. *IEEE Transactions on Evolutionary Computation*, *5*(4), 349–358. doi:10.1109/4235.942529

O'Neill, M., & Ryan, C. (2003). *Grammatical evolution: Evolutionary automatic programming in an arbitrary language*. Norwell, MA, USA: Kluwer Academic Publishers. Available from http://portal.acm.org/citation.cfm?id=862025

Ochi, L. S., Vianna, D. S., Drummond, L. M. A., & Victor, A. O. (1998). A parallel evolutionary algorithm for the vehicle routing problem with heterogeneous fleet. *Future Generation Computer Systems*, *14*(5-6), 285–292. doi:10.1016/S0167-739X(98)00034-X

Ogryczak, W. (2000). Inequality measures and equitable approaches to location problems. *European Journal of Operational Research, 122*, 374–391. doi:10.1016/S0377-2217(99)00240-4

Oh, S. C., & Haghani, A. (1997). Testing and evaluation of a multi-commodity multi-modal network flow model for disaster relief management. *Journal of Advanced Transportation, 31*(3), 249–282. doi:10.1002/atr.5670310304

OIG-06-32 (2006, March). Office of Inspector General, Department of Homeland Security: "A Performance Review of FEMA Disaster Management Activities in Response to Hurricane Katrina. Retrieved April 29, 2006 from http://www.dhs.gov/xoig/assets/mgmtrpts/OIG_06-32_Mar06.pdf

OIG-08-11 (2008, January). Department of Homeland Security Inspector General, Major Management Challenges Facing the Department of Homeland Security. Retrieved February 10, 2009 from http://www.dhs.gov/xoig/assets/mgmtrpts/OIG_08-11_Jan08.pdf

Okutani, I., & Stephanedes, Y. J. (1984). Dynamic prediction of traffic volume through Kalman filtering theory. *Transportation Research Part B: Methodological, 18*(1), 1–11. doi:10.1016/0191-2615(84)90002-X

Oloruntoba, R., & Gray, R. (2006). Humanitarian aid: an agile supply chain. *Supply Chain Management: an International Journal, 11*(2), 115–120. doi:10.1108/13598540610652492

Onut, S., Tuzkaya, U. R., & Dogac, B. (2008). A particle swarm optimization algorithm for the multiple – level warehouse layout design problem. *Computers & Industrial Engineering, 54*, 783–799. doi:10.1016/j.cie.2007.10.012

Osborne, M. J., & Rubinstein, A. (1994). *A Course in Game Theory*. Cambridge, MA: MIT Press.

Ozdamar, L., Ekinci, E., & Kucukyazici, B. (2004). Emergency logistics planning in natural disasters. *Annals of Operations Research, 129*, 217–245. doi:10.1023/B:ANOR.0000030690.27939.39

Ozdamar, L., & Yi, W. (2008). Greedy Neighborhood Search for Disaster Relief and Evacuation Logistics. *IEEE Intelligent Systems, 23*(1), 14–23. doi:10.1109/MIS.2008.7

Pan, F., & Nagi, R. (2010). Robust supply chain design under uncertain demand in agile manufacturing. *Computers & Operations Research, 37*(4), 668–683. doi:10.1016/j.cor.2009.06.017

Panayiotou, C. G., & Cassandras, C. G. (1999). Optimization of kanban - based manufacturing systems. *Automatica, 35*(3), 1521–1533. doi:10.1016/S0005-1098(99)00074-6

Pang, H., Wei, Y., Wang, S., & Liu, X. (2009). Research on multi – time period production plan of supply chain under demands uncertainty. *Proceedings of the 6th International Symposium on Neural Networks on Advances in Neural Networks* (Vol. 5551, pp. 1098-1106).

Pankratz, G. (2005). A grouping genetic algorithm for the pickup and delivery with time windows. *OR-Spektrum, 27*, 21–41. doi:10.1007/s00291-004-0173-7

Papageorgiou, L. G. (2009). Supply chain optimisation for the process industries: advances and opportunities. *Computers & Chemical Engineering, 33*(12), 1931–1938. doi:10.1016/j.compchemeng.2009.06.014

Park, D., Messer, C. J., & Urbanik, T. (1998). Short-term freeway traffic volume forecasting using radial basis function neural networks. *Transportation Research Record, 1651*, 39–47. doi:10.3141/1651-06

Park, D., Rilett, L. R., & Han, G. (1999). Spectral basis neural networks for real-time travel time forecasting. *Journal of Transportation Engineering, 125*(6), 515–523. doi:10.1061/(ASCE)0733-947X(1999)125:6(515)

Parlar, M. (1997). Continuous-Review Inventory Problem with Random Supply Interruptions. *European Journal of Operational Research, 99*, 366–385. doi:10.1016/S0377-2217(96)00165-8

Parlar, M., & Perry, D. (1996). Inventory Models of Future Supply Uncertainty with Single and Multiple Suppliers. *Naval Research Logistics*, *43*, 191–210. doi:10.1002/(SICI)1520-6750(199603)43:2<191::AID-NAV3>3.0.CO;2-5

Parsopoulos, K. E., Skouri, K., & Vrahatis, M. N. (2008). Particle swarm optimization for tackling continuous review inventory models. In *Applications of Evolutionary Computing* (*Vol. 4974*, pp. 103–112). Berlin, Heidelberg: Springer. doi:10.1007/978-3-540-78761-7_11

Pasandideh, S. H. R., & Niaki, S. T. A. (2008). A genetic algorithm approach to optimize a multi-products EPQ model with discrete delivery orders and constrained space. *Applied Mathematics and Computation*, *195*(2), 506–514. doi:10.1016/j.amc.2007.05.007

Pasia, J. M., Doerner, K. F., Hartl, R. F., & Reimann, M. (2007). Solving a bi – objective vehicle routing problem by pareto – ant colony optimization. In *Engineering Stochastic Local Search Algorithms. Designing, Implementing and Analyzing Effective Heuristics* (*Vol. 4638*, pp. 187–191). Berlin, Heidelberg: Springer. doi:10.1007/978-3-540-74446-7_15

Paternina – Arboleda, C. D, & Das, T. K. (2001). Intelligent dynamic control policies for serial production lines. *IIE Transactions*, *33*, 65–77. doi:10.1080/07408170108936807

Pawlikowski, K. (1990). Steady state simulation of Queuing Processes. *ACM Computing Surveys*, *22*(2), 123–170. doi:10.1145/78919.78921

Peidro, D., Mula, J., Poler, R., & Lario, F.-C. (2009). Quantitative models for supply chain planning under uncertainty: a review. *International Journal of Advanced Manufacturing Technology*, *43*(3-4), 400–420. doi:10.1007/s00170-008-1715-y

Peleg, B. (1984). *Game Theoretic Analysis of Voting in Committees*. Cambridge University Press.

Peleg, B. (1992). Axiomatizations of the Core. In R. Aumann & S. Hart (Eds.), *Handbook of Game Theory with Economic Applications*. Amsterdam, North-Holland: Elsevier.

Pellegrini, P., Favaretto, D., & Moretti, E. (2007). Multiple ant colony optimization for a rich vehicle routing problem: a case study. In *Knowledge-Based Intelligent Information and Engineering Systems* (*Vol. 4693*, pp. 627–634). Berlin, Heidelberg: Springer. doi:10.1007/978-3-540-74827-4_79

Perantonis, S. J., & Karras, D. A. (1995). An efficient constrained learning algorithm with momentum acceleration. *Neural Networks*, *8*(2), 237–239. doi:10.1016/0893-6080(94)00067-V

Perboli, G., Pezzella, F., & Tadei, R. (2008). EVE-OPT: a hybrid algorithm for the capacitated vehicle routing problem. *Mathematical Methodologies in Operational Research*, *68*, 361–382. doi:10.1007/s00186-008-0236-7

Perry, G. L. (1966). *Unemployment, Money Wage Rates, and Inflation*. Cambridge, MA: MIT Press.

Petersen, K., Ragatz, G., & Monczka, R. (2005). An examination of collaborative planning effectiveness and supply chain performance. *The Journal of Supply Chain Management*, *41*(2), 14–25. doi:10.1111/j.1055-6001.2005.04102002.x

Phelan, M., & McGarraghy, S. (2007). Mitigating the bullwhip effect in supply chains using grammatical evolution. In *Proceedings of the Systems Dynamics Society Conference*.

Pinto, P. C., Runkler, T. A., & Sousa, J. M. (2007). *Ant Colony Optimization and its Application to Regular and Dynamic MAX – SAT Problems* (pp. 285–304). Advances in Biologically Inspired Information Systems.

Pop, P. C., Pintea, C. M., & Sitar, C. P. (2007). An ant based heuristic for the railway traveling salesman problem. In *Applications of Evolutionary Computing* (*Vol. 4448*, pp. 702–711). Berlin, Heidelberg: Springer.

Prestwich, S. Tarim, S. A., Rossi, R. & Hnich, B. (2008). A steady-state genetic algorithm with resampling for noisy inventory control. in *Parallel Problem Solving from Nature-PPSN X* (Vol. 5199, pp. 559-568). Berlin Heidelberg: Springer.

Prins, C. (2004). A simple and effective evolutionary algorithm for the vehicle routing problem. *Computers & Operations Research, 31*, 1985–2002. doi:10.1016/S0305-0548(03)00158-8

Prins, C., & Bouchenoua, S. (2006). A memetic algorithm solving the VRP, the CAPR and general routing problems with nodes, edges and arcs. In *Studies in Fuzziness and Soft Computing* (*Vol. 166*, pp. 65–85). Berlin, Heidelberg: Springer.

Prins, C., Prodhon, C., & Calvo, R. W. (2006). A memetic algorithm with population management (MA|PM) for the capacitated location – routing problem. In *Evolutionary Computation in Combinatorial Optimization* (*Vol. 3906*, pp. 183–194). Berlin, Heidelberg: Springer. doi:10.1007/11730095_16

Psaraftis, H. N. (1995). Dynamic Vehicle Routing: Status and Prospects. *Annals of Operations Research, 611*, 143–164. doi:10.1007/BF02098286

Puris, A., Bello, R., Martinez, Y., & Nowe, A. (2007). Two – stage ant colony optimization for solving the traveling salesman problem. In *Nature Inspired Problem-Solving Methods in Knowledge Engineering* (*Vol. 4528*, pp. 307–316). Berlin, Heidelberg: Springer. doi:10.1007/978-3-540-73055-2_33

Qu, L., & Sun, R. (1999). A synergetic approach to genetic algorithms for solving traveling salesman problem. *Information Sciences, 117*, 267–283. doi:10.1016/S0020-0255(99)00026-2

Rabelo, L., Helal, M., & Lertpattarapong, C. (2004, Jan). Analysis of supply chains using system dynamics, neural nets, and eigenvalues. In J. S. S. R.G. Ingalls M. D. Rossetti & B. A. Peters (Eds.), *Proceedings of the 36th winter simulation conference.*

Rao, R. V. (2007). Vendor selection in a supply chain using analytic hierarchy process and genetic algorithm methods. *International Journal of Services and Operations Management, 3*(3), 355–369. doi:10.1504/IJSOM.2007.013097

Ray, J. (1987). *A multi-period linear programming model for optimally scheduling the distribution of food-aid in West Africa.* MS Thesis, University of Tennessee, Knoxville, TN.

Rego, C., & Rucairol, C. (1995). Using tabu search for solving a dynamic multi-terminal truck dispatching problem. *European Journal of Operational Research, 83*, 411–429. doi:10.1016/0377-2217(95)00016-J

Reimann, M. (2007). Guiding ACO by problem relaxation: a case study on the symmetric TSP. In *Hybrid Metaheuristics* (*Vol. 4771*, pp. 45–56). Berlin, Heidelberg: Springer. doi:10.1007/978-3-540-75514-2_4

Reimann, M., Doerner, K., & Hartl, R. F. (2004). D-Ants: Savings Based Ants divide and conquer the vehicle routing problem. *Computers & Operations Research, 31*, 563–591. doi:10.1016/S0305-0548(03)00014-5

Reimann, M., & Ulrich, H. (2006). Comparing backhauling strategies in vehicle routing using Ant Colony Optimization. *Central European Journal of Operations Research, 14*, 105–123. doi:10.1007/s10100-006-0163-8

Renna, P., & Argoneto, P. (2008). Capacity Allocation in Multi-Site Factory Environment: a Multi Agent Systems Approach. Intelligent Computation in Manufacturing Engineering Innovative and Cognitive Production Technology and Systems, 23-25 July, Naples, Italy.

Reyes, L. C., Orta, J. F. D., Barbosa, J. J. G., Jimenez, J. T., Huacuja, H. J. F., & Cruz, B. A. A. (2008). An ant colony system algorithm to solve routing problems applied to the delivery of bottled products. In *Foundations of Intelligent Systems* (*Vol. 4994*, pp. 329–338). Berlin, Heidelberg: Springer. doi:10.1007/978-3-540-68123-6_36

Rezaei, J., & Davoodi, M. (2008). A deterministic, multi-item inventory model with supplier selection and imperfect quality. *Applied Mathematical Modelling, 32*(10), 2106–2116. doi:10.1016/j.apm.2007.07.009

Rezg, N., Xie, X., & Mati, Y. (2004). Joint optimization of preventive maintenance and inventory control in a production line using simulation. *International Journal of Production Research*, *42*(10), 2029–2046. doi:10.1080/00207540310001638235

Rice, M. (2004). Computational Intelligence Algorithms for Optimized vehicle routing applications in Geographic information systems. Thesis Proposal.

Rizzoli, A. E., Oliverio, F., Montemanni, R. & Gambardella, L. M. (2004). Ant Colony Optimization for vehicle routing problems: from theory to applications. IDSIA, Technical Report.

Roodbergen, K. J., Sharp, G. P., & Vis, I. F. A. (2008). Designing the Layout Structure of Manual Order Picking Areas in Warehouse. *IIE Transactions*, *40*(11), 1032–1045. doi:10.1080/07408170802167639

Rosenschein, J. S., & Zlotkin, G. (1994). *Rules of Encounter*. Cambridge, MA: MIT Press.

Rosenthal, R. E. (2008). *GAMS: A User's Guide*. Washington, D.C.: GAMS Development Corporation.

Rumelhart, D. E., Hinton, G. E., & Williams, R. J. (1986). Learning internal representations by error propagation. *Parallel distributed processing: explorations in the microstructure of cognition* (Vol. 1. *Foundations*, 318–362.

Sabri, E. H., & Beamon, B. M. (2000). A multi-objective approach to simultaneous strategic and operational planning in supply chain design. *Omega*, *28*(5), 581–598. doi:10.1016/S0305-0483(99)00080-8

Samanlioglu, F., Ferrell, W. G. Jr, & Kurz, M. E. (2008). A memetic random – key genetic algorithm for a symmetric multi – objective traveling salesman problem. *Computers & Industrial Engineering*, *55*, 439–449. doi:10.1016/j.cie.2008.01.005

Sandholm, T., Larson, K., Andersson, M., Shehory, O., & Tohme, F. (1999). Coalition structure generation with worst case guarantees. *Artificial Intelligence Journal*, *11*, (1), 209–238. doi:10.1016/S0004-3702(99)00036-3

Santoso, T., Ahmed, S., Goetschalckx, M., & Shapiro, A. (2005). A stochastic programming approach for supply chain network design under uncertainty. *European Journal of Operational Research*, *167*(1), 96–115. doi:10.1016/j.ejor.2004.01.046

Sarkar, S. (2009). A Real-option Rationale for Investing in Excess Capacity. *Managerial and Decision Economics*, *30*, 119–133. doi:10.1002/mde.1446

Savelsbergh, M. W. P., & Sol, M. (1998). Drive: Dynamic routing of independent vehicles. *Operations Research*, *46*, 474–490. doi:10.1287/opre.46.4.474

Schmitt, L. J., & Amini, M. M. (1998). Performance characteristics of alternative genetic algorithmic approaches to the traveling salesman problem using path representation: An empirical study. *European Journal of Operational Research*, *108*, 551–570. doi:10.1016/S0377-2217(97)00206-3

Schneeweiss, C. (2003). *Distributed Decision Making* (2nd ed.). Berlin: Springer-Verlag.

Schneider, J., Froschhammer, C., Morgenstern, I., Husslein, T., & Singer, J. M. (1996). Searching for backbones – an effective parallel algorithm for the traveling salesman problem. *Computer Physics Communications*, *96*, 173–188. doi:10.1016/0010-4655(96)00062-8

Schoemaker, P. J. H. (1993). Multiple scenario development: its conceptual and behavioral foundation. *Strategic Management Journal*, *14*(3), 193–213. doi:10.1002/smj.4250140304

Scholz-reiter, B., Delhoum, S., Zschintzsch, M., Jagalski, T., & Freitag, M. (2006). Inventory Control in Shop Floors, Production Networks and Supply Chains Using System Dynamics. In *Proceedings of the 12th ASIM Conference on Simulation in Production and Logistics* (pp. 273-282)

Schwarz, E. S., & Trigeorgis, L. (Eds.). (2001). *Real options and investment under uncertainty: classical readings and recent contributions*. Cambridge, MA: MIT Press.

Sena, G. A., Megherbi, D., & Isern, G. (2001). Implementation of a parallel genetic algorithm on a cluster of workstations: traveling salesman problem, a case study. *Future Generation Computer Systems, 17*, 477–488. doi:10.1016/S0167-739X(99)00134-X

Shah, N. (2003). Pharmaceutical supply chains: key issues and strategies for optimisation. In *Proceedings of 4th international conference on foundations of computer-aided process operations* (pp. 73-85).

Shahabudeen, P., Gopinath, R., & Krishnaiah, K. (2002). Design of bi-criteria kanban system using simulated annealing technique. *Computers & Industrial Engineering, 41*(4), 355–370. doi:10.1016/S0360-8352(01)00060-2

Shahabudeen, P., & Krishnaiah, K. (1999). Design of a Bi-Criteria kanban system using Genetic Algorithm. *International Journal of Management and System, 15*(3), 257–274.

Shapiro, J. F. (1999). On the connections among activity-based costing, mathematical programming models for analyzing strategic decisions, and the resource-based view of the firm. *European Journal of Operational Research, 118*(2), 295–314. doi:10.1016/S0377-2217(99)00027-2

Shapiro, A. (2003). Monte Carlo Sampling Methods. In Raszczynski & Shapiro (Eds.), *Stochastic Programming, Handbooks in OR-MS 10*. Amsterdam: Elsevier.

Shapiro, J. F. (2003). Challenges of strategic supply chain planning and modelling. In *Proceedings of 4th international conference on foundations of computer-aided process operations* (pp. 27-34).

Shapley, L. S. (1953a). *Additive and non-additive set functions*. PhD thesis, Department of Mathematics, Princeton University.

Shapley, L. S. (1953b). A value for n-person games. *Annals of Mathematics Studies*, 28, 307-317. Reprint in A.E. Roth (Ed.) (1988), 31-40.

Sheffi, Y. (2005). *The Resilient Enterprise: Overcoming Vulnerability for Competitive Advantage*. Cambridge, MA: MIT Press.

Sheffi, Y., Rice Jr, J.B., Caniato, F., Fleck, J., Disraelly, D., Lowtan, D., Lensing, R. & Pickett, C. (2003). *Supply Chain Response to Terrorism: Creating Resilient and Secure Supply Chains*. Supply Chain Response to Terrorism Project – Interim Report, MIT Center for Transportation and Logistics.

Shen, Z., Dessouky, M., & Ordonez, F. (2005). Stochastic vehicle routing problem for large-scale emergencies (Technical Report 2005-06). Department of Industrial and Systems Engineering, University of Southern California.

Shi, X. H., Liang, Y. C., Lee, H. P., Lu, C., & Wang, Q. X. (2007). Particle swarm optimization – based algorithms for TSP and generalized TSP. *Information Processing Letters, 103*, 169–176. doi:10.1016/j.ipl.2007.03.010

Silva, C. A., Runkler, T., & Sousa, J. M. (2007). Optimization of logistic systems using fuzzy weighted aggregation. *Fuzzy Sets and Systems, 158*, 1947–1960. doi:10.1016/j.fss.2007.04.008

Silva, C. A., Runkler, T., & Sousa, J. M. (2008). Rescheduling and optimization of logistic processes using GA and ACO. *Engineering Applications of Artificial Intelligence, 21*, 343–352. doi:10.1016/j.engappai.2007.08.006

Silva, C. A., Runkler, T., Sousa, J. M., & Palm, R. (2002). Optimization of logistic processes using ant colonies. In. *Proceedings of Agent-Based Simulation, 3*, 143–148.

Silva, C. A., Runkler, T., Sousa, J. M., & Palm, R. (2005). Soft Computing optimization methods applied to logistic processes. *International Journal of Approximate Reasoning, 40*, 280–301. doi:10.1016/j.ijar.2005.06.004

Silva, C. A., Runkler, T. A., Sousa, J. M., & Sa da Costa, J. M. (2003). Optimization of Logistic Processes in Supply-Chains Using Meta-heuristics. In *Progress in Artificial Intelligence* (*Vol. 2902*, pp. 9–23). Berlin, Heidelberg: Springer. doi:10.1007/978-3-540-24580-3_9

Silva, C. A., Sousa, J. M., Runkler, T., & Sa da Costa, J. M. G. (2005). Ant-based distributed optimization for supply chain management. In *Adaptive and Natural Computing Algorithms* (pp. 357–360). Vienna: Springer. doi:10.1007/3-211-27389-1_86

Silva, C. A., Sousa, J. M., Runkler, T., & Sa da Costa, J. M. G. (2009). Distributed supply chain management using ant colony optimization. *European Journal of Operational Research, 199*, 349–358. doi:10.1016/j.ejor.2008.11.021

Silva, C. A., Runkler, T. A., Sousa, J. M., & Palm, R. (2002). Ant Colonies as Logistic Processes Optimizers. In *Proceedings of the ANTS 3rd International conference on Ant Algorithms* (Vol. 2463, pp. 76-87).

Sim E., Jung, S., Kim, H., & Park, J. (2004). A generic network design for a closed-loop supply chain using genetic algorithm. In *Genetic and Evolutionary Computation-GECCO 2004* (Vol. 3103, pp. 1214-1225).

Sivanandam, S. N., & Deepa, S. N. (2007). Introduction to Genetic programming. In *Genetic Programming* (pp. 131–163). Berlin, Heidelberg: Springer.

Skaruz, J., Seredynski, F., & Gamus, M. (2006). Nature – inspired algorithms for the TSP. In *Intelligent Information Processing and Web Mining* (*Vol. 31*, pp. 319–328). Berlin, Heidelberg: Springer.

Smith, K. R. (1969). The effect of uncertainty on monopoly price, capital stock and utilization of capital. *Journal of Economic Theory*, *1*, 48–59. doi:10.1016/0022-0531(69)90011-8

Smith, G. C., & Smith, S. S. F. (2002). An enhanced genetic algorithm for automated assembly planning. *Robotics and Computer-integrated Manufacturing*, *18*(5-6), 355–364. doi:10.1016/S0736-5845(02)00029-7

Smith, B. L., & Demetsky, M. J. (1994). Short-term traffic flow prediction: neural network approach. *Transportation Research Board*, *1453*, 98–104.

Smith, B. L., & Demetsky, M. J. (1996). Multiple-interval freeway traffic flow forecasting. *Transportation Research Record*, *1554*, 136–141. doi:10.3141/1554-17

Smith, B. L., & Demetsky, M. J. (1997). Traffic flow forecasting: comparison of modelling approaches. *Journal of Transportation Engineering*, *123*(4), 261–266. doi:10.1061/(ASCE)0733-947X(1997)123:4(261)

Smith, B. L., Williams, B. M., & Oswald, R. K. (2002). Comparison of parametric and nonparametric models for traffic flow forecasting. *Transportation Research Part C, Emerging Technologies*, *10*, 303–321. doi:10.1016/S0968-090X(02)00009-8

Smith, B. L., Williams, B. M., & Oswald, K. R. (2000). Parametric and nonparametric traffic volume forecasting. In *Proceedings of the 80th TRB Annual Meeting*, Washington, DC

Snyder, L. V. (2006). Facility location under uncertainty: a review. *IIE Transactions*, *38*, 537–554. doi:10.1080/07408170500216480

Snyder, L.V., Scaparra, P.M., Daskin, M.S., & Church, R.L. (2006). Planning for Disruptions in Supply Chain Networks. *Tutorials in Operations Research*, 234-256.

Sparling, D. (2002). Simulations and supply chains: strategies for teaching supply chain management. *Supply Chain Management: An International Journal*, *7*(5), 334–342. doi:10.1108/13598540210447782

Spearman, M. L., Woodruff, D. L., & Hopp, W. J. (1990). CONWIP: a pull alternative to kanban. *International Journal of Production Research*, *28*, 879–894. doi:10.1080/00207549008942761

Srinivas, D. Y., Choudhary, A. K., Harding, J. A. & Tiwari, M. K. (2005). A Cooperative Multi Colony Ant Optimization Based Approach to Efficiently Allocate Customers to Multiple Distribution Centers in a Supply Chain Network. In *Computational Science and Its Applications-ICCSA 2005* (Vol. 3483, pp. 680 – 691). Berlin Heidelberg: Springer.

Stathopoulos, A., & Karlaftis, M. G. (2003). A multivariate state-space approach for urban traffic flow modelling and prediction. *Transportation Research Part C, Emerging Technologies*, *11*(2), 121–135. doi:10.1016/S0968-090X(03)00004-4

Stenger, A. J. (1996). Reducing inventories in a multi-echelon manufacturing firm: a case study. *International Journal of Production Economics*, *45*(1-3), 239–249. doi:10.1016/0925-5273(94)00146-4

Sterman, J. D. (1989). Modeling managerial behavior: Misperceptions of feedback in a dynamic decision making experiment. *Management Science*, *35*(3), 321–339. doi:10.1287/mnsc.35.3.321

Sterman, J. D. (1992). Teaching takes off: flight simulators for management education. *OR/MS Today*, *19*(5), 40-44.

Strozzi, F., Bosch, J., & Zald, J. M. (2007). Beer game order policy optimization under changing customer demand. *Decision Support Systems*, *42*(4), 2153–2163. doi:10.1016/j.dss.2006.06.001

Su, C. T., & Wong, J. T. (2008). Design of a replenishment system for a stochastic dynamic production / forecast lot – sizing problem under bullwhip effect. *Expert Systems with Applications*, *34*, 173–180. doi:10.1016/j.eswa.2006.08.010

Sugimori, Y., Kusunoki, K., Cho, F., & Uchikawa, S. (1977). Toyota production system and kanban system materialization of just-in-time and respect-for-humans systems. *International Journal of Production Research*, *15*(6), 553–564. doi:10.1080/00207547708943149

Syarif, A., Yun, Y. S., & Gen, M. (2002). Study on multistage logistic chain network: a spanning tree-based genetic algorithm approach. *Computers & Industrial Engineering*, *43*(1-2), 299–314. doi:10.1016/S0360-8352(02)00076-1

Syntetos, A., & Boylan, J. (2001). On the bias of intermittent demand estimates. *International Journal of Production Economics*, *71*(1-3), 457–466. doi:10.1016/S0925-5273(00)00143-2

Tan, K. C., & Chew, Y. H. (2006). A hybrid multiobjective evolutionary algorithm for solving vehicle routing problem with time windows. *Computational Optimization and Applications*, *34*, 115–151. doi:10.1007/s10589-005-3070-3

Tang, C. S. (2006). Perspectives in Supply Chain Risk Management. *International Journal of Production Economics*, *103*, 451–488. doi:10.1016/j.ijpe.2005.12.006

Taniguchi, K., & Terano, T. (2004). Analyzing dynamics of a supply chain using logic-based genetic programming. In *Knowledge-Based Intelligent Information and Engineering Systems* (*Vol. 3213*, pp. 464–471). Berlin, Heidelberg: Springer.

Tarakanov, A., & Dasgupta, D. (2000). A formal model of an artificial immune system. *Bio Systems*, *55*, 151–158. doi:10.1016/S0303-2647(99)00093-3

Tarantilis, C. D., Ioannou, G., & Prastacos, G. (2005). Advanced vehicle routing algorithms for complex operations management problems. *Journal of Food Engineering*, *70*, 455–471. doi:10.1016/j.jfoodeng.2004.09.023

Tasgetiren, M. F., Suganthan, P. N., & Pan, Q. K. (2007). A discrete particle swarm optimization algorithm for the generalized traveling salesman problem. In *Proceedings of the 9th annual conference on Genetic and evolutionary computation* (pp. 158 – 165).

Teixeira, J. F., Brito, A. C., & Saw, R. (2004, 7-9 June). Distributed application for supply chain management training. In J. Marin & V. Koncar (Eds.), *Proceedings of International Simulation Conference* (p. 335). University of Malaga, Malaga, Spain: EUROSIS.

Teng, S. Y., Ong, H. L., & Huang, H. C. (2006). Heuristic algorithms for visiting the customers in a rolling schedule environment. *OR-Spektrum*, *28*(2), 241–266. doi:10.1007/s00291-005-0002-7

Teodorovic, D. (2008). Swarm intelligence systems for transportation engineering: Principles and applications. *Transportation Research Part C, Emerging Technologies*, *16*, 651–667. doi:10.1016/j.trc.2008.03.002

Thomas, A. S. (2003). *Humanitarian Logistics: Enabling Disaster Response*. Fritz Institute. Retrieved July 4, 2008 from http://www.fritzinstitute.org/PDFs/WhitePaper/EnablingDisasterResponse.pdf

Thomas, A. S., & Kopczak, L. R. (2005). *From Logistics to Supply Chain Management: The Path Forward in the Humanitarian Sector*. Fritz Institute. Retrieved July 4, 2008 from http://www.fritzinstitute.org/PDFs/WhitePaper/FromLogisticsto.pdf

Ting, C. J., Tsai, C. Y., & Yeh, L. W. (2007). The use of particle swarm optimization for order allocation under multiple capacitated sourcing and quantity discounts. *Proceedings of the IEMS*, *6*(2), 136–145.

Tombuş, O., & Bilgiç, T. (2004). A column generation approach to the coalition formation problem in multi-agent systems. *Computers & Operations Research*, *31*, 1635–1653. doi:10.1016/S0305-0548(03)00112-6

Tomlin, B. (2006). On the Value of Mitigation and Contingency Strategies for Managing Supply Chain Disruption Risks. *Management Science*, *52*(5), 639–657. doi:10.1287/mnsc.1060.0515

Tomlin, B. (2009). Disruption Management Strategies for Short Life-Cycle Products. *Naval Research Logistics*, *56*(4), 318–347. doi:10.1002/nav.20344

Tomlin, B., & Wang, Y. (2005). On the Value of Mix Flexibility and Dual Sourcing in Unreliable Newsvendor Networks. *Manufacturing & Service Operations Management*, *7*(1), 37–57. doi:10.1287/msom.1040.0063

Toth, P., & Vigo, D. (2002). *The vehicle routing problem*. USA: SIAM Monographs on Discrete Mathematics and Applications.

Tricoire, F. (2006). *Optimisation Des Tournées De Véhicules Et De Personnels De Maintenance: Application A La Distribution Et Au Traitement Des Eaux*. PhD Thesis, Université de Nantes

Tricoire, F. (2007). Vehicle and personnel routing optimization in the service sector: application to water distribution and treatment. *4OR*, 5, 165-168

Trigeorgis, L. (1996). *Real Options: Managerial Flexibility and Strategy in Resource Allocation*. Cambridge, MA: The MIT Press.

Tsai, C. Y., & Yeh, S. W. (2008). A multiple objective particle swarm optimization approach for inventory classification. in *International Journal of Production Economics*, *114*(2), 656-666.

Tsiakis, P., Shah, N., & Pantelides, C. C. (2001). Design of multi-echelon supply chain networks under demand uncertainty. *Industrial & Engineering Chemistry Research*, *40*(16), 3585–3604. doi:10.1021/ie0100030

Tsou, C. S. (2008). Multi-objective inventory planning using MOPSO and TOPSIS. *Expert Systems with Applications*, *35*(1-2), 136–142. doi:10.1016/j.eswa.2007.06.009

Tsou, C. S. (2009). Evolutionary pareto optimizers for continuous review stochastic inventory systems. *European Journal of Operational Research*, *195*, 364–371. doi:10.1016/j.ejor.2008.02.039

Tully, S. (2000). The B2B tool that really is changing the world. *Fortune Magazine*, *141*(6), 132–145.

Turowski, K. (2002). Agent-based e-commerce in case of mass customization. *International Journal of Production Economics*, *75*, 69–81. doi:10.1016/S0925-5273(01)00182-7

Tzeng, G. H., Cheng, H. J., & Huang, T. D. (2007). Multi-objective optimal planning for designing relief delivery systems. *Transportation Research Part E, Logistics and Transportation Review*, *43*, 673–686. doi:10.1016/j.tre.2006.10.012

Ugur, A., & Aydin, D. (2009). An interactive simulation and analysis software for solving TSP using Ant Colony Optimization algorithms. *Advances in Engineering Software*, *40*, 341–349. doi:10.1016/j.advengsoft.2008.05.004

Ukkusuri, S. V., & Yushimoto, W.F. (2008). Location Routing Approach for the Humanitarian Prepositioning Problem. *Journal of Transportation Research Record*, 18-25.

Urban, T. L. (1998). An inventory-theoretic approach to product assortment and shelf-space allocation. *Journal of Retailing*, *74*(1), 15–35. doi:10.1016/S0022-4359(99)80086-4

Van der Vorst, J. G. A. J. (2006). Performance Measurement in Agri-Food Supply Chain Networks. In Ondersteijn, C. J. M. (Eds.), *Quantifying the Agrifood Supply Chain* (pp. 15–26). The Netherlands: Springer. doi:10.1007/1-4020-4693-6_2

Van Mieghem, J. (2007). Risk Mitigation in Newsvendor Networks: Resource Diversification, Flexibility, Sharing, and Hedging. *Management Science*, *53*(8), 1269–1288. doi:10.1287/mnsc.1070.0700

Van Wassenhove, L. N. (2006). Blackett memorial lecture - humanitarian aid logistics: supply chain management in high gear. *The Journal of the Operational Research Society*, *57*(5), 475–489. doi:10.1057/palgrave.jors.2602125

Vapnik, V. (1998). *The nature of statistical learning theory*. New York: Wiley.

Vapnik, V., Golowich, S. E., & Smola, A. J. (1996). *Support vector method for function approximation, regression estimation and signal processing* (pp. 281–287). Nips.

Vassiliadis, V., & Dounias, G. (2009). Nature – Inspired Intelligence: A review of selected methods and applications. *International Journal of Artificial Intelligence Tools*, *18*(4), 487–516. doi:10.1142/S021821300900024X

Veatch, M. H., & Wein, L. M. (1992). Monotone control of queueing networks. *Queueing Systems*, *12*, 391–408. doi:10.1007/BF01158810

Veeraraghavan, S., & Scheller-Wolf, A. (2008). Now or Later: a Simple Policy for Effective Dual Sourcing in Capacitated Systems. *Operations Research*, *56*(4), 850–864. doi:10.1287/opre.1080.0552

Venkatraman, S., & Yen, G. G. (2005). A generic framework for constrained optimization using genetic algorithms. *IEEE Transactions on Evolutionary Computation*, *9*(4), 424–435. doi:10.1109/TEVC.2005.846817

Vivo-Truyols, G., Torres-Lapasio, J. R., & Garcıa-Alvarez-Coque, M. C. (2001). A hybrid genetic algorithm with local search: I. Discrete variables: optimisation of complementary mobile phases. *Chemometrics and Intelligent Laboratory Systems*, *59*, 89–106. doi:10.1016/S0169-7439(01)00148-4

Vlachogianni, E. I., Colias, J. C., & Karlaftis, M. G. (2004). Short-term Traffic Forecasting: Overview of Objectives and Methods. *Transport Reviews*, *24*(5), 533–557. doi:10.1080/0144164042000195072

Vlachos, D., & Dekker, R. (2003). Return Handling Options and Order Quantities for Single Period Products. *European Journal of Operational Research*, *151*, 38–52. doi:10.1016/S0377-2217(02)00596-9

Wang, H. S. (2009). A two – phase ant colony algorithm for multi – echelon defective supply chain network design. *European Journal of Operational Research*, *192*, 243–252. doi:10.1016/j.ejor.2007.08.037

Wang, J. Q., Tong, X. N., & Li, Z. M. (2007). An improved evolutionary algorithm for dynamic vehicle routing problem with time windows. In *Computational Science-ICCS 2007* (*Vol. 4490*, pp. 1147–1154). Berlin, Heidelberg: Springer. doi:10.1007/978-3-540-72590-9_171

Wang, K., & Wang, Y. (2008). Applying Genetic Algorithms to Optimize the Cost of Multiple Sourcing Supply Chain Systems-An Industry Case Study. In *Success in Evolutionary Computation* (*Vol. 92*, pp. 355–372). Berlin, Heidelberg: Springer. doi:10.1007/978-3-540-76286-7_16

Wang, K. J., & Chen, M. J. (2009). Cooperative capacity planning and resource allocation by mutual outsourcing using ant algorithm in a decentralized supply chain. *Expert Systems with Applications*, *36*, 2831–2842. doi:10.1016/j.eswa.2008.01.089

Wang, W., Wu, B., Zhao, Y., & Feng, D. (2006). Particle swarm optimization for open vehicle routing problem. In *Computational Intelligence* (*Vol. 4114*, pp. 999–1007). Berlin, Heidelberg: Springer. doi:10.1007/978-3-540-37275-2_126

Wang, S., & Archer, N. (2007). Business-to-business collaboration through electronic marketplaces: An exploratory study. *Journal of Purchasing and Supply Management*, *13*, 113–126. doi:10.1016/j.pursup.2007.05.004

Wang, R. C., & Chuu, S. J. (2004). Group decision-making using a fuzzy linguistic approach for evaluating the flexibility in a manufacturing system. *European Journal of Operational Research*, *154*(3), 563–572. doi:10.1016/S0377-2217(02)00729-4

Wang, W. P. (2009). Toward developing agility evaluation of mass customization systems using 2-tuple linguistic computing. *Expert Systems with Applications*, *36*(2), 3439–3447. doi:10.1016/j.eswa.2008.02.015

Wang, L. (2005). *Support vector machines: Theory and applications (studies in fuzziness and soft computing)*. Secaucus, NJ, USA: Springer-Verlag New York, Inc.

Wang, Y., & Gerchak, Y. (2000). Input Control in a Batch Production System with Lead Times, Due Dates and Random Yields. *European Journal of Operational Research*, *126*, 371–385. doi:10.1016/S0377-2217(99)00295-7

Wang, G., Liu, Y. & Zheng, M. (2009). Fuzzy two – stage chain problem and its intelligent algorithm (Vol. 5552, pp. 15 – 24).

Wang, H. S., Che, Z. H. & Wu, C. (2009). Using analytic hierarchy process and particle swarm optimization algorithm for evaluating product plans. *Expert Systems with Applications*.

Webb, A. R. (2002). *Statistical pattern recognition* (2nd ed.). Wiley. doi:10.1002/0470854774

Weber, R. J. (1979). Subjectivity in the valuation of games. In Moeschlin, O., & Pallaschke, D. (Eds.), *Game theory and related topics* (pp. 129–136). Amsterdam: North-Holland.

Weber, R. J. (1988). Probabilistic values for games. In Roth, A. E. (Ed.), *The Shapley Value: Essays in Honor of Lloyd S. Shapley* (pp. 101–119). Cambridge University Press. doi:10.1017/CBO9780511528446.008

Wei, J. D., & Lee, D. T. (2006). Priority – based genetic local search and its application to the traveling salesman problem. In *Simulated Evolution and Learning* (*Vol. 4247*, pp. 424–432). Berlin, Heidelberg: Springer. doi:10.1007/11903697_54

Weise, T. (2009). Global Optimization Algorithms: Theory and Applications (2nd ed.). Retrieved from http://www.it-weise.de

Wen, M., Cordeau, J.-F., Laporte, G., & Larsen, J. (in press). The Dynamic Multi-Period Vehicle Routing Problem. *Computers & Operations Research*.

Wets, R. J.-B. (1996). Challenges in stochastic programming. *Mathematical Programming*, *75*(2), 115–135. doi:10.1007/BF02592149

Whittaker, J., Garside, S., & Lindeveld, K. (1997). Tracking and predicting network traffic process. *International Journal of Forecasting*, *13*, 51–61. doi:10.1016/S0169-2070(96)00700-5

Williams, B. M., Durvasula, P. K., & Brown, D. E. (1998). Urban traffic flow prediction: application of seasonal autoregressive integrated moving average and exponential smoothing models. *Transportation Research Record*, *1644*, 132–144. doi:10.3141/1644-14

Wilson, M. C. (2007). The Impact of Transportation Disruptions on Supply Chain Performance. *Transportation Research Part E, Logistics and Transportation Review*, *43*(4), 295–320. doi:10.1016/j.tre.2005.09.008

Winston, G. C. (1974). The theory of capital utilization and idleness. *Journal of Economic Literature*, *74*, 1301–1320.

Wong, J. T. (2009). The distribution processing and replenishment policy of the supply chain under asymmetric information and deterioration: Insight into the information value. *Expert Systems with Applications*.

Wu, T., Blackhurst, J., & O'Grady, P. (2007). Methodology for supply chain disruption analysis. *International Journal of Production Research*, *45*(7), 1665–1682. doi:10.1080/00207540500362138

Xanthopoulos, A., Vlachos, D., & Iakovou, E. (2010). Newsvendor Disruption Management Policies for a Two-Echelon Supply Chain. Working paper, Aristotle University of Thessaloniki.

Xia, Y., Yang, M. H., Golany, B., Gilbert, S. M., & Yu, G. (2004). Real-Time Disruption Management in a Two-Stage Production and Inventory System. *IIE Transactions*, *36*, 111–125. doi:10.1080/07408170490245379

Xiao, T., & Qi, X. (2008). Price Competition, Cost and Demand Disruptions and Coordination of a Supply Chain with one Manufacturer and Two Competing Retailers. *Omega: The International Journal of Management Science*, *36*(5), 741–753. doi:10.1016/j.omega.2006.02.008

Xiao, T., & Yu, G. (2006). Supply Chain Disruption Management and Evolutionarily Stable Strategies of Retailers in the Quantity-Setting Duopoly Situation with Homogeneous Goods. *European Journal of Operational Research*, *173*, 648–668. doi:10.1016/j.ejor.2005.02.076

Xie, J., & Dong, J. (2002). Heuristic genetic algorithms for general capacitated lot-sizing problems. *Computers & Mathematics with Applications (Oxford, England)*, *44*(1-2), 263–276. doi:10.1016/S0898-1221(02)00146-3

Xing, L. N., Chen, Y. W., Yang, K. W., Hou, F., Shen, X. S., & Cai, H. P. (2008). A hybrid approach combining an improved genetic algorithm and optimization strategies for the asymmetric traveling salesman problem. *Engineering Applications of Artificial Intelligence*, *21*, 1370–1380. doi:10.1016/j.engappai.2008.01.003

Xu, N., & Nozick, L. (2009). Modeling supplier selection and the use of options contracts for global supply chain design. *Computers & Operations Research*, *36*(10), 2786–2800. doi:10.1016/j.cor.2008.12.013

Yadav, S. R., Dashora, Y., Shankar, R., Chan, F. T. S., & Tiwari, M. K. (2008). An interactive particle swarm optimisation for selecting a product family and designing its supply chain. *Int. J. Comput. Appl. Technol.*, *31*(3/4), 168–186. doi:10.1504/IJCAT.2008.018155

Yager, R. R. (1995). An approach to ordinal decision making. *International Journal of Approximate Reasoning*, *12*(3-4), 237–261. doi:10.1016/0888-613X(94)00035-2

Yamamoto, H., Qudeiri, J. A., & Marui, E. (2008). Definition of FTL with bypass lines and its simulator for buffer size decision. *International Journal of Production Economics*, *112*(1), 18–25. doi:10.1016/j.ijpe.2007.03.007

Yamamoto, J., & Sycara, K. (2001). A Stable and Efficient Buyer Coalition Formation Scheme for E-Marketplaces. *International Conference on Autonomous Agents (Agents 2001),* Montreal Canada, May 28-June 1.

Yang, J., Shi, X., Marchese, M., & Liang, Y. (2008). An ant colony optimization method for generalized TSP problem. *Progress in Natural Science*, *18*, 1417–1422. doi:10.1016/j.pnsc.2008.03.028

Yang, J., Wu, C., Lee, H. P., & Liang, Y. (2008). Solving traveling salesman problems using generalized chromosome genetic algorithm. *Progress in Natural Science*, *18*, 887–892. doi:10.1016/j.pnsc.2008.01.030

Yang, L., & Stacey, D. A. (2001). Solving the traveling salesman problem using the enhanced genetic algorithm. In *Advances in Artificial Intelligence* (*Vol. 2056*, pp. 307–316). Berlin, Heidelberg: Springer. doi:10.1007/3-540-45153-6_30

Yang, S., Yang, J., & Abdel-Malek, L. (2007). Sourcing with Random Yields and Stochastic Demand: A Newsvendor Approach. *Computers & Operations Research*, *34*, 3682–3690. doi:10.1016/j.cor.2006.01.015

Yang, T., Kuo, Y., & Cho, C. (2007). A genetic algorithms simulation approach for the multi-attribute combinatorial dispatching decision problem. *European Journal of Operational Research*, *176*(3), 1859–1873. doi:10.1016/j.ejor.2005.10.048

Yang, J. (2005). Using Immune Algorithms for Inventory Model with Reverse Logistics. Master Thesis.

Yang, M. F. & Lin, Y. (2009). Applying the linear particle swarm optimization to a serial multi – echelon inventory model. *Expert Systems with Applications*.

Yang, S., Wang, M., & Jiao, L. (2004b, 19-23 June). A novel quantum evolutionary algorithm and its application. In *Proceedings of IEEE Congress on Evolutionary Computation 2004 (CEC 2004)* (Vol. 1, pp. 820-826). IEEE Press, New Jersey.

Yang, S., Wang, M., & Jiao, L. (2004a, 31 August—4 September). A genetic algorithm based on quantum chromosome. In *Proceedings of IEEE International Conference on Signal Processing (ICSP 04)* (pp. 1622-1625). IEEE Press.

Yano, C., & Lee, H. L. (1995). Lot Sizing with Random Yields: a Review. *Operations Research, 43*(2), 311–334. doi:10.1287/opre.43.2.311

Yao M. J., & Chu, W. M. (2008). A genetic algorithm for determining optimal replenishment cycles to minimize maximum warehouse space requirements. *Omega, 36*(4), 619–631. doi:10.1016/j.omega.2007.01.007

Yao, M. J., & Hsu, H. W. (2008). A new spanning tree-based genetic algorithm for the design of multi-stage supply chain networks with nonlinear transportation costs. *Optimization and Engineering, 10*(2), 219–237. doi:10.1007/s11081-008-9059-x

Yeh, W. C. (2004). A hybrid heuristic algorithm for the multistage supply chain network problem. *International Journal of Advanced Manufacturing Technology, 26*(5-6), 675–685. doi:10.1007/s00170-003-2025-z

Yeo, K. T., & Qiu, F. (2003). The value of management flexibility – a real option approach to investment evaluation. *International Journal of Project Management, 21*, 243–250. doi:10.1016/S0263-7863(02)00025-X

You, F., & Grossmann, I. E. (2008). Design of responsive supply chains under demand uncertainty. *Computers & Chemical Engineering, 32*(12), 3090–3111. doi:10.1016/j.compchemeng.2008.05.004

Yu, Y.-W., Yu, H.-C., Itoga, H., & Lin, T.-R. (2008). Decision-making factors for effective industrial e-procurement. *Technology in Society, 30*, 163–169. doi:10.1016/j.techsoc.2007.12.004

Yuan, Q., He, Z., & Leng, H. (2008). A hybrid genetic algorithm for a class of global optimization problems with box constraints. *Applied Mathematics and Computation, 197*, 924–929. doi:10.1016/j.amc.2007.08.081

Yun, S.-Y., Namkoong, S., Rho, J.-H., Shin, S.-W., & Choi, J.-U. (1998). A performance evaluation of neural network models in traffic volume forecasting. *Mathematical and Computer Modelling, 27*(9–11), 293–310. doi:10.1016/S0895-7177(98)00065-X

Zadeh, L. A. (1985). Syllogistic reasoning in fuzzy logic and its application to usuality and reasoning with dispositions. *IEEE Transactions on Systems, Man, and Cybernetics, SMC-15*, 754–765.

Zadeh L. A. (1975). The concept of a linguistic variable and its application to approximate reasoning. *Information Science*, 8, 199–249 (pt. I), 301–357(pt. II)

Zegordi, S. H., & Nia, M. A. B. (2009). Integrating production and transportation scheduling in a two-stage supply chain considering order assignment. *International Journal of Advanced Manufacturing Technology, 44*(9-10), 928–939. doi:10.1007/s00170-008-1910-x

Zhang, G. Q., & Lai, K. K. (2006). Combining path relinking and genetic algorithms for the multiple-level warehouse layout problem. *European Journal of Operational Research, 169*(2), 413–425. doi:10.1016/j.ejor.2004.08.007

Zhang, J. L., Zhao, Y. W., Peng, D. J., & Wang, W. L. (2008). A hybrid quantum – inspired evolutionary algorithm for capacitated vehicle routing problem. In *Advanced Intelligent Computing Theories and Applications. With Aspects of Theoretical and Methodological Issues* (*Vol. 5226*, pp. 31–38). Berlin, Heidelberg: Springer. doi:10.1007/978-3-540-87442-3_5

Zhang, X., & Tang, L. (2009). A new hybrid ant colony optimization algorithm for the vehicle routing problem. *Pattern Recognition Letters, 30*, 848–855. doi:10.1016/j.patrec.2008.06.001

Zhang, G., Patuwo, B. E., & Hu, M. Y. (1998). Forecasting with artificial neural networks: the state of art. *International Journal of Forecasting, 14*, 35–62. doi:10.1016/S0169-2070(97)00044-7

Zhang, H. M. (2000). Recursive prediction of traffic conditions with neural networks. *Journal of Transportation Engineering*, *126*(6), 472–481. doi:10.1061/(ASCE)0733-947X(2000)126:6(472)

Zhang, T., Tian, W. X., Zhang, Y. J. & Liu, S. X. (2008). Improved ant colony system for VRPSPD with maximum distance constraint. *Systems Engineering – Theory & Practice, 28*(1).

Zhao, F., Li, S., Sun, J., & Mei, D. (2009). Genetic algorithm for one – commodity pickup-and-delivery traveling salesman problem. *Computers & Industrial Engineering*, *56*, 1642–1648. doi:10.1016/j.cie.2008.10.014

Zhou, G., Min, H., & Gen, M. (2002). The balanced allocation of customers to multiple distribution centers in the supply chain network: a genetic algorithm approach. *Computers & Industrial Engineering*, *43*(1-2), 251–261. doi:10.1016/S0360-8352(02)00067-0

Zimmermann, H.-J. (1991). *Fuzzy set theory and its applications* (2nd ed.). Dordrecht: Kluwer.

About the Contributors

Ioannis Minis is a Professor in the Department of Financial and Management Engineering of the University of Aegean. He conducts research in design, production and operations systems, including supply chain management. Dr. Minis holds a Ph.D. degree from the University of Maryland in Mechanical Engineering, and has held the positions of Assistant and Associate Professor of Mechanical Engineering at the same University (1988-1997). He is conducting research in Operations for over 20 years and has authored two edited volumes, several book chapters, over 45 journal articles and over 60 articles in conference proceedings. Dr. Minis has been the recipient of the 1993 Earl E. Walker Outstanding Young Manufacturing Engineer Award from the Society of Manufacturing Engineers (SME).

Vasileios Zeimpekis is Adjunct Lecturer in the Department of Financial & Management Engineering at the University of the Aegean. He is also Senior Research Officer at the Design, Operations, & Production Systems (DeOPSys) Lab situated at the same University. His interests focus on road transportation & logistics with emphasis on decision support systems and telematics. He has published 3 edited volumes and more than 40 papers in the area of supply chain and transportation. Vasileios, holds a BEng(Hons) in Telecommunications Engineering from the University of Essex, (UK). He has also been awarded with an MSc in Mobile & Satellite Communications from the University of Surrey (UK) and an MSc with Distinction in Engineering Business Management from the University of Warwick (UK). He earned his PhD from the Department of Management Science & Technology at the Athens University of Economics & Business.

Georgios Dounias holds a Production and Management Engineering Diploma and a Doctoral Diploma both from the Technical University of Crete, Dept. of Production Engineering & Management. Since 2003 he is with the Department of Financial & Management Engineering, University of the Aegean, Chios, Greece (Full Professor since May 2010). He has served as Head of the Department (2008-2010), Head of the Postgraduate Studies in Financial and Management Engineering (2005-2008) and he is also Director of the Management and Decision Engineering Laboratory (2005-today). His research interests are related to Computational & Nature Inspired Intelligence, Management Engineering, Financial Decision Making, Medical Decision Making and Fault Diagnosis of Complex Dynamic Systems. George Dounias has participated in more than 25 national and international funded research programs in the last 20 years. He has published over 150 research reports and papers in journals, books and conferences, within 1993-2010 and he has served as editorial board member, guest editor or reviewer of 28 refereed international journals and as organizing / program committee in more than 60 international conferences, summer schools and special research events.

Nicholas Ampazis holds a BEng (Hons) degree from the Department of Electrical Engineering, Imperial College London (1992), an MSc degree with Distinction in Information Processing and Neural Networks from the Department of Mathematics, King's College London (1995), and a PhD with Distinction from the Department of Electical and Computer Engineering, National Technical University of Athens (2001). From 1996 to 2001 he was a scholar with the Institute of Informatics at the National Center from Scientific Research "Demokritos", Athens, Greece. From 2002 to 2005 he was an adjunct professor at the Department of Financial and Management Engineering (FME), University of the Aegean, and since 2005 he is an assistant professor (computer science) at the same department. He is also the director of the Intelligent Data Exploration and Analysis Laboratory (IDEAL) at the FME departhment. His research interests include computational intelligence algorithms (with emphasis in neural networks), data mining, information retrieval, recommender systems and supply chain management, and has published over 40 papers journal and conference papers in these research areas.

* * *

Theodore Athanasopoulos is currently a PhD candidate and research associate at the Department of Financial Management & Engineering. He holds a diploma on Production Engineering & Management from the Technical University of Crete. His research focuses on transportation management, routing and scheduling problems and mathematical programming. He has published more than 10 papers in scientific journals and conferences in the area of supply chain and transportation. On the past he has worked as a business consultant in major transportation organization as well in other public and private organizations, in strategic and business planning and business process re-engineering.

Pierluigi Argoneto received his Master of Science in Mechanical Engineering, year 2003, obtained summa "cum laude" from the Faculty of Engineering of the University of Basilicata, Italy. From the DTMPIG of the University of Palermo, Italy, he holds a doctoral degree in Production Engineering, year 2007. During and after his Ph.D., thematic concerning the analysis, the design and the negotiation protocol tests for e-procurement applications have been investigated. A second research interest has been the analysis of competitive environment, with a particular focus on the decision support methodologies at strategic level, mainly based on a game theoretic approach. Another research line concerns the formalization and the study of networked enterprises by using Real Options and cooperative games as tools for decisional support systems. Nowadays he works at the Healthcare Department of the Regione Basilicata at the office of strategic investments and management of financial resources of the healthcare system.

Vlachos Dimitrios is an Assistant Professor of the Department of Mechanical Engineering at the Aristotle University of Thessaloniki (AUTH). He received Diplomas in Electrical Engineering and in Mechanical Engineering and a Ph.D. in Mechanical Engineering, all from AUTH. He has also been a post-doctoral fellow at the Erasmus University in Rotterdam. His research interests include quantitative analysis of supply chains and inventory systems, risk management, green logistics and reverse logistics. His papers have been published among other journals in Management Science, IIE Transactions, European Journal of Operations Research, International Journal of Production Economics and Production in Operations Management.

Dimitrios M. Emiris is an Associate Professor at the Department of Industrial Management and Technology, University of Piraeus, Greece. He obtained the Diploma in Electrical Engineering from the National Technical University of Athens, in 1987. He obtained the M.Sc. and the Ph.D., in 1988 and 1991, respectively, from the Department of Electrical Engineering, University of Rochester. From 1997 to 2001 he served as an Assistant Professor of the Production Systems Division at the Department of Production Engineering and Management, of the Technical University of Crete. He has published over 100 articles in international journals and conferences and is the author of three books. His research interests lie in the areas of computational intelligence, logistics, project and production management.

Michael C. Georgiadis is an Associate Professor in the Department of Engineering Informatics and Telecommunications, at University of Western Macedonia, Greece and honorary senior research fellow in the Centre for Process Systems Engineering at Imperial College London. He was manager of academic business development for Process Systems Enterprise Ltd, UK. He obtained his Chemical Engineering Diploma from Aristotle University of Thessaloniki, Greece and an MSc and PhD from Imperial College London. Dr. Georgiadis has co-authored over 60 papers and seven books. He has a long experience in the management and participation of more than 20 collaborative research contracts and projects and consults to Process Systems Enterprise Ltd and Parametric Optimization Solutions Ltd.

Soumia Ichoua is an Associate Professor of Computer Science at the Department of Computer Science and Engineering in Johnson C. Smith University , Charlotte, NC. She is also an adjunct Professor at the Department of Operations & Decision Systems in Laval University , Canada and an associate member of Interuniversity Research Centre on Enterprise Networks, Logistics and Transportation (CIRRELT), Canada. Her research interests lie in the application of dynamic-stochastic optimization techniques and parallel algorithms to supply chain networks, logistics, industrial scheduling and distribution systems management. Dr. Ichoua has been supervising several undergraduate and graduate students in projects related to these fields. Some of her research papers have been published in leading journals in the field of transportation and Operations Research including Transportation Science, European Journal of Operational Research, and Computers and Operations Research.

Dimitrios E. Koulouriotis received his PhD in Intelligent Systems from Department of Production and Management Engineering, Technical University of Crete, Greece, in 2001. He received the Diploma in Electrical and Computer Engineering at the Democritus University of Thrace and the M.S. in Electronic and Computer Engineering at the Technical University of Crete, in 1993 and 1996 respectively. He is currently in the Department of Production and Management Engineering, Democritus University of Thrace, as an Associate Professor. His research interests include computational intelligence, machine learning and pattern recognition and their applications in vision, image and signal processing, robotics, production engineering and management. He has published over 150 research papers, and he served as reviewer in numerous conferences and journals.

Pantelis Longinidis is a PhD student in the Department of Engineering Informatics and Telecommunications, at University of Western Macedonia, Greece. He received a BSc in Economics from Aristotle University of Thessaloniki, Greece, an MSc in Logistics and Supply Chain Management from the same university, and an MBA in Financial Management from the University of Macedonia, Greece. His postgraduate studies have been supported from various national scholarships foundations.

His research interests are focused in supply chain management and optimization, logistics, enterprise resource planning systems, financial econometrics, and time series modeling.

Seán McGarraghy is a lecturer in the MIS subject area at the Smurfit School of Business, University College Dublin, and a member of the UCD Natural Computing Research and Applications (NCRA) group. His PhD is in mathematical quadratic form theory. His research interests include: Natural Computing, in particular Evolutionary Algorithms and Physically-inspired Algorithms; applications to Business Analytics and Supply Chain Management; and Quadratic Forms and related topics. He is co-author of a forthcoming book on Natural Computing Algorithms.

Michael Phelan is a PhD student at the Smurfit School of Business, University College Dublin. His PhD is in the area of supply chain optimisation using nature-inspired algorithms. The core of his research involves the development of Grammatical Evolution (GE) grammars using hybrid meta-heuristics including Genetic Algorithms (GA), Particle Swarm Optimisation and Quantum Inspired GA. These meta-heuristics can employ the use of statistical forecasting techniques, inventory control policies and complex conditional statements to derive supply chain ordering policies for each agent in a supply chain. Michael is currently working for Dell Inc. in forecasting and also has a Masters in Management Science from the Smurfit School of Business, UCD and a BSc. in Applied Mathematics & Computing from University of Limerick.

Paolo Renna is an Assistant Professor at Department of Environmental Engineering and Physics in the Engineering Faculty of Basilicata University (Italy). He took Ph.D. degree at Polytechnic of Bari in Advanced Production Systems. His academic researches principally deal with the development of innovative negotiation and production planning in distributed environments and manufacturing scheduling in dynamic environment. Several contributions have been presented on design Multi Agent Architecture and test by discrete event simulation in Business to Business environment. Among the contributions, he is co-author of two research books about e-marketplaces and production planning in production networks. Moreover, he has developed coordination approaches in multi-plant production planning environment and innovative scheduling approaches in flexible and reconfigurable manufacturing systems.

Athanasios Skarlatos obtained the B.Sc. Degree from the Department of Industrial Management and Technology, University of Piraeus, in 2006, and the M.Sc. Degree in Logistics from the same University in 2009. Mr. Skarlatos has been active in the area of Logistics with emphasis in Warehouse Management and currently holds a managerial position in one of the largest Greek firms in this industry.

Vassilios Vassiliadis has a diploma on Financial Engineering and Management (University of the Aegean, 2005). Since 2007, he is a candidate PhD of the same faculty. His doctorate thesis is "Nature-Inspired Intelligence in Financial Decision Making", under the supervision of professor George Dounias (Professor on the Department of Financial Engineering and Management). Specifically, the main field of his expertise is the development of nature-inspired algorithmic methodologies (neural networks, genetic algorithms, swarm intelligence etc.) and the use of these methods in solving dynamic financial problems (dynamic portfolio management). From 2006 till 2008, he had been working as a researcher in a program, whose main aim is the development of models and algorithms for the study of financial markets and the development of investment strategies

Alexandros Xanthopoulos was born in Athens, Greece, in 1982. He received the degree of Production and Management Engineer from the Engineering School of the Democritus University of Thrace, Greece, in 2006. He is currently a PhD student at the Department of Production and Management Engineering of the Democritus University of Thrace (DUTH). He has published articles on evolutionary optimization and production/inventory control of stochastic manufacturing systems in refereed scientific journals. His research interests focus on computational intelligence, primarily evolutionary optimization, Reinforcement Learning, Fuzzy logic, and its application to industrial/manufacturing systems and discrete event systems modelling and control.

Index

Q

R

S

Breinigsville, PA USA
07 February 2011
255010BV00006B/1-84/P

9 781615 206339